PROVIDING PEACEKEEPERS

Providing Peacekeepers

The Politics, Challenges, and Future of United Nations Peacekeeping Contributions

Edited by
ALEX J. BELLAMY AND PAUL D. WILLIAMS

OXFORD
UNIVERSITY PRESS

OXFORD
UNIVERSITY PRESS

Great Clarendon Street, Oxford, OX2 6DP,
United Kingdom

Oxford University Press is a department of the University of Oxford.
It furthers the University's objective of excellence in research, scholarship,
and education by publishing worldwide. Oxford is a registered trade mark of
Oxford University Press in the UK and in certain other countries

First Edition published in 2013

Impression: **4**

British Library Cataloguing in Publication Data
Data available

Library of Congress Cataloging in Publication Data
Data available

ISBN 978-0-19-967282-0

Printed and bound in Great Britain by Clays Ltd, St Ives plc

Acknowledgements

This book has benefited from the help of several people and we are pleased to acknowledge them here.

Corey Brodsky deserves a special note of thanks for his excellent logistic and organizational skills as well as his research assistance. Corey also compiled the index.

The project would not have been possible without the generous funding provided by the Elliott School of International Affairs at the George Washington University and the Griffith Asia Institute/Centre for Governance and Public Policy at Griffith University.

We are also grateful to a wide range of officials in the United Nations Department of Peacekeeping Operations for taking the time to discuss with us various aspects of this project. We hope the final product is helpful in the important work that they do.

Our contributors deserve thanks for participating in the workshop, agreeing to address the long list of questions demanded by our framework, and responding so positively to our requests for revisions.

At Oxford University Press we are grateful to Dominic Byatt, Sarah Parker, and Joanna North for their help in shepherding us through the publication process. We are also grateful to the anonymous reviewers for their insightful feedback.

Contents

List of Figures and Tables

List of Abbreviations

ACOTA	African Contingency Operations Training and Assistance
AFD	Armed Forces Division (Bangladesh)
AHC	ad hoc coalition
AKP	Justice and Development Party (Turkey)
AMIB	African Union Mission in Burundi
AMIS	African Union Mission in Sudan
AMISOM	African Union Mission in Somalia
ANC	African National Congress (South Africa)
APC	armoured personnel carrier
ASEAN	Association of Southeast Asian Nations
AU	African Union
BIPSOT	Bangladesh Institute of Peace Support Operation and Training
C34	Special Committee on Peacekeeping Operations (UN)
CAR	Central African Republic
CCOPAB	Brazilian Joint Centre for Peace Operations Training
CEMAC	Economic Community of Central African States
CIAA	Commission for the Investigation of Abuse of Authority (Nepal)
CIS	Commonwealth of Independent States
CNDP	National Congress for the Defence of the People (DRC)
COE	contingent owned equipment
CoESPU	Center of Excellence for Stability Police Units (Italy)
CORF	Collective Operational Reaction Forces (Central Asia)
CRDF	Collective Rapid Deployment Force (Central Asia)
CRF	Central Readiness Force (Japan)
CSDP	Common Security and Defence Policy (EU)
CSTO	Collective Security Treaty Organization
DAPKOP	Director of Army Peacekeeping Operations (Ghana)
DC	Designated Unit Contributor
DFA	Department of Foreign Affairs (South Africa)
DFID	Department for International Development (UK)
DFS	Department of Field Support (UN)
DIG	Deputy Inspector General of Police (Bangladesh)

DIPSO	Director of International Peacekeeping Support Operation (Ghana)
DIRCO	Department of International Relations and Cooperation (South Africa)
DPKO	Department of Peacekeeping Operations (UN)
DRC	Democratic Republic of the Congo
ECOMOG	ECOWAS Monitoring Group
ECOWAS	Economic Community of West African States
EU	European Union
FARDC	Armed Forces of the Democratic Republic of Congo
FCO	Foreign and Commonwealth Office (UK)
FOCAC	Forum on China and Africa Cooperation
FPU	Formed Police Unit
G8	Group of Eight
G20	Group of Twenty
G77	Group of Seventy-Seven
GAF	Ghana Armed Forces
GDP	Gross Domestic Product
GPOI	Global Peace Operations Initiative
GPS	Ghana Police Service
IAPTC	International Association of Peacekeeping Training Centres
IBSA	India–Brazil–South Africa
ICITAP	International Criminal Investigate Training Assistance Program (US)
IFOR	Implementation Force
IISS	International Institute for Strategic Studies
INTERFET	International Force (East Timor)
IPCHQ	International Peace Co-operation Headquarters (Japan)
IRD	International Relations Directorate, Ghana Police Service
ISAF	International Security Assistance Force (Afghanistan)
KAIPTC	Kofi Annan International Peacekeeping Training Centre (Ghana)
KFOR	Kosovo Force
MNF	Multinational Force
MOD	Ministry of Defence
MOFA	Ministry of Foreign Affairs (Japan)
MOHA	Ministry of Home Affairs (Bangladesh)
MOOTW	Military Operations Other Than War
MOU	Memorandum of Understanding
MRE	Ministry of External Relations (Brazil)

MSA	Mission Subsistence Allowance
MSDF	Maritime Self Defence Force (Japan)
NAM	Non-Aligned Movement
NATO	North Atlantic Treaty Organization
NEPAD	New Partnership for Africa's Development
NEP BATT	Nepalese Battalion
NGO	non-governmental organization
NIS	new independent states
NOCPM	National Office for the Coordination of Peacekeeping Missions (South Africa)
NSC	National Security Council
OAU	Organization of African Unity
OMP	overall military potential
OOD	Overseas Operations Directorate (Bangladesh)
OSCE	Organisation for Security and Co-operation in Europe
OWAC	overlapping Western agendas cluster (of contributing countries)
PCC	police-contributing country
PDD	Presidential Decision Directive (US)
PEP	Partnership for Effective Peacekeeping
PKK	Kurdistan Workers' Party
PKSOI	US Army Peacekeeping and Stability Operations Institute
PLA	People's Liberation Army (China)
PRC	People's Republic of China
PTSD	post-traumatic stress disorder
R2P	responsibility to protect
RUF	Revolutionary United Front (Sierra Leone)
SAAF	South African Air Force
SADC	Southern African Development Community
SADF	South African Defence Force
SAN	South African Navy
SANDF	South African National Defence Force
SAPS	South African Police Service
SAPSD	South African Protection Service Detachment
SCO	Shanghai Cooperation Organization
SDF	Self-Defence Force (Japan)
SEA	sexual exploitation and abuse
SFOR	Stabilization Force

SINOMAPA	National System for the Support of Peacekeeping Operations (Uruguay)
SIPRI	Stockholm International Peace Research Institute
SMC	Strategic Military Cell
STF	Special Task Force
TAF	Turkish Armed Forces
TCC	troop-contributing country
TNPF	Turkish National Police Force
UAV	unmanned aerial vehicles
UN	United Nations
UNC	United Nations cluster (of contributing countries)
UNHCR	United Nations High Commissioner for Refugees
UNMO	United Nations Military Observer
UNPOL	United Nations Police
UNSAS	United Nations Standby Arrangement System
WEOG	Western European and Others Group (UN)

List of Contributors

Adekeye Adebajo is the Executive Director of the Centre for Conflict Resolution, Cape Town, South Africa and has served on United Nations missions in South Africa, Western Sahara, and Iraq.

Kwesi Aning is Head of the Department of Research at the Kofi Annan International Peacekeeping Training Centre, Accra, Ghana.

Festus K. Aubyn is a Senior Research Fellow at the Kofi Annan International Peacekeeping Training Centre, Accra, Ghana.

Maj. Gen. Dipankar Banerjee (Ret'd) is the Founding Director of the Institute of Peace and Conflict Studies, New Delhi, India.

Alex J. Bellamy is Professor of International Security in the Asia Institute at Griffith University, Australia.

Niloy R. Biswas is Lecturer in the Department of International Relations at the University of Dhaka, Bangladesh.

Katharina P. Coleman is Associate Professor in the Department of Political Science at the University of British Columbia, Canada.

Donald C. F. Daniel is a Professor in the Security Studies Program of the School of Foreign Service at Georgetown University, Washington, DC, and a fellow in the School's Center for Security Studies.

Cedric de Coning is a Research Fellow with the Norwegian Institute of International Affairs (NUPI) and a peacekeeping and peacebuilding adviser for the African Center of the Constructive Resolution of Disputes (ACCORD). He is also a special adviser to the Head of the Peace Support Operations Division of the African Union and a member of the Advisory Group for the UN Peacebuilding Fund.

Bates Gill, the Director of the Stockholm International Peace Research Institute (SIPRI) from 2007 to 2012, is the Chief Executive Officer of the United States Studies Centre at the University of Sydney, Australia.

Chin-Hao Huang is an Associate Research Fellow with the Stockholm International Peace Research Institute (SIPRI) China and Global Security Programme and currently completing his Ph.D. at the University of Southern California, USA.

Katsumi Ishizuka is Professor in the Department of International Business Management at Kyoei University, Japan.

Kai Michael Kenkel is Assistant Professor at the Institute of International Relations of the Pontifical Catholic University of Rio de Janeiro, Brazil.

Walter Lotze works in the Peace Support Operations Division of the African Union Commission. Prior to joining the African Union, he worked for civil society and research organizations focused on peace and security in Africa.

Inam-ur-Rahman Malik is serving as Superintendent of Police in the Police Service of Pakistan and has served in the United Nations mission in Timor-Leste.

Alexander Nikitin is Director of the Centre for Euro-Atlantic Security of the Moscow State Institute of International Relations and President of the Russian Political Science Association.

Nil S. Satana is Associate Professor in the Department of International Relations at Bilkent University, Ankara, Turkey.

Adam C. Smith is a Research Fellow in the International Peace Institute, New York City, USA.

Arturo C. Sotomayor is Assistant Professor in the Department of National Security Affairs, School of International Graduate Studies at the Naval Postgraduate School, Monterey, USA.

Thierry Tardy is Faculty Member and Head of Research at the Geneva Centre for Security Policy (GCSP), Switzerland.

Paul D. Williams is Associate Professor in the Elliott School of International Affairs at the George Washington University, Washington DC, USA.

Rashed Uz Zaman is Associate Professor in the Department of International Relations at the University of Dhaka, Bangladesh.

Introduction: The Politics and Challenges of Providing Peacekeepers

Alex J. Bellamy and Paul D. Williams

Once again, United Nations (UN) peacekeeping stands at a political crossroads: it faces a future characterized by 'strategic uncertainty' and the need to consolidate its operations after the dramatic surge experienced during the 2000s.[1] During the first decade of the twenty-first century, the rising demand for peacekeepers saw the UN operate at a historically unprecedented tempo, with increases in the number and size of missions as well as in the scope and complexity of their mandates. The need to deploy over 120,000 UN peacekeepers and the demands placed upon them in the field have threatened to outstrip the willingness and to some extent capacity of the UN's member states. As UN Secretary-General Ban Ki-moon acknowledged in February 2011, 'Securing the required resources and troops [for UN peacekeeping] has consumed much of my energy. I have been begging leaders to make resources available to us.'[2]

This situation raises the questions of why states contribute forces to UN-led missions and, conversely, what factors inhibit them from doing more?[3] This book is an attempt to answer these questions. In this introductory chapter we do three things: first, we examine the challenges the UN faces when generating forces for its peacekeeping operations; second, we explain

[1] See Bruce Jones et al., *Building on Brahimi: Peacekeeping in an Era of Strategic Uncertainty* (New York: NYU Center on International Cooperation, April 2009) and 'UN peacekeeping in consolidation phase, says top official', UN News Centre, 6 August 2010 at http://www.un.org/apps/news/story.asp?NewsID=35558&Cr=le+roy&Cr1

[2] Ban Ki-moon, Cyril Foster Lecture, University of Oxford, 2 February 2011, at http://www.un.org/News/Press/docs/2011/sgsm13385.doc.htm

[3] Among the most relevant book-length studies are Trevor Findlay (ed.), *Challenges for the New Peacekeepers* (Oxford: Oxford University Press/SIPRI, 1996); David S. Sorenson and Pia Christina Wood (eds.), *The Politics of Peacekeeping in the Post-Cold War Era* (Abingdon: Frank Cass, 2005); Donald C. F. Daniel et al. (eds.), *Peace Operations: Trends, Progress, and Prospects* (Washington, DC: Georgetown University Press, 2008).

why attempts to develop a general, causal theory of why states provide peacekeepers have proved unsatisfactory; and, third, we outline the approach taken in the rest of the book. In two concluding chapters, we develop a new framework for analysing these issues based on the material presented in the book's case study chapters and we offer some recommendations about how the UN can broaden and deepen its pool of contributors in order to meet its future peacekeeping challenges.

THE CHALLENGE

The task of providing peacekeepers continues to be met in a highly unequal manner with well over two-thirds of all UN uniformed personnel coming from just twenty or so countries. Among the top ten contributors of uniformed personnel to UN missions during the twenty-first century are four South Asian states (Pakistan, Bangladesh, India, and Nepal), three African states (Nigeria, Ghana, and Kenya), and one each from the Middle East (Jordan), South America (Uruguay), and the former Soviet Union (Ukraine).[4] Of these top ten, one of the largest contributors (Pakistan) was beset with major internal armed conflict and domestic strife and five others faced serious domestic problems or armed conflicts (India, Nepal, Bangladesh, Kenya, and Nigeria). Over the same time period, the world's most stable and prosperous governments in the Western world—which also possess most of the world's high-end military capabilities—significantly reduced the numbers of troops they contributed to UN-led peace operations.[5]

Fulfilling the demand for more and better peacekeepers poses a serious challenge for the future of UN peacekeeping. As Birger Heldt has put it,

> contributions to UN operations mainly come from a handful of large and poor countries.... [S]hould these countries change their policies, the UN will face a challenge to find replacements for their contributions. This means that the UN needs to consider how to diversify the pool of its contributors so that it becomes less dependent on a few countries. This is one of the larger issues for the future of peacekeeping.[6]

[4] Based on data provided by the UN Department of Peacekeeping Operations at http://www.un.org/en/peacekeeping/contributors/. This ranking was calculated by taking the number of uniformed personnel contributed by a state to UN-led peacekeeping operations during each month of December for the years 2000 through 2010. Points were awarded to each contributor in the top ten for each year (i.e., 10 for 1st place, 9 for 2nd place, etc.). The combined total of these scores were then ranked to produce the top ten contributor states.

[5] Alex J. Bellamy and Paul D. Williams, 'The West and Contemporary Peace Operations', *Journal of Peace Research*, 46:1 (2009), pp. 39–57.

[6] Birger Heldt, 'Trends from 1948 to 2005: How to View the Relation between United Nations and Non-UN entities', in Daniel et al. (eds.), *Peace Operations*, p. 26.

In addition, as Donald Daniel points out in Chapter 1 of this volume, the available pool of UN peacekeepers is heavily influenced by the fact that there is a relatively fixed stock of global military resources suitable for UN peacekeeping. This stock is significantly smaller than often surmised with Daniel estimating that the ceiling might be around 210,000 troops. Key limiting factors include the presence of large numbers of conscripts in many armies, rotation demands, the increasing training and expertise requirements associated with UN peacekeeping, and the suitability of forces for peacekeeping.

Political decisions about whether to contribute forces to UN peacekeeping must also be considered because states have choices about where to send their troops. While the 2000s saw a significant increase in the number of peacekeepers deployed by various coalitions of states and international organizations—including the UN, NATO, the European Union, and the African Union—the range of alternative institutional vehicles for conducting peacekeeping operations means the UN has to compete for personnel. The UN's principal competitors are NATO, the European Union, Western-led coalitions of the willing, and, to a lesser extent, the African Union. The result, according to the former Under-Secretary-General for Peacekeeping, Alain Le Roy, is that, 'it is probably inevitable that the UN will be the organization of last resort, when others either cannot gain the necessary consensus, or maintain the staying power over the long term, or indeed where no one major actor has enough abiding interest but the world must nevertheless act'.[7]

The UN's leadership and at least some of its member states seem to understand the problem. The Secretary-General, for example, warned that while 'those who mandate [UN] missions, those who contribute uniformed personnel and those who are major funders are separate groups . . . tensions and divisions are inevitable, with potentially negative impacts on our operations'.[8] Guatemala's Permanent Representative to the UN described the situation in less diplomatic terms, as 'an accident waiting to happen'.[9] It was in this context that the UN's Departments of Peacekeeping Operations (DPKO) and Field Support (DFS) launched their 'New Horizon' initiative which in 2009 called for 'an expanded base of troop- and police-contributing countries . . . to enhance collective burden-sharing and to meet future requirements'.[10] The following year, the General Assembly's Special Committee on Peacekeeping Operations (C34) also emphasized the need to 'expand the available pool of capabilities' for peacekeeping. To achieve

[7] Alain Le Roy, 'Look Forward: Peace Operations in 2020', in Thierry Tardy (ed.), *For a Renewed Consensus on UN Peacekeeping Operations* (Geneva: GCSP, 2011), p. 21.

[8] Speech to the UN Security Council, 26 August 2011, at www.un.org/apps/news/infocus/sgspeeches/statments_full.asp?statID=1275

[9] S/PV.6603, 26 August 2011, p. 24.

[10] *A New Partnership Agenda: Charting a New Horizon for UN Peacekeeping* (New York: UN DPKO/DFS, July 2009), p. vi.

this goal, the Committee called upon the UN Secretariat to analyse 'the willingness and readiness' of contributing countries and 'to develop outreach strategies' in order to strengthen contacts and longer-term relationships with current or potential contributing countries, encourage further contributions from existing contributors, and provide practical support to emerging contributors.[11]

In our view, 'expanding the pool of available capabilities' for UN-led operations means doing four main things. First, persuading more countries to move from making primarily token contributions[12] to becoming major contributors of UN peacekeepers, namely, being able to provide sustained contributions of more than 2,000 troops/police. Second, persuading Western (and other) states with relevant capabilities—such as the European Union's battle groups—to deploy them in order to fulfil specialist peacekeeping functions. Third, persuading current major contributors to sustain or expand their contributions while also improving the performance capabilities of their deployed forces. Fourth, persuading some contributors to purchase or develop relevant specialist/niche capabilities which they either do not currently possess or do not have in surplus, and to contribute them to UN peacekeeping operations. If the UN is to achieve these goals and expand the pool of peacekeepers to meet the challenges of the twenty-first century it will need to understand the factors that motivate or inhibit contributions producing such varied outcomes among its member states. The following section summarizes existing attempts to theorize about why states provide UN peacekeepers.

(PROBLEMATIC) GENERAL EXPLANATIONS

There have been numerous attempts to develop a general theory of UN peacekeeping contributions. We think all of them have failed. Some simply fail to cope with the profound variation in state behaviour related to peacekeeping. Other accounts which are presented as general theories are really descriptions of past behaviour translated into predictions about future behaviour and confuse statistical correlations with causal explanations.[13] Indeed, the

[11] Report of the Special Committee on Peacekeeping Operations 2010 substantive session (22 February–19 March 2010), General Assembly Official Records 64th Session, Supplement No. 19 (A/64/19, 2010), paragraph 75. See also Report of the Special Committee on Peacekeeping Operations 2011 substantive session (22 February–18 March and 9 May 2011), General Assembly Official Records 65th Session, Supplement No. 19 (A/65/19, 2011), paragraph 74.

[12] In Chapter 2 of this book, Katarina Coleman defines tokenism as providing fewer than 40 people to a mission who do not form a specialized team/unit.

[13] For instance, finding a correlation between democracy and peacekeeping contributions, James Lebovic claimed that 'a country's level of democracy explains both its [peacekeeping]

persistent attempts to construct a general theory probably owe as much to the professional incentive structure in academic International Relations, which pushes scholars to claim generalizable conclusions, than to any genuine conviction that such a theory is possible.[14]

This section examines four of the most prominent approaches and suggests that while they offer useful insights each falls short of offering a persuasive general theory. This suggests to us that while much can be learned by understanding general patterns and trends the quest for a general *causal* explanation is illusory. Ultimately, this is because decisions are shaped by the particular political context in which they are taken, derive from multiple factors which change over time, are made by individuals, and therefore display a significant degree of idiosyncrasy.[15] Consequently, the best we can hope for is an approach which can convey the types of structures and processes that inform decision-making and provide a framework for comparison across cases that facilitates better understanding of how decisions are taken in individual countries as well as any general trends or patterns.

Realist-Inspired Accounts

Realist-inspired explanations hold that states provide peacekeepers for self-interested reasons.[16] As Trevor Findlay put it, states participate because it is 'decidedly in their national security interests'.[17] Such self-interest is commonly expressed in two ways. First, because peacekeeping contributions are understood to be more a traditional exercise of foreign policy than a charitable act, states whose interests are better served by maintaining the prevailing status quo are thought more likely to participate in peace operations than those whose interests favour fundamental change. Second, states are also likely to provide peacekeepers as a 'self-interested action to establish, preserve or increase [their] position and power base in the world'.[18]

From this perspective, states see peacekeeping as a relatively inexpensive way of enhancing their prestige. Hence relatively 'safe' missions such as

participation and contribution levels'. James H. Lebovic, 'Uniting for Peace? Democracies and United Nations Peace Operations after the Cold War', *Journal of Conflict Resolution*, 48:6 (2004), p. 928.

14 See J. Samuel Barkin, *Realist Constructivism: Rethinking International Relations Theory* (Cambridge: Cambridge University Press, 2010), p. 150.

15 See, for example, the case of Nigeria in Chapter 11 of this book.

16 Laura Neack, 'UN Peace-keeping: In the Interest of Community or Self?', *Journal of Peace Research*, 32:2 (1995), pp. 181–96; Laura Neack, 'Multilateral Responses to Risky States: The Case of UN Peacekeeping', in Gerald Schneider and Patricia A. Weitsman (eds.), *Risky States and the Intergovernmental Management of Conflict* (New York: St. Martin's Press, 1997).

17 Trevor Findlay, 'Introduction', in Findlay (ed.), *Challenges for the New Peacekeepers*, p. 8.

18 Neack, 'UN Peace-keeping', p. 188.

UNAVEM II in Angola and UNMIH in Haiti were oversubscribed with willing contributors.[19] Moreover, peace operations were dominated by Western 'middle powers' during the Cold War because these states calculated that their material interests were best served by the status quo and participation would bring international recognition of their special role in world politics, thereby enhancing their position in the international system.[20] 'Middle powers' such as Canada, Sweden, Norway, and Australia thus became reliable contributors to UN peace operations because they believed it was a 'positional good'. The prestige derived from providing peacekeepers bolstered their influence on international security issues and facilitated the pursuit of foreign policy goals, including participation in exclusive clubs like the G8 or G20 or the acquisition of Security Council membership that would otherwise have been beyond their reach.[21]

Realist-inspired approaches offer similar self-interested explanations for why non-Western states provide peacekeepers. Thus, India's participation is explained by reference to the enhanced 'international status' it derived from such activities.[22] Likewise, Nigeria's decision to shoulder the burden of peace enforcement and peacekeeping in Liberia and Sierra Leone has been explained by reference to its ambition for a permanent seat on the UN Security Council.[23]

[19] Findlay, 'Introduction', p. 9.

[20] As Richard Bruneau points out, there is an internal contradiction here. On the one hand, middle powers are assumed to be supporting the status quo. On the other, however, they are trying to reform the international system to increase their own influence. They are therefore purportedly both pro-status quo and reformist at the same time. Richard Bruneau, *Selfishness in Service of the Common Good: Why States Participate in UN Peacekeeping* (Canada: Norman Paterson School of International Affairs, 24 November 2004), p. 16.

[21] See Andrew Cooper, *Niche Diplomacy: Middle Powers After the Cold War* (New York: St. Martin's Press, 1997); Sean M. Maloney, *Canada and UN Peacekeeping* (St. Catherine's: Vanwell Publishing, 2001); Hans Kammler, 'Not for Security Only: The Demand for International Status and Defence Expenditure', *Defence and Peace Economics*, 8:1 (1997), pp. 1–16; Ugurhan G. Berkok, 'Third-Country Demand for Peacekeeping', *Defence and Peace Economics*, 17:5 (2006), p. 474.

[22] For instance, Ramesh Thakur, 'Peacekeeping and Foreign Policy: Canada, India and the International Commission in Vietnam, 1954–1965', *British Journal of International Studies*, 6 (1980), pp. 125–53; Swadesh Rana, 'Changing Indian Diplomacy at the United Nations', *International Organization*, 24:1 (1970), pp. 48–73; Kabilan Krishnasamy, 'Recognition for Third World Peacekeepers: India and Pakistan', *International Peacekeeping*, 8:4 (2001), pp. 56–76; Kabilan Krishnasamy, 'The Paradox of India's Peacekeeping', *Contemporary Southeast Asia*, 12:2 (2003), pp. 263–80. While the pursuit of prestige and influence was clearly significant, Nehru's political philosophy with its doctrine of non-alignment and commitment to the UN was also surely important. See Alan Bullion, 'India and UN Peacekeeping Operations', *International Peacekeeping*, 4:1 (1997), pp. 98–114.

[23] Eric G. Berman, 'The Security Council's Increasing Reliance on Burden-Sharing: Collaboration or Abrogation?', *International Peacekeeping*, 5:1 (1998), p. 4. Other accounts suggest that regional political considerations were more important. See Adekeye Adebajo, *Liberia's Civil War* (Boulder, CO: Lynne Rienner, 2002) and *Building Peace in West Africa* (Boulder, CO: Lynne Rienner, 2002).

Finally, realist-inspired accounts suggest that states provide peacekeepers to influence UN decision-making to their advantage. As Laura Neack put it, 'these states use their control over the UN to keep it out of regions considered to be their own spheres of influence and thus controllable'.[24]

We think realist-inspired accounts suffer from several major problems. First, they do not explain variations in the behaviour of 'middle powers' and non-Western countries that might be thought likely to benefit from international prestige.[25] If 'middle powers' advanced their interests by participating in peace operations what accounts for the significant variation in their behaviour? According to Neack's dataset, Canada participated in seventeen Cold War peace operations, whereas the Netherlands participated in seven and Belgium only four. Sharp variations were also evident between Nordic states during the 1990s: Iceland barely participated; Denmark contributed to a small number of missions and exhibited a clear geographic preference but when it did contribute it deployed significant numbers of troops; Finland's contribution was similar to Denmark's; Norway contributed significant numbers of personnel to many missions that were widely dispersed; Sweden also contributed to many missions that were geographically dispersed, but its contributions tended to be small.[26] Realism cannot explain why states with similar characteristics—and therefore presumably similar interests—have such different peacekeeping records.[27] Similarly, if the pursuit of international prestige and influence during the Cold War was a key motivating factor for non-Western states how do we explain major disparities between India (eleven missions) and Pakistan (four missions)?[28] And after the Cold War, what explains why so many countries decided to participate in UN peace operations for the first time?

Second, there is little direct evidence that contribution decisions are guided by self-interest alone. Sometimes evidence points in the opposite direction—that soldiers are dispatched in the absence of core national interests, a fact which can create its own problems when troops are deployed into hostile environments.[29] For example, even if Canada developed its 'middle power'

[24] Neack, 'UN Peace-keeping', p. 168.

[25] A problem noted by Arturo C. Sotomayor Velásquez, 'Why Some States Participate in UN Peace Missions While Others Do Not: An Analysis of Civil–Military Relations and its Effects on Latin America's Contributions to Peacekeeping Operations', *Security Studies*, 19:1 (2010), p. 169.

[26] See Andreas Andersson, 'The Nordic Peace Support Operations Record, 1991–1999', *International Peacekeeping*, 14:4 (2007), pp. 476–92.

[27] See Bellamy and Williams, 'The West'.

[28] Although it participated in UN missions, only after the end of the Cold War did UN peacekeeping become a significant feature of Pakistani foreign and defence policy. See Krishnasamy, 'Recognition for Third World Peacekeepers', p. 57.

[29] See the discussion in Nicholas J. Wheeler, *Saving Strangers: Humanitarian Intervention in International Society* (Oxford: Oxford University Press, 2000), pp. 299–310.

doctrine in order to extend its international influence—a view which is contested—there is little evidence that other so-called 'middle powers' such as the Nordic states or Ireland were driven primarily by a desire to extend influence.[30] In the absence of direct evidence, the realist-inspired case draws upon inferences, one of the most significant being the uneven geographic distribution of peace operations, which is taken as evidence that the great powers protect their own areas of influence from UN involvement while utilizing the UN in contested regions. But in pointing to the geographic distribution of UN peace operations, the realist-inspired position confuses permanent membership of the Security Council with participation in peace operations. The US and Soviet Union both clearly preferred to keep the UN out of their spheres of influence but their capacity to do this derived from their status as permanent members of the UN Security Council and was entirely unrelated to their level of participation in peacekeeping operations themselves (which was non-existent).[31] Moreover, this line of argument may be convincing in the Western hemisphere and Eastern Europe during the Cold War, but is much less so in other regions such as Africa and Southeast Asia.[32] In the latter regions, regional groupings and ad hoc coalitions of states engaged in peace operations and the reluctance to pursue peacekeeping through the UN was as much a product of local concerns about the principle of non-interference and preferences for regional responses as it was a product of great power reticence or blocking. Finally, the realist-inspired claim is contradicted by analysis which suggests that the UN was *more likely* to deploy peacekeepers

[30] Laura Neack's realist-inspired account of middle power peacekeeping is almost entirely derived from inferences from the Canadian case. She makes particular use of J. L. Granastein, 'Peacekeeping: Did Canada Make a Difference and What Difference Did Canada Make to Peacekeeping?' in John England and Norman Hillmer (eds.), *Making a Difference: Canada's Foreign Policy in a Changing World Order* (Toronto: Lester Publishing, 1992). Walter Dorn offers a different perspective and suggests that Canadian participation was largely driven by a belief that UN operations could strengthen international peace and security. See Walter A. Dorn, 'Canadian Peacekeeping: Proud Tradition, Strong Future?', *Canadian Foreign Policy*, 12:2 (2005), pp. 7–32. Evidence from Ireland suggests that a genuine commitment to the UN system as a source of international peace and security was critical. See Norrie MacQueen, *Peacekeeping and the International System* (London: Routledge, 2006), pp. 16–17; Ray Murphy, 'Ireland, the United Nations and Peacekeeping Operations', *International Peacekeeping*, 5:1 (1998), pp. 22–45. Norway, meanwhile, viewed peacekeeping as an important element of peacemaking. See Torunn Laugen Haaland, 'Participation in Peace Support Operations for Small Countries: The Case of Norway', *International Peacekeeping*, 14:4 (2007), p. 496.

[31] This was recognized at the time. See Francis O. Wilcox, 'Regionalism and the United Nations', *International Organization*, 19:3 (1965), pp. 789–811 and John Ruggie, 'Contingencies, Constraints and Collective Security: Perspectives on UN Involvement in International Disputes', *International Organization*, 28:2 (1974), pp. 498–503. Towards the end of the Cold War, the US administration blocked the proposed deployment of UN peacekeepers to Guatemala. See William J. Durch, 'Introduction', in William J. Durch (ed.), *The Evolution of UN Peacekeeping* (New York: St. Martin's Press, 1993).

[32] Neack makes this claim in 'UN Peace-keeping', p. 168.

in internal conflicts where permanent members of the Security Council thought their national interests were at stake.[33]

Third, the realist-inspired argument is circular and at best simply rules out the possibility that states will intentionally act contrary to their perceived interests. Rather than explaining behaviour, it begs fundamental questions about how states define their interests in the first place. As constructivist scholars have shown, social actors do not have pre-given interests.[34] Rather, interests are socially constructed, that is, they are forged in the interplay between material conditions and ideational factors such as identity (we cannot know what we want until we know who we are), normative values (we cannot know what we want until we know what we cherish), and shared local, regional, and global norms (we cannot know what we want until we know what it is appropriate for an actor with a given identity to want).[35] To understand variation in peacekeeping contributions we must understand variation in the way states construct their interests.

An argument related to the realist-inspired account suggests that some states, especially developing states such as Bangladesh and Fiji, contribute troops to UN peace operations for financial reward, namely, UN compensation rates might be higher than deployment costs and participation gives the added bonus of access to foreign currency.[36] Some countries, such as Finland and Nigeria, pass these benefits onto their peacekeepers in the form of additional allowances while others channel them, in whole or in part, into the national accounts.[37] But while financial benefits may be a significant factor for some states they are not a general cause of peacekeeping contributions more broadly. First, some developing states that contribute peacekeepers see it as an additional burden on scarce resources.[38] Specifically, the higher demands

[33] Chantal de Jonge Oudraat, 'The United Nations and Internal Conflicts', in Michael E. Brown (ed.), *The International Dimensions of Internal Conflict* (Cambridge, MA: MIT Press, 1996), pp. 518–19.

[34] See Alexander Wendt, *Social Theory of International Relations* (Cambridge: Cambridge University Press, 1999), pp. 169–70.

[35] As Martha Finnemore put it, 'states are embedded in dense networks of transnational and international social relations that shape their perceptions of the world and their role in that world. States are socialised to want certain things.' Martha Finnemore, *National Interests in International Society* (Ithaca, NY: Cornell University Press, 1996), p. 2.

[36] Ramesh Thakur, 'Ministate and Macrocooperation: Fiji's Peacekeeping Debut in Lebanon', *Review of International Studies*, 10:4 (1984), p. 284. Thakur does recognize other factors are important too, including Fiji's realization that the protection of small states depends on the viability of the UN. By 1996, Bangladesh had received a total of $154 million in UN payments. Kabilan Krishnasamy, 'Bangladesh and UN Peacekeeping: The Participation of a "Small" State', *Commonwealth and Comparative Studies*, 41:1 (2003), p. 37.

[37] See Alex Morrison, 'UN Peacekeeping Reform: Something Permanent and Stronger', *Brown Journal of World Affairs*, 3:1 (1996), pp. 95–110.

[38] Referring to Argentina at the beginning of the twenty-first century, see Cynthia A. Watson, 'Argentina', in Sorenson and Wood (eds.), *The Politics of Peacekeeping*, p. 64.

placed on peacekeepers require investment in training and equipment that are not wholly covered by the UN's compensation scheme.[39] Moreover, the UN's almost permanent financial crisis causes delays in reimbursements, making it an unreliable source of income and forcing contributing countries to bear financial risks in the interim. As Trevor Findlay concluded, 'the UN is usually so slow in paying and the amount so relatively niggardly that this cannot be a sole motivating factor' for peacekeeping contributions.[40] For example, in 2000, Pakistan was owed some $50 million in unpaid reimbursements and Bangladesh received around 25 per cent of its reimbursement three years late.[41] Second, up to the mid-1990s, per capita UN reimbursements were significantly higher than the marginal costs of deploying troops even from advanced Western states. This made it virtually impossible to determine which examples of state behaviour were affected by reimbursement rates and which were not.[42] Third, with the exception of very small states such as Uruguay and Nepal, the revenue raised by peacekeeping is negligible relative to the size of national economies.[43] Finally, if peacekeeping was a lucrative business for contributors then why were more developing states not engaged in peacekeeping earlier? For example, if Fiji profited financially by providing UN peacekeepers, why did Tonga not contribute at all and why have Vanuatu and Samoa contributed only a handful of police officers?

[39] The UN offers two broad categories of compensation payments for countries participating in peacekeeping operations: payments to individuals and payments for equipment and assets. Peacekeeping troops are paid by their home governments according to their own national rank and salary scale. Their governments are reimbursed by the UN at a flat rate of just over US$1,028 per soldier per month (approved by the General Assembly in 2002). All international civilian staff, civilian police, and military observers assigned to a UN peacekeeping operation are entitled to a Mission Subsistence Allowance (MSA). This is a daily allowance paid by the UN for living expenses incurred in the field in connection with their temporary assignment to the mission. MSA rates vary according to the mission in question. With regard to equipment and assets, since 1996, every troop- and police-contributing country (TCC/PCC) signs a memorandum of understanding with the UN for every formed military or police united deployed to a peacekeeping operation. The memorandum details the major equipment, self-sustainment services, and personnel for which the contributing country is entitled to be financially reimbursed. A distinction is usually made between 'wet lease' arrangements, whereby TCCs/PCCs would provide major equipment and maintenance, and 'dry lease' arrangements, whereby TCCs/PCCs provide only major equipment with the UN or another third party assuming responsibility for maintenance.

[40] Findlay, 'Introduction', p. 9.

[41] Kabilan Krishnasamy, 'Pakistan's Peacekeeping Experience', *International Peacekeeping*, 9:3 (2002), p. 112; Krishnasamy, 'Bangladesh and UN Peacekeeping', p. 37.

[42] Victoria K. Holt, 'Reforming UN Peacekeeping: The US Role and the UN Financial Crisis', *Brown Journal of World Affairs*, 3:1 (1996), pp. 125–34.

[43] Krishnasamy, 'Recognition for Third World Peacekeepers', p. 57; Krishnasamy, 'Pakistan's Peacekeeping Experience', p.112. In the late 1990s, compensation rates delivered $12–15 million per 1,000 troops deployed for twelve months. This has since increased, but not at a rate faster than inflation.

An alternative variant on the same theme has suggested that since most peacekeepers came from developing (aid-receiving) states, contributions to UN missions could be explained by an 'aid imperative' wherein the troop contributors were 'increasingly driven by financial and development motives'.[44] This approach, though, suffers from similar problems to those identified above: it cannot explain why the aid motive works for some developing states but not others; nor can it explain why this imperative became operative only in the past twenty years.

Liberal accounts

Unlike realists, liberals focus on principled considerations to explain peacekeeping contributions. They believe progress is possible and that states will cooperate for mutual gain, even when the burdens and benefits are distributed unequally.[45] Liberal accounts emphasize that democratic states are more likely to participate in peace operations than non-democratic states and that the increased number of troop-contributing countries after the Cold War is connected to the global spread of democracy.[46] One strand of this literature suggests that democratic states are particularly likely to view participation in UN peacekeeping as offering political benefits and hence 'a country's level of democracy accounts for why and how much countries contributed' to peace operations.[47]

Democratic peace theory posits three reasons why democracies have particular incentives to provide peacekeepers. First, their legitimacy derives from liberal principles so they more readily accept the proposition that individuals have inalienable rights that must be promoted and protected everywhere. Second, democratic theorists and leaders typically believe that democracy and humanitarianism can be exported and that these principles are not easily separated from self-interest.[48] That is because democratic governments have a shared interest in creating the conditions in which 'peace, prosperity and democracy' can thrive. Third, democracies are thought to be more likely to

[44] James H. Lebovic, 'Passing the Burden: Contributions to UN Peace Operations in the Post-Cold War Era', unpublished paper, July 2010, on file with the authors.

[45] See Robert Keohane and Lisa Martin, 'The Promise of Institutionalist Theory', *International Security*, 20:1 (1995), pp. 39–51.

[46] On this empirical point, see Donald C. F. Daniel, Katrin Heuel, and Benjamin Margo, 'Distinguishing Among Military Contributors', in Daniel et al (eds.), *Peace Operations*, pp. 27–46. See also Lebovic, 'Uniting for Peace?' and Donald C.F. Daniel and Leigh C. Caraher, 'Characteristics of troop contributors to peace operations and implications for global capacity', *International Peacekeeping*, 13:3 (2006), pp. 297–315. It should be noted that the authors do not tie this to a liberal account of why states contribute.

[47] Lebovic, 'Uniting for Peace?', p. 910.

[48] Lebovic, 'Uniting for Peace?', p. 912.

join international organizations and to cooperate with each other to achieve common goals, such as peace and security.[49]

Democratic governments are therefore well-disposed towards peacekeeping because they believe it fosters peace and helps spread democracy and human rights.[50] But such a disposition does not always translate into peacekeeping contributions. As such, the link between democracy and participation in peace operations is 'probabilistic' at best.

Democracies were the principal contributors of troops during the Cold War and remain an important, though significantly diminished, source of troops.[51] Andersson claims that the level of participation in UN peace operations increases as the level of democracy within contributing states increases.[52] But this approach cannot explain variation across democracies, inconsistent contributions by one democracy, or the contributions of non-democracies. It is also difficult to isolate democracy from other potential factors such as regional security cultures. For example, the assertion that the post-Cold War spread of democracy was associated with an increase in the number of countries willing to provide UN peacekeepers relies on the proliferation of Eastern European troop contributors. But how do we know that it was *democratization* within these countries rather than, for example, their incorporation into Western Europe's regional security architecture that encouraged these states to contribute peacekeepers? Finally, the democracy thesis was disputed by a recent study of UN and non-UN peacekeeping contributions by forty-seven sub-Saharan African countries. This concluded that 'states that are poorer, with lower state legitimacy and lower political repression, participate more often in regional peacekeeping'. Specifically, the profile of an African state most likely to contribute to peacekeeping was 'a poor, less repressive, former British colony with low state legitimacy and a large military'.[53]

[49] See Jon C. Pevehouse, 'Democracy from the Outside-In? International Organizations and Democratization', *International Organization*, 56:3 (2002), pp. 515–49; Edward D. Mansfield and Jon C. Pevehouse, 'Democratization and International Organizations', *International Organization*, 60:1 (2006), pp. 137–67. On why states of all types find efficiencies in cooperating through international organizations see Kenneth W. Abbott and Duncan Snidal, 'Why States Act Through Formal International Organizations', *Journal of Conflict Resolution*, 42:1 (1998), pp. 3–32.

[50] See John M. Owen, 'How Liberalism Produces Democratic Peace', p. 118 and Christopher Layne, 'Kant or Cant: The Myth of the Democratic Peace', p. 198, both in Michael E. Brown, Sean M. Lynn-Jones, and Sean E. Miller (eds.), *Debating the Democratic Peace* (Cambridge, MA: MIT Press, 1996).

[51] See Andreas Andersson, 'United Nations Intervention by United Democracies? State Commitment to UN Intervention, 1991–1999', *Cooperation and Conflict*, 37:4 (2002), pp. 363–86, Daniel and Caraher, 'Characteristics of Troop Contributors'; and Daniel, Heuel, and Margo, 'Distinguishing Among Military Contributors', p. 32.

[52] The principal and very striking difference is between these two types and autocracies. See Andersson, 'United Nations Intervention'.

[53] Jonah Victor, 'African Peacekeeping in Africa', *Journal of Peace Research*, 47:2 (2010), pp. 217, 227.

Liberal institutionalists emphasize that multilateral cooperation through endeavours such as UN peace operations spreads the risks and costs, offers advantages of scale and efficiency, provides political legitimacy through the legitimating functions of international organizations, dilutes potential opposition, and allows states to monitor and control the behaviour of other participants.[54] Such cooperation helps achieve long-term gains, which explains why states are sometimes prepared to forgo short-term advantages by contributing. Most obviously, from this perspective, cooperation in peace operations helps maintain international order and establish the conditions needed for mutual prosperity through trade.

Liberal institutionalism does offer a general explanation for why states cooperate to foster peace in ways that do not deliver direct pay-offs: it helps maintain international peace and security. Allied concepts such as 'free-riding' (whereby some states choose to benefit from collective goods without contributing to their provision) and 'bandwagoning' (whereby some states simply follow the lead of more powerful states) go some way to explaining why, if cooperation and peacekeeping are self-evident collective goods, some states contribute while others do so only symbolically or not at all. But to the extent that these concepts explain variation, they beg rather than answer the key questions. *Why*, for instance, do some states free-ride while other, similar, states contribute more than their fair share? Why do some states contribute peacekeepers in one situation but not in another like-situation? Why do some states make token contributions to avoid the appearance of free-riding while others make larger contributions?

Impure public goods

Public goods theory suggests that states might produce collective goods through self-interested behaviour. If so, it overcomes the sharp distinction between self-interest and common interest that informs realist-inspired and, to a lesser extent, liberal approaches.[55] Pure public goods are joint and non-excludable: jointness means that consumption of the good by one actor does not diminish the amount of the good available for consumption by other

[54] See Keohane and Martin, 'The Promise of Institutionalist Theory', and Lisa Martin, 'Interests, Power and Multilateralism', *International Organization*, 46:4 (1992), pp. 765–92. On the legitimating effects of international organizations, specifically regional organizations, see Katharina P. Coleman, *International Organizations and Peace Enforcement* (Cambridge: Cambridge University Press, 2007).

[55] This is an account put forward by Davis B. Bobrow and Mark A. Boyer, 'Maintaining System Stability: Contributions to Peacekeeping Operations', *Journal of Conflict Resolution*, 41:6 (1997), pp. 723–48.

actors; non-excludability means that the good is available to all.[56] Bobrow and Boyer argue that in theory peace operations are pure public goods—their purpose is to halt armed conflict and prevent its recurrence. But if peace operations are pure public goods, they confront the collective action problem, i.e. while everyone would benefit from the provision of a collective good someone has to pay to provide it and therefore self-interested actors will either not provide the goods (because they do not want to bear the costs) or will provide an insufficient amount of the good.[57] This would seem to militate against states providing UN peacekeepers.

Others thought states were likely to contribute to the production of public goods when doing so brought them private benefits.[58] In relation to peacekeeping, private benefits may include the resolution of conflicts that directly damage a state's interests by harming trade; creating refugee flows or destabilizing political relations; the protection of friendly governments or rebel groups; and/or the acquisition of economic or social benefits. In this scenario, the goods provided are not pure public goods, but they are still public goods—Bobrow and Boyer describe them as 'impure public goods'. An additional source of impurity comes from the uneven geographical distribution of the goods produced by peace operations. Because individual peace operations are deployed in geographically limited areas, the peace and stability they produce are enjoyed more directly by those closest to them and only indirectly by those further away. Moreover, the public goods produced by peacekeeping (stability, creation of conditions conducive to trade, democracy, etc.) are disproportionately enjoyed by the dominant powers.[59]

States will thus provide peacekeepers when the provision of a public good is thought likely to also produce private goods for the contributor. According to Bobrow and Boyer, this means that those that are more likely to extract private good—according to them the great powers and so-called middle powers—are more likely to provide peacekeepers. So the increased participation of African states in UN peacekeeping since the end of the Cold War might be explained by the private benefits they draw from resolving violent conflicts in their neighbourhoods.[60] But it is important to recall that providing 'impure public

[56] The standard text on public goods on which this distinction is based is Richard Cornes and Todd Sandler, *The Theory of Externalities: Public Goods and Club Goods* (Cambridge: Cambridge University Press, 1996).

[57] See Mancur Olson, *Logic of Collective Action: Public Goods and the Theory of Groups* (Cambridge, MA: Harvard University Press, 1965).

[58] Todd Sandler, 'The Impurity of Defense: An Application to the Economics of Alliances', *Kyklos*, 30 (1977), pp. 443–60.

[59] Bobrow and Boyer, 'Maintaining System Stability', p. 727.

[60] This is in line with research showing a link between trading activity with the conflict region and likelihood of peacekeeping contributions. See J. Khanna, Todd Sandler, and H. Shimizu, 'The Demand for UN Peacekeeping: 1975–1996', *Kyklos*, 52:3 (1999), pp. 345–68. However, it is also important to note that the growth of African peacekeeping contributions owed a great deal

goods for the vast majority of affected parties' is 'different from [providing] purely private goods for a very few parties'.[61]

Public goods theory exposes the fallacy of thinking that self-interest and community-interest are mutually exclusive by reminding us that states often have mixed motives. Its principal weakness lies in the lack of empirical evidence for its central finding vis-à-vis great and middle powers.[62] Not only have some great powers contributed much less than their size and military capacity would lead us to expect, since the end of the Cold War middle powers have also been eclipsed as the principal source of troops.[63] A further weakness is its assumption that decisions to provide peacekeepers are primarily self-interested. Some qualitative research has concluded that, periodically, some of these states believed UN peacekeeping to be contrary to their interests.[64]

Bureaucratic disposition: civil–military relations

A fourth, more recent, theory suggests that decisions to deploy troops to UN peace operations are 'a result of internal processes', specifically 'civil-military and bureaucratic considerations'.[65] There is also a related argument that the size, quality, and posture of a state's armed forces are related to its contribution to UN peace operations, although clearly this is just one factor among several.[66] Sotomayor's bureaucratic explanation holds that where militaries are unwilling to participate, this serves as a powerful brake and forces political and civilian authorities to offer them enticements. Armed forces may be reluctant to participate in peace operations for several reasons, including a doctrinal focus on internal security or national defence from external threats, the lack of professional inducements, peacekeeping's focus on low-intensity operations and concomitant equipment, worries about UN command and control and force structure mechanisms, as well as the tendency to create difficult mandates in hostile environments. On the other hand, where the armed forces support peacekeeping—whether because it serves the national interest, enhances prestige, strengthens operational capacity, or delivers

to various forms of training and assistance packages provided by Western states, principally the US, UK, France, and the EU.

61 Bobrow and Boyer, 'Maintaining System Stability', p. 729.

62 Sotomayor, 'Why Some States Participate', p. 170.

63 Bellamy and Williams, 'The West'.

64 In the case of France, see Thierry Tardy, 'French Policy Towards Peace Support Operations', *International Peacekeeping*, 6:1 (1999), pp. 55–78. In 1958, the French President went so far as to declare the UN itself to be contrary to French interests.

65 Sotomayor, 'Why Some States Participate', p. 162.

66 Daniel, Heuel, and Margo, 'Distinguishing Among Military Contributors', p. 39; Donald C. F. Daniel, 'Why So Few Troops from Among so Many?' in Daniel et al. (eds.), *Peace Operations*, pp. 47–61.

financial rewards—it is more likely that the state will contribute.[67] In short, variations in the level of commitment to UN peacekeeping across countries can be explained in terms of the extent to which the military sees itself as externally oriented and how far defence and foreign policies are integrated.[68]

Although its evidence comes principally from three Latin American cases, this approach offers some important new insights. In particular, it stresses the interaction between international and domestic structures, the connection between a state's own threat environment and its proclivity to contribute peacekeepers, how military culture and civil–military relations constrain or enable contribution decisions, and that military institutions influence the level of commitment. But it does not explain everything, which is perhaps why Sotomayor describes it as a 'probabilistic' theory.[69]

First, some militaries that confront internal and external threats are major contributors to UN peace operations: Pakistan, Rwanda, Nepal, Nigeria, Ethiopia, Bangladesh, Sri Lanka, Indonesia, and South Korea stand out in this regard. Indeed, according to one account the growth of Pakistani peacekeeping after the Cold War coincided with a deterioration of its internal and external security situation.[70] So did Nepal's.[71] Second, the distinction between externally and internally oriented security doctrines is vague and difficult to operationalize globally. Many contributing countries employ their militaries for internal security while simultaneously contributing to peace operations. Third, the link between externally oriented security doctrines and peacekeeping contributions is not always clear. Ireland and New Zealand, for example, provide UN peacekeepers but do not actively seek to extend their influence overseas. Others that are more active around the world, militarily, diplomatically, and economically, have a patchier record when it comes to peacekeeping—the US, Russia, the UK, and China in particular. Fourth, while the armed forces contribute to policy-making, they do not determine it, except in military regimes. In the early 1990s, Argentina began participating in UN peace operations despite objections from the military, though over time the military came to endorse this new role through a combination of socialization

[67] On the potential military rewards from peacekeeping see Charles C. Moskos, *Peace Soldiers: The Sociology of a United Nations Military Force* (Chicago: University of Chicago Press, 1976); Findlay, 'Introduction', p. 9; Laura L. Miller, 'Do Soldiers Hate Peacekeeping? The Case of Preventive Diplomacy Operations in Macedonia', *Armed Forces and Society*, 23:3 (1997), pp. 415–19. Fiji presents a particularly useful case study of the various types of rewards, including financial, material, professional, and social. See Katsumi Ishizuka, 'Fiji: A Micro-State and its Peacekeeping Contribution', *Peacekeeping and International Relations*, 28:3 (1999), pp. 18–21.

[68] Sotomayor, 'Why Some States Participate', p. 162.

[69] Sotomayor, 'Why Some States Participate', p. 194.

[70] Krishnasamy, 'Recognition for Third World Peacekeepers', p. 57.

[71] See Chapter 13 this volume.

and domestic legitimation, institutional learning about how peacekeeping strengthened military professionalism, and material rewards.[72]

There are several other variants of institutionally focused explanations. Some see peacekeeping as attractive because it provides 'invaluable overseas experience' for the personnel concerned.[73] Others see participation in peacekeeping as a way of keeping the armed forces in praetorian states 'occupied outside of the country rather than meddling in domestic affairs' and perhaps rehabilitating them after a period of authoritarianism.[74] An alternative argument is that peacekeeping participation provides militaries with an acceptable, even prestigious role, thereby insulating them from full exposure to what might have been a more significant series of cuts brought on by the post-Cold War peace dividend. Sandra Whitworth goes as far as suggesting that 'Peacekeeping provides the rationale for a number of militaries that otherwise have no raison d'être.' In cases such as Argentina, Ireland, and Japan, 'peacekeeping serves as a form of insurance for post-Cold War militarism'.[75] A final variant of the institutional argument suggests that UN peacekeeping contributions exhibit a degree of path dependency inasmuch as peacekeeping activism can become a bureaucratic/institutional habit for particular states.[76] (This has been made easier by the increasing number of peacekeeping training centres which have been established around the globe since the mid-1990s.[77])

Summary

Our survey of the existing literature suggests that previous attempts to theorize why states provide UN peacekeepers are incapable of accounting for the wide variations in state behaviour largely because they rely on one or two causal factors. This is a fundamental flaw because, as Sotomayor argued, decisions about contributions are shaped by the interaction of a wide range of factors including domestic political forces, bureaucratic interests, personal idiosyncrasies, policies and relations, regional security cultures and contexts, and broader global facts, as well as a whole set of demand-side factors. Although some general trends and patterns are discernible, these factors

[72] Deborah L. Norden, 'Keeping the Peace, Outside and In: Argentina's UN Missions', *International Peacekeeping*, 2:3 (1995), pp. 330–49.

[73] Findlay, 'Introduction', p. 9.

[74] Findlay, 'Introduction', p. 9.

[75] Sandra Whitworth, *Men, Militarism and UN Peacekeeping: A Gendered Analysis* (Boulder, CO: Lynne Rienner, 2004), p. 25.

[76] Bobrow and Boyer, 'Maintaining System Stability', p. 731.

[77] For a list, see the International Association of Peacekeeping Training Centres at www.iaptc.org

interact in multiple ways in different contexts to produce varied outcomes. Hence the best way to proceed is to develop a framework that distinguishes the range of factors involved, posits suggestions about their relationship, but also includes empirical analysis of particular decision-making contexts. The following section outlines how we organized our attempt to develop such a framework.

RATIONALES FOR PROVIDING PEACEKEEPERS

In light of the preceding survey, we identified five clusters of potential (and non-mutually exclusive) motivating rationales for providing peacekeepers related to political, economic, security, institutional, and normative concerns. Each author of the case study chapters was asked to analyse their country's experience in light of the relative significance of these rationales. Particularly in countries without a recent track record of providing UN peacekeepers we adopted an inductive approach by inviting the contributors to reflect upon the principal inhibiting factors. We also suggested that it might be useful to distinguish between the *predispositions* states hold towards the UN and peacekeeping in general, and the specific *decisions* taken by their governments with respect to particular missions (a theme we return to in chapter 19). A positive disposition towards the UN or peacekeeping in general does not determine individual decisions about contributing to particular missions; these depend on specific state policies and commitments at particular moments in time. In similar fashion, even states which are not positively predisposed to UN peacekeeping might contribute if the right circumstances present themselves.

Political rationales: States might participate in peacekeeping because it helps them fulfil other political objectives. For example, a variety of states are said to find in UN peacekeeping missions, 'a niche that brings them greater respect and authority in international institutions, especially the UN, allowing them more voice in international security issues than they otherwise would'.[78] There are many political reasons why states might provide peacekeepers. Among the most prominent are: pressure or persuasion by allies, great powers, or the UN Secretary-General or Secretariat, and perceptions that peacekeeping contributions enhance the country's 'national prestige' or might strengthen its bid to acquire a non-permanent seat on the UN Security Council (or for some states, their bid for a permanent seat on a reformed Council).[79]

[78] Kimberly Zisk Marten cited in Sotomayor, 'Why Some States Participate', p. 169.
[79] Findlay, 'Introduction', pp. 7–9.

Economic rationales: The central argument here is that economic incentives represent an important rationale for providing UN peacekeepers.[80] One important element of this argument is the existence of the UN's system of compensation payments for member states which provide peacekeepers, which stands in stark contrast to most international organizations which have adopted a 'costs lie where they fall' approach. As we discussed above, while financial considerations often play a role in contribution decisions, we need to be clear about who precisely is meant to be benefiting. When discussing economic rationales for providing peacekeepers it is thus useful to distinguish between four principal types of beneficiary. First, national governments, particularly in developing states with small economies, might use UN compensation payments to support national budgets and their search for foreign currency. Second, national defence and security sectors might see in UN compensation payments for peacekeeping an opportunity to augment their budgets. Third, individuals, especially military and police officers, can benefit economically from UN peacekeeping deployments through mission subsistence allowances (especially for staff officers, military observers, and some police) and if the portion of the UN's compensation payment of $1,028 per soldier per month they receive from their national government significantly augments their domestic salary. Fourth, private firms and national corporations can profit from UN procurement contracts for goods as diverse as beef, bottled water, and air transportation.

Security rationales: Although UN-led peacekeeping operations are not typically associated with national defence or core national security interests, states are commonly thought to be more likely to provide peacekeepers when they believe this promotes their broader national security interests.[81] Thus the level of perceived threat posed by a particular conflict could be a major driver of contribution decisions.[82] Such threat mitigation can assume several forms including insuring against a bad outcome in a particular armed conflict—perhaps by supporting one of the conflict parties—or by helping to contain it (geographically or in terms of casualty levels). Geographical proximity is assumed to play a prominent role with peace operations being more likely to receive contributions from states in the immediate neighbourhood or region than those further afield. However, larger powers or those with more internationalist mindsets might understand their security interests in more global terms.

[80] See, for example, David Axe, 'Why South Asia Loves Peacekeeping', *The Diplomat*, 20 December 2010 at http://the-diplomat.com/2010/12/20/why-south-asia-loves-peacekeeping/

[81] Findlay, 'Introduction', p. 8.

[82] Vincenzo Bove and Leandro Elia, 'Supplying Peace: Participation in and Troop Contribution to Peacekeeping Missions', *Journal of Peace Research*, 48:6 (2011), pp. 699–714.

Institutional rationales: Participation in UN peacekeeping can stem from motives related to the country's armed forces, security sector, and bureaucratic dynamics. After all, decisions to engage in UN operations are usually taken within the context of a nation's civil–military relations and are therefore affected by it.[83] There is also an argument that the size, quality, and posture of a state's armed forces are related to its contribution to UN peace operations, although clearly this is just one factor among several.[84] Moreover, some militaries see peacekeeping operations as attractive because they provide 'invaluable overseas experience' for the personnel concerned while others might view peacekeeping as a way of keeping the 'armed forces occupied outside of the country rather than meddling in domestic affairs' or of rehabilitating them after a period of authoritarian rule.[85] Alternatively, participation in UN peacekeeping operations could be seen as providing the armed forces in a variety of states (including Argentina and Uruguay) with a prestigious post-Cold War role, thereby insulating them from full exposure to what might have been a more significant series of cuts brought on by a post-Cold War peace dividend.[86]

Normative rationales: Countries might provide UN peacekeepers for normative reasons. Specifically, states with self-images as 'global good Samaritans', 'good international citizens', or as members of a 'non-aligned' group of states that supports the UN as an alternative to great power hegemony might be disposed to provide peacekeepers in part because they believe that it is the right thing to do. A variety of subtly different normative rationales can be identified. 'Good Samaritans' identify with the suffering of others and contribute to peacekeeping efforts because it promotes the greater good.[87] For example, since the genocide in 1994, Rwanda has sought to champion the norm of genocide prevention, reflected in the fact that it has deployed over 90 per cent of its UN peacekeepers to help protect civilians in the Darfur region of Sudan.[88] Alternatively, some states maintain a principled commitment to the UN as they see it as the most legitimate system of conflict management and wish to play a supportive role as 'good international citizens'. Ghana stands out in this regard as a contributor that is normatively committed to the UN's peace and security goals to such an extent that it is written in the country's

[83] Sotomayor, 'Why Some States Participate'.

[84] Daniel, Heuel, and Margo, 'Distinguishing Among Military Contributors', p. 39; Daniel, 'Why So Few Troops'; and Daniel's contribution to this volume.

[85] Findlay, 'Introduction', p. 9. See also Elizabeth Dickinson, 'For Tiny Burundi, Big Returns in Sending Peacekeepers to Somalia', *Christian Science Monitor*, 22 December 2011.

[86] Whitworth, *Men, Militarism and UN Peacekeeping*, p. 25.

[87] Alison Brysk, *Global Good Samaritans: Human Rights as Foreign Policy* (Oxford: Oxford University Press, 2009).

[88] For a discussion, see Danielle Beswick, 'Peacekeeping, Regime Security, and "African Solutions to African Problems": Exploring Motivations for Rwanda's Involvement in Darfur', *Third World Quarterly*, 31:5 (2010), pp. 739–54.

constitution (see Chapter 12). A related view sees the UN system as worthy of support because it offers a fairer and preferable alternative to great power hegemony. India perhaps stands out as a contributor that sees the UN as an alternative to great power hegemony and vehicle for a non-aligned approach to peace and security but this view is increasingly apparent within other rising powers, especially Brazil and China.

STRUCTURE OF THIS BOOK

If the UN is to meet the challenges of twenty-first century peacekeeping by 'expanding the base' of its contributors, it will need a sophisticated understanding of why states do, or do not, provide peacekeepers. This book attempts to develop such an understanding. Although earlier attempts to develop general explanations have generated some important insights, none are wholly convincing. This is because contribution decisions are informed by a large number of often highly context-dependent factors. Consequently, the best analytical strategy is to develop a framework for analysis that identifies the key factors and provides a basis for comparison.

The framework developed in the book's concluding section emerged in light of the material presented in the following general and case study chapters. Part I of the book provides two chapters which analyse prominent general patterns: the first discusses how the provision of UN peacekeepers fits into broader trends in peace operations conducted by international institutions other than the UN; while the second discusses the pronounced pattern of token contributions to UN peacekeeping operations.

Parts II, III, and IV analyse the experience of three groups of contributing countries. Part II analyses the permanent five members of the UN Security Council, namely, the United States, the United Kingdom, France, the People's Republic of China, and the Russian Federation. Part III then analyses seven of the top contributors of uniformed peacekeepers during the first decade of the twenty-first century, namely, Bangladesh, Pakistan, India, Nigeria, Ghana, Nepal, and Uruguay. Part IV focuses on four 'emerging' or potentially more significant contributors, namely, Brazil, Turkey, South Africa, and Japan.

After reflecting on their country's experience, we also asked our authors to examine other issues. Specifically, we asked them to summarize the relevant historical background and the process by which national decisions about the provision of peacekeepers were made. While the former illuminates the role of past experience in shaping how different states view the merits and demerits of UN peacekeeping, the latter provides insights into the roles of relevant individuals, bureaucracies, and other aspects of domestic politics. The authors were also asked to consider those factors which had inhibited greater participation and to identify future challenges or opportunities that might affect the country's willingness to provide UN peacekeepers in the future.

In Part V, we begin with a chapter which outlines a new framework for understanding the central questions addressed in this book, namely, why do states contribute forces to UN missions and, conversely, what factors inhibit them from doing more? In the final chapter we offer some recommendations for how the UN might approach force generation issues so as to meet the foreseeable challenges of twenty-first-century peacekeeping and improve the quantity and quality of its uniformed peacekeepers.

Part I

Context

1

Contemporary Patterns in Peace Operations, 2000–2010

Donald C. F. Daniel

This chapter provides the backdrop for this book's analyses of the politics, challenges, and future of contributions of uniformed personnel to United Nations (UN) peacekeeping operations. Its starting point is that contributor countries have choices as to which organizations and missions to send their troops. Since the sharp rise in the number of peace operations in the 1990s and again in 2003, official decision-makers and informed observers have regularly lamented a lack of troops and resources relative to expressed mission requirements. As a result, the choices the contributors make are consequential to the UN. The UN wants to be chosen, and from that perspective, it is in a zero-sum competition with other organizations and choices. Observers and analyses that reflect this competitive perspective often decry the UN's lack of troops and resources compared with the troops and resources deploying to non-UN missions.[1] This chapter argues for a more nuanced view that justifies another perspective, one that posits that the UN has an impressive record of being chosen and that the key to better meeting mission requirements includes a cooperative (as opposed to a zero-sum) relationship between the UN and the non-UN entities that undertake peace operations. This perspective is grounded in the UN's comparative advantages in peacekeeping and on its indispensable role in a global division of peace operations labour.

[1] This is a long-standing theme. The next two citations summarize the comments made by UN troop contributors in two international meetings, one held in Washington in 2001 and the other at the United Nations in 2011. The venues and spokesmen were different, but the remarks were essentially identical. Donald C. F. Daniel, 'The Future of International Peace Operations', Report on international workshop held at the US Institute of Peace, Washington, DC, 9 and 10 July 2001. Co-sponsored by the National Intelligence Council, the UN Association of the USA, and the US Institute of Peace. UN Department of Public Information, 'Delegates Stress the Need to Correct Imbalance in "Division of Labour" as Special Committee on Peacekeeping Operations Concludes General Debate', loose minutes of the 219th and 220th Meetings of the (C34) Special Committee on Peacekeeping Operations, United Nations, New York, 23 February 2011.

Working from a database of designated contributors and contributions from 2001 through 2010, this chapter aggregates the mission choices made by contributor countries into three sets: (1) UN missions; (2) an interlaced group of 'Western' agendas missions; and (3) a mixed set of generally small and idiosyncratic missions that, with some notable exceptions, drew mostly on local contributors. The contributors to each set are collectively compared for their national military profiles—assessed by their ground force size and overall military potential—and their deployment profiles—defined by contributor weight (a composite of the size of a nation's contribution and the number of years it contributed), the global versus local orientation of contributors, and the number of states that de facto 'committed' to a choice. The UN's assemblage of contributors generally fared well except for overall military potential, a conclusion in line with the observations of those unhappy with the UN's inability to obtain more of the troops and resources that go to non-UN missions.

A focus on contributor 'commitments' underscores that it is unrealistic to consider these troops and resources as consistently available to the UN in any case. The reason is simple: there is no global pool of contributors per se. There are really three separate pools: a UN cluster (UNC), an overlapping Western agendas cluster (OWAC), and a small miscellaneous third set—too atomized to earn the term 'cluster'—that includes two subsets. One subset consists almost exclusively of small contributors committed to African organizations while the second is made up of states that so spread their forces about as to preclude characterizing them as committed to a particular organization over the decade. States in the commitment clusters largely eschewed significant participation in the missions of other clusters, and states in the third set either did not much participate in either the UN or the OWAC missions, or so spread their forces around as to preclude labelling them as 'committed' to any one choice over the decade.

That states clustered with their own kind could be very undesirable if the UN and OWA missions performed exactly the same sets of tasks, but they do not. The UN's brand is complex peacekeeping; even though its committed contributors possess only modest overall military potential, their operational experience goes far to suit them to that type of mission. In contrast, the OWAC takes on the missions that tend more to the hard military tasks such as peace enforcement (see Table 1.5). Not all OWAC states place themselves in the forefront of such tasks, but they support those that do. Thus, there seems to be a de facto division of labour between the UNC and the OWAC. It does not mean that UNC states will always sign up to do complex peacekeeping or that OWAC states will always volunteer to undertake muscular or robust missions. But it underscores that as a practical reality, it makes little sense to ask the UN to do what the OWAC is better suited to do or to expect the OWAC states will give up their agenda-driven missions and shift to those of the UN. If the past is prologue (for the next five years at least), the UN, even with states of modest military potential, will remain the indispensable go-to choice for complex peacekeeping and the OWAC organizations and states the go-to entities for enforcement. Indeed, what change may occur would probably involve the UN moving 'down' to lighter footprint missions and not 'up' to more muscular peacekeeping and peace enforcement.

This chapter presents ten propositions that flesh out its findings and arguments. Before doing so, however, we turn to a brief description of the designated unit contributor database upon which this analysis is based.

1.1 DESIGNATED UNIT CONTRIBUTOR DATABASE

Much of the analysis in this chapter builds on data drawn from the Designated Unit Contributor (or DC) Database put together at the Center for Peace and Security Studies (CPASS) of Georgetown University and covering the years 2001 through 2010.[2] A designated unit contributor (as opposed to a 'token' or non-contributor) is a country that provided at least 100 troops (the low end of a company) to at least one of the operations listed in the yearly compilations of peace missions found in the Stockholm International Peace Research Institute (SIPRI) database.[3] That database attends to operations conducted either under the direct authority of the United Nations or by another entity—a regional organization, alliance, or an ad hoc coalition—whose activities were sanctioned by the UN Security Council.

The CPASS database tracks each designated contributor's yearly troop numbers. UN mission numbers were drawn from the UN's detailed database. Obtaining non-UN mission numbers involved cross-checking SIPRI's numbers (most of which are as at 31 December of each year) against those found in the International Institute for Strategic Studies' (IISS) annually published *The Military Balance*, as well as information provided by organizations, coalitions, nations, or news accounts. Because of the skewing effect from the very large US troop deployments to the Multinational Force in Iraq (MNF-I) and to the International Security Assistance Force (ISAF) in Afghanistan, these US deployments are excluded from the database and associated calculations.[4]

[2] Found at http://cpass.georgetown.edu/center/research/peacekeeping/

[3] Basic mission data are found in published SIPRI yearbooks. More detailed contribution data are found at http://www.sipri.org/databases/pko/pko

[4] SIPRI dealt with the statistical outlier issue by excluding Multinational Force-Iraq personnel numbers and by providing two versions of aggregate data, one including and one excluding personnel numbers in the International Security Assistance Force in Afghanistan. See, e.g., *SIPRI Yearbook 2001* (Oxford: Oxford University Press, 2011), p. 110, footnote 3 and p. 112.

1.2 INITIAL BACKGROUND AND FRAMEWORK FINDINGS

1. *Unprecedented contributor highs characterized the 2001–2010 decade in peace operations.*

There are 44 peace operations in the designated unit contributor database for 2001 through 2010. As seen in Table 1.1, the UN undertook eighteen missions, more than twice as many as the next generic organizational choice, ad hoc coalitions, and three times as many as the next busiest standing organization, NATO.

There were 101 designated contributors and, depending on how one calculates, the former encompassed nearly two-thirds to three-quarters of all the potential unit contributors.[5] From fifty DCs in 2001, the total rose steadily to an unprecedented high of eighty-three in 2007, dropping to seventy-nine by 2010. Troop contributions generally followed the same trajectory: a low of 100,000 in 2002, an unprecedented high of 146,000 in 2007, and levelling off to 140,000 after. The post-2006 trends suggest that international society may now be at its limit in terms of contributors and troops.[6]

2. *Most contributors were more willing to give time than to give troops, thereby causing the peace operations enterprise to rest on a narrow base.*

A positive feature of the 2001–10 peace operations picture was the willingness of most contributors to stay the course once they signed on. Of the fifty contributors in 2001 and of the eighty-three in 2007, forty-one (or 82 per cent) and seventy-two (or 87 per cent) respectively remained in that capacity continuously through 2010. A less positive development is that 84 per cent of all troops came from less than one-third of the contributors, a trend that makes for a sharply sloping distribution.

Table 1.2 employs both the time and troop variables to divide the 101 contributors by 'weight'. Each nation's position reflects the number of years it was a DC and the average number of troops deployed in those years. Only about one-fifth of contributors are in the heavyweight tiers, five and six; one-third

[5] For most of the decade the UN had 192 members, but only a subset possessed ground forces large enough to view them as potential unit contributors. A minimum of 800 soldiers—the number possessed by the designated contributor (Gambia) with the smallest ground force, makes for 159 potential unit contributors. A minimum of 4,000—a number shown in previous analysis to be a more representative cutoff for troop providers, makes for 139 potential contributors. See Donald C. F. Daniel, 'Partnering for Troop Supply', *International Peacekeeping*, 18:5 (2011), p. 550 and p. 557, footnote 8.

[6] One can predict that for the foreseeable future the maximum hypothesized (but unrealizable) limit for troops is 210,000. This number was arrived at by adding together each contributor's highest yearly troop deployment during the decade. It is unrealizable because it is implausible to assume that all 101 states would contribute their maximum in one year, and if they did there would surely be a subsequent letdown.

Table 1.1 Designated Unit Contributor Missions, 2001–2010, by Organization and Macro Choice*

UN	AHC	NATO	EU	AU	ECOWAS	CIS	CMAC/CEEAC
UNKOM							
UNFICYP							
UNDOF							
UNIFIL							
UNTAET							
UNMISET							
UNAMSIL							
MONUC							
MONUSCO							
UNMEE							
UNMIL	*MFO-Sinai*						
UNOCI	**ISAF**						
ONUB	*SAPSD-Burundi*	**SFOR**					
MINUSTAH	*RAMSI*	**KFOR**	**Concordia**	*AMIB*			
UNMIS	**MNF-Iraq**	**Essential Harvest**	*Artemis-Congo*	*AMIS*			
UNAMI-DPA	*MNF-Haiti*	**Amber Fox**	**ALTHEA**	*AMISEC*			
UNAMID	*Licorne*	**Allied Harmony**	*EUF-DRC*	*AMISOM*	*ECOMIL*		
MINURCAT	*ISF-Timor*	**ISAF**	*EUF-CHAD*	*MAES*	*ECOMICI*	*JCCPF Moldova*	*FOMUC/MICOPAX*
Total = 18	8	6	5	5	2	1	1

*Macro choices indicators: Underline: UN Missions; **Bold: OWA Missions**; *Italicized: Third Set Missions*

Table 1.2 Contributor Rankings Determined by Number of Years as a Designated Unit Contributor and Average Number of Troops Deployed in Those Years

Tier 1	Tier 2	Tier 3	Tier 4	Tier 5	Tier 6
Azerbaijan	Albania	Argentina	Austria	Australia	Bangladesh
Burk Faso	Bolivia	Belgium	Brazil	Canada	France
Cambodia	Chad	Benin	China	Ethiopia	Germany
Cameroon	Chile	Bulgaria	Denmark	Ghana	India
Congo	Colombia	Burundi	Egypt	Nepal	Italy
Croatia	Congo	Czech Republic	Greece	Netherlands	Nigeria
Dominican Republic	El Salvador	Fiji	Jordan	Poland	Pakistan
Estonia	Gabon	Finland	Kenya	Rwanda	United Kingdom
Guatemala	Gambia	Georgia	Morocco	Spain	United States
Honduras	Guinea	Hungary	Romania	Turkey	
Macedonia	Guinea-Bissau	Indonesia	Senegal	Uruguay	
Malawi	Japan	Ireland	South Africa		
Mali	Latvia	Norway	South Korea		
Mozambique	Lithuania	Portugal	Uganda		
Nicaragua	Malaysia	Russia	Ukraine		
Qatar	Mongolia	Sri Lanka			
Sierra Leone	Namibia	Sweden			
Singapore	New Zealand	Thailand			
Sudan	Niger	Zambia			
Tanzania	Peru				
	Philippines				
	Slovakia				
	Slovenia				
	Switzerland				
	Togo				
	Tunisia				
	United Arab Emirates				
20 DCs	27 DCs	19 DCs	15 DCs	11 DCs	9 DCs
DCs in tier 1 averaged 100–499 troops/year and 2.8 years of contributions.	DCs in tier 2 averaged 100–499 troops/year and 6.7 years of contributions.	DCs in tier 3 averaged 500–999 troops/year and 8.7 years of contributions.	DCs in tier 4 averaged 1000–1999 troops/year and 8.9 years of contributions.	DCs in tier 5 averaged 2000–2999 troops/year and 9.5 years of contributions.	DCs in tier 6 averaged 3000 + troops/year and contributed 10 years.

are in the middleweight tiers, three and four, and nearly one-half in the lightweight tiers, one and two. Thus, many contributors were in for the long haul, but the troop numbers rested on a narrow base of providers.

3. *The macro level choices open to contributors for deploying troops fell into three mission sets: UN missions, an interlaced set of overlapping Western agendas (OWA) missions, and a third, mixed set of generally small idiosyncratic missions that, with notable exceptions, drew mostly local contributors.*
4. *The vast bulk of contributors and troops went to UN and OWA missions, but trends indicate a relative increase in dependence on the UN for peace operations generally.*

The starting point for arriving at three macro sets was analysis of the eight specific organizational choices made by contributors between 2001 and 2010. (Table 1.1 identifies which missions fall under which macro choice.) As seen in Figure 1.1 and Figure 1.2, the UN (in first rank), NATO (second), and ad hoc coalitions or AHCs (third) drew by far the largest number of contributors and troops, an outcome partly reflecting a full ten years' worth of choices in each category and a global (as opposed to strictly regional) array of missions.

The UN's performance is impressive. Not only did it have the largest number of missions (underlined in Table 1.1), it also had the most contributors (seventy-four) and, at 589,000 troops overall, better than 40 per cent of all troops provided to organizations[7] from 2001–2010. Most notable is that the

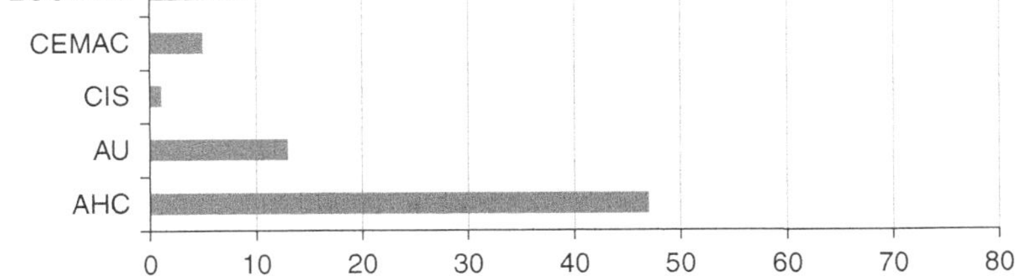

Figure 1.1 Number of Dedicated Contributors by Organization, 2001–2010

[7] The point is made of all troops provided to organizations because a straight organizational count modestly exaggerates the actual number of troops deployed because of rollover. That is, one mission with a set of troops may be re-authorized under another name within the same organization or may be transferred (again with a new name) to another organization. The troops in the new mission are usually the same as the troops in the old, but from an organizational

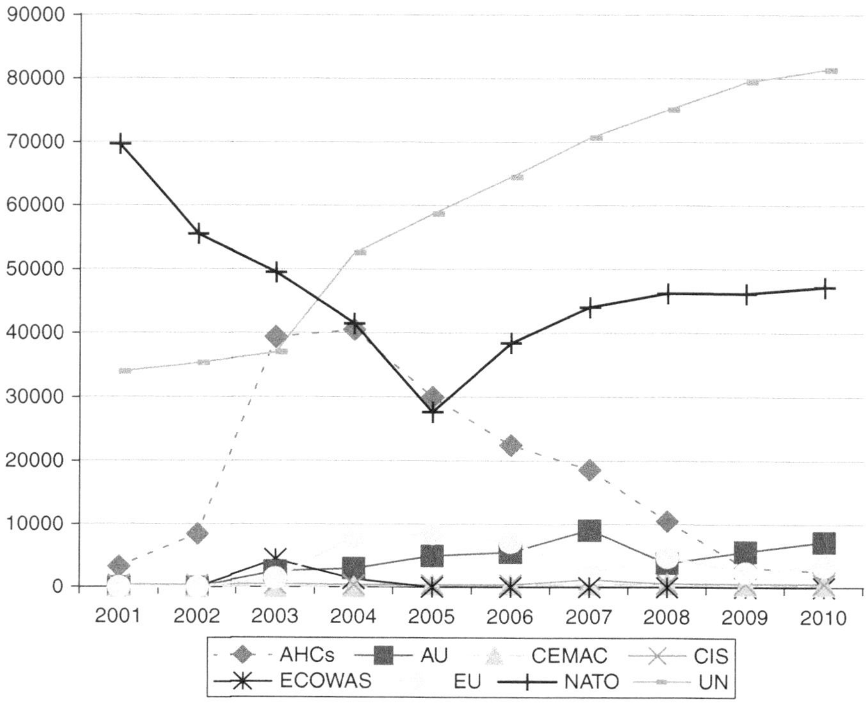

Figure 1.2 Number of Troops Deployed to Organization by Year

steady increase in UN deployed troops contrasts with the trend curves for all other organizational choices in Figure 1.2. The curves indicate a relative increase in dependence on the UN for peace operations generally. It is the only organization that justifiably constitutes a stand-alone macro choice.

The second macro choice is an inductive construct—the overlapping Western agendas (OWA) set—that sought to account for the up and down nature of the NATO and AHC curves, with one dropping as the other increased only to reverse the pattern beginning in 2005. These movements suggested a hydraulic relationship between these choices, i.e., as the number of troops increased in some missions, the rise seemed to come at the expense of troops in others since, presumably, the contributors only had so many troops available and had to shift them about as agenda priorities changed. A crosscheck of the geographic regions where troops deployed (Figure 1.3) shows interlaced curves for Europe, the Middle East, and South Asia that drew attention to the NATO missions in Europe and South Asia and the ad hoc missions in the

mission count, they are counted again in the organizational counts. Doing so is necessary in order to track the relative importance of missions and organizations.

Middle East and South Asia. A mission-by-mission enquiry into the contributors to those missions clarified, as expected, that the core of the relationship revolved around the deployment of Western contributors and their key Asian allies.[8] Extending the enquiry into all missions where these states deployed surfaced a broader set of missions that, because they drew such significant numbers of Western and allied states and troops, justified viewing them as part of an overlapping 'Western' agendas group. These included NATO's KFOR operation in Kosovo, NATO's SFOR and the EU's follow-on *Althea* operations in the Balkans, NATO's *Operation Essential Harvest* in Macedonia and its three follow-ons: *Amber Fox*, *Allied Harmony*, and the EU's *Concordia*, the AHC Multinational Force in Iraq, and ISAF, initially an AHC and then a NATO mission in Afghanistan.[9] Consistent with the same criteria of wide participation and high troop numbers, the UN's Lebanon

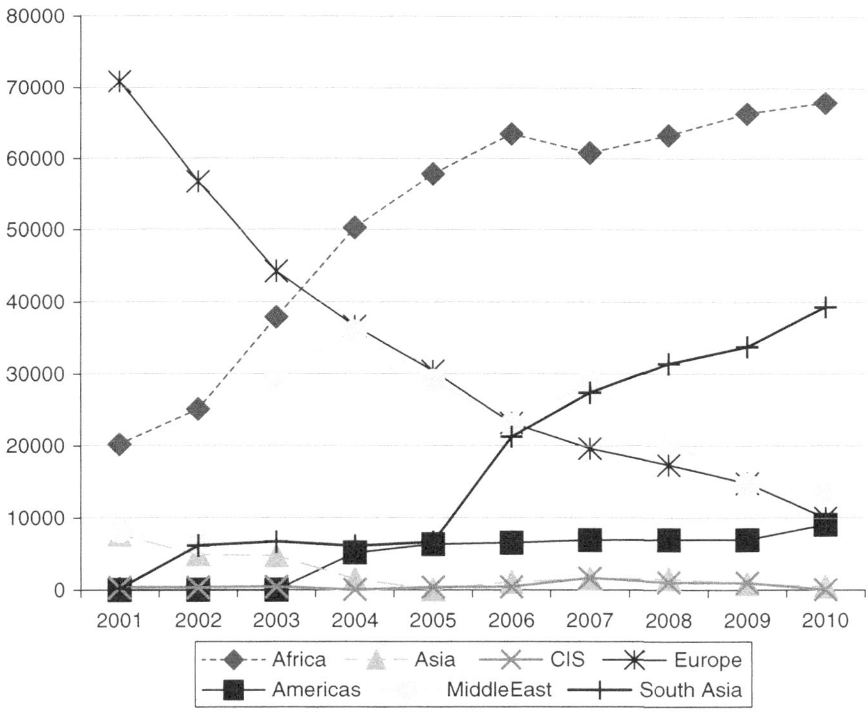

Figure 1.3 Number of Troops Deployed to Region by Year

[8] The Western state set was made up of the DCs that were full members of NATO and the EU as well as Australia, Japan, New Zealand, and South Korea. There were thirty-five in total.

[9] MNF-I involved twenty-one states and a high of 27,000 troops in 2003; the ISAF series (consisting of the AHC and NATO versions) involved thirty-two states and a high of 38,000 in

mission (UNIFIL) from 2006 on was added due to a ramp-up in Western participation from two states and 440 troops in 2005 to a high of thirteen nations and 8,600 Western troops in 2007. Also added were two UN missions to East Timor (UNTAET and UNMISET). Though the number of Western states including allies was only five, they deployed nearly 10,000 troops over four years, and, more importantly, the missions were direct follow-ons to the INTERFET coalition (not included in the database because it was completed by 2001) that had drawn 12,000 or more personnel (including extensive naval as well as air contingents) from twelve Western and allied states from September 1999 to February 2000, at which time the mission rolled over to UNTAET.[10]

While Westerners (including Asian allies) were at the core, this mission set drew sixty-four contributors in total and 694,000 or 50 per cent of all troops provided to organizations from 2001 through 2010. As seen in Figure 1.4, the

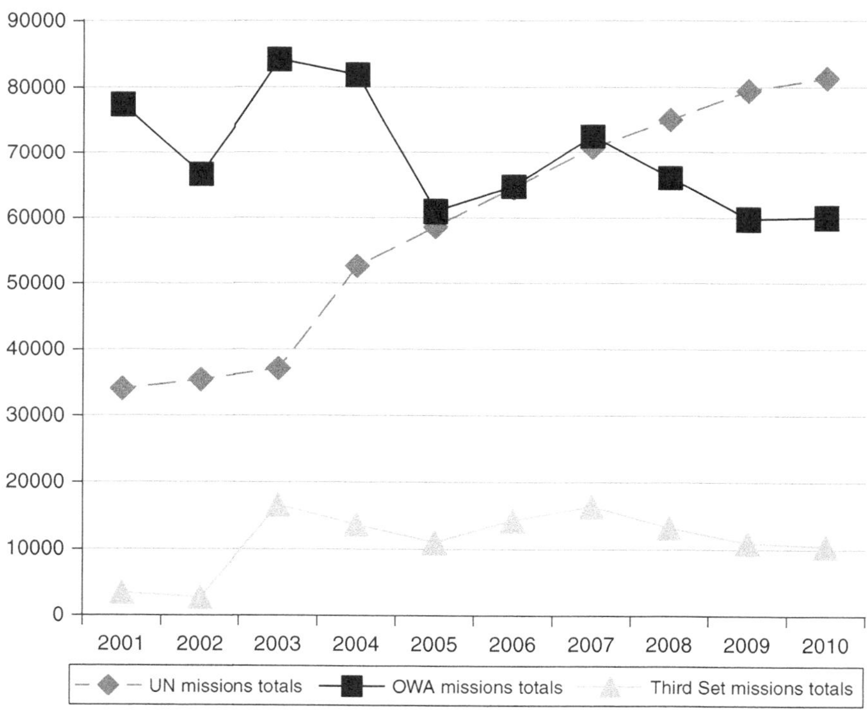

Figure 1.4 Number of Troops Deployed by Macro Choice

2010; the SFOR/Althea series drew twenty-five states and a high of nearly 20,000 troops in 2001; KFOR drew twenty-five states and a high of 37,000 in 2001; and the Macedonia series (Operations *Essential Harvest*, *Amber Fox*, and *Allied Harmony*) drew twelve states and a high of nearly 5000 in 2001.

[10] All other missions that Western states participated in usually drew only three or fewer of them and troop totals of less than 1,000.

OWA set had its annual high of 84,000 early in the decade and declined thereafter to 60,000 at its end. In contrast, the UN trend line started out relatively low but then moved up to reach its high of 81,000 at the end of the decade, thereby underscoring the point made earlier about rising dependence on the UN in general.

The OWA mission conglomerate is, of course, an analytic construct, but one can argue that it reflects genuine cross-cutting concerns among the participating states such as ensuring the stability of critical regions and nations in crisis, limiting the spread of terrorist groups, affirming the importance of NATO and the EU, establishing one's bona fides to serve as a member of these organizations, currying favour from the United States, paying it back for past favours, and giving in to US pressure.[11]

A third mission set consists of the remaining eighteen operations (italicized in Table 1.1). These were undertaken by the AU, the CEMAC/CEEAC, the CIS, the ECOWAS, the EU, and by ad hoc coalitions not already accounted for in the OWA set. They were omitted from the OWA set because they attracted insufficient Western contributors. This mixed group encompassed forty-three contributors and 112,000 troops in total. Unlike the UN and OWA sets, there is no unifying feature to these missions overall, and as seen in Figure 1.1, all the standing organizations have comparatively low yearly troop totals (which is the case as well with the remainder AHC missions) which have been drifting down since 2007, a trend that mildly reinforces the UN's growing relative prominence. Most of the missions drew a handful or less of contributors.

These three mission sets provide the framework for much of the remaining analyses. As opposed to eight choices, they constitute a less cluttered and a more representative picture of reality and of the UN's place in it.

1.3 COMPARING THE MISSION CATEGORIES

5. *In comparisons of contributor profiles, the UN fares well in most dimensions but falls especially short in overall military potential.*

Which macro choice gets the best of the DCs? Which get the rest? Comparisons were made of the military and deployment profiles of the contributors to each macro mission set. Two measures of the military profiles of a country are the size of its active ground forces—which forces are the main military

[11] See Daniel, 'Partnering for Troop Supply', pp. 543–4; and Donald C. F. Daniel and Tromila Wheat, 'Transregional Military Dimensions of Civilian Protection: A Two-Part Problem with a Two-Part Solution', *Journal of International Peacekeeping*, 15 (2011), pp. 329–30.

elements of peace operations—and the overall potential of its military. Size data are readily obtainable and straightforward. Data to measure overall military potential are also readily at hand when the proxy is defence spending per active military personnel.[12] The higher the per capita spending, the greater the probability of a fully professional (as opposed to conscript) military whose level of training is high and whose inventory of military equipment is broad and technically advanced.

For ease of comparison across these dimensions, the measurements utilize a scale from one to six, six being the top score. Each state was ranked in decreasing order from that with the largest ground force to that with the smallest and that with the highest potential to that with the lowest.[13] Those at the mean and above are in the top ranks, five and six; those between the median and the mean are in the middle ranks, three and four; and those below the median are in the bottom ranks, one and two. Each of these groupings was divided at the halfway point in order to establish which states get a ranking of 6 versus 5 and the like.

Two deployment profile measures are contributor weight, a variable introduced earlier, and global versus local orientation, i.e., the degree to which a country deploys its forces out of region versus keeping them in-area. The one to six scaling standard is applied for contributor weight with nations at six being those that gave the highest average yearly amounts for the greatest number of years. The nations at one gave the smallest amounts and for the shortest periods. As for orientation, a state that deployed two-thirds of its forces out of region over the decade was credited with having a (mostly) global orientation; one that deployed two-thirds or more in-region was credited with having a (mostly) local orientation; and one that fell in between was labelled mid-range. A global orientation is not necessarily better than a local one, especially when a region's need is great, but ceteris paribus, it provides a sorely needed flexibility since, as requirements for troops rise, no region (except possibly the CIS) can meet all of its own requirements. Outside help is a must.[14] Global and mid-range states are very important from that perspective.

As per Table 1.3, the collective of UN contributors compares favourably in ground force size and contributor weight vis-à-vis the collectives that went to OWA and third set missions. The UN's relatively lower global percentage reflects its role as Africa's primary peace operations organization and its reliance in that capacity on the participation of twenty African contributors,

[12] Data are for 2008 and taken from IISS, *The Military Balance 2009* (Abingdon: Routledge, 2009).

[13] The measurements involved not only designated but also nominal and non-contributors (i.e., all 159 states labelled as potential unit contributors).

[14] Daniel, 'Partnering for Troop Supply', pp. 546–7.

Table 1.3 Collective Characteristic Scores for Dedicated Unit Contributors per Macro Choice

Macro Choices	Ground Force Size	Overall Military Potential	Contributor Weight	% of countries going global	% mid-range	% remaining local
74 UN DCs	3.32	3.35	3.32	38	26	35
64 OWA DCs	3.39	4.16	3.31	58	29	14
43 Third Set DCs	3.17	3.17	3.26	24	17	60

all but one of which were entirely or mostly local. While twenty-eight (or 38 per cent) of the UN's contributors were mostly or entirely global, the number for the smaller OWA set is thirty-eight (58 per cent). Only nine (14 per cent) of the OWA contributors were mostly or entirely local.

Where the UN collective fared poorly was in overall military potential. Fully thirty-two (or 43 per cent) of its providers were in the bottom two quality tiers; only sixteen (or 25 per cent) of the OWA contributors were so positioned. The UN's heavy reliance on troops from developing nations impacted heavily.

6. *Roughly equal numbers of states 'committed' to participation in the UN and the OWA missions, and when their profiles are compared, the contrast in overall military potential becomes even sharper.*

An additional deployment profile measure is whether a state is willing effectively to commit to the UN, to the OWA mission conglomerate, or to the specific organizations (such as the AU or CEEAC) that undertook the remaining missions. There were two tests for de facto commitment. One was whether a state deployed two-thirds or more of its troops, over all the years it contributed, to one of these choices. The second was whether a state committed to the same choice for at least three-fifths of the years it contributed or, if it contributed less than three years, whether it deployed entirely to that choice. A state had to meet both the troop and time requirements in order to be considered committed.

Applying these criteria resulted in thirty-seven members of a UN cluster[15] (the UNC) and forty-two in an OWA cluster[16] (OWAC). UNC and OWAC

[15] Argentina, Bangladesh, Benin, Bolivia, Brazil, Burkina Faso, Cambodia, Chile, China, Egypt, Ethiopia, Ghana, Guatemala, Guinea, Guinea-Bissau, India, Indonesia, Jordan, Kenya, Malawi, Malaysia, Morocco, Namibia, Nepal, Niger, Nigeria, Pakistan, Peru, Philippines, Qatar, Senegal, Sierra Leone, Sri Lanka, Togo, Tunisia, Uruguay, Zambia.

[16] Albania, Australia, Azerbaijan, Belgium, Bulgaria, Canada, Croatia, Czech Republic, Denmark, Dominican Republic, El Salvador, Estonia, Finland, Georgia, Germany, Greece, Honduras,

states deployed 477,000 and 578,000 to their respective mission sets. In the third missions set, nine states committed to specific organizations (one to an ad hoc coalition, three to the AU, and five to CEMAC/CEEAC) with modest troop contributions in each case.[17] Beyond the states associated with these three mission sets are fifteen contributors[18] that so spread their forces around as to preclude being able to label them as committed to any set, resulting in the formation of a no-commit category. Most of the no-commit states are small contributors, but it is worth noting that France is part of this group and that it alone accounts for nearly half of the aggregate contributions of the entire fifteen.[19]

The de facto committers were the core contributors to the UN and the OWA missions and were responsible for four-fifths of all troops deploying to each set. Since 2007, the spread between UNC and OWAC troops deployed has steadily increased in favour of the UNC, which had 20,000 more troops in the field in 2010 than did the OWAC, a trend that underscores yet again the UN's critical importance to the peace operations enterprise (see Figure 1.4).

When profile comparisons are restricted to the committers, the UN improves its relative standing slightly in contributor weight and global orientation. It also pulled ahead of the OWAC in ground force size, but fared even worse in overall military potential (see Table 1.4). This is due to the dearth of Western state committers to the organization. Nearly all of them committed to the OWA set instead. There was no top rank overall military potential (OMP) contributor to the UN set and only two of its contributors were in the second best tier. In contrast, twenty-eight OWAC states were in the top two OMP ranks.

The nine states that committed to the third mission set compared favourably only in the ground force size category. Eight of them were African. The fifteen non-committers were a varied mix of advanced and developing Western, Asian, Eurasian, and African states. Their best showing, in overall military potential, involved a roughly even spread among the six quality rankings.

Hungary, Italy, Japan, Latvia, Lithuania, Macedonia, Malaysia, Netherlands, Nicaragua, Norway, Poland, Portugal, Qatar, Romania, Singapore, Slovenia, South Korea, Spain, Sweden, Switzerland, Thailand, Turkey, United Arab Emirates, United Kingdom, United States.

17 Columbia (AHC), Burundi (AU), Sudan (AU), Uganda (AU), Cameroon (CEMAC), Chad (CEMAC), Congo (CEMAC), Congo DR (CEMAC), Gabon (CEMAC). The overall troop numbers amounted to less than 25,000 for the decade.

18 Austria, Fiji, France, Gambia, Ireland, Mali, Mongolia, Mozambique, New Zealand, Russia, Rwanda, Slovakia, South Africa, Tanzania, Ukraine.

19 The careful reader has realized that the totals in this paragraph add up to 103 DCs, two more than the number of DCs specified under proposition 1. The reason is that the UN and OWA mission sets both included the UNTAET, UNMISET, and post-2005 UNIFIL operations. The overlap meant that two states, Malaysia and Qatar, were credited with committing to each.

Table 1.4 Collective Characteristic Scores for Dedicated Unit Contributors per Commitment Choice

Commitment Choice	Ground Force Size	Overall Military Potential	Contributor Weight	% of countries going global	% mid-range	% remaining local
37 UNC	3.38	2.22	3.11	46	8	46
42 OWAC	3.12	4.62	3.02	52	36	12
9 committers in third set	3.33	1.78	2.00	11	0	89
15 Non-Committed	2.53	3.33	2.87	47	0	53

1.4 ANOTHER COMPARISON AND THE DIVISION OF LABOUR IN PEACE OPERATIONS

7. *Mission specialization makes for an additional comparison that mutes somewhat the UN's relatively low overall military potential status.*

In the period up to the end of the Cold War, the UN specialized in traditional peacekeeping. These were observation and interposition missions where the peacekeepers, in the aftermath of a cease-fire, aimed to defuse tensions between state belligerents, reduce the prospects of conflict reignition, and reinforce expectations that peace (the absence of war) could be maintained. The Cold War's end saw the United Nations shift increasingly to missions in the midst of or in the aftermath of internal conflict between substate groups where the peacekeepers engaged in complex or multidimensional peacekeeping that aimed to help (1) restore basic services for the population buffeted by unrest; (2) re-establish background security so that indigenous populations and UN and NGO personnel, including humanitarian aid workers, could move freely; (3) buttress the rule of law through security sector reform; (4) disarm, demobilize, and reintegrate soldiers; (5) protect civilians under imminent threat; (6) promote human rights; (7) foster political dialogue and national reconciliation; (8) facilitate free and fair elections; (9) extend the geographical writ of whatever government is deemed legitimate; (10) clear land mines; and (11) act as an objective source of public information. Many of these tasks fall under the rubrics of peacebuilding or statebuilding with UN military peacekeepers working alongside police contingents and civilian personnel. As Sherman and Tortolani put it in 2009, 'Multidimensional operations are now the rule . . . with UN peacekeeping operations currently tasked to implement some 300 individual functions that fall under twenty-one broad categories' such as those outlined in this paragraph.[20]

A fundamental principle of UN peacekeeping is obtaining consent of the local parties amongst which the peacekeepers must operate, but consent is often fragile. In the face of spoilers, UN troops at times have had to move to a posture of robust peacekeeping especially when undertaking to protect civilians and extend a government's authority. Speaking in 2011, the then Under-Secretary-General for Peacekeeping observed that the number of robust missions 'has increased over the last ten years and now includes MONUSCO [in the DR Congo], UNOCI [in Côte d'Ivoire], UNAMID [in Darfur], UNIFIL [in Lebanon], and MINUSTAH [in Haiti]'.[21] He also acknowledged the stress that such missions placed on UN forces, and since the 1990s both UN officials and policy documents have underscored the limits on the UN's capacity for robust peacekeeping.[22] The latter is contrasted with peace enforcement, a task that they describe as going beyond the writ of UN peacekeeping. The UN's Principles and Guidelines for Peacekeeping make this distinction:

> United Nations peacekeeping operations are not an enforcement tool... Although on the ground they may appear similar, robust peacekeeping should not be confused with peace enforcement... [It] involves the use of force at the tactical level... and consent of the host nation and/or the main parties to the conflict. By contrast, robust peace enforcement does not require the consent of the main parties and may involve the use of... force at the strategic or international level.[23]

The main troop contributors to UN peacekeeping have made abundantly clear their disquiet with undertaking even robust peacekeeping. A summary of the 2010 meeting of the UN's Special Commission on Peacekeeping Operations contained this observation:

> While the EU group of countries pushed for the concept of robust peacekeeping, the Non-Aligned Movement Group (NAM), which includes nearly all the major personnel contributors to UN operations, expressed huge resistance, invoking the lack of resources to implement robust mandates—particularly the failure of well-equipped Northern states to contribute [to UN missions]—and arguing that such

[20] Jake Sherman and Benjamin Tortolani, 'Implications of Peacebuilding and Statebuilding in United Nations Mandates', in *Robust Peacekeeping: The Politics of Force* (New York: New York University Center for International Cooperation, 2010), p. 15.

[21] Statement by Alain Le Roy, Under-Secretary-General for Peacekeeping Operations, 2011 Substantive Session of the Special Committee on Peacekeeping Operations, 22 February 2011, p. 8.

[22] See Alex J. Bellamy and Paul D. Williams, 'Conclusion: What Future for Peace Operations? Brahimi and Beyond', *International Peacekeeping*, 11:1 (2004), pp. 183–212.

[23] *United Nations Peacekeeping Operations: Principles and Guidelines* (New York: UN DPKO/DFS, 2008), p. 34.

> mandates jeopardized the integrity of the peacekeeping principles [of consent of the parties, impartiality, and use of force only in self-defence].[24]

Former Under-Secretary-General Le Roy acknowledged the consequences of the NAM position when he stated, 'UN peacekeeping will never go to peace enforcement . . . No country contributing to peacekeeping will accept [having] "Blue Helmets" involved in peace enforcement.'[25]

The reference in the above paragraph to the EU is intellectually catalytic since European states make up the vast bulk of the OWAC. While the line between robust peacekeeping and peace enforcement is blurred, the fact is that the OWA mission set contains clear cases of peace enforcement broadly understood: KFOR, SFOR, IFOR, ISAF, and MNF-I.[26] Not all members of the OWAC readily operate at the spear's sharp end, but those that do not do so nevertheless support those who do, committing themselves to the OWAC agendas and not to the UN. Like their UN counterparts, they too engage in peacebuilding, but as a group their value-added lies in engaging in or buttressing large-scale and sustained peace enforcement. It is a specialization of the OWAC.

The significance of UN and OWAC specializations puts in relief the UNC's low standing in overall military potential. The latter crudely measures the capacity of a state to perform military tasks generally. While the UNC states may not have the capacity to do peace enforcement or robust peacekeeping on other than an episodic and limited basis, their inclinations and experiences (and that of the UN Secretariat) suit them to do largely consensual complex peacekeeping. Their operational experience trumps overall military potential, and for complex operations, it goes a long way in a world where the 'Western' (or globally Northern) states contribute to UN operations only in a minor or by exception basis.

8. *Mission specialization is the foundation for an informal but practical division of labour that has arisen in peace operations.*

Analysts at New York University's Center on International Cooperation have provided a useful categorization of how organizations partner on troop deployments.[27] One category is that of sequential operations (where one organization deploys first and then passes the baton to other); another is parallel

[24] Thierry Tardy, 'Peace Operations: The Fragile Consensus', in *SIPRI Yearbook 2011* (Oxford: Oxford University Press, 2011), p. 94.

[25] UN News Centre, 'Interview with Under-Secretary-General for Peacekeeping Operations, Alain Le Roy', 10 August 2011, at http://www.un.org/apps/news/newsmakers.asp?NewsID=40

[26] See Alex J. Bellamy and Paul D. Williams with Stuart Griffin, *Understanding Peacekeeping* (Cambridge: Polity Press, 2nd edition, 2010), Chapters 9 and 12.

[27] See A. Sarjoh Bah and Bruce D. Jones, *Peace Operations Partnerships: Lessons and Issues from Coordination to Hybrid Arrangements* (New York: New York University Center on International Cooperation, May 2008).

Table 1.5 Simplified List of Linked Missions Involving UN and OWAC States or France

First Year	UN mission	Western or French mission
1992	UNOSOM 1→	UNITAF
1993	UNOSOM 2 +	US offshore support
1994	UNMIH +	←US led MNF-Haiti-1994
1995	UNPROFOR→	Operation Deliberate Force→NATO IFOR
1996	UNTAES +	NATO IFOR
1999	UNMIK +	NATO KFOR
1999	UNTAET	←Australian-led INTERFET
2000	UNAMSIL +	UK Operation Palliser
2002	UNAMA (DPA) +	ISAF AHCs
2003	UNOCI +	French Operation Licorne
2003	UNAMI (DPA) +	US-led MNF-Iraq
2003	MONUC +	EU Operation Artemis
2004	MINUSTAH	←US-led MNF-Haiti-2004
2006	UNOTIL (DPA) +	Australian-led Operation Astute AHC
2006	MONUC +	EUFOR RDC
2009	MINURCAT +	EUFOR Tchad/RCA

(Arrows designate sequential missions and direction. Plus signs parallel missions.)

operations (where independent entities coordinate the tasks to be done in the same area at the same time by the troops each deploys). There are long histories of such operations involving the UN partnering with the OWAC states and/or France with the former undertaking complex peacekeeping and the latter providing the military muscle necessary to enforce a peace.

Table 1.5 is a select list of linked UN (including Department of Political Affairs) and non-UN Western states missions: each of the former entailed complex peacekeeping; each of the latter entailed Western forces that either performed or were, if circumstances required, ready to undertake peace enforcement. All the non-UN missions received Security Council authorization with an understanding that the UN and non-UN entities would divide the labour.

A rich example of the symbiosis took place in East Timor. In August 1999 the UN's special political operation, UNAMET, was active assisting local authorities administer a referendum on Timorese independence. The referendum's passage triggered a violent backlash from non-Timorese Indonesians. UNAMET's writ did not extend to dealing with violence. That task was taken on by an Australian-led ad hoc coalition of states. With UN authorization, the coalition restored peace, after which, as noted earlier, it passed the baton back to the UN to carry out an ambitious complex mission, UNTAET, designed to bring about self-rule. Progressively smaller UN complex peacekeeping and special political missions followed on after UNTAET, but a reflash of violence caused Australia again to lead another temporary multinational force in 2006.

In short, when violence occurred, the UN stepped aside to let Australian-led coalitions step up, after which the coalitions stood down in favour of the UN again.

There are other variations on mutual troop deployment cooperation between the UN and Western states. One is exemplified by two similar cases occurring almost simultaneously. In 2003 France and the United States intervened directly in Côte d'Ivoire and Liberia respectively in order to restore stability all the while laying the groundwork for follow-on ECOWAS enforcement missions (ECOMICI and ECOMIL) that were succeeded in turn by UN complex peacekeeping missions (UNOCI and UNMIL). Another variation is the UNIFIL case in 2006. In the aftermath of anti-Hezbollah Israeli incursions in Lebanon, the Security Council authorized a rapid infusion of several thousand additional peacekeepers. Italy, France, and Spain provided the bulk of the initial tranches. The UN and the EU sorted out special arrangements for these deployments, including the formation of a dedicated cell to handle command and communications issues between New York and the field.[28] 'In its earliest phase, the upgraded UNIFIL looked like an EU-led multinational force operating under a UN logo.'[29] And while UNIFIL was not a peace enforcement mission, the 'speed, scale, and sophistication of the deployment diminished the necessity of using force—the deployment itself changed the calculation of forces on the ground'.[30]

9. *UN Secretariat endeavours to formalize partnerships with Western organizations and nations (among others) run afoul of another perception about the 'division of labour', a perception that ironically may be a reaction to yet another 'Western agenda'.*

UN officials readily admit that it is 'sometimes... absolutely necessary to be supported by national militaries'.[31] To their credit they are working to make the division of labour between the UN and Western (and other) entities less informal and ad hoc. The capstone peacekeeping document 'supports a vision of a system of inter-locking capabilities in which the roles

[28] 'It was France that publicly began the debate in 2006 by making the presence in New York of a true UNIFIL strategic military command a condition for its participation in the operation.' Patrice Sartre, *Making UN Peacekeeping More Robust: Protecting the Mission, Persuading the Actors* (New York: International Peace Institute, 2011), pp. 26, 28. See also *Annual Review of Global Peace Operations, 2008* (Boulder, CO: Lynne Rienner, 2008), pp. 65–8. UN General Assembly, 'Comprehensive Review of the Strategic Military Cell', at http://daccess-dds-ny.un.org/doc/UNDOC/GEN/N07/320/28/PDF/N0732028.pdf?OpenElement

[29] *Annual Review of Global Peace Operations, 2007* (Boulder, CO: Lynne Rienner, 2007), p. 9.

[30] Bruce Jones, Richard Gowan, Jake Sherman et al., *Building on Brahimi: Peacekeeping in an Era of Strategic Uncertainty* (New York: New York University Center on International Cooperation, April 2009), p. 20.

[31] Loose minutes of Press Conference of Senior Secretariat Officials on Peacekeeping Issues (New York: UN Department of Public Information, 15 April 2011).

and responsibilities of comparative advantages of the various partners are clearly defined'.[32] Among the partners are 'Non-United Nations led military formations deployed nationally, under the aegis of a regional organization or as part of an ad hoc coalition'.[33] The UN's ongoing 'New Horizon' initiative is dedicated to that end, and its foundation document specifically identifies the European Union (in addition to the African Union) as a 'key' partner with which to reinforce interoperability.[34] Among the document's many recommendations are those that intend to improve coordination associated with the transfer of authority from a non-UN to a UN mission.[35]

The consensus-building process for implementing these recommendations is very slow.[36] As highlighted earlier in the summary of the 2010 meeting of the Special Commission on Peacekeeping Operations, differences between the Western states and the NAM are a major obstacle. To the NAM a 'division of labour' means that the Western states pay the bulk of UN peacekeeping financial costs while NAM states do the heavy lifting in the field.[37] Western states sometimes share the troop burden—that is the point of Table 1.5—but the NAM perspective is that they do not do so nearly enough. Employing careful diplomatic language, Under-Secretary-General Le Roy reiterated the NAM's case when he held up UNIFIL—an operation with many European troops—as a model for application 'especially in Africa' where UN 'peacekeepers are very much tested to the limit and... taking big risks. That is very worrying.'[38] The UNIFIL build-up, however, only exacerbated NAM disquiet because of the privileged arrangements put in place to secure major European participation.[39]

Addressing trends in contemporary UN peacekeeping, Richard Gowan highlighted an ironic development in light of the categories employed in this

[32] *United Nations Peacekeeping Operations Principles and Guidelines*, p. 10. See also Ross Fetterly, 'The Demand and Supply of Peacekeeping Troops', *Defence & Peace Economics*, 17:5 (2006), pp. 457–71.

[33] *United Nations Peacekeeping Operations Principles and Guidelines*, p. 73.

[34] *A New Partnership Agenda: Charting a New Horizon for UN Peacekeeping* (New York: UN DPKO/DFS, July 2009), p. vi.

[35] *A New Partnership Agenda*, p. 10.

[36] *The New Horizon Initiative: Progress Report No. 1* (New York: UN DPKO/DFS, October 2010). See inter alia, p. 13. See also Björn Hettne and Fredrik Söderbaum, 'The UN and Regional Organizations in Global Security: Competing or Complementary Logics?', *Global Governance*, 12:3 (2006), pp. 227–32.

[37] 'Delegates Stress Need to Correct Imbalances in "Division of Labour" as Special Committee on Peacekeeping Operations Concludes General Debate', Loose Minutes of 219th and 220th Meetings of the Special Committee on Peacekeeping Operations (New York: UN Department of Public Information, GA/PK/207, 23 February 2011).

[38] 'UN Peacekeeping Enters Consolidation Phase: Interview with Alain Le Roy, Under-Secretary-General for Peacekeeping Operations', in UN Department of Peacekeeping Operations, *United Nations Peace Operations Year in Review 2010* (New York, March 2011), pp. 6, 9.

[39] 'Strategic Summary 2006', in *Annual Review of Global Peace Operations, 2007*, p. 9.

chapter.[40] He observes that 'peacekeeping veterans' link the operational difficulties of 'heavy peacekeeping' with overambitious aims. Specifically, 'the UN has been accused of pursuing a *Western agenda* . . . with [its] strong emphasis on democracy, human rights and international justice rather than adapting to local power dynamics' (emphasis added). Thus, he asks whether heavy peacekeeping will give way to 'lighter civilian missions' that do not try to impose the values of the powers that mandate (and pay) for the UN's missions but rather work within the power realities that exist among the domestic protagonists to mediate a solution. Participants at a 2010 experts meeting in Berlin concluded that such a trend—while 'obscure'—was already evident.[41]

That such a trend has arisen should not be surprising. One example, which played out in the Democratic Republic of Congo, makes the point:

> There, the UN deployed [MONUC] to help implement . . . a . . . flawed . . . peace agreement, helped organize . . . elections and—with the EU's help—tamped down two major episodes of renewed violence. Now, the UN is . . . fighting a war . . . alongside the elected government . . . whose political program is . . . uncertain and whose army's human rights record is abysmal—but whose opponents have shown an even more callous disregard for human life.[42]

What peacekeepers would be enthusiastic to find themselves in such a briar patch, especially after the EU's troop mission (EUFOR-DRC) left in 2006? Adding insult to injury was the DRC's dissatisfaction with the mission, triggering its being downgraded and renamed MONUSCO in 2010.

1.5 A CONCLUDING PROPOSITION

10. *For the near term, episodic and informal cooperation between the UN and Western states may be the best that can be expected in an era where lighter footprint UN missions may become more the trend.*

UNIFIL-type arrangements may be the price that will have to be paid if the Western states are to return to the UN's fold after they draw down from

[40] Richard Gowan, *Five Paradoxes of Peace Operations* (Berlin: Zentrum für International Friedensatze, Policy Briefing, September 2011), pp. 3–4.

[41] 'Beyond Heavy Peacekeeping: Alternative Mission Models for Building the Rule of Law', Meeting Note of Expert Seminar, Berlin, Germany, 2 June 2010 (Berlin: Zentrum für International Friedensatze, 2011). A summary of Security Council dynamics underscores the disquiet of many council members and major UN troop contributors with protection of civilian mandates. Security Council Report, *Protection of Civilians* Update Report of 3 May 2011, at www.securitycouncilreport.org

[42] Bruce Jones, 'Preface', in *Robust Peacekeeping: The Politics of Force*, p. ii.

Afghanistan between now and 2014.[43] The UN has already included that arrangement in its lessons learned.[44] But even an Afghan drawdown may not open much of a window of opportunity. American, Canadian, and European defence budgets are severely stressed. The European Union seemingly remains willing to undertake relatively small peacebuilding missions alongside the UN in Africa, but it struggled mightily to launch the EUFOR Tchad/RCA mission in 2008.[45] It remains to be seen when the next such parallel mission will occur. Should the Balkans, Haiti, Timor Leste, Lebanon, or a former colony flare up again, the interests of the Western states may be engaged enough to draw them in temporarily, but absent that condition, the only real hope for better Western participation may be the very long and tedious process of consensus-building at the UN.

The rest of the chapters in this volume speak to that process. Whatever the outcome, the UN's brand today remains complex peacekeeping, and one can opine that if it moves off from that centre, it will almost certainly be 'down' in the direction of lighter footprint missions Gowan speaks of and not 'up' towards heavier missions. The latter will remain a specialty of OWAC states and France. No amount of politicking will change that fact.

[43] UN Department of Public Information, Verbatim transcript of Interview with the Under-Secretary-General for Peacekeeping Operations, Alain Le Roy, New York, 10 August 2011. Le Roy specifically referenced the drawdown in Afghanistan as a period when Western states might return. See also Naveed Bandali, 'Committed to Keeping the Peace', *Journal of International Peace Operations*, 6:1 (2010), p. 21.

[44] Alain Le Roy, statement made at 'Peacekeeping on the Ground' conference, Berlin, Germany, 7 November 2011. This meeting was sponsored by the German Foreign Office and four other organizations. Notes in author's possession.

[45] See Richard Gowan, *The Future of Peacekeeping Operations: Fighting Political Fatigue and Overstretch* (Berlin: Friedrich Ebert Stiftung, Dialogue on Globalization Briefing Paper 3, 2009), p. 4. The EU's Chad experience included problems of transition with the UN due to the UN's difficulty in generating necessary forces and training of local police. Dijkstra believes such problems have contributed to making joint UN-EU operations less likely. Hylke Dijkstra, 'The Military Operation of the EU in Chad and the Central African Republic: Good Policy, Bad Politics', *International Peacekeeping*, 17:3 (2010), pp. 395–407.

2

Token Troop Contributions to United Nations Peacekeeping Operations

*Katharina P. Coleman**

The range in the size of troop contributions to United Nations (UN) peacekeeping operations is remarkable. In August 2011, at one extreme, India contributed 3,913 military personnel (and 255 police officers) to the UN Stabilization Mission in the Democratic Republic of Congo (MONUSCO). At the other extreme, twenty-seven states made troop contributions to UN peacekeeping operations that consisted of a single officer.[1] It is therefore misleading to conceptualize state decisions about whether to contribute to UN peacekeeping operations as a binary choice between participation and non-participation, without drawing distinctions based on troop contribution size. It is also misleading to study state motivations for participating in UN missions exclusively by analysing their reasons for making large troop contributions: there is no reason to assume that state motivations are constant across different contribution sizes, or indeed across different types of similarly sized troop contributions.

This chapter begins the work of disaggregating national troop contributions to UN peacekeeping operations by size and subsequently by type.[2] In particular, it focuses on very small ('token') troop contributions, which are remarkably common. In August 2011, states made 322 troop contributions (i.e., national contributions of at least one military personnel to a particular UN

* Research funding from the Social Sciences and Humanities Research Council of Canada is gratefully acknowledged.

[1] UN Department of Peacekeeping Operations (DPKO), *UN Mission's [sic] Summary Detailed by Country, Month of Report: 31-August-11*. At http://www.un.org/en/peacekeeping/resources/statistics/contributors.shtml. 'Military personnel' here refers to both 'troops' and 'experts on mission' in the UN categorization of troop contributions.

[2] I focus exclusively on troop contributions: police contributions lie outside the scope of the present analysis.

mission) to substantial UN peacekeeping operations, i.e., operations deploying a total of more than 300 troops.[3] Of these contributions, 220 included less than forty troops and 179 included less than ten. Of the ninety-seven troop-contributing countries (TCCs), ninety made at least one contribution of less than forty troops and eighty made at least one contribution of less than ten. The chapter begins by arguing that token troop contributions have become a distinctive mode of participation in UN peacekeeping operations. It then offers a typology of token troop contributions to UN peacekeeping operations and examines state motivations for choosing each token contribution type. Finally, it suggests that the emergence of token contributions as a distinctive participation form hampers ongoing UN efforts to expand the organization's base of (substantial) peacekeeping contributors.

2.1 TOKEN CONTRIBUTIONS AS A DISTINCTIVE MODE OF PARTICIPATION IN UN PEACEKEEPING OPERATIONS

As Figure 2.1 illustrates, token contributions of forty or less troops have become increasingly common in UN peacekeeping operations both in absolute terms and as a percentage of all national troop contributions.[4] Moreover, token contributions represent a deliberately chosen and distinctive mode of participation. This distinctiveness is rarely recognized, because tokenism is widely and uncritically attributed to resource scarcity: states are simply assumed to make token contributions only because they cannot make more substantial ones. As one UN official put it, states 'contribute what they can . . . they will release what they can afford'.[5] However, the notion that token contributions are simply 'ordinary' contributions scaled down to reflect resource constraints does not stand up to closer scrutiny, for three main reasons.

First, the sheer number of token contributions militates against viewing tokenism as a residual category of troop contributions. As noted, 220 of the 322 national troop contributions deployed in UN peacekeeping operations in August 2011 were token contributions comprising less than forty military personnel, and 179 of these included less than ten military personnel. In this

[3] UN DPKO, *UN Mission's Summary 31-August-11*. Operations numbering less than 300 total military personnel are excluded because the definition of tokenism and the impact of one or two military officers will differ in very small and/or pure observer peacekeeping operations.

[4] Data from International Institute for Strategic Studies (IISS), *The Military Balance* (London: IISS); annual editions 1990–1 through 2008–9. Data are considered only for UN peacekeeping operations including at least 100 troops in order to exclude (almost) pure observer missions.

[5] Confidential interview with UN DPKO official, July 2010.

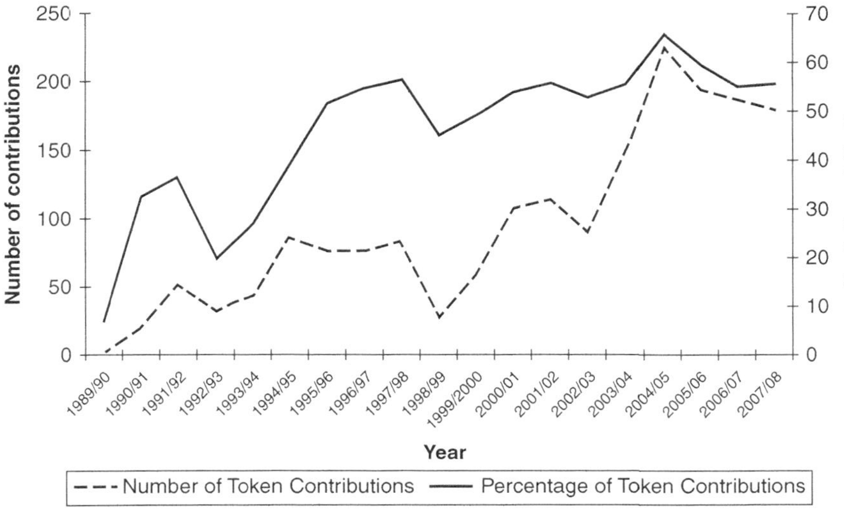

Figure 2.1 Tokenism in UN Peacekeeping Operations

sense, token contributions are not variants of 'ordinary' contributions but *constitute* the most ordinary contribution type.

Second, the number and nature of countries making token troop contributions contradict the notion that tokenism is reserved for states facing absolute constraints on their military or financial resources. In August 2011, ninety of the UN's ninety-seven TCCs (fully 92.8 per cent) made at least one contribution of less than forty troops. Of these ninety token troop contributors, forty-one (45.6 per cent) had a 2010 per capita GDP above the global median and twelve (13.3 per cent) were in the global top 10 per cent in terms of per capita GDP. Forty-seven token troop contributors (52.2 per cent) were above the global median in terms of the size of their armed forces, and eight (8.9 per cent) were in the global top decile by this measure.[6]

Finally, the 'portfolios' of troop contributions that most TCCs maintain confirm that tokenism has emerged as a distinctive contribution type. Very few states make only one troop contribution at a time. In August 2011, seventy-two of the UN's ninety-seven TCCs participated in more than one UN mission. Of the remaining twenty-five states, seventeen contributed troops to non-UN operations such as the NATO-led forces in Kosovo (KFOR) and Afghanistan (ISAF) or the Economic Community of Central African States deployment in the Central African Republic (MICOPAX).[7]

[6] Calculations based on data from the World Bank's *World Development Indicators* database. At http://databank.worldbank.org/ddp/home.do?Step=1&id=4.

[7] NATO, *NATO Kosovo Force (KFOR) Placemat*, 5 October 2011, online at http://www.nato.int/kfor/. NATO, *International Security Assistance Force (ISAF): Key Facts and Figures*,

Thus only eight UN TCCs made a single international troop contribution (in seven cases a token one), while the remaining eighty-nine states (91.8 per cent of UN TCCs) held 'portfolios' of multiple simultaneous troop contributions to different operations.

The vast majority of these portfolios suggest that token troop contributions represent a deliberate strategy to spread a state's military resources over more multilateral operations. Four broad portfolio categories can be distinguished. First, some states make only substantial troop contributions to UN peacekeeping operations, declining to avail themselves of the option of making token contributions. States can move from one portfolio type to another over time, of course, but in August 2011, only six TCCs (Argentina, Italy, Morocco, Portugal, Slovakia, and South Africa) fell in this category, representing just 6.7 per cent of states making multiple simultaneous troop contributions to multilateral missions.[8] Second, some states make only token troop contributions to UN peacekeeping operations and do not participate militarily in any other operations. In August 2011, this included ten TCCs: Guinea, Kyrgyzstan, Mali, Moldova, Namibia, Serbia, Tunisia, Yemen, Zambia, and Zimbabwe.[9] Five of these TCCs made four or more token contributions, and Yemen and Zambia led the group with six token contributions each. Third and most commonly, TCCs' portfolios can include both token and non-token contributions to various UN peacekeeping operations. Fifty-one of the eighty-nine portfolios observed in August 2011 (57.3 per cent) fall in this category. Finally, in August 2011, twenty-two states (24.7 per cent of portfolios) made only token contributions to UN peacekeeping operations but also participated militarily in non-UN peace operations. Three of these (Luxembourg, Cameroon, and Montenegro) arguably made token contributions to their respective non-UN operations,[10] but the remaining nineteen combined token contributions to UN peacekeeping operations with often far more substantial troop contributions to non-UN missions. Most strikingly, the United States deployed 90,000 ISAF troops but only nineteen UN peacekeepers distributed over three peacekeeping operations.

16 August 2011. At http://www.isaf.nato.int/isaf-placemat-archives.html. IISS, *The Military Balance 2012* (London: IISS, 2012).

[8] South Africa and Argentina did not contribute troops to non-UN missions, but Italy, Portugal, and Slovakia made substantial troop contributions to ISAF, and Morocco deployed 162 troops with KFOR.

[9] Zambia and Yemen did, however, make non-token police contributions to UN peacekeeping operations.

[10] Montenegro deployed thirty-six troops in ISAF, however, coming close to the upper limit of the numerical definition of token contributions used in this chapter. NATO, *International Security Assistance Force (ISAF): Key Facts and Figures*, 16 August 2011. At http://www.isaf.nato.int/isaf-placemat-archives.html.

Thus contemporary UN TCCs almost universally broaden their contribution portfolios by making token troop contributions to at least some UN peacekeeping operations: fully 93.3 per cent of the portfolios observed in August 2011 (83 out of 89) exhibit this pattern. States committing few troops overall to multinational operations tend to use token contributions to parse these resources into several UN peacekeeping operations. Moldova, for example, deployed only seven troops in August 2011 but participated in three separate UN peacekeeping operations. States that can and do make substantial troop contributions—either to select UN peacekeeping operations or to non-UN missions—supplement these commitments with token troop contributions to additional missions. There is very little tendency to concentrate national resources in a single mission and very few states have declined to make token contributions to UN missions. This strongly suggests that tokenism is deliberately used by contemporary states as a distinctive tool to expand their contribution portfolios.

2.2 A TYPOLOGY OF TOKEN CONTRIBUTIONS IN UN PEACEKEEPING OPERATIONS

Once the UN Security Council has mandated a UN peacekeeping operation, the task of force generation (i.e., building the peacekeeping force from member states' troop contributions) falls largely to the UN's Department of Peacekeeping Operations (DPKO). Within DPKO, the Office of Military Affairs includes a Military Planning Service that produces a Concept of Operation for the mission and derives a list of Force Requirements, disaggregating the total number of personnel authorized by the Security Council into component units (headquarters staff, infantry battalions, engineer companies, etc.) assigned specific tasks within the deployment.[11] The Office's Force Generation Service negotiates with potential TCCs to secure the military capabilities envisioned in the Force Requirements document. These negotiations cover a host of issues including the number and nature of the troops to be contributed. Once an agreement is reached between the TCC and DPKO, its details are captured in a legal Memorandum of Understanding (MOU). In contemporary UN peacekeeping operations, three basic types of token troop contributions have emerged from the interactions between DPKO and TCCs.

[11] Col. William Stutt, 'Force Generation in the United Nations', *Blue Helmet Review 2006*, pp. 85–6.

2.2.1 Staff Officer Contributions

The military chain of command for UN peacekeeping operations includes three types of officer. First, at the apex, the Force Commander and other top officials are directly appointed and employed by DPKO to ensure their responsiveness to UN rather than national directives. Thus although states often vigorously promote their nationals for these senior positions, the officers selected are UN appointees and do not constitute a national troop contribution. Second, there are officers within virtually every formed troop contingent that states contribute to an operation. The UN provides guidelines about the command structures within different contingent types, and a TCC's Memorandum of Understanding with the UN will specify the number of officers envisioned for the contingent.[12] Third, there are staff officers who work at the mission headquarters and, if applicable, in forward or regional force headquarters. These include senior officers such as the mission's Chief of Staff and Chief Operations Officer as well as a plethora of lower-ranking officers. Many of these officers hail from the mission's major TCCs. Large contingent contributors typically insist on filling a significant share of the most influential staff positions, and are expected to furnish their share of the less glamorous lower-ranking officers: 'basically, if you look at a pyramid, whatever percentage you have of the troops on the ground, in the vertical slice going up to the top, that determines at what level within the staff you're entitled to fill positions'.[13] However, not all staff officer positions are allocated to the mission's large TCCs. Token contributions also occur, where states participate in a particular operation by sending only a small number of staff officers. In August 2011, for example, Canada deployed a single staff officer in the UN Force in Cyprus (UNFICYP) and the UK deployed five staff officers in MONUSCO.

2.2.2 Military Observers

UN military observers (UNMOs) are unarmed officers whose tasks within a peacekeeping operation often include monitoring a cease-fire, supervising the disarmament of militias, observing conditions in potential conflict areas, and/or reporting alleged human rights abuses.[14] Effective UNMOs must thus

[12] UN, *Manual on Policies and Procedures Concerning the Reimbursement and Control of Contingent-Owned Equipment of Troop/Police Contributors Participating in Peacekeeping Missions (COE Manual)* (A/C.5/63/18, 29 January 2009), Chapter 9. UN DPKO, *Standby Arrangements in the Service of Peace: Tables of Organization and Equipment, 1998* (New York: UN internal document, 1998).

[13] Confidential interview with UN peacekeeping officer, November 2010.

[14] UN, *United Nations Military Observer Handbook* (New York: DPKO, 2001), p. 33.

combine core military capabilities (knowledge of infantry operations, weapons identification, patrolling, etc.) with investigation, inspection, and reporting skills and the ability to accurately assess potentially dangerous military and political situations.[15] In addition, they must be able to communicate effectively in the operation's working language, be experienced vehicle drivers to ensure their own mobility, and have negotiation and conflict resolution skills to 'de-escalate situations . . . without using or showing any force'.[16]

UNMOs are an integral part of the UN peacekeeping forces in which they serve, but they typically live and work separately from the operation's formed military contingents. They are often deployed in small teams to relatively isolated positions, where their role is to interact with the local population and extend the UN's monitoring presence. To facilitate such autonomous deployments, UNMOs receive a Mission Subsistence Allowance from the UN that is designed to allow them to find their own accommodation and sustenance in the local economy, independently of the logistic arrangements sustaining formed contingents.

UNMO teams are typically highly multinational: often every officer is drawn from a different country. This helps ensure that reporting is not biased by particular national predispositions or priorities, and it reinforces UNMO teams' symbolic status as representatives of the UN as a whole. One important side effect is that states are presented with an opportunity to make token troop contributions: they can provide a handful of officers—or even a single officer—to fill individually allocated UNMO positions. In August 2011, for example, Mongolia deployed two UNMOs in MONUSCO, Moldova fielded one in South Sudan, and Niger contributed one to the UN force in Lebanon.

2.2.3 Troops Integrated in Another TCC's Formed Contingent

The operational units identified within a UN operation's Force Requirements list (infantry battalions, support companies, etc.) are normally recruited as formed contingents. DPKO force generators are generally reluctant to accept units formed by contributions from more than one state, because such composite units are prone to interoperability challenges: national differences in language, training, and equipment may seriously erode the unit's military effectiveness. As former Under-Secretary-General for Peacekeeping Operations Jean-Marie Guéhenno put it,

[15] UN, *Peacekeeping Training: United Nations Military Observer Course—Curriculum* (New York: DPKO, 1995), p. 59. UN, *Selection Standards and Training Guidelines for United Nations Military Observers* (New York: DPKO, 2002), p. 16.

[16] UN, *Peacekeeping Training*, p. 59.

> As a rule of thumb you can say that a homogeneous brigade will be more effective than a heterogeneous brigade and a homogeneous battalion will be more effective than a heterogeneous battalion. There's no question about that. In terms of military efficiency, the more homogeneity at a high level the better . . . I tried to resist as much as possible having too small units. In particular, I think having composite battalions is a bad idea, a very bad idea.[17]

However, if UN force generators are not able to secure all the units identified in a Force Requirements list from individual TCCs, they may have to contemplate composite units. Their calculation of whether to accept such units is affected by their estimation of how well the contributing states can be expected to cooperate: a history of joint deployments or joint training makes the composite unit more attractive. The conflict environment into which the unit is expected to deploy also matters: the more volatile the area of deployment, the more undesirable it becomes to deploy a composite unit potentially weakened by interoperability challenges. By contrast, there is less of a premium on military effectiveness in relatively benign conflict environments and correspondingly less reluctance within DPKO about accepting composite units. As one UN official commented,

> it all depends on the operation. Let's take the DRC, where in Eastern DRC you have jungle and other types of terrain, large terrain, difficult terrain, you've got a plethora of armed groups, many of whom are potential spoilers and may shoot at you. In those circumstances, what you really want are homogenous units or formations . . . Now take Cyprus, where frankly it's not the most dangerous of missions . . . Now there, frankly, you don't have to have formed units and a brigade of one nation. The tempo of operations and the level of difficulty are not such that you need that. So you can multinationalize to your heart's content.[18]

Conflict environments vary within missions as well as across them, however: within a given mission, some areas of deployment will be more risky than others. Thus in 2011, the Ituri region of the DRC was considered less volatile than North or South Kivu.

Thus despite DPKO's general reluctance to deploy composite units, some UN peacekeeping forces do feature such units, and some of these composite units include token forces. In 2011, for example, the Argentinian contingent in UNFICYP included token contributions of fifteen and fourteen troops, respectively, from Chile and Paraguay.[19]

[17] Telephone interview with Jean-Marie Guéhenno, Under-Secretary-General for Peacekeeping Operations, UN DPKO, 2000–8, 15 July 2010.

[18] Confidential interview with a DPKO official, 13 July 2010.

[19] *Report of the Secretary-General on the United Nations Operation in Cyprus* (S/2011/746, 30 November 2011), p. 9.

2.3 STATE MOTIVATIONS FOR MAKING TOKEN CONTRIBUTIONS TO UN PEACEKEEPING OPERATIONS

As Bellamy and Williams conclude in Chapter 19 and chapters on individual TCCs confirm, states make decisions about troop contributions for a variety of reasons and on a case-by-case basis. National cultures and institutions interact with the particular policy context to produce unique decisions about whether to participate in a given operation—and if so, with how many troops. Nevertheless it is possible to identify both general factors that render all token contributions attractive to potential TCCs and particular factors that may incline states towards specific types of token contributions.

2.3.1 General Advantages of Token Contributions

Token contributions offer general advantages in each of the three dimensions of decision-making identified by Bellamy and Williams in Chapter 19. At the level of *policies*, token contributions expand the options available to states: instead of a binary choice between non-participation and the commitment of substantial military and financial resources to a peacekeeping operation, states enjoy a tripartite menu of choice including non-participation, substantial troop commitments, and token contributions. Thus if the policy context militates against substantial troop deployments (e.g., because the mission is risky, national interests are not perceived to be engaged, domestic support for the operation is low, and/or national forces are committed to other operations), policy-makers can still choose tokenism over non-participation. Token contributions also offer an advantage for future policy-making: they establish a state as a troop contributor, giving it access to operational and political information circulated within the mission and the right to attend UN meetings on the mission. As Canada's lone UNFICYP officer noted, 'As long as there is a Canadian contribution, the Canadian ambassador to the UN goes to all the meetings, is privy to all the information, and has a say in what happens with the mission. Whether your contingent is a thousand or it's one, you still have a voice.'[20]

At the level of state *institutions*, token contributions have distinctive cost and capacity implications. These are not always positive, because substantial troop contributions to UN peacekeeping operations can be more profitable than token ones. The UN compensates states for the deployment of their

[20] Interview with Capt. Lorne Cooper, Operational Intelligence Section, UNFICYP. Nicosia, 19 November 2010.

troops, and a TCC can reap a profit if UN compensation rates exceed its military salaries. Moreover, although the UN does not directly pay for equipment purchases, it pays states for the use of contingent-owned equipment, which can help TCCs amortize equipment purchases. Where such financial benefits exist, military and civilian bureaucracies may favour substantial troop contributions over token ones. As one UN force generator put it, 'if [states] are financially driven then they want [to contribute] either a unit that has lots of people—because people pays—or lots of equipment, because equipment pays'.[21]

As several case studies in this book document, however, the scope for reaping financial profits from large UN troop contributions is limited (see, for example, Chapters 9 and 10). Substantial troop contributions represent a financial loss for states where troop salaries are higher than UN rates and/or where standard military contingents are larger or more expensively equipped than UN guidelines prescribe.[22] For other states, the risk that arrears to the UN peacekeeping budget will impede or delay compensation to troop contributors diminishes the financial attractiveness of making large troop commitments. In both cases, civilian bureaucracies mindful of national budget constraints and military bureaucracies keen to preserve their resources may prefer token to substantial troop contributions.

Moreover, states that have a long-term financial incentive to make substantial rather than token troop contributions may lack the institutional capacity to do so. This is not always simply a problem of resource scarcity: the difficulty often lies in the *kinds* of resources the UN requires. In particular, DPKO has specific expectations about how various kinds of troop contingents must be equipped, which are becoming more stringent as it shifts from a focus on the absolute number of deployed troops towards a more 'capability driven' approach to force generation.[23] Many states find these equipment standards onerous:

> Most people think that, OK, you take one unit from your country and move to a UN mission. It's not so simple. You have maybe to get additional equipment. The standard of equipment of UN is not equal of national equipment. Because maybe in my country a battalion is doing their [sic] task every day with this equipment, standard equipment, but when you try to be in a UN mission you have to follow big, big rules regarding equipment. A soldier has to have everything—boots, dress, first aid equipment, it's a big list, and it's a big difference from your country to the UN... [In addition,] when the UN requests a company or battalion, the first six months it has to be self-sustaining. Nothing is provided by the UN at the

[21] Confidential interview with a DPKO Force Generation Service official, 30 June 2010.

[22] UN, *COE Manual* (New York, 29 January 2009).

[23] UN DPKO and DFS, *A New Partnership Agenda: Charting a New Horizon for UN Peacekeeping* (New York: UN, July 2009), pp. 29–33.

beginning . . . so you have to bring your equipment, your accommodation, at least for the first six months. And it's really a big, big deal to get all this stuff.[24]

For some TCCs that might otherwise have both the ability and a financial incentive to make substantial troop contributions, these requirements are prohibitive. Thus five states that deployed troops to Liberia in 2003 under the aegis of the Economic Community of West African States (ECOWAS) had to reduce or eliminate their commitments in the follow-on UN mission at least in part because they did not meet UN standards.[25]

Acquiring the capacity to deploy substantial contingents of UN peacekeepers through equipment purchases is costly, and attempting to amortize these purchases through long-term UN deployments is risky because the UN may find that it no longer requires a particular troop contribution. A DPKO official acknowledged, 'when we see the reactions of countries that are pulled out of a mission at the inappropriate time, it means that the investment has not been covered. They are not getting a financial benefit of [sic.] what they've been doing.'[26] States can mitigate this risk by specializing in areas where the UN struggles to meet its needs (e.g., mobility, intelligence, or mine-clearing capacities), but specialization typically generates additional costs and may not correspond to national defence priorities.

In short, despite the UN reimbursement system, cost considerations and/or capacity constraints can make substantial troop contributions unattractive to states. When this is the case, token contributions offer an alternative participation strategy, the precise financial and capacity implications of which vary by token contribution type and are therefore discussed in more detail below.

While cost and capacity calculations within state institutions may explain a state's preference for making a token contribution instead of a substantial one, however, they fail to explain the choice of tokenism over non-participation or the pattern of multiple token and non-token contributions observed among contemporary TCCs. The sections below highlight that a variety of advantages specific to distinct token contribution types help account for this choice and pattern. In addition, however, all token contributions to the UN present one key advantage which appeals at the level of state *cultures*: TCCs gain prestige by making token contributions to UN peacekeeping operations.

A 2010 UN-commissioned report highlighted prestige as a 'strong motivation' for several prolific UN troop contributors.[27] UN officials concur:

[24] Confidential interview with UN diplomat, July 2010.

[25] Katharina P. Coleman, 'Innovations in "African Solutions to African Problems": The Evolving Practice of Regional Peacekeeping in sub-Saharan Africa', *Journal of Modern African Studies*, 49:4 (2011), p. 538.

[26] Confidential interview with DPKO official, July 2010.

[27] GfK Roper Public Affairs & Corporate Communications (GfK Roper), *Opinion Leader Research: Report of Findings from In-depth Interviews; Troop Contributing Countries*

'serving with the UN is also a prestige issue for many of our TCCs. It shows their engagement and their positive participation in the global security equation.'[28] As Bellamy and Williams note, whether and to what extent states pursue prestige depends on the embedded practices that help constitute their national cultures. How they pursue prestige is also idiosyncratic. In August 2011, ninety-six of the UN's 193 member states chose not to provide troops to (non-observer) UN peacekeeping operations, regardless of the prestige implications of doing so. Yet the avenues through which it is possible to gain international prestige also depend on international factors—and a concurrence of two such factors currently allows states to reap prestige through token contributions to UN operations.

First, UN peacekeeping itself is almost universally respected as a legitimate (albeit occasionally insufficiently effective) international use of military force. Contributing to a UN operation is therefore widely recognized as an act of good global citizenship.

Second, although the most prolific TCCs enjoy a special position within the UN system, token contributions attract a positive recognition that is often disproportionate to their military impact. Actors outside of the UN system, including domestic publics, often have limited information about the size of national troop contributions and/or care principally about whether their country is participating, rather than at what level. Token contributions allow states to claim participation in a mission. Reflecting on the lone Canadian officer in UNFICYP, the mission's Senior Adviser noted that outside UNFICYP headquarters 'the Canadian flag flies as proudly as the Argentinian or British or Slovak flag. Because flags don't distinguish between the numbers of contributing countries' troops.'[29] The officer in question concurred, and noted the cumulative effect of making several small contributions: 'It allows us to say yes, we're participating in all these missions. Well, there's only one there, but you don't have to tell them that. The statistics look better, the flag flies in more places.'[30] UN officials acknowledge this as a general dynamic: 'it sounds better if you say that we're contributing to ten different missions, and you don't have to go into the details of how many people you send'.[31]

Yet token contributions also garner prestige within the UN system, where information about troop contribution size is more readily available. UN procedures designed to provide positive recognition for TCCs rarely draw formal distinctions between large and small troop contributors. Thus

(TCC)—Bangladesh, Ghana, Jordan (Prepared for United Nations DPKO Public Affairs Section, June 2010), p. 4.

[28] Interview with Nick Birnback, Chief, Public Affairs Section, UN Department of Peacekeeping Operations, 7 July 2010.

[29] Interview with Wlodek Cibor, Senior Adviser, UNFICYP. Nicosia, 17 November 2010.

[30] Interview with Lorne Cooper, 19 November 2010.

[31] Confidential interview with DPKO official, July 2010.

any TCC, regardless of contribution size, is entitled to join the Special Committee on Peacekeeping (C34). Token contributions also allow states to appear on the UN's much-circulated troop contributors lists. As a UN diplomat explained, using the example of Brazil: 'The UN prepares monthly reports, and in this monthly report you can see the countries providing troops . . . And when you read UNFICYP, you can see Brazil. Just because it's one [sic]. But if there is nobody there, there's no Brazil in UNFICYP . . . It's just one, but you are there.'[32] Moreover, most UN officials are quick to defend the operational value of even small troop contributions, often suggesting that they provide 'niche' capacities. Indeed, their focus is frequently on the fact, and not the size, of participation: 'every time that you have a high-level meeting, you put down a list of which missions does this country contribute to. And you know, you don't always bring in exactly how many.'[33]

2.3.2 Advantages of Token Staff Officer Contributions

Token staff officer deployments offer several specific advantages in addition to the benefits common to all token troop contributions. Contributing senior staff officers allows a state to exercise considerable influence on the mission. As one DPKO official explained:

> If you send a company . . . of say 150 or 200 people, it's one coherent unit which can have influence over a very small area on the ground, as part of the bigger picture. If you send five staff officers, you can have, perhaps, Chief Planner, Chief of Staff, the Senior Military Adviser and so on. By positioning a very small group of senior officers you can have very much greater influence over the mission.[34]

Staff officers also have privileged access to information about a peacekeeping force's activities and about developments in the mission's host country, which they can convey to their governments. Thus token staff officer contributions in part reflect the fact that 'some countries' policy is to have maximum influence with minimum engagement, or at least maximum situational awareness with minimum engagement'.[35]

In addition, staff officers in UN peacekeeping operations can gain valuable professional experience: 'officers get multinational and international experience and they get linguistic experience, they learn how to be interoperable with militaries from the rest of the world. We send back better officers than we

[32] Interview with Col. Ricardo Antonio De Biase, Military Adviser, Permanent Mission of Argentina to the UN, New York, 12 July 2010.

[33] Confidential interview with UN official, July 2010.

[34] Confidential interview with DPKO official, June 2010.

[35] Interview with Col. Gerard Hughes, Chief of Staff, UNFICYP. Nicosia, 17 November 2010.

get.'[36] Officers deployed in mission headquarters may hone their skills in planning and conducting military operations, enhance their ability to operate in multinational environments, and develop their understanding of UN peacekeeping practices. Their government can call on this expertise to refine its policies towards UN peacekeeping, their armed forces can draw on it to update military training processes, and they build up the credentials that may allow them to compete for such UN high-profile posts as Force Commander. One senior DPKO official indicated, 'what I have said to a number of countries, if you think about getting one day a senior position in a mission, send officers in the staffs . . . Because it's also a requirement for selection to have UN experience.'[37]

Finally, staff officers are relatively inexpensive to deploy. TCCs are responsible only for identifying the staff officer and providing his/her personal equipment. Transport into the mission can often be largely achieved through commercial airlines. Once deployed, staff officers draw a Mission Subsistence Allowance directly from the UN, with which they are expected to find their own accommodation and food locally, and which also covers incidental expenses. If security conditions do not allow staff officers to live autonomously, the mission will rent and secure a building for them.[38] The UN is responsible for building and equipping the mission headquarters and provides vehicles for staff officers as required. In short, TCCs are not responsible for their staff officers' logistic support.

However, not all states are able to make token staff officer contributions to UN missions, for two main reasons. First, staff officer positions (especially at more senior levels) require high-ranking, highly trained, and experienced personnel. TCCs whose militaries include few such officers struggle to fill these positions, notably because these officers must be rotated (i.e., repatriated and replaced) on a regular basis. Second, there is intense competition for staff officer positions, particularly the more senior ones. An operation's large troop contributors typically demand a substantial proportion of these positions. Among the states that are unwilling or unable to make large troop contributions, only those with substantial political influence and/or a reputation for exceptional officers are likely to secure influential staff positions. One UN force generator acknowledged, 'I need particular TCCs to bring that experience into the headquarters, otherwise the headquarters won't run properly . . . So it's a two-way street: they want influence, I need their experience.'[39]

[36] Interview with Nick Birnback, 7 July 2010.

[37] Confidential interview with DPKO official, July 2010.

[38] The accommodation portion of the MSA would then be withheld. Confidential interview with a logistics officer in the UN Department of Field Support, July 2010.

[39] Confidential interview with DPKO FGS official, June 2010.

2.3.3 Advantages of Token Military Observer Contributions

UNMOs are less able to influence a mission's direction than senior staff officers, and because they are not deployed at mission headquarters they have less immediate access to operational information. Nevertheless making a token UNMO contribution brings informational advantages: by the nature of their task, UNMOs generate information about the political and military situation in their area of deployment, and they are included in both the formal information-distribution system and informal discussions within the mission. Yet it is primarily a combination of financial and access reasons that makes UNMO contributions popular, especially among developing states.

Like staff officers, UNMOs are relatively easy to transport to their missions, they deploy with only their personal equipment, and the UN provides vehicles where necessary. Like staff officers, moreover, UNMOs receive, a Mission Subsistence Allowance which not only releases the TCC from responsibility for providing logistic support but can also constitute a major financial boon for the deployed officer. In 2008, standard rates ranged from US$54/day in MINURSO in Western Sahara to US$169/day in MONUC in the DRC.[40] For officers from developing states this can mean receiving the equivalent of their regular monthly salary every few days. Thus 'a one-year assignment on one of these missions is your pension. It's like winning the lottery.'[41] For many TCCs, therefore, token UNMO contributions enable the distribution of highly desirable rewards among deserving (or well-connected) officers.[42]

UNMO positions are also more easily obtained than most staff officer positions. The competition for posts among a mission's large troop contributors and states with highly sophisticated militaries tends to focus on the senior staff positions: 'when it comes to observers, it's more open, the chances of deploying observers even if you have no large contingent are absolutely existent'.[43] Moreover, although the UN sets clear training and competency standards for UNMOs, it largely relies on TCCs to apply these standards. While many UNMOs are highly competent, therefore, anecdotes of officers deployed without appropriate training, language skills, or even the ability to drive are not infrequent.

[40] UN data, available at http://www.un.org/depts/OHRM/salaries_allowances/allowances/msa.htm.

[41] Confidential interview with a UN peacekeeper, November 2010.

[42] See Chapter 9 for evidence that similar considerations can affect the selection of police officers for UN missions.

[43] Confidential interview with a former senior DPKO official, March 2011.

2.3.4 Advantages of Troops Integrated in Another TCC's Formed Contingent

Troops deployed within another TCC's formed contingent generate little influence since they are largely subordinate to their contingent commander.[44] Given the constraints of operating within a formed military unit, they offer few informational advantages beyond establishing their state as a troop contributor. They are also ineligible for a Mission Subsistence Allowances, eliminating this financial benefit of contribution. Nevertheless, this form of token contribution presents two core advantages.

First, troops that are integrated into larger operational units are relatively cheap to deploy because they can draw on the host unit's logistic support, including accommodation, transport, medical support, etc. As an Argentinian diplomat remarked with respect to the multinational contingent his country leads in UNFICYP: 'these small contingents, the Paraguayan, the Chilean, and the Brazilian, they moved just personnel, with small equipment. And all the major equipment and self-sustainment equipment is provided by the Argentinian contingent. So it's so easy to participate in this way in this mission.'[45]

Second, co-deployment in a single operational unit provides personnel from different TCCs with a unique opportunity for professional exchanges and joint training. This is a key consideration behind Argentina's acceptance of other South American troop contributions into its UNFICYP contingent:

> we have many regional agreements. But most of the exercises we do every year are just for a small period of time, maybe two weeks. But when you start working together every year on a daily and weekly basis, that improves your relationship a lot. Chileans know how we work, we know how they work, and it's the same with Brazilians and with Paraguayans. You come to have friends in other armed forces, you understand their policy, their, strategy, everything, their military procedures. So I think most of the big reasons to work together start from this point. Partnership.[46]

These motivations are generalizable to other UN operations and indeed beyond the UN framework. Thus within the ISAF framework, Estonia has been willing to deploy a rifle company to Helmand province in part because it perceives military and political benefits in co-deploying with the UK.[47] These joint training advantages, combined with the burden-sharing benefits from joint deployment, explain why states are far more enthusiastic about composite units than UN force generators.

[44] The chain of command is less absolute in multinational forces than in single-state ones, but despite the reservations asserted by sovereign states it nevertheless exists.

[45] Interview with Col. De Biase, 12 July 2010.

[46] Interview with Col. De Biase, 12 July 2010.

[47] Confidential interview with an Estonian diplomat, July 2011.

2.4 CONCLUSION: TOKEN CONTRIBUTIONS AND FORCE GENERATION

States' motivations for contributing to UN peacekeeping operations are varied and complex, but this chapter has highlighted several general factors that shape participation decisions. The first is how large a troop contribution is required for participation. All other things being equal, given the financial and capacity constraints potential TCCs face, participation rates will be lower if only substantial formed contingents are accepted into a peacekeeping operation and higher if token troop contributions are accepted. The emergence of tokenism as a distinctive form of participation in UN peacekeeping has broadened the range of policy choices available to states and facilitated their participation in missions they might not otherwise have contributed to.

A second set of factors comprises the general benefits states derive from making token troop contributions in the current UN system. In addition to the cost and capacity advantages they present for some states, token troop contributions produce access and information advantages: regardless of contribution size, all UN TCCs receive operational information about the mission they are participating in and every TCC has a voice in diplomatic meetings about the deployment. Most importantly, however, token troop contributions tend to generate international prestige. Although highly prolific troop contributors may garner special recognition, all UN TCCs bolster their claims of good international citizenship both vis-à-vis external/domestic audiences and within the UN system itself. Moreover, token contributions allow states to spread their military resources over a wider range of UN (and potentially non-UN) missions, multiplying the prestige garnered from participation.

The final set of factors relates to the specific advantages states can derive from each of the three distinct types of token contributions to UN peacekeeping operations (staff officers, UNMOs, troops integrated into another TCC's formed contingent) and the constraints they face in exercising this option. Staff officer contributions, especially at senior levels, generate special influence and information for their TCC while requiring only a limited expenditure of national resources, given how few officers are involved and the fact that they receive a Mission Subsistence Allowance. However, intense international competition makes it very difficult for states to secure senior staff positions. UNMO positions are easier to secure, relatively inexpensive to fill, and offer some informational advantages to TCCs. UNMOs are also entitled to the UN's Mission Subsistence Allowance, which makes these positions extremely attractive to officers in many developing countries and therefore a useful reward for governments and/or military bureaucracies to distribute. Finally, deploying a token number of troops within another state's formed contingent permits extended interactions that allow the militaries involved to deepen professional ties and enhance their interoperability.

From the point of view of UN force generation, however, the phenomenon of token troop contributions poses a critical problem. UN officials have long stressed the need to distribute the military burden of UN peacekeeping more evenly among member states. The seminal 2009 'New Horizon' report reiterated this need: 'UN peacekeeping cannot rely heavily on a small number of significant contributors. An expanded base of troop- and police-contributing countries is required to enhance collective burden-sharing and to meet future requirements.'[48] In practice, 'expanding the base' means two things. One is increasing the number of developing states that make substantial troop contributions to UN missions, which requires further capacity-building through training and equipment purchases, assisted by the UN and/or developed states.[49] The other is bringing Western states back into the ranks of major troop contributors. The percentage of UN peacekeeping troops coming from OECD countries has steadily declined from 43 per cent in 1998 to 6 per cent in 2005.[50] However, the emergence of tokenism as a distinctive form of participation in UN peacekeeping operations has decreased both sets of states' incentives to become more substantial troop contributors.

In many Western states, public opinion is broadly supportive of the UN and would frown on a complete disengagement from UN peacekeeping. Even in the United States, where 'recent years [have] shown significant dissatisfaction with the UN's performance', overall support for the institution and for peacekeeping remains robust: in a 2006 poll, 69 per cent of respondents felt that US support of UN peacekeeping was 'important and worthwhile' compared to only 24 per cent who felt it was 'a waste of resources'.[51] Many Western states are also sensitive to their international reputation as good global citizens and supporters of UN peacekeeping, and recognize that this reputation is difficult to sustain without contributing at least some troops to UN operations. Within the UN, debate about the distribution of peacekeeping burdens has become acrimonious, and developing countries have increasingly argued that financial contributions alone cannot establish a state's good citizenship with regards to UN peacekeeping. As Guatemala's representative put it in the Security Council's 2011 open debate on peacekeeping,

> so long as roughly 90 per cent of the budget is provided by less than 10 industrialized countries, while roughly 90 per cent of the troops are provided by a different set of 10 developing countries, we will have a great deal of accumulated

[48] UN DPKO and DFS, *A New Partnership Agenda*, p. vi.

[49] UN DPKO and DFS, *A New Partnership Agenda*, pp. 31–2.

[50] Ramesh Thakur, *The United Nations, Peace and Security* (Cambridge: Cambridge University Press, 2006); p. 46. See also Alex J. Bellamy and Paul D. Williams, 'The West and Contemporary Peace Operations', *Journal of Peace Research*, 46:1 (2009), pp. 39–57.

[51] Council on Foreign Relations, 'Chapter 10: U.S. Opinion on International Institutions', *Public Opinion on Global Issues*, p. 1. At http://www.cfr.org/world/us-opinion-international-institutions/p20131.

> tension . . . it is not useful to view peacekeeping as a large-scale outsourcing exercise through which developed countries contract lower-cost troops from developing countries to carry out the hard and dangerous work. Among other things, this is quite degrading for troop-contributing countries.[52]

Token troop contributions allow Western states to assure domestic publics and international interlocutors that they continue to participate in UN peacekeeping with 'boots on the ground' as well as with financial resources. The fact that many of these 'boots' belong to token numbers of staff officers is not uncontroversial: 'you can't have a group of countries that is good enough to command the others, and the others are just good enough to follow the orders'.[53] Yet Western diplomats counter that their officers make a critical contribution to UN peacekeeping: 'we do punch significantly above our weight, because we've got . . . tremendous breadth and depth of experience, and . . . world class staff education'.[54] Critics retort that such contributions are insufficient, that Western states should also provide larger military units, and that developing countries can also provide outstanding officers. Nevertheless, they often concede the point, albeit partially and reluctantly: 'I mean it's better than nothing. And sometimes, from a technical standpoint, they have some experienced officers who can contribute to the effectiveness of a mission. So that is valuable.'[55] Thus, strategic token contributions allow Western states to attenuate (though not eliminate) critiques that they are not sufficiently supportive of UN peacekeeping. Their incentives to increase their UN troop commitments diminish correspondingly.

For developing states, too, the incentives to progress from token to substantial troop contributions are limited. UN officials do stress, 'We have good examples of countries that started at a very humble level and which step by step developed their capacity . . . A new contributor can become a stronger contributor tomorrow.'[56] They can point, for example, to Mongolia, which progressed from two UN peacekeepers in August 2002 to 262 in August 2007.[57] Yet unless the UN or another international actor directly finances equipment purchases, building the military capacity to deploy (and rotate) substantial formed contingents remains costly for developing states. Moreover, if they do acquire this capacity, states often face strategic choices as to where to deploy it—and despite the UN's unique advantage in reimbursing

[52] S/PV.6603, 26 August 2011, p. 24.

[53] Confidential interview with former senior DPKO official, March 2011.

[54] Confidential interview with Western UN diplomat.

[55] Interview with former senior DPKO official, July 2010, remarks not for closer attribution.

[56] Interview with Brig. Gen. Jean Baillaud, Chief of Staff, Office of Military Affairs/DPKO, New York, 14 July 2010.

[57] Jargalsaikhan Mendee, *Mongolia's Peacekeeping Commitment: Training, Deployment, and Evolution of Information Capabilities* (Washington, DC: National Defense Intelligence College, 2007), p. iii.

deployment costs their calculations do not always favour the global organization. Regional organizations may have the edge in addressing conflicts closer to home, allowing large contributors greater freedom to pursue national aims, and/or exerting political pressure to elicit larger troop contributions from their members. ISAF is a prime example of the latter phenomenon: while some TCCs (e.g., Austria, Ireland) have consistently maintained token troop contributions, new and aspiring NATO members have felt considerable pressure to increase their troop commitments in order to demonstrate their value as Alliance members. Thus between January 2007 (when ISAF had just expanded its area of operations to cover all of Afghanistan) and October 2011, Albania, Bulgaria, Croatia, the Czech Republic, Estonia, Hungary, Latvia, Lithuania, Poland, Romania, and Slovakia each dramatically increased their troop contributions, bringing their combined total of ISAF troops from 1,815 to 7,569.[58] By contrast, tokenism has emerged as such a common, stable, and acceptable participation form within UN peacekeeping that states feel little pressure to prove their commitment to the organization by increasing their troop contributions.

The fourth type of troop contribution portfolio described above is particularly evocative of the challenges UN force generation faces. As noted, in August 2011 twenty-two states (24.7 per cent of observed portfolios) made only token contributions to UN peacekeeping operations but also contributed troops to non-UN operations, and in nineteen of these cases they made substantial contributions to at least one non-UN mission. This group includes Australia, Canada, Finland, New Zealand, Norway, Sweden, and the United States, states that in late 1992 accounted for 11,875 UN peacekeepers but in August 2011 contributed only ninety-four UN peacekeepers—but 93,337 ISAF troops.[59] It also includes Bosnia-Herzegovina, Bulgaria, the Czech Republic, Slovenia, Poland, and Romania, who in August 2011 jointly contributed 5,883 ISAF troops but only seventy-three UN peacekeepers. The four African states in the group (Burundi, Cameroon, Chad, and Uganda) accounted for twenty-eight UN peacekeepers and 9,741 troops deployed in African continental and sub-regional operations.[60]

As long as a significant subset of UN troop contributors feel that their national interest is best served by concentrating their military resources in non-UN missions while taking advantage of the prestige and other benefits of making token contributions to UN missions, DPKO will struggle to achieve its

[58] Data from NATO, *International Security Assistance Force*, placemat, 29 January 2007 and NATO, *International Security Assistance Force: Troop Contributing Nations*, placemat, 18 October 2011.

[59] Data from IISS, *The Military Balance 1993–1994* (London: IISS, 1993); NATO, *International Security Assistance Force (ISAF): Key Facts and Figures*, 16 August 2011; and UN DPKO, *UN Mission's Summary 31-August-11*.

[60] Data from IISS, *The Military Balance 2012* (London: IISS, 2012).

goal of expanding its base of substantial troop contributors. The emergence of tokenism as a distinctive mode of participating in UN peacekeeping operations has expanded the options of potential TCCs and enhanced state participation in UN missions, but it has negative implications for the size of the troop contributions the UN is able to elicit from its members.

Part II

The Permanent Five

3

United States of America

Adam C. Smith

Since the beginning of the twenty-first century, the United States has played a limited operational role in United Nations (UN) peacekeeping operations, choosing to contribute only a small number of its uniformed personnel to a handful of missions. Over the same period, however, the US has advocated for, and proven instrumental in, the exponential growth of UN peacekeeping. This ambivalence derives from a number of interrelated cultural, historical, political, and bureaucratic factors that affect America's general predisposition towards UN peacekeeping as well as its short- to mid-term policies on whether or not to contribute American troops. The ways these factors interact with the disparate entities that comprise the US government help explain the paradox of sustained US government support for UN peacekeeping—through essential funding, diplomacy, capacity-building, and training initiatives—and its concurrent reluctance to consider contributing American troop contingents to those same missions.

This chapter begins by taking stock of US engagement in UN peacekeeping over the last decade, set within the context of its military commitments elsewhere. It argues that since 2000, the US has been one of the member states—if not *the* member state—most integral to the growth of UN peacekeeping. US support also remains essential for the sustainability of multilateral peacekeeping efforts, especially those taking place in Africa. The basis of this support lies in American cultural and normative values, augmented in the first decade of the twenty-first century with pragmatic national security concerns. The next sections highlight those factors that have constrained US military and police contributions to the UN. Here, cultural factors are important, notably an exceptionalist American worldview that champions the principles of collective security, but sets itself apart, leading to a selective application of those principles. America's occasional use of unilateral military force, its preference for engaging in operations through ad hoc coalitions or NATO rather than the UN, as well as its objection to the idea of foreigners commanding US troops (despite a long history of such practice dating back to the American Revolutionary War) are examples of this selectivity. The domestic political environment that often militates against the deployment of US troops as UN peacekeepers can also be seen as a reflection of American culture.

Various aspects of American institutions—their organizational design, culture, and embedded practices—also impede contributions of US troops and police to UN-led missions. These aspects include the separation of powers between the President and Congress, the complex bureaucracy and institutional silos of the Pentagon and the Department of State, the lack of a national police force or gendarmerie, the lack of career incentives for US military personnel to serve with the UN, and an implicit understanding that the US military's comparative advantage is its advanced war-fighting capabilities, and that therefore troops from other countries can best execute the world's peacekeeping tasks. Finally, there are proximate causes that affect policy choices to contribute or not. These include policy shifts in response to significant events; the geopolitical context that currently makes US participation in peacekeeping politically problematic for the UN; and the exigencies of and capacity constraints resulting from other US national security priorities, such as the wars in Iraq and Afghanistan.

Looking to the near future, the likelihood of seeing many US soldiers wearing Blue Helmets remains quite low. Any potential shift in this regard, due perhaps to a change in the political composition of the US Congress or Presidency, would ultimately be constrained in either direction by the same underlying factors that prevented George W. Bush from abandoning the UN, or Barack Obama from fully embracing it. Neither the broad scope of US security interests, nor the pressing need for burden-sharing are likely to change significantly in the near future.

3.1 US TROOP CONTRIBUTIONS IN CONTEXT, 2000–2010

The total number of uniformed Americans serving in UN-led operations has remained low throughout the post-Cold War period, with the exception of a spike in contributions from November 1992 to March 1996, when the US sent significant numbers of personnel to UN missions in Somalia (UNOSOM II), Haiti (UNMIH), and the former Yugoslavia (UNPROFOR and UNPREDEP). At the start of 2001, the US had 44 military and 844 police personnel serving in UN missions, the majority of which were privately contracted civilian police clustered in Kosovo (600 in UNMIK), Bosnia (164 in UNMIBH), and East Timor (80 in UNTAET). Of the forty-four military personnel, forty-three were observers (milobs). The US contribution made up 2.3 per cent of the total uniformed personnel in UN peacekeeping at the time and ranked the United

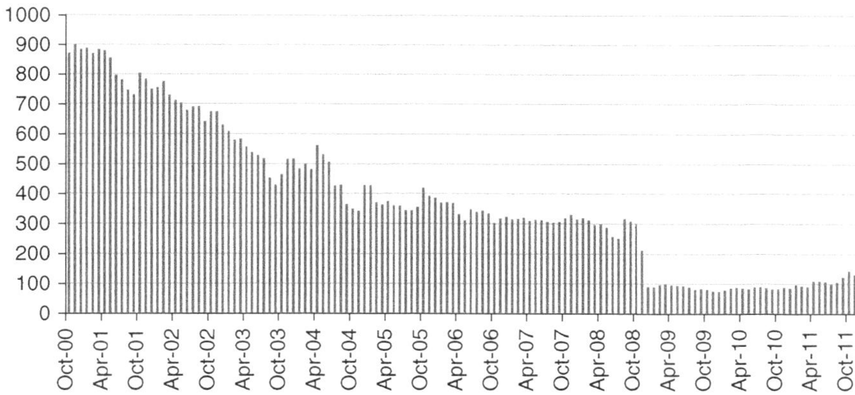

Figure 3.1 US Uniformed Personnel in UN Peacekeeping Operations, 2000–2011

States 14th out of the 90 troop-contributing countries (TCCs). It also made the US the top TCC among the permanent five members of the Security Council, which combined accounted for 2,377, or 6.1 per cent, of total UN forces.

Figure 3.1 shows the steady reduction in US contributions over the decade, to a low of seventy-five in December 2009. The closure of UNMIBH in December 2002 (the result of a US veto) and the steady drawdown of UNMIK through November 2008 were the principal sources of the reductions. By the end of the decade, eighty-seven personnel remained (sixty-one civilian police, thirteen troops, and thirteen milobs) in six UN missions, with the majority stationed in Haiti (MINUSTAH), a short distance from the US mainland. By that point—December 2010—the US ranked 70th among UN troop contributors, providing 0.09 per cent of the UN's 98,638 uniformed peacekeepers.

The contribution of US troops to UN peacekeeping operations was also low in relation to overall US military capacity, which hovered around 1.4 million active personnel throughout the decade. Of course, as a global superpower with broad strategic interests, much of that capacity was not sitting idle. Approximately 263,000 American troops (19 per cent) were stationed in 140 countries across the globe in 2001, even before operations in Afghanistan and Iraq began. The majority of those soldiers were deployed to forward operating bases (40,000 in Japan, 70,000 in Germany, over 11,000 in Kuwait, Bahrain, and Saudi Arabia), and at sea (53,000).[1] Some of these troops were engaged in

[1] Statistics on troop levels can vary greatly, even from the same institutional source, such as the US Department of Defense. For instance, while some figures count only 'boots on the ground' (BOG), higher counts include military personnel located in neighbouring countries providing theatre-wide support. In the US context, the difference can be great. The figures in this section mostly refer to the higher, theatre-wide counts. For more on troop level source differences, see Amy Belasco, *Troop Levels in the Afghan and Iraq Wars, FY2001–FY2012: Cost and Other Potential Issues* (Washington, DC: Congressional Research Service, 2 July 2009), pp. 3–5.

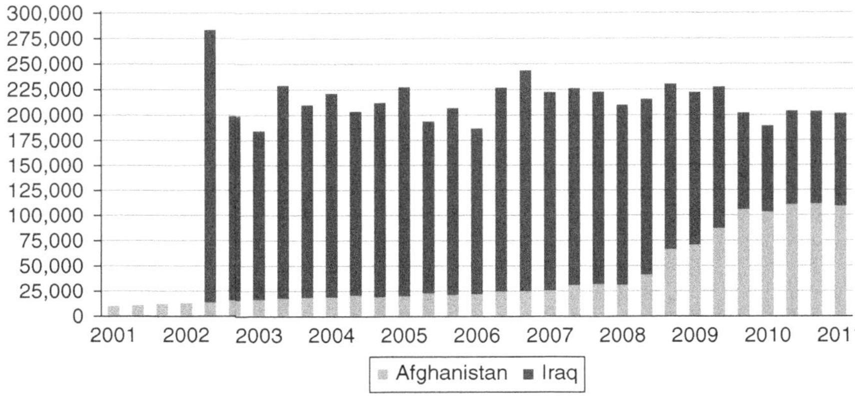

Figure 3.2 Total US Troop Deployments to Iraq and Afghanistan, 2001–2011[2]

stability operations, either in NATO missions, as part of a multinational force, or unilaterally. Roughly 36,000 were stationed in South Korea, over 9,000 were in the former Yugoslavia under both US and NATO command, and 500 were with the Multilateral Force (MFO) in the Sinai.[3]

The focus of the US military shifted significantly following the attacks on New York and Washington, DC in September 2001. *Operation Enduring Freedom* commenced the following month, with approximately 8,800 US soldiers engaged in combat operations in Afghanistan. In March 2003, a US-led coalition invaded Iraq, employing at its peak 285,000 US personnel in support of the initial operation. Instability and attacks on coalition forces followed soon after the overthrow of the Iraqi regime, and through mid-2009, the US kept no less than 165,000 soldiers in and around Iraq. At the same time, troop levels in Afghanistan increased from 20,000 in 2006 to 100,000 by mid-2010.[4] Figure 3.2 shows the US deployment figures to Iraq and Afghanistan from 2001 to 2011.

In total, during the decade following September 2001, an estimated 2,333,972 individual US military personnel served tours in Iraq, Afghanistan, or in both places.[5] Thus, while the US did maintain a high level of military capacity throughout the first decade of the twenty-first century, much of that capacity and, importantly, the collective attention of the US military and policy-makers were occupied with matters other than UN peace operations.

[2] Figures available through 2011 are taken from International Institute for Strategic Studies, *The Military Balance* (Abingdon: Routledge, annual 2001–11)

[3] 'Active Duty Military Personnel Strengths by Regional Area and by Country: December 31, 2000', US Office of the Under Secretary of Defense for Acquisition, Technology, and Logistics. At http://siadapp.dmdc.osd.mil/personnel/M05/hst1200.pdf

[4] Belasco, *Troop Levels*.

[5] Luis Martinez and Amy Bingham, 'US Veterans: By the Numbers', *ABC News*, 11 November 2011, at http://abcnews.go.com/Politics/us-veterans-numbers/story?id=14928136#all

3.2 UN PEACEKEEPING'S STRONGEST SUPPORTER?

A case can be made, however, that even if it only contributed few personnel to UN forces, the US was the most instrumental UN member state in supporting the expansion of UN peacekeeping after 2000. From 2001 to 2010, the number of uniformed UN peacekeepers deployed rose from 37,733 to nearly 100,000 while the annual UN peacekeeping budget rose from $2.8 billion to $7.8 billion.[6] As a permanent member of the Security Council, the United States can exercise its veto power over any resolutions mandating peace operations, as it did in 2002 when it vetoed a mandate renewal for UNMIBIH.[7] It also wields significant influence over the mandates of all UN peacekeeping missions, not least because the ten elected members of the Security Council as well as China and Russia often stay on the sidelines during initial resolution drafting processes, letting the so-called P-3 first come to agreement on mandate language.[8] Perhaps most importantly, the US *paid* for the expansion of peacekeeping, far more than any other member state. In 2000 the US contributed $498 million for UN peacekeeping. As the Security Council expanded the UN's peacekeeping operations that figure steadily rose, hitting $1 billion in 2006 and more than doubling to $2.13 billion by 2010.[9] As is true for all permanent members of the Security Council, the US pays a premium for its privileged position and is assessed at a higher rate for the peacekeeping budget than for the regular UN budget. The US was assessed 27.1 per cent of the annual peacekeeping budget in 2005–9, down from a *nominal* high of nearly 32 per cent in the mid-1990s, but still more than the other four permanent members of the Security Council combined.[10]

[6] See UN Department of Peacekeeping website, at http://www.un.org/en/peacekeeping/resources/statistics/contributors.shtml

[7] The US vote against renewing the mandate of UNMIBH was not necessarily about UNMIBH per se, but rather a product of the Bush administration's concerns that US personnel serving in UNMIBH could be prosecuted for crimes by the International Criminal Court. The Security Council did not agree to give American personnel immunity from ICC prosecution, which led to the US 'no' vote. See Frederick Rawski and Nathan Miller, 'The United States in the Security Council: A Faustian Bargain?' in David M. Malone (ed.), *The UN Security Council* (Boulder, CO: Lynne Rienner, 2004), p. 363.

[8] See 'The Working Methods of the Security Council: Politics, Procedures, and Progress', UN Studies Program at Columbia University, School of International and Public Affairs, May 2009, p. 26.

[9] Looked at from another angle, of course, the US contribution to the UN peacekeeping budget in 2010 was only 0.3 per cent of the US defence budget.

[10] The US contribution to UN budgets has often been a contentious subject in Congress. In 1995, the US Congress imposed a 25 per cent cap on annual US contributions to the UN peacekeeping budget, which led to significant arrears when the UN continued to assess the US at a higher rate. The US nearly lost its vote in the UN General Assembly in 1999 because of such arrears. In 2000, the Helms-Biden act allowed for the payment of arrears in exchange for a reduction in US assessments to both the peacekeeping and regular UN budgets. Of late, Congress has annually authorized raising its assessment cap for that year from 25 per cent to 27.1 per cent,

Yet, the US did more during the decade than passively approve and finance UN peacekeeping missions; it also pushed actively on the diplomatic front to both expand and strengthen UN peacekeeping. From the outset of his term as US Ambassador to the UN, Richard Holbrooke focused his attention on the UN's peacekeeping work in Africa. The US presidency of the Security Council in January 2000 was devoted to this issue, and later that year the US led a Security Council delegation mission to Africa.[11] Despite its reputation for unilateralism, the Bush administration also actively supported the expansion of the UN mission in the Democratic Republic of the Congo in 2002—what was to become the UN's most expensive mission—and lobbied for new operations in Liberia, Côte d'Ivoire, and Haiti.[12] It also campaigned publicly for the deployment of large new missions, most notably in Sudan's Darfur region in 2006, when it recommended doubling the number of troops and transferring command from the African Union to the UN, and in Somalia, when in late 2008 the US pushed strongly for UN budgetary and logistics support to the AU mission there under the pretext of an eventual transition to a UN force.

If the enthusiasm for the UN itself was at times tacit during the Bush administration, it was made explicit from the outset of the Obama administration. From the start of his presidential campaign in 2007, Obama drew a stark line between his own multilateral leanings and what he saw as the go-it-alone tendencies of his predecessor, promising 'to rebuild the alliances, partnerships, and institutions necessary to confront common threats and enhance common security'.[13] Highlighting the key role played by the largest troop-contributing countries to UN peacekeeping, the new US president held a private meeting with the leaders of those states at his first trip to the UN General Assembly in 2009. Obama claimed that 'UN peacekeeping can deliver important results by protecting civilians, helping to rebuild security, and advancing peace around the world.' But he also made clear that his administration's approach to UN peacekeeping would not differ much from previous administrations. Obama, like Bush before him, limited US engagement to diplomatic and financial support, as well as training, equipping, and capacity-building efforts. In terms of American personnel, he said the US would be 'willing to consider contributing civilian police, civilian

allowing the US to pay all of its assessed contribution. See Marjorie Ann Browne, *United Nations System Funding: Congressional Issues* (Washington, DC: Congressional Research Service, 14 January 2011).

[11] John Hirsch, 'Sierra Leone', in Malone (ed.), *The UN Security Council*, p. 530.

[12] Victoria K. Holt and Michael G. Mackinnon, 'The Origins and Evolution of US Policy towards Peace Operations', *International Peacekeeping*, 15:1 (2008), p. 28.

[13] Barack Obama, 'Renewing American Leadership', *Foreign Affairs*, 86:4 (2007), p. 11.

personnel, and military staff officers' to the UN. Absent from his endorsement was any consideration to contribute American troop contingents.[14]

The focus on supporting other countries' troop contributions, rather than providing its own, is a key feature of the US government's engagement strategy for UN peacekeeping. Beginning with the Clinton administration's African Crisis Response Initiative in 1997, the US has been funding training programmes for potential UN TCCs, primarily in Africa. The Global Peace Operations Initiative (GPOI) was established in 2004, and since then the US has spent between $85–115 million annually to train and equip peacekeepers from other countries, provide equipment and transportation for peacekeeping missions, and build peacekeeping skills and infrastructure. This makes the US the largest bilateral capacity-builder of any UN member state. About half of that funding is focused on 25 African states, and managed separately by the African Contingency Operations Training and Assistance (ACOTA) programme. GPOI has also supported the training of nearly 2,000 police trainers from 29 countries at the Italian-run Center of Excellence for Stability Police Units (CoESPU). The State Department runs GPOI, but collaborates closely with the Department of Defense (DoD), which implements roughly 50 per cent of GPOI activities. Funding and policy decisions are made jointly by State and DoD. Starting in 2010, the programme's emphasis shifted from direct training to self-sufficiency, i.e., training national trainers so as to build the capacity of nations to develop and sustain their own peacekeeping infrastructure and capabilities.[15]

The US has also been the leading provider of financing, air lift, training, and equipment for African Union missions in Darfur and Somalia. For example, from 2004 to 2006, the US government spent $280 million to build and maintain the camps that housed AU forces throughout Darfur,[16] and from 2007 to 2010, spent an estimated $230 million to provide logistics support, equipment, and pre-deployment training for AMISOM troop contributors; all in addition to its assessed contribution to the mission.[17] Programmes in the US Department of State like GPOI also work to fill gaps in peacekeeping by supporting the development of policy and guidance, for instance by funding work on the development of military training standards and guidance on tasks

[14] Barack Obama, 'Strengthening UN Peacekeeping to Meet 21st Century Challenges', Statement to Leaders of Top Troop-Contributing Countries, New York, 23 September 2009.

[15] Nina M. Serafino, *The Global Peace Operations Initiative: Background and Issues for Congress* (Washington, DC: Congressional Research Service, 11 June 2009).

[16] United States Government Accountability Office, 'Darfur Crisis: Progress in Aid and Peace Monitoring Threatened by Ongoing Violence and Operational Challenges', November 2006, p. 45.

[17] Lauren Ploch, *Countering Terrorism in East Africa: The US Response* (Washington, DC: Congressional Research Service, 3 November 2010), p. 29.

like the protection of civilians, as well as funding studies on key issues like the UN's shortage of critical air assets.

The US government has also provided additional operational support. In 2002, US Special Forces provided critical pre-deployment training to battalions from Nigeria, Senegal, and Ghana to reinforce the UN peacekeeping operation in Sierra Leone, and in 2003, US Marines anchored off the coast of Monrovia provided 'over-the-horizon' support to UN peacekeepers in Liberia. The most recent example was the quick and substantial American military response to the 2010 Haitian earthquake, when at its peak, the US had 22,000 DoD personnel, 58 aircraft, and 33 ships providing emergency humanitarian and disaster relief, and logistics and rule of law capacity. Despite early tension between the parties, such support helped ease the emergency response burden on a UN peacekeeping operation missing over 100 staff members, including its civilian head.[18]

On US soil, at least during the Obama administration, the White House and the Department of State have played the role of UN cheerleader, making great efforts to convince Congress and the Washington foreign policy establishment of the utility of UN peacekeeping and its importance to US national security. For example, in her testimony to the House Foreign Affairs Committee in 2009, Susan Rice, the US Permanent Representative to the UN, made the case that UN peacekeeping operations advanced 'U.S. national security interests' by among other things helping to protect the borders of war-torn states, police their territory, halt the flow of illicit arms, drugs and trade, and deny sanctuary to transnational terrorist groups such as al-Qaeda.[19] The Obama administration also managed to ensure that Congress fully funded American peacekeeping assessments to the UN, including the payment of $721 million in arrears.

Despite its multifaceted support for UN peacekeeping, however, the US has sometimes been a fickle friend. It is not uncommon for the US government to withhold crucial financial and political support for the resources and capacities the UN needs to accomplish the ambitious mandates set by the Security Council.[20] Moreover, when things do not go well, the US Congress has been a particularly vocal critic of the UN. In those cases, the White House rarely

[18] P. K. Keen, Matthew G. Elledge, Charles W. Nolan, and Jennifer L. Kimmey, 'Foreign Disaster Response: Joint Task Force Haiti Observations', *Military Review* (November–December 2010), p. 85.

[19] Susan E. Rice, written testimony submitted to the House Foreign Affairs Committee, Washington, DC, 29 July 2009.

[20] See for instance, Stewart Patrick, 'A Return to Realism? The United States and Global Peace Operations since 9/11', *International Peacekeeping*, 15:1 (2008), pp. 133–48; or Frederick Rawski and Nathan Miller, 'The United States in the Security Council: A Faustian Bargain?' in Malone (ed.), *The UN Security Council*, pp. 357–71.

spent precious political capital to defend the world body. This sometimes schizophrenic approach to peacekeeping is in large part a product of the interplay of the many different parts and competing interests that make up the American government.

There are, of course, practical, self-interested reasons behind any country's decision to provide UN peacekeepers, and the US is no exception. However, incentives that can appeal to other TCCs, such as financial reimbursements, or increased prestige, decision-making influence, or operational experience, are not particularly relevant to the United States. In general, US support for the UN is deeply rooted in American cultural values that are supportive of the principles on which the UN was founded. But this is strongly conditioned by specific geopolitical circumstances and the evolving understanding of America's national security interests.

American support for the UN derives first from normative factors. The US government's peacekeeping activism in the Security Council has, at times, resulted almost exclusively from domestic lobbying by groups of well-meaning Americans. The Darfur crisis is perhaps the most well-known example of the influence of the American public on UN peacekeeping. Here, Christian groups, students, and other grassroots campaigns put political pressure on the Bush administration to make the establishment of a UN peacekeeping mission in Darfur a priority.[21]

American presidents from Woodrow Wilson and Franklin Roosevelt to George H. W. Bush and Bill Clinton made normative arguments to justify American involvement and leadership in such things as the First and Second World Wars, the United Nations, and to respond to humanitarian crises in Somalia and the Balkans in the 1990s. To them and many other Americans, America's proper role is to lead international efforts in resolving conflict, ending suffering, and expanding democracy. This idealistic expression of American exceptionalism has often led to an ambitious foreign policy 'drawn with sweeping, at times messianic, strokes'.[22] It surely influenced Franklin Roosevelt and the early American architects of the United Nations, and continues to serve as a counterweight to those who see in the UN a threat to US sovereignty. This normative foundation helps prevent the US from ever abandoning the UN, even during the lowest points in US–UN relations.

Despite this general underlying support of the United Nations, US engagement in UN peacekeeping has varied according to the strategic concerns of the day. Interest peaked at the start of the post-Cold War period when George

[21] See Rebecca Hamilton, *Fighting for Darfur: Public Action and the Struggle to Stop Genocide* (New York: Palgrave Macmillan, 2011).

[22] Edward C. Luck, *Mixed Messages: American Politics and International Organization: 1919–1999* (Washington, DC: Brookings Institution Press, 1999), p. 18.

H. W. Bush famously championed the establishment of a 'New World Order'.[23] By the time of the October 1993 Black Hawk Down disaster in Somalia though, such optimism had run its course. A period of retrenchment from 1994 until late 2001 followed, in which US political and military leaders questioned both the utility of UN peacekeeping and the strategic importance of those areas of the world where UN peacekeepers were engaged. The attacks of 9/11, however, challenged this strategic outlook by showing that major threats to US national security could emanate from the poorest, most remote places on earth.

An improved US understanding of the strategic significance of those countries hosting UN peacekeepers came with a realization that despite its overwhelming military capacity, the US did not have the means, money, or will to police the globe. It therefore had a need for burden-sharing that UN peacekeeping could, at least in part, provide. The need was made more pressing as wars in Iraq and Afghanistan dragged on and a global economic downturn strained resources further.

3.3 THE CULTURE AND POLITICS OF AMERICAN AMBIVALENCE

If, as described above, the US public and its leaders generally prize the values of the UN and often see both normative and strategic value in UN peacekeeping, why does Washington not contribute its own troops—arguably the most capable and well-equipped in the world—to UN-led missions? This section explores two sets of underlying factors that work against potential troop contributions: cultural factors, which play out through America's highly charged domestic politics, and institutional factors, specific to the structure and processes of the US government's bureaucracy and its political system. The final section describes the proximate factors that affect short-term decisions, as well as short- to mid-term policy, not to contribute troops to the UN.

Ambivalence has been a standard feature of America's engagement in international organizations for many years. It results in part from cultural and historical factors, not least American exceptionalism. These factors help explain American support for universal rights and international

[23] Among many references, George H. W. Bush, Address to the 46th Session of the UN General Assembly, New York City, 23 September 1991.

norms, but also the friction that occurs when the institutions established to maintain those principles are perceived to be encroaching on American sovereignty.[24]

Cultural traits ultimately reduce the range of options for US government support to UN peacekeeping in three central ways. First, an isolationist impulse, an outgrowth of America's founding narrative and its geographical separation from other nations, remains a particularly vocal undercurrent of American politics. The first US President, George Washington, famously warned against forming foreign political alliances, arguing instead for isolationism, in part because US geography made it possible. Referring to Europe, he stated, 'it must be unwise for us to implicate ourselves by artificial ties in the ordinary vicissitudes of her politics, or the ordinary combinations and collisions of her friendships or enmities. Our detached and distant situation invites and enables us to pursue a different course.'[25] That same mistrust of foreign governments and guarded defence of American sovereignty have stoked domestic opposition to American involvement in two world wars, membership in both the League of Nations and the United Nations, and the participation of US troops in UN peacekeeping. The sentiment still resonates strongly with a segment of American society (and its representatives in Congress) overtly hostile to US engagement with the UN, particularly when it comes to military matters and whether US troops should be placed under foreign command. US officials point out that American military personnel serving in a UN peacekeeping mission operate only under UN *operational control*, remaining under US command at all times.[26]

A second factor influenced by American history and geography is the general lack of knowledge about the United Nations among the American public, which hampers the formation of any broad-based pro-UN constituency. In part this derives from America's status as a world power and cultural hegemon: for instance, Americans need not learn a foreign language to

[24] For thorough analysis on American exceptionalism and its effect on US behaviour towards the UN, see Luck, *Mixed Messages* and Steward Patrick and Shepard Forman (eds.), *Multilateralism and U.S. Foreign Policy* (Boulder, CO: Lynne Rienner, 2002).

[25] 'Farewell Address', George Washington, 1796.

[26] Perhaps nothing vividly underlines the strong sentiment that still exists on this subject more than the court-martial case of US Army Specialist Michael New. While serving in the 1/15 Battalion of the 3rd infantry Division of the US Army in 1995, Spt. New refused to wear a UN beret and arm patch as part of the US contingent serving in Macedonia (UNPREDEP). New held steadfast and was court-martialled as a result of his actions. He challenged his court-martial on the grounds that the chain of command was unconstitutional, but the verdict was upheld through several appeals processes. See *Peacekeeping: Military Command and Control Issues* (Washington, DC: Congressional Research Service, Report RL 31120, 1 November 2001).

travel internationally. It also comes from America's relative geographic isolation from other countries and its ability to be self-sufficient when necessary, thanks to its abundant resources. Hence, Americans may voice general support for UN principles, but often know little about its actual workings. In one poll, 49 per cent of Americans could not name one activity of the UN other than peacekeeping. In another poll, less than half (49 per cent) could identify the American city in which the UN is headquartered.[27] The little news about UN peacekeeping in American newspapers often consists of either specific scandals or general criticism. US and UN failure in Somalia in 1993 (featured in a best-selling book and a Hollywood film) made a lasting impression on American audiences. Other highly publicized incidents during the 1990s, such as the 'oil-for-food' scandal and the failure to prevent genocide in Rwanda, also left their mark on the UN's reputation with many Americans.[28]

Given this superficial understanding of the UN, there is no broad domestic constituency in the US to pressure political leaders to increase US involvement in UN peacekeeping. Likewise, there is no significant constituency to defend the UN when it is attacked by the particularly vocal minority that instinctively opposes it. Certain members of Congress and presidents from both political parties have at times found it politically expedient to blame the UN for failures. Thus, episodes such as Somalia or Rwanda are well remembered as failures of the UN, not necessarily of the United States. Such a political landscape is a major constraint on US politicians who might want to put UN peacekeeping engagement high on their agenda.

Finally, cultural factors play a role in how America perceives the proper role of its military. Despite its years of global hegemony, Americans rarely think of the US as an empire, and in fact, polls show that Americans have no appetite for empire.[29] The US military, therefore, was never envisioned or designed with large-scale nation-building or governance tasks in mind (unlike the armed forces of some colonial powers). Rather, it was designed to win conventional wars that might threaten the peace of the United States and—as the 'benevolent superpower'—its allies around the world.[30] There is thus a feeling that UN peacekeeping can—and therefore should—be performed by

[27] Luck, *Mixed Messages*, p. 264.

[28] Ironically, of course, it was in large part the pressure from the US government that prevented the UN from reinforcing its peacekeeping force in Rwanda to try to end the genocide. See Colin Keating, 'An Insider's Account', in Malone (ed.), *The UN Security Council*, pp. 500–11.

[29] Joseph S. Nye, Jr., 'Soft Power and American Foreign Policy', *Political Science Quarterly*, 119:2 (2004), p. 264.

[30] This is notwithstanding DoD Directive 3000.05, of November 2005, 'Military Support to Security, Stability, Transition and Reconstruction Operations' (updated September 2009). This directive codified that stability operations are 'a core US military mission that the Department of Defense shall be prepared to conduct with proficiency equivalent to combat operations'. It also states that DoD should be prepared to support 'stability operations activities led by other U.S. Government departments or Agencies [...] foreign governments and security forces, international governmental organizations, or when otherwise directed'.

militaries that do not carry such a great, and challenging, burden. This rationale is likely to be further reinforced as the US military has to operate in the context of major budget cuts, which are estimated to be almost 22 per cent by 2017 from its peak in 2010.[31]

3.4 INSTITUTIONAL ROADBLOCKS

American resistance to providing troops to UN peacekeeping is not only cultural and political. It is also exacerbated by specific features of the US government and its military. One potent factor that limits decisive UN engagement by a US president is the structure of the US government, which gives significant power to the legislative branch (i.e., Congress), and features a strong system of checks and balances (for instance, the President has the authority to order American troops into battle, but only Congress can issue a declaration of war).

With its control over US government spending, the Congress can—and will—withhold US assessments to UN peacekeeping. Antipathy towards the UN from many in Congress has been influenced by the perception of the institution and many of its member states as being anti-Israel. The perception became prevalent following the infamous General Assembly Resolution 3379 (1975) that equated Zionism with racism. Although the resolution was subsequently revoked in 1991, criticism of Israel and, in particular, its actions with regard to the Occupied Palestinian Territory, can be a recurrent theme in UN fora.

Within the US government, even when one party controls both the Presidency and Congress, certain checks are in place, such as the Senate filibuster, to give significant obstructive power to the minority party. US legislators who may represent only a small fraction of the US population—often the fraction least engaged in foreign affairs—can wield disproportionate influence over those affairs. As such, foreign policy issues like UN peacekeeping are often subject to the parochial interests of a powerful member of Congress. The frequent battle to cut US funding to the UN, led for many years by a US Senator from North Carolina, Jesse Helms, is a well-known example of this phenomenon. A more recent example took place in 2011, as Representative Ileana Ros-Lehtinen of Florida, the head of the House Foreign Affairs Committee, proposed a law that would mandate US opposition to any new or expanded peacekeeping missions unless her stringent set of proposed reforms

[31] US Department of Defense, 'Defense Budget Priorities and Choices', January 2012, p. 2.

were enacted at the UN. The powerful role played by the US Congress—and a few determined individuals in it—can therefore amplify the voices of a strident anti-UN minority in the American public. On the whole, however, the separation of powers and checks and balances within the US government also prevents a radical departure in the general course of America's foreign policy when the presidency shifts from one political party to another.

Inside the US government bureaucracy, challenges to quick and effective decision-making on UN affairs also exist. Engagement with the United Nations is led by the US Department of State, but all matters military must have the active cooperation of the Department of Defense. Interaction with the UN on peacekeeping should occur primarily through the US Mission to the UN, with its State Department staff and the military advisers and liaisons from DoD who serve in the Mission. However, the picture gets more complex when considering the informal communication that also occurs between the UN and State Department offices in Washington, primarily the Bureau of International Organization Affairs, but also with the Bureau of Political-Military Affairs, which houses the Global Peace Operations Initiative, and others.

In DoD, there are multiple sources of engagement and points of contact, which is not surprising for a truly immense entity which was never organized with regard to how it might best support UN peacekeeping. Organizationally, the Office of the Secretary of Defense is at the top, which directs the Joint Chiefs of Staff, the three branches of the military (Army, Navy, and Air Force) and the nine unified combatant commands (e.g., US Central Command, US Africa Command, US Special Operations Command, etc.). With regard to policy, there are specific sub-components that have UN peacekeeping in their orbit, such as the Director for Plans and Policy of the Joint Chiefs of Staff, the Office of the Deputy Assistant Secretary of Defense for Partnership Strategy and Stability Operations, and the Office of the Assistant Secretary of Defense for Special Operations/Low-Intensity Conflict. There are also specific operational and support entities such as the US Army Peacekeeping and Stability Operations Institute (PKSOI), which develops doctrine, lessons-learned and training programmes, and the US Military Observer Group–Washington, which provides command authority and administrative support to the US military personnel in UN missions. At present, there are 'operations officers' in the US Military Observer Group–Washington to coordinate support to US personnel in UN Missions in Haiti, Iraq, Liberia, Israel/Egypt (UNTSO), and the Multinational Force and Observers (MFO) in the Sinai.[32]

The US foreign policy bureaucracy, beyond the State Department and the Pentagon, is complex. After the President, the most influential individual voices on UN engagement are those of the Secretary of State, the Secretary

[32] US Army website: www.g357extranet.army.pentagon.mil/usmog-w/ (accessed January 2012).

of Defense, and the US Ambassador to the UN (who was re-elevated to cabinet-level rank in 2009 by President Obama). The President relies on a National Security Adviser and the National Security Council (NSC) to help make decisions and develop policy on national security issues. The NSC is advised on military matters by the Chairman of the Joint Chiefs of Staff among others, while the Director of National Intelligence represents the US intelligence community (comprised of sixteen separate intelligence agencies) on the NSC, and a host of senior thematic and regional advisers might weigh in on UN matters, such as the Senior Director for Multilateral Affairs or the Senior Director for Africa, for example. This does not, of course, include the various influential committees that relate to UN affairs in Congress, such as the Senate Foreign Relations Committee, Senate Armed Services Committee, the House Committee on Foreign Affairs, or the House Appropriations Committee. Civilian peacekeeping matters, including civilian police—an increasingly large part of UN peacekeeping—are handled jointly by the State Department and the US Agency for International Development.

Given such a complex bureaucracy—combined with other strategic priorities, the general ambivalence of the US public, and the tricky domestic political calculations—it is perhaps unsurprising that requests from the UN can get lost in the shuffle. One example of this rather deliberate process working through the US bureaucracy came in 2009, early into the Obama administration, when the US Mission to the UN requested that the UN Department of Peacekeeping Operations provide it with a list of critical equipment and personnel gaps in UN peacekeeping operations. The expectation was that the new administration could help fill some of the key capability gaps hobbling UN peacekeeping missions. After receiving the list, however, it took the US Mission to the UN nearly nine months to respond to it formally, and in the end, found it could not directly provide anything.[33] Unlike some countries, the US government has not yet developed a system or specific processes to efficiently respond to operational requests from UN peacekeeping.[34]

Likewise, the provision of American police to UN peacekeeping is hampered by organizational and bureaucratic constraints, not least the lack of a national police force or gendarmerie. This limitation was highlighted by the US experience in Haiti (1994–5), where the US had to contribute contingents to a coalition (the Multinational Force, MNF) and the UN police force (UNMIH). According to Robert Perito, this experience 'exposed the problems created by the extremely decentralized US system of over 18,000 state, county, and municipal police departments'. The Department of State, tasked with both

[33] Author's interview with UN official, New York, 22 February 2011.

[34] For a detailed explanation of the process by which requests from the UN are typically handled in the US Government, see Nancy Soderberg, 'Enhancing US Support to UN Peacekeeping', *Prism*, 2:2 (2011), p. 18.

finding the personnel and guiding policy in the absence of a national police force, outsourced the job to private security companies.[35] This practice worked as poorly in Haiti as it did later in Bosnia, where DynCorp personnel were implicated in, among other things, a sex trafficking ring. A separate initiative of the Department of Justice, the International Criminal Investigate Training Assistance Program (ICITAP), has been around since 1986, and, in Bosnia at least, proved more successful in its efforts to rebuild a local police force.[36] Although it employs nearly 400 personnel at its headquarters and in the field, ICITAP is non-operational and can provide assistance only by working in conjunction with embassies.[37] Recent innovations, such as the 2005 creation of the Civilian Reserve Corps, have not led to an increase in US contributions of civilian police to UN operations. The Civilian Response Corps, in fact, does not have the capacities to perform actual policing functions.[38] Even the State Department's Bureau of International Law Enforcement and Narcotics Affairs, the central agency working on these issues, employs relatively few police professionals on its staff.

Along with the lack of a national police force, a key constraint in efforts to deploy US civilian police is said to be the recruitment of qualified personnel. As Durch and England explain, 'Police officers operate very differently from military personnel. Very few officers expect deployment abroad for extended periods of time; they accept positions abroad for additional income prior to retirement, and one year is often the maximum many will accept.'[39] Furthermore, there is little to no official US government outreach to police associations to promote international policing.

Unlike the institutional constraints facing the provision of American civilian police, with American soldiers there is a central and influential institution—the Pentagon—that oversees policy, recruitment, training, and support. Yet despite the change in Pentagon policy that now proclaims stabilization operations to be a core function of US military, it is far from certain that the military establishment views participation in peacekeeping favourably.[40] This seems to be a

[35] Robert M. Perito, 'Police in Peace and Stability Operations: US Policy and Practice', *International Peacekeeping*, 15:1 (2008), p. 56.

[36] Perito, 'Police in Peace and Stability Operations', p. 59.

[37] William J. Durch and Madeline L. England, *International Police: Improving Effectiveness and Responsiveness* (Washington, DC: Stimson Centre Issue Brief, September 2009), p. 7.

[38] Durch and England, *International Police*, p. 7.

[39] Durch and England, *International Police*, p. 6.

[40] It is also uncertain whether this emphasis on stability operations—in either official policy or actual practice—will remain post-Afghanistan. As William Flavin rightly points out, the long history of US stabilization/nation-building/peacekeeping efforts is significant, but the lessons learned from them are often forgotten and the doctrine abandoned until a new need for it arises. As he puts it, 'these flirtations with peace operations in the past were transitory, as the focus remained on big conventional conflicts. The world has changed but the question remains of whether the change in US doctrine will be permanent or a temporary shift driven by immediate

significant constraint, as the counsel of US military leaders is influential in both the Executive Office and inside the halls of Congress. The concerns of the military cited below are also quite significant factors with regard to the American preference for pursuing its military objectives—when it must do so multilaterally—through NATO or 'coalitions of the willing', rather than through the UN.

Aside from the cultural factors that relate to concerns with foreign command of US troops, there are several institutional factors as to why the military generally resists increased engagement in peacekeeping. First, there are the mixed institutional (if not personal) memories of the US military's peacekeeping experiences with the UN in Somalia, Haiti, and Macedonia and with NATO in Bosnia and Kosovo. Somalia's 'Black Hawk Down' incident is still seen as a low point in recent US military history. A second constraint is the nature of peacekeeping itself (often misunderstood however, by the US military) and its supposed effect of degrading the war-fighting capability of US soldiers. This was a more common argument pre-Iraq and Afghanistan, as many in the military now value certain skills needed in stabilization operations that can be acquired through experience in UN peacekeeping missions. It is unclear, however, if the US military as an institution has made this connection. The debate on the proper role of the US military is still prevalent in discussions on whether stabilization operations should remain a 'core task' of the US military post-Iraq and Afghanistan.[41]

A third reason for reluctance is the practical observation that increased US military support to UN peacekeeping may be unwelcome by many UN member states, particularly those of the Non-Aligned Movement (NAM). Indeed, the US has, in the past, been prevented from providing gratis military staff officers to UN Headquarters or Missions by other countries concerned about increased American influence over UN operations.[42] Fourth, there are few incentives for individual military officers to serve in UN operations, in terms of their career development. It has even been said that 'assignment to the UN is deadly to careers'.[43] Finally, one should not underestimate the influence of the defence sector lobbying on policy matters in Congress and in the Pentagon. Compared to other tasks and needs of the US military, UN

events.' See William Flavin, 'US Doctrine for Peace Operations', *International Peacekeeping*, 15:1 (2008), p. 49.

[41] This is not to say that 'stabilization' operations and 'peacekeeping' are one and the same, although there are many similarities in how the two are defined in US military doctrine. However, the 'operational effectiveness' argument against refocusing or restructuring the US Army towards asymmetric operations like those in Afghanistan are similar to those arguments against US military involvement in peacekeeping—and typically come from the same people.

[42] See Nancy Soderberg, 'US Support for UN Peacekeeping: Areas for Additional DOD Assistance', Center for Technology and National Security Policy, National Defense University, September 2007, p. 15. This view was also confirmed in the author's telephone interview with a US official, 25 January 2012.

[43] Soderberg, 'US Support for UN Peacekeeping', p. 19.

peacekeeping offers relatively few large contracts to profit a US company (or jobs to profit a Congressman's district). Without much 'arms industry' constituency, there is no accompanying lobbying or pressure for increased UN engagement, unlike for other areas of US military engagement. However, it is possible that after the drawdown of the US military presence in Afghanistan, the large community of American-operated private security contractors may see UN peacekeeping as a promising source of revenue.

3.5 PROXIMATE CONSTRAINTS TO AMERICAN PARTICIPATION

Cultural and institutional factors may predispose the US against contributing troops or police to UN peacekeeping, but there are proximate causes that have had the most immediate effect on specific decisions and policies to not contribute troops. These include: the shift in official US peacekeeping policy that resulted in large degree from the US experience in Somalia; the current geopolitical context that complicates US military participation in many if not most UN peacekeeping operations; and the exigencies of other US national security priorities—in other words, the capacity constraints that result from US priorities elsewhere, notably Iraq and Afghanistan.

Any explanation of US peacekeeping policy would be insufficient without taking into account the brief period of US engagement with UN peacekeeping in the immediate post-Cold War era, which left an immediate mark on US policy (through Presidential Decision Directive 25), and, as mentioned above, a lasting impression on US policy-making elite, the US military establishment, and the American public. The US experience in Somalia from 1992–4 proved particularly deterministic in this regard. The well-publicized deaths of eighteen US soldiers in October 1993, along with the numerous difficulties of the broader operation, gave ammunition to those eager to criticize a Democratic president with little foreign policy experience, and quickly burst the optimistic post-Cold War embrace of peacekeeping. Although those US troops were killed while carrying out a mission commanded by US officials, this experience encouraged the view that the US military should work outside of the strictures of UN command and focus on those areas that were traditionally considered of core strategic interest: Europe, the Middle East, and East Asia. The new approach was documented in official policy in the form of an executive order, Presidential Decision Directive (PDD) 25, signed by Bill Clinton on 6 May 1994.

PDD 25, the product of an interagency review to define US policy on peace operations, was initiated by Clinton shortly after his election. Given the administration's declared appetite for 'assertive multilateralism', what emerged was something of a surprise: a policy 'designed to impose discipline on both the UN and the US', in the words of the State Department. While it did affirm, in principle, the value of UN peace operations in serving America's interests, PDD 25 set a goal to reduce the US financial commitment to UN peacekeeping, established seventeen 'factors for consideration' to qualify US support to and participation in a UN operation, and clarified US policy against foreign command or control of US troops. (PDD 25 would, curiously, be criticized from both sides, as some feared its criteria for participation were too lax or open for interpretation, while others saw the criteria as so restrictive as to essentially prohibit any future participation of US troops in UN peacekeeping.) Belying an ambivalence that would continue to characterize US engagement in UN peacekeeping for years to come, PDD 25 closed with the dual warnings that 'the US cannot be the world's policeman. Nor can we ignore the increase in armed ethnic conflicts, civil wars and the collapse of governmental authority in some states—crises that individually and cumulatively may affect US interests.'[44]

As Holt and Mackinnon argue, 'the mission to Somalia and the accompanying debate in Washington proved to be a watershed, marking the start of a new era of US restraint and caution'.[45] Unfortunately, this new cautious approach could not have been more poorly timed. It was only months later when the UN Security Council was confronted with reports of mass killings in Rwanda. Once the genocide began in earnest and UN peacekeepers from Belgium were targeted and killed, the US response in April 1994 was to argue strenuously *against* reinforcing the small UN contingent on the ground, partly for fear of a repeat of Somalia.[46] PDD 25 has not been mentioned much since those days, but it would be hard to deny that since PDD 25 was issued, US peacekeeping policy with regard to the participation of its own personnel has been anything other than cautious.[47]

The second proximate factor regards the specific geopolitical context in which decisions are made. If the events of 9/11 awakened America's interest in the stabilization of fragile states, ironically the US response to 9/11 (principally its invasion of Iraq) ensured that it would become much more difficult, politically, for the US to actually take part in stabilization efforts abroad. Particularly in Islamic states, the presence of American troops in a peacekeeping mission

[44] 'Clinton Administration Policy on Reforming Multilateral Peace Operations (PDD 25)', Bureau of International Organizational Affairs, US Department of State, 22 February 1996.

[45] Holt and Mackinnon, 'The Origins and Evolution', p. 20.

[46] See Keating, 'An Insider's Account', pp. 500–11.

[47] See Holt and Mackinnon, 'The Origins and Evolution'.

could serve as a lightning rod for international terrorist recruitment and attacks. In the words of one American official, there is a keen understanding that a US military presence in a UN mission 'instantly changes the political dynamic'.[48] Privately, UN officials also confirm this same view. Few in the UN Secretariat have forgotten the fate of the UN headquarters in Iraq—destroyed in a terrorist attack, and its vibrant leader Sergio Viera de Mello killed along with twenty-three others. It was targeted in part because of its cooperation with the American military. Of course, even absent a specific association with US personnel, Islamic extremists can violently oppose the UN and its core principles, as seen in the deadly terrorist attack on the UN offices in Algiers in 2007 and Nigeria in 2011.

Outside of the Islamic world, in other parts of Africa for instance, increased US engagement on the continent has been met with scepticism, in part because of the perception that its renewed interest is motivated almost entirely by counter-terrorism objectives.[49] Combined with the perceived hostility of NAM countries towards greater American influence in UN peacekeeping, the US strategy of late has deliberately been one of quiet, behind-the-scenes support, rather than a visible operational role in the field.

Finally, and perhaps most importantly, a key proximate factor that has limited US military cooperation with the UN has been the low priority assigned to UN peacekeeping relative to other potential uses of the US military. Despite an acknowledgement of the threats posed by fragile and failed states, the US, by and large, still does not view the countries which host UN peacekeeping missions, such as the DRC or Sudan, as core security concerns.[50] It is no surprise then that starting in 2001 efforts in Afghanistan and Iraq took centre stage (and remained there). As explained above, the capacity and the collective attention of the US military were occupied by those conflicts for most of the decade, which remained the case with the transition from Bush to Obama. Following the drawdown of the coalition presence in Iraq, attention has shifted to the instability in the broader Middle East, in places like Egypt and Yemen.

As the US plans for an eventual withdrawal from Afghanistan, cuts to the defence budget in the context of a global economic recession and a massive national debt will likely affect its peacekeeping contributions. Although the precise level of cuts has yet to be agreed, estimates from the Pentagon target a

[48] Author's interview with a US official, New York, 13 January 2012.

[49] See A. Sarjoh Bah and Kwesi Aning, 'US Peace Operations Policy in Africa: From ACRI to AFRICOM', *International Peacekeeping*, 15:1 (2008), pp. 118–32.

[50] According to the 2010 National Security Strategy, the top of the list of security priorities are: 'the pursuit of nuclear weapons by violent extremists', and the fight against al-Qaeda and its affiliates, where the 'frontline is Afghanistan and Pakistan' (p. 4). Further down the list are more UN-related tasks, like 'supporting the development of institutions within fragile democracies' and shaping 'an international order that promotes a just peace' (p. 5). The White House, 'National Security Strategy', May 2010.

22 per cent reduction by 2017 from its 2010 level.[51] Such a fiscally constrained environment will only exacerbate the already-challenging domestic political context and could move UN peacekeeping further down the list of the US military's priorities.

3.6 CONCLUSION

> Building partnership capacity elsewhere in the world also remains important for sharing the costs and responsibilities of global leadership. Across the globe we will seek to be the security partner of choice, pursuing new partnerships with a growing number of nations—including those in Africa and Latin America—whose interests and viewpoints are merging into a common vision of freedom, stability, and prosperity. Whenever possible, we will develop innovative, low-cost, and small-footprint approaches to achieve our security objectives, relying on exercises, rotational presence, and advisory capabilities.[52]

When considering the future of US military contributions to UN peacekeeping, one increasingly relevant issue is how the budgetary pressures will affect the development of US defence strategy. The above quote from the Obama administration's 2012 Defense Strategic Guidance (DSG) points to a more nimble and lower cost approach to US defence strategy moving forward, an approach on display in recent years in the US military's increased dependence on Special Operations units and unmanned aerial vehicles (UAVs). The deployment of 100 US military personnel to central Africa to assist the governments of the region in their pursuit of the Lord's Resistance Army is consistent with this vision of adaptable, bilateral partnerships and light footprints. Indeed, signalling a strategic shift, the guidance document explicitly states that 'in the aftermath of the wars in Iraq and Afghanistan, the United States will emphasize non-military means and military-to-military cooperation to address instability and reduce the demand for significant US force commitments to stability operations'.[53]

The large, conventional, light infantry battalion on which the UN typically relies to man its peacekeeping operations is not entirely consistent with this approach. No matter how high UN peacekeeping comes to rank on the list of US priorities, unless the UN also begins to embrace a higher-tech, lighter footprint approach to UN peacekeeping, the level of participation of US military will be inherently limited. It is worth noting, however, that as part of the recent 100-man

[51] 'Defense Budget Priorities and Choices', US Department of Defense, January 2012, p. 2.
[52] The White House, 'Sustaining US Global Leadership: Priorities for 21st Century Defense', January 2012, p. 3.
[53] The White House, 'Sustaining US Global Leadership', p. 6.

US deployment to central Africa, the US did station two military personnel as advisers within the UN's stabilization mission in the Democratic Republic of the Congo (MONUSCO). This kind of token contribution to UN missions can have a multiplier effect when it comes from the US, in terms of the encouragement of other TCCs to contribute their own personnel, and the logistical and intelligence support that the Pentagon provides to its personnel in the field.[54]

If, in fact, the most the UN can hope for in terms of uniformed US personnel contributions is one or two American staff officers or military advisers in its missions, the more important question is perhaps whether changes in the domestic political equation could lead to a dramatic shift in US funding of UN (and African Union) peacekeeping, or in its critical programmes to train, equip, and provide lift for current and future UN TCCs. Given the underlying factors detailed above, any sea change in this regard would be unlikely. A worst case scenario for the UN would occur in the event of both increased fiscal pressures and an unfavourable political context in the US (i.e., Republican control of both chambers of Congress and the Presidency). Such a scenario would likely result in heavy cuts to, or dissolution of, programs like the Global Peace Operations Initiative. It would be much more difficult, however, to decrease the US share of the assessed UN peacekeeping budget significantly due to both global and domestic pressures. Despite this, American officials could surely insist on even more stringent cost-cutting measures in peacekeeping operations, accelerated drawdowns in current missions, and for any new missions, the use of even lighter footprints, or non-military Special Political Missions in place of the more costly multidimensional peacekeeping operations.

Conversely, a best case scenario, in a more sympathetic political and fiscal context, would see funding of US training programmes continue at their current levels past 2014, combined with additional operational assistance, facilitated by the US military drawdown in Afghanistan. Such assistance would be most impactful were it to include the provision of key enablers, such as airlift and sealift, military utility helicopters and land transport (APCs), and intelligence and logistics support. This could be augmented by increased funding of State Department, US Agency for International Development, and Justice Department initiatives to develop reliable, rapidly deployable rosters of specialized policing and rule of law experts, as well as initiatives to support developing countries in the recruitment, training, and use of indigenous capacities.

[54] Soderberg, 'Enhancing US Support', p. 22.

4

The United Kingdom

Paul D. Williams[*]

In mid-1995, as the United Nations (UN) was wrapping up its peace operation in Bosnia and Herzegovina, UNPROFOR, Britain ranked as the organization's top troop-contributing country (TCC) with over 10,000 of its soldiers wearing the UN's Blue Helmets. During the 2000s, however, the number of British Blue Helmets rarely crept above 600. Most of them served in the UN missions in Cyprus and the Balkans. Britain's leading role in the Cyprus mission, UNFICYP, dated from the 1960s, the result of its colonial legacy, the importance of its military areas on the island, and its sense of political responsibility for mitigating the conflict. Britain's presence in the UN's Kosovo mission, UNMIK, derived from a combination of more recent normative and security commitments: having been a leading proponent of humanitarian intervention to stop ethnic cleansing in the Federal Republic of Yugoslavia in 1998–99, it was not surprising that Britain deployed troops to stabilize the situation afterwards.

This chapter describes the pattern of Britain's contribution to international peace operations during the 2000s in order to explain why so few UK uniformed personnel (troops, military experts, and police) were deployed on UN-led, Blue Helmet missions. The small number of British UN peacekeepers was not because UK officials thought UN peacekeeping was always ineffective: in appropriate circumstances, peacekeeping clearly works and British governments regularly acknowledged as much.[1] Rather, the central explanations lie in a series of interrelated factors. First, a principal concern for successive British governments at the UN was to continue to use their position as a permanent member of the Security Council to wield strategic influence over the direction of peacekeeping operations without having to deploy many of

* Thanks go to Alex Bellamy and Thierry Tardy for their helpful comments on earlier versions of this chapter.

[1] See Virginia Page Fortna, *Does Peacekeeping Work? Shaping Belligerents' Choices after Civil War* (Princeton, NJ: Princeton University Press, 2008); *The National Security Strategy of the United Kingdom* (London: Stationery Office, Cm 7291, March 2008), pp.17, 41, 48, 50.

their own personnel in the process. Second, with regard to achieving Britain's broader foreign policy goal, UN peacekeeping was only ever seen as one among many tools, and only rarely was it considered the most important or effective. During the 2000s, Britain's principal foreign policy problems demanded other tools and UK officials were not sufficiently moved to provide peacekeepers out of a general obligation to support the UN or maintain international peace and security. In this sense, Britain's strategic priorities simply diverged from those of UN peacekeeping, which was conducted primarily in Africa, Lebanon, and Haiti. Third, Britain preferred to deploy its armed forces under other frameworks: unilaterally, in coalitions with valued partners, or through NATO and later European Union (EU) multilateral frameworks. In part, this was because important sections of the British military and political establishment retained a deep scepticism about the effectiveness of UN multidimensional peacekeeping, especially related to questions concerning force structure, command and control, rules of engagement, and national caveats. As a consequence, although Britain entered the twenty-first century led by a Labour government determined to use its military as 'a force for good' in world politics, this did not translate into a commitment to provide peacekeepers for UN-led Blue Helmet missions.[2] Such concerns fed into a brand of British exceptionalism which saw UK troops as too highly trained and equipped to be wasted as rank and file UN peacekeepers. Worse still, they might actively lose their warrior skills if they engaged in too much UN peacekeeping. Finally, both at home and abroad, there were few voices pushing British governments to provide more UN peacekeepers. Consequently, successive UK governments did not have to work hard to defend their record on UN peacekeeping from critics calling for them to do more.

To address these issues, the chapter proceeds in three parts. The first summarizes UK contributions to UN-led and UN-authorized peace operations during the 2000s. The second section provides an overview of the British government's decision-making process with respect to UN-led peacekeeping missions. The third section discusses the interrelated factors noted above which help explain the relatively small number of UK troops deployed on Blue Helmet operations. Looking to the future, the conclusion discusses whether the British withdrawal from Afghanistan is likely to lead to an increase in contributions to UN-led peacekeeping. In sum, Britain is unlikely to provide many Blue Helmets, especially in the form of infantry battalions. However, it is more likely to seek to bolster its credibility as a leading political voice on the strategic direction of UN peacekeeping by continuing to make various token contributions and providing more specialist, niche capabilities to enhance the effectiveness of UN operations.

[2] Ministry of Defence, *The Strategic Defence Review* (London: Stationery Office, Cm 3999, 1998), para.19.

4.1 UK CONTRIBUTIONS TO UN-LED AND UN-AUTHORIZED PEACE OPERATIONS

Britain's contribution of uniformed personnel to UN-led, Blue Helmet missions has varied significantly over time. From being, albeit briefly, the UN's top TCC in mid-1995 with over 10,000 peacekeepers deployed, between 2000 and 2011 very few British soldiers were deployed as UN Blue Helmets (see Figure 4.3).[3] This was in stark contrast to the large numbers of British troops dispatched to UN-authorized crisis management operations, principally in the Balkan, Afghan, and (post-invasion) Iraq theatres.

This section summarizes these international deployments before providing an overview of the UK's contributions to UN-led peacekeeping missions. Here, Britain's contributions can be summarized as: (1) its leading role in the UN Security Council's decision-making process and its support for the post-Brahimi Report reform agenda for peacekeeping; (2) its financial contributions to the UN peacekeeping budgets as well as other voluntary contributions; and (3) the deployment of its uniformed personnel to UN peacekeeping operations, principally in Cyprus and the Balkans.

In the 2000s, the vast majority of Britain's military contributions to UN-authorized (but not UN-led) peace operations came in the Balkans (primarily Bosnia and Herzegovina[4] and Kosovo[5]), the International Security Assistance Force (ISAF) in Afghanistan, and the multinational stabilization force in the aftermath of the US-led invasion of Iraq. For much of this decade, Britain had over 12,000 troops deployed in these missions (see Figure 4.1). Taking rotation issues into account, the UK military was operating at a very high tempo with a high proportion of its forces (see Figure 4.2).[6] This led to the widespread perception that Britain's military was stretched too thin to achieve its objectives in Afghanistan and Iraq and certainly had no spare capacity to devote to additional UN-led missions.

UK officials have cited three main reasons for Britain's preference for participating in UN-authorized over UN-led, Blue Helmet missions.[7] First,

[3] During the 1990s, the UK also provided several *gratis* intelligence officers to serve in DPKO's Information and Research Unit. This used information from the field to draft threat assessments and scenarios for UN missions and facilitated intelligence-sharing between its members. The unit was disbanded in 1999 by a UN General Assembly resolution after the UN decided that the use of *gratis* officers gave unfair advantages to already powerful developed states but that the organization could not afford to fund non-*gratis* posts for the unit.

[4] During the 2000s, Britain contributed approximately 3,000 troops to the SFOR mission and then, from 2004, about 700 of the 7,000 troops in EUFOR Althea.

[5] In the early 2000s, Britain contributed approximately 3,000 troops to KFOR in Kosovo, down from its initial deployment of 19,000.

[6] For every soldier deployed on active duty another two are required to make operations sustainable (one training for deployment and one on leave after deployment).

[7] FCO sources cited in Ralph Wilde, 'Characteristics of International Administration in Crisis Areas: Aspects of UK Government Policy', *Electronic Journal of Comparative Law*, 10:3 (December 2006), p. 8. At http://www.ejcl.org/103/article103-15.pdf

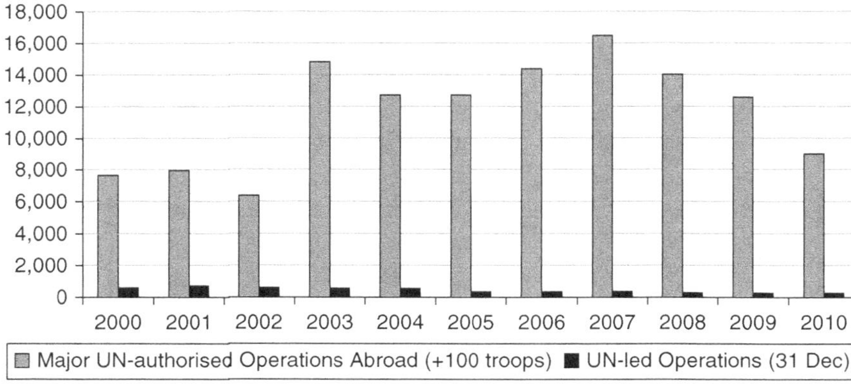

Figure 4.1 UK Major Military Operations Abroad, 2000–2010[8]

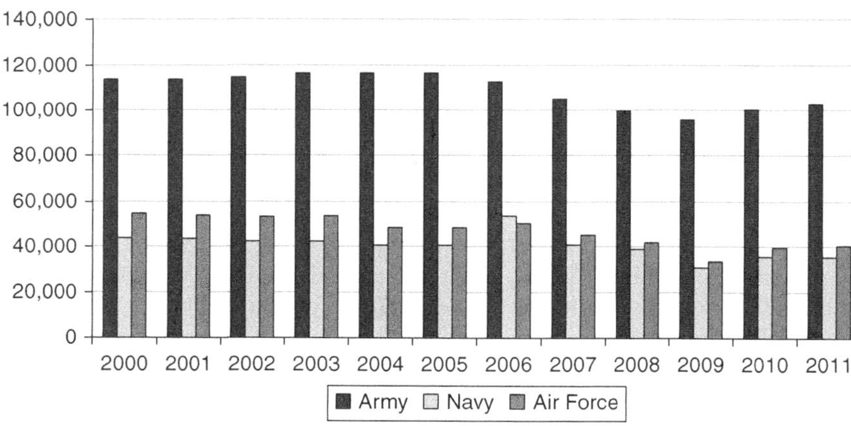

Figure 4.2 Active Personnel in the UK Armed Forces, 2000–2011[9]

was the belief that Britain could wield more influence over coalition missions than UN-led operations. Second, it was stressed that the UK had particular obligations with regard to crisis management arising from its membership of NATO and the EU which generally trumped considerations about participating in UN missions. Third, UK troops were thought to be better suited for high

[8] International Institute for Strategic Studies, *The Military Balance* (Abingdon: Routledge annual 2000–10). Debate continues over whether the Iraqi no-fly zones, Operations *Northern* and *Southern Watch* were authorized by the UN Security Council. They were not authorized explicitly in resolutions 687 or 688 but are included in this figure. They account for 1,104 personnel in 2000 and 2001, and 1,365 personnel in 2002.

[9] International Institute for Strategic Studies, *The Military Balance* (Abingdon: Routledge annual 2000–11).

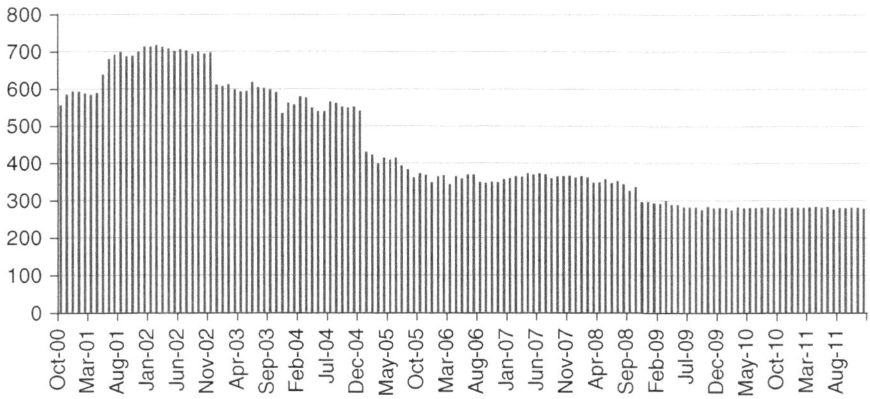

Figure 4.3 UK Uniformed Personnel in UN Peacekeeping Operations, 2000–2011

intensity/combat missions that were generally not carried out by UN Blue Helmet operations.

Britain's emphasis on UN-authorized operations carried out as coalition, NATO, and sometimes EU missions left relatively little room for military contributions to UN-led peacekeeping. When Britain did contribute uniformed personnel to these Blue Helmet missions it did so with a small number of troops, various token contributions (such as staff officers and military observers), and training support packages for other UN troop- and/or police-contributing countries (TCC/PCCs).

The UK's troop deployments were primarily in Cyprus (UNFICYP) and Kosovo (UNMIK), operations that Britain had a particular political stake in (see Figure 4.3). Britain's deployment of troops to UNFICYP in March 1964 was its first participation in UN peacekeeping—and it remains there today. In this case, Britain, which had assumed responsibility for security on the island, was keen to divest itself of those responsibilities and spread the burden by calling for a UN peacekeeping operation. Its Cyprus contributions are also partly about the UK's commitment to the sovereign base areas on the island. In recent years, military personnel have also acknowledged that there is a certain amount of rest and relaxation in a UNFICYP deployment because the level of threat is so low.[10] The several hundred British troops in UNFICYP have also helped to bolster the UK's overall UN contribution numbers to a less embarrassing level: without the UNFICYP deployment, Britain would have slid well down the rankings of UN TCCs, making it the lowest ranked P-5 member. Even so, senior British officials have debated whether to withdraw their troops. Although some participants have framed this as an economic issue, others have

[10] Author's interview with a UK official, London, 12 October 2011.

been keen to focus on whether UNFICYP's presence is helping the Cyprus peace process and conflict resolution.[11] The UK believes that all UN peacekeeping operations should be kept under periodic review and that they should only continue if they advance conflict resolution and a political settlement. It is not clear if UNFICYP is having that effect.

In Kosovo, the deployment of UK ground troops followed in the wake of NATO's *Operation Allied Force*, the aerial bombardment of the Federal Republic of Yugoslavia in 1999. Initially, nearly 20,000 British soldiers were deployed as part of the 50,000-strong UN-mandated but NATO-led Kosovo Force (KFOR). However, in the early 2000s approximately 150 British uniformed personnel were also deployed as part of the UN Mission in Kosovo, UNMIK. By the end of 2008, following Kosovo's unilateral declaration of independence in February that year, the British presence in UNMIK had been reduced to just one police officer.

In addition to troop contingents, Britain also deployed a variety of staff officers and military observers to UN peacekeeping missions.[12] Although some sections of the British military viewed such postings as an irritating distraction from the priority campaigns in Iraq and Afghanistan, others had more positive views.[13] The UK government certainly saw several benefits in these token contributions.[14] One advantage was that they helped the overall efficacy of UN missions. Second, placing a colonel (or several) in various field mission headquarters or within DPKO could generate greater strategic influence over the missions than if the UK deployed a couple of infantry companies. These staff officers might also provide access to potentially useful military intelligence. They certainly afforded British officers the chance to work with counterparts from non-NATO and non-EU countries, and sometimes to gain experience of operating one or two levels above their British Army rank. Finally, the British Army's significant surplus of colonels and other officers provided an opportunity for some of them to gain detailed knowledge of contemporary UN operational procedures, as well as different—but still useful—operational experiences than those available in Iraq and Afghanistan.[15]

[11] Author's interview with a UK official, New York, 14 November 2011.

[12] Once a decision was taken by the UK to support or bid for a staff slot on a UN mission then the relevant background, training, and experience requirements were identified and the job advertised on the British Army's intranet site. These UN appointments were advertised alongside all other operational appointments on the regular appointment sheets. British officers then volunteered and a representative was selected.

[13] Author's interview with Lieutenant-General Jonathon Riley, 21 December 2011.

[14] See also Katharina Coleman's chapter in this volume.

[15] Author's interviews with UK officials in London and New York, 12 October, 8 December, and 23 December 2011.

The principal aim of these token deployments was to help Britain influence the strategic direction of UN peacekeeping operations through the quality rather than the quantity of its contributions. As a government document made clear in 2006:

> Given limited resources and other UK military commitments/priorities, our approach is based on quality over quantity. Our aim is to place Staff Officers in influential strategic positions, usually in the mission headquarters, where their experience and quality can best add value to the effectiveness of a mission. We also have three senior UK military officers serving in the Department of Peacekeeping Operations in New York serving on long-term contracts.[16] We also contribute through short-term (up to 3 months) deployments of staff expertise for specific tasks.[17]

Britain did not always acquire all the staff officer posts it wanted to fill. Sometimes, candidates from other countries were selected. At other times, UK personnel faced political obstacles. For example, having maintained approximately five staff officers in the UNAMID operation in Darfur, these had to be withdrawn in late 2009 after the Government of Sudan refused to renew their visas—this was part of Khartoum's broader concerted strategy to use the fact that UNAMID should retain a 'predominantly African character' as an excuse to expel competent non-African personnel, thereby reducing the mission's overall effectiveness.

The UK has also deployed police officers to a variety of UN missions. However, this has raised several challenges. The House of Commons Defence Select Committee summarized the issue in the following manner:

> Policing within the UK is undertaken by over 50 forces covering three legal jurisdictions [Home Office (England and Wales), the Scottish Executive, and the Northern Ireland Office] .... Additionally the Ministry of Defence Police is an executive agency of MoD. This makes 'recruitment' for international missions very difficult. The FCO and DFID have a roster of police officers willing to go on missions, but while many junior officers volunteer, senior officers rarely do so. Ultimately, decisions to 'free' officers for international deployments are made by the UK's Chief Constables, not the Home Secretary. The Chief Constables will give greater priority to fulfilling their obligations at home than to international deployments. Overseas police commitments are considered marginal activities in the context of the Home Office's agenda. This amounts to a disincentive to the constabularies to volunteer police officers, especially senior ones, to international missions.[18]

[16] Of course, UK military officers serving in DPKO become UN officials when they are there. At times, this has generated some friction inasmuch as they are not always doing the UK government's bidding.

[17] *The United Kingdom in the United Nations* (London: Stationery Office, Cm 6892, July 2006), para. 196.

[18] House of Commons Defence Select Committee, *Iraq: An Initial Assessment of Post-Conflict Operations: Sixth Report of Session 2004–05* (London: Stationery Office, HC 65-I March 2005),

An additional problem was that UK police forces are predominantly staffed by officers with no firearms training, and since UN peacekeeping operations often called for armed police this raised further administrative and training issues which had to be overcome. Nevertheless, despite such hurdles, it is also important to recall that UK police forces have the type of senior officers—not 'beat cops'—who could be very useful at the strategic level of UN missions, i.e., recently retired officers who have experience of setting up new forces, payroll structures, mentoring, etc.[19]

The UK government also provided training packages for other country's peacekeepers. Specifically, British military advisory and training teams (BMATT) operated in around ten countries worldwide while the Ministry of Defence (MOD) also provided short-term training teams (STTT) in other areas of the world, typically for between two and six weeks.

Beyond deployments of uniformed personnel, Britain also made several other contributions to UN peacekeeping. As a permanent member of the Security Council, the UK played an important political role in the significant increase in the number and complexity of UN peace operations in the 2000s. Britain also wielded veto power over the establishment of all UN peacekeeping operations. Although it did not cast its veto during this period, in late 2008 Britain argued strongly against establishing a UN peacekeeping operation in Somalia when the outgoing George W. Bush administration in the US pushed for such a mission to take over from the beleaguered African Union force, AMISOM.[20]

Under successive Labour governments (1997–2010), Britain was also a vocal advocate of the post-Brahimi Report reform agenda for peacekeeping and other relevant thematic priorities, notably protection of civilians, protection of children in armed conflict, and women, peace, and security. On the crucial issue of civilian protection, the Foreign Secretary argued shortly after the release of the Brahimi Report that UN peacekeepers must never 'stand aside while serious crimes against humanity are committed'.[21] By the end of the decade, the UK's focus was on strengthening the strategic relationship

paras 163–64. At http://www.publications.parliament.uk/pa/cm200405/cmselect/cmdfence/65/6508.htm

[19] Author's interview with a UK official, New York, 14 November 2011.

[20] See, for example, Wikileak Cables from the US Embassy in London numbers 08 LONDON2898 and 08LONDON3038 on Somalia, at http://wikileaks.org/cablegate.html. The British rationale was that there was no peace to keep and it would be extremely difficult to find adequate numbers of peacekeepers with sufficient training/skills in the necessary tasks. As a consequence, the UK position was that 'It would be "irresponsible" to put ill-trained and poorly equipped troops in such a complicated peacekeeping operation.'

[21] Robin Cook and Menzies Campbell, 'Revised role in humanitarian tragedies' (3 September 2000), at http://www.globalpolicy.org/security/peacekpg/lessons/cook.htm

between the peacekeeping and peacebuilding functions of UN operations.[22] As part of this agenda, Britain also tried to 'develop a supply of suitable civilian personnel and deploy them into hostile environments, and to identify lessons to feed into policy, doctrine and training'.[23] In a joint initiative with France released in early 2009, Britain also stressed the importance of ensuring effective strategic oversight of peacekeeping; achieving efficient missions within existing resource constraints; and learning lessons from field experience.[24]

UN peacekeeping did not receive greater attention under the Conservative-led coalition government which assumed office in May 2010. Indeed, the coalition government argued that nurturing key *bilateral* relationships held the key to achieving Britain's foreign policy objectives. Its first National Security Strategy made no mention of peacekeeping, except to state that Britain was 'the third largest financial contributor to UN peacekeeping'.[25]

In financial terms, Britain was a leading contributor to the UN's peacekeeping budgets, which cover compensation for TCCs/PCCs, mission-specific headquarters funding, and field support/logistics. In mid-2001, the UK's contribution on the UN peacekeeping scale of assessments was 7.0 per cent. By mid-2003 it had dropped to 6.8 per cent but by the end of the decade it had risen to 8.15 per cent. Britain was also one of the most generous funders of the UN's Peacebuilding Fund established in October 2006. As of early 2010, the UK had deposited nearly $53 million in the Peacebuilding Fund, more than any other state except Sweden, and had pledged an additional £11 million in 2011–12.[26]

Britain's financial contributions to UN peacekeeping were met from an annually managed budget which is a call on the Treasury's central contingency reserve, but which formed part of the Africa and Global Conflict Prevention Pools maintained by the Foreign and Commonwealth Office (FCO), the Department for International Development (DFID), and the MOD. Major (military) operations in crisis areas (e.g., Afghanistan and Iraq) were funded through ad hoc bids to the Treasury submitted by the MOD (the extraordinary budget had to be voted for by Parliament).This financial set up meant that if the UK government had wanted to contribute a few more personnel to UN

[22] *The National Security Strategy of the United Kingdom: Update 2009* (London: Stationery Office, Cm 7590, June 2009), p. 70.

[23] Richard Teuten (then head of the Stabilisation Unit), 'Stabilisation and Civil–Military Relations in Humanitarian Response: Mission Integration', paper for the NGO–Military Contact Group, London, 29 January 2009, http://www.stabilisationunit.gov.uk/index.php/about-us/key-documents/67-stabilisation-unit-speeches/120-nmcg-conference-stabilisation-and-civil-military-relations-in-humanitarian-response-missionintegration

[24] Non-Paper on UN peacekeeping released jointly by the UK and France in January 2009, at http://www.franceonu.org/IMG/pdf_09-0116-FR-UK_Non-Papier_-_Peacekeeping_2_-2.pdf

[25] *A Strong Britain in an Age of Uncertainty: The National Security Strategy* (London: Stationery Office, Cm 7953, October 2010), p. 22.

[26] Mr Duncan, *Hansard*, House of Commons, Written Answers, 14 March 2011, column 42.

peacekeeping operations it would have been at the budgetary expense of some of its other conflict management-related programmes operating with Conflict Prevention Pool funds. Ironically, this might not have been the case if Britain had decided to make a major troop contribution to a UN peacekeeping operation (e.g., of several thousand soldiers). In that scenario, the Treasury would probably have considered such a deployment a major operation and funded it directly from the contingency reserve.[27] In practice, of course, such a deployment was not discussed during the period under review here.

Despite the financial constraints, British officials were keen to emphasize that political imperatives, not financial concerns, drove their decisions on peacekeeping. As government minister and former senior UN official Lord Malloch-Brown stated in late 2009, when the UK's contribution to UN peacekeeping was higher than initially expected, this meant the government had to dip 'into the budgets of the FCO, DFID and the MOD to make up the shortfall'. Nevertheless, he continued, 'the political, security and strategic arguments for a peacekeeping operation must always prevail and . . . we must work out how to pay for it subsequently. Otherwise, we would have a terrible inversion of the priorities we must have when moving on peacekeeping operations.'[28]

4.2 UK DECISION-MAKING MECHANISMS FOR UN PEACEKEEPING

Historically, British governments have viewed UN peacekeeping as a potentially useful political tool to promote their foreign policy objectives. As a result, the Foreign Office, not the Ministry of Defence, had the main responsibility for handling it. Since the Suez Crisis (1957), the FCO has adopted a broadly positive attitude although it realized long ago that 'a UN peacekeeping operation was not just a tool of the member states but could also play a role as an independent actor'. This lesson was first learned the hard way when Britain failed to generate any real leverage over UNEF in the aftermath of the Suez crisis.[29] In this context, UN peacekeeping occupied at best a niche role in Britain's Cold War policies but it did prove useful in several respects: it helped preserve stability in regions where Britain had interests; it was used to help Britain save face (as in the UNEF operation); it could be a useful scapegoat to

[27] Author's communication with UK official, London, 31 January 2012.

[28] Lord Malloch-Brown, *Hansard*, House of Lords, 6 July 2009, column 446. Later that year, Baroness Kinnock also confirmed that the UK government 'would not block a UN mission in the Security Council on financial grounds alone'. *Hansard*, House of Lords, 7 December 2009, column 887.

[29] Neil Briscoe, *Britain and UN Peacekeeping, 1948–67* (Basingstoke: Palgrave Macmillan, 2003), pp. 230, 227.

conceal an ineffectual policy; it could be a temporary expedient tool until a better approach was found; and it offered a means of burden-sharing (e.g., UNFICYP) or burden-passing (e.g., UNTSO).[30]

Within the Ministry of Defence, UN peacekeeping has rarely been a priority. It was not treated particularly seriously during the Cold War. Indeed, the first Army Field Manual on Peace Keeping Operations was only produced in 1988. UN peacekeeping was thrust to prominence in the early 1990s, however, especially after Britain provided the UNPROFOR Force Commander and briefly became the UN's top TCC because of its contributions in Bosnia and Herzegovina. Nevertheless, it was not until 1994 that the subject was included in the syllabus for the initial Army Officer training at the Royal Military Academy Sandhurst, although it had been addressed at the intermediate and advanced staff courses well before then.[31] Like UN peacekeeping more generally, its status in Whitehall entered the doldrums between 1995 and 1999.

In late 1999, the Defence Secretary clarified to Parliament that Britain had made available to the UN forces from its pool of Joint Rapid Reaction Forces. These forces would be available for operations across the entire crisis spectrum and under national, NATO, EU, OSCE, coalition, or UN auspices under the UN Standby Arrangement System. If the UN requested UK military support, and if it received ministerial agreement, the Defence Secretary confirmed that his ministry would decide how that support could best be provided and which unit(s) from the Joint Rapid Reaction Forces to engage.[32]

By the mid-2000s, decisions about whether and how to contribute to UN peacekeeping operations were assessed within the overall context of the UK's international priorities. Since 2003, these priorities were made explicit in a series of documents and national security strategies.[33] Compared to the post-9/11 counter-terrorism agenda, the invasion of Iraq, and a sustained focus on the commercial aspects of diplomacy, UN peacekeeping was a long way down the list of the UK's international priorities.

In 2006, in response to a questionnaire distributed by the International Congress on Comparative Law, UK officials stated that the decision of whether or not the government would participate in a UN peacekeeping mission was

30 Briscoe, *Britain and UN Peacekeeping*, pp. 231–2.

31 See Tom Woodhouse and Alexander Ramsbotham, 'The United Kingdom', in David Sorenson and Pia Christina Wood (eds.), *The Politics of Peacekeeping in the Post-Cold War Era* (London: Frank Cass, 2005), pp. 96–7.

32 Geoff Hoon, *Hansard*, House of Commons, Written Answers, 4 November 1999, column 252.

33 *UK International Priorities: A Strategy for the FCO* (London: FCO, December 2003). This determined that for 2003–6 the FCO had four specific policy responsibilities: (1) promoting the security of the UK within a safer, more peaceful world; (2) improving prosperity in the UK and worldwide through effective economic and political governance globally; (3) promoting a strong role for the UK in a strong Europe responsive to people's needs; and (4) making sure that UK Overseas Territories are secure and well governed.

based on three main factors: security concerns (i.e., what was the level of threat posed by the crisis in question both for domestic UK security and international stability more generally); humanitarian concerns; and the historical links between Britain and the recipient country in question. Geographical considerations were said to be immaterial to the decision-making process. The likelihood of other countries contributing to the mission was apparently a relevant but not decisive factor.[34]

The decision on whether to contribute was driven from the top down, dictated by the political intent of the government after considering recommendations from the FCO, MOD, and DFID. Once the political decision to contribute was made, the Ministry of Defence would submit options to the UN for consideration alongside other TCCs. The size, composition, and modalities of the UK's contribution depended upon a risk assessment wherein the risk to UK personnel was balanced against the severity of the situation.[35] This would vary according to whether it was civilian or military personnel being deployed.[36]

The Foreign Office has remained the lead department in this process although it kept in constant dialogue with the MOD and DFID. To facilitate coordination in this area, in 2005 the Cross Whitehall Peacekeeping Action Plan was established. This entailed a working group involving FCO, MOD, and DFID personnel to coordinate their activities and commission initiatives on issues such as strengthening the capacity of regional organizations to conduct peace operations, supporting the UN's peacekeeping capabilities through help with doctrine-writing, and coordinating Britain's approach to specific peacekeeping operations. By the end of the decade, however, this Action Plan had been replaced by less centrally coordinated cross-governmental meetings on different strands of the peace and security agenda, including revisions to and implementation of Britain's National Action Plan on UN Security Council Resolution 1325 and support to UN and regional peacekeeping from the multi-departmental Conflict (funding) Pool.[37] Since mid-2010 with the arrival of the Conservative-led coalition government, political decisions have been funnelled through the National Security Council. Before that, the Defence and Overseas Policy Committee played a similar role as it was responsible for the strategic direction of UK defence and overseas policy.

[34] Cited in Wilde, 'Characteristics of International Administration in Crisis Areas', p. 3.

[35] The document does not make clear the criteria the government uses to judge either 'risk' or 'severity'.

[36] FCO sources cited in Wilde, 'Characteristics of International Administration in Crisis Areas', p. 3.

[37] Whereas the FCO currently has a seven-person team to cover peacekeeping issues, the MOD's support to the UN is just two people. At UK–UN, approximately a dozen officials work on peacekeeping issues—this includes those who work on geographic desks where peacekeeping operations are deployed, those who work on relevant cross-cutting issues, and the military team.

In this bureaucratic context, it is the UK Mission to the UN in New York that acts as Britain's initial point of regular interface with UN DPKO, receiving its requests for troops and other capabilities, and whose personnel engage with the relevant UN mechanisms such as the Special Committee on Peacekeeping Operations (C34), the Security Council's Working Group on Peacekeeping Operations, and the General Assembly's Administrative and Budgetary Fifth Committee. From the UK's perspective, part of the challenge is that unlike its commitments to provide standby forces for NATO's response force and the EU's battle groups, there is no obligation to retain standby forces earmarked solely for use in UN peacekeeping operations. As noted above, even British troops placed under the UN Standby Arrangement System were not solely available for UN missions.

Until 2009, DPKO's outreach was distinctly ad hoc and based around needs arising from specific missions. Since 2009, however, DPKO has circulated 'Gap Lists' summarizing the authorized but still missing capabilities within all of the UN's ongoing peacekeeping operations. These lists were faxed to the UK–UN mission on a regular, sometimes monthly, basis. Perhaps because it already knew the answer would be 'no', DPKO rarely asked British officials for troop contributions but instead pitched its requests for niche capabilities and enablers such as aviation units, APCs, medical support, senior staff officers, etc. The UK–UN mission would then pass this information to Whitehall with any additional comments it thought were relevant. It is not clear what level of attention these requests received in Whitehall but the widespread feeling among the British government was that the Iraq and Afghan campaigns left the armed forces with very little spare capacity. One UK official, for example, suggested that the question of supplying British infantry to UN missions simply did not appear on the political radar screen for most of the decade.[38] Sometimes, however, UN DPKO communicated its needs more emphatically. In the summer of 2010, for example, the Under-Secretary-General for Peacekeeping, Alain Le Roy, visited the UK and explicitly asked for a response to DPKO's requests.[39]

DPKO also regularly approached Britain for senior mission personnel and staff officers. This apparently stimulated British efforts to develop a better system for feeding such requests. For most of the 2000s, these requests focused on military personnel, but as noted above, towards the end of the decade the UK's Stabilisation Unit started initiatives to enable Britain to provide more personnel to fill senior mission civilian roles.[40]

[38] Author's interview with UK official, London, 12 October 2011.

[39] Author's interview with UK official, London, 27 October 2011.

[40] Author's interview with UK official, London, 27 October 2011; Teuten, 'Stabilisation and Civil–Military Relations'.

4.3 EXPLAINING UK CONTRIBUTIONS AND NON-CONTRIBUTIONS

Seven interrelated factors help explain the small number of British peacekeepers in UN-led peacekeeping operations during the 2000s. The order in which these factors are discussed below is not meant to suggest a clear hierarchy: in practice, these issues interrelate in complex ways which vary according to the missions and requests in question.

4.3.1 Alternative Strategic Priorities

The principal explanation is that during the twenty-first century Britain had more pressing security/foreign policy priorities. Specifically, UN-authorized or non-UN operations in the Balkans, Afghanistan, and Iraq soaked up the vast majority of political attention, military resources, and public support for overseas campaigns. In sum, UK foreign policy priorities did not converge with the UN's Blue Helmet missions. In this context, anyone broaching the subject of increasing UK contributions to UN-led missions would need to preface their pitch to the MOD with "after Iraq and Afghanistan . . . " or be laughed out of the room.[41] (Whether this means that in the absence of the Iraq and Afghanistan campaigns Britain would have deployed several thousand troops on UN-led missions is certainly open to doubt.)

This explanation suggests that when the UN needed UK military support, *realpolitik* dictated a negative response. One example was the UK's decision in 2006 not to send troops to participate in the revamped UN mission in Lebanon, UNIFIL II. London did apparently offer to provide a UK-manned AWACS surveillance aircraft, although the UN had to reject the offer because of cost considerations.[42] UNIFIL II was the one UN mission during the 2000s to which a number of major EU powers deployed troops, in large part because a distinct Strategic Military Cell was established to overcome some of their concerns about UN command and control issues. Nevertheless, Britain's strategic interests lay elsewhere and it came at a time when the UK military was stepping up its operations in Helmand, Afghanistan. Another relevant episode occurred in late 2008 when UN peacekeepers in Goma, DRC, came under sustained assault from Laurent Nkunda's CNDP fighters. At the time, Britain was one of the countries on the EU battle group standby roster. Yet during the crisis its officials argued strongly against the idea that an EU force should temporarily reinforce the beleaguered UN peacekeeping operation,

[41] Author's interview with a UK official, London, 12 October 2011.

[42] A. Walter Dorn, *Keeping Watch: Monitoring Technology and Innovation in UN Peace Operations* (New York: UN University Press, 2011), p. 188.

MONUC. Instead, the UK argued that MONUC should be bolstered from other sources precisely because it did not want to have to activate the EU battle group and hence deploy British troops. While the FCO apparently saw some merit in deploying British troops as part of an EU bridging force in the eastern DRC, the MOD was much less keen on such a mission given the prospect of additional commitments in Afghanistan.[43] Not only did this reveal the low priority accorded to the UN (and the EU battle group concept) by senior UK officials but the justification used—that Britain lacked spare capacity—also raised the serious question of whether it should have put itself on the EU battle group standby roster if it knew this.[44]

4.3.2 Alternative Institutional Preferences for Crisis Management

A related explanation suggests that although Britain was committed to the idea of international crisis management, this did not necessarily mean it would always provide peacekeepers to UN operations. As discussed above, during the 2000s, Britain deployed significant numbers of troops on coalition, NATO and even some EU missions but few to the UN (see Figure 4.1). This reflected the fact that British ministers were primarily focused on commitments arising from UK membership of NATO, which were given greater priority than those to the EU and certainly to the UN. As a consequence, the Ministry of Defence was heavily engaged in crisis management issues but not through UN structures. Officials within the UK–UN mission were keenly aware that this argument—'we're doing peacekeeping, just not UN peacekeeping'—did not go down well at the UN. They therefore regularly suggested that the UK should deploy a contingent of troops (say 300 strong) which would help strengthen a particular UN mission on the ground but which would also help increase British influence and credibility in a variety of debates at the UN. Apparently, ministers and senior officials in Whitehall were not receptive to this idea.[45]

4.3.3 Military Concerns

A third explanatory factor is scepticism about aspects of UN peacekeeping within the British military establishment. This scepticism has revolved around

[43] See Richard Gowan, 'From Rapid Reaction to Delayed Inaction? Congo, the UN and the EU', *International Peacekeeping*, 18:5 (2011), pp. 593–611.

[44] Author's interviews with UK officials, London, 12 October; New York, 14 November 2011.

[45] Author's interview with a UK official, New York, 14 November 2011.

concerns about costs but more prominently about UN command and control mechanisms.

Financially, UN compensation rates do not cover the costs of UK military deployment—the incremental costs (actual costs minus UN reimbursements) are thus prohibitive. Behind the scenes, for example, there have been frequent debates within the UK government over the cost of the UNFICYP deployment although it has always been concluded that the political consequences of withdrawal would be greater than the financial savings.[46] In an attempt to allay some of these costs and to free up army regulars for other missions, by December 2008 Britain's contribution to UNFICYP, *Operation Tosca*, was being conducted by members of the Territorial Army.[47] As noted above, however, British ministers have always been at pains to stress that cost would not be a prohibitive factor if national interests were thought to be at stake.

While broadly comfortable with UN command and control procedures for traditional peacekeeping missions, the British military had significant concerns about the UN's structures for more complex multidimensional missions, especially those which might require the use of force. In one sense, all alliance or coalition operations threaten unity of command—hence the military's long-standing suspicion of multinational operations and its preference for national operations or those based on a 'framework'/lead state model.[48] (These concerns do not apply solely to the military. In one recent case, the UK was planning to send some police officers to the UN missions in Sudan but it was worried that they would not receive adequate duty of care (i.e., their personal safety being assured) in the field because of problems with the UN chain of command.[49])

Within British military circles, if multinational operations are unavoidable, coalitions or NATO are the preferred vehicles, the EU comes a rather distant third and the UN even lower. In some sections of the British military the legacy of the UK's experiences in UNPROFOR continues to stain perceptions of the UN. As one current UK senior military officer who had been a commander in the eastern 'safe area' of Gorazde put it,

> After UNPROFOR, we took the view 'never again' unless the environment is truly benign. The British armed forces should only do enforcement in a coalition

[46] Author's interview with a UK official, London, 12 October 2011.

[47] In the previous nine years, Territorial Army personnel were only sent as individual augmentees (approximately ten such augmentees per year were deployed during this period). Bob Ainsworth, *Hansard*, House of Commons, Written Answers, 12 January 2009, column 89.

[48] Richard P. Cousens, 'Amritsar to Basra: The Influence of Counter-Insurgency upon the British Perspective of Peacekeeping', in Rachel E. Utley (ed.), *Major Powers and Peacekeeping* (Farnham: Ashgate, 2006), p. 59; Briscoe, *Britain and UN Peacekeeping*, p. 233.

[49] Author's interview with a UK official, New York, 14 November 2011.

> framework, preferably with a mandate from the UN. Right the way through the army there was a feeling that 'we will not wear that [UN] badge of shame again'.[50]

This episode was said to have exposed the UN's fundamental problems with force structure, command and control, mandates and rules of engagement issues, as well as the unwillingness of many field contingents and staff at UN headquarters to engage in anything other than consensual peacekeeping. The subsequent mythology in the British Army was that its forces were left unable to defend themselves because of the UN, which led to the problems of hostage taking and attacks on UK contingents. In fact, UNPROFOR did have a mandate to use force but the principal problem was that when UK (and other UN) forces engaged in combat they were regularly outgunned, in part because Western states, including Britain, were reluctant to accept the costs and risks that military escalation would have entailed.[51] In the end, UNPROFOR stimulated major debates in the UK's doctrine-writing circles which eventually produced the 'wider peacekeeping' publication.[52]

In some respects, this negative view of the UN was only compounded further with the British military's experience in Sierra Leone from 2000. This case provides a good illustration of the MOD/military perspective on UN peacekeeping at the start of the twenty-first century. Here, the UK recognized the UN force, UNAMSIL, was in a dire predicament but decided to assist by conducting a unilateral mission rather than put British troops under UN command. There were several reasons why Tony Blair's government deployed troops to Sierra Leone. Not only did many international eyes turn to Britain as the former colonial power but there was a need to protect British citizens; there was the humanitarian impulse to 'do something' as Sierra Leone teetered on the brink of a crisis that could be averted by the use or threat of military force; a democratically elected government needed help; Blair's party had widely touted the need for British foreign policy to emphasize its 'ethical dimension'; and there was a widespread perception that the future credibility of UN peacekeeping operations was at stake, particularly in Africa.[53]

The central lesson drawn by the British military from this episode was that unilateral UK help was sufficient to rescue the UN—there was no need for Britain to assume command of the UN mission or deploy troops within it.[54] The Foreign Office, on the other hand, was more worried that Britain's

[50] Author's interview with Lieutenant-General Jonathon Riley, 21 December 2011.

[51] For example, the British government rejected repeated proposals by the UN Secretary-General to replace UNPROFOR with a more robust Multinational Force.

[52] See MOD, *Wider Peacekeeping* (London: TSO, 1995) and for an overview of its genesis and the debates see Rod Thornton, 'The Role of Peace Support Operations Doctrine in the British Army', *International Peacekeeping*, 7:2 (2000), pp. 41–62.

[53] Paul D. Williams, 'Fighting for Freetown: British Military Intervention in Sierra Leone', *Contemporary Security Policy*, 22:3 (2001), pp. 140–68.

[54] Andrew M. Dorman, *Blair's Successful War: British Military Intervention in Sierra Leone* (Farnham: Ashgate, 2009), p. 13.

decision to remain outside UNAMSIL might undermine the UN mission.[55] So was the UK's UN Association which remained 'disappointed that they [the British troops] were not placed within the UNAMSIL structure'.[56]

Britain decided not to join UNAMSIL for three main reasons. First, it did not trust the competence of UN command and control, which in this case was initially led by an Indian Force Commander with the biggest TCCs being India, Nigeria, and Jordan. Consequently, British officials felt they would have to take full command of UNAMSIL, or keep UK forces out. The Ministry of Defence also argued that because of these concerns it would have to deploy a full brigade in order to become the largest TCC and thus be able to guarantee its pick of force commander for the UN mission. Instead, Blair's government opted to provide an over-the-horizon rapid response brigade.[57] Second, domestic public opinion did not favour a long British deployment. Indeed, the Conservatives and Liberal Democrats were deeply sceptical about committing British armed forces at all and at one point called for their withdrawal.[58] Keeping with tradition, the House of Commons was not given a vote on the deployment. Third, in May 2000, Britain had not figured out what its longer-term military commitment to Sierra Leone would be and hence did not want to tie itself into any sustained obligations.[59]

4.3.4 UK Exceptionalism

A fourth factor is the widely held self-image that Britain is a special power, not an ordinary UN TCC. As discussed above, British officials have correctly concluded that they gain significant strategic influence over UN peacekeeping through the permanent seat at the Security Council and various token contributions. British decision-makers thus routinely conclude that their troops would be wasted as rank and file infantry in UN operations because other states can provide such forces more effectively and cheaply.[60] Instead, the UK military is best used for high-end military operations like those in Sierra Leone, Afghanistan, or Iraq. This was one of the ways Blair's government justified the small number of British peacekeepers in UN-led missions: as one of the few states that could provide troops capable of conducting robust, 'first-in' expeditionary missions in 'challenging circumstances', it 'would expect to

[55] Dorman, *Blair's Successful War*, p. 78.
[56] *Memorandum by the United Nations Association of Great Britain and Northern Ireland* (March 2004) at http://www.publications.parliament.uk/pa/cm200304/cmselect/cmdfence/465/4042011.htm
[57] Dorman, *Blair's Successful War*, p. 117.
[58] Dorman, *Blair's Successful War*, p. 107.
[59] Dorman, *Blair's Successful War*, pp. 88–9.
[60] Author's interview with a UK official, London, 27 October 2011.

play a lesser part in enduring operations where many other countries can contribute'.[61] Such views echoed earlier sentiments that the British military was able to perform such tasks precisely because it had not geared itself up for peacekeeping. In the late 1990s, for example, the chairman of Parliament's Select Committee on Defence, Bruce George, endorsed the argument 'that the only reason why we [Britain] can provide such excellent troops in their present shape is that they have retained a high-intensity war-fighting capability, which can then be flexed into other shapes, whereas if we had designed our troops around a peacekeeping or gendarmerie function, they would be nothing like as good at peacekeeping'.[62]

While these descriptions of the UK's military capabilities were probably accurate they did not sit comfortably with the fact that the majority of British soldiers deployed in UN missions were in UNFICYP, one of the most 'enduring' and least militarily demanding of all UN peacekeeping operations.[63] Nor did they play well at the UN because, as one British official acknowledged, this argument was tantamount to saying 'your infantry are more expendable than ours'.[64]

4.3.5 The Africa Factor

Although not discussed explicitly in these terms and often rejected as a significant factor by UK officials who point to British operations in Sierra Leone, the fact that the majority of UN peacekeeping during the 2000s occurred in sub-Saharan Africa was significant. In particular, it reinforced the view that the UN tended to operate in areas that were not Britain's strategic priorities. It is a long-standing feature of Britain's post-Cold War security policy that Africa is not a major strategic concern, the partial exception being counter-terrorism arguments related principally to Somalia.[65] As a result, during the 1990s it was widely thought that 'a UK presence in major operations is unlikely outside Europe'.[66] British operations in Sierra Leone from 2000 appear to be the exception that confirms this rule. Beyond this case, Britain deployed only a handful of staff officers to UN missions and some small contingents (less than 100 soldiers) to some of the EU missions in the

[61] *Delivering Security in a Changing World: Supporting Essays* (London: TSO Cm 6041-II, December 2003), p. 3.

[62] Cited in Nigel D. White, *Democracy Goes to War: British Military Deployments under International Law* (Oxford: Oxford University Press, 2009), p. 157.

[63] Paul D. Williams, *British Foreign Policy under New Labour, 1997–2005* (Basingstoke: Palgrave Macmillan, 2005), p. 177.

[64] Author's interview with a UK official, New York, 14 November 2011.

[65] See Paul D. Williams, 'Britain and Africa in the Twenty-First Century', in Jack Mangala (ed.), *Africa and the New World Era* (New York: Palgrave Macmillan, 2010), pp. 37–51.

[66] Tom Woodhouse, 'The Gentle Hand of Peace? British Peacekeeping and Conflict Resolution in Complex Political Emergencies', *International Peacekeeping*, 6:2 (1999), pp. 28–9.

DRC. This raises the interesting counter-factual question of whether Britain would have contributed significantly to Blue Helmet operations if they had been authorized in more strategically important locales such as the Balkans, the Mediterranean, or the Middle East. As it turned out, Britain was never confronted with the question of how to contribute to a UN peacekeeping operation being deployed to an area of real strategic interest.

4.3.6 Difficult Domestic Politics

A sixth factor was the lack of a significant domestic constituency pushing Britain to provide more UN peacekeepers. This factor has several dimensions. First, while Britain's military is widely seen as one of its principal foreign policy assets, there were few voices in British domestic politics calling for it to be used more frequently in UN peacekeeping operations. Second, Britain's elected representatives have not seen UN peacekeeping as a priority. Indeed, it has rarely been debated in the House of Commons or House of Lords. By one count, between 1992 and 2006 there were only eight substantive debates on the UN as a whole in the House of Commons.[67] Nor was there much support for the idea within British academia. For example, in one of the few books explicitly intended to flesh out the contours of a 'progressive' UK foreign policy for Gordon Brown's government, 'peacekeeping' did not even warrant an entry in the index let alone a substantive discussion (nor did the UN Security Council for that matter).[68] The UK's UN Association was arguably the only group to consistently advocate that Britain should provide more UN peacekeepers. In December 2003, for instance, the Association wrote to the Defence Secretary to express concern that there was no reference in the Defence White Paper or the FCO White Paper on *UK International Priorities* to Britain's anticipated role in supporting UN peacekeeping operations. It also stressed that after the reforms outlined in the Brahimi Report (2000), which Britain strongly endorsed, 'we hoped that the response of the UK and its NATO partners would have been to enhance rather than to diminish their inputs'. It concluded that 'With British troops not being committed to work within UN Forces, we believe that Her Majesty's Government is failing to fulfill a major obligation placed upon its shoulders through its permanent membership of the UN Security Council.'[69]

[67] Simon Burall, Brendan Donnelly, and Stuart Weir, *Not In Our Name: Democracy and Foreign Policy in the UK* (London: Politico's, 2006), p. 162.

[68] David Held and David Mepham (eds.), *Progressive Foreign Policy: New Directions for the UK* (Cambridge: Polity Press, 2007).

[69] *Memorandum by the United Nations Association of Great Britain and Northern Ireland* (March 2004) at http://www.publications.parliament.uk/pa/cm200304/cmselect/cmdfence/465/4042011.htm

4.3.7 No International Pressure

A final factor was the lack of any significant international pressure on Britain to do more. In sum, there were no real short-term costs to the small number of British Blue Helmets. As several UK officials acknowledged, there was no indication that major UN troop/police contributing countries were willing to make this a major issue in their bilateral relations with Britain. Some speculated that perhaps Britain's official discourse might have been different if other UN members said, 'either you contribute more troops or we will stop contributing our troops'. If for example, India had made this a major bilateral issue and raised it with the British Prime Minister or Foreign Secretary then the UK government would have had to provide a public response. This did not happen and so Britain was never really publicly challenged on this issue.[70]

4.4 CONCLUSIONS

The main rationales for Britain's troop contributions to Cyprus, Bosnia and Herzegovina, and Kosovo and its various token contributions to UN-led missions elsewhere were a combination of political and security concerns. In this sense, Britain has used UN peacekeeping as one tool among many for advancing its foreign policy objectives, and not since the mid-1990s has it been considered a top priority. To the extent that successive UK governments saw generic value in UN peacekeeping this was only strong enough to drive financial contributions. Interestingly, compared to the often explicit debate amongst French officials, British officials rarely suggested that contributing UN peacekeepers might be a way to legitimize Britain's continued permanent seat on the UN Security Council.[71]

While there was some evidence of normative support for the idea of UN peacekeeping—recall that a significant rationale for the Sierra Leone deployment was to help the beleaguered UN mission—and especially recent peacekeeping reforms, this did not alter the fact that Britain's strategic priorities lay elsewhere. Thus Britain has been good at advancing relatively cost-free initiatives to stimulate peacekeeping reform without leading by example in the field.[72] To the extent that any institutional rationales were evident during the 2000s, they played a largely constraining role inasmuch as important sections

[70] Author's interviews with UK officials, London, 12 October; New York, 14 November 2011.

[71] See Thierry Tardy's chapter in this volume.

[72] See, for example, the Non-Paper on UN peacekeeping released jointly by the UK and France in January 2009, at http://www.franceonu.org/IMG/pdf_09-0116-FR-UK_Non-Papier_-_Peacekeeping_2_-2.pdf

of the British political and especially military establishment remain deeply sceptical about the lack of appropriate structures and competence levels at the UN. Economic factors did not weigh particularly heavily on the British debate about peacekeeping, although once again, their net effect was prohibitive.

Looking to the future, however, there is certainly room for Britain to increase its contributions to UN-led operations after the withdrawal from Afghanistan in 2014. In the post-Afghanistan era of financial austerity, senior figures in the British military might just conclude that a 'use it or lose it mentality' will prevail among UK politicians whereby the armed forces may come under pressure to use certain assets or lose their funding. During the 2000s, the British military did not need UN peacekeeping to make a case for relevance or the relevance of particular assets. But if the UK military is put under pressure to find business, UN peacekeeping operations might become a more attractive proposition, especially if they were to take place in strategically important areas for Britain such as the Middle East and Mediterranean.

In the interim period the British government is debating how it can best contribute to future UN peacekeeping operations. Given that Britain is unlikely to deploy many infantry contingents to Blue Helmet missions, the central practical question is what alternative types of capabilities it might provide. Naturally, this will depend on the type of armed forces that emerge in the post-Afghanistan era and how the coalition government implements the 2010 Strategic Defence and Security Review. Perhaps of most relevance for the future of peacekeeping are the UK government's priority areas for UN reform, especially its call for a more representative Security Council, greater UN budget discipline and more equitable allocation of UN costs among member states, a greater role for conflict prevention alongside peacekeeping and peacebuilding efforts, greater integration of UN efforts across the political, security, development and humanitarian sectors, and better UN coordination with NATO and the EU, including more strategic dialogue and cooperation on planning operations.[73] For early 2012, Britain's current priorities are said to focus on providing niche capabilities to UN peacekeeping missions such as in the information and surveillance areas, and providing training and training support, specifically developing a new type of pre-deployment mission-specific training package that will increase the effectiveness of newly deployed UN peacekeepers.[74] Other areas under consideration are medical and evacuation capabilities for missions.

[73] *Securing Britain in an Age of Uncertainty* (London: Stationery Office, Cm 7948, October 2010), pp. 61–2. The sixth priority referred to ensuring the appropriate governance of cyber space.

[74] Author's interview with a UK official, New York, 23 December 2011.

5

France

*Thierry Tardy**

French policy towards United Nations (UN) peacekeeping offers a mixed picture of what France wants to achieve in the field of conflict management and through what institutional frameworks. On the one hand, France is greatly involved in the design and decision-making process of contemporary UN-led peacekeeping operations. On the other hand, after having been equally present in the field during the early 1990s (in operations in the former Yugoslavia, Cambodia, and Somalia in particular), France underwent a major policy shift that led it to distance itself from UN-led operations. Drawing on the difficulties encountered in Bosnia and Herzegovina, France developed a rather dismissive approach towards the UN as a peacekeeping actor and began to favour other institutions as vehicles for crisis management, such as NATO as of 1995 and then the European Union (EU) as of 2003.

This chapter offers an assessment of French policy and perceptions in relation to the virtues and limits of UN peacekeeping operations in the twenty-first century. It starts with an overview of the strategic relationship between France as a medium-sized power and the UN—its Security Council in particular—as a relic of France's past grandeur as well as a vehicle of French security policy. This leads to the dichotomy between, on the one hand, the political role that France plays at the Security Council in peacekeeping-related debates among others, and on the other hand, a very selective and relatively small contribution to UN field missions.

The chapter focuses on the rationale for this dichotomy and the security, political, and institutional factors that explain French policy. While France's often leading role in debates about the mandating and management of peacekeeping operations is partly aimed at justifying France's permanent seat in the Security Council, its feeble participation in field missions raises

* I am grateful to Megan Chester for her research assistance.

questions about its status at the UN. The chapter asks whether France is being weakened at the UN because of its absence from UN operations and how it responds to criticisms of its low-key field presence. Finally, it explores how likely and under what conditions France might increase its involvement in UN-led peacekeeping operations, especially in a post-Afghanistan era.

5.1 FRANCE AND THE UN: A STRATEGIC RELATIONSHIP

The UN plays an important role in shaping France's identity and policy on the international scene primarily by allowing France to act beyond the limits of its material power, but also because the type of norms and values that are conveyed by the UN are consistent with French political culture. More specifically, France's permanent seat at the UN Security Council simultaneously offers an important platform for French foreign policy and gives France an international status that it would not enjoy otherwise. Given the country's De Gaulle-inherited obsession for maintaining its position in international politics, France's presence in the club of great powers compensates for its inexorable relative decline since the inception of the UN. This observation appears somewhat paradoxical when put in the context of De Gaulle's dismissive view about the role of the UN as an actor of security governance.[1] Yet all presidents of the Fifth Republic have recognized the strategic importance of the UN and have tried to take advantage of France's special status at the UN Security Council.[2]

This has been particularly true since the end of the Cold War and the concomitant outbreak of new conflicts—notably in Europe—and revitalization of the UN Security Council. In this context, the French narrative established a link between France's position at the UN and the notion of responsibility in world affairs. Together with 'vital interests' and 'strategic interests', the third category of 'national interests' was defined by the 1994 *White Paper on Defence* as 'interests that correspond to [France's] international responsibilities' that 'derive from its obligations as permanent member of the UN Security Council and its particular vocation'.[3] The necessity

[1] De Gaulle had a state-centric approach to international politics and was therefore distrustful vis-à-vis the UN, especially in the context of decolonization when the UN General Assembly tried to interfere into French Algerian politics.

[2] See Rachel Utley, *The French Defence Debate: Consensus and Continuity in the Mitterrand Era* (Basingstoke: Macmillan, 2000), p. 187.

[3] *White Paper on Defence 1994* (Paris, 10/18, 1994), p. 50.

to both take advantage of the privilege and justify France's position in the club is well understood within the French foreign policy apparatus.

In a context of slow decline, by the early twenty-first century France was probably best described as a medium-sized power. Yet it has done relatively well in maintaining its profile as an actor that still counts in world security governance. Arguably, France is maximizing its Security Council position in a way that is similar to the United Kingdom. France is extremely active in the Council (see below), developing an agenda on many country-specific or thematic issues to the extent that it may contend that it deserves the inherited permanent seat. No other foreign policy asset gives France a similar position on the world scene. The only one approaching such importance is its nuclear status, but it is too contested to offer the same kind of benefits. Over the last decade, examples abound—from Iraq to Libya, but also Lebanon, Chad, and Côte d'Ivoire in the peacekeeping area—where France took advantage of its permanent position at the Security Council to ensure a centrality in decision-making that would otherwise not be guaranteed.

Beyond its permanent membership of the Security Council, France is also eager to develop and act through multilateral instruments that, again, allow Paris to shape the foreign policy environment in a way that bilateral relations would not permit. In doing so, France combines a realist agenda that pushes it to promote and defend narrowly defined national interests and a liberal approach to foreign policy, whereby it advocates the development of international relations based on some agreed norms and values.[4]

These parameters have a direct impact on France's policy vis-à-vis peace operations. In general terms, French participation in these operations is one of the key dimensions of the country's response to security threats. By contributing to peace operations, France intends to meet security challenges such as regional conflicts, refugee flows, organized crime, humanitarian emergencies, and violations of human rights. Peace operations thus appear as tools of France's security policy to influence events in areas where it has strategic or historical interests. At the same time, these operations are a way for France to raise its profile as a political and military power. In this sense, notwithstanding the propensity of democratic states to participate in peace operations, participation in such missions appears to be a political imperative for France.[5]

However, French policy towards the UN as a peacekeeping actor has been shaped by current and past perceptions of the UN's effectiveness and efficiency, as well as by the evolving priorities, concerns, and institutional

[4] See Thierry Tardy, 'France: Between Exceptionalism and Orthodoxy', in E. Kirchner and J. Sperling (eds.), *Global Security Governance* (London: Routledge, 2007), pp. 32–3.

[5] See Andreas Andersson, 'Democracies and UN Peacekeeping Operations, 1990–1996', *International Peacekeeping*, 7:2 (2000), pp. 1–22.

preferences of French conflict management policy. In this context, the French position is characterized by a dichotomy between the importance it attaches to the UN as a security institution and its relative absence from the main operational instrument at the UN's disposal, namely, peacekeeping operations.

5.2 LESSONS FROM THE 1990S: FROM LEADERSHIP TO RETRENCHMENT

5.2.1 UNPROFOR in Bosnia and Herzegovina: France's Responsibility and Losses

In the post-Cold War era, French policy towards the UN as an operational instrument of conflict management oscillated between unconditional support in the early 1990s and sustained mistrust as of the mid-1990s.[6] After the Cold War, the UN's revitalization was received positively by France, which saw the organization as both a valuable tool of conflict management and a foreign policy instrument. Subsequently, France played a key political role at the Security Council and made major contributions to UN operations in the former Yugoslavia (in which it was one of the largest three troop contributors), Somalia, and Cambodia. Indeed, in early 1994, France was the largest troop contributor to all UN missions (see Table 5.1). This was consistent with its foreign policy narrative on the necessity of holding its rank on the Security Council by living up to its responsibilities.[7]

However, the difficulties encountered by the UN Protection Force (UNPROFOR), and therefore by France, in Bosnia and Herzegovina between 1992 and 1995, which culminated with the fall of the safe area of Srebrenica and the subsequent massacre of more than 7,000 civilians by Bosnian Serb forces, had a direct impact on French perceptions of the role of the UN in conflict management.[8] More specifically, a major lesson learned through the Bosnian experience (and reinforced by the Rwandan episode, 1990–94), both for France and for the majority of Western countries, was that the UN was not an appropriate tool for complex and multidimensional peace operations in situations of ongoing violence, and therefore had to be replaced by other instruments such as regional arrangements, ad hoc coalitions, or unilateral initiatives. As stated by former French Defence Minister François Léotard, the

[6] See Thierry Tardy, 'French Policy Towards Peace Support Operations', *International Peacekeeping*, 6:1 (1999), pp. 55–78.

[7] See *White Paper on Defence 1994*, pp. 50–1.

[8] See Helge Brunborg and Henrik Urdal, *Report on the Number of Missing and Dead from Srebrenica* (The Hague: International Criminal Tribunal for former Yugoslavia, February 2000).

only way out of the Bosnian quagmire was to 'move away from the UN system'.[9]

France lost seventy soldiers in Bosnia and Herzegovina and had between 600 and 700 wounded.[10] It also experienced the inadequacy of a UN peace-keeping operation where there was 'no peace to keep' and where, most importantly, the Blue Helmets could do very little in the face of humiliations by the local forces. Paradoxically, there was a widespread perception that France had become the victim of an operation for which it had itself designed the mandate at the UN Security Council, and in which it had secured most of the key positions (such as Force Commanders). Yet the trauma was particularly acute within the military, which combined well-founded critiques and a scapegoat approach to conceal their own miscalculations on the nature of such 'new' peace operations.

Despite the fact that France was involved at all levels of the UN structure during UNPROFOR, its disavowal of the mission stemmed from distrust of the UN's command and control structure itself. Furthermore, French criticism focused on the very nature of peace operations and the role of military force in their implementation. What was at stake here was the compatibility of the key principles of UN peacekeeping operations (consent of the host state, impartiality, and non-resort to force except in self-defence) with those of the imperatives of decisive military action.[11] For the French military, the norms of peacekeeping contradicted the principles of military action and therefore increased the vulnerability of soldiers whilst limiting their freedom of action.[12] Moreover, the French military came to the view that the principled and rigid distinction between peacekeeping and peace enforcement was problematic. The fact that, by definition, one could not move from the peacekeeper's impartial posture to a more coercive one without jeopardizing the long-term nature of the international presence—which was by and large the French position throughout the Bosnian war—was strongly contested by the military. This difference of opinion was evident even during the operation in Bosnia, where the ambiguities of the UNPROFOR mandate led to tension between

[9] Testimony of François Léotard, *Srebrenica: rapport sur un massacre. Volume 2: Hearings* (Joint Information Mission, French National Assembly, report No. 3413, 2001), p. 260.

[10] Testimony of Alain Juppé and Testimony of François Léotard, *Srebrenica: rapport sur un massacre*, pp. 103 and 256 respectively.

[11] The Joint Concept on the Employment of Armed Force defines five principles of military action: freedom of action, concentration of effort, economy of resources, surprise, and the controlled use of force; see *Joint Concept on the Employment of Armed Force* (Paris: Centre Interarmées de Concepts, de Doctrines et d'Expérimentations, French Ministry of Defence, January 2010), pp. 28–30.

[12] See 'Enseignemants Tactiques. Les opérations terrestres de l'armée de terre des années 90—Témoignages', in *Cahier de la réflexion doctrinale* (Paris: Centre de Doctrine d'Emploi des Forces, French Ministry of Defence, 2005), pp. 37–8.

some of the French Force Commanders and their political counterparts in Paris, to the extent that the military also considered themselves as paying for the mistakes made at the political level (in France and at the UN).[13]

Beyond Bosnia and Herzegovina, French policy vis-à-vis UN peace operations has since the end of the Cold War focused on managing these ambiguities and contradictions inherent in multidimensional peacekeeping. In this effort, France has oscillated between different positions: on the one hand, it has embraced the activity of peace missions as it participated in many such operations through various institutional frameworks (UN, NATO, EU, coalitions of states); on the other hand, France—or rather the French military—have been keen to maintain the primacy of the combat functions of its soldiers, which they argued must not be undermined by participation in peace operations.

5.2.2 Policy Shift: Moving Away from the UN

In the mid-1990s, these various considerations led to a reorientation of French crisis management policy towards a stricter definition of the conditions for French engagement paralleled by a change in institutional preferences and a form of re-nationalization. France remained committed to peace operations (see below), but moved away from the UN and instead favoured frameworks—such as NATO, the EU, or coalitions of states—that better suited its political and military requirements in terms of strategic cultures, command and control structures, or conception of the use of force. The institutional channels that were favoured were also perceived as minimizing the dangers of the aforementioned ambiguities on the nature of peace operations. This policy shift was endorsed by the 1994 *White Paper on Defence*, which indicated that the UN Security Council may ask regional organizations to share the burden of crisis management and further stated that the 'participation of French forces will be contemplated only if the mandate and the operation match certain political and military criteria', including 'the hierarchy of our strategic priorities and the interests which we intend to defend in the world' as well as 'the modalities of mission implementation, in particular the rules of engagement [that] will need to be approved at the political level, national and multinational'.[14]

All subsequent doctrinal and policy documents that draw upon lessons from the early 1990s operations follow this rationale, insisting on the necessity to better define the conditions for French engagement so as not to repeat past

[13] Author's interviews as part of his doctoral research with French senior officers, 1994 to 1997. See also Thierry Tardy, *La France et la gestion des conflits yougoslaves (1991–1995). Enjeux et limites d'une opération de maintien de la paix de l'ONU* (Brussels: Bruylant, 1999).

[14] *White Paper on Defence*, pp. 75–6.

errors. As an example, a Chief of Staff's document issued in January 1995 stated that whenever multidimensional peace operations were deployed in semi-permissive environments, the 'French component should, as much as possible, remain under national or allied command so as to guarantee the effectiveness of action and allow for identical rules of engagement'.[15] In the same vein, while considering complex peace operations, a French parliamentary inquiry conducted after the Rwandan genocide made the point that the intervention mode that had proven its effectiveness was 'the establishment of a force under national or international command, at the request of the Security Council', where the 'responsibility for running the operation falls on a lead-nation or a defence regional organisation', i.e., not the United Nations.[16]

Equally important in this policy development was the reference to Chapter VII of the UN Charter in Security Council resolutions.[17] This became a criterion for French participation, regardless of which institution took the lead. UNPROFOR's resolutions mainly fell within Chapter VII, but the consensual spirit of the operation was considered one of the main sources of the difficulties encountered. For the French military in particular, clear rules of engagement that unambiguously referred to Chapter VII and allowed the use of force in cases other than self-defence were seen as necessary to keep control of the situation on the ground in semi-permissive environments.[18]

In practice, missions such as *Operation Turquoise* in Rwanda during the summer of 1994 or the Rapid Reaction Force in Bosnia and Herzegovina in June 1995 corresponded to this new approach.[19] In both cases, the effectiveness of military operations was to be ensured by national oversight as opposed

[15] See *Doctrine Lanxade. Orientations pour la conception, la préparation, la planification, le commandement et l'emploi des forces françaises dans les opérations militaires fondées sur une résolution du Conseil de Sécurité de l'ONU* (Paris: French Chief of Staff, March 1995). The same approach is expressed in the French Aide-Mémoire to the UN Secretary-General's *Supplement to the Agenda for Peace* (1995), as well as in the Parliamentary report on Rwanda (see *Rapport d'information sur les opérations militaires menées par la France, d'autres pays et l'ONU au Rwanda entre 1990 et 1994* (Paris: National Assembly, No. 1271, 1998).

[16] *Rapport d'information sur les opérations militaires menées par la France . . .*

[17] The French Aide-Mémoire to the UN Secretary-General's *Supplement to the Agenda for Peace* states that 'The decision to launch [peace restoration] operations must be based on Chapter VII of the Charter of the United Nations.' See 'Letter dated 18 January 1996 from the Permanent Representative of France to the United Nations addressed to the Secretary-General' (UN document, A/50/869-S/1996/71, 30 January 1996).

[18] Interestingly enough, UN Security Council Resolution 1701 (2006), which strengthened UNIFIL in Lebanon and led to greater French contributions, did not refer to Chapter VII due to the opposition of the Lebanese government. Nevertheless, it authorized UNIFIL 'to take all necessary action' (para. 12) to implement its mandate, which France saw as an acceptable compromise.

[19] In June 1995, following numerous Blue Helmets being taken hostage in several places in Bosnia and Herzegovina, France, the United Kingdom, and the Netherlands assembled a multinational force mandated by the Security Council to protect UNPROFOR, principally around Sarajevo.

to UN command. Later, the NATO-led operations during the implementation of the Dayton Peace Agreement (IFOR/SFOR) as of 1996, and then throughout the stabilization of Kosovo (KFOR) as of June 1999, as well as the EU-led operations in Africa as of 2003, fell within the same logic. In all cases, the UN still played the key role in legitimizing the operations—through Security Council resolutions—but, contrary to the immediate post-Cold War period, it was no longer the preferred operational institution. While the UN remains an important forum for French policy development and expression, the consensus among the political class, i.e., well beyond the military establishment, is that it is ill-suited for the type of operations that the so-called 'new wars' call for.[20]

This policy shift from the UN to ostensibly more effective regional organizations (or coalitions) along with the insistence on a better definition of the conditions for French engagement poses the question of a possible concomitant evolution from a liberal 'milieu goals' to a more realist 'possession goals' approach.[21] In other words, is the shift a sign of an inclination towards a clearer interest-based security policy that regional institutions would be better placed to deliver?[22] The answer is positive to a certain extent: France indeed wants to be more selective and to intervene where clear security interests have been identified, which may be in contradiction with the idea of collective security as understood by the UN. In the meantime, the defence of 'milieu goals' is not mutually exclusive with pursuit of 'possession goals'—the former may indeed serve the latter inasmuch as the liberal approach implies national interests of a different nature rather than the absence of such interests. Furthermore, both the 1990s UN operations (in Cambodia and former Yugoslavia) and the three UN operations to which France contributed during the 2000s (in Lebanon, Côte d'Ivoire, and Chad and the Central African Republic, see below) are clear cases where a French geopolitical agenda drove engagement. Conversely, some EU-led operations—such as the two operations in the Democratic Republic of Congo (DRC)—may also be seen as falling within the liberal agenda of promoting international stability rather than buttressing directly threatened interests. Thus, in the end, we should conclude that the shift in French thinking evident in the second half of the 1990s was less an evolution of the French vision of the ultimate purpose of crisis management than a quest for improving effectiveness of the military implementation of Security Council mandates.

[20] See Rachel Utley, 'A Means to Wider Ends? France, Germany and Peacekeeping', in Rachel Utley (ed.), *Major Powers and Peacekeeping* (Aldershot: Ashgate, 2006), pp. 66–7.

[21] See Arnold Wolfers, *Discord and Collaboration* (Baltimore: Johns Hopkins University Press, 1962), pp. 73–4.

[22] On the issue of realist versus liberal states' motivations in UN peace operations, see James Lebovic, 'Uniting for Peace? Democracies and United Nations Peace Operations after the Cold War', *Journal of Conflict Resolution*, 48:6 (2004), pp. 910–36.

5.3 THE SMALL FRENCH PRESENCE IN UN-LED PEACEKEEPING OPERATIONS

A stricter definition of the conditions for French engagement in peace operations led to a decreased presence in UN missions. In general terms, the number of French personnel deployed in UN operations significantly decreased in the second half of the 1990s. There were 13,955 personnel deployed (in sixteen UN operations) in January 1999, versus 63,504 (in seventeen operations) in January 1995.[23] Over the same period, the French contribution decreased from 5,082 (8 per cent of the total) to 580 (4.15 per cent of the total) (see Table 5.1 and Figure 5.1). In the decade that followed (see Table 5.1 and Figure 5.2), while the number of personnel deployed started again to increase at the turn of the century, with the creation in 1999–2000 of large operations in Sierra Leone, Kosovo, and the DRC, to reach 39,061 in January 2001, the French contribution remained at a low level, with 501 personnel in 2001 (1.28 per cent of the total), and even 320 in January 2004 (0.65 per cent), ranking France as the thirtieth largest contributor of troops and police to UN peacekeeping operations that year. Most notably, France did not make more than a token contribution to the large operations of Sierra Leone, Liberia, and the DRC.

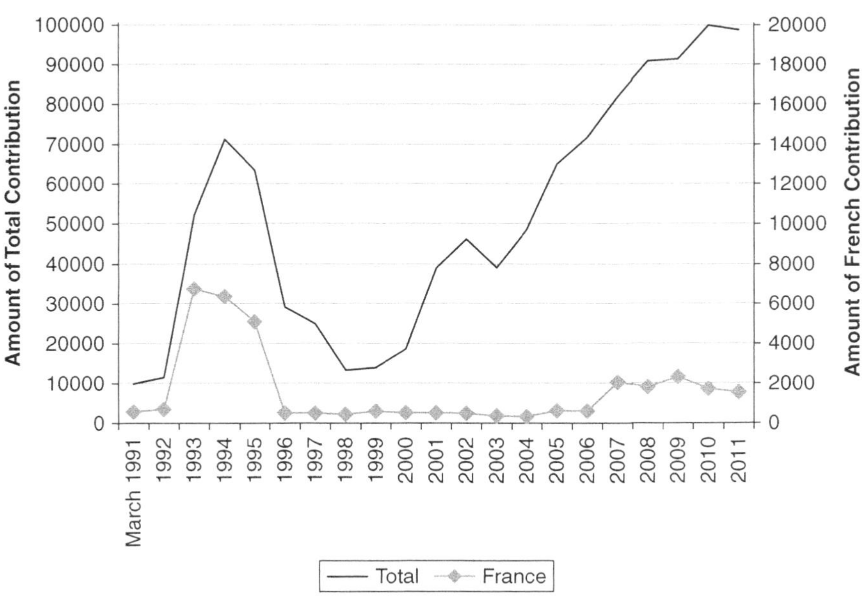

Figure 5.1 French Versus Total UN Peacekeeping Contributions

[23] All figures given in the following pages and tables come from the UN website, accessible at http://www.un.org/en/peacekeeping/resources/statistics/contributors.shtml (from 2011) and http://www.un.org/en/peacekeeping/resources/statistics/contributors_archive.shtml (before 2011).

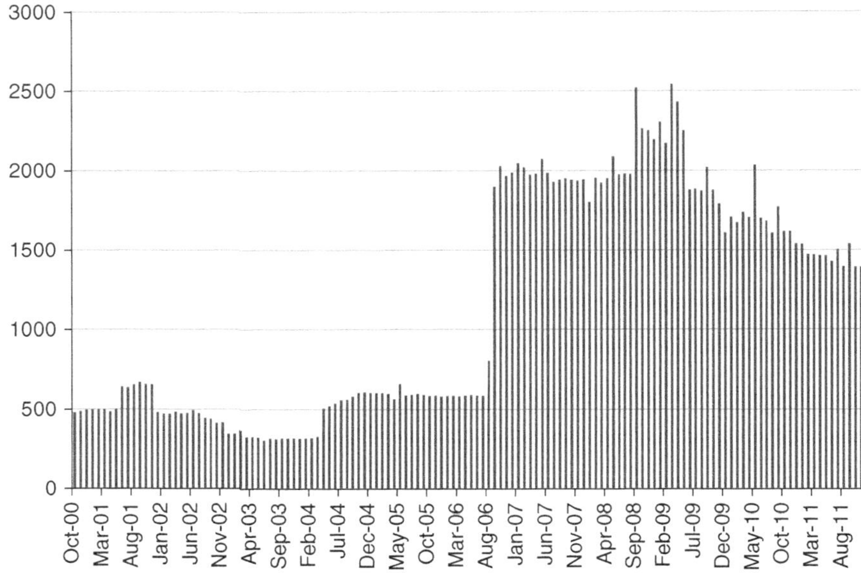

Figure 5.2 French Uniformed Personnel in UN Peacekeeping Operations, 2000–2011

In this context of weak operational engagement, in 2004 France started to return to UN peacekeeping, in a select number of operations, notably in Côte d'Ivoire, Lebanon, and Chad. France participated in the UN Operation in Côte d'Ivoire (UNOCI) from its inception in April 2004 with an initial contribution at 185 troops (engineer unit) that was by and large constant until its withdrawal in March 2009 (see Table 5.2).[24] In Lebanon, the French contingent was significantly reinforced with the establishment of UNIFIL II in August 2006 (from 432 personnel in August to 1,531 personnel in September), and increased to 2,177 personnel in September 2008 (see Table 5.3), making France the second largest troop contributor after Italy. As for Chad and the Central African Republic (CAR), in March 2009 France 're-hatted' some of its soldiers that had been deployed in the EU bridging operation (EUFOR Chad/CAR) into the UN operation (MINURCAT 2) (see Table 5.4).[25] This commitment was maintained until early 2010, when France started to withdraw its troops from MINURCAT.

[24] See 'UN Mission's Summary detailed by Country', 30 April 2004. At http://www.un.org/en/peacekeeping/resources/statistics/contributors_archive.shtml

[25] From March 2008 to March 2009, the EU deployed a UN-mandated military mission in Chad and CAR as a bridging operation before the UN took over in March 2009 with the MINURCAT 2.

Table 5.1 French Contributions to UN Peacekeeping Operations, 1991–2011

	*2011**	*2010*	*2009*	*2008*	*2007*	*2006*	*2005*	*2004*	*2003*	*2002*	*2001*
French contribution	1537	1709	2308	1803	2049	586	606	320	348	473	501
Rank	19	16	13	15	10	22	21	30	27	27	28
Total	98,837	99,943	91,382	90,883	81,992	71,811	65,050	48,590	39,147	46,239	39,061
Percentage	1.55	1.71	2.52	1.98	2.5	0.81	0.93	0.65	0.88	1.02	1.28

* 31 January of each year

	*2000**	*1999*	*1998*	*1997*	*1996*	*1995*	*1994*	*1993*	*1992*	*March 1991*
French contribution	507	580	429	486	494	5,082	6,356	6,737	684	558
Rank	15	12	13	24	22	2	1	1	10	11
Total	18,643	13,955	13,329	24,952	29,140	63,504	71,303	52,127	11,495	9,927
Percentage	2.71	4.15	3.21	1.94	1.69	8.0	8.91	12.92	5.95	5.62

* 31 January of each year

Table 5.2 French Contributions to UNOCI (Côte d'Ivoire)

April 2004*	October 2004	April 2005	October 2005	April 2006	October 2006	April 2007	October 2007	April 2008	October 2008	March 2009	April 2009
185	195	199	199	199	197	199	195	198	194	192	20

* end of each month

Table 5.3 French Contributions to UNIFIL (Lebanon)

August 2006*	September 2006	September 2007	September 2008	September 2009	September 2010	September 2011
432**	1,531	1,587	2,177	1,585	1,575	1,439

* Re-enforcement of UNIFIL that becomes UNIFIL 2; ** end of each month

Table 5.4 French Contributions to MINURCAT (Chad/CAR)

March 2009*	April 2009	May 2009	June 2009	July 2009	August 2009	September 2009	October 2009	November 2009	December 2009	January 2009	February 2010	March 2010	April 2010
802**	839	686	319	320	325	324	310	224	51	19	50	47	16

* The UN operation takes over the EU-led mission; ** end of each month

Along with these three operations, France regularly contributed to between four and nine other peace operations throughout the 2000s.[26] More specifically, it sent gendarmerie personnel (between 80 and 100) to UNMIBH in Bosnia-Herzegovina until the termination of the operation in late 2002, as well as to UNMIK in Kosovo (about eighty personnel until the mid-2000s before the contribution was slowly reduced until UNMIK gave way to the EU mission EULEX). It also deployed gendarmes to MINUSTAH in Haiti (particularly in the sixteen months following the January 2010 earthquake, with up to 212 personnel in June 2010). However, it is worth noting that the overall French police contribution was cut by 57 per cent between 2000 and 2011 (from 212 in January 2000 to 92 in January 2011), whereas the percentage of the police contribution against the total French personnel deployed decreased from 41.8 per cent in 2000 to 5.9 per cent in 2011, mainly due to the increase in troops in Lebanon that was not paralleled by an equivalent police deployment. One interesting aside is that the French ratio of female-to-male personnel was 7.59 per cent in September 2011 (117 out of 1,540), to be compared with an average of 6.46 per cent for the permanent members of the Security Council, or an average of 5.81 per cent in the European Union.

Apart from Haiti and Kosovo, all other personnel commitments—military and police—consisted of less than twenty individuals. Most notably, the French contribution to MONUC in the DRC never exceeded twenty people.

By the end of February 2012, France ranked eighteenth out of the UN's troop and police contributing countries with 1,398 personnel out of 98,926. This ranked it first out of the 'Western European and Others Group' (WEOG). The fact that the WEOG's top contributor was ranked only eighteenth overall illustrates the 'commitment gap', discussed in the introduction to this volume, whereby 'Northern' countries contribute relatively few personnel to UN operations. France's contribution should also be analysed in light of its presence in Lebanon which accounts for 1,302 of its personnel, or 93 per cent, leaving less than 100 personnel for the other six UN operations to which France contributes.

5.4 RATIONALE FOR FRENCH ENGAGEMENT: SECURITY AND INSTITUTIONAL PARAMETERS

This brief overview of French commitments to UN peacekeeping operations poses the question of why France participated in the three aforementioned

[26] MINURSO in Western Sahara; MONUC/MONUSCO in the DRC; UNMEE in Ethiopia-Eritrea; UNMIL in Liberia; UNOMIG in Georgia; UNTSO in Israel; UNAMID in Sudan (Darfur); MINUSTAH in Haiti; and UNMIK in Kosovo.

missions in Africa and Lebanon but not others. Was French policy driven by security or political interests, or was it the result of a broader commitment to the UN role in the maintenance of international peace and security? In any case, how do these contributions square with France's overall distrust towards the UN as an operational actor described earlier?

5.4.1 Côte d'Ivoire, Lebanon, and Chad: Strategic Interests and UN's Comparative Advantage

The answers to these questions seem to reveal both a narrow interest-driven approach and the need to take account of institutional considerations. Furthermore, in each case, particular circumstances allowed France to overcome the underlying issues in its UN policy. First, through its contribution to the UN operations in Côte d'Ivoire, Lebanon, and Chad, France committed troops in places that clearly fell within its areas of strategic interest.[27] These three countries were seen as crucial to France's economic and political interests in the Middle East (Lebanon) and Africa (Côte d'Ivoire and Chad), to the extent that their stability had to be secured through a series of commitments, including of a military nature. As soon as the prospect of a UN operation for these countries was placed on the table, the French principled position towards the institution was inevitably modified.

Furthermore, in the two African cases, a national military presence preceded the deployment of a UN operation. In Côte d'Ivoire, the French UN deployment took place in parallel with—and was therefore facilitated by—the presence of *Operation Licorne*. The French-led (and UN-mandated) *Operation Licorne* was deployed in February 2003 to help stabilize the country following the Linas-Marcoussis Agreement and to protect French citizens in the country.[28] As the events of April 2011 showed, where French contingents used force alongside UNOCI to resolve a political impasse and protect civilians imperilled by a potential relapse into civil war, *Licorne* provided a rapid reaction capacity for the UN operation (including its French component) and a degree of force protection that the UN could not necessarily guarantee. In addition, the nature of the unit deployed in UNOCI—an engineering unit—limited the risks of possible misuse by the UN.

Chad/CAR was different in several respects but was of equal strategic importance. France has a long-standing military presence in Chad (*Operation Epervier*) in support of President Deby as well as in the CAR ('*détachement Boali*'), and pushed in 2007 for the establishment of a UN—and then EU—

[27] See Michael Gilligan and Stephen John Stedman, 'Where Do the Peacekeepers Go?', *International Studies Review*, 5:4 (2003), pp. 37–54.

[28] Its deployment preceded the UNOCI creation in April 2004.

operation on the frontier with Darfur. Although officially mandated to provide security and facilitate the delivery of humanitarian assistance in the eastern part of Chad and the CAR, the EU and UN operations were from the start suspected by the host government of being instruments of French policy in the region.[29] The French contribution to EUFOR Chad/CAR and *a fortiori* MINURCAT cannot be understood without reference to these considerations. Furthermore, although *Operation Epervier* was not in support of the UN mission, it implicitly offered a security guarantee to French units placed under UN command.

In this context, in both Côte d'Ivoire and Chad/CAR, the French contribution to UN operations can be interpreted as a means to ensure a certain degree of credibility for the missions, the success of which was instrumental to the stability of the countries concerned and therefore to the French position there. In the Chad/CAR case, French backing for the UN mission was also aimed at consolidating what had been achieved by the EU bridging operation.

This being said, the extent to which the French contributions to these two missions indeed served national interests is not obvious given the limited size and short duration of France's commitment. Also, because France already had a military presence in these two countries, the question is raised as to why it decided to contribute to the parallel UN operations. In Côte d'Ivoire in particular, it might be asked what was gained by contributing engineers to UNOCI that could not be achieved through *Operation Licorne*? This suggests that there are limits to what can be explained by reference to the interests-driven approach.

This leads to the second set of reasons that explain the French presence in UN operations: institutional considerations. In both Côte d'Ivoire and Chad, French policy and narratives about the need for long-term stabilization instruments could hardly have been squared with a concomitant absence from the UN operations. In Chad, given French involvement in establishing the EU mission and the subsequent UN force, there was significant pressure to 're-hat' French troops when MINURCAT took over. In other words, at the point of the transition to MINURCAT, France could maintain a plausible commitment to pursuing collective crisis management in that country only through a direct contribution to the UN. Arguably, the specificity of these circumstances and the pressure exerted on France in these two countries was not observed in other cases of UN deployments, most notably in the DRC.

Lebanon offers a slightly different picture, due to the longer-term French commitment to UNIFIL, but also because institutional considerations were less prominent. Lebanon has long been a place of strategic interest for French Middle East policy that has justified a military presence in a peacekeeping format since 1978 when UNIFIL was established. UNIFIL was created at the

[29] See Hylke Dijkstra, 'The Military Operation of the EU in Chad and the Central African Republic', *International Peacekeeping*, 17:3 (2010), pp. 395–407.

initiative of France. There was little doubt at the time that France's presence in UNIFIL was aimed at buttressing narrowly defined interests rather than 'milieu goals'. These considerations remained throughout the 2000s and were central to the French position in 2006. As stated by the French Foreign Minister at the UN Security Council when the resolution on UNIFIL II was adopted, 'France has played a very active part in the search for a solution' as it is 'linked to Lebanon by deep historical and cultural ties and by strong and ongoing relations with the countries of the region'.[30]

In terms of institutional preferences, options other than the UN were examined by European countries when considering how to strengthen UNIFIL in order to facilitate an Israeli withdrawal from Lebanon in the summer of 2006. Yet the UN was eventually chosen as UNIFIL was already present on the ground, and the UN framework met both the preferences of Lebanese actors (any other Western arrangement would have been unacceptable to Hezbollah in particular), and those of large troop contributors such as India or China. However, the increased French commitment was made possible by the establishment of the Strategic Military Cell (SMC) within the UN Department of Peacekeeping Operations (DPKO), which gave the French military optimum control over the use of their units.[31] What France sees as the imperfect nature of the UN was therefore partly remedied by the creation of this mechanism.

Overall, what this shows is that France's participation in UN operations is linked to specific circumstances that can in some circumstances lead to increased contributions. Such contributions have tended to be relatively selective and short-term, however. With the exception of Lebanon, there has been no long-term commitment to any of the other UN-led operations. French participation in Lebanon was the result of particular circumstances—namely its historical presence in the country, its role in the creation of UNIFIL in 1978, and the establishment of the Strategic Military Cell—and should not therefore be interpreted as a sign of a more general French return to UN operations.

In the meantime, these three cases also show that the UN may offer an institutional crisis management framework that cannot be ignored by France. It is certainly not seen as the best option, but the circumstances can, by default rather than by design, make the UN a temporary or ad hoc instrument of French peacekeeping policy. In this analysis, both narrow security interests and broader institutional reasons can justify the provision of French

[30] Philippe Douste-Blazy in S/PV.5511, 11 August 2006, p. 7.

[31] See Alain Pellégrini, *Un été de feu au Liban. 2006, les coulisses d'un conflit annoncé* (Paris: Economica, 2010), pp. 131–34; Richard Gowan and Alexandra Novosseloff, 'Le renforcement de la Force intérimaire des Nations Unies au Liban: Etude des processus décisionnels au sommet', *Annuaire français de relations internationales*, 11 (2010), pp. 245–67.

peacekeepers, not least because UN operations have sometimes deployed where France has limited institutional alternatives.

Finally, the DRC case attests to the type of institutional choices that France makes when contemplating its involvement in peace operations. While France has never gone beyond a symbolic presence in the MONUC/MONUSCO, it pushed twice—or even three times if one includes the 2008 failed operation[32]—for the deployment of EU-led missions to which it provided the bulk of the troops.[33] In all these cases, the EU was perceived to be better-suited than the UN for handling the complex and possibly hostile situation; the decision was therefore taken not to strengthen the MONUC through a direct French contribution but instead to create a parallel structure to facilitate a short-term intervention. Furthermore, in the case of *Operation Artemis* in 2003, France refused to 're-hat' its troops from the EU-led operation to MONUC; the type of political engagement that in Côte d'Ivoire and Chad justified a contribution to the UN mission was not apparent in the DRC.

5.4.2 Overcoming the Critique on France's Weak Troop Contribution

One could wonder to what extent the weak presence in UN operations undermines France's overall position at the UN. If medium-sized states justify their position at the Security Council in part by contributing to UN-led peace and security activities, then how does France overcome the paradox of its position? Three elements come into play here.

First, one argument is that France is a larger contributor than most other permanent members of the Security Council and European countries. As of September 2011, it came second among the five permanent members after China (which ranked 15th) and was well ahead of the United Kingdom (47th), Russia (50th), and the United States (60th). France was also well ahead of Germany—which ranked 48th. In other words, France occupies a position closer to that of China or Brazil when it comes to providing peacekeepers, than to the UK or Germany.

Second, despite its weak engagement in UN operations (or maybe precisely because of it), France often—and somewhat fallaciously—presents

[32] In November 2008, France considered the deployment of an EU-led operation in support of the MONUC following the *Congrès National pour la Défense du Peuple* (CNDP) offensive around the city of Goma. The operation was never established.

[33] In 2003, the EU deployed its first autonomous military operation (*Operation Artemis*) in the Ituri Province of DRC. This served as a bridging operation before MONUC took over. In 2006, the EU deployed another military operation (*Operation EUFOR DRC*) to support MONUC during the presidential election.

itself as one of the main contributors to UN operations, invoking both its financial participation—as the fifth largest contributor to the UN peacekeeping budget[34]—and the fact that it is a major contributor to UN-mandated—as opposed to UN-led—peace operations.[35] Beyond the contentious nature of the argument, France indeed remains very committed to peace operations mandated by the UN but run through other institutional channels, with an average of 5,000 to 9,000 personnel deployed in such missions over the last decade.[36] This is noticeable as it attests to a partial disavowal of the UN as an operational framework rather than a withdrawal from UN-mandated peace operations that still constitute the great majority of French military engagement.[37]

Third, as discussed below, France palliates its weak presence in UN operations by taking an active role in shaping policy. Taken together, these three sets of arguments allow France to be relatively successful in its positioning at the UN. There exists some pressure from the UN Secretariat and the main TCCs, yet France is in a position to refute its critics and, ultimately, to appear as an important conflict management actor.

5.5 CURRENT AND FUTURE TRENDS

5.5.1 Presidential Prerogatives on Military Engagements

Under the Fifth Republic, the French foreign policy decision-making process has largely been in the hands of the president. This has been constant regardless of the political orientation of the president and of the prime minister. Insofar as military contingents deployed on UN peace operations are concerned, decisions are made by the president but are to a large extent shaped by the ministers of foreign affairs and defence. As in the foreign affairs field more generally, the parliament plays a limited role in this process. In 2008, Article 35 of the Constitution was amended to make it mandatory for the executive power to 'inform the Parliament of its decision to deploy armed

[34] France paid 7.55 per cent of the UN peacekeeping budget in 2011–12.

[35] See for example, remarks by France at the Security Council's debate on peacekeeping, S/PV.6603, 26 August 2011, p. 12. See also Emmanuel Bonne, 'Western States and UN Peacekeeping: What Participation in a Post-Afghan Era?' in Thierry Tardy (ed.), *For a Renewed Consensus on UN Peacekeeping Operations* (Geneva: Geneva Paper—Conference Series No. 23, October 2011), p. 46.

[36] In 2011, France was mainly involved in four UN-mandated but not UN-led peacekeeping missions: ISAF (NATO) in Afghanistan (about 4,300 personnel); KFOR (NATO) in Kosovo (about 430); *Operation Licorne* in Côte d'Ivoire (about 1,100); and *Operation Atalanta* (EU) in the Gulf of Aden (about 280). See French National Assembly, Foreign Affairs Committee, Report on Defense, Vol. IV, No. 3775, 12 October 2011, p. 8.

[37] The operations in Libya and Afghanistan do not qualify as peacekeeping operations as defined in this volume.

forces abroad, at the latest three days after the beginning of the intervention' and to ask for the 'authorization of the Parliament' to prolong the length of the intervention after a period of four months. Such a vote was cast on 28 January 2009 on the operations in Côte d'Ivoire (*Operation Licorne*), Lebanon (UNIFIL), Kosovo (NATO's operation), and Chad/CAR (the EU operation). However, this provision has not significantly modified the decision-making process or degree of parliamentary oversight.

Overall, a broad consensus across the political spectrum has presided over the nature of French involvement in UN operations. Some divergences have existed, for example, on the rationale for the French presence in UNPROFOR in Bosnia and Herzegovina during the *cohabitation* (1993–95), which led to a policy shift in 1995 when Jacques Chirac was elected president, and on the choice of institutional alternatives to the UN, such as NATO in particular. However, these debates have not historically called into question the broad agreement about French policy in UN operations.

Over the last fifteen years, the military has presented UNPROFOR as the prime example of what should not be done. Particularly, many of the current senior officers who had command responsibilities in UNPROFOR twenty years ago have been the most anxious not to put French soldiers under UN command and have played a key role in advocating alternatives to the UN command and control structure, notably regional organizations, coalitions, or national operations. In the case of Lebanon in 2006, while the UN framework was used at the political level, the military pushed for the establishment of the Strategic Military Cell within the UN DPKO to ensure—in the end not necessarily successfully—better national control of the use of French troops.

In the end, while the UN remains, as reiterated in the 2008 White Paper on National Defence and Security, at the centre of the international security architecture, including in its legitimizing role of peacekeeping operations, it is still perceived as structurally ill-adapted to France's conception of crisis management.[38] French officials tend to see the UN through the lens of the early 1990s, although it is difficult to distinguish whether this perception is the result of current assessments of UN capacity, or if it is the product of historically based anguish rooted in UNPROFOR's failures twenty years ago. Furthermore, there are few if any discernible UN advocates in France challenging this position or demanding a debate to revisit the issue.

5.5.2 Policy-shaping at the UN

France's relatively modest troop and police presence within UN-led operations contrasts with its role at the political level, particularly at the UN

[38] *White Paper on National Defence and Security* (Paris: Odile Jacob, 2008), pp. 114–16.

Security Council where France actively participates in debates and resolution drafting. France is in the lead at the Security Council on the operations in Côte d'Ivoire, the DRC, Lebanon, and Burundi (as well as Chad/CAR until its withdrawal). Over the last three years, France has proposed/supported (alone or with others) an average of almost two-thirds of the draft resolutions dealing with peacekeeping subsequently adopted by the Security Council (16 out of 26 in 2009; 22 out of 36 in 2010; 25 out of 40 in 2011).[39] This is more than any other Security Council member.[40]

France is also active in thematic discussions both at the Security Council and in other political bodies such as the Special Committee on Peacekeeping Operations (C34), the Fifth Committee (Administrative and Budgetary issues), and the Security Council Working Group on Peacekeeping Operations. In 2009, following difficulties encountered by MONUC in particular (when facing fighting between the Congolese armed forces and Laurent Nkunda's rebels in November 2008), France, together with the United Kingdom, launched an initiative to improve the overall effectiveness of operations, and in particular their political and military direction.[41] Its three main points related to the strategic oversight of operations, the implementation of mandates, and the insertion of peacebuilding tasks (with the definition of benchmarks) into exit strategies, but the initiative also included reference to the management of administrative, logistical, and financial aspects of missions, civilian protection and robust peacekeeping, and Security Council working methods. Those issues have been taken to different UN bodies in relation to the parallel DPKO/DFS New Horizon Agenda and the work that followed, including seminars, policy papers, and inter-governmental meetings.[42] Overall, France has, through these debates, managed to ensure a certain level of visibility and deflect criticism about its weak field presence. France may be reluctant to commit troops to UN operations but cannot be accused of being disinterested in what it presents as 'one of the most important and certainly most symbolic activities of the United Nations'.[43]

[39] Author's calculations based on the number of resolutions each year which dealt explicitly with peacekeeping and which country had proposed them (while taking account of resolutions supported by several countries).

[40] The United Kingdom proposed/supported 10 out of 26 draft resolutions dealing with peacekeeping in 2009, 17 out of 36 in 2010, and 17 out of 40 in 2011; the United States: 12 out of 26 in 2009, 20 out of 36 in 2010, 21 out of 40 in 2011; the Russian Federation: 5 out of 26 in 2009, 8 out of 36 in 2010, 7 out of 40 in 2011; and China: 2 out of 26 in 2009, 5 out of 36 in 2010, 3 out of 40 in 2011.

[41] See Franco-British Non-Paper on Peacekeeping, January 2009. At http://www.franceonu.org/IMG/pdf_09-0116-FR-UK_Non-Papier_-_Peacekeeping_2_-2.pdf

[42] See *A New Partnership Agenda: Charting a New Horizon for UN Peacekeeping* (New York: UN DPKO/DFS, 2009); *The New Horizon Initiative* (New York: DPKO/DFS, Progress Report No. 1 (October 2010), and Progress Report No. 2 (December 2011).

[43] Remarks by France at the Security Council's debate on Peacekeeping, S/PV.6592, 27 July 2011, p. 22.

Interestingly enough, this type of engagement is not backed by sustained policy debate among the French think tank or academic community. UN security and peacekeeping studies remain under-developed in France and neither official bodies nor the research community appear willing to address this lacuna. French officials and scholars have a very low profile in the various policy and academic conferences dealing with peacekeeping. Furthermore, France's level of activity in official debates contrasts with a parsimonious presence in UN DPKO, where France has emphasized its retention of the position of Under-Secretary-General (USG) rather than on 'placing' French citizens at intermediary levels (P5 to D2 positions).[44] Although UN civil servants are not supposed to seek or receive instructions from any government, this raises the issue of whether a French strategy of influence exists.

5.5.3 The Unlikely Return to UN Peacekeeping

One of the objectives of the 2000 Brahimi Report on UN peace operations was to restore the trust in UN peacekeeping that many countries had lost due to events in Bosnia and Herzegovina, Somalia, and Rwanda. It was hoped that by reforming the UN and making it a more efficient conflict management actor, the UN could entice countries that formerly distanced themselves from the institution to reconsider their position and possibly return to UN operations. In the same vein, a possible interpretation of France's push, in the first decade of the twenty-first century, for reforms to the UN command and control structure, more robust operations, and clearer exit strategies, could be that it wished to create the conditions for a possible return to UN-led missions. As UN operations are unlikely to disappear or totally give way to those conducted by regional organizations and as France will most likely remain an important actor in international conflict management, it would be logical to strengthen an institution that one day might again become an option for French military projection. Furthermore, while the UN might not be the preferred option, the recent history of conflict management practices—with the UN in Lebanon, Côte d'Ivoire, or Chad, but also with other organizations, from Afghanistan to Libya—has demonstrated how scenarios that seemed unlikely at a given moment could become a reality. In other words, scenarios where France would contribute significantly to a UN-led operation cannot be ruled out a priori and this, as a result, creates a need to actively engage with and improve command and control, doctrinal and other aspects of UN peacekeeping.

[44] The DPKO has been headed by a French representative since 1997 when Bernard Miyet took over from Kofi Annan. The position was then held by Jean-Marie Guéhenno (2000–8) and Alain Le Roy (2008–11). In September 2011, French diplomat Hervé Ladsous replaced Alain Le Roy.

Nevertheless, there is little indication of a more pronounced policy shift. Not only does mistrust of the UN remain evident, especially among military officers, but operational and financial constraints (mainly budget reductions) further limit support for participation in UN-led operations. In reference to the post-Afghan context, French diplomat Emmanuel Bonne emphasized the 'fatigue' that Afghanistan has created 'in the public opinion of many Western countries', and concluded that 'it is not guaranteed that the experience of Afghanistan and the entry into a post-Afghan era . . . will produce any dramatic change in the way Western countries, at least France, approach peacekeeping'.[45]

Furthermore, the French position is complicated by the constant suspicion held by other actors—in Africa in particular, where two-thirds of UN peacekeepers are deployed—that France has a hidden agenda whenever it intervenes. The French colonial legacy and its ambiguous role during and immediately after the 1994 Rwandan genocide fuel local perceptions of a French 'Trojan Horse' strategy.[46] Part of the political equation for France, therefore, is to find a path between being criticized for its absence in UN operations in Africa and criticized for the alleged malevolence and neo-colonial aspects of its presence (a criticism aired in relation to both Côte d'Ivoire and Chad).[47] The point here is not to exonerate France for the ambiguities of its foreign and defence policies—critiques are often well-founded—but to flag the parameters that French decision-makers need to take into account when reviewing conflict management policy. In this analysis, the UN can be seen as a legitimizing body for French presence, as was the case with *Operation Turquoise* in Rwanda in 1994 and more recently with *Operation Licorne* in Côte d'Ivoire. Nonetheless, France is likely to remain circumspect about long-term involvement in a UN operation in Africa.

At the same time, recent evolutions in peacekeeping have produced configurations that better suit French peacekeeping requirements. In particular, the model of establishing a rapid reaction force to support a UN operation whilst remaining operationally distinct is one that receives support in France and has become a common feature in practice. Be it in the DRC in 2006 with the EU-led operation EUFOR DRC, or more specifically in Côte d'Ivoire with *Operation Licorne* providing operational support to UNOCI, this type of cooperation is more likely to be reproduced and developed in the future. Through operations that can be national, NATO- or EU-led, or run by a

[45] Bonne, 'Western States', p. 49.

[46] See Adekeye Adebajo, *Building Peace in West Africa* (Boulder, CO: Lynne Rienner, 2002), p. 31.

[47] See Lansana Gberie and Prosper Addo, *Challenges of Peace Implementation in Cote d'Ivoire* (Berlin: Center for International Peace Operations Report 08/04, 2004); Charlemagne, 'Colonial Baggage: The Lessons of Europe's Muddle over its Military Mission to Chad', *The Economist*, 7 February 2008; and Dijkstra, 'The Military Operation of the EU in Chad'.

coalition of states, France can simultaneously contribute to stabilization imperatives under its own conditions while also supporting parallel UN missions. But this model also accentuates the distinction between two types of military operations. In its analysis of the role of *Operation Licorne* in stabilizing the situation in Abidjan in April 2011, French Defence Minister Gérard Longuet insisted on the 'unity of command' as a key comparative advantage of the French-led force, whereas 'the contingents of the United Nations were not capable to handle this type of situation'.[48]

This is also to a large extent how France approaches the emerging EU–UN partnership—as a substitute for direct EU participation in UN operations but with the idea that Common Security and Defence Policy (CSDP) missions could support the UN's broader role in maintaining international peace and security. It is in the same spirit that France is involved in African peacekeeping capacity-building programmes which train and support African contingents (e.g., in Togo and Benin). In the future, France is more likely to favour these different types of support (perhaps including seconding military officers in UN operations headquarters or having a French officer as Force Commander) than it is to contemplate the full deployment of a battalion in a UN-led mission.

5.6 CONCLUSION

France's position and policy at the UN is similar in many respects to that of the United Kingdom, but not with that of any other UN member. France sees its permanent seat at the UN Security Council as a relic of its great power status, which needs to be preserved, and has simultaneously developed a narrative about its role in international politics through the UN. The French approach to peacekeeping operations developed in this context. France is active on the political front, but the main lesson from UNPROFOR in the early 1990s was a reappraisal of the UN's capacity to run complex and multidimensional peace operations, causing a subsequent French withdrawal from UN-led peacekeeping.

Twenty years after the Bosnian episode, a broad consensus remains that the UN is not the best option for French engagement in crisis management. Some reforms have been launched, in part due to French initiatives, and the centrality of the political and legal role of the UN remains intact in French eyes. France has also remained very active at the Security Council and other UN bodies on peacekeeping issues. However, when it comes to providing

[48] Gérard Longuet, Defence Minister of France, debate organized by *La Revue des deux mondes*, Paris, 27 October 2011.

peacekeepers, France still regards regional organizations or coalitions of states as preferable conflict management tools.

In the meantime, France contends that it remains one of the major players in UN operations by emphasizing its financial contribution and its presence in UN-mandated operations, as opposed to UN-led missions. By doing so, France tries to fix the contradiction coming from its central political role and its weak operational presence. Two difficulties may arise from this position. The first is France's ability to maintain the illusion of a major presence while staying away from most UN-led operations. Second, the French position, and with it that of other EU member states, carries the risk of aggravating the divide between the countries that decide and pay on the one hand, and the countries that implement UN missions on the other hand. Providing support to UN operations might be an appropriate short-term answer, yet in the long run the dichotomy is likely to be detrimental both to the UN's capacity and to the central position that France aspires to keep.

6

The People's Republic of China

Bates Gill and Chin-Hao Huang

Since the mid-1990s, the foreign policy of the People's Republic of China (China or PRC) has evolved to become more pragmatic and in some respects more convergent with global norms of cooperation.[1] In particular, Chinese armed forces—including the People's Liberation Army (PLA) and elements of China's domestic security forces—have been increasingly exposed to, and supportive of, the global norms of United Nations (UN) peacekeeping, not least through expanded participation in UN peace operations.[2] By the end of 2011, the active deployment of Chinese troops—in the form of engineers, military observers, transport and logistical support units, civilian police, and medical staff—to UN peacekeeping operations had seen a twenty-fold increase since the early 2000s and China had nearly 2,000 Blue Helmet troops and civilian staff stationed across twelve UN missions. This ranked China sixteenth among UN member states contributing to UN peace operations, higher than any other permanent member of the Security Council and higher than any NATO or other European country. As such, China is increasingly in a position to strengthen peace operations, contribute to stability and security in Africa and beyond, and expand its multilateral military cooperation. In turn,

[1] See David C. Kang, *China Rising: Peace, Power, and Order in East Asia* (New York: Columbia University Press, 2007); Alastair Iain Johnston and Robert Ross (eds.), *New Directions in the Study of China's Foreign Policy* (Stanford, CA: Stanford University Press, 2006); Bates Gill, *Rising Star: China's New Security Diplomacy* (Washington, DC: Brookings Institution Press, revised edn. 2010); Evan Medeiros and M. Taylor Fravel, 'China's New Diplomacy', *Foreign Affairs*, 82:6 (2003), pp. 22–35; Robert Sutter, *Chinese Foreign Relations* (Lanham, MD: Rowman & Littlefield, 2008).

[2] See Bates Gill and Chin-Hao Huang, *China's Expanding Role in Peacekeeping* (Stockholm: SIPRI, 2009); Chin-Hao Huang, 'Principles and Praxis in Chinese Peacekeeping', *International Peacekeeping*, 18:3 (2011), pp. 259–72; International Crisis Group (ICG), *China's Growing Role in UN Peacekeeping* (Brussels: ICG, 2009); Stefan Staehle, 'China's Shifting Attitude Towards UN Peacekeeping Operations', *The China Quarterly*, 195 (2008), pp. 631–55; Shogo Suzuki, 'Seeking "Legitimate" Great Power Status in Post-Cold War International Society: China's and Japan's Participation in UNPKO', *International Relations*, 22:1 (2008), pp. 45–63.

these activities raise the prospects for China to become even more integrated internationally as a responsible major power.

Given these important developments and their implications for the future of peace operations, this chapter examines China's evolving approach to UN peace operations. After a background section describing China's changing approach to peacekeeping, the chapter then identifies the key factors which motivate those changes. The chapter also provides an overview of some of the most important outcomes which have arisen as a result of China's changing approach to peacekeeping, including a greater Chinese flexibility and pragmatism on issues of sovereignty and humanitarian intervention. Our central argument is that while Chinese contributions to UN peacekeeping have increased markedly in recent years, ongoing debates within China's policy-making and elite circles will likely contribute to a cautious and selective approach towards future UN peace operations.

6.1 CHINA'S CHANGING APPROACH

Since its founding in 1949, the PRC's views on and ultimately participation in UN peacekeeping have gradually evolved in a more positive direction, but with significant twists and turns in policy and practice along the way. Throughout the 1970s and much of the 1980s—the first two decades after it joined the UN in 1971—China viewed UN peacekeeping with a significant degree of scepticism, maintained a low profile on peacekeeping issues, and refrained from taking substantive actions in the Security Council debates on peacekeeping.[3] This cautious approach reflected a traditional and narrow interpretation of positive international law and its application with regard to sovereignty: China upheld the inviolable principle of state sovereignty and often questioned the necessity of external interventionism in areas of conflict, even if a particular operation was sanctioned by the Security Council and was operating under the auspices of international peacekeeping forces. In addition, China's scepticism was in no small part coloured by its earlier experiences and encounters, particularly during the 1950–53 Korean War where the PLA fought UN forces under a US command. It thus harboured—and as we shall see, continues to harbour—serious concerns about the nature and legitimacy of interventionist operations, particularly those that are Western-led.

A shift in China's position on peacekeeping became more evident in the 1980s. In 1988, Beijing applied to and became a member of the UN Special

[3] See Samuel Kim, 'China's International Organization Behavior', in Thomas Robinson and David Shambaugh (eds.), *Chinese Foreign Policy* (Oxford: Oxford University Press, 1995), pp. 420–2; Yin He, *China's Changing Policy on UN Peacekeeping Operations* (Stockholm: Institute for Security and Development Policy, 2007).

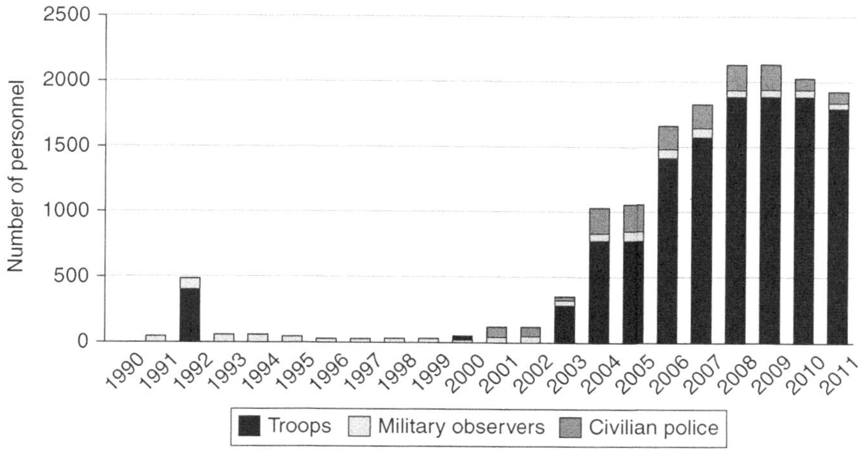

Figure 6.1 Chinese Contributions to UN Peacekeeping Operations, 1990–2011 (data for 2011 are for January–October)

Source: UN DPKO, at www.un.org/Depts/dpko/dpko/contributors/

Committee on Peacekeeping Operations, paving the way for increased engagement in multilateral peacekeeping activities. As one senior Chinese official put it at the time, all states should lend 'powerful support' to peacekeeping, setting a new tone for Chinese pronouncements in support of the UN peacekeeping regime.[4] Subsequently, it deployed twenty military observers to the UN Transition Assistance Group (UNTAG) to help monitor elections in Namibia. This was followed by the deployment of five military observers to the UN Truce Supervision Organization (UNTSO) in the Middle East. Perhaps the most significant break with past practices came with the decision to deploy 400 engineering troops and 49 military observers to the UN Transitional Authority in Cambodia (UNTAC) in 1992. In spite of its relatively underdeveloped power projection capability at the time, Chinese peacekeepers were deployed largely as a result of factors beyond realist assumptions. Chinese decision-makers were more concerned with China's image and reputation, particularly after the Tiananmen crackdown in 1989, and sought regional confirmation of its status as a peaceful neighbour.

During the late 1990s and early 2000s, China's participation in peacekeeping activities expanded and diversified. After the withdrawal of UNTAC, Chinese contributions to UN peacekeeping remained between 50 to 100 peacekeepers in the decade from 1993 to 2002, and then quickly grew in 2007–8 to around 2,000 personnel deployed, a contribution that has remained relatively constant since (see Figure 6.1). The majority of the Chinese troops

[4] See Kim, 'China's International Organization Behavior'.

deployed with UN peacekeeping operations provide engineering, transport, or medical support, though China began to deploy police in 1999 (to East Timor) and as of November 2011 had 91 police deployed in Haiti, Liberia, South Sudan, and Timor-Leste. China also had 50 military experts in five UN missions. According to China's Defence White Paper published in 2011, Chinese peacekeepers have 'built and repaired over 8,700 km of roads and 270 bridges, cleared over 8,900 mines and various explosive devices, transported over 600,000 tons of cargo across a total distance of 9.3 million km, and treated 79,000 patients'. The White Paper notes that as of the end of 2010, China had sent 17,390 military personnel to nineteen UN peacekeeping operations, nine of whom lost their lives in the line of duty.[5]

6.2 EXPLAINING CHINA'S CHANGING APPROACH

A number of factors help explain the evolution of China's views towards UN peacekeeping, with both normative and practical factors playing a role. Perhaps one of the most important is the country's increasing socialization and engagement in international institutions and debates.[6] China's more active participation in UN peacekeeping came at a time of growing debates about how international society should reconcile the imperatives of global stability and justice and strike the right balance between state sovereignty and human rights. From these debates, a loose consensus emerged by the early 2000s, especially in the West, that there is political and moral currency for the 'international community' to take exceptional measures at times of need in addressing human rights concerns, especially when the host state does not fulfil its responsibility to protect its citizens.[7] Although China was a relative newcomer to these debates, the issue gained a degree of traction within China as well, with a number of international law scholars and foreign policy experts pointing to the changing nature of peacekeeping and the circumstances that warrant a more flexible interpretation and understanding of the principles related to sovereignty.[8] In October 1998, at a conference commemorating the 50th anniversary of the Universal Declaration of Human Rights, the former

[5] *China's National Defense in 2010* (Beijing: State Council Information Office, March 2011), section IV.

[6] On socialization arguments, see Alastair Iain Johnston, *Social States: China in International Institutions 1980–2000* (Princeton, NJ: Princeton University Press, 2008).

[7] Taylor Seybolt, *Humanitarian Military Intervention* (Oxford: Oxford University Press, 2007). See also, Gareth Evans, 'Responding to Atrocities: The New Geopolitics of Intervention', in *SIPRI Yearbook 2012* (Oxford: Oxford University Press, 2012), chapter 1.

[8] Allen Carlson, 'China's Approach to Sovereignty and Intervention', in Johnston and Ross (eds.), *New Directions in the Study of China's Foreign Policy*, pp. 217–41.

Chinese Foreign Minister Qian Qichen said that there was a global recognition of the 'universality of human rights' and that all nations 'observe the same international norms on human rights'. Qian added that 'We all recognize that no country's human rights situation is perfect, and that all countries are confronted with a weighty task of further promoting and protecting human rights.'[9] This important acknowledgement underlined the emergence and growing relevance of human rights values in the Chinese foreign policy lexicon.

More importantly, a widening circle of policy elites began to debate issues such as state sovereignty and conditions for interventionism. Of particular interest is the increasing number of influential Chinese academic, scholarly, and policy-oriented journals that printed and circulated these discussions. Such journals include: *Zhongguo Faxue* (中国法学 Chinese Legal Studies); *Xibu Faxue Pinglun* (西部法学评论 Western Law Review); *Fazhi yu Shehui* (法制与社会 Legal System and Society); and *Wuda Guojifa Pinglun* (武大国际法评论 International Law Review of Wuhan University). These journals printed an increasing number of articles discussing state obligations to their citizens and arguing that a failure to uphold these responsibilities warrants intervention by the 'international community' to protect those individuals.[10] Other articles have also argued that human rights are moral issues increasingly shaped by the 'international community' and that all states have a right to monitor these concerns.[11]

Allen Carlson's research led him to conclude that an increasing number of Chinese researchers, scholars, experts, and policy-makers have adopted more

[9] 'Qian Qichen Urges Further Promotion of International Human Rights', *Xinhua News* (Beijing), 20 October 2008 [trans. BBC Monitoring Service, International Reports].

[10] See for example Cheng Hao [程浩], 'Lianheguo Weihe Xingdongzhong de Zhuquan Rangdu Wenti Fenxi' [联合国维和行动中的主权让渡问题分析] [An Analysis on UN Peacekeeping Operations and Sovereignty], *Fazhi yu Shehui* [法制与社会] (*Legal System and Society*), 5 (2009), pp. 1–7; Zeng Lingliang [曾令良], 'Lun lengzhan hou shidai de guojia zhuquan' [论冷战后时代的国家主权] [A Discussion of State Sovereignty in the Post-Cold War Era], *Zhongguo faxue* [中国法学] (*Chinese Legal Studies*), 1 (1998), pp. 109–20; Xu Guojin [徐构进], 'Guojia lüxing guoji renquan yiwu de xiandu' [国家履行国际人权义务的限度] [The Limits on State Performance of Human Rights Obligations], *Zhongguo faxue* [中国法学] (*Chinese Legal Studies*), 2 (1992), pp. 13–20; Yan Haiyan [颜海燕], 'Baohu de Zeren Jiesi' [保护的责任解析] [An Analysis on the Responsibility to Protect], *Xibu Faxue Pinglun* [西部法学评论] (*Western Law Review*), 1 (2010), pp. 125–9.

[11] See Liu Jie [刘杰], *Renquan yu Guojia Zhuquan* [人权与国家主权] (*Human Rights and State Sovereignty*) (Shanghai: Shanghai Renmin Chubanshe, 2004); Allen Carlson, *Unifying China, Integrating with the World* (Stanford, CA: Stanford University Press, 2005); Li Buyun [李步云], 'Renquan de liangge lilun wenti' [人权的两个理论问题] (Two Theoretical Human Rights Issues), *Zhongguo faxue* [中国法学] (*Chinese Legal Studies*), 3 (1999), pp. 38–42; Cheng Shuaihua [成帅华], 'Guojia zhuquan yu guoji renquan de ruogan wenti' [国家主权与国际人权的若干问题] (Issues Involving International Human Rights and State Sovereignty), *Ouzhou* [欧洲] *(Europe)*, 1 (2000), pp. 32–5; Shi Yinhong [时殷弘], 'Lun ershi shiji guoji guifan tixi' [论二十世纪国际规范体系] (A Discussion of the System of International Norms in the Twentieth Century), *Guoji luntan* [国际论坛] (*International Forum*), 6 (2000), pp. 8–10.

flexible views of sovereignty and the conditions under which UN peacekeeping operations should be sanctioned to help enforce the peace in conflict regions and protect civilians. Moreover, Carlson found that some of these policy elites gained important access to key policy-makers and top leaders within the Chinese foreign and security policy apparatus and that they shaped the foreign policy discourse on peacekeeping.[12] In 2005, for example, President Hu Jintao announced that China would endorse a 'comprehensive strategy featuring prevention, peace restoration, peacekeeping and post-conflict reconstruction'.[13] Understanding the increasing complexity and evolving nature of peacekeeping, Hu further noted that '[i]n areas emerging from conflict, ensuring the rule of law and justice should become an integral part of the overall effort to achieve peace and stability, protecting the fundamental interests of local populations and serving the overall interests of social stability'.[14] It is too early to gauge whether China has internalized and accepted these global norms, but Chinese official policy and rhetoric with regards to sovereignty, intervention, and peacekeeping have become more flexible. China increasingly understands the value and importance of aligning its national interests with these emerging global conventions because active participation in peacekeeping also helps to burnish China's image and reputation. More importantly, China does not want to be seen as a global outlier and would prefer to be recognized as a contributor to, or at least not an inhibitor of, global peace and stability.

Equally important, China's expanding participation and evolving role in UN peacekeeping activities in the last two decades also helps to project a positive and constructive side to its rising prominence and power on the global stage. The Chinese leadership is acutely aware that many countries, particularly in its region, remain uncertain and wary about the PLA's military capabilities and the country's overall strategic intentions. Hence, concerned with its image and global reputation, it is understood in Beijing that China needs to be more responsive to international expectations, minimize tensions and conflict, and make tangible contributions to international peace and security. Peacekeeping has thus become an important priority, and helps to put into action the call by senior Chinese officials for the country to demonstrate its 'peaceful development' and commitment to a 'harmonious world'.[15] Its increased peacekeeping activity provides an opportunity to display a more positive side of the PLA's military capabilities, reassuring neighbours about its peaceful intentions, and at the same time signalling that China is trying to act

[12] Carlson, 'China's Approach to Sovereignty and Intervention'. See also his book, *Unifying China, Integrating with the World* (Stanford, CA: Stanford University Press, 2005).

[13] S/PV.5261, 14 September 2005.

[14] S/PV.5225, 12 July 2005.

[15] 'Hu Jintao Says China Pursues Peaceful Development', *People's Daily* (Beijing, 3 September 2005 [trans. BBC Monitoring Service, International Reports].

as a responsible power.[16] China also believes that participation will give it greater influence over the direction of peacekeeping and hopes that over time it can contribute more actively to debates about peacekeeping doctrine and strategy, steering it towards greater moderation and tempering calls for what it sees as excessive interventionism.

As China becomes increasingly engaged with the UN peacekeeping regime, a widening array of voices within the Chinese academy and policy-making circles have also called for Chinese foreign and security policy to be defined beyond material power interests. An editorial in the widely read Chinese Communist Party domestic and foreign affairs journal, *Liaowang*, pointed out:

> Compared with past practices, China's diplomacy has indeed displayed a new face. If China's diplomacy before the 1980s stressed safeguarding of national security and its emphasis from the 1980s to early this century is on the creation of excellent environment for economic development, then the focus at present is to take a more active part in international affairs and play a role that a responsible power should on the basis of satisfying the security and development interests.[17]

A senior Chinese official remarked at the 2007 Munich Conference on Security Policy that China's increasing involvement in UN peacekeeping missions 'reflected China's commitment to global security given the country's important role within the international system and the fact that its security and development are closely linked to that of the rest of the world'.[18] There is a growing recognition that as China's international role evolves and expands, its interests will likewise become more global in nature. Its national security is thus becoming intrinsically linked to a stable and peaceful international environment, and this in turn is an important factor in China taking a more cooperative stance and supportive role in UN peacekeeping.

Peacekeeping, anti-piracy missions, rescue-and-relief operations, counter-terrorism exercises, and post-conflict reconstruction contributions have all become components of China's increasingly complex and dynamic international strategy.[19] These activities are broadly defined as non-traditional

[16] See Jing-Dong Yuan, 'Multilateral Intervention and State Sovereignty: Chinese Views on UN Peacekeeping Operations', *Political Science*, 49:2 (1998), pp. 275–95; Wang Yizhou [王逸舟] (ed.), *Mohe zhong de jiangou: zhongguo yu guoji zuji guanxi de duoshijiao toushi* [磨合中的建构：中国与国际组织关系的多视角透视] *(Construction in Contradiction: A Multiple Insight into Relationships Between China and International Organizations)* (Beijing: China Development Press, 2003).

[17] 'PRC's "new diplomacy" stress on more active international role', *Liaowang* (Beijing), 11 July 2005 [trans. World News Connection].

[18] John Hill, 'China Bolsters Peacekeeping Commitment', *Jane's Defence Weekly*, 14 February 2007.

[19] See Zhongying Pang, 'China's Changing Attitude to UN Peacekeeping', *International Peacekeeping*, 12:1 (2005), pp. 87–104; Wang Jisi [王缉思], 'Guanyu Gouzhu Zhongguo Guoji Zhanlue de Jidian Kanfa' [关于构筑中国国际战略的几点看法] (Some Thoughts on Building a Chinese International Strategy), *Guoji Zhengzhi Yanjiu* [国际政治研究] (*International Political*

security issues, and their growing importance parallels the PLA's interest in mobilizing its resources and preparing for military operations other than war (MOOTW) both at home and abroad. This reflects President Hu Jintao's call for the security forces to more adequately perform and engage in MOOTW as part of the PLA's 'new historic mission'.[20] Doing so would help safeguard national interests as well as contribute to regional and global peace, security, and development. In May 2009, the PLA General Staff Department announced that it would strengthen the PLA's emergency response system and rapid deployment capacity to respond to the various MOOTW, including peacekeeping activities.[21] In June 2009 the Central Military Commission, the PLA, and five of the seven military area commands met in Beijing to strengthen and improve the PLA's peacekeeping role, discussing ways to streamline the selection, organization, training, and rotation of Chinese peacekeepers.[22]

In addition to hopes of burnishing the Chinese military's image abroad, the deployment of Chinese troops in UN peacekeeping missions carries inherent practical benefits for the Chinese security forces as well. Training and operating alongside other troop-contributing countries' forces provides an invaluable experience that allows Chinese troops to improve their responsiveness, riot control capabilities, coordination of emergency command systems, and ability to carry out MOOTW more effectively. Over time, participation in peacekeeping missions abroad will also help to modernize and professionalize the security forces. For example, a sustained effort to deploy troops in Africa has meant that PLA forces are gaining greater operational knowledge of different operating environments. It also provides them with 'more knowledge about logistics, ports of debarkation, lines of communication, lines of operation, operational intelligence, local "atmospherics" and modus operandi and means of sustaining forces in Africa over prolonged periods'.[23] All these measures allow the Chinese security forces to display their professionalism and operational competence on the one hand, while also demonstrating its growing deterrent capability on the other.[24]

Studies), 25 (2007), pp. 1–5; 'Chinese Expert Views Army Counteracting Non-Traditional Security Threats', *Zhongguo Xinwen She* (Beijing), 20 June 2007 [trans. BBC Monitoring Service, International Reports].

[20] James Mulvenon, 'Chairman Hu and the PLA's "New Historic Missions"', *China Leadership Monitor*, 27 (2009), pp. 1–11; Cynthia Watson, 'The Chinese Armed Forces and Non-Traditional Missions: A Growing Tool of Statecraft', *China Brief*, 9:4 (2009), pp. 9–12.

[21] 'PLA Constructs MOOTW Arms Force System', *People's Liberation Army Daily* (Beijing), 14 May 2009 [trans. BBC Monitoring Service, International Reports].

[22] 'PLA Peacekeeping Work Conference Held in Beijing', *People's Liberation Army Daily*, 26 June 2009 [trans. BBC Monitoring Service, International Reports].

[23] Philip Rogers, 'China and UN Peacekeeping Operations in Africa', *Naval War College Review*, 60:2 (2007), p. 89.

[24] 'The Deterrence Function of Launching Military Training Exercises', *People's Liberation Army Daily* (Beijing), 29 April 2008 [trans. Open Source Center].

In sum, it appears that China's evolving approach towards UN peacekeeping is motivated by a combination of factors. Through increasing interactions within international society, China has become more willing to accept global norms and to contribute to peace and stability. At the same time, participation in peacekeeping also allows China to professionalize its armed forces, to test its power projection capabilities through MOOTW, and to help attain its aspirations for becoming a major global power.

6.3 CHINESE PEACEKEEPERS IN ACTION: WHAT OUTCOMES?

6.3.1 Greater Capabilities and Professionalism

The PLA has been working to professionalize and improve the calibre of its peacekeeping troops, getting them better prepared with the standard operating procedures maintained by the UN Department of Peacekeeping Operations (DPKO).[25] Chinese troops' English and French language proficiency is generally weak, limiting their interaction with other contingents and local populations. Chinese officials appear to have recognized these shortcomings and are placing increased emphasis on preparation for peacekeeping. As part of the PLA budget, Chinese policy-makers have sought to improve and expand Chinese peacekeeping training facilities. In June 2009, China unveiled a new peacekeeping training centre in Huairou in a suburb northeast of Beijing.[26] The new facility is used for pre-deployment training and also serves as the main venue for international exchanges on peacekeeping. The facilities include simulation rooms, shooting and driving ranges, and simulated UN peacekeeping camps and de-mining training grounds. In Langfang, a city to the southeast of Beijing, the Ministry of Public Security has also established the Civilian Peacekeeping Police Training Centre to train police officers and formed police units (FPU).

In addition, in recent years, the PLA has become more open to interfacing with foreign counterparts to help expand its peacekeeping capacity. In total, as of December 2010, the PLA had held 44 joint military training exercises with foreign forces.[27] Chinese security personnel have participated in joint peacekeeping training and exchanges with other countries, including Australia,

[25] 'Chinese Deputy Military Chief on Raising Army's Peacekeeping Role', *Zhongguo Xinwen She*, 22 June 2007 [trans. BBC Monitoring Service, International Reports].

[26] 'China Opens First Peacekeeping Training Center', *China Daily*, 25 June 2009 [trans. BBC Monitoring Service, International Reports].

[27] *China's National Defense in 2010.*

Bangladesh, Canada, France, Germany, India, Indonesia, Mongolia, New Zealand, Romania, Singapore, South Africa, Sweden, Switzerland, Thailand, and the UK.[28] In 2009, China sent a military medical team for a joint exercise with Gabon, where the team also provided medical care to local residents. In 2010, a Chinese military medical detachment was dispatched to Peru to practise humanitarian assistance and emergency rescue operations.[29] Through these joint training exercises, the PLA has requested foreign military counterparts to provide more in-depth pre-deployment training assistance programmes and joint training and simulation drills.[30]

China has also hosted a number of international seminars on peacekeeping, bringing in foreign experts, scholars, and practitioners to exchange views and share lessons learned from previous peacekeeping experiences. The international seminars with the UK, as well as with Norway and Sweden, for example, have opened avenues for joint collaboration in peacekeeping. The International Committee of the Red Cross has also been asked by the Chinese government to provide pre-deployment briefings for peacekeepers to help train and better prepare personnel on issues related to international humanitarian law.[31]

Regionally, China is stepping up coordination for multilateral peacekeeping activities, sponsoring and taking part in such events as the China–Association of Southeast Asian Nations (ASEAN) peacekeeping seminar in 2007.[32] China has also engaged in a series of drills and simulation exercises with Russia and Central Asian countries under the umbrella of the Shanghai Cooperation Organization (SCO). These exercises, under the name 'Peace Mission', are described as 'counter-terrorism military exercises' by the Chinese, and have been held four times: in 2005, 2007, 2009, and 2010. The 'Peace Mission 2005' was one of the largest joint military exercises China has ever carried out.[33] The exercise involved nearly 10,000 army, air force, and naval personnel and included headquarters and command-post exercises in Vladivostok, coordination of battleship movements around the Shandong Peninsula, as well as amphibious landings. While counter-terrorism training with Russia and other

[28] Ping Zhang, 'Remarks on the People's Liberation Army's Participation in UN Peacekeeping Operations', speech at conference on Multi-Dimensional and Integrated Peace Operations: Trends and Challenges, Beijing, 26–27 March 2007.

[29] *China's National Defense in 2010.*

[30] Ping Zhang, 'Remarks on the People's Liberation Army's Participation'.

[31] International Committee of the Red Cross, *Annual Report 2009* (Geneva, May 2010), pp. 3–4.

[32] 'Defense Ministry Touts Deepened China-ASEAN Security Cooperation', *Xinhua News*, 30 March 2009 [trans. BBC Monitoring Service, International Reports].

[33] Alyson J. K. Bailes, *The Shanghai Cooperation Organization* (Stockholm: Stockholm International Peace Research Institute, 2007); Marc Lanteigne, 'Security, Strategy and the Former USSR: China and the Shanghai Cooperation Organization', in Shaun Breslin (ed.), *A Handbook of Chinese International Relations* (London: Routledge, 2010), pp. 166–76.

Central Asian states may not be directly related to UN peacekeeping per se, it helps the PLA to improve its mobilization capabilities and to conduct a range of operation types that could be applicable to multilateral peacekeeping missions, encouraging China to provide more contributions to peace operations, particularly troops, as the PLA's capabilities and the calibre of its troops improve. Some observers also suggest that such military exercises are contingency plans for managing a possible humanitarian crisis in neighbouring North Korea.[34]

As the Chinese Defence White Paper issued in 2011 put it, these exchanges and exercises are 'conducive to promoting mutual trust and cooperation, drawing on useful lessons, and accelerating the PLA's modernization' and 'improve [the PLA's] capabilities in responding to humanitarian emergencies'.[35] Uncertain, however, is whether political cadres in Beijing will sustain these efforts and see peacekeeping as an important policy priority. On the one hand, this would mean devoting greater financial and human resources to the PLA General Staff Department, the Ministries of Defence, Public Security and Foreign Affairs, the National Defence University, and the peacekeeping training establishments. On the other hand, it would also require the political leadership to encourage and facilitate greater exchanges, dialogues, joint exercises, and simulations with other international, regional, and national actors aimed at strengthening Chinese peacekeeping capacities as well as building up greater expertise within the peacekeeping epistemic community in China.

6.3.2 UN Politics and Contributions

In 2002, China's interest in contributing to the management of peacekeeping was marked by an agreement to join the UN Standby Arrangement System. Under this arrangement, the Chinese Ministry of Defence placed a 525-strong engineering battalion, a 25-strong medical unit, and two 160-strong transport companies on standby and ready for deployment with other UN forces within 90 days.[36] In recent years, Chinese peacekeepers have been increasingly commended for their discipline and professionalism: as of 2011, no allegation of misconduct had been lodged against Chinese personnel in UN peacekeeping operations. This is important for the UN, as reports of misconduct by peacekeepers, including corruption, sexual abuse, and exploitation, have

[34] Stephen Blank, 'Peace Mission 2009: A Military Scenario beyond Central Asia', *China Brief*, 20 August 2009, pp. 7–9.

[35] *China's National Defense in 2010.*

[36] 'Chinese Peacekeepers in Action', *People's Liberation Army Daily*, 15 January 2003 [trans. BBC Monitoring Service, International Reports].

tainted and even jeopardized UN missions.[37] In August 2007, UN DPKO approved China's Major General Zhao Jingmin as force commander for the Mission in Western Sahara (MINURSO), the first time a Chinese national held such a senior position.[38] Subsequently, Major General Chao Liu became the second Chinese national to serve as force commander when he was appointed to head the UN Peacekeeping Force in Cyprus (UNFICYP) in January 2011.[39] Elsewhere, PLA colonels are increasingly solicited as senior level staff officers in DPKO as well as in missions.[40]

Notwithstanding these positive acknowledgements and contributions, Chinese officials stress that the ratio of Chinese appointments to senior ranking posts in DPKO remains lower than that of other major powers. This is a legitimate concern as the burden of troop contributions have increasingly fallen on developing countries, while Western countries tend to deploy fewer troops but occupy key decision-making and support posts in DPKO and in UN missions (see Coleman's chapter in this volume). UN officials are likely to continue working closely with Chinese counterparts to see that China's interest in increasing its contributions is sustained. Chinese officials could play a more active role in policy planning, force generation, coordination, and other leadership positions. As former Under-Secretary-General for Peacekeeping Operations, Jean-Marie Guéhenno, argued, such appointments would mark an important recognition of China's positive role and growing importance in peacekeeping.[41]

On the whole, however, China needs to engage more substantively in UN peacekeeping operations. In terms of financial contribution, China provides about 3 per cent of the peacekeeping budget, significantly less than most of the other permanent members of the UN Security Council. According to the UN Multi-Donor Trust Fund Office, China has also contributed a total of $4 million to the UN Peacebuilding Fund from 2006 to 2012, but has yet to provide financial support for other aid programmes or trust funds.[42] Consequently, China will need to increase its financial contributions if it wishes to

[37] Sharon Wiharta, 'The Legitimacy of Peace Operations', in *SIPRI Yearbook* 2009 (Oxford: Oxford University Press, 2009), pp. 95–116.

[38] 'UN Secretary-General Appoints Major General Zhao Jingmin of China as Force Commander for Western Sahara Mission', press release, UN Department of Public Information, 28 August 2007, at www.un.org/News/Press/docs//2007/sga1089.doc.htm

[39] 'Secretary-General Appoints Major General Chao Liu of China to Head United Nations Peacekeeping Force in Cyprus', press release, UN Department of Public Information, 13 January 2011, at http://www.un.org/News/Press/docs/2011/sga1276.doc.htm

[40] Gill and Huang, *China's Expanding Role in Peacekeeping.*

[41] 'UN Official Commends China's role in Peacekeeping', *Xinhua News*, 16 January 2007 [trans. BBC Monitoring Service, International Reports].

[42] 'Contributor/Partner Fact Sheet', United Nations Development Group, 1 February 2012, at http://www.unpbf.org/donors/contributions/

play a role commensurate with its Security Council responsibilities and global status.

Moreover, China's increasing role in UN peacekeeping may create higher expectations for China to expand its troop commitments in areas where there are critical needs. China initially offered to deploy 'combat' troops (as opposed to logistical support units) to Lebanon in 2006, and officials are on record as saying that China remains open to the idea of deploying such troops if DPKO requested them, though it remains to be seen whether China would respond favourably.[43] Likewise, some UN officials have called for China to contribute such force enablers as light tactical and transport helicopters and more ground transport units to help sustain and facilitate operations. In short, as China seeks to play a more active role in shaping and influencing UN peacekeeping affairs, it could consider increasing personnel, financial, and logistical contributions.

6.4 CHINESE PEACEKEEPING IN AFRICA

Nearly three-quarters of China's peacekeeping contributions are currently based in Africa, providing critical support for post-war reconstruction in Liberia, the DRC, Southern Sudan, and Côte d'Ivoire. Moreover, the 2009 Forum on China and Africa Cooperation (FOCAC) action plan stated that China had agreed to step up its work to address security issues on the continent. The action plan stated, in part:

> The Chinese Government will continue to support the United Nations Security Council in playing a constructive role in solving conflicts in Africa and continue to support and participate in UN peacekeeping missions there. It will strengthen cooperation with countries concerned in the UN Peace Building Commission and support countries in their post-war reconstruction processes . . .
>
> The Chinese Government . . . will continue to support the efforts of the AU [African Union], other regional organizations and countries concerned to solve regional conflicts, and will intensify cooperation with African countries in peace-keeping theory research, peacekeeping training and exchanges and in supporting the building of peacekeeping capacity in Africa.[44]

[43] 'Chinese combat troops "can be part of UN peacekeeping"', *China Daily*, 7 July 2010, at http://english.peopledaily.com.cn/90001/90776/90883/7055042.html; 'China Considers Deploying Combat Troops to UN Mission in Lebanon', *People's Daily*, 28 September 2006 [trans. BBC Monitoring Service, International Reports].

[44] 'FOCAC Sharm el Sheikh Action Plan 2010–2012', Forum on China–Africa Cooperation, 12 November 2009, at www.focac.org/eng/dsjbzjhy/hywj/t626387.htm

China and the AU have also facilitated interaction by establishing the Strategic Dialogue Mechanism as a regularized measure to exchange views on relations and security issues. This effort further complements the multilateral process at the UN where Chinese and African foreign ministers jointly decided to launch a political consultation mechanism in September 2007 to ensure a more calibrated approach in addressing regional security issues. Such mechanisms have increased regular exchanges, opening the door to greater consultation on areas of convergence and divergence. More importantly, these interactive processes have introduced Chinese foreign policy-makers to regional and global norms that are pertinent to bringing peace and stability to Africa. China's attempts to identify more closely with the developing world, particularly in Africa, and to seek external confirmation of its status as a responsible, major power have been important considerations behind this socialization process.

As the China–Africa relationship deepens, China's expanding military, political, and economic ties in Africa will need to be managed to complement China's contributions to peacekeeping in Africa. UN officials report some frustration at their lack of access to information about bilateral military ties between China and African countries where their peacekeepers are also deployed (such as the DRC, Liberia, and Sudan).[45] It is therefore unclear whether those arrangements complement China's peacekeeping activities and UN efforts to provide greater security and stability in Africa. Since 2008 UN officials have been exploring with the Chinese UN mission in New York ways of supporting security sector reform and issues related to disarmament, demobilization, and reintegration of ex-combatants in African states. The Chinese delegation has reportedly not been obstructive; but nor has it taken any major initiatives in this regard.[46]

Likewise, as China's diplomatic and business interests deepen in Africa, crafting appropriate policies to balance them is likely to become more complicated. The goodwill earned by Chinese peacekeeping contingents repairing roads, improving state infrastructure, and offering medical assistance could be undermined by other bilateral activities of the Chinese government, state-owned companies, entrepreneurs, and émigrés across the continent. As African states emerge from protracted internal conflicts, China wants to be recognized as a partner in African development. One high-profile example is the Chinese-financed construction of the new AU headquarters building in Addis Ababa, which opened for business in 2012. The challenge then will be to improve oversight and coordination to ensure that bilateral military engagements and a widening array of commercial links in the continent not only

[45] Authors' interviews with UN officials, Kinshasa, March–April 2009.
[46] Authors' interviews with UN officials, Kinshasa, March–April 2009.

complement the Chinese peacekeeping presence but also contribute to development and stability in Africa.

6.4.1 Balancing Sovereignty and Intervention

When confronted with important questions related to foreign policy and international security, Chinese policy-makers tend to take a case-by-case approach. As such, although rhetoric and government policies seem to have supported UN peacekeeping, traditional ideas about state sovereignty persist. There are instances when China has supported operations on humanitarian grounds, including in East Timor in 1999, though this operation initially was by a UN-authorized force led by Australia which enjoyed Indonesia's formal consent. China also contributed a civilian police contingent to support the subsequent UN mission in East Timor. In 2003, in response to growing instability in the DRC and Liberia, the Ambassador to the UN, Zhang Yishan, argued that the UN should intervene in such conflict areas 'earlier, faster and more forcefully'.[47]

Traditionally, China has objected to authorizing or extending the mandates of UN peacekeeping missions in countries that recognized Taiwan. In January 1997, China vetoed a proposed mission to Guatemala until the Guatemalan government gave assurances that it would no longer support a General Assembly vote on admitting Taiwan to the UN.[48] In 1999, China vetoed the continuation of the UN Preventive Deployment in Macedonia (UNPREDEP) two weeks after suspending diplomatic ties with the country over its recognition of Taiwan, bringing an end to that conflict prevention work.[49] Some Chinese peacekeeping specialists later acknowledged that this was a 'difficult lesson for China' and that the government should have 'considered Macedonia's interests more than its own national interests'.[50]

In 1999, at the height of the crisis in the Balkans, China initially opposed authorizing a peacekeeping force for Kosovo. Chinese opposition was in large part accentuated by the mistaken bombing of the Chinese embassy in Belgrade by NATO warplanes in May that year. Chinese objections turned to indignant

[47] 'China Takes on Major Peacekeeping Role', *Jane's Intelligence Review*, 1 November 2003.

[48] 'Security Council Authorizes Deployment of UN Military Observers to Verify Implementation of Cease-Fire Agreement in Guatemala', press release, UN Department of Public Information, 20 January 1997, at www.un.org/News/Press/docs/1997/19970120.sc6314.html; International Security and Institutions Research Group, *Vetoed Draft Resolutions in the UN Security Council 1946–2009* (London: Foreign and Commonwealth Office, August 2009).

[49] 'Taiwan Criticizes China UN Veto', *BBC News*, 26 February 1999, at http://news.bbc.co.uk/2/hi/285835.stm

[50] Pang, 'China's Changing Attitude'.

outrage as the Chinese general public as well as the regime insisted that the US-led NATO bombing was deliberate and intended to contain China.

China supported the UN peace operations mission in Haiti from 2004 to 2010 with deployments of a Formed Police Unit, in spite of the fact that Haiti diplomatically recognizes the Republic of China (Taiwan) and not the PRC. However, China apparently used the threat of curtailing the mission to warn Haiti against any high-profile diplomatic exchanges in support of Taiwan. Some observers contend that Haiti's continued recognition of Taiwan was a reason for the withdrawal in 2010, while others have indicated that China was 'uncomfortable' with the overwhelming US civilian and military presence following the earthquake.[51] The Haiti case indicates that there are still gaps in and limitations to China's overall commitment to peacekeeping. As in Kosovo, the resurgence of *realpolitik* ideology seemed to have trumped the broader underlying trend of more active engagement and participation in peacekeeping operations.

Beijing's position on the Darfur question, however, provides a prominent example of constructive engagement where China yielded to widespread regional and international pressure. Responding to mounting criticism of its relations with the Sudanese government, in 2006 China began exerting diplomatic pressure on Sudan to allow UN as well as AU peacekeepers into Darfur.[52] In November 2006, with the humanitarian situation worsening, the former Chinese Ambassador to the UN, Wang Guangya, was widely credited in gaining Sudanese acceptance of the UN/AU hybrid peacekeeping force of 20,000 troops in Darfur. Subsequently, China also became the first permanent member of the UN Security Council to commit and deploy 315 troops there and was widely applauded by African leaders.[53] In February 2007, President Hu Jintao visited Sudan and met President Omar al-Bashir. The visit drew widespread criticism internationally, particularly from the United States, since China was seen as abetting alleged genocidal acts committed in Darfur. However, Hu reportedly intervened to press al-Bashir to abide by international commitments, and he delivered a rare public statement that outlined the basis for China's approach towards resolving the Darfur crisis, stating '[i]t is imperative to improve the situation in Darfur and living conditions of local people'.[54] While this could be interpreted as mere rhetoric, that is about as close as a Chinese leader has come to publicly chiding a foreign leader.

[51] Authors' interviews with Chinese scholars and officials, Beijing, June 2010; 'Analysis: UN Refocuses Haiti Mission', *United Press International*, 16 February 2007.

[52] Chin-Hao Huang, 'U.S.-China Relations and Darfur', *Fordham International Law Journal*, 31:4 (2008), pp. 827–42.

[53] Edward Cody, 'China Given Credit for Darfur Role', *Washington Post*, 13 January 2007, at www.washingtonpost.com/wp-dyn/content/article/2007/01/12/AR2007011201924.html

[54] 'Hu Puts Forward Principle on Darfur Issue', *Xinhua News*, 5 February 2007 [trans. BBC Monitoring Service, International Reports].

What the senior-level leadership says on these sensitive issues is important because it reflects its changing behaviour and understanding of peacekeeping and non-interventionism. China's quest to play a leadership position in the developing world, particularly in Africa, means that it needs to be more attentive to African public opinion and concerns. As seen here with its peacekeeping contributions to Darfur, ideational factors thus altered China's foreign policy calculus and its own identity and interests so that they are more consistent, or at least not at odds, with regional and global norms.

6.5 CONCLUSION

Looking ahead, China will most likely be cautious and selective in its future participation in UN peace operations, indicating that its stance on peacekeeping, sovereignty, and intervention does not follow a linear, predetermined path. If the UN turns to China more often, it should temper its expectations with a view to seeing a measured and gradual involvement on China's part. Practical matters of political, military, and bureaucratic will and capacity are sure to slow China's responsiveness. With about 2,000 troops deployed on UN missions, an equal number of troops are currently undergoing training to prepare for troop rotation. This figure is not insignificant, given such constraints as the shortage of well-trained personnel with English or French language skills. Likewise, the PLA's limited air- and sea-lift capacities further restrict its ability to provide rapid deployment of troops over long distances. Chinese officials also acknowledge that the PLA and the police force need to improve their understanding of peacekeeping standard operational procedures, international humanitarian law, and UN military regulations and manuals.

There are ways to address gaps in China's peacekeeping capabilities and to help enlarge China's role and commitment to international peacekeeping. Providing greater leadership opportunities for Chinese peacekeepers in field missions and in DPKO would engage China more closely in decision-making processes. There are also prospects for inviting Chinese delegations to participate more actively in (or at least observe) training and simulation exercises organized by other countries. Such constructive engagement could be important in seeing China become more cognizant of and familiar with UN peacekeeping norms and procedures.

More importantly, over the last two decades, China's engagement in international institutions has exposed it to normative values concerning human rights and conflict resolution that are gaining traction and being factored into its foreign policy discourse. It is still at an early stage to determine how far China has accepted these norms; what is increasingly clear, however, is that, in spite of China's rise on the global stage, its options and actions are still influenced by the views and policies of other important actors, particularly the United States and its allies and partners. When there has been broad international consensus regarding a specific operation, as in Darfur, China has tended to lend its support, rather than be viewed as obstructionist.

However, the epistemic community currently addressing peacekeeping remains small in China. There are few practitioners and scholars who have relevant expertise. Given China's emerging international roles and its increasingly socialized behaviour, it has yet to consistently demonstrate how far and for what purposes a rising China will exert its influence in the conduct of international affairs. Moreover, whether these changes in its normative behaviour will reverse is still unclear. There is growing awareness, however, that peacekeeping is fast emerging as an important issue, and more is likely to be done within Chinese academic and other quasi-governmental institutions to help build and expand this epistemic community.[55] Regularized international delegation visits and exchanges can foster this process. There are precedents in other areas such as arms control and non-proliferation, cooperation on pandemics, and international trade where increasing interaction with external actors over time helps foster and sustain a more constructive approach by China consistent with global normative consensus.[56] Last but not least, there is a need to understand that Chinese decision-making is heavily shaped by calculations of interests. It should be noted that the socialization process remains incomplete. China's approach to peacekeeping is still open to internal debate. It has made significant contributions but there are continued limitations, including China's at times less supportive policies regarding peacekeeping. In particular, the episodic reversals in Chinese normative behaviour tend to occur when China displays a more confident and assertive self-image, complemented with strained relations abroad. We may be entering such a period in the coming years.

An effective strategy of embedding China more closely into the set of global norms and institutions related to peacekeeping must make a convincing case that China's commitment to becoming a more responsible stakeholder and a legitimate great power is not only in the interests of international society, but is equally or even more so in China's interests. By and large, China's current leadership appears to recognize the value of multilateral security and confidence-building measures, conforming to regional and global norms, and measured steps to demonstrate constructive intentions. To be sure, on

[55] Authors' interviews with Chinese scholars and officials, Beijing, June 2010; remarks by Chinese participants at a conference on 'China and Multilateral Peace Operations', Oslo, 18–19 March 2010.

[56] Quansheng Zhao, 'Policymaking Processes of Chinese Foreign Policy: The Role of Policy Communities and Think Tanks', in Breslin (ed.), *A Handbook of Chinese International Relations*, pp. 22–34.

peacekeeping, there remains plenty of work ahead to convince the Chinese to sign on more actively to this aspect of the global agenda. This has much to do with China's oft-expressed perception that peacekeeping operations merely cloak ambitions to impose democratic governance, human rights, and regime change. With conservative and nativist voices at home—and with some these voices on the rise in recent years—there will be continued ambivalence and perhaps deepening scepticism. Understanding how Chinese decision-makers balance and reconcile these conflicting interests is critical and merits continued observation and sustained engagement with a broader range of Chinese policy elites on peacekeeping affairs.

7

The Russian Federation

Alexander Nikitin

As one of the five permanent Security Council members, the Russian Federation by definition is involved in all peacekeeping-related debates and decisions in the United Nations (UN). As a great power (first by territorial size and within the top ten global powers by the size of its economy and reserves/exports of key natural resources), Russia perceives itself as a state with global interests and responsibilities, and has a record of involvement in international crises. At the same time, Russian participation in UN peacekeeping remains modest and exhibits features similar to those that may be observed in the peacekeeping contributions of the European permanent members of the Security Council, the UK and France. The main factors which limit Russian participation in UN peacekeeping are its domestic situation in the immediate post-Soviet era, its focus on conflict resolution in the post-Soviet space, and a tendency to pursue these activities outside the auspices of the UN. Russia experimented in the 1990s with 'simulative peacekeeping'—operations with various legal underpinnings but not UN mandates. In Russia's view, these missions resembled impartial UN disengagement or 'traditional peacekeeping' operations. They involved the substantial use of Russian military force in several conflicts in the 'near abroad', including in Tajikistan, Abkhazia/Georgia, South Ossetia/Georgia, and Moldova.

In the post-Cold War era, Russia proceeded from disorganized ad hoc peacekeeping efforts in the post-Soviet space towards the creation of a relatively sophisticated system of legal regulation for peacekeeping based on national legislation and treaties developed through the Commonwealth of Independent States (CIS). The prospects for Russian involvement in future UN peacekeeping operations are deeply interconnected with the new regional format of the Collective Security Treaty Organization (CSTO) which has created its own peacekeeping structures. Economic constraints and the reform of the military in the early twenty-first century have further complicated Russia's capacity and willingness to participate in UN peacekeeping.

This chapter proceeds in three main parts. The first provides an overview of developing Soviet and Russian attitudes towards UN peacekeeping. The second examines how Russia takes decisions about whether and when to commit forces to peacekeeping operations. The third section considers why Russia's contribution to UN peacekeeping has been modest, focusing on the place of domestic politics, the country's strategic priorities and its preference for using non-UN instruments for addressing conflicts in its own neighbourhood—the latter of which is partly attributed to negative past experiences with UN peacekeeping. This section returns to the theme of regional alternatives to UN peacekeeping and suggests that Russian policy on contributing to UN peacekeeping is likely to be shaped by the direction of the CSTO.

7.1 SOVIET/RUSSIAN CONTRIBUTIONS TO INTERNATIONAL PEACE OPERATIONS

Soviet/Russian attitudes to UN peace operations have moved from full rejection of early UN peacekeeping practices to intensive involvement in some operations. Although the Soviet Union was one of the founders of the UN and from the very beginning held a permanent seat in the Security Council, under Stalin the Soviet leadership distrusted the new interstate organization, seeing it as a vehicle for advancing US interests—a perspective shaped by the fact that the US could count on reliable majorities in both the Security Council and General Assembly. Stalin believed that the great powers should resolve crises by direct diplomacy and/or the use of force, and that strong powers should not conduct their diplomacy in the public debates of the UN General Assembly. Superpowers, in his view, should create and impose, not follow international rules. Table 7.1 demonstrates this antipathy by showing the Soviet Union's voting on collective operations in conflict areas during the first decade after start of the first UN peacekeeping operations.

Table 7.1 USSR Votes and Participation in UN Peacekeeping, 1947–1958

Operation	Vote	Provided Peacekeepers?	Provided Finances?
Greece/Bulgaria, Albania, Yugoslavia, 1947	Veto	No	No
UNCI, 1947, Indonesia	Abstained	No	No
UNTSO, since 1948, Middle East	Abstained	Observers (1973–)	No
UNMOGIP, 1949, India–Pakistan	Abstained	No	No
UNEF I, 1956–67, Middle East	Abstained	No	No
UNOGIL, 1958, Lebanon	Abstained	No	No

It is notable that the Soviet Union either abstained or cast its veto in votes about peacekeeping operations during the first decade of the UN. Moreover, Moscow provided neither financial support for such operations nor personnel. The absence of personnel was consistent with an emerging norm that none of the permanent members of the Security Council should contribute troops to peacekeeping operations because, as powers with global interests, they could not be disinterested peacekeepers. On several occasions Western powers tried to circumvent Moscow's veto by moving votes on operations to the General Assembly, where, together with current and former colonies they had a majority. This shift to the General Assembly contradicted, in Moscow's view, the share of responsibilities given to the Council and Assembly by the UN Charter.[1] After Stalin's death, the Soviet Union under Khrushchev changed its approach to UN peacekeeping and became more accommodating. The Soviet Union began to offer political support to most operations, while still not providing finances or sending Russian military or civilian personnel (see Table 7.2).

During the Brezhnev era in the 1970s and early 1980s, the USSR followed the same policy, with Moscow and the West generally appearing on opposite ends of conflicts by their respective proxies. But Moscow provided a modest amount of financial support for UN peacekeeping operations in the Middle East (see Table 7.3).

In the mid-1980s, Moscow's attitude towards UN operations changed once again. The reformist leader, Mikhail Gorbachev, withdrew Soviet forces from Afghanistan in 1989 and removed the Russian veto for an international operation there. He also stopped military assistance to Angola and allowed international involvement in resolving its civil war (see Table 7.4).

On the brink of the collapse of the Soviet Union in 1990–91, Moscow started to support almost every UN peace operation not only politically, but

Table 7.2 USSR Votes and Participation in UN Peacekeeping, 1960–1970

Operation	*USSR vote*	*Provided Peacekeepers?*	*Provided Finances?*
ONUC, 1960, Congo	Support (then oppose)	Airlift food supply	No
UNSF, 1962, New Guinea	Support	No	No
UNYOM, 1963, Yemen	Abstained	No	No
UNFICYP, 1964, Cyprus	Support	No	No
DOMREP, 1965, Dominican Republic	Support	No	No
UNIPOM, 1965–66, India–Pakistan	Support	No	No

[1] Various models of the share of responsibilities in peace operations between the UN Security Council, General Assembly, and other UN structures are discussed in detail in V. F. Zaemsky, *United Nations and Peacekeeping* (Moscow: International Relations, 2008), pp. 77–105.

also with financial support. It provided $6.5 million to UN operations in Central America, $6.3 million to the UN operation in El Salvador (ONUSAL), $16 million to the operation in Iraq/Kuwait (UNIKOM), and $17 million to MINURSO in Western Sahara. Moscow also contributed military observers to eight UN operations during this period (see Table 7.5).

During the post-Soviet period, Russian participation in UN peacekeeping operations remained at quite a low level considering the country's great power status and permanent membership of the UN Security Council. Russia's most significant contribution to UN-led and UN-mandated peacekeeping was its provision of troops to the various peace operations in the former Yugoslavia, beginning in 1992. Russia participated together with Western peacekeepers in operations in the former Yugoslavia, which gradually advanced from

Table 7.3 USSR Votes and Participation in UN Peacekeeping, 1970–1980

Operation	USSR Vote	Provided Peacekeepers?	Provided Finances?
UNEF II, 1967–79, Middle East	Support	Airlift (1973) to Finnish troops	US$10m (for two operations)
UNDOF, 1974, Middle East	Support	No	
UNIFIL, 1978, Lebanon	Abstained (1978) Support (1986–)	No	1993

Table 7.4 USSR Votes and Participation in UN Peacekeeping, 1988–1990

Operation	USSR Vote	Provided Peacekeepers?	Provided Finances?
UNIIMOG, 1988–91, Iran–Iraq	Support	Airlift to Canadian Peacekeepers	No
UNGOMAP, 1988–90, Afghanistan–Pakistan	Veto 1988 Support late 1988–	No	No
UNAVEM I, 1989–91	Support	No	US$15m

Table 7.5 USSR Votes and Participation in UN Peacekeeping, 1990–1991

Operation	USSR Vote	Provided Peacekeepers?	Provided Finances? (US$m)
Namibia 1989–90	Support	Military observers	No
Central America, 1989–92	Support	No	6.5
El Salvador, 1991–95	Support	No	6.3
Iraq/Kuwait, 1991	Support	Military observers	16
Western Sahara, 1991	Support	Military observers	17
Cambodia, 1991–92	Support	Military mediators	No

relatively traditional peacekeeping to peace enforcement mandates. The Russian presence in the Balkans grew from 900 soldiers in 1992 to 1,500 in 1994 during the UNPROFOR operation in Croatia and Bosnia and Herzegovina. Russia also contributed around 1,340 peacekeepers to the NATO-led IFOR/SFOR operations in Bosnia and Herzegovina from 1996. The Russian brigade in Bosnia and Herzegovina, which consisted of airborne troops, had an area of responsibility of 1,750 square kilometres, including 75 kilometres of the inter-entity boundary line. Russia also contributed 1,500 troops to the NATO-led KFOR operation in Kosovo from 1999.

After withdrawal from Yugoslavia, Russia's contributions declined. During this period Russian participation in UN operations was geographically spread and comprised a series of token contributions (see chapter 2). Russian peacekeepers participated in the missions in the Democratic Republic of Congo (DRC), Sudan, Western Sahara, Liberia, Côte d'Ivoire, Haiti, East Timor, Kosovo, and in the Middle East.

During the 2000–2011 period, Russian contributions to UN-led peacekeeping operations fluctuated between 220 and 370 uniformed (military and police) peacekeepers, remaining on basically the same level and disposition (i.e., multiple token contributions) achieved after the withdrawal of Russian peacekeeping contingents from the former Yugoslavia (see Figure 7.1). No civilian (non-uniformed) experts or observers were sent to UN operations during this period.[2] In early 2012, Russia's contribution of peacekeepers in UN contingents dropped to 209 soldiers and police officers. After the end of March

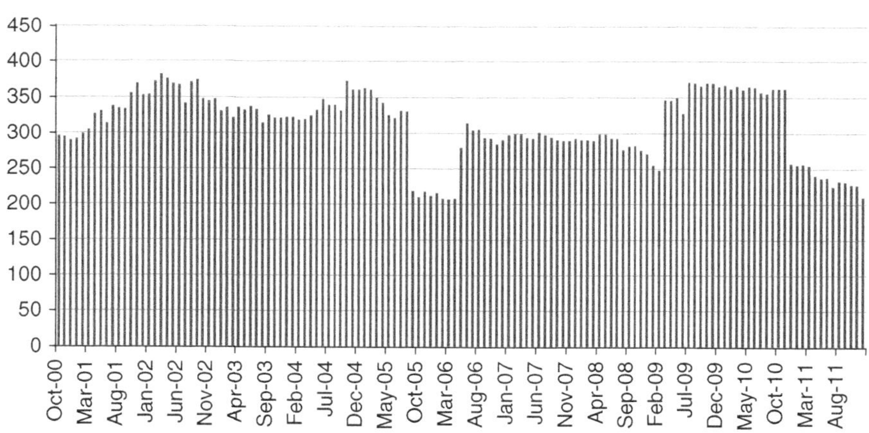

Figure 7.1 Russian Federation Uniformed Personnel in UN Peacekeeping Operations, 2000–2011

[2] Data from the Russian Ministry of Foreign Affairs, at http://www.mid.ru/bdomp/ns-dmo.nsf. For comparison, according to the Berlin-based ZIF Center, in 2010 there were more than 10,000

2012, when Russia withdrew its peacekeepers (planning rotation in the future) from South Sudan, Moscow's contribution dropped to just eighty-three persons (thirteen of them police officers), leaving Russia ranked in 66th place among UN contributor countries.

Russia's financial contribution to UN peacekeeping activities in the fiscal year 2010/11 was $160 million or approximately 2 per cent of the UN peacekeeping budget. This was an insignificant increase (a growth of $2 million from the previous financial year) compared to Russia's financial contributions in the period between 2001 and 2009. This reflects the fact that while Russia pays its assessed contributions for UN peacekeeping it does not make significant additional voluntary contributions. However, although Russia's contribution of uniformed personnel remains quite modest, Russia is the second largest supplier of contractor services to UN peacekeeping operations. In 2011, Russian companies held contracts from the UN worth $382 million, which composed 14 per cent of UN peacekeeping services.[3] Almost all of this is comprised of aviation transportation services provided by Russian aviation and cargo companies.

7.2 EXPLAINING RUSSIA'S CONTRIBUTIONS: THE ROLE OF NON-UN OPERATIONS

As with the three Western permanent members of the Security Council, Russia tends to view UN peacekeeping as only one among several possible crisis management tools, with contributions to UN operations balanced against its other international commitments. In Russia, it is typically perceived that UN-led peacekeeping operations and UN-mandated peace enforcement operations performed by international coalitions, including Russian troops, are components of the same species of operations understood as 'UN-mandated operations' or 'international operations in conflict areas'. The same notion of 'international peace operations in conflict areas' was applied by Russian politicians, public, and the media to operations in the post-Soviet space that did not have a Security Council mandate, namely operations in Tajikistan, South Ossetia/Georgia, Abkhazia/Georgia, and Transdnestria/Moldova. It is important to understand that all the above-mentioned conflicts erupted in 1991–92, either immediately prior to or immediately after the dissolution of the Soviet Union. These missions were perceived by politicians in the CIS and by the

international civilians serving in about sixty operations worldwide—about 8,300 civilians in UN operations and about 3,000 civilians in EU operations. See Jens Behrendt, 'Civilian Personnel in Peace Operations: From Improvisation to Sytems?' *ZIF Policy Briefing*, Berlin (April 2011).

[3] Data provided at a briefing at the Russian Foreign Ministry, November 2011.

public as 'internal' or 'internally rooted' conflicts and therefore not relevant to external, UN-centred mechanisms designed for interstate conflict resolution. Only by the mid-1990s did post-Soviet elites start to perceive these conflict resolution efforts as international in character, where the presence or absence of UN mandates was an appropriate consideration.

Although Russia made only a modest contribution of uniformed personnel to UN peacekeeping before the Yugoslav operations, it made several significant international deployments in the post-Soviet space, comprising around 10,000 troops in total, to missions it generally saw as peace operations, but which were neither led nor mandated by the UN.

Up to 6,950 Russian troops participated in the 1992–2000 operation aimed at stopping a civil war in Tajikistan. This took place under a mandate from the CIS. The operation involved troops from four countries (Russia, Kazakhstan, Kyrgyzstan, and Uzbekistan) and had no formal UN mandate. However, the mission regularly reported its activities to UN authorities and over time the CIS came to interpret the operation as a case of regional peacekeeping under Chapter VIII of the UN Charter. On a parallel track, about 130 UN military observers from thirteen countries were deployed in Tajikistan as part of the UN-mandated observation mission, UNMOT. The absence of a UN mandate for the CIS operation was caused by the UN Security Council's preference for avoiding interference in a civil war in which there was no peace to keep and which contained a number of armed groupings. The UN tended towards a more cautious and classical interpretation of peacekeeping and was not ready to propose solutions for conflicts in what in 1992 was widely interpreted as 'Russia's backyard'.

Another 1,750 Russian troops were involved in the CIS-mandated disengagement operation in Abkhazia/Georgia from 1994 until 2008. As in Tajikistan, the UN established a parallel observation operation in Abkhazia/Georgia (UNOMIG originally comprised of 131 military, 94 international civilian personnel, and 186 local civilian personnel). Thus, CIS-mandated peacekeeping operations in Tajikistan and Georgia worked alongside UN observation missions but were not formally connected to them. As in Tajikistan, the goals of the CIS contingent in Georgia/Abkhazia were to disengage warring parties and prevent further bloodshed (the tasks were 'Chapter Six-and-a-Half' in nature, based on Dag Hammarskjöld's formulation), while the purposes of UN-mandated observation missions were mainly fact-finding and reporting to the UN on the pattern of conflicts and ways towards political solutions.

In the West, some analysts argued that Russia was trying to keep the UN at a distance from these conflict management initiatives in order to retain control over the area and the political outcomes of the civil war in Tajikistan.[4] This

[4] See, for example, Kevin O'Prey, 'Keeping the Peace in the Borderlands of Russia', in William Durch (ed.), *UN Peacekeeping, American Policy and The Uncivil Wars of the 1990s* (New York: Palgrave Macmillan, 1996), pp. 409–65.

assumption has some merit but overestimates both the rationality of Russian politics and the readiness of the UN to step in if it had been invited. In the mid-1990s, the UN was overwhelmed with difficult operations in the former Yugoslavia, witnessed unusually high losses in peace operations, and was not prepared to embark on another complex mission in the post-Soviet Central Asia, especially because many Western leaders—specifically those in Germany and France—believed that engagement in this area was not a priority and was widely viewed as being the prerogative of Moscow. At the same time, the new Russian Federation became involved in conflict resolution efforts in Tajikistan not by strategic rational choice but rather because of the flow of events: removing the former Soviet contingents of Division 201 and Russian border-guards from Tajikistan would have meant opening CIS borders to Afghanistan and risking significant instability.

In general, CIS contingents interfaced cooperatively with UN observers, while UN teams tended to provide information in return only through official UN–Ministry of Foreign Affairs channels. In Tajikistan, the UN was invited to take part as official observers at the negotiating and concluding of the Tajik Peace Accords (1997), and UN Special Envoy Charles Merriam co-signed those peace agreements together with Tajik President E. Rakhmon and the leader of the Tajik United Opposition Mekhmed Nouri.

In Abkhazia, interaction between CIS and UN operations involved occasional tensions. At the start of the operation, the Georgian government hoped that Russian peacekeepers would help to suppress 'Abkhazian separatism' (Russia was itself combating separatist trends in Chechnya, just across the border) and ensure the return of displaced Georgians. But Russian peacekeepers considered such tasks to be outside their CIS mandate, which they interpreted simply as providing a buffer between the parties. In response, Georgia started to appeal to the UN mission as a counterbalance to the CIS mission.[5]

From 1992 until 2008, around 500 Russian troops participated in the so-called 'Trilateral Peacekeeping Forces' on the disengagement line between South Ossetia and Georgia. They comprised Russian, Georgian, and South Ossetian forces with a combined strength of 1,500 troops. The Trilateral Forces were created on the basis of the written agreement between Georgia and Russia signed by Presidents Shevardnadze and Yeltsin in 1992. Their task was to stabilize the unofficial border ('disengagement belt') between Georgian and Ossetian held territories using loyal military contingents from the warring parties and a Russian peacekeeping contingent.

[5] Heidi Tagliavini, former Head of the UNOMIG Mission to Georgia and Special Representative of the UN Secretary-General in Georgia, discussed the modalities and achievements of the UN mission in Heidi Tagliavini, 'The Main Principles of Peace Support and the Role of the UN/UNOMIG in Resolving the Conflict in Abkhazia/Georgia', in Alexander Nikitin (ed.), *Peace Support Operations, Parliaments and Legislation* (Moscow: Aslan Publishers, 2004), pp. 67–75.

Immediately before the five-day Russian–Georgian war in 2008, the Georgian President withdrew his consent to the mission, making Russian peacekeepers *persona non grata*. However, Russia argued that because, at the beginning of the conflict, Georgian forces killed fifteen Russian soldiers in an artillery attack, its operations in South Ossetia and Abkhazia could not be considered peacekeeping. Moreover, after Russia's unilateral recognition of both territories as independent states in September 2008, Russian contingents in these territories became 'military bases' governed by bilateral agreements.

Russia also contributed to a 'Trilateral Force' on the border between the self-proclaimed Transdnestrian Republic and Moldova (1992–present). Initially, Russia contributed three battalions (up to 1,600 troops) but by 1995 the situation had stabilized and the size of the Russian element was reduced to a single battalion (less than 500 troops on a rotational basis) and remained at this level throughout the 2000s. In some Western studies, the operation in Moldova is interpreted as 'an instrument of unilateral interference in a separatist conflict in order to further Moscow's neo-imperialist interests, and probably with the ultimate aim of forcing the newly independent state to accept a Russian military base upon its territory'.[6] But this interpretation underestimates the trilateral character of the forces and the fact that the operation was requested by the Moldovan authorities. Moldovan President Mircha Snegur co-signed with Russian President Yeltsin an agreement on the trilateral character of the peacekeeping contingent. Equally, the Moldovan side did not request the quick withdrawal of the Russian element, preferring that it remain until the Russian army had removed from Transdnestria the former Soviet arsenals held by the Fourteenth Army. This was because Chisinau was afraid that these huge arsenals might fall into the hands of the Transdnestrian army and various militia groups and transnational criminal gangs.

Only the multilateral operation in Tajikistan was considered a full-scale CIS peacekeeping operation, with the operation in Abkhazia/Georgia being purely Russian despite receiving CIS approval. The operations in Tajikistan and Abkhazia were based on a mandate authorized by the heads of CIS states. Moreover, in the operation in Tajikistan, the command chain was subordinated to the CIS Military Cooperation Staff and politically the operation was subordinated to the CIS Council of Heads of State, the Council of Foreign Affairs Ministers, and the Council of Defence Ministers. The operation was administered not by national ministries of defence, but by the international staff for CIS Military Cooperation, which appointed commanders on a rotational basis. From this point of view, only this operation can be properly understood as a regional CIS peacekeeping operation. Other missions, such as

[6] Trevor Waters, 'Russian Peacekeeping in Moldova', in John Mackinlay and Peter Cross (eds.), *The Paradox of Russian Peacekeeping* (Tokyo: United Nations University Press, 2003), p. 150.

those in Georgia/South Ossetia and Moldova/Transdnestria, were trilateral operations initially based on host state consent.

From the Russian and CIS/CSTO perspective, to date there have been no cases of peace enforcement in the post-Soviet space composed of New Independent States (NIS) and thus no need for a UN mandate despite the withdrawal of host state consent in some cases. From this perspective, Chapter VIII of the UN Charter legitimized the CIS and CSTO as regional security organizations able to provide peacekeeping based upon regional mandates. However, these missions have provoked international debate for a number of reasons.[7]

One notable factor, though, is the lack of external authorization for these operations, especially from the UN Security Council. This has become a particular source of tension in the wake of Georgia's withdrawal of consent to the deployment of Russian troops and Russia's recognition of secessionist territories as new independent states. From the Russian perspective, Western criticism on these grounds is misplaced because NIS governments support regional conflict resolution initiatives. They regularly inform the UN about the status of the operations in Tajikistan, Georgia, and Moldova. In addition, the UN continued to express great doubts concerning its readiness to undertake formal international peacekeeping missions on NIS territory that go beyond the deployment of small numbers of unarmed observers.[8]

NIS conflict resolution practices are innovative because they involve the opposing sides in the peacekeeping processes. For example, in the case of South Ossetia, both Georgian and South Ossetian military battalions patrolled alongside Russian troops. In Transdnestria, three Moldovan and three Transdnestrian battalions composed the peacekeeping force in collaboration with Russian battalions. This proved useful when, at early stages of conflicts, when such trilateral forces were created, the hostilities involved not organized violence between coherent groups but, rather, poorly organized violence perpetrated by various armed groups on both sides. In this context, the political authorities on both sides were not able properly to control their own supporters. Thus the mechanism of trilateral patrols was established to build confidence, maintain order, and prevent the escalation of conflict by

[7] See Western disagreement with Russian interpretations of NIS peacekeeping in Terry McNeill, 'Humanitarian Intervention and Peacekeeping in the Former Soviet Union and Eastern Europe', *International Political Science Review*, 18:1 (1997), pp. 95–113; Frederick H. Fleitz, *Peacekeeping Fiascos of the 1990s* (Westport, CT: Praeger, 2002); and E. Gross, D. Hamilton, C. Major, and H. Riecke (eds.), *Preventing Conflict, Managing Crisis* (Washington, DC: Center for Transatlantic Relations, 2011).

[8] That was the essence of the UN reaction to the letter submitted to the UN Secretary-General in 1995 by the five presidents of the CIS states (Russia, Tajikistan, Kirgizstan, Uzbekistan, and Kazakhstan) in which they requested that the UN consider the possibility of a full-scale UN stabilization operation in Tajikistan (to substitute for the CIS operation). However, the UN limited its involvement to the small UNMOT observation team.

unauthorized armed groupings. In this respect, joint patrolling between opposing parties was relatively successful during the early stages of the conflicts in Moldova/Transdnestria and Ossetia/Georgia, though such arrangements took significant effort to establish. In the longer term, however, this approach failed to foster conflict resolution, giving rise, among other things, to the 2008 war in Georgia.

Another area where NIS peacekeeping operations have been innovative has been in the use of force and military technology. NIS operations were sometimes criticized for the use of heavy weapons, war-like tactics, and the use of standard armed forces in civilian areas, instead of using specially trained and equipped peacekeeping contingents or acting in a manner consistent with core peacekeeping principles such as impartiality and minimum use of force. In the early years of NIS peacekeeping, when there was a visible lack of specifically trained soldiers and officers, such tactics were extremely common. However, the situation changed after 1994: special training facilities were expanded, and Russian conscripts were no longer sent to external conflict zones. Throughout the 2000s, all Russian military peacekeeping units were assembled on a voluntary basis and underwent training aimed at securing compliance with UN standards.

7.3 RUSSIAN DECISION-MAKING AND TRAINING FOR PEACEKEEPING

During the Soviet years, decisions on participation in UN peacekeeping operations involved clear ideological elements (Moscow tried to keep the UN out of conflicts where the USSR had vested interests or proxies) and were products of interaction between the International Department of the Central Committee of the Communist Party and the International Organizations Department of the Ministry of Foreign Affairs, sometimes with the direct intervention of leaders like Stalin or Khrushchev.

However, from 1991 until the mid-1990s, the period of collapse of the Soviet Union and the emergence and reorganization of the Russian Federation, there were no systematic decision-making mechanisms relating to external conflict resolution activities and conflicts in the so-called 'Far Abroad' were perceived as being of lesser priority than those in the 'Near Abroad' (the former Soviet space). Various contingents of the former Soviet Armed Forces remained on the territory of now newly independent states (Tajikistan, Moldova, Georgia, etc.) and were sometimes involved by the flow of events in regional conflicts, without clear central planning or coordination. Reflecting on this period, Dov Lynch rightly observed that, 'Russian operations do not reflect an organized programme following clear mandates and peacekeeping doctrines, instead varying according to the nature of the conflict, the requirements perceived by the Russian government, and the resources available to Russia at the time of deployment.'[9]

The situation that commanders of the former Fourteenth Soviet Army faced in Moldova/Transdnestria was quite characteristic of how the practice of peacekeeping evolved without clear political oversight or strategy. After several failed attempts to get clear instructions from Moscow, and in a context of bloody riots and civil war in Transdnestria, General Lebed and General Zhurbenko decided themselves to place tanks between the warring sides. This initiative was criticized by the Russian Ministry of Foreign Affairs as 'uncoordinated' but it nevertheless succeeded in stemming the violence. It also proved popular with the public, with General Lebed being elected to the Russian Parliament under the nickname (and electoral slogan) of 'Peacekeeper'. This characteristic episode took place before Moldova and Russia co-signed a formal agreement on the deployment of a trilateral peace operation along the disengagement line between Moldovan and Transdnestrian forces. It is worth noting that the Moldovan authorities insisted that the Russian contingent not be comprised of soldiers from the former Fourteenth Army but, for the sake of neutrality, draw on troops from other parts of Russia. Moscow agreed and the first rotation was brought from Leningrad/St Petersburg.

The period between 1991 and 1994–95 was also characterized by schemes for keeping the armed forces of the now divided former Soviet republics under the unified or collective command of the CIS authorities. A Joint CIS Military Staff was created, and CIS-mandated operations in Tajikistan and Abkhazia/Georgia formally went under its international chain of command, though in practice they were technically supervised by the Russian (former Soviet) General Staff.[10]

7.3.1 Legal Grounds: The 1995 Russian Federal Law and 2005 CIS Model Law

By the mid-1990s it had become clear that no unified CIS conflict resolution system would be created because of political differences among CIS leaders. Russia decided to codify conflict resolution practices unilaterally and in 1995 a

[9] Dov Lynch, 'Post-Imperial Peacekeeping: Russia in the CIS', paper for the Norwegian Institute for Defence Studies, IFS info 2/2003, at http://brage.bibsys.no/fhs/bitstream/URN:NBN:no-bibsys_brage_21515/1/IFSInfo0203.pdf

[10] The peace support role of the CIS Military Staff is discussed in General Vladimir Yakovlev, 'Peace Support Activities of the CIS and the Role of the Staff for the Coordination of Military Cooperation', in Nikitin (ed.), *Peace Support Operations*, pp. 61–7.

new Federal Law was adopted. The Law 'On the Order of Providing Military and Civil Personnel of the Russian Federation for Participation in Peacekeeping Operations and Enforcement of International Peace and Security Operations and other Types of Peacekeeping Activities', as its title supposes, was designed to cover cases not only of 'classical' UN peacekeeping but also new types of coercive Chapter VII operations (such as Iraq in 1991 and Bosnia in 1994–95), as well as operations with or without the UN mandate in the post-Soviet space.[11]

In its Preamble, the Law postulates that Russia may participate in operations mandated by the UN, OSCE, and the CIS 'as permitted by the Chapters VI, VII and VIII of the UN Charter', as well as by 'international treaties obligations of the Russian Federation'.[12] Responsibility for peace operations is shared between the President, the Government, and the Council of Federation (upper Chamber of the Parliament). Decisions on sending individual soldiers or military observers to UN missions are to be taken by the President based on presentations from the ministries of Foreign Affairs and Defence, while decisions to contribute civilian personnel to UN operations are a prerogative of the Government. The deployment of a contingent (brigade or other sized formations) to operations abroad requires a vote on the decision by the Council of Federation, although in practice this has not always occurred prior to deployment (see below). Such a decision must specify the size of contingent, weaponry, and the terms and length of stay. Parliament's blessing is required for Russia to respond positively to requests for contingents by the UN. When the proposed operation is a peace enforcement mission, the Council of Federation must approve the operation and the Lower Chamber (State Duma) must be informed (though no vote is required).[13]

The Federal Law includes an important clause (in Article 10) on the necessity of forming within the armed forces a specially equipped and trained permanent peacekeeping contingent (Peacekeeping Forces of the Russian Federation), financed through a 'separate budget line'. However, this was implemented only partially through the designation of additional peacekeeping training functions to the Fifteenth Samara Division of the Russian Armed Forces.

The adoption of the Federal Law, which remains a key regulatory document, was partially motivated by the need to legitimize the dispatch of Russian

[11] The text of the Federal Law along with comments is available in Alexander Nikitin, *Peace Operations: Concepts and Practice* (Moscow: Moscow Public Scientific Foundation, 2000), pp. 178–84.

[12] Nikitin, *Peace Operations*, p. 178.

[13] For points of comparison on the role of parliaments see an article by the former Vice-President of the NATO Parliamentary Assembly and member of the Netherlands Senate, Wim F. van Ekelen, 'The Parliamentary Dimension of Oversight over the Military', in Nikitin (ed.), *Peace Support Operations*, pp. 152–74.

contingents to Bosnia in 1995. Voting on this issue (the first practical application of the Law) in the Council of Federation went smoothly. However, voting on the Russian military operation in Abkhazia/Georgia produced heated debates among parliamentarians and a negative vote. Parliamentarians insisted that other CIS states should allocate contingents and finances for the implementation of CIS decisions on Abkhazia, and not place the entire burden on Russia. The difficulty of this situation was increased by the fact that at the time of the negative vote, the Russian contingent was already situated in Abkhazia (a legacy of Soviet times). As a result of the vote, use of this contingent in the CIS-mandated operation became illegitimate for half a year, until it was finally approved by the Council of Federation.

The next important stage in advancing legal grounds for the participation of Russian and other CIS states in peacekeeping was marked by the adoption of a Model Law of the Commonwealth of the Independent States 'On Participation of a State in Peace Support Operations'.[14] This law was adopted in 2004 by the CIS Inter-Parliamentary Assembly. It aims to unify legislation on peacekeeping across CIS member states. It provides standard legal definitions, formulations, and clauses on the mechanisms that may be applied by any CIS state in its national legislation if and when it plans to join or undertake peace operations, either under UN auspices or under the auspices of the CIS or any other regional organizations. After discussing modes of participation in UN peacekeeping and peace enforcement operations and in peacekeeping operations of regional organizations (CIS and others), the law also specifies as a separate type 'local peacekeeping operations' under bilateral or multilateral interstate agreements.

The model law sets out the responsibilities of Presidents, Governments, and Parliaments in relation to the deployment of military and civilian personnel to peacekeeping operations. It sets out minimal training requirements for peacekeepers and modes of interaction between national authorities, the UN, and other international organizations on peacekeeping issues. It requires that national authorities implement International Humanitarian Law and International Human Rights Law in the course of peacekeeping activities. It also suggests limitations on the use of force in peacekeeping operations. Although the model law is not binding, discussion of it among parliamentarians and ministries, which lasted three years, significantly improved the acquaintance and legal literacy of parliamentarians and officials in relation to peacekeeping.

[14] See M. Krotov and Alexander Nikitin, 'Introductory Comments', in M. Korotov and Alexander Nikitin, *On Participation of a State in Peace Support Operations: Commonwealth of the Independent States (CIS) Model Law* (Moscow: Aslan Publishers, 2004).

7.3.2 Training Russian Peacekeepers

Between the 1970 and 1990s, the training of Soviet/Russian participants in UN peacekeeping operations was organized by the Ministry of Defence through a system of special UN Military Observers training courses in the city of Solnechnogorsk. This changed in the mid-1990s when military peacekeepers assigned to the Ministry of Defence (and designated for both UN-mandated and regional peacekeeping operations) were concentrated in the Fifteenth Motorized Infantry Division (based near the city of Samara). This division was assigned the specific function of training personnel for peace operations. In the late 2000s the training system was reformed again. Under these reforms, soldiers eligible for deployment as peacekeepers would be nominated by their division and those designated to join UN contingents would undergo training in a Ministry of Defence training centre in Narofominsk, near Moscow. Since June 2005 military cadres from CSTO states became entitled to train and be certified in Russian defence academies and institutions at no cost to their governments. Joint programmes for the training of peacekeepers, anti-terror, and anti-drug specialists from all CSTO countries were organized by Russian military academies.

The training of Russian police peacekeepers is organized on the basis of the All-Russian Institute for Continuous Education of the Ministry of Interior in Domodedovo, near Moscow. The whole process of the selection and training of police personnel for international functions is supervised by the Ministry of Interior Department of Cadres Supply. The Domodedovo Centre also provides training for foreign police. For example, around 200 police peacekeepers from several African countries underwent six months of training in 2009, and 300 police from Afghanistan underwent training under an agreement with the UN.

Generally, the process of selecting, training, and assigning both military and police peacekeepers to UN operations is managed by the Department of International Organizations of the Russian Foreign Ministry and Departments of Cadres of Ministry of Defence and Ministry of Interior, with the Security Council of the Russian Federation playing a supervisory role.

As a sign of a growing national constituency in favour of peacekeeping, in the early 2000s former Soviet/Russian veterans of UN operations established a National Association of Peacekeepers and in 2009 published records relating to Russian participation in UN peacekeeping.[15] The association launched educational and information projects aimed at promoting a 'peacekeeping culture' in Russia. Such projects included 'Modelling UN Peacekeeping' and

[15] See V. Gergel (ed.), *On the Service of Peace, 1973–2008* (Moscow: Textbooks Publishers, 2009).

'Young Peacekeepers' aimed at acquainting college and university students with UN activities in peacekeeping. Basically a 'former peacekeepers lobby group', the association also interacts with the ministries of Foreign Affairs and Defence through the Russian UN Association and UN Information Centre in Moscow. It also established a Russian Museum of Peacekeeping.

7.4 MOTIVATIONS FOR RUSSIAN PEACEKEEPING POLICIES

There are several clusters of factors that may explain the relatively low level of Russian participation in UN peacekeeping. These principally relate to security rationales (Russia's priorities lay in the NIS space) and political rationales (difficult domestic politics, disputes with the West over the legitimacy of different types of peacekeeping activities, and a preference for working with regional institutions).

7.4.1 Security Priorities: Domestic Threats and the Near Abroad

Russia's security priorities are focused on domestic issues and the post-Soviet space. Since the collapse of the Soviet Union in late 1991, the security agenda of the Russian Federation has been preoccupied with a combination of domestic threats and challenges in the post-Soviet space. A joint study convened in November–December 2010 by the Institute of Sociology of the Russian Academy of Sciences and the ZIRCON Group identified Russian perceptions about security threats.[16] Experts were invited to evaluate the relative importance of seventy potential threats and challenges. The main conclusion was that the most acutely felt threats, according to experts, were of a domestic nature. The most significant overall threat was identified as corruption within domestic institutions while the most significant international challenge identified by the study was the global economic and financial crises, which appeared in twenty-first place. Another study, conducted by the VZIOM Centre showed that only 7 per cent of the sample of members of the Russian public associated Russian 'greatness' with the return of its control over the territories of the former Soviet Union.[17] Another 7 per

[16] 'National Security of Russia Estimated by Experts', study of November–December 2010, results published in February 2011. At http://www.zircon.ru/upload/File/russian/publications/1/Nacionalnaja.bezopasnost.Rossii.v.ocenkah.jekspertov_28-02-11.pdf

[17] VZIOM Center. Press issue No. 1601, 12 October 2010, at http://www.wciom.ru (in Russian).

cent argued that great power status required Russia to become a world centre of influence able to resolve international conflicts. Another 10 per cent thought that 'revival of the national spirit' was necessary for a great power. Only 4 per cent thought great power status for Russia required reaffirming its role as a 'civilizational bridge between Europe and Asia'. Such attitudes reveal the public's focus on largely domestic concerns. Various other surveys showed that Russians were preoccupied with the 'Near Abroad' and were relatively uninterested in the 'Far Abroad'. Combined, these attitudes remain a major reason for Russia's limited involvement in UN peacekeeping activities in Africa, Asia, and the Middle East: the contemporary Russian public, in contrast to Soviet times, does not consider international power projection and overseas involvements to be important components of Russia's global role.

7.4.2 Political Rationales: Disputes with the West

Russian apprehension towards UN peacekeeping is shaped somewhat by disputes with the West, especially in relation to the use of coercive force. Coercive operations with or without UN mandates by NATO or US-led coalitions (for example, in Kosovo, Afghanistan, Iraq, and Libya) on one side and Russian involvement in certain conflicts (without UN mandates, but sometimes with CIS authorization) have provoked mutual recriminations and accusations. There are numerous examples of Western academics criticizing Russian peacekeeping on various grounds. For example, British researcher Terry McNeill concluded in relation to Russia's post-Soviet peacekeeping 'experiments' that '[t]he very vagueness of the concepts of peacekeeping and humanitarian intervention creates serious ambiguities which can be exploited—as Russia has been doing—to cover hegemonic ambitions.'[18] Trevor Findlay meanwhile complained that 'Russia launched them [peacekeeping operations] without a peacekeeping doctrine, with little prior experience.'[19] Johnson goes even further in estimating that these operations were 'without proper mandate, with partiality, and a high level of force'.[20]

Russian experts, in their turn, widely criticize many aspects of Western-led peacekeeping and peace enforcement practices, especially in the cases of UN-mandated missions in Kosovo, Iraq, and Libya.[21] These negative assessments feed into understandings of UN peacekeeping because much of the Russian

[18] McNeill, 'Humanitarian Intervention', p. 95.

[19] Trevor Findlay, *The Use of Force in UN Peace Operations* (Oxford: Oxford University Press/SIPRI, 2002), p. 409.

[20] L. Johnson, 'In Search of a Doctrine: Russian Interventionism in Conflicts in its "Near Abroad"', *Low Intensity Conflict and Law Enforcement*, 5:3 (1996), p. 440.

[21] See Alexander Nikitin and A. Kazantsev (eds.), *In Search of New Role: International Security Organizations in Euro-Atlantic and Eurasian Regions* (Moscow: MGIMO, 2011) and

academic literature does not distinguish UN peacekeeping from the coercive use of force (as in Iraq, Afghanistan, and Libya) either with or without UN mandates. These sorts of disputes breed mistrust, especially in relation to issues such as the use of force for civilian protection, and militate against the Russian government making larger contributions to UN operations, which are widely perceived as being in the same basket as other, more controversial, operations.

7.4.3 Difficult Domestic Politics and Institutional Reform

Another important factor that limits Russian readiness to participate in UN peacekeeping operations is what may be described as a 'post-imperial' syndrome that influenced the country's political culture after the collapse of the Soviet Union. This syndrome is reminiscent of the 'post-Vietnam syndrome' in the US, which deterred leaders and public opinion from foreign policy activism. In Russia during the 1990s, it was commonly understood that Russia was not simply a smaller Soviet Union and widely thought that Moscow should not repeat its predecessor's mistake of ideological involvement in the 'Far Abroad'. Self-perceptions of Russia as a large but regional power prevailed over previous perceptions of itself as a global power.

This view was supported by the perception that Russia was militarily and geostrategically weak. Russia's military force proved to be far from decisively strong in domestic conflicts in Chechnya and other Caucasian regions, contributing to a general reluctance to employ military capabilities overseas. It was only closer to the end of the 2000s that the national mentality started to recover from these post-Soviet syndromes and the country's leadership started gradually to re-establish a global presence. But while perceptions of weakness receded in the twenty-first century, significant military reforms, including the most recent and deepest round in 2010–11, kept military and police forces from prioritizing the provision of peacekeepers. The latest military reform proposed major cuts in the general size of Russia's armed forces, including increasing the percentage of contracted officers, shrinking the number of conscripts, and eliminating non-commissioned officers as a class. The reforms are also premised on the restructuring of forces along a functional rather than a regional basis and introducing intensive 'vertical' rather than 'horizontal' aggregation (i.e., establishing combined task brigades instead of territorial 'armies'). These reforms, while raising the potential effectiveness of the armed forces, diminished their ability to keep contingents for long periods in latent conflict areas of the 'Far Abroad'. The best equipped

I. Yurgens, A. Dynkin, and V. Baranovsky (eds.), *Architecture of Euro-Atlantic Security* (Moscow: Econ-Inform, 2009).

and trained national military forces were already involved in regional conflict resolution efforts in Central Asia and the Caucasus. Within the military, this strengthened arguments that contributing forces to assist 'somebody else's conflicts' in Africa or Asia was a poor use of resources when set against the demands of domestic conflicts.

7.4.4 Negative Experiences of UN and NATO Peacekeeping

Russian attitudes towards UN peacekeeping have been influenced by negative experiences of peacekeeping with NATO in Kosovo and the limited role of the UN in the post-Soviet space. The collapse of the former Yugoslavia and split of the former Soviet Union happened almost simultaneously. Russian politicians and the public paid a significant amount of attention to conflict resolution efforts in the Balkans, from operations in Bosnia and Herzegovina to the current situation around Albania and Kosovo. This was partly because of the simultaneity of Yugoslavia's problems with that of Russia, partly because of historic ties with Serbia, and partly due to the strategic proximity of the former Yugoslavia. As noted above, Russia supported UN peacekeeping and peace enforcement in the former Yugoslavia and sent a brigade to participate jointly with NATO troops in missions in Bosnia and Herzegovina and Kosovo. However, both missions proved difficult and controversial, so that while they may have contributed to practical interoperability, in other respects they discouraged future Russian participation in joint operations.

Peacekeeping was conducted without much success by UNPROFOR while peace enforcement proved relatively more successfully through the NATO-led IFOR/SFOR and KFOR missions. However, these missions received mixed reviews in Russia. For some, they represented a sign of real and positive change in the role of NATO and its relations with Russia. But others were deeply critical for several reasons.[22] First, critics accused NATO of being biased against the Serbs. With a certain degree of overstatement it might be said that some Russians believed themselves and NATO to be on different sides of the Yugoslav conflict.[23] Second, many Russian politicians believed that NATO violated or at least misinterpreted the UN mandate when it undertook

[22] In the lower chamber of the Parliament the 'Anti-NATO Coalition' was formed during the Yugoslavian operation, and more than 200 out of 500 parliamentarians became members of it. The coalition undertook numerous propagandistic actions and lobbied for anti-Western amendments in several foreign policy legislations, including postponements of ratification of the START-2 Treaty.

[23] Strong criticism on this point was expressed, among others, by Konstantin Zatulin, Deputy Chair of the CIS Affairs Committee of the State Duma (Parliament), and Dmitri Rogozin, leader of the Congress of Russian Communities Party, who was later nominated as the Russian Permanent Representative (Ambassador) to the NATO and NATO–Russian Council.

Operation Deliberate Force in 1995. Third, in relation to Kosovo in particular, while NATO was effective in performing military functions it proved unable to find a political settlement. Negative attitudes were only hardened by the experience in Kosovo, where Russia argued that NATO failed to be neutral, protected Albanians, and mistreated Serbs. Russia withdrew its military contingent from the UN-mandated operation in Kosovo early, stressing that it disagreed with NATO's interpretation of the operation's mandate.

Despite a serious impasse in Russia–NATO relations caused by these differences in the former Yugoslavia, the crises there allowed Russia and NATO to gain some joint experience of field peacekeeping. The Russia–NATO Council went so far as to develop a concept of joint Russian–NATO peacekeeping operations. It was the result of three years of consultations in a special working group set up for the purpose. Unfortunately, the subsequent document has never been formally adopted.

7.4.5 Preference for Regional Instruments of Crisis Management

The Russian Federation's ambivalent attitude towards UN peacekeeping is to a significant extent shaped by its preference for using regional instruments to address conflicts in the NIS—a tendency that is likely to continue as those instruments become stronger. In September 2002, the charter of a new regional interstate organization came into effect, marking a significant change in the geostrategic situation of the NIS region, namely, the conversion of the Collective Security Treaty into the Collective Security Treaty Organization (CSTO).[24]

The CSTO was in part a response to the common threat to the security of Russia and Central Asia posed by the Taliban and associated groups in and around Afghanistan. In May 2001, before the creation of the CSTO, a decision was made to form a Collective Rapid Deployment Force (CRDF) for the Central Asian Region of Collective Security under CIS auspices. In the summer of 2001, the force consisted of 1,500 troops with battalions from Kazakhstan, Kyrgyzstan, Russia, and Tajikistan. In 2004, the CRDF was upgraded to eleven battalions, with its military headquarters in Bishkek and the air force base in Kant. The base in Kant contains an international staff of up to 800, which greatly contributes to CRDF mobility during outbreaks of violence. The CSTO Secretary-General explained that, 'the time for decision-making concerning the use of the CRDF does not exceed one hour-and-a half to two hours in case of a sharpening of the local situation. Just several more

[24] Signed in 1992, it entered into force in 1994. The treaty text is at http://dkb.gov.ru/start/

hours would be required by the military to relocate the contingent into the conflict region.'[25]

On 6 October 2007, an agreement for the creation of the Joint CSTO Peacekeeping system was signed by heads of seven CSTO states. The system includes the formation of the CSTO Collective Peacekeeping Forces which were de facto formed in 2011, numbering 4,500 military and police personnel. These forces are mandated for use under either a UN or regional mission. On 15 June 2009 the President of Russia approved a decree assigning the Russian Peacekeeping Contingent to the CSTO Peacekeeping Forces. The Russian component included a separate motorized infantry brigade, special tasks police forces (150 policemen), and observers and advisers from the Ministry of Interior.

The assigning of large Russian military and police components to regional peacekeeping tasks is a significant determinant of Russia's capacity to contribute more to UN peacekeeping and an indication of its willingness to do so. These assigned integrated forces must undergo special training for peacekeeping-type operations, which, in turn, requires the establishment of a peacekeeping training system. The new system will expand the current capacity for training 200–300 peacekeepers at a time to a capacity to train up to 2,500 military and police personnel simultaneously. Nevertheless, by relating these capacities to the CSTO, Moscow is clearly signalling that it intends to continue to prefer providing its peacekeepers to regional arrangements rather than to the UN.

Another instrument for regional conflict management is the Collective Operational Reaction Forces (CORF, comprising 15,000 soldiers), which may be used in the territories of the CSTO during social emergencies or in cases of external threat. The principal external threat is thought to be the infiltration of Islamists into Central Asia from Afghanistan after the withdrawal of NATO forces there in 2014. It has to be noted that personnel for both CORF and peacekeeping forces remain under national jurisdiction during peace time and unite in combined international brigades only during regular joint exercises or in cases of emergency, and at the discretion of the national government.

In summary, therefore, Russia's relatively low level of participation in UN peacekeeping derives from a combination of factors that it holds in common with the West—most notably its security priorities, a preference for operating outside the UN, and unhappy experiences with UN operations. Additional factors unique to Russia's context include its difficult domestic politics, institutional reform of its military, and profound disagreements with NATO on the interpretation and implementation of peacekeeping mandates. Moves to

[25] Interview of CSTO Secretary-General N. Bordyuzha with RIA-Novosti Agency, 10 August 2004.

strengthen regional peacekeeping through the CSTO suggest that these tendencies are likely to continue to outweigh the positive influences described earlier.

7.5 CONCLUSION

After its deep military reform, Russia is systematizing the training of its peacekeepers and special-forces elements and may have the capacity to slightly increase its contribution to UN peacekeeping, especially in peacekeeping-related services (like transportation). However, like many Western states, Russia prefers to deploy its forces within missions organized by regional organizations or ad hoc coalitions of the willing, and does not see a UN mandate as essential for authorizing these operations.

These tendencies have pushed Russia to concentrate on efforts to create a regional CSTO-based system of conflict resolution and peacekeeping. Moscow continues to perceive NATO and, to a lesser extent, the European Union as rivals to its own integrative efforts, and the expansion of NATO- and EU-based crisis management and peacekeeping efforts serve as additional motivations for the creation of CSTO peacekeeping capabilities. In addition, since the UN is unlikely to play a major role in conflict resolution initiatives in the post-Soviet space, this makes Russia's emphasis on regional peacekeeping instruments more realistic.

Although Russia and the NIS gained both specific and general experience with respect to peace operations in the 1990s and 2000s, there is still much debate as to how to classify these missions and certainly disagreement with some of the categorizations used by Western scholars. In this regard, conflict management activities in the NIS have not developed in a manner that is easily translated into Western typologies. While some operations do not qualify as peace support missions, others fit UN peacekeeping standards even though a formal UN mandate was not issued. At the same time, if one compares NIS activities to all varieties of UN-mandated operations, 'coalition operations', NATO-led missions, and unilateral and UN-mandated actions of international coalitions in conflict areas, they do not seem so different after all.

Part III

Top Contributors (2000–2010)

8

Bangladesh

Rashed Uz Zaman and Niloy R. Biswas

Over the past two decades Bangladesh, a country usually associated with floods, natural disasters, and poverty, has been able to project a positive international image through its participation in United Nations (UN) peacekeeping operations. Indeed, in the twenty-first century, Bangladesh can claim to be one of the UN's largest contributors of uniformed peacekeepers; a considerable source of pride for the Bangladesh armed forces and the country alike. But how is it that Bangladesh came to assume such a leading role in UN missions? What are the rationales behind its provision of peacekeepers? And what are the implications of such a policy for Bangladesh's armed forces and the country?

To address these questions the chapter is divided into five main parts: Section 8.1 presents a brief history of Bangladesh's participation in UN peacekeeping missions from its humble beginnings in 1988. Sections 8.2 and 8.3 cover more recent trends as well as analysing the decision-making process through which troops are sent abroad and the training such personnel receive. Section 8.4 explores Bangladesh's decisions to participate in so many UN missions with reference to the country's political, social, and economic history. Section 8.5 looks at the challenges facing Bangladesh as it becomes more involved with peacekeeping missions. While providing peacekeepers has brought Bangladesh political kudos, considerable ambiguity remains about the impact of UN peace missions on Bangladesh's domestic sphere.

8.1 BANGLADESH IN UN PEACEKEEPING MISSIONS: A BRIEF HISTORY

In 1988, just 17 years after Bangladesh's bloody and violent separation from Pakistan and the creation of an army virtually from the scratch, Dhaka sent

31 military observers to the UN Iran–Iraq Military Observation Group (UNIIMOG) mission.[1] Over the years, Bangladesh contributed more peacekeepers to more missions. In 1989, 25 observers from the Army and 34 from the Bangladesh Police joined the UN Transition Assistance Group (UNTAG) in Namibia.[2] Bangladesh also contributed a total of 2,193 soldiers as part of US-led coalition forces in the Gulf War (1990–91).[3] In 1992, it sent its first battalion-sized contingent to the UN Transitional Authority in Cambodia (UNTAC). The sincerity and impartiality of Bangladeshi troops and police in these early missions earned them a good reputation and helped carve a space for further peacekeeping activities. Within a short period of time Bangladesh became a leading provider of UN peacekeepers and as of early 2012 has participated in 45 missions in 35 countries.[4]

In the past eleven years, Bangladesh's contribution of troops increased by about 400 per cent (see Figure 8.1). As of May 2011, Bangladesh had contributed a total of 99,653 troops and police personnel in UN peacekeeping missions (see Table 8.1). The army contributed 88.36 per cent and the police 7.44 per cent of this total. One hundred and three Bangladeshi uniformed peacekeepers have died while serving under the UN flag (and more than 130 have been seriously injured in its ongoing deployments, see Table 8.1).[5]

In the 1990s, Bangladesh participated in UN peacekeeping missions in Cambodia, Rwanda, Mozambique, Somalia, Haiti, Angola, Sierra Leone, Congo, East Timor, and parts of the former Yugoslavia. Between 1990 and 2000, Bangladeshi troops served in three major concurrent UN missions: Mozambique (February 1993–December 1994), Rwanda (October 1993–February 1994), and Somalia (July 1993–February 1995).[6]

A total of 1,967 Bangladeshi soldiers participated in the UN Mission in Somalia (UNOSOM) where they succeeded in maintaining cordial relations with the locals.[7] There were no major combat-related casualties in this

[1] See UN, *Iran-Iraq UNIIMOG: Background*, http://www.un.org/en/peacekeeping/missions/past/uniimogbackgr.html (accessed 27 April 2012).

[2] Armed Forces Division, *Bangladesh in UN Peacekeeping Missions*, AFD website, http://www.afd.gov.bd/?q=node/25 (accessed 25 April 2012).

[3] Syed Fatemy Ahmed Roomy, 'The United Nations and South Asia: Bangladesh's Contribution to UN Peacekeeping', in Ramesh Thakur and Oddny Wiggen (eds.), *South Asia in the World* (Tokyo: UN University Press, 2004), p. 117.

[4] Armed Forces Division, *Bangladesh in UN Peacekeeping Missions* at http://www.afd.gov.bd/?q=node/2S.

[5] The Bangladesh Army has lost 91 officers and soldiers, including two mid-ranking officers of lieutenant colonel rank. See Armed Forces Division, 'Our Supreme Sacrifices', AFD website, http://www.afd.gov.bd/?q=node/28 (accessed 26 April 2012).

[6] Kabilan Krishnasamy, 'Bangladesh and UN Peacekeeping: The Participation of a "Small" State', *Commonwealth and Comparative Politics*, 41:1 (2003), p. 32.

[7] Ilyas Iftekhar Rasul, 'Bangladesh's Contribution to United Nations Peacekeeping Missions in Africa', paper presented at a seminar on 'Look Africa: An Emerging Foreign Policy Option for Bangladesh' (Dhaka: Bangladesh Institute of International And Strategic Studies, 2 December 2010), p. 4.

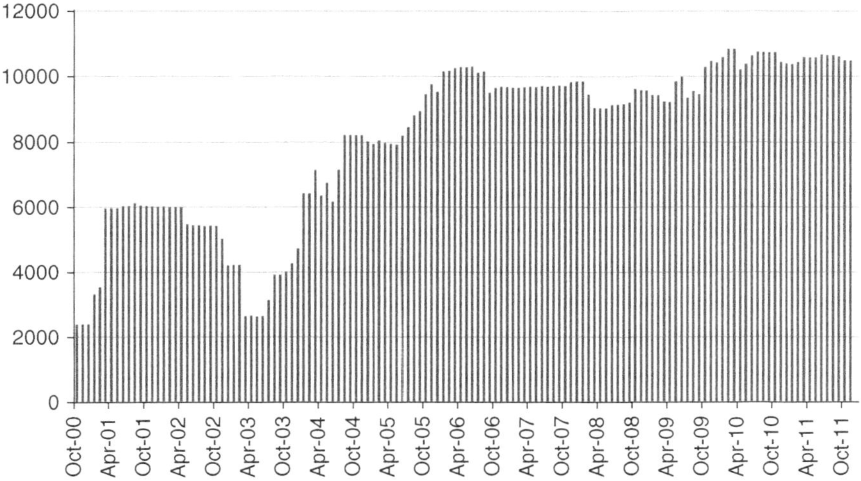

Figure 8.1 Bangladeshi Uniformed Personnel in UN Peacekeeping Operations, 2000–2011[8]

Table 8.1 Bangladesh in UN Peacekeeping Operations (45 missions in 35 countries)[9]

Event	*Army*	*Navy*	*Air Force*	*Police*	*Total*
Number of peacekeepers (completed missions)	88,056	1,523	2,659	7,415	99,653
As of May 2011	Ten Missions in Nine Countries				
Deployed peacekeepers	7,369	526	518	2,051	10,734
Deceased peacekeepers	91	1	3	8	103
Injured peacekeepers	125	1	5	6	137

mission. In Rwanda, however, Bangladeshi troops were severely criticized in the volatile and challenging UN Assistance Mission in Rwanda (UNAMIR). Canadian force commander General Dallaire complained about Bangladeshi national contingents disobeying orders. General Dallaire issued letters to senior Bangladeshi army officers and UN headquarters concerning the consistent disregard of the Bangladeshi contingent to his orders on protecting civilians in Rwanda.[10] This created misunderstanding and adversely affected

[8] The graph was collected from an interview with the DPKO officer deputed from the Bangladesh Army. It is compiled from the yearly reports available at http://www.un.org/en/peacekeeping/resources/statistics/contributors_archive.shtml

[9] Armed Forces Division, *Special Supplement on International Day of UN Peacekeepers 2011*, 29 May 2011, http://www.afd.gov.bd/?q=node/56 (accessed 5 April 2012).

[10] Paul D. Williams, *War and Conflict in Africa* (Cambridge: Polity Press, 2011), pp. 199–200.

the chain of command between multinational troops in other units and the UN mission headquarters.

In late 1999 Bangladesh contributed troops to the UN Assistance Mission in Sierra Leone (UNAMSIL). While some states withdrew their peacekeepers following disputes within the mission, Bangladesh deployed a brigade size force within the shortest possible time and its peacekeepers played a crucial role in taking control of rebel-controlled territories and ensuring some semblance of order in Sierra Leone.[11] In recognition of the overall contribution of Bangladeshi peacekeepers, Bengali was declared the second language of Sierra Leone by its government.[12] In 2003, the President of Sierra Leone visited Bangladesh to express his gratitude for the efforts made by the country's peacekeepers.[13]

8.2 ONGOING PEACEKEEPING OPERATIONS

Between January and March 2012, Bangladesh contributed approximately 10 per cent of all uniformed personnel deployed in UN-led peacekeeping operations. Over 90 per cent of these troops were deployed in Africa with Côte d'Ivoire and Liberia hosting the most Bangladeshi peacekeepers. As of March 2012, Bangladesh was participating in ten UN peacekeeping operations (seven in Africa, two in Asia, and one in the Caribbean) with a total of 10,245 uniformed personnel (the armed forces contribute 79 per cent, the police make up 20 per cent, and 1 per cent are observers; see Table 8.2). Bangladesh also deployed its first naval contribution to a UN mission in May 2011: a frigate and an offshore patrol vessel to the UN Interim Forces in Lebanon (UNIFIL).[14]

The Bangladesh police force first contributed to UN peacekeeping in 1989 through the UN Transition Assistance Group (UNTAG) in Namibia.[15] Since then Bangladeshi police officers have participated in all the major peacekeeping missions where the UN has deployed police. Between 2001 and 2011, there was a huge increase in the numbers of Bangladeshi police personnel in UN missions (see Table 8.3). These have deployed as individual police experts and

[11] Rasul, 'Bangladesh's Contribution', p. 4.

[12] 'The Dedicated Peace Makers', *Star Weekend (The Daily Star)*, Vol. 10, Issue 47, 16 December 2011, http://www.thedailystar.net/magazine/2011/12/03/cover1.htm (accessed 19 May 2012).

[13] 'Freetown seeks investment in garment, textile, President Kabbah leaves today, thanks Dhaka for peacekeeping in Sierra Leone', *The Daily Star*, 23 October 2003, http://www.thedailystar.net/2003/10/23/d3102301022.htm (accessed 19 May 2012).

[14] Authors' communication with DPKO officer, January 2012.

[15] Motiar Rahman, 'Blue Beret in the UN Peacekeeping Process: The Case of Bangladesh Police', *Indian Journal of Politics*, 14:1 (2009), p. 36.

Table 8.2 Bangladeshi Participation in UN Peacekeeping (as of March 2012)[16]

Mission	*Experts on mission*			*Individual police*			*Formed police units*			*Troops*			*Total*
	M	F	T	M	F	T	M	F	T	M	F	T	
MINURSO	9	0	9	–	–	–	–	–	–	17	3	20	29
MINUSTAH	–	–	–	10	0	10	353	122	475	–	–	–	485
MONUSCO	34	0	34	–	–	–	314	76	390	2,516	6	2,522	2,946
UNAMID	10	0	10	115	13	128	558	0	558	395	2	397	1,093
UNIFIL	–	–	–	–	–	–	–	–	–	325	0	325	325
UNMIL	13	0	13	13	0	13	–	–	–	1,432	6	1,438	1,464
UNMISS	–	–	–	3	0	3	–	–	–	1,205	4	1,209	1,212
UNMIT	3	0	3	39	0	39	105	0	105	–	–	–	147
UNOCI	13	0	13	1	0	1	360	0	360	2,164	6	2,170	2,544
Total	82	0	82	181	13	194	1,690	198	1,888	8,054	27	8,081	10,245

[16] UN DPKO, *UN Mission's Summary detailed by Country*, http://www.un.org/en/peacekeeping/contributors/2012/March12_3.pdf (accessed 9 April 2012).

Table 8.3 Bangladeshi Police Officers in UN Missions, 2001–2011[17]

Year	2001	2002	2003	2004	2005	2006	2007	2008	2009	2010	2011
Number	178	103	92	108	478	787	947	1,102	1,614	1,862	2,083

Formed Police Units (FPU) in East Timor, Congo, Côte d'Ivoire, Darfur (Sudan), and Haiti. One officer of Additional Inspector General of Police rank had served in the UN Department of Peacekeeping Operations (DPKO) headquarters. This is the second highest position in the Bangladesh Police. As of May 2011, four Deputy Inspector Generals of Police (DIG) and twenty-one Superintendents of Police (SP) had served in UN missions.[18]

The number of female police officers participating in peace missions has also increased. A Bangladeshi female police contingent, the first of its kind from a Muslim-majority nation, was deployed in Haiti (MINUSTAH) in May 2010.[19] Prior to that, the only all-female FPU was deployed in Liberia (UNMIL) in January 2007 by India. The goal of sending a female FPU in Haiti was to provide humanitarian services in the post-earthquake areas—ensuring primary education and healthcare, and preventing violence against women. In May 2012, a Bangladeshi FPU made up of 120 police personnel received the United Nations Medal for significant contribution in MINUSTAH.[20]

Prior to their deployment on UN missions, Bangladeshi police officers go through a two-week tailor-made induction training course in Sardah Police Training Academy. The training includes information on the geopolitical importance and general history of the mission-country as well as personal safety, peace-building tactics such as mediation and negotiation strategies, and hostage rescue. Inspired by the ongoing success and future prospects in UN missions, the Bangladesh Police has strengthened its ongoing reform programme funded by the UN Development Programme and the UK's Department for International Development and in 2012 hosted the Asia Region Women Police Conference at Dhaka.[21] Bangladesh plans to commit more resources and training to female police officers to enable them to serve in UN peace missions.

The financial package offered for UN peacekeeping is an attractive incentive for a developing country like Bangladesh. For example, between 2009 and

[17] The figures in the table show numbers of police personnel in UN missions in the month of December of each stated year. See 'Troops and police contributors archive (1990–2011)', United Nations Peacekeeping Website, http://www.un.org/en/peacekeeping/resources/statistics/contributors_archive.shtml (accessed 9 April 2012).

[18] Bangladesh Police Website, http://www.police.gov.bd/index5.php?category=206 (accessed 9 April 2012).

[19] Selim Mia, 'Bangladesh deploys female UN peacekeepers', *BBC News Online*, 12 May 2010, http://news.bbc.co.uk/2/hi/8678561.stm

[20] 'Bangladeshi peacekeepers get UN medal in Haiti', *New Age*, 16 May 2012, http://www.newagebd.com/detail.php?date=2012-05-16&nid=10477 (accessed 19 May 2012).

[21] Police Reform Programme website, http://www.prp.org.bd/ (accessed 2 May 2012).

Table 8.4 UN Reimbursement of Money (as of July 2010)[22]

Fiscal year	*Equipment reimbursement ($)*	*Troops cost reimbursement ($)*	*Total reimbursement ($)*
	E	C	C + E
2001–2	16,118,800.47	81,639,026.00	97,757,826.47
2002–3	37,432,740.09	67,051,154.00	104,483,894.09
2003–4	44,296,416.36	46,713,064.00	91,009,480.36
2004–5	31,606,099.37	93,794,400.06	125,400,499.43
2005–6	84,182,738.40	161,861,802.37	246,044,540.77
2006–7	79,046,617.94	136,366,902.22	215,413,520.16
2007–8	49,200,697.85	105,686,967.55	154,887,665.40
2008–9	27,844,530.37	95,053,666.20	122,898,196.57
2009–10	48,936,327.81	80,945,156.00	129,881,483.81
Total	418,664,968.66	869,112,138.40	1,287,777,107.06

2011, Bangladesh earned $917 million from its participation in the UN peacekeeping missions.[23] This amount is 8 per cent of the total remittances earned by Bangladesh during the same time period. From 2001 to 2010, UN compensation amounted to a total of approximately $1.28 billion, which includes 72 per cent troop costs with the rest as equipment cost reimbursement (see Table 8.4).

8.3 HOW DOES BANGLADESH RESPOND TO UN PEACEKEEPING REQUESTS?

Bangladesh sends troops and police personnel to UN missions based on the Memorandum of Understanding (MoU) signed as part of the UN Standby Arrangement System (UNSAS).[24] Having been made operational in 2000, since September 2010 the UNSAS database provides opportunities for

[22] 'Role of BD Armed Forces in UN Peacekeeping Missions', restricted Bangladesh Army document (no date, anonymous author).

[23] Agence France-Press, 'Peacekeeping pays: Bangladeshi soldiers secure billion-dollar niche in global economy', 26 April 2012, http://www.interaksyon.com/article/30416/peacekeeping-pays-bangladeshi-soldiers-secure-billion-dollar-niche-in-global-economy (accessed 2 May 2012) and 'Shantirokkha Mission e Bochor e Bangladesher Aai Aarai Hazar koti taka', *Bangladeshnews24.com online*, 26 April 2012, http://www.bangladeshnews24.com/2012/04/26/33011.htm (accessed 29 April 2012).

[24] The UN Standby Arrangements System (UNSAS) was established in 1993. It provides the UN with 'a database detailing the military units and the equipment which some Member States are willing, in principle, to make available to the Organization at short notice'. See, UN, 'Issues Related to Deployment of Peace Operations', in *UN Peace Operations: Year in Review 2003*, http://www.un.org/en/peacekeeping/publications/yir/2003/index.htm (accessed 25 April 2012).

troop-contributing countries (TCC) to upload their own pledges and contributions.[25] Bangladesh is currently one of the 93 states in UNSAS that fall into Level 3.[26] In December 1997, Bangladesh signed a generic MoU on Standby Arrangements with the UN. The mission-specific MoUs specify resources provided, response times, conditions for employment, and technical data or requirements regarding contributions.

The Bangladesh armed forces finalized their troop structure in 2004 and as per the MoU with the UNSAS, pledged to contribute three Brigade Groups (nine infantry battalions). The total strength earmarked for UN peacekeeping, including military observers and staff, was 12,000. This force structure was revised in 2005, in line with new requests from DPKO as well as with the growing ability of the Bangladesh Army to contribute further. One more Brigade Group was added, raising the total strength to approximately 15,000. Bangladesh remains prepared to deploy a team of 370 troops to the mission headquarters within 30 days, and a brigade group within 100 days from the day of notification.[27] In addition, Bangladesh is committed to contributing significant naval components, for example, frigates, patrol craft, and mine sweepers. It also pledged a helicopter squadron.[28] As of May 2012, Bangladesh was providing the UN with nine utility helicopters and one C-130 transport aircraft.[29] Such pledges have created further pressure to modernize the Bangladeshi armed forces to deliver on the country's commitment to UN peacekeeping.

Bangladesh's procedures for deciding when to provide peacekeepers for UN operations are clearly devised and top-down in nature. Bangladesh receives a request for any new peacekeeping operations from UN DPKO/Department of Field Support (DFS). Dhaka's Permanent Mission at the UN receives this request on behalf of the Ministry of Foreign Affairs (MoFA). It examines the request in light of Bangladesh's foreign policy priorities and existing international commitments. The Defence Attaché in the Permanent Mission in New York deals with the bureaucratic procedures and subsequently forwards the requests to the relevant agencies in Bangladesh. Requests relating to troops are directed to the Armed Forces Division (AFD), which is the coordinating

[25] Cited from the PowerPoint presentation at UN, *UN Force Link Website*, https://cc.unlb.org/UNSAS%20Documents/Forms/AllItems.aspx?RootFolder=%2fUNSAS%20Documents%2fKEY%20DOCUMENTS&FolderCTID=&View=%7bE2B2C6EC-22B3-4BA7-88F0-B3B89FDCC0D7%7d (accessed 25 April 2012).

[26] Level 3 contributions involve a signed generic Memorandum of Understanding (MoU) on standby arrangements with the UN. The MoU specifies the resources provided, response times, and conditions for employment. An attachment to the MoU provides details on technical data or requirements regarding the contributions. See UN, *United Nations Stand-by Arrangement System: Military Handbook* (New York: UNDPKO, 2003), p. 7.

[27] Roomy, 'The UN and South Asia', p. 121.

[28] Roomy, 'The UN and South Asia', p. 121.

[29] Authors' telephonic conversation with a serving officer of the Bangladesh Air Force (henceforth identified as Officer C), Dhaka, 21 May 2012.

headquarters of the Army, Navy, and Air Force. The Overseas Operations Directorate (OOD) deals with peacekeeping operations in the Army Headquarters in Dhaka.[30] Requests for naval and air force components are transferred to the respective Navy and Air Force Headquarters in Dhaka, which then issue necessary directives for the upcoming peacekeeping operations. For troops, the OOD issues the necessary instructions to all other concerned branches of the armed forces for the requisite preparations. This involves selection of personnel, provision of equipment, and training. The Ministry of Home Affairs (MoHA) receives requests related to the deployment of the police personnel for UN missions. After the initial notification, the MoHA transfers the order to Police Headquarters in Dhaka to take decisions on the selection of personnel.

In addition to the decisions at the operational level—i.e., the deployment of forces on UN operations—diplomats from the Bangladesh Permanent Mission in New York play an active political role in UN peacekeeping. They have been active in Fourth and Fifth Committee meetings to endorse the rights, safety, and security of the peacekeepers. Bangladesh has served as Chair of the UN Peacebuilding Commission and has led the drafting of two significant documents: the 2010 Review of Peacebuilding Architecture, and the 2010 Review of International Civilian Capacity.[31] In finalizing the documents, Bangladesh successfully convinced other parties to incorporate issues like south–south cooperation and women's empowerment. In an interview with a senior diplomat from the Bangladesh Permanent Mission, it was also revealed that Bangladesh had played a leading role in the 2001–2 administrative and budgetary meetings to raise the monthly stipends for the peacekeepers to the current level of $1,028 per month.[32] Bangladesh exploits its leadership skills from its experience of leading roles in the G77 and other least developed country platforms.

At the operational level, the task of forming troop contingents is given to the OOD. In many instances the contingent units are modified to meet the operational requirements of a particular UN peacekeeping operation. A colonel from the Bangladesh Army commands the contingent unit, equipped with necessary personnel and equipment. All the infantry battalions of the Bangladesh Army have now performed peacekeeping operations in various missions at least once,

[30] The Overseas Operations Directorate was set up in 2005 in order to free the Military Operations Directorate from the added responsibility of UN missions for the Bangladesh Army. Authors' communication with DPKO officer, January 2012.

[31] Lokman Hussain, 'Bangladesh in Maintenance of International Peace and Security: Rethinking Its Role in a Changing Environment', *Special Supplement on International Day of UN Peacekeepers 2011*, 29 May 2011, http://www.afd.gov.bd/?q=node/56 (accessed 4 April 2012).

[32] Authors' interview with a senior diplomat of the Bangladesh Permanent Mission to the UN, New York, 3 May 2012. The official also mentioned the leadership role of Bangladeshi negotiators to conclude the provision of a 'one-time supplemental payment' of $85 million to troop-contributing countries between July 2011 and June 2012. See UN General Assembly, A/RES/65/289, 8 September 2011, p. 9.

some of them twice.[33] Based on demands, small contingents of engineers, signals, and military police units are also frequently deployed in UN missions.

Contingents from Bangladesh are selected for two types of assignments—the regular rotation of contingents for already deployed missions, and for newly established missions.[34] In each case, troops undertake intensive training exercises and other related preparations. Each outgoing unit receives training based on the recommendations provided by the reconnaissance teams who visit the mission area to identify requirements. Preparation for a contingent/unit to a new mission is more complicated than rotation of troops for an existing mission. For the rotation duty, once the rotation of contingents is approved by the UN DPKO, the necessary warning order is given to the units previously earmarked by the OOD. Preparation of any unit for rotation takes minimum effort as logistics are already organized in the mission area.[35] The training courses address these complicated issues.

The Bangladesh Institute of Peace Support Operation and Training (BIPSOT) provides specialized training to potential UN peacekeepers.[36] BIPSOT was established in 1999 as the 'Peacekeeping Operations and Training Centre' (PKOTC) to address the skills required for a new generation of peacekeepers, which would be different to the routine combatant skills of military personnel. In 2002 it was remodelled and renamed with more capacities and resources.

BIPSOT conducts regular Pre-deployment Training for the selected contingent members.[37] Apart from the regular peacekeeping troops, a number of officers are sent to peacekeeping operations as observers. They also receive training and guidelines at BIPSOT.[38] BIPSOT pioneered e-learning for the Bangladesh Armed Forces by conducting the UN Military Observer Course (UNMOC) online in June 2011. So far, it has trained a total of 4,733 personnel including 887 foreign students from 25 countries.[39] BIPSOT hosted the Annual Conference of the International Association of Peacekeeping Training Centres (IAPTC) in 2010. Since then, the Commandant of BIPSOT has served

[33] Authors' communication with DPKO officer, January 2012.

[34] Authors' communication with DPKO officer, January 2012.

[35] Authors' communication with DPKO officer, January 2012.

[36] For details, see BIPSOT's website, http://www.bipsot.net

[37] Some of the main subjects of Pre-Deployment Training are: an overview of the mission area; handling of situations they are likely to face; the UN mandate for that mission; details regarding Rules of Engagement; personnel safety; health and hygiene; and a language course.

[38] Other courses conducted at BIPSOT are UN Contingent Commanders Course (UNCCC), UN Military Observer Course (UNMOC), UN Staff Officers Course (UNSOC), UN Logistic Officers Course (UNLOC), Junior Officers Peace Support Operation Course (JOPSOC), UN Contingent Member Course (UNCMC), Train the Trainer Course on International Humanitarian Law (IHL), and Short Course on French Language. For details on BIPSOT's training and *Shanti Doot 3*, see BIPSOT, *Shanti Doot 3* (Dhaka: BIPSOT/GPOI/Bangladesh Army/USPACOM, March 2012), http://www.bipsot.net/download/Magazine_SD3.pdf (accessed 29 April 2012).

[39] See BIPSOT website and BIPSOT, *Shanti Doot 3*.

as president of the IAPTC and BIPSOT as the Interim Secretariat of the Association of Asia-Pacific Peace-Operation Training Centres.

8.4 RATIONALES FOR PROVIDING UN PEACEKEEPERS

Bangladesh's turbulent history and the political, economic, and social challenges it faces can help us understand why the country has achieved such an enviable record as a provider of UN peacekeepers. A cursory official response to why Bangladesh provides so many UN peacekeepers would include the following points:

- First, participation in UN peace operations fulfils the country's constitutional and international obligations.
- Second, involvement with such missions allows troops and officers of the Bangladesh Army to interact with members of foreign armed forces and improve their professional skills. Such multinational exposure helps them gain operational expertise and first-hand knowledge of the latest doctrines and military equipment.
- Third, financial incentives are a powerful reason why Bangladesh takes part in UN missions. They allow the Bangladesh Army to purchase and maintain military equipment which it would not be able to obtain under normal circumstances and to reward its personnel. In other words, peace operations help subsidize Bangladesh's armed forces.[40]

It should be mentioned here that Bangladesh does not face any significant external security threat. Of course, there are some internal security challenges but they are not severe enough to hamper deployment of Bangladesh armed forces to UN peacekeeping missions. Nevertheless, analysts have offered additional reasons as to why Bangladesh provides so many UN peacekeepers. Dipankar Banerjee, for example, identified the fulfilling of international obligations, the need to project a positive image of the country, diverting the army's attention away from any praetorian desire, subsidizing the army with the reimbursement obtained from peacekeeping missions, and the financial benefit brought to members of the armed forces as reasons compelling Bangladesh to adopt such a policy.[41] In a similar vein, C. S. R. Murthy emphasized

[40] On Bangladesh's interests in participating in UN peacekeeping missions see Muhammad Aminul Islam, 'Peacekeeping Operations and Its Legal Implications', *Bangladesh Army Journal* (January 2001), pp. 50–8; Md Rashidul Islam, 'UN Peacekeeping by Bangladesh: Rationales and Attainments', *Special Supplement on International Day of UN Peacekeepers 2011*, 29 May 2011, http://www.afd.gov.bd/?q=node/56 (accessed 8 May 2012).

[41] Dipankar Banerjee, 'South Asia: Contributors of Global Significance', in Donald C. F. Daniel, Patricia Taft, and Sharon Wiharta (eds.), *Peace Operations* (Washington, DC: Georgetown University Press, 2008), pp. 195–6.

the financial imperative and the fact that the army is now unwilling to overthrow the civilian government and usurp power by taking advantage of the volatile political situation prevailing within the country.[42]

While we agree with these sentiments, we also argue that the particular characteristics of the Bangladesh Army play an integral role in explaining the country's policy towards UN peacekeeping. We organize our discussion of Bangladesh's participation in UN missions under the headings of economic, normative, and political–institutional rationales.

8.4.1 Economic Rationales

Bangladesh is a low-income developing country with a gross national income per capita of $700 (between 2007 and 2011).[43] While the country has enjoyed economic growth over the last two decades and has achieved impressive progress in terms of attaining the Millennium Development Goals, it is still a small country with a very high population density and limited economic resources. This means that domestic economic opportunities are limited, pushing governments to look for economic opportunities abroad. It is thus not surprising that UN compensation rates for peacekeeping operations are attractive to Bangladeshi soldiers and police. Banerjee points out that the financial benefits accrued by the Bangladeshi forces play an important role in supporting the economy.[44] This contention is strongly supported by a series of interviews we conducted with Bangladesh Army officers. All of the interviewees reiterated strongly that it was financial considerations which made the Bangladesh Army eager for UN duties. One officer identified pecuniary benefits as the sole criterion for the Bangladesh Army opting for peacekeeping duties.[45] While other officers pointed out the importance of financial incentives as one of the underlying causes, one officer also drew attention to the fact that while UN peacekeeping missions were previously financially attractive to officers of the Bangladesh Army, the situation had changed. He believed that with the gradual strengthening of the Bangladeshi economy and rising economic opportunities offered by the increasingly developed private sector, officers were no longer

[42] C. S. R. Murthy, 'Unintended Consequences of Peace Operations for Troop-Contributing Countries from South Asia', in Chiyuki Aoi, Cedric de Coning, and Ramesh Thakur (eds.), *Unintended Consequences of Peacekeeping Operations* (Tokyo: UN University Press, 2007), p. 160.

[43] World Bank Country Data, at http://data.worldbank.org/country/bangladesh (accessed 8 May 2012).

[44] Banerjee, 'South Asia', p. 195. See also Krishnasamy, 'Bangladesh and UN Peacekeeping', p. 37.

[45] Authors' interview with a retired officer of the Bangladesh Army (henceforth identified as Officer A), Dhaka, 1 May 2012.

seeing UN missions as quite so financially lucrative as they did in the past. Of course, the situation is different for soldiers and non-commissioned officers and they are inclined towards UN missions more than ever.[46]

The financial inducements for Bangladesh Air Force members are particularly high. One officer who flew UN aircraft in peacekeeping operations pointed out that he earned $3,000 per flying hour and that this was in addition to other perks and benefits.[47] Such statements corroborate Krishnasamy's contention that at the national level, UN compensation brought in additional revenues to the country's foreign exchange coffers and thereby played a positive role in the country's economy.[48] Indeed, official sources indicate that during 2001–10, the government received a total of $1.28 billion from the UN as compensation for troop contribution, contingent-owned equipment, and other forms of compensation (see Table 8.4).

8.4.2 Normative Rationales

But economic incentives are not the whole story. Bangladesh has also provided UN peacekeepers in order to promote a positive image of the country. Political leaders and army officials never fail to point out how Bangladesh's performance in peacekeeping operations has served to depict the country in a positive light. In her address on the occasion of the International Day of UN Peacekeepers in 2011, Prime Minister Sheikh Hasina expressed her gratitude to Bangladeshi peacekeepers for elevating the country's image in the international arena.[49] So did UN Secretary-General Ban Ki-moon.[50] Norrie MacQueen points out that for many countries, contributing to peacekeeping operations came to form part of their essential international identity.[51] Bangladesh can be understood as one such country. As *The Economist* pithily observed, donning Blue Helmets gave Bangladeshis the chance to be known for something other than bad politics and natural disasters.[52]

[46] Authors' interview with a serving officer of Bangladesh Army (henceforth identified as Officer B), Dhaka, 2 April 2012.

[47] Authors' interview with Officer C, Dhaka, 18 April 2012.

[48] Krishnasamy, 'Bangladesh and UN Peacekeeping', p. 37.

[49] Prime Minister Sheikh Hasina's message, *Special Supplement on International Day of UN Peacekeepers 2011*, 29 May 2011, http://www.afd.gov.bd/?q=node/56 (accessed 9 May 2012).

[50] 'Dhaka, UN for newer areas of partnership', *New Age*, 14 November 2011, http://newagebd.com/newspaper1/archive_details.php?arcid=40076 (accessed 9 May 2012).

[51] Norrie MacQueen, *Peacekeeping and the International System* (London: Routledge, 2006), pp. 16–17.

[52] 'Supply-side peacekeeping: The UN finds an unusual way to exert influence', *The Economist*, 21 February 2007, http://www.economist.com/node/8730316 (accessed 9 May 2012).

8.4.3 Political–Institutional Rationales

We think a good case can be made that political and institutional imperatives also play a major role in Bangladesh's decisions to provide UN peacekeepers. Murthy, for instance, categorically states that the Bangladeshi government used peacekeeping missions as a way of keeping the Army from meddling in domestic politics.[53] Similarly, a Bangladeshi scholar observed that participation in UN missions has induced the Army to 'remain out of any scheme of taking over the State [*sic*] power' and that military takeovers have ceased as an 'indirect' outcome of such missions.[54] The fact that Bangladesh has not experienced any military coups since 1990 would seem to support these observations. We differ slightly from the existing literature inasmuch as we argue that it is the peculiar characteristics of the Bangladesh Army which have led it to embrace peacekeeping missions. To substantiate this point we need to briefly describe the genesis and development of the Army.

Bangladesh gained independence from Pakistan on 16 December 1971 after a vicious and bloody struggle which lasted for about nine months. During the war a good number of Bengali officers and soldiers of the Pakistan Army rebelled and it was around this nucleus of trained fighters that the independence movement gathered and coalesced into a fighting force.[55] What is important for this chapter is the impact this struggle had upon the men who went on to form the new Bangladesh Army.

The 1971 war, like other civil wars, blurred the distinction between soldiers and civilians and did away with the traditional barriers between officers and men. A difficult-to-pin-down homogeneity replaced the conventional army's traditional hierarchy. Such bonds, tempered by war, turned the majority of soldiers into an exclusive fraternity which posed a serious challenge to the peacetime chain of command when it was restored after the war. The war also saw egalitarian socialist ideals become attractive to many guerrillas. The brutal nature of the war and the tremendous political consciousness arising from it enveloped most of the Bangladeshi participants. An important section of the newly established Bangladesh Army was thus more influenced by the searing experience of a vicious war than by the regimental traditions of peacetime

[53] Murthy, 'Unintended Consequences', p. 159. See also Banerjee, 'South Asia', p. 195.

[54] Shekh Mohammad Altafur Rahman, 'Impact of Human Security Approach in the Post UN Peace Keeping Mission: A Case Study of Bangladesh', paper presented at 'The 4th International Conference on Human Rights & Human Development Critical Connections: Human Rights, Human Development and Human Security', 18–19 June 2011 (Thailand, University of Mahidol, 2011), p. 10, http://www.humanrights-mu.org/attachments/article/88/Altaf_Paper.pdf (accessed 28 March 2012).

[55] For a description of the rebellion and formation of Liberation Forces in the 1971 war, see Talukdar Maniruzzaman, *The Bangladesh Revolution and its Aftermath* (Dhaka: The University Press Limited, 2nd impression, 2003), pp. 103–25.

traditional soldiering. They brought to the Bangladesh Army a degree of politicization not seen in either the Indian or Pakistani armies.[56]

To this heavily politicized army was added another unique characteristic: the issue of 'repatriated' officers, Bengali officers who remained in West Pakistan during the war.[57] This was arguably the principal division within the army.[58] It led to further inequalities and divisions in the ranks of the newly formed army. The multiple divisions within the Bangladesh Army and the failure of the Awami League government to effectively deal with the many challenges facing the newly independent nation led to a profound sense of disillusionment within the country. It was under such circumstances that a group of disgruntled army officers staged a military coup on 15 August 1975 which resulted in the assassination of the country's Prime Minister Sheikh Mujibur Rahman along with most of his family members.

Bangladesh underwent a period of violent uncertainty in the days following the August 1975 killings. The military officers spearheading the putsch put a pseudo-civilian government in charge but it was obvious the real authority lay with the men with the tanks and guns. The situation further divided the army. Serious disputes arose among senior military commanders with Chief of Army Staff Major General Ziaur Rahman not forcing the coup leaders to return to the barracks and the Chief of the General Staff, Major General Khaled Musharraf, insisting they do so. Such divisions triggered a counter-coup in November 1975 which saw Musharraf depose both the President of the country and the Chief of Army Staff. In the violence that followed, several officers, including Musharraf, were killed. A series of uprisings and mutinies convulsed the military.[59]

The reassertion of civilian control over the military and the country came under the leadership of Major General Ziaur Rahman who sought to 'tame' the Army. While a series of mutinies did take place during Zia's term of office, he dealt severely with them and was able to establish order within the Army, though a lot of blood—mostly military—was shed in the process. The Army was expanded, professionalized, and modernized, which yielded

[56] S. Mahmud Ali, *Understanding Bangladesh* (New York: Columbia University Press, 2010), pp. 118–19.

[57] Jeremie Codron, 'Putting Factions "Back in" the Civil–Military Relations Equation, Genesis, Maturation and Distortion of the Bangladeshi Army', *South Asia Multidisciplinary Academic Journal*, 18 October 2007, http://samaj.revues.org/230?&id=230#authors (accessed 9 May 2012).

[58] Craig Baxter and Syedur Rahman, 'Bangladesh Military: Political Institutionalization and Economic Development', *Journal of Asian and African Studies*, 26:1–2 (1991), p. 44.

[59] For a description of the August coup and the events following the killings see Zillur R. Khan, 'Politicization of the Bangladesh Military: A Response to Perceived Shortcomings of Civilian Government', *Asian Survey*, 21:5 (1981), pp. 551–64; and Ali, *Understanding Bangladesh*, pp. 55–129.

positive results. However, the divisions which had plagued the Bangladesh Army since its inception did not totally disappear and Zia was assassinated in one such feud on 30 May 1981.

A brief period of civilian rule bridged the hiatus between the military regimes of General Zia and General Hussain Muhammad Ershad. The latter assumed the reins of government between 1982 and late 1990. The process of militarizing the civilian administration, a process initiated by Zia, was accelerated under the new regime. General Ershad also took measures to safeguard the corporate interest of the military. A handsome salary, lucrative fringe benefits, ever-increasing military budget, and the prospects of rapid promotions within an expanding military all helped to keep the military reasonably satisfied.[60] General Ershad's regime came to an end on 6 December 1990 when the Bangladesh Army top brass refused to confront the democratic activists who were calling for Ershad's resignation.[61]

What concerns us is that in the decades since the overthrow of Ershad's rule and the introduction of democratic rule in Bangladesh, the Bangladesh Army has not been able to remain above politics and the resulting factionalism.[62] Both the Awami League and the Bangladesh Nationalist Party (which have ruled the country alternately over the past 21 years) attempted to establish groups of officers who would potentially support particular party-political lines. This has led to a deepened factionalism among the senior and mid-level commissioned ranks. However, it must be noted this factionalism is less motivated by ideological leanings and more by personal interests and professional ambitions.[63] While this factionalism continues, both the army and Bangladeshi politicians find it beneficial for the army to focus on peace missions. A sort of a concordance seems to have emerged whereby politicians and the senior military figures have agreed on a situation in which factionalism and cleavages are introduced into the army through the confrontational politics practised by the two main political parties.[64] However, this factionalism is not allowed to lead to a situation where the army reverts back to its pre-1980s form and peace missions perform a critical role in channelling the army's attention away from such praetorian aspirations. Whether this will work in the long run remains to be seen as it raises some significant challenges.

[60] Muhammad A. Hakim, 'Bangladesh: The Beginning of the End of Militarised Politics?' *Contemporary South Asia*, 7:3 (1998), p. 286.

[61] See William B. Milam, *Bangladesh and Pakistan: Flirting with Failure in South Asia* (Dhaka: The University Press Limited, 2010), pp. 106–8.

[62] Baxter and Rahman, 'Bangladesh Military', p. 59.

[63] Ali, *Understanding Bangladesh*, pp. 189–249.

[64] On concordance theory and its relevance for explaining civil–military relations see Rebecca L. Schiff, 'Civil–Military Relations Reconsidered: A Theory of Concordance', *Armed Forces and Society*, 22:1 (1995), pp. 17–24.

8.5 CHALLENGES

Although Bangladesh has made many positive strides in the realm of domestic development, including women's empowerment and microcredit schemes, the country is wracked by endemic poverty and political instability. It has also not managed to deal with all its corruption problems. In addition, allegations of the armed forces being hostile towards ethnic minorities in the Chittagong Hill Tracts and the nationwide extrajudicial killings by the elite security agencies have raised questions about the compliance of such forces with global human rights standards.[65] In short, Bangladesh continues to confront several issues which might affect its participation in UN peacekeeping operations.

First, the standard of Bangladeshi troops and the state of their equipment was a real concern during the first decade of their participation in peacekeeping missions. In Rwanda (1993–94) Bangladeshi peacekeepers faced logistics and equipment problems as well as the disputes with Force Commander Dallaire noted above.[66] In 1995, a total of 1,000 Bangladeshi troops in UNPROFOR in the former Yugoslavia became trapped in the UN 'safe area' of Bihac. 'Not only were they poorly equipped to defend themselves, being armed only with rifles, but they had not anticipated being in a situation of virtual all out war in which withdrawal was impossible.'[67] However, Bangladesh responded to such setbacks in its second decade of UN missions by significantly increasing the skills and professionalism of its troops. Budget constraints mean that equipment problems still endure, however. In addition, the linguistic capability of Bangladesh's troops, especially with regard to French and Arabic languages, remains poor.

Second, UN peacekeeping has had an enormous impact on Bangladeshi defence institutions. The armed forces now accommodate peace-based modules and post-war state-building components in their training discourse. Such modules focus on 'human' rather than simply 'national' security and combat roles. They therefore pose a challenge for more traditionally oriented militaries.[68] After 25 years of UN peacekeeping, the Bangladesh armed forces have to balance their role as peacekeepers with the need to perform more traditional national defence tasks.[69] So far, little or no thought has been given to how the transformation brought on by peacekeeping has impacted the capacity of the Bangladesh armed forces to carry out traditional combat missions in the future.

[65] Hana S. Ahmed, 'Disregarding the Jumma', *Himal South Asia*, July 2011, http://www.himalmag.com/component/content/article/4528-disregarding-the-jumma.html (accessed 12 May 2012).

[66] Krishnasamy, 'Bangladesh and UN Peacekeeping', p. 42.

[67] Trevor Findlay, 'Introduction', in Trevor Findlay (ed.), *Challenges for the New Peacekeepers* (Oxford: SIPRI/Oxford University Press, 1996), p. 27.

[68] Authors' interview with a serving officer of Bangladesh Army (henceforth identified as Officer D), Dhaka, 2 April 2012.

[69] Rahman, 'Impact of Human Security', p. 11.

Third, peacekeeping has also influenced defence budgeting and the procurement of equipment, as Bangladesh has started equipping its Blue Helmet contingents with modern weapons and materiel. The money reimbursed as equipment costs through 'wet lease' agreements with the UN provides a significant incentive for Bangladesh and the armed forces regularly revise their budget to comply with the UN's requirements. The government of Bangladesh approved an increment in its defence-related budgetary allocation from $1.3 billion in 2010–11 to $1.5 billion in 2011–12.[70] On the basis of this increase, it finalized a procurement deal for 44 tanks, three armed recovery vehicles (ARV), and two helicopters.[71] These new assets should ensure the necessary logistical support to Bangladeshi contingents in UN missions. Despite the fact that such expenditures will be reimbursed, these procurements could be affected by two main challenges: (a) the government's defence purchases often overlook transparency and produce political and strategic repercussions, and (b) the government adjusts the extra money allocated to the defence budget by ignoring other priority sectors. This could adversely influence overall macroeconomic development. In addition, the Armed Forces Division has not developed future plans for this expensive equipment. The question may also be posed as to why Bangladesh is spending so much money procuring defence equipment which will be of little or no use in future combat operations.[72] This raises important issues about defence budgeting and procurement in the light of Bangladesh's considerable participation in UN peace operations.

Fourth, the increasing involvement of multidimensional peacekeeping operations with issues of civil administration may encourage peacekeepers to become more interested in participating in civilian institutions back home, challenging the uneasy civil–military relationship described earlier. Furthermore, civil–military relations in Bangladesh have taken on a new dimension in recent years. The civilian legislature's control of the military has diminished as can be seen in the inactive role of the Parliamentary Standing Committee on Defence Affairs.[73] In contrast, the presence of military personnel in civilian administration has not declined sharply from the authoritarian era of 1975–90. The outcome is a blurring of the traditional division between civil and

[70] Hasan Jahid Tusher, 'Army to get 44 tanks: 2 helicopters also on purchase list', *Daily Star*, 27 June 2011, http://www.thedailystar.net/newDesign/news-details.php?nid=191737 (accessed 30 March 2012).

[71] Tusher, 'Army to get 44 tanks'.

[72] Authors' interview with DPKO officer, January 2012.

[73] Ahmed has explained the role of the Parliamentary Standing Committee on Defence during 1998–2001. However, the defence-related parliamentary committees are also largely absent in the consecutive parliaments. See Syed Imtiaz Ahmed, 'Civilian Supremacy in Democracies with "Fault Lines": The Role of the Parliamentary Standing Committee on Defence in Bangladesh', *Democratization*, 13:2 (2006), pp. 283–302.

military institutions.[74] This may have a significant bearing on the future of democratization in Bangladesh and its contributions to UN peacekeeping.

There is a prevailing idea that participation in UN peacekeeping will reduce the desire of the Bangladesh armed forces to take over state power.[75] But during the 2007 political crisis, the Army indirectly intervened to topple the caretaker government and set up an Army-backed interim government. In January 2007, this prompted a private warning from the UN to senior Bangladeshi military officers that if they did not hold the scheduled controversial elections, 'this might "have implications" for its lucrative involvement in UN peacekeeping contracts'.[76] The President declared an emergency, dismissed the cabinet, and delayed the elections. The military actively supported forming a non-political cabinet to create a level-playing field for the political parties. The army was not neutral and the whole episode was a reminder of the fragility of civilian rule.[77] However, the military was successful in rebuilding certain institutions and performing some crucial tasks. For example, it prepared voter lists and issued identity cards all over the country very effectively. It also cooperated with the election commission to ensure the holding of elections. Although the period ended with parliamentary elections, the army's role proved deeply divisive and reminds us that key issues about the military's role in politics remain unresolved.

Fifth, discipline and management are critical for minimizing health, safety, and security risks to troops. Bangladesh shows zero tolerance in dealing with sexual exploitation and abuse by peacekeepers. For example, in 1997, one soldier was immediately sent home from Haiti after misbehaving with a US service woman.[78] The armed forces apply strict rules in prohibiting both sexual exploitation and abuse (SEA) and consensual relationships during missions, and punish the offenders. There are twenty-two SEA cases recorded so far by the Bangladesh Army and one case by the Bangladesh Navy.[79] Dismissal from the service was the punishment in most of these cases.[80] The 2010 incident of a virulent cholera epidemic in Haiti brought on by UN peacekeepers from Nepal also raises new challenges for the Bangladesh Army. It now has to ensure its peacekeepers are not vectors for diseases which may wreak havoc in their respective theatres of operation. Any lapse on the part of the army could

[74] Schiff, 'Civil–Military Relations', p. 12.

[75] Rahman, 'Impact of Human Security', p. 12.

[76] *Economist*, 'Supply-side peacekeeping'.

[77] Nurul Islam, 'The Army, UN Peacekeeping Mission and Democracy in Bangladesh', *Economic & Political Weekly*, 45:29 (17 July 2010), pp. 81–2.

[78] Krishnasamy, 'Bangladesh and UN Peacekeeping', p. 42.

[79] In total there are 23 complaints. Authors' communication with DPKO officer, January 2012.

[80] In his interview, Officer B pointed out that none of the offences was severe enough for prison terms but since the Bangladesh Army follows a zero-tolerance on SEA cases, the perpetrators were dismissed from service.

have a detrimental effect upon the prestige of Bangladesh and, of course, put the UN under severe stress as the Haiti episode clearly showed.

Sixth, financial issues will continue to impact the future of Bangladeshi peacekeeping. At the micro level, it is notable that financial gain has become the primary reason why many join the military.[81] This could be seen as a type of brain-drain that wastes precious (often educated and trained) human capital on the military. This is because participation in UN missions seems to be more lucrative as an option than serving on any other assignment and officers often leave or retire early after completing a UN mission.[82] There are also two broad financial impacts at the macro level. First, UN peacekeeping enables Bangladesh to maintain a force structure of around 10,000 soldiers at no cost to the government.[83] Second, the money earned contributes to the overall remittance flow, and hence strengthens the national economy. Nevertheless, the national financial benefit does not appear to be as clear as it for the individuals.[84] Indeed, any national impact is hard to quantify. Interviews with returned peacekeepers have found that UN mission earnings were normally spent in non-productive sectors, for example, in consumption goods and real estate. Some invested money in small and medium enterprises, and in stock markets.

Although there is no concrete evidence to support the contention, competition for placement in UN peacekeeping creates grievances among those not selected. For example, it was widely publicized that the 2009 Bangladesh Rifles mutiny against its officers was an outburst of such frustration among a group of non-commissioned officers and soldiers.[85] However, the government and the Armed Forces Division deny such allegations and emphasize they are committed to providing equal opportunities to all members of law-enforcement institutions as and when positions on UN missions are available.

8.6 CONCLUSION

Bangladesh has traversed a long road since 1988 when it first sent troops to a UN peacekeeping mission. Since then, more than 100,000 Bangladeshis have

[81] Officer A elaborated further on this matter when he pointed out that participation in UN peace missions at times leads to venality among some officers who became too involved with money-making ventures like investing in shares and buying real estate. Such activities, at times, tend to divert officers away from soldiering and hamper the professionalization of the military.

[82] Authors' communication with DPKO officer, January 2012.

[83] David Axe, 'Why South Asia Loves Peacekeeping', 20 December 2010, *The Diplomat Online*, http://the-diplomat.com/2010/12/20/why-south-asia-loves-peacekeeping/?all=true (accessed 28 March 2012).

[84] Murthy, 'Unintended Consequences', p. 163.

[85] Islam, 'The Army', p. 80.

donned the Blue Helmet and faithfully performed a wide range of duties. In the process, the armed forces of the country have managed to present a positive image of a country which seldom receives good media coverage. The UN missions have also provided an opportunity for Bangladesh to earn much sought-after foreign currency. This monetary windfall has helped the country tide over economic and financial challenges though a critical study of this phenomenon is yet to be written. More importantly, the missions have also helped Bangladesh to maintain a semblance of nearly uninterrupted democratic government since 1991.

While such achievements have made both Bangladeshi soldiers and civilians proud, several challenges remain and it is imperative that Bangladesh's policy planners, both in the civil and military sectors, pay attention to them. Of these challenges, the question of civil–military relations remains crucial. If peacekeeping is perceived to be a way of weaning the army away from praetorian ambition then it is time for policy planners to think about what a reduced commitment to peacekeeping operations might imply for the state of Bangladesh's democracy. Moreover, the importance given to peacekeeping operations also raises questions about the orientation and focus of the country's armed forces. This, in turn, can have serious implications for the country's security. The issues of equipment procurement for the armed forces, which have become a priority as participation in UN missions has increased, show no signs of abating. They are of crucial importance in a country where good governance is more of an aspiration than a reality. Such challenges in no way demean Bangladesh's impressive achievements in the field of peacekeeping but if left unattended they could jeopardize the country's unique achievements in this area.

9

Pakistan

*Inam-ur-Rahman Malik**

Since the early 1990s especially, Pakistan has emerged as one of the largest and most consistent contributors to UN peacekeeping operations. It has established itself as 'a major stakeholder with considerable experience' in the enterprise and takes pride in this, seeing 'UN peacekeeping as an instrument of international peace'.[1] In 2005, Pakistan's Prime Minister, Shaukat Aziz, noted that a 'strong UN system' was at the top of Pakistan's vision of 'the basic tenets' of a 'just' global order. He further stated that his country believed that although 'sobered by the tumultuous experience of global wars and confrontations, humanity is moving to a new order of peace and harmony . . . where the collective will of humanity—manifested through a reformed United Nations—will ensure fair play and a level playing field for interstate relations'.[2] By 2010, Pakistan had fifty years of UN peacekeeping experience. Over this period, more than 100,000 Pakistanis have participated in forty-one UN peacekeeping missions and more than 100 have made the ultimate sacrifice by laying down their lives in the cause of peace.[3]

This chapter begins with a historical overview of Pakistan's participation in UN peacekeeping. It then examines how Pakistan decides whether or not to contribute peacekeepers. Thereafter, various rationales for Pakistan's major involvement in UN peacekeeping are discussed. The chapter then investigates Pakistan's stance on current peacekeeping trends. The final section reflects on lessons learnt from the country's peacekeeping endeavour: Pakistan's

* The views expressed in this chapter are those of the author and do not necessarily reflect the official policy of the Pakistan Army or Government of Pakistan.

1 Amjad Hussain B. Sial, Acting Permanent Representative of Pakistan to the UN, remarks to Special Committee on Peacekeeping Operations, 22 February 2011.

2 Conference address by Shaukat Aziz, 'Dynamics of Pakistan's Foreign Policy in the New World Order', IRRI-KIIB, Brussels, 26 January 2005.

3 In comparison, since 2001, the Pakistan Army and the Frontier Corps have suffered 3,109 'martyrs' and 9,681 injured personnel in the war against terrorism. See the Pakistan Army's official website, http://www.pakistanarmy.gov.pk/AWPReview/HomePage.aspx

experience highlights the importance of building wider community support along with 'staying power' as major planks for mission success. However, it is lamentable that there exists no formal mechanism through which the growing community of peacekeepers could learn from Pakistan's vast and varied UN peacekeeping experiences.

9.1 HISTORICAL OVERVIEW

Pakistan's first engagement with UN peacekeeping began in 1949 when military observers were deployed to supervise the cease-fire line (later renamed the 'Line of Control') between India and Pakistan in the disputed territories of Jammu and Kashmir. Eleven years later, Pakistan deployed its first contingent of 800 personnel to the UN mission in the Congo. Although Pakistan portrays itself as a traditional UN peacekeeper, it contributed to only four UN missions during the Cold War. Its active and large-scale contribution to UN peacekeeping started in the 1990s when these operations became a 'vehicle for promotion and cultivation of national interests on the global scene' and Islamabad identified UN peacekeeping 'as a top priority in its foreign policy agenda'.[4] By the mid-1990s, Pakistan had deployed 10,000 of its troops to thirteen UN peacekeeping operations throughout the world. The trend initiated in the 1990s kept its momentum in the first decade of the twenty-first century, as is evident from Figure 9.1.

UN missions to which Pakistan made major contributions during the period 2000–10 include Sierra Leone (UNAMSIL), Liberia (UNMIL), and Democratic Republic of Congo (MONUC/MONUSCO). The relative increase in Pakistan's peacekeeping deployments post-2003 can be attributed to:

- the de-escalation of Indian–Pakistani hostilities in late 2002 in the Indian subcontinent following one of the largest military mobilizations since the Second World War;[5]
- the increased number of UN peacekeeping missions and the new missions being located in Africa which is considered 'safe' by Pakistani policy-makers from the point of view of great power politics;[6]

[4] The quotes are from 'Pakistan and Contemporary Peacekeeping—A National Perspective', *The Citadel* (Rawalpindi), 12:1 (1995), p. 15; and Kabilan Krishnasamy, 'UN Peacekeepers as "Reliable" Forces: Pakistan's Somalia Experience', *Islamabad Policy Research Institute Journal*, 11:1 (2002), p. 104.

[5] The nascent peace process between India and Pakistan was initiated subsequently in 2003. Although Pakistan reduced its peacekeeping deployments at the height of the 2001–2 tensions with India, it did not entirely withdraw its UN peacekeepers in spite of the eyeball-to-eyeball troop deployment against India along its eastern border.

[6] Author's interview with Ministry of Foreign Affairs officer, July 2011. Whereas Africa as a peacekeeping destination seems to be the unproclaimed no-go area for many Western powers,

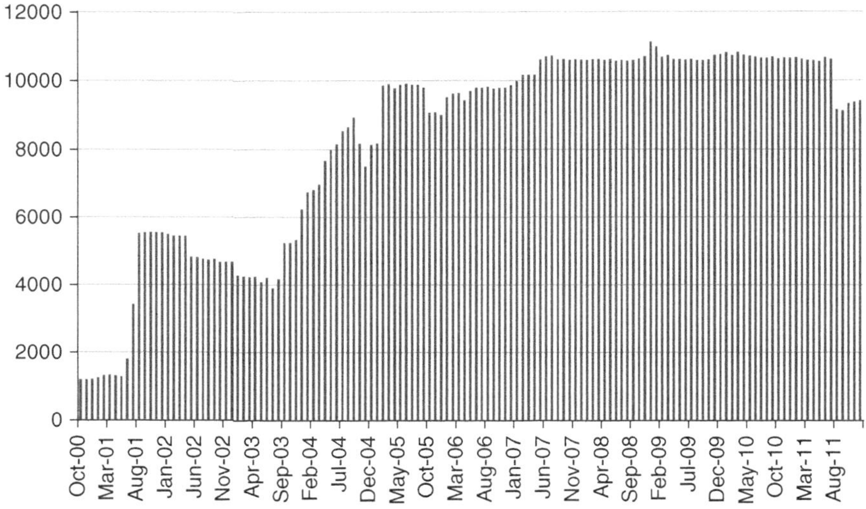

Figure 9.1 Pakistan's Uniformed Personnel in UN Peacekeeping Operations, 2000–2011

- the eagerness of Pakistan's military to contribute peacekeepers as evident from General Pervez Musharraf's statement that 'we would like to contribute as many troops as possible anywhere in the world';[7]
- the greater need for, and acceptance of, Pakistani troops by the UN primarily as a result of Pakistan's determination exhibited during UNAMSIL's darkest phase in 2000 and its contribution in turning the mission from a 'basket case' to a potential role model in twenty-first-century peacekeeping.[8]

9.2 DECISION-MAKING

Upon receiving a request for peacekeepers from the UN Secretariat, Pakistan's Ministry of Foreign Affairs makes a policy decision on how to respond. Its

Pakistan considers it a 'safe' area as there are comparatively few great power rivalries in the region in the post-Cold War era. It is also pertinent to mention that Pakistani peacekeepers have not suffered any major combat casualties in Africa or elsewhere ever since the tragic loss of 24 peacekeepers in Somalia in 1993.

[7] Quoted in Colum Lynch, 'Providing UN Peacekeepers', *Washington Post*, 15 November 2000. Since Musharraf assumed power in a coup in 1999, the timing of this statement reveals a desire on his part to legitimize his rule and gain favours with the rest of the world through UN peacekeeping.

[8] Pakistan provided a composite force of three infantry battalion groups, one engineering battalion with a host of supporting elements to UNAMSIL in 2001.

calculations are made in reference to five considerations, *inter alia*.[9] First, the need for a clear mandate based on judicious interpretation of the UN Charter and relevant international laws. Second, the extent of political will among the parties to the conflict to respect agreements and permit UN personnel to carry out their tasks. Third, the geopolitical interests of states in close proximity to the conflict zone in question, especially the willingness and anticipated cooperation of influential neighbouring states. The final two considerations are the strength of political support from the relevant international actors and the provision of resources necessary to achieve the operation's objectives.

Once the decision to participate in a UN mission is taken, Pakistan's senior officers decide the scope and scale, logistics and operational details of the Pakistani contingent based on input generated by the specialized Peacekeeping Cell within the Military Operations Directorate at the General Headquarters (GHQ).[10] The contribution to UN Police (UNPOL) is primarily dealt with by the Ministry of Interior as well as the provincial and federal police set-ups although the Economic Affairs Division, the Ministry of Foreign Affairs, the Cabinet Division, and the Establishment Division are also involved in the selection and deployment process of Pakistani UNPOL. Figure 9.2 summarizes the primary decision-making entities involved in Pakistan's peacekeeping contributions to the UN.

In Pakistan's case, it is the military–bureaucratic nexus that plays the pivotal role in making decisions regarding the country's contributions to UN peacekeeping. The government in power balances the political ramifications and calls the final shots through the Ministry of Foreign Affairs. For example, Pakistani bureaucrats in the Ministry of Foreign Affairs were reluctant initially to contribute troops to the AU–UN hybrid mission to Darfur in late 2007 due to Pakistan's traditionally strong bilateral relations with Khartoum as well as friendly relations in the context of the Organization of Islamic Cooperation.[11] Nevertheless, despite a reluctant Ministry of Foreign Affairs, Pakistan did commit personnel to Darfur. Thus, strong political decisions do play a part in decision-making. However, parliament is kept out of decisions on peacekeeping issues and there is hardly any domestic debate about Pakistan's involvement in UN peacekeeping as such issues have traditionally been hidden

[9] *Report of the Standing Committee on Defence and Defence Production on 60th Peacekeepers Day (29 May 2008)* (Islamabad: Senate Secretariat, 2008). See also Mr Tarar, S/PV.6603 (Resumption 1), 26 August 2011, pp. 3–4.

[10] Maria Kiani, 'Pakistan's Contribution to UN Peacekeeping', *Strategic Studies*, 24:3 (2004), pp. 56–7.

[11] The Organization of Islamic Conference was renamed the Organization of Islamic Cooperation in 2011.

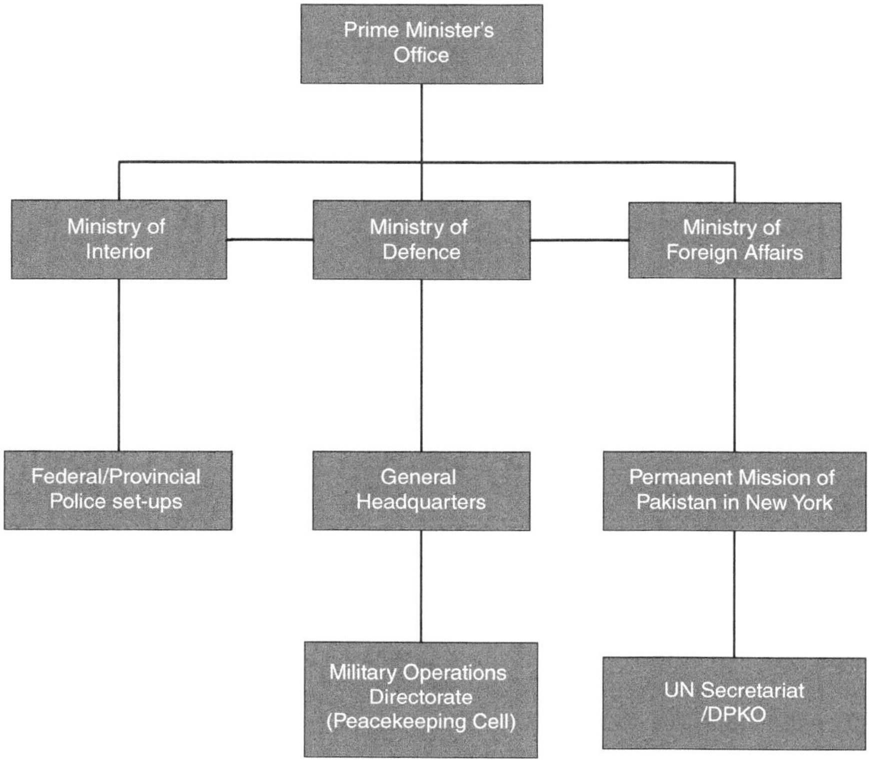

Figure 9.2 Pakistan's Decision-Making Structures for UN Peacekeeping

from the public eye.[12] The only two prominent exceptions have been Somalia (1993) and debates about Iraq (2003).

Following coordinated attacks on Pakistani peacekeepers in Somalia in June 1993 in which twenty-four were killed, the government faced intense domestic criticism. The Pakistani press published articles lamenting that Pakistan had fallen into 'America's peacekeeping trap' and that it had meekly yielded to the treatment of its soldiers as cannon fodder or 'America's foot soldiers'.[13] Pakistan, however, remained steadfast in Somalia until the end of the mission in 1995, despite the domestic backlash.[14] More recently, in the case of Iraq, there was a debate in 2003 over whether a UN peacekeeping mission should be deployed in the aftermath of the US-led occupation. Pakistan under General

[12] See *UN Peacekeeping Operations and Pakistan* (Islamabad Policy Research Institute, Factfile, 2006), p. 78.

[13] Quoted in Krishnasamy, 'UN Peacekeepers', p. 99.

[14] Kabilan Krishnasamy, 'Pakistan's Peacekeeping Experiences', *International Peacekeeping*, 9:3 (2002), p. 109.

Pervez Musharraf weathered pressure from the Bush administration and did not commit its troops to Iraq citing domestic opposition and lack of a mandate from the UN or a regional organization for the US-led occupation.[15] In an interview with ABC News in September 2003, President Musharraf defended his decision by saying that it would have been 'much easier' for his government to send Pakistani troops to Iraq 'under the United Nations cover'.[16]

9.3 EXPLAINING PAKISTAN'S UN PEACEKEEPING CONTRIBUTIONS: POLITICAL RATIONALES

The history of Pakistan's independence movement is essentially one of struggle of the minority against the majority and a quest to throw off the yoke of colonialism. Since becoming independent, Pakistan's strong alignment with the concept of UN-led 'collective security', which underwrites the spirit of UN peacekeeping, can be seen as continuation of its commitment to the same struggle for oppressed people the world over, carried out by the UN usually through peaceful means. Pakistan's adherence to the principles of the UN Charter, and as a corollary to peacekeeping, can also be traced to the foundations of Pakistan's foreign policy. Quaid-e-Azam Muhammad Ali Jinnah, the founder of Pakistan and its first Governor General, in a broadcast to the people of America in February 1948, outlined the following goals of Pakistan's foreign policy:

> Our foreign policy is one of friendliness and goodwill towards the nations of the world. We do not cherish aggressive designs against any country or nation. We believe in the principle of honesty and fair play in national and international dealings and are prepared to make our utmost contribution to the promotion of peace and prosperity among the nations of the world. Pakistan will never be found lacking in extending its material and moral support to the oppressed and suppressed peoples of the world, and in upholding the principles of the United Nations Charter.[17]

In line with these sentiments, idealist explanations for Pakistan's strong commitment to UN peacekeeping are common.[18] For example, peacekeeping

[15] 'Pakistan to wait for appropriate time: Troops for Iraq', *The Dawn*, 9 July 2003.

[16] Interview with Peter Jennings of ABC News, September 2003, http://abcnews.go.com/WNT/story?id=129411&page=1

[17] *Foreign Office Yearbook 2008–09* (Islamabad: Ministry of Foreign Affairs, 2009), p. 12, http://www.mofa.gov.pk/Publications/Year_Book_2008-09.doc

[18] Kabilan Krishnasamy, 'Recognition for Third World Peacekeepers: India and Pakistan', *International Peacekeeping*, 8:4 (2001), p. 57.

has been described as 'a noble calling'[19] and the 'most vital achievement and lasting legacy of the United Nations'.[20] Pakistan's Ministry of Foreign Affairs justifies its contributions to UN peacekeeping by asserting that its 'policy . . . is based on the conviction that peacekeeping is an essential tool for maintaining international peace and security'.[21]

Participation in UN operations has helped Pakistan demonstrate its credibility as a good international citizen and its commitment to peace around the globe, notwithstanding the internal conflicts it has to grapple with.[22] Recognition of this commitment was evident in the UN Secretary-General's remarks on his visit to Pakistan in March 2001. He said:

> Thanks to the thousands of Pakistani soldiers who have served under the United Nations flag . . . Pakistan can truly call itself a leader in the work of the international community . . . your soldiers have made the ultimate sacrifice in the service of world peace, and the United Nations. I salute this record of global idealism because I believe it reflects a determination among the Pakistani people to serve the world.[23]

The timing of these comments was significant as these were uttered prior to 11 September 2001 when General Musharraf was Chief Executive and was struggling to gain domestic and international legitimacy for his military regime.[24]

Pakistan's participation in UN peacekeeping can also be viewed through the prism of the international prestige and influence it generates for the participating countries, particularly within the UN itself. The pre-eminence of the UN as the most visible and legitimate international organization is undisputed. Sovereign equality in the UN, however, is confined to matters not concerned with international security and the composition of the UN Security Council gives a select few states indefinite great power status. While UN

[19] Ambassador Munir Akram, Permanent Representative of Pakistan in the General Debate of the Special Political and Decolonization (4th) Committee on Agenda Item 32: Comprehensive Review of the Whole Question of Peacekeeping Operations in all their Aspects, 24 October 2005.

[20] Riaz Khokhar, Pakistan's Foreign Secretary, seminar on 'Pakistan in UN Peacekeeping Operations' held by Ministry of Foreign Affairs, Pakistan and the UN Information Centre in Islamabad on 28 May 2004.

[21] *Foreign Office Yearbook 2005–06* (Islamabad: Ministry of Foreign Affairs, 2006), pp. 107–8, http://www.mofa.gov.pk/Publications/Year_Book_2005-06.doc

[22] Krishnasamy, 'Pakistan's Peacekeeping Experiences', p. 113. Pakistan's military has used its peacekeeping profile as image-builder at the domestic level as well. Military officers wearing blue berets were featured on the front cover of Pakistan's official armed forces magazine, *al-Hilal*, in its March 2011 issue. Pakistani peacekeepers also featured in an Urdu documentary titled *Aman ke Safeer* ('Ambassadors of Peace'), aired on the official Pakistan Television network.

[23] Excerpt from the text of the toast delivered by Secretary-General Kofi Annan at the official banquet hosted by the Chief Executive, General Perez Musharraf, in Islamabad, Pakistan, on 11 March 2001, http://www.un.org.pk/sg/statements.htm

[24] General Musharraf was later elected as the President of Pakistan for five years through a referendum held on 30 April 2002.

peacekeeping attracted many Western middle powers for a time, the experiences of the mid-1990s (see chapters on the UK and France in this volume), the 'Somalia syndrome', and changing foreign policy priorities prompted these states to shy away from UN peacekeeping. The resulting vacuum in the supply of peacekeepers coupled with the unprecedented demand for new missions created opportunities for action by smaller and middle-power states and opened up space for countries like Pakistan to display their credentials on the global terrain.

UN peacekeeping not only helps Pakistan project its middle-power credentials to the outside world and garner much-needed international goodwill, it also enhances Pakistan's diplomatic profile at the UN where 'India–Pakistan rivalry is taken for granted'.[25] It also helps Pakistan weaken India's quest to become 'a favourable candidate for a permanent seat on the Security Council'.[26] The correlation between large contributions to UN peacekeeping and enhanced prospects of securing a permanent seat on the Security Council was echoed by the President of the United States. In supporting India's candidature for a permanent seat on an enlarged Security Council in November 2010, US President Barack Obama, speaking at the *LokSabha* saluted 'India's long history as a leading contributor to United Nations peacekeeping missions' and in the same breath, welcomed 'India as it prepares to takes its seat on the United Nations Security Council'.[27]Although the move was largely symbolic with no prospect of imminent reform and likely stiff Chinese opposition, the statement was not received well in Pakistan.[28] Two days later, the federal cabinet in Pakistan passed a resolution expressing its concern about US support for India's bid for a permanent seat on a reformed Security Council which, it argued, would have 'grave ramifications for the . . . prospects of *the system of multilateral cooperation* as envisaged by the . . . UN Charter'.[29] In an op-ed article in the Indian newspaper *The Hindu*, Pakistani columnist Ejaz Haider was quick to remind the readers that 'Statistically, Pakistan is the largest contributor to UN peacekeeping missions followed by Bangladesh and then India.'[30]

[25] Munir Akram, 'Bid for UNSC seat', *The Dawn*, 9 October 2011. Ambassador Munir Akram is the former Permanent Representative to the UN from Pakistan and has served for two terms as President of the UN Security Council.

[26] Kabilan Krishnasamy, 'The Paradox of India's Peacekeeping', *Contemporary South Asia*, 12:2 (2003), p. 263.

[27] Full text of President Obama's speech to the *LokSabha*, the lower house of the Parliament of India, 8 November 2010, http://www.indianexpress.com/news/barack-obamas-speech-at-the-parliament/708277/0

[28] 'A wake-up call for Pakistan', *Express Tribune*, 11 November 2010.

[29] http://www.pakun.org/press-releases/2010/11102010-01.php (emphasis added).

[30] 'Not so beautiful from this angle', *The Hindu*, 11 November 2010.

9.4 SECURITY RATIONALES

Pakistan's 'policy making elite tends to define threats to national security mainly in terms of the perceived peril from New Delhi'.[31] The practical manifestation as well as a living reminder of this threat is the Siachen glacier, the highest and costliest battlefield in the world at an altitude of over 20,000 feet with temperatures averaging 50 degrees below zero where, in spite of the perpetually frozen terrain which holds no conceivable military advantage to either side, the two states have maintained a permanent military presence since 1984 and where more deaths have occurred due to the extreme weather conditions than to armed hostilities.[32] This historical hostility towards India has established 'the primacy of the national security agenda' in Pakistan where policy-makers remain 'uncomfortable with India's urge to gain regional or global prominence. Any reference to India acquiring a prominent role in world affairs, especially as a result of its comparatively greater military capacity is seen as a potential threat and as inherently antithetical to Pakistan's interests.'[33] Pakistan therefore wants not to be outdone by India in its UN peacekeeping profile and views its UN blue berets as a counterweight to Indian regional as well as global ambitions.

Pakistan's peacekeeping credentials have also enabled it to raise what it considers the unresolved issue of Kashmir, consistently and more effectively at the UN Security Council. Safeguarding the country's security and geostrategic interests, including Kashmir, is Pakistan's number one proclaimed foreign policy priority.[34] The military establishment and the policy-making elite view the Kashmir issue as critical for Pakistan's security.[35] The quintessential importance of Kashmir in Pakistan's security paradigm can be gauged from General Pervez Musharraf's statement to *Time* correspondent Lally Weymouth that Kashmir 'is our national interest'.[36] Pakistan therefore attaches great importance to both the 'symbolic value and substantive contribution' of UNMOGIP, which monitors the Line of Control in the disputed area of

[31] Ayesha Siddiqa, *Military Inc.: Inside Pakistan's Military Economy* (Karachi: Oxford University Press, 2007), p. 62.

[32] 'Demilitarization of Siachen', *Daily Times*, 25 July 2010. Over 5,000 Indian and 3,000 Pakistani soldiers have perished in the 50 miles of the inhospitable terrain of Siachen glacier between April 1984 and April 2012. See 'Siachen tragedy—Day 4: Rescuers search desperately as weather turns foul', *Express Tribune*, 11 April 2012.

[33] Siddiqa, *Military Inc.*, p. 63. This India-centric threat perception dates back to Pakistan's inception as 70 per cent of Pakistan's first budget was allocated to defence.

[34] *Foreign Office Yearbook 2008–09* (Islamabad: Ministry of Foreign Affairs, 2009), p. 14, http://www.mofa.gov.pk/Publications/Year_Book_2008-09.doc

[35] Siddiqa, *Military Inc.*, p. 63.

[36] Robert G. Wirsing, *Precarious Partnership: Pakistan's Response to U.S. Security Policies* (Hawaii: Asia-Pacific Center for Security Studies, 2003), p. 5.

Jammu and Kashmir.[37] This is because, 'as long as the United Nations retains its military presence along the Line of Control, the Kashmir issue will continue to be characterized as an international dispute', to the chagrin of Indian policy-makers.[38]

Pakistan has also had a long, fractured, love–hate relationship with the United States. There exists a wide chasm between Pakistan's perception of its national interests and the security policies of the dominant superpower. The distrust of US security policies has led Pakistanis to 'generally hold the view that U.S. security policy in Asia, including what they see as Washington's progressive shift towards an Indo-centric strategic design, is neglectful of Pakistan's basic national interests'.[39] It is interesting to note that Pakistan's initial surge in peacekeeping contribution in the early 1990s coincided with the United States imposing military and economic sanctions against Pakistan, primarily because of its nuclear programme. In June 2005, the United States signed a ten-year defence framework agreement with India aimed at a new era of bilateral cooperation in addition to participation in multinational military operations.[40] Pakistan expressed 'serious concern' over the agreement and its potential ramifications.[41]Around the same time, Pakistan's Minister for Foreign Affairs described multilateralism as the panacea for festering global issues and underscored the need to make the UN an effective institution. In his words, 'we believe that only multilateral cooperation, in a world based on principles of liberty and law, and an effective UN system can ensure peace, security and harmony between cultures, countries and faiths. Pakistan is making its contribution towards the achievements of these objectives'.[42] More recently, in 2011, in the aftermath of Osama Bin Laden's killing, which the United States conducted without taking Pakistan's military onboard, the Raymond Davis incident, and the Salala tragedy, the already strained US–Pakistan relationship took a nosedive. As one leading Pakistani nuclear physicist-cum-political analyst put it, 'in the [Pakistan] military's mind, the

[37] Riaz Kohkhar, Seminar on 'Pakistan in UN Peacekeeping Operations' held by the Foreign Ministry of Pakistan and the UN Information Centre in Islamabad on 28 May 2004.

[38] Ishtiaq Ahmad, 'US experts ignore Kashmir realities', *The Nation* (Lahore), 30 November 1997.

[39] Wirsing, 'Precarious Partnership', p. 1. This distrust is mutual. See Blake Hounshell, 'Did the United Sates use the Kashmir Earthquake to Send Intelligence Operatives into Pakistan?', *Foreign Policy Blog*, 13 February 2012.

[40] C. Raja Mohan, *India: The Ultimate Test of Free Market Democracy*. Reaction to working paper for the Stanley Foundation's Powers and Principles Project, October 2008, p. 32.

[41] Ihtashamul Haque, 'Concern Voiced over Indo-US Defense Accord', *Dawn* (Karachi), 24 July 2005.

[42] *Foreign Office Yearbook 2005–06* (Islamabad: Ministry of Foreign Affairs, 2006), pp. 4–5, http://www.mofa.gov.pk/Publications/Year_Book_2005-06.doc

Americans are now a threat, equal to or larger than India'.[43] Pakistan's participation in UN peacekeeping can therefore be seen as one of the levers in its diplomatic toolkit to serve as a hedge against what Pakistani policy-makers see as Washington's see-saw relationship with Pakistan and its growing romance with its arch-rival, India.

9.5 INSTITUTIONAL RATIONALES

The military in Pakistan is a voluntary service comprising 650,000 personnel.[44] However, the approximate strength totals around one million personnel, if paramilitary forces and coastguards are included.[45] This makes Pakistan's military one of the top ten largest armed forces in the world.[46] The sheer size of Pakistan's military is, however, a manifestation of regional security dynamics and underscores the South Asian subcontinent's military surplus.[47] Since Pakistan's independence in 1947, its military has governed the country outright three times and has exerted a strong political influence even when not in power.[48] In part, this dominance stems 'from the fact that the Pakistani military is the only institution that works more or less as it is meant to, as measured against the generally accepted standards of a modern state institution'.[49] However, prolonged military rule has affected policy-making procedures. 'The various legal and constitutional provisions introduced during ten years of [Gen.] Zia ul Haq's rule [1977–88] and consolidated by the Musharraf regime transformed the military from a tool for policy implementation to an equal

[43] Pervez Hoodbhoy, 'Pakistan's Rush for more Bombs—Why?' *Express Tribune*, 29 January 2012. For a recent account of how Pakistan views its relations with the United States, see Bill Keller, 'The Pakistanis have a Point', *New York Times Magazine*, 14 December 2011.

[44] Siddiqa, *Military Inc.*, p. 59.

[45] These paramilitary formations include the Frontier Corps (Khyber Pakhtunkhwa and Balochistan), Pakistan Rangers (Punjab and Sindh), Northern Area Scouts, and Frontier Constabulary. Since Pakistan's peak peacekeeping contributions have hovered around 10,000 uniformed personnel in the 2000s, only 1 per cent of Pakistan's uniformed personnel were deployed as UN peacekeepers at a given point during this decade.

[46] Riaz Ahmed Shaikh, 'Pakistani Military's Role in the Asian Context', in Giuseppe Caforio (ed.), *Advances in Military Sociology: Essays in Honor of Charles C. Moskos* (Bingley, UK: Emerald Group Publishing, 2009), p. 284.

[47] Mohan, *India: The Ultimate Test of Free Market Democracy*, p. 32. Keeping in view the dismal social and human development indicators of South Asian countries, it is in the interest of the regional states to transform their policy orientation from 'military surplus' to 'production surplus'. This is only possible if the countries bury the hatchet and pursue 'smart power'—by integrating political and economic tools with their military muscle—so that the region's people are able to realize their true potential, which unfortunately remains grossly suppressed.

[48] This threat of direct military intervention has, however, markedly receded in recent years. See Reza Sayah, 'Five reasons why the army won't takeover Pakistan', *CNN*, 16 January 2012.

[49] Anatol Lieven, 'Military Exceptionalism in Pakistan', *Survival*, 53:4 (2011), p. 53.

partner in policy making.'[50] This has led some commentators to assert that the 'defence and foreign policies of the country are normally decided by the armed forces of Pakistan as per their own priorities'.[51] Participation of Pakistan's military in UN peacekeeping cannot therefore be seen as a compulsion dictated by the political leadership. To the contrary, it is in the institutional interest of the military to support and contribute to UN peacekeeping efforts.

It is pertinent to mention that owing to prolonged stretches of direct military rule, Pakistan's military 'considers itself as an alternative institution capable of contributing to [the country's] socioeconomic and political development'.[52] Over the years, the Pakistan Army has played significant state-building roles in various sectors of Pakistan's economy such as transportation, communication, flood rehabilitation, and disaster relief. It also has the experience of initiating quick-impact projects in troubled zones within the country. For example, army engineers are currently constructing a highway in north-western Pakistan aimed at linking the restive South Waziristan area to the central economy, the target completion date of which is 2013.[53] Thus Pakistan's military 'is increasingly flexible to fit into civilian-oriented activities—a major advantage for post-Cold War peacekeeping operations'.[54] It is also therefore well placed to undertake critical peacebuilding tasks which now form part of at least ten out of the sixteen current UN peacekeeping operations.

Pakistan's UN peacekeeping endeavours have also provided vital international exposure for its military in emergency medical and engineering services, aviation, de-mining, and other essential professional techniques. The professional and organizational benefit to Pakistan's military accruing from UN peacekeeping has been summed up as providing 'Pakistan's forces with an opportunity to be exposed to operational procedures of other forces; learn new techniques of planning; logistics and communications skills; command and control structures; methods of coordination and use state of the art weaponry and machinery. This military training and exposure has proved to be invaluable to the Pakistan Army.'[55]

Pakistan's participation in UN peacekeeping missions also has the potential to open up avenues for exposure to comparatively more robust non-UN peacekeeping missions. For example, Pakistan was the only non-European state among the fourteen non-NATO countries which contributed 1,000 troops

[50] Siddiqa, *Military Inc.*, p. 139.

[51] Shaikh, 'Pakistani Military's Role in the Asian Context', p. 283.

[52] Siddiqa, *Military Inc.*, p. 64.

[53] 'Pakistan looks to South Waziristan highway to fight militancy', *Express Tribune*, 4 November 2011. See also 'South Waziristan: Military assures support for IDPs', *Express Tribune*, 31 October 2011.

[54] Krishnasamy, 'Pakistan's Peacekeeping Experiences', p. 116.

[55] Kiani, 'Pakistan's Contribution to UN Peacekeeping', p. 45.

in the NATO-led Implementation Force (IFOR) in Bosnia-Herzegovina.[56] Pakistan had earlier justified its participation in UNPROFOR in the former Yugoslavia, the precursor to IFOR, on the basis of public opinion in Pakistan having been 'greatly incensed at the systematic campaign of "ethnic cleansing" in Bosnia'.[57] IFOR was NATO's first-ever ground force operation, its first-ever deployment 'out of area', and its first-ever joint operation with other non-NATO countries. Joining IFOR 'provided Pakistan with a proverbial foot in the door into the higher echelons of NATO representing the territory of Europe. That participation exposed the Pakistani military personnel to modern and state-of-the-art machinery, equipment and communication systems; cohesive planning of military combat and patrols and various facets of greater inter-operationalablilty [sic].'[58]

In addition to professional grooming and institutional strengthening, peacekeeping deployments also have vital welfare connotations. Pakistan's military, which takes pride in its journey 'from scratch to nuclear power',[59] recognizes the significance of providing welfare for its personnel like all modern and professional armed forces.[60] This provision of welfare is, in part, a legacy of the British colonial empire. Yong argues that 'it was in the soldier's homes and villages, and not in the regiments, that the "loyalty" of the army was won or lost'.[61] As a result, Pakistan's military works on the principle of taking care of its personnel 'from cradle to grave' and has a well-structured welfare system for its serving and retired personnel and their dependants.[62] Peacekeeping deployment serves as a unique 'gratis' welfare-cum-professional tool for the Pakistan military owing to the financial bonus attached to it at no additional financial cost to the country as well as the ample avenues it offers for professional grooming of its personnel. This tool is, however, selectively employed to chisel only the best and the brightest service members and Pakistan's military 'has developed a rigid selection process that places emphasis on personal qualities such as patience, sensitivity to gender and differing cultures, understanding, calmness and self-discipline'.[63]

[56] The fourteen non-NATO states which participated in IFOR in Bosnia-Herzegovina were Austria, Czech Republic, Estonia, Finland, Hungary, Latvia, Lithuania, Pakistan, Poland, Romania, Russia, Slovakia, Sweden, and Ukraine. See http://www.afsouth.nato.int/archives/operations/IFOR/IFORFactSheet.htm

[57] Statement of Pakistan's representative S. M. Khan at the UN Security Council, cited in Daniel Bethlehem and Mark Weller (eds.), *The Yugoslav Crisis in International Law*, Cambridge International Document Series 5 (Cambridge: Cambridge University Press, 1997), p. 155.

[58] Kiani, 'Pakistan's Contribution to UN Peacekeeping', p. 53.

[59] 'A Journey from Scratch to Nuclear Power' is the title of one of Pakistan Army's official web-pages: http://www.pakistanarmy.gov.pk/AWPReview/TextContent.aspx?pId=18&rnd=157

[60] Siddiqa, *Military Inc.*, p. 208.

[61] Cited in Siddiqa, *Military Inc.*, p. 218.

[62] Siddiqa, *Military Inc.*, p. 218.

[63] Krishnasamy, 'UN Peacekeepers as "Reliable" Forces', p. 103.

In an empirical study conducted on 172 Pakistani peacekeepers, 'financial advantage and professional grooming' were reported by participants as benefits of the peacekeeping deployment.[64] The commissioned officers of the Pakistan Army consider UN assignments as 'prestigious and as a boost to personal image and identity'.[65] Pakistani officers serving as force commanders in UN peacekeeping missions gain vital command exposure in complex multinational environments and almost invariably rise to strategically important positions upon end of their assignment. And since deployment in UN peacekeeping operations often entails the first trip abroad for the average Pakistani soldier, families take pride in their relative's service to the cause of peace, 'miles away from home'.[66] This accolade is not limited to the local level; on the national level, Pakistan's foreign secretary glorified Pakistani peacekeepers by saying 'we salute our peacekeepers—our brave soldiers—who have upheld the cause of peace in different parts of the world and in so doing have earned prestige and honour for themselves and their country'.[67]

On the flipside, peacekeeping entails individual and institutional costs as well. Deployment on UN peacekeeping missions in inhospitable environments, far away from home, can exact a heavy toll on the psychology and mental health of peacekeepers and result in their becoming stress-prone. Meta-analysis of twelve studies reporting Post-Traumatic Stress Disorder (PTSD) among peacekeepers has revealed wide heterogeneity of outcomes but has highlighted the importance of the creation of standards for PTSD evaluation among peacekeepers.[68] The only such study carried out on Pakistani peacekeepers concluded that 'lack of recreational facilities, separation from family and risk of getting infectious diseases were common stressors' among Pakistani peacekeepers.[69] These individual stressors can have an impact at the institutional level as well. However, no study has been carried out yet to determine these effects.

[64] Nadeem Ahmed et al., 'Psychiatric Morbidity in Pakistan Peacekeepers and their Perception about Deployment in Liberia', *Pakistan Armed Forces Medical Journal*, 60:2 (2010), p. 208.

[65] Krishnasamy, 'Pakistan's Peacekeeping Experiences', p. 114.

[66] The local phrase is '*saat samundar paar*' which means 'across seven seas'. Unfortunately, Pakistan's public sector, including the military, lags far behind in gender mainstreaming. However, significant steps have been taken in recent years to redress the imbalance, including reservation of a 10 per cent quota for women in all government jobs. Female officers have also recently been commissioned as officers in the Pakistan Army, Pakistan Air Force, and Pakistan Navy.

[67] Riaz Khokhar (Pakistan's foreign secretary) at a seminar on 'Pakistan in UN Peacekeeping Operations' held by the Ministry of Foreign Affairs, Pakistan and the UN Information Centre, Islamabad, 28 May 2004.

[68] Wanderson Fernandes Souza et al., 'Posttraumatic Stress Disorder in Peacekeepers: A Meta-Analysis', *Journal of Nervous and Mental Disease*, 199:5 (2011), p. 309.

[69] Ahmed et al., 'Psychiatric Morbidity in Pakistan Peacekeepers', p. 208.

9.6 ECONOMIC RATIONALES

Since member states make voluntary contributions to UN peacekeeping and since it is a global impure public good, financial remuneration to contributing countries is a *sine qua non* to compensate the states which place their troops in harm's way and also to differentiate between contributing and non-contributing or 'free-riding' countries.[70] The latter have also been referred to as 'willing to pay but not play'.[71] A financial incentive is also essential to raise the morale of troops serving abroad and to keep them motivated to serve under risky, volatile, and stressful conditions.[72] Countries volunteering uniformed personnel are compensated by the UN at a flat rate of around US $1,028 per soldier per month. Peacekeepers are paid by their respective governments according to their national rank and salary scale. Military Experts on Mission (formerly Military Observers) and UN Police personnel receive a Monthly Subsistence Allowance (MSA) of between US$100 and $300 per day directly in their bank accounts from the peacekeeping budgets established for each operation. The foreign currency inflows received as compensation from the UN and the foreign currency denominated savings of individual peacekeepers remitted through formal banking channels enhance the recipient country's foreign exchange reserves.

On the microeconomic level, the benefits accruing from participation in peacekeeping operations can be broadly separated into tangible and non-tangible benefits. With regard to the former, it is important to point out that remuneration for serving in peacekeeping is in addition to the regular monthly salaries which all uniformed peacekeepers continue to receive from their respective countries. For a typical Pakistani soldier and for his counterparts from developing countries, the pecuniary benefits, though not huge, represent a once-in-a-career opportunity to generate savings and gain some financial stability. It is noteworthy that Pakistani authorities do not deduct their own slice from this remuneration or death/disability claims of peacekeepers. All payments are payable to the individual peacekeeper, which is not the case for every troop contributing country. To manage the incentives the Pakistan Army, as a matter of policy, does not deploy its soldiers 'in

[70] From an economic perspective, paradoxically, the free-rider incentives of non-participation in endeavours like UN peacekeeping 'are particularly strong for conditions under which cooperation would generate large global welfare gains'. In view of the increasing demand for peacekeepers over the last decade, the main challenge to UN peacekeeping, therefore, is to shape an incentive structure for sovereign states to participate in peacekeeping, principal guidelines of which may come from coalition theory, a field of game theory. See Christoph Bohringer, *The Kyoto Protocol: A Review and Perspectives* (Manheim: Centre for European Economic Research (ZEW), Discussion Paper No. 03-61, 2003), pp. 6–7.

[71] Alfonso J. Motta Allen, *United Nations Peacekeeping Operations: Mexico's Response to an Emerging International Security Paradigm* (Canada: Dalhousie University, 2008), p. 61.

[72] Kiani, 'Pakistan's Contribution to UN Peacekeeping', p. 45.

more than one external assignment throughout their military career'. This helps ensure that soldiers do not look to peacekeeping as 'a potential money-making venture' which might compromise their professionalism in the longer term. The intangible benefits include, but are not limited to, professional exposure to military skills as practised in other countries, exposure to foreign environments, interaction with other militaries, and an opportunity for tourism.

Of course, it should be recalled that the amount paid to peacekeepers as allowance has remained practically frozen since 1992, although there was an ad hoc increase in 2002 and another one-time increase in 2011. Before 1992, troop cost was adjusted to consumer price indices and inflation—incidentally this was the time when the leading contributors to UN peacekeeping were France, Canada, Italy, and the UK. After the mid-1990s, when South Asian and African states came to dominate the peacekeeping scene, the trend changed. This has recently prompted some major contributors to argue that they are being obliged to contribute to 'subsidized peacekeeping'. Pakistan has also taken strong exception to these moves. For example, its acting permanent representative informed the Security Council in October 2011 that, 'While expenditure and remunerations for other UN activities are adjusted to inflation and cost-of-living fluctuations, the peacekeepers are expected to work on fixed and archaic rates. It is no longer sustainable for TCCs to subsidize UN peacekeeping.'[73]

On the macro level, economic gains accrue primarily from the flat-rate reimbursement per soldier contributed and compensation for equipment provided and for certain services rendered. Since there is considerable delay in reimbursement for services rendered by the troop-contributing countries and the compensation provided by the UN, the foreign exchange earnings may fluctuate from year to year, based on actual UN reimbursements released. The total estimated foreign exchange earned by the Pakistani government on account of participation in UN peacekeeping amounts to $220 million per annum. The amount may be termed huge for a small-sized economy; for the middle-sized economy of Pakistan, however, which allocates $20 per capita per annum to military spending, the amount is quite modest. Given that the total external debt and liabilities owed by Pakistan stood at $60,116 million[74] at the end of fiscal year 2010–11 and total annual remittances received from expatriate Pakistanis totalled $11,201 million[75] in 2011 alone, the macroeconomic impact of the amount earned from peacekeeping, though not insignificant, is no more than a few drops in the ocean of Pakistan's external balance of payments and should not be seen as a major motivation

[73] Mr Tarar, S/PV.6603 (Resumption 1), 26 August 2011, p. 4.
[74] Economic Affairs Division, Ministry of Finance, Government of Pakistan.
[75] State Bank of Pakistan, http://www.sbp.org.pk/ecodata/homeremmit/remittance.pdf

on the part of Pakistani policy-makers to board the UN peacekeeping bandwagon. According to alliance theory, 'states are more likely to contribute to the provision of impure public goods [including UN peacekeeping operations] when higher levels of private benefits are possible'.[76] From a realist standpoint, Pakistan, like almost all other states, is no exception and it can be argued that microeconomic and institutional spin-off benefits are most important.

9.7 POLICE CONTRIBUTIONS

Pakistan has also emerged as one of the UN's top police contributing countries since it first sent its police personnel to Namibia (UNTAG) in 1989. Pakistan's police contribution enables it, *inter alia*, to play a more effective role in missions with protection of civilians (POC) mandates.[77] An individual seconded Pakistani police peacekeeper deployed in UN peace operations typically receives a monthly Mission Subsistence Allowance (MSA) from the UN which is between six and twelve times more than the salary s/he receives in Pakistan. 'Generous even for officers from developed states', the MSA serves as the primary motivation for individual Pakistani police officers to volunteer for UN Police service.[78] In the case of individual seconded police officers, no direct economic benefit accrues to the government of Pakistan.[79] However, the government receives monetary reimbursement from the UN for police personnel deployed as part of a Formed Police Unit. Service in UN peacekeeping is looked down upon by certain senior police officers as in their view, having served a year or more as peacekeepers, the police personnel become 'spoiled' and 'too soft' to handle the tough realities of policing back home in Pakistan. However, a more common view is that UN missions serve as a vital opportunity for police personnel to gain financial stability and an avenue for infusing modern concepts pertaining to human rights, gender mainstreaming, the handling of vulnerable persons, and community policing.[80]

[76] Richard Bruneau, *Selfishness in Service of Common Good: Why States Participate in UN Peacekeeping* (Canada: Norman Paterson School of International Affairs, 2004), p. 5.

[77] Author's interviews with military officers, July 2011. Based on their experience in domestic internal security duties, many Pakistan military officers consider police peacekeepers to be better suited to handle situations in which protection of civilians is involved.

[78] William Durch et al., *Enhancing United Nations Capacity to Support Post-Conflict Policing and Rule of Law* (Washington, DC: Henry L. Stimson Center, 2010), p. 27.

[79] As stated earlier, the foreign currency denominated savings remitted by individual peacekeepers through formal banking channels do have an indirect effect of contributing, albeit insignificantly, to the recipient country's foreign exchange reserves.

[80] Author's interviews with senior Police Service of Pakistan officers, August 2011.

9.8 LESSONS LEARNED

UN peacekeepers have traditionally been deployed to situations where there was a peace to keep. In the early 1990s, however, Pakistan and the UN had to make a major departure from traditional peacekeeping as UN peacekeepers found themselves deployed in situations (e.g., Somalia, Bosnia-Herzegovina, Rwanda) where there was essentially no peace to keep. The Somalia venture (1992–95) was a watershed in Pakistan's UN peacekeeping profile which had two significant impacts. First, being the only country to have served in all the various phases of the missions and being the first country to arrive and the last to leave, Pakistan's peacekeepers gave a practical demonstration of their 'staying power' in various phases of the peace mission despite suffering numerous casualties in the often hostile environment of war-ravaged Somalia.[81] This unfaltering commitment over a prolonged period as the single largest contributor cemented Pakistan's credentials as 'one of UN's most reliable peacekeepers'.[82] Second, the Somalia fatalities proved to be a catalyst in reforming Pakistan's peacekeeping doctrine and strategic thinking on these issues within the higher echelons of Pakistan's military.

In Somalia, the Pakistan Army got embroiled in 'the US "Rambo" style of peacekeeping' by becoming preoccupied with Aideed's capture—but lost the confidence of the locals in the process, which is essential for ensuring success in any peace operation. Based on this experience, 'building wider community support' has become the cardinal building-block for Pakistan's military contingents in all post-Somalia peacekeeping deployments.[83] The strategy adopted by the Pakistan Army in the UNAMSIL mission in Sierra Leone, now widely considered as a successful peacekeeping mission, is illustrative in this regard.[84] There, the Pakistani battalion in the newly disarmed Kono district successfully adopted the 'hearts and minds' approach to peacekeeping by providing medicines 'from their own supplies', rehabilitating schools, mosques, and churches, and even 'cut their own rations in order to provide food to vulnerable Sierra Leoneans'. A senior Pakistan Battalion (PakBat) officer described the humanitarian approach in the following manner: 'We have civil projects to win the heart and minds of the people. It's part of our policy to win the hearts and minds of the people. For example, it used to take 5–6 hours to get from Kenema to Daru. Now it takes 2 hours because of the road improvements we made . . . We have distributed 10,000 footballs

81 Krishnasamy, 'UN Peacekeepers as "Reliable" Forces', p. 94.
82 Krishnasamy, 'UN Peacekeepers as "Reliable" Forces', p. 94.
83 Krishnasamy, 'Pakistan's Peacekeeping Experiences', p. 110.
84 See Funmi Olonisakin, *Peacekeeping in Sierra Leone* (Boulder, CO: Lynne Rienner, 2008).

(soccer balls) to schools and children.'[85] Pakistani troops executed a similar strategy in Liberia when they deployed in Lofa County, providing humanitarian and medical assistance to 20,000 people.[86] This has all happened despite there being significant 'limits set on how much a peacekeeping mission can reach out to civil society without undermining the legitimacy of the host government'.[87]

It is pertinent to mention that in spite of its rich and diversified peacekeeping track record, Pakistan has yet to establish a formal institutionalized system of capturing, internalizing, and learning from the experiences of its individual peacekeepers and replicating the best practices employed by its contingents upon their return from UN assignments. This is especially true of police officers who serve in UN missions. Training for military peacekeepers is currently being conducted at the Peacekeeping Training Cell in the School of Infantry and Tactics, situated in Quetta.[88] Some pre-deployment briefings are imparted to the departing military peacekeepers, as well. Courses on peacekeeping are also part of the curricula for almost all promotion courses for military officers. However, the training of peacekeepers is not apparently accorded due priority and is not conducted in a systematic and proactive manner.[89] Training for police peacekeepers is almost entirely non-existent, with Pakistani UNPOL officers learning the tricks of the trade only upon arrival in the mission area by trial-and-error or from their peers on an informal basis.[90] Establishment of a dedicated peacekeeping training institute for the military and a centre of excellence for police peacekeepers in Pakistan would be of immense benefit not only for institutional learning but it would also better enable Pakistani peacekeepers to perform the tasks required in

[85] Clifford Bernath and Ayre Nyce, *UNAMSIL—A Peacekeeping Success Lessons Learned: Report on the United Nations Mission in Sierra Leone* (Washington, DC: Refugees International, 2002), p. 14. For similar strategies successfully employed by Pakistan Army contingents in Bosnia-Herzegovina and Haiti, see Krishnasamy, 'Pakistan's Peacekeeping Experiences', pp. 110–11.

[86] Mr Kasuri, S/PV.4970, 17 May 2004.

[87] *Annual Review of Global Peace Operations, 2011* (New York: Lynne Rienner/Center on International Cooperation, 2011), p. 13.

[88] The seriousness accorded by Pakistan military to training its peacekeeping personnel can be gauged by the fact that 'Peacekeeping Operations' is mentioned at the very bottom of the list of various courses offered at the School webpage, http://www.pakistanarmy.gov.pk/AWPReview/TextContent.aspx?pId=273&rnd=480

[89] One military officer interviewed pointed out that 'stress management', 'familiarization with the local culture', and 'communication in the local language' are not properly incorporated in the pre-departure training and briefings. This is perhaps because the Pakistan Army still views UN peacekeeping through a largely 'infantry-based' prism.

[90] A brief mission-specific induction training is imparted to all incoming UNPOL officers by the UN. However, this training can have the desired efficacy only if preceded by thorough Pre-Deployment Training (PDT) imparted in Pakistan before departure to UN missions. This PDT is required to be imparted by all member states to all personnel provided to UN peacekeeping operations in accordance with General Assembly resolution A/RES/49/37.

multifarious UN assignments. These tasks are becoming more challenging with each passing year, demanding a specialized and tailored response commensurate with the complex and multidimensional requirements of twenty-first-century peacekeeping.[91] Since there is little sharing of peacekeeping experiences with other contributing countries, such an enterprise would not only enrich Pakistan's peacekeeping-related learning and exposure through representation at the AIPTC and enable Pakistan to better conform to the UN Peacekeeping Pre-deployment training (PDT) standards but it would also help emerging and potential contributors to learn from Pakistan's hands-on and varied peacekeeping capabilities.[92]

9.9 PAKISTAN'S STANCE ON CURRENT PEACEKEEPING TRENDS

Pakistan lays particular emphasis on enhanced triangular cooperation between the Security Council, TCCs, and the Secretariat.[93] It is against the politicization of the protection of civilians (POC) concept and considers this the 'primary responsibility of the host government, which can be complemented by a peacekeeping mission depending on resources at its disposal. Working with local government is the key for protecting civilians.'[94] As for the legal accountability of peacekeepers, the process is well enshrined in Pakistani military manuals. Allegations of gold smuggling by Pakistani peacekeepers deployed in DRC were denied by Pakistani authorities and the UN inquiry into the matter also did not implicate the Pakistani peacekeepers in smuggling. Professionalism demands zero tolerance of sexual exploitation and abuse, and this, Pakistani officials say, is practised not to please anyone but to keep

[91] Pakistan 'actively considered' establishing a peacekeeping training centre in 2005. However, it did not materialize on the ground. See 'Pakistan Eyes Peacekeeping Training Centre', *Jane's Defence Weekly*, 15 June 2005.

[92] AIPTC is an acronym for Association of International Peacekeeping Training Centres. In the absence of a dedicated peacekeeping training centre, Pakistani peacekeepers are also missing out on vital skills-enhancing collaborative arrangements being undertaken by various peacekeeping training centres around the globe. It is noteworthy to mention that the other two top UN peacekeeping contributors from South Asia, i.e., India and Bangladesh, which are the subject of this study, have already established vibrant peacekeeping training centres offering courses and expertise to national as well as international potential peacekeepers.

[93] Raza Bashir Tarar, Acting Permanent Representative of Pakistan to the UN, in S/PV.6603 (Resumption 1), 26 August 2011, pp. 3–4.

[94] Statement by Raza Bashir Tarar, Deputy Permanent Representative of Pakistan in the Special Political and Decolonization (Fourth) Committee on Comprehensive review of the Whole Question of Peacekeeping Operations in all their Aspects, 27 October 2011, http://pakun.org/statements/Fourth_Committee/2011/10272011-01.php

the high standards of Pakistan's military.[95] Recently, three members of the Pakistani Formed Police Unit serving with the UN Stabilization Mission in Haiti (MINUSTAH) were subjected to court martial proceedings in accordance with Pakistani laws in Port-au-Prince and were found guilty. These members were immediately repatriated, dishonourably discharged from service with loss of benefits, and imprisoned.[96] As regards future challenges, Pakistan has the requisite political will and capacity to play its part in the surge in demand and growing complexity of mandates. However, Pakistan's recipe for success for future peacekeeping operations lies in 'strict adherence to the UN Charter and abiding by the guiding principles of UN Peacekeeping—namely, consent of the parties concerned, non-use of force except in self-defence and strict neutrality'.[97]

9.10 CONCLUSION

The preceding discussion illustrates that Pakistan has become a reliable and effective UN peacekeeper. Motivated by various rationales, the signs are that Pakistan is likely to continue to provide a large-scale contribution to UN peacekeeping operations, at least in the near future. The only two major caveats are the country's internal security threats which may 'crowd out' the Pakistan military's external deployments and the ever increasing challenges to the state of Pakistan's economy which may prompt a strategic rethink of Pakistan's existing security and foreign policy paradigm. There is little evidence to suggest that debates about POC or 'robust peacekeeping' will impact negatively on Pakistan's willingness to contribute forces—at least for the foreseeable future. Owing to its large and consistent peacekeeping profile, Pakistan along with other large contributors would not, however, remain content with a place in the seating compartment in the global train of peacekeeping. Instead, it would like itself to be represented in the driving cabin where it can help steer strategic decisions on UN peacekeeping.

[95] Ambassador Munir Akram, Permanent Representative of Pakistan in the General Debate of the Special Political and Decolonization (Fourth) Committee on Agenda Item 32: Comprehensive Review of the Whole Question of Peacekeeping Operations in all their Aspects, 24 October 2005.

[96] See 'Haiti: Three UN Peacekeepers Repatriated for Sexual Abuse', UN News Centre, 13 March 2012, http://www.un.org/apps/news/story.asp?NewsID=41538&Cr=Haiti&Cr1=

[97] Statement by Raza Bashir Tarar, 27 October 2011.

10

India

Dipankar Banerjee

India was among the earliest troop contributors to United Nations (UN) peacekeeping operations. By the end of 2011, it had contributed a total of 163,000 personnel and participated in forty-three missions.[1] It was the first country to field a unit composed entirely of women police officers to the UN mission in Liberia (UNMIL) in January 2007, which at the time of writing continues to be rotated annually.[2] India has so far provided one military adviser and one deputy military adviser to the UN Department of Peacekeeping Operations (DPKO), thirteen force commanders in various UN missions and one division commander in Congo (1961–2). India has also paid the highest price in terms of the number of peacekeepers that have lost their lives in the line of duty, suffering 143 fatalities on UN missions by 31 January 2012.

Overall and without much variation, India's share of UN peacekeepers has varied between 7 and 12 per cent of the whole. In the twenty-first century, India has consistently been the third largest troop-contributing country (TCC) after Bangladesh and Pakistan, contributing around 8,000 soldiers and police at any given time. Since 2004, when UN missions in Africa increased dramatically, India's contribution also increased in absolute terms, though its overall share of peacekeepers did not, as Figure 10.1 shows.

In the twenty-first century the bulk of India's UN peacekeepers have been deployed in Africa. India's initial major contribution came in Sierra Leone where it provided the first force commander in UNAMSIL and deployed some 3,000 soldiers. This was later surpassed by its contribution in the Democratic Republic of the Congo under MONUC/MONUSCO where by early 2012 India had over 4,000 uniformed personnel deployed, roughly half of

[1] Data based on the assessment of the UN Section of the Army Headquarters, Department of UN Peacekeeping, Deputy Director General of Staff Duties. Author's interview, 17 January 2012.

[2] Lieutenant General Satish Nambiar, *For the Honour of India: A History of Indian Peacekeeping* (New Delhi: Centre for Armed Forces Historical Research, United Services Institute of India, 2009), p. 500.

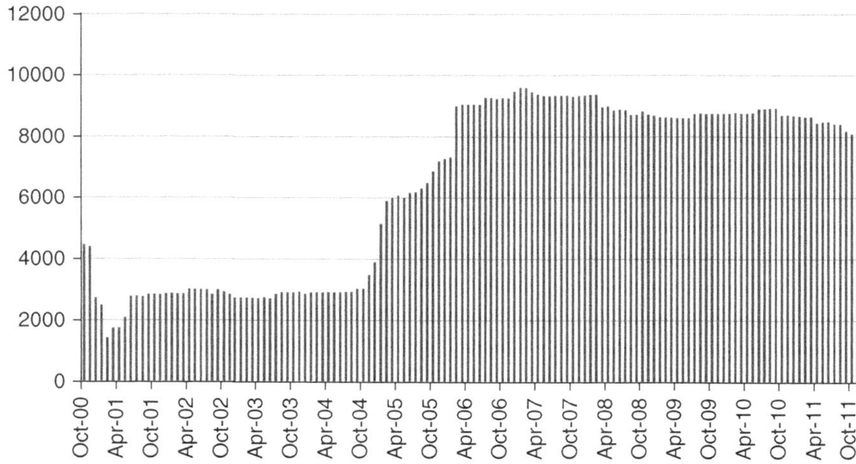

Figure 10.1 Indian Uniformed Personnel in UN Peacekeeping Operations, 2000–2011

its entire contribution of uniformed UN peacekeepers. This was a country where India had also played a role in the ONUC operation during the early 1960s. The big change in tempo in the DRC came in November 2004 when India deployed three infantry battalions under 301 Infantry Brigade and a helicopter unit consisting of Mi 17 and Mi 25 helicopters with its local protection unit.[3] Elsewhere, India made a major contribution to the mission between Ethiopia and Eritrea (UNMEE) from 2000–8 with some 1,600 soldiers consisting of one infantry battalion, military engineers, military observers, and staff officers.[4] Finally, India deployed an infantry battalion and allied troops totalling about 1,000 personnel in the UN Mission in Sudan (UNMIS) after 2005.[5] In terms of police contributions, India contributes the second largest number of civilian police to UN peacekeeping after Bangladesh with over 1,000 police officers deployed by early 2012, of which about 150 were female. India also deployed a range of around 100 military experts (staff officers and observers) around the world.

This chapter explores why India has provided so many UN peacekeepers and why UN peacekeeping has been popular in India. As Ramesh Thakur and I observed a few years ago, there were three broad historical reasons why the UN looked to India to provide peacekeepers: the size and professionalism of India's armed forces, the lack of such forces in most developing countries until

[3] Nambiar, *For the Honour of India*, pp. 226–53.
[4] Nambiar, *For the Honour of India*, pp. 294–317.
[5] Nambiar, *For the Honour of India*, pp. 318–35.

the 1990s, and India's influence in world affairs through its leading role in the Non-Aligned Movement (NAM).[6] As the Cold War ended, the situation changed. More countries now had armies with surplus troops and were willing to contribute to UN peacekeeping. To incentivize participation, the UN paid for the services of soldiers and in 1996 enhanced its reimbursement rates.[7] But well-trained, competently led armies that could also field advanced combat support weapons and systems were still few in number and India remained a preferred choice for the UN in situations that were likely to be difficult.

Why did India agree to take part in so many UN operations? The short answer is that India's sense of being a great power in the making was a key factor: as India's founding Prime Minister Jawaharlal Nehru put it, 'We cannot shed the responsibilities that go with a great country.'[8] This helps explain India's chairmanship of the three Indochina commissions in the 1950s, which it saw as being 'one of the necessities of the settlement . . . our refusal would have meant imperiling the whole agreement'. Just as important was the Prime Minister's conviction that, as a result of the Geneva Agreements for Indochina, there were better prospects for peace and stability in Asia as a whole.[9] This conviction—that India's contribution helped maintain regional peace and stability—was perhaps the dominant reason for participation in UN peacekeeping in the early years. That it also served India's foreign policy objectives was an additional bonus.

But it did not automatically follow that India would remain so committed to UN peacekeeping missions. Indeed, what makes UN peacekeeping an acceptable proposition in India in the twenty-first century when it is increasingly unpopular in much of the developed world? What policy objectives does India perceive to further through such participation? Will India's favourable attitude towards peacekeeping continue and if so why? And what are the anxieties and concerns that may affect India's peacekeeping contributions in the future?

One place to start is with the commitment to international peace and security written into the Indian Constitution. Coupled with this was a long-term foreign policy commitment to supporting the process of decolonization after the Second World War. Finally, having participated in peacekeeping from the outset, by the end of the twentieth century India had developed a sort of peacekeeping habit whereby successive governments saw (and continue to see) participation in UN peacekeeping operations as the country's major

[6] Ramesh Thakur and Dipankar Banerjee, 'India: Democratic, Poor, Internationalist', in Charlotte Ku and Harold Jacobson (eds.), *Democratic Accountability and the Use of Force in International Law* (Cambridge: Cambridge University Press, 2003), pp. 176–20.

[7] 'How Peacekeeping Works', *BBC News*, 17 April 2007, at http://news.bbc.co.uk/2/hi/6524867.stm

[8] Cited in Thakur and Banerjee, 'India', p. 179.

[9] Thakur and Banerjee, 'India', p. 179.

contribution to the world body and a significant part of justifying its case for permanent membership of a reformed UN Security Council.

Although unlikely to change radically in the short term, India's commitment to UN peacekeeping in the future could be adversely affected by several conditions. One set of issues has to do with the structure of peacekeeping itself. Relevant factors here include the effectiveness or otherwise of mandates, the morale of those charged with implementing them, India's representation in the UN's Department for Peacekeeping Operations/Department of Field Support (DPKO/DFS), and opportunities to participate in profitable logistics support functions. Another set of issues relates to UN policy on Jammu and Kashmir. A third issue may have to do with the growing impression that troop contributions for UN peacekeeping are a 'developing country' responsibility and not a matter for the 'major powers'—a factor which becomes more important as India comes to see itself as a major rather than emerging power. A fourth set of issues emerge from the question of the legitimacy and structure of the UN and India's aspiration to become a permanent member of a reformed Security Council. Finally, India has expressed concern at the direction of contemporary UN peacekeeping. In 2009, for example, its representative told the Security Council that: 'Peacekeeping mandates have become too broad and too all-encompassing. These difficulties are compounded by the fact that robust peacekeeping has not been properly defined.' Echoing Brazilian sentiments, it called for a refocusing on the developmental and capacity-building side of the agenda, arguing that 'India believes that the future of peacekeeping, and at least a part of peace building, lies in the development of police and rule of law capacities in United Nations missions.'[10]

This chapter first provides a brief history of India's participation in UN peacekeeping, highlighting the reasons for its participation. Next, it describes the policies and processes that shape New Delhi's decisions about the commitment of troops. Finally, it considers the contingencies and challenges that may affect India's future peacekeeping contributions.

10.1 INDIAN PEACEKEEPING: A BRIEF HISTORY

Even before India's independence in 1947, Ms Vijayalakshmi Pandit, leader of the Indian delegation to the UN General Assembly's first session in New York (October–December 1946) and sister of Prime Minister Nehru, pledged India's 'commitment to the principles of peace and justice as enshrined in

[10] S/PV.6153 (Resumption 1), 29 June 2009, pp. 13–14.

the United Nations Charter'.[11] Since then, India has accorded a high priority in its foreign policy to participating in UN peacekeeping. Indeed, this international commitment is included in India's Constitution promulgated on 26 November 1949. Specifically, Article 51 under the section Directive Principles of State Policy, states that:

> The State shall endeavour to—
>
> (*a*) promote international peace and security;
> (*b*) maintain just and honourable relations between nations;
> (*c*) foster respect for international law and treaty obligations in the dealings of organized peoples with one another; and
> (*d*) encourage settlement of international disputes by arbitration.

Though not an enforceable part of the Constitution, the Directive Principles are a powerful statement of national policy that the state endeavours to implement. This statement provides a rationale for, and even some influence over, the procedure for India's participation in UN peacekeeping operations.

Having gained independence ahead of other colonized countries in Asia and Africa, India made it a foreign policy priority to support freedom for other colonies. Many of the conflicts that subsequently ensued in these two continents were a consequence of post-colonial struggles and required some degree of UN involvement to assist their resolution. India felt a strong commitment to support this effort.

A key question that arose in these early years related to India's capacity to play such a role on the world stage. Two conflicts in Asia in the 1950s involving the UN, neither of which involved Blue Helmet peacekeeping missions, helped remove any doubts. First, was the Korean War (1950–3), then the wars in Indochina, where India has served as Chair of the International Commission (noted above). In the Korean War, which was a Chapter VII military operation authorized by the UN Security Council, India contributed a Field Ambulance (medical unit including a field hospital) of twenty-six medical officers and 300 soldiers to the multinational force.[12] This unit received numerous commendations including a Bronze Star and a Unit Citation from General Douglas MacArthur.[13] But, India's more significant contribution was the International

[11] K. P. Saksena, 'India and the Evolving United Nations', in Satish Kumar (ed.), *The UN at 50: An Indian View* (New Delhi: India International Centre, 1995), p. 4.

[12] The officers quoted here and later include both officers and junior commissioned officers (JCOs). The latter category is peculiar to India and Pakistan and has as its tradition the British Indian Army where platoon commanders were found from among native officers who were commissioned by the Viceroy and not the King of England. This distinction has continued in both armies since then. For the purpose of this chapter and in the interest of conformity both are being included under the category of 'officers'.

[13] 'Soldiers with Red Hats', *Sainik Samachar*, New Delhi, 1–15 January 2004, p. 14.

Custodian Force (ICF, 1953–4) in Korea. This consisted entirely of Indian soldiers and was deployed to facilitate exchange of prisoners of war and implement the armistice. India deployed 434 officers and 5,696 soldiers for this task under the Neutral Nations Repatriation Commission (NNRC), set up by the UN and chaired by India. India succeeded in this delicate civil–military task and earned international appreciation for its mediation and facilitation. In a letter to Prime Minister Nehru, US President Dwight Eisenhower commended the ICF, writing, 'no military unit in recent years has undertaken a more delicate and demanding peacetime mission than that faced by the Indian forces in Korea . . . . The performance of these officers and their troops was fully in keeping with the high reputation of the Indian Army.'[14]

Successful participation in these operations helped establish India's peacekeeping credentials and its capability. It provided confidence to India's political leaders that its armed forces were able to undertake complex international tasks with competence. It also highlighted the foreign policy benefits of participation in terms of furthering a positive image of India and generating international prestige. In turn, when demands were made by the UN for troops these mostly received a welcome acceptance in Delhi.

A major area of Indian contribution in this early period was in maintaining the peace in the Gaza Strip and Sinai via UNEF I (from November 1956 to May 1967). This followed a conflict that involved forces from the UK and France and where the UN General Assembly first authorized the deployment of armed military contingents, with the host state's (Egypt) consent. Eleven battalions in rotation for a year each involved a contribution from India of a total of 802 officers and 12,383 soldiers to this operation, and India also provided two generals who served as force commanders. The short-term success of this mission encouraged the UN to agree to the deployment of a larger armed contingent in the Congo where the situation suddenly worsened in 1960.

UN peacekeepers in the Congo had to contend with widespread violence and an attempted secession by the mineral-rich province of Katanga supported by Belgian-backed mercenaries. Indian forces played a major role in preventing this by deploying a composite brigade under the command of Major General Dewan Prem Chand. The enforcement operations led to a significant military action in which the Indian contingent suffered thirty-nine fatalities.[15] Over a period of four years from 14 July 1960 to 30 June 1964, two Indian brigades were deployed in succession totalling 871 officers and 11,354 soldiers. It is worth recording that during this period India faced a major war with China (20 October to 21 November 1962) in which it suffered

[14] At http://hofars.com/public/project_page_disp.php?escort=54&wish_me_luck=e4505f67d496ff1ec1fae02ce276e0e1&escort_extend=30

[15] UN DPKO website at http://www.un.org/en/peacekeeping/fatalities/documents/StatsByNationalityMission_2.pdf

a serious reverse. Despite this, there was never any question of withdrawing the forces from the Congo and they remained there until the end of operations in 1964.

An important question that might have affected India's troop contribution to the UN at this time was the conflict over Jammu and Kashmir. This issue generated armed hostilities between India and Pakistan in 1947 and was referred to the UN by India, resulting in the enactment of a cease-fire from 1 January 1949 and deployment of a UN Observer Mission (UNMOGIP). India had expected that the UN would respond more forcefully to what it saw as Pakistani aggression. When this failed to happen, Nehru was severely criticized in parliament for referring the matter to the UN when the Indian Army seemed poised to secure a military victory. To date, however, this has not affected India's participation in UN peacekeeping operations. But, should there be any change in the situation there for whatever reason, this could have the potential to impact adversely on future participation.

The end of the Cold War brought about a veritable explosion of UN peacekeeping and with it increased demand for Indian peacekeepers. A good example was UNOSOM II in Somalia (1993–5). When the observers deployed under UNOSOM I could not stem the conflict and concomitant famine, disease, and pilfering of humanitarian assistance by rival militias, the UN adopted a more assertive mandate. This was first enforced through a US-led multinational force (UNITAF) and then through UNOSOM II. Indian peacekeepers were deployed in Somalia between August 1993 and March 1995. At the height of its commitment, the Indian contingent consisted of a composite force of a brigade group with additional supporting troops numbering about 5,000 soldiers under the command of Brigadier Bhagat. The Indian contingent also included a helicopter unit and for the first time a sizeable naval task force deployed off the coast of Somalia. The Indian troops were located west and south of Mogadishu and hence avoided some of the most vicious attacks by armed militias in the capital. But, long distances, difficult lines of maintenance, lack of effective central authority in the country, and intense factional and tribal fighting posed significant challenges to peacekeeping. The Indian contingent focused on humanitarian and developmental tasks in addition to trying to keep the peace. This was well suited to the role that the Indian Army was familiar with in countering insurgencies at home, and Indian peacekeepers contributed to the improvement of conditions in the areas to which they were deployed.[16] UNOSOM II posed a series of difficult challenges for its peacekeepers: there was no peace to keep and there were plenty of arms and hostile factions who had substantial combat experience. It was obvious

[16] Nambiar, *For the Honour of India*, pp. 255–77.

that UN peacekeeping had entered a new phase calling for a comprehensive review.

India was called upon to play a major role in several of the post-Cold War peacekeeping operations. As a matter of policy, it decided not to be involved in regions where other states had more pressing strategic interests and hence were willing to commit troops. The Balkans in the early 1990s was one such region and Yugoslavia posed another complication for India. Marshal Tito, socialist Yugoslavia's erstwhile leader whose death in 1981 began the country's spiral towards dissolution, had been co-founder of the Non-Aligned Movement and Yugoslavia enjoyed close friendly ties with India. New Delhi was neither asked nor wanted to get involved in Yugoslavia's disintegration. But, when UN Secretary-General Boutros Boutros-Ghali asked India for a competent and impartial senior general to head the force it readily agreed. Lieutenant General Satish Nambiar was thus sent as both the overall Force Commander and Head of Mission at UNPROFOR from March1992 to March 1993.[17] The general and his staff officer were the only two Indians in that mission. At the end of a year-long contract he declined an extension and returned to the Indian Army. Haiti was another example where the devastating earthquake of January 2010 required deployment of UN forces to maintain peace and facilitate development. Because of its distance from India and closeness to several states with significant military capacity, India decided that other neighbouring countries were better placed to commit troops and so refrained from contributing to MINUSTAH.

India continued to provide UN peacekeepers in Asia during the 1990s. In Cambodia, it contributed a battalion to both the UNAMIC (1991–2) and UNTAC (1992–3) missions. In Timor-Leste, India was initially unwilling to participate, fearing that the mission would lead to the secession of a part of Indonesia, a non-aligned country with whom New Delhi had good relations. However, with the mission enjoying Indonesia's consent, it later contributed two Special Representatives of the Secretary-General and observers to UNMIT from 2006.

10.2 PARTICIPATION IN TWENTY-FIRST CENTURY UN PEACEKEEPING: THE CASE OF SIERRA LEONE

The increasingly complex challenges faced by UN peacekeeping became evident in Africa at the turn of the century, where most of the new UN peacekeeping operations were deployed. Several states were undergoing difficult political and

[17] Author's interview with Lt. Gen. Satish Nambiar (Retd.), 12 March 2012.

economic readjustments leading to severe internal instabilities. Security forces in many parts of the continent were limited in numbers and in some cases lacked training, discipline, and equipment. In addition, Africa was largely underdeveloped with poor communication and infrastructure, posing severe challenges to troop deployment and sustenance. The sheer difficulty of the operating environments encountered may have been one reason why developed countries tended to stay away from twenty-first century UN peacekeeping operations in Africa, leaving the field almost entirely (with the notable exceptions of an Irish detachment in Liberia) to regional forces and South Asian troops.

Arguably India's most controversial engagement with UN peacekeeping during this phase was in the UN mission in Sierra Leone (UNAMSIL) between 1999 and 2002. The mission was mandated to help implement the Lomé Peace Accord and assist in the implementation of the disarmament, demobilization, and reintegration (DDR) plan. In the wake of Nigeria's withdrawal of its troops from the earlier ECOMOG mission (see chapter 11), a UN force of some 6,000 soldiers was authorized in October 1999. UNAMSIL was to include troops from Nigeria, Ghana, and Guinea 're-hatted' from the ECOMOG mission, some additional Kenyan soldiers, and a composite brigade group from India of about 3,000 soldiers.[18]

UNAMSIL did not get off to a good start with sporadic deployment and a number of contingents experiencing severe shortage of appropriate equipment. The two battalions from Nigeria and the one from Ghana, which had joined UNAMSIL from ECOMOG, lacked not only logistics and communications assets but also vehicles and basic military equipment: none of them therefore met the UN's self-sustainment requirements.[19] This was because under ECOMOG they were provided logistics support by an American company, Pacific Architects and Engineers, on contract with the UN, and when they became a part of UNAMSIL this support was withdrawn.[20] The Indian contingent loaned vehicles and communication equipment to these contingents.[21]

Despite the Lomé Accord, it soon became apparent that the Revolutionary United Front (RUF) in particular was unlikely to stick to its terms, especially the disarmament provisions. Consequently, in late April and early May 2000 as the UN stepped up its attempts to implement the disarmament programme,

[18] For an Indian perspective of these operations see Shalini Chawla, 'United Nations Mission in Sierra Leone: A Search for Peace', December 2000, at http://www.idsa-india.org/an-dec-00-10.html

[19] Eric G. Berman and Melissa T. Labonte, 'Sierra Leone', in William J. Durch (ed.), *Twenty-First-Century Peace Operations* (Washington, DC: US Institute of Peace Press, 2006), p. 170.

[20] Author's interview with Lt. Gen. Vijay Jetley (Retd.), 1 May 2012.

[21] Author's confidential interviews conducted at the Director General Staff Duties office with officers responsible for peacekeeping, February and March 2012.

violent confrontations between RUF fighters and peacekeepers occurred around several of the DDR camps, especially those that were closer to the diamond-rich areas dominated by the RUF. By mid-May, rebel forces had killed several UNAMSIL peacekeepers and taken hostage and confiscated the equipment of nearly 500, including the entire newly deployed Zambian battalion and a company of Nigerians in Kambia.[22] Kenyan contingents in Makeni and Magburaka were also encircled and running dangerously low on ammunition. By this stage the Indian troops were also suffering their own problems; most notably twenty-three Indian peacekeepers were detained by the RUF en route to the Indian contingent at Kailahun whose 200 troops as well as military observers from over a dozen countries were surrounded by RUF forces.

In response to these various challenges, Major General Vijay Jetley, UNAMSIL's Indian Force Commander, planned a rescue operation, which involved deploying the Indian Quick Reaction Company (QRC) to assist the Kenyans in Magburaka. He also dispatched the newly deployed Zambian battalion to relieve the Kenyans in Makeni. Unfortunately, the entire Zambian battalion of some 430 troops was unable to execute this task and was instead taken hostage by the RUF and relieved of their weapons and vehicles.[23]

In the wake of the hostage crisis a high-level assessment team, led by a former Assistant Secretary-General in the DPKO, Manfred Eisele, was dispatched to Sierra Leone. Although its findings were never publicly released, the UN Secretary-General later summarized them as confirming the dire state of UNAMSIL, including serious management problems in the mission and a lack of common understanding of the mandate and rules of engagement. The assessment mission also noted that some of UNAMSIL's military units lacked proper training and equipment.[24] Media coverage of UNAMSIL was also rather unhelpful as it often sought to blame the mission's weaknesses solely on the failure of individual troop-contributing countries rather than taking into account other political factors.

On 11 May 2000 a meeting was held at the UN to address the crisis and determine further action. The Indian representative urged the Council 'not to consider withdrawing as an option' and promised the rapid deployment of a second Indian battalion that would enable UNAMSIL to do what was necessary to reassert control over the situation. 'We must stay there for two reasons', he argued: 'First, because to leave now would be to abandon the people of Sierra Leone to a terrible fate, and second, because the credibility of

[22] Funmi Olonisakin, *Peacekeeping in Sierra Leone: The Story of UNAMSIL* (Boulder, CO: Lynne Rienner, 2008), pp. 54–8.

[23] Berman and Labonte, 'Sierra Leone', pp. 178–80.

[24] *Fifth Report of the Secretary-General on the United Nations Mission in Sierra Leone*, S/2000/751, 31 July 2000, p. 9. See also Berman and Labonte, 'Sierra Leone', p. 171.

the United Nations is at stake.' He further urged the Security Council to authorize the use of force but in a side-swipe at the deployment of British troops outside of UNAMSIL's command structure, he warned strongly against these non-UN troops taking military action in a theatre 'where peacekeepers are deployed'.[25] A week after this debate, UNAMSIL's strength was increased to 13,000 troops.

With requisite reserves in place by July 2000, Jetley responded to relieve the encircled UN forces. *Operation Khukri* was launched and succeeded in rescuing more than 200 UN troops held in Kailahun, inflicting major losses on the RUF, and resulting in only one UN fatality. This operation demonstrated conclusively that given the right mandate and adequately equipped troops, albeit with some logistical support from the UK, even UN peacekeeping operations in less than ideal conditions could still employ force successfully.

Not surprisingly the crisis generated tensions between the UN's political and military leadership even before a confidential report written by General Jetley in May 2000 was leaked to the international media in September.[26] In the report, Jetley accused senior Nigerian military and political officials of attempting to sabotage UNAMSIL by colluding with RUF rebels to prolong the conflict in order to benefit from Sierra Leone's illicit diamond trade. No evidence was provided for these allegations. Tremendous political damage was, however, done to UNAMSIL: Nigeria refused to place its peacekeepers under Jetley's command and the UN Secretary-General and Sierra Leone's President Kabbah tacitly backed the Nigerians. Under these circumstances Jetley offered to relinquish his appointment as force commander. The government of India took the view that faced with such deteriorating relations and having lost the full support of the UN but having completed most of the tasks set out for UNAMSIL in the Lomé Accord it could now disengage. It decided to withdraw its 3,000-strong contingent in September 2000 after giving three months' notice.[27] This development also prompted the departure of the Jordanian peacekeepers, with Amman citing the refusal of Britain to put its own troops under UN command as the reason.[28]

UNAMSIL demonstrated some of the considerable challenges of working with other contingents with different levels of training, capability, and rules of engagement, and varying perceptions of a mission's mandate. The experience was disappointing for India, but although it generated some short-term criticism it did not have any lasting adverse impact on India's commitment

[25] 'Secretary-General pleads with Council not to fail people of Sierra Leone, Africa', Security Council Press Release, SC/6857, 11 May 2000.

[26] Olonisakin, *Peacekeeping in Sierra Leone*, pp. 83–6.

[27] 'Sierra Leone Peacekeeping Crisis', *BBC News*, 22 September 2000, at http://news.bbc.co.uk/2/hi/africa/937080.stm

[28] John Hirsch, 'Sierra Leone', in David M. Malone (ed.), *The UN Security Council* (Boulder, CO: Lynne Rienner, 2004), p. 528.

to international peacekeeping. Throughout the first decade of the twenty-first century India consistently supported UN peacekeeping in Africa and Asia with substantial all-round force capability. Specific decisions, of course, remained subject to overall national interest and force availability, which was highlighted by India's decision, announced in 2010, to withdraw its helicopters from peacekeeping missions in the Democratic Republic of Congo (DRC).

As noted above, in late 2004, India had significantly increased its contribution to the MONUC force by deploying over 3,000 troops. India had also deployed helicopter units to the mission. By 2010, India had a total of seventeen helicopters—eight Mi 25/35 armed helicopters and nine Mi 17 medium lift helicopters—in the UN missions in the DRC and Sudan. Yet following a government announcement in mid-2010, these were withdrawn by July 2011 and weeks later were replaced by six light utility helicopters.[29] The official reason given by Manjeev Singh Puri, India's Deputy Ambassador to the UN, was that India needed its helicopters and their existing 'contract has ended'.[30] The real reason, however, was more to do with meeting India's internal security requirements, particularly in its struggle against Maoist rebels.[31] India is among the very short list of countries that do provide helicopters to UN peacekeeping, but it cannot continue to do so indefinitely especially when national interests call for their use at home.[32]

10.3 POLICIES AND PROCESSES FOR PEACEKEEPING TROOP CONTRIBUTIONS

While decisions about contributing to specific peace operations are influenced by the context of each mission, the principal underlying factors determining Indian participation have remained relatively constant during the period under review.

First, upon receiving requests, the Indian government imposes two tests: is there a peace to keep and is the Security Council committed to supporting the mission? India has tended to accept the judgement of the Security Council and has accepted its decision as conclusive evidence of the 'do-ability' of a mission.

[29] 'Indian helicopters back in UN peacekeeping', *Pragmatic Euphony blog*, 8 September 2011, at http://pragmatic.nationalinterest.in/2011/09/08/indian-helicopters-back-in-un-peacekeeping/

[30] 'India withdrawing helicopters from U.N.'s Congo mission', *The Hindu*, 16 June 2011, at http://www.thehindu.com/news/national/article2107605.ece

[31] 'No conspiracy to snub the UN', *Pragmatic Euphony blog*, 11 September 2010 at http://pragmatic.nationalinterest.in/2010/09/11/no-conspiracy-to-snub-the-un/

[32] For more details about helicopter utilization in UN operations, see Jake Sherman, Alischa Kugel, and Andrew Sinclair, 'Overcoming Helicopter Force Generation Challenges for UN Peacekeeping Operations', *International Peacekeeping*, 19:1 (2012), pp. 77–92.

It has also always considered a Security Council decision as sufficient legitimacy to warrant the provision of Indian peacekeepers. Though it generally prefers to deploy its forces with authorization from the UN Security Council, it has on one occasion (Sri Lanka in 1987) been prepared to dispatch peacekeepers on the basis of host state request alone.

Second, the government takes account of whether the proposed mission involves countries with traditional or friendly ties with India which may be a party to the conflict and whose interests may be directly or indirectly affected. Former Yugoslavia and Timor-Leste can be seen as areas where India did not find it convenient to participate initially. Third, the government considers whether there are any domestic religious or ethnic sensitivities that need to be taken into account. India is committed to secularism as state policy and its soldiers are multi-faith and ethnically diverse. It has the world's third largest Muslim population of around 150 million. Any fundamental clash with these values or where the interest of concerned groups may be directly or indirectly affected would need to be considered for their potential negative impact within the country. Though not specifically requested to contribute to peace operations in Iraq, Afghanistan, or the Middle East, these would come under the latter category and would be seriously examined.

Decisions about whether to participate in peacekeeping operations follow a set procedure that has evolved over time. Requests for troops are received from the DPKO by the Permanent Mission, India (PMI) at the UN in New York, which transmits this request to the Ministry of External Affairs in Delhi. Since late 2010 an army officer of the rank of colonel has been posted at the PMI. He is charged with simultaneously reporting this request to the Service Headquarters in Delhi and beginning planning and coordination with the UN DPKO, thus shortening the process of deployment and decision-making.

The political angle is simultaneously vetted and cleared at the foreign office in Delhi. This is a necessary first step even though no formal request has been turned down on these grounds in recent years. India has declined some requests to participate in non-Blue Helmet operations, perhaps most notably the request from Colombo in 2002 after the Tamil Tigers had captured the 'Elephant Pass' from the Sri Lankan army two years earlier, and from Washington, DC in 2003 to join the coalition forces in Iraq. Both cases were discussed informally in the Indian parliament and were turned down because they did not generate a consensus. India was also very reluctant to commit its troops to a potential UN peacekeeping operation or international stabilization force in Mogadishu, Somalia which was proposed by the Americans and UN Secretary-General in late 2008.

After the foreign policy clearance to participate has been granted, this decision is then conveyed to the Ministry of Defence where a tri-service joint board examines the proposal in detail under the Director General of Staff Duties (DGSD) at the Army Headquarters. Quite often preliminary consultation under the DGSD may be undertaken simultaneously in anticipation of political clearance. Each case is examined from the following perspectives:

- Political factors: does the proposed mission fit with India's national interests or further them? Are there any other issues of national concern affecting India's participation?
- Force availability and commitment: well-trained infantry and police contingents are available and can be spared if a decision is made, but this issue will still need to be specifically examined in each case.
- All aspects of participation are further examined in detail and ground reconnaissance carried out if required. Units selected and earmarked for deployment in advance are next sent to the Centre for United Nations Peacekeeping Operations near Delhi. Here they receive advanced orientation and training normally for three months before embarkation.
- Requirements for helicopters, naval ships, or specialist vehicles have to be assessed against domestic requirements. India does not have an unlimited number of these assets and domestic contingencies, such as natural calamities including floods or earthquakes, or internal disturbances have to be taken in to account. For obvious reasons, domestic requirements are likely to prevail. However, once committed to the UN these assets are rarely withdrawn (although see the episode described above in relation to the DRC).

In light of these discussions, the final decision on each UN mission is taken by a Cabinet Committee on Security based on a note prepared by the Cabinet Secretary. In India's parliamentary system, this means the ultimate decider is the Prime Minister and this decision need not be referred formally to Parliament. (With respect to India's participation in non-UN missions, however, the political climate is such that these would probably require parliamentary approval.)

Police forces have in recent years been a major element in India's contributions to UN peacekeeping. The procedure followed in their case remains the same except that the Home Ministry instead of the Ministry of Defence is the key ministry involved in the process. The Indian armed forces are prepared to contribute troops at short notice should these be required. Since 1993, through a memorandum of understanding with the UN, India has maintained a Standby Brigade Group for UN peacekeeping operations with a comprehensive all-round capability numbering 4,056 all ranks. An infantry battalion group is deployable within thirty days, and the remainder of the brigade within eight weeks after final clearance of troop deployment is received.[33]

[33] Author's interviews with senior officers of the concerned branch at the Army HQ in Delhi, 15 March 2012.

The benefits of this carefully laid out process for deployment are felt in three specific ways. First, it has made it unnecessary for parliament to constantly debate the issue of India's participation in international peacekeeping and has allowed the executive (i.e., the Cabinet) to decide. Second, by providing legitimacy to peacekeeping and its inclusion in the Indian Constitution as one of the legitimate responsibilities of the state, it has reduced the necessity for detailed deliberation. Third, it has simplified the procedure for obtaining approval. After a decision is made, an announcement is then normally made in the parliament as a *suo moto* statement by the foreign minister.

Issues related to international peacekeeping have occasionally been raised in parliament but these have usually concerned the timely payment of dues, welfare measures, and administrative issues. The Indian parliament has seldom challenged the legitimacy of India's participation under the UN flag, although it would be more likely to occur in situations where a prime minister headed a coalition government or had only a marginal majority. It can be questioned whether the absence of parliamentary debate strengthens India's political support to UN peacekeeping. Debate is not the only means of obtaining parliamentary sanction. As in most parliaments around the world, informal consultations, discussions at the foreign policy subcommittee level, and meetings between party leaders are some of the measures adopted in the Indian parliament to ascertain and build political consensus. Finally, should it ever be felt necessary, the opposition can always call for a debate in parliament through a notice to the Speaker. So far, a formal parliamentary debate on UN peacekeeping has never been required or called. However, in other situations, such as consideration for providing peacekeeping troops to non-UN operations, the government in power may find it necessary to seek parliamentary approval, as occurred in the two cases of Sri Lanka (2002) and Iraq (2003) noted above.

Politically, therefore, India's provision of UN peacekeepers has not been a contentious domestic issue. The armed forces have enjoyed considerable public support, which cuts across the national political spectrum. India's armed forces have always remained out of the state decision-making structure. Policies on defence are framed entirely by the civilian bureaucracy in the Ministry of Defence (MOD), to which no serving military officer has ever been deputed. The MOD of course almost always consults and receives military advice before a decision is taken. But, final government decisions are framed by the MOD and conveyed to the Services Headquarters for implementation. This procedure eliminates the potential of intervention by the military in direct policy formulation in the government.

10.4 INDIA'S RATIONALES FOR PROVIDING PEACEKEEPERS

There are multiple reasons why India provides UN peacekeepers. Unlike some other countries, India does not see UN peacekeeping as providing vital military training and experience for its soldiers and police. Indeed, it is notable that upon returning from UN peacekeeping operations, Indian soldiers go on leave for two months, reassemble, and then are sent on a year-long individual and collective training cycle before they are deployed for operational roles back home.

Arguably the main general rationales for Indian peacekeeping are normative and political and involve a commitment to maintaining international peace and security which is embedded in the country's Constitution. Over the years, India has come to accept that UN peacekeeping has had a major positive impact on India's image abroad and has helped to further its foreign policy objectives.

India has also used its strong peacekeeping credentials as a major justification for a larger role within the UN. India's official position in relation to the question of Security Council reform is that expansion should be based on normative criteria, especially principles of democratic representation. While New Delhi's financial contribution to the UN is relatively modest, its peacekeeping credentials are strong. This has emerged as one of the principal bases for India's bid for a permanent seat on a reformed UN Security Council. The Indian Foreign Secretary, Nirupama Rao, emphasized this at a speech at Harvard in the United States in 2010:

> In the United Nations system, there is today a majority view in favour of reform of the United Nations, and especially its major organs like the Security Council, which is responsible for collective peace and security. India has been at the forefront of this move, seeking an enhanced global role as a permanent member of the reformed Security Council, commensurate with its size, capabilities, contribution to UN peacekeeping operations and impeccable track record in upholding the UN system.[34]

The potential role of economic rationales is more complex.[35] Here it is useful to distinguish between economic benefits that accrue to the Indian national economy as a whole and those that accrue to participating individual members of the armed forces or police. India's annual GDP as of 2012 is US$1.7

[34] Address by the Foreign Secretary at Harvard, on 'India's Global Role', 20 September 2010, at http://www.indianconsulate.com/2PressAndPublicity/AddressbyForeignSecretaryatHarvard092010.pdf

[35] For a simplistic and misguided view see David Axe, 'Why South Asia loves peacekeeping', *The Diplomat*, 20 December 2010, at http://the-diplomat.com/2010/12/20/why-south-asia-loves-peacekeeping/

trillion.[36] Its defence budget for the fiscal year 2012–13 is US$40.44 billion.[37] The compensation that Indian forces might receive for equipment use, though varying enormously year to year depending on equipment (particularly helicopters) provided and its utilization and allowances for peacekeeping personnel, comes to about two hundred million dollars a year.[38] Besides the laborious procedure and inevitable delay—sometimes of several years before payments are realized—the operational costs of UN peacekeeping have prompted questions in India's parliament about whether the country should continue financing these operations. For example, in reply to a question in parliament on 30 November 2011, India's Minister of State for External Affairs acknowledged that a total of approximately US$52.40 million in UN reimbursements was outstanding, of which US$15.24 million was for troop and police costs and US $37.16 million for the cost of equipment.[39]

The UN's compensation rates to individual participants do benefit Indian soldiers and police officers and this is still a significant motivating factor for them. But, the impact of compensation is diminishing. The UN per diem rates were fixed in 1996 and have not kept pace with either rising costs or rising salaries in India. Moreover, with conditions inside the Indian Army improving significantly, deployments in places like Sudan and the DRC are becoming less attractive to Indian soldiers. Therefore, the effect of UN compensation on the motivation of individuals to become peacekeepers has to be understood in this context. The current monthly UN contribution rates are:

- $1,028 for pay and allowances for soldiers and a larger amount for officers
- $303 supplementary pay for specialists
- $68 for personal clothing, gear, and equipment
- $5 for personal weaponry.[40]

Indian military pay has twice been revised substantially since 1996 in keeping with both living costs and a growing economy. Unlike some UN troop

[36] World Bank data for 2012, accessed at http://www.google.co.in/publicdata/explore?ds=d5bncppjof8f9_&met_y=ny_gdp_mktp_cd&idim=country:IND&dl=en&hl=en&q=india%27s+gdp

[37] 'India's Defence Budget 2012–13', *IDSA Comment*, 20 March 2012 at http://www.idsa.in/idsacomments/IndiasDefenceBudget2012-13_LaxmanBehera_200312

[38] The calculations are based on very complex formulae for working out depreciation costs, helicopter flight times, scales allocated, etc. According to the author's discussion with the Pay and Accounts Branch of the MOD, this was an approximate annual figure for India over the last seven years.

[39] Lok Sabha Unstarred Question No.1561, at http://www.mea.gov.in/mystart.php?id=220218628. No details were provided as to the period for which these payments were due. The global shortfall of peacekeeping reimbursements on 31 March 2012 was US$2.18 billion. See http://www.un.org/en/peacekeeping/operations/financing.shtml

[40] Rates are as of April 2007 and they have not changed since then. 'How Peacekeeping Works', *BBC News*, 17 April 2007, at http://news.bbc.co.uk/2/hi/6524867.stm

Table 10.1 Indian and UN Peacekeeper Allowances (rupees)

	Indian pay and allowances	Additional UN allowance
Soldiers	20–30,000	52,000
Junior officers (JCOs)	40,000	80,000
Officers	75,000	110,000

Notes: Approximate and mean monthly pay in Indian rupees; exchange rate based on March 2012 @ 50 Indian rupees to one US dollar.

contributing countries, the Indian government does not deduct any amount for maintenance or miscellaneous from the UN allowances and pays its soldiers the amount in full when received from the UN. An approximate comparison of UN allowances and domestic pay per month—converted into Indian rupees at March 2012 exchange rate—is given in Table 10.1.

There is a variation in the UN daily compensation rate for military observers and staff officers. However, while unit personnel have their costs covered (accommodation, food, etc.), staff officers and observers bear their own expenses. In the countries of deployment these costs have risen fairly dramatically. After meeting these expenses, soldiers sometimes do not have a significant surplus.

The amount also fails to compensate sufficiently for prolonged absence from families and homes. Hence most troops from India now serve for six months at a time and are then rotated. Over a six-month period this does not constitute sufficient compensation to affect a soldier's motivation to serve away from home and family. At present only about 8,000 Indian soldiers serve at any one time in UN peacekeeping operations. This figure, when compared to the overall army strength of approximately 1,250,000, is about 0.7 per cent. Of the police participants the percentage serving in the UN is even smaller. Therefore, whatever financial gain an Indian soldier may receive, it accrues to a negligible number. Today, these conditions do not constitute a major incentive for the Indian armed forces and are not an important reason for participation in UN peacekeeping.

Finally, a major critique of participation that is gathering momentum in India is that increasingly UN peacekeeping is being viewed as a mission for underdeveloped countries to conduct but not one suitable for major powers or Western countries. It has been noticed in India that developed countries and permanent members of the Security Council are only willing to contribute forces to UN peacekeeping for a short duration and in very small numbers, unless they have other interests at stake. Where they have deployed in larger numbers, such as the UNIFIL II mission in Lebanon, they have pushed for special changes to be made to the UN's command and control structures. Among the P5 countries, China contributes the largest number of uniformed personnel to UN peacekeeping but still only about 2,000, i.e., a quarter or less of the number provided individually by Bangladesh, Pakistan, and India. This lends itself to the conclusion that as India becomes a great power it should become less inclined to contribute to UN peacekeeping, with some commentators already arguing that continued participation damages the country's international image by linking it to the category of less developed countries.[41] Indeed, in 2009, India argued in the UN Security Council that:

> There is no scarcity of the personnel and capacities of the type that the United Nations requires. There are enough troops, enough policemen, enough civilian experts, enough capacities and enough helicopters available to the international community. That is not the problem. The problem is that there is reluctance on the part of Member States to make these available to the United Nations.[42]

10.5 CONCLUSION

India has been a major and consistent participant in UN peacekeeping around the world since the 1950s and remains so today. This is unlikely to change in the near future. India has a very large pool of well-trained soldiers and police personnel many of whom can be spared for UN peacekeeping. Its procedures for participation allow for quick response to urgent requirements. The contingents India provides are well equipped, well led and are trained specifically in advance for the roles they are required to perform. Large numbers of senior officers from India have now played leading roles in UN peacekeeping missions or held senior appointments at DPKO. As long as the UN remains an effective body assuring peace around the world and enjoying global legitimacy, India can be expected to continue to make a major contribution of its uniformed personnel.

However, concerns about the direction of peacekeeping, political sensitivities around the Jammu and Kashmir issue, concerns about India's level of representation inside the UN, and the absence of developed countries from the peacekeeping rank and file could challenge this consensus in the future. Partly because of these concerns, India utilized its temporary membership of the Security Council in 2010–12 to initiate an open debate on the future of peacekeeping when it circulated a concept note titled *Peacekeeping: taking stock and preparing for the future.* Convening this session on 26 August 2011 during India's presidency of the Security Council, its Permanent Representative, Hardeep Puri, assured the Council of India's continued commitment to

[41] This is one of several comments that have begun to be articulated in policy circles in India in the last few years. See 'Time to abandon UN peacekeeping', *Pragatic Euphony blog*, 8 January 2008, at http://pragmatic.nationalinterest.in/2008/01/08/time-to-abandon-un-peacekeeping/

[42] S/PV.6153 (Resumption 1), 29 June 2009.

the ideals and goals of peacekeeping. But the special session also highlighted the many challenges peacekeeping currently faced around the world and proposed some means to address them. A principal theme was improving communications between the troop- and police-contributing countries, the UN Secretariat, and other stakeholders, so as 'to foster a spirit of partnership, cooperation, confidence and mutual trust and to ensure that the Security Council has the benefit of the views of those serving in the field when making its decisions about peacekeeping mandates'.[43] Convening the meeting was thus both an expression of India's continued support for UN peacekeeping operations and a signal about its principal areas of ongoing concern.

[43] The concept note is available at http://www.securitycouncilreport.org/atf/cf/%7B65BFCF9B-6D27-4E9C-8CD3-CF6E4FF96FF9%7D/PKO%20S%202011%20496.pdf

11

Nigeria

Adekeye Adebajo

Since its independence in 1960, over 150,000 Nigerian soldiers have been deployed to international peacekeeping missions, and the country has contributed troops to about forty major United Nations (UN) and regional peacekeeping missions in Africa, Asia, Europe, and the Middle East. In February 2012, Nigeria had 5,726 UN peacekeepers deployed in UN missions in Sudan's Darfur region, Liberia, Côte d'Ivoire, the Democratic Republic of Congo (DRC), South Sudan, Western Sahara, Haiti, Lebanon, and East Timor. This ranked it the fifth largest contributor after Bangladesh, Pakistan, India, and Ethiopia.

This peacekeeping activism has been part of a *Pax Nigeriana*: Nigeria's historical quest to pursue a hegemonic leadership role and to secure a permanent seat on a reformed UN Security Council. In addition, Nigeria's foreign policy has historically been guided by the idea of 'concentric circles'. The innermost circle represents Nigeria's own security, independence, and prosperity and is centred on its immediate neighbours—Benin, Niger, Chad, and Cameroon; the second circle revolves around Nigeria's relations with the Economic Community of West African States (ECOWAS); the third circle focuses on continental African issues of peace, development, and democratization; while the fourth circle involves Nigeria's relations with organizations, institutions, and states outside Africa.[1] In practical terms, Nigeria's diplomacy has often emphasized the importance of creating a 'zone of peace' in West Africa.[2]

This chapter explains Nigeria's peacekeeping contributions with reference to the three factors of culture, institutions, and individual decision-makers.

[1] See, for example, Ibrahim Gambari, 'From Balewa to Obasanjo: The Theory and Practice of Nigeria's Foreign Policy', in Adekeye Adebajo and Abdul Raufu Mustapha (eds.), *Gulliver's Troubles: Nigeria's Foreign Policy After the Cold War* (Scottsville: University of Kwazulu-Natal Press, 2008), pp. 58–80.

[2] Telephone interview with Segun Apata, Deputy Permanent Representative of Nigeria to the UN, 1999–2003, 13 May 2012.

Culture was important in shaping Nigeria's national identity and place in the world within the idea of *Pax Nigeriana*, as well as its self-image as a responsible regional hegemon. The key institution was the Nigerian military which shaped the advice provided to policy-makers but did not play a decisive role in this process. Rather, key individuals largely dictated Nigeria's involvement in peacekeeping activities, all of whom had military backgrounds, namely, Generals Ibrahim Babangida, Sani Abacha, and Olusegun Obasanjo. Although there was a political and military elite which shared some of the views of these three powerful individuals, I argue that their dominant and idiosyncratic role in policy-making was more important than official institutions or policies in determining Nigeria's peacekeeping role in the three most important UN missions in Sierra Leone (1999–2005), Liberia (2003–present), and Sudan's Darfur region (2007–present) on which this chapter will largely focus.

The chapter begins by setting out the types, challenges, and rationales of Nigeria's contributions to UN peacekeeping since 1960. It then explains the concept of *Pax Nigeriana* and highlights the role of three powerful generals in the country's participation in peacekeeping missions. While this book's focus is on the twenty-first century, it is important to provide a synopsis of the Nigerian-led ECOMOG (the ECOWAS Ceasefire Monitoring Group) operations in Liberia and Sierra Leone between 1990 and 1999, not least because they involved 368 and 50 UN military observers, respectively, led to the deaths of an estimated 1,500 Nigerian peacekeepers, and involved some $8 billion of national funds. These two missions laid the foundation for Nigeria's continued peacekeeping contributions to countries under the UN flag during the 2000s, and the subsequent extension of these efforts to Darfur in 2004. I then assess how, after 1999, a civilian Nigerian government under General Olusegun Obasanjo pushed for greater burden-sharing by the UN, insisting that the world body take over the ECOMOG mission in Sierra Leone and later the mission in Liberia. The chapter concludes by restating the main arguments of why Nigeria consistently contributed to UN peacekeeping efforts over five decades and analyses the implications of this role for future governments.

11.1 NIGERIA'S CONTRIBUTIONS TO UN PEACEKEEPING

Nigeria first contributed 5,000 troops and police (rotated over four years) to the UN peacekeeping mission in the Congo (ONUC, 1960–4).[3] Between 1978

[3] See Festus Ugboaja Ohaegbulam, *Nigeria and the UN Mission in the Democratic Republic of the Congo* (Tampa: University Presses of Florida, 1982).

and 1983, Nigeria contributed 7,000 troops (rotated over five years)—including a 100-strong naval contingent—to UNIFIL in Lebanon. This contingent was withdrawn by the civilian regime of Shehu Shagari following Israel's invasion of Lebanon. Nigerian troops also served on UN missions in India/Pakistan, Iran/Iraq, Iraq/Kuwait, Angola, Mozambique, Somalia, Cambodia, Yugoslavia, and Rwanda. Nigeria further deployed police contingents to Namibia, Western Sahara, Liberia, Sierra Leone, Côte d'Ivoire, Sudan, Burundi, Bosnia, Haiti, East Timor, Kosovo, and Afghanistan.[4] Three Nigerians have served as Special Representatives of the UN Secretary-General: Ibrahim Gambari (Angola and Darfur); Olu Adeniji (Central African Republic [CAR] and Sierra Leone); and Margaret Vogt (CAR). Six Nigerians also served as UN force commanders: Johnson 'Ironside' Aguiyi-Ironsi (the Congo); Chis Garuba (Angola); Chikadibia Isaac Obiakor (Liberia; and later Chief Military Adviser at the UN Secretariat); Joseph Owonibi (Liberia); Martin Luther Agwai (Darfur); and Moses Bisong Obi (South Sudan).

Nigeria provided UN peacekeepers initially because it wanted to play a leadership role in Africa, but UN missions also provided practical training for Nigerian soldiers and police. There have, however, been disagreements within the Nigerian military about whether peacekeeping enhances the professionalism of its soldiers or erodes their battle-readiness by involving them in 'police' duties.[5] Nigeria's contributions to UN peacekeeping have been consistent over the last five decades, the main change being the increase in police officers, particularly after the success of its police force in the UN mission in Namibia (1989–90). Its contribution of uniformed personnel to the UN in the twenty-first century is depicted in Figure 11.1.

Every Nigerian government since 1960—whether military or civilian—has supported the country's role in UN peacekeeping. Since Nigeria was under military rule for twenty-nine out of its fifty-two years of independent statehood, this group has often dominated decisions to deploy UN peacekeepers. Furthermore, General Olusegun Obasanjo served as an elected civilian leader between 1999 and 2007, meaning that leaders with military backgrounds effectively ruled the country for thirty-seven of fifty-two years. Three Nigerian heads of state—General Johnson Aguiyi-Ironsi (January–July 1966); General Yakubu Gowon (1966–75); and General Olusegun Obasanjo (1976–9 and 1999–2007)—were also part of the UN mission in the Congo, which was a

[4] See Julie G. Sanda, 'Nigeria's Global Role in Peacekeeping', in Attahiru M. Jega and Jacqeline W. Farris (eds.), *Nigeria at Fifty* (Abuja: Shehu Musa Yar'Adua Foundation, 2010), pp. 79–98; Ibrahim A. Gambari, *Nigeria at Home and Abroad* (New York: Chaneta International, 2007), pp. 295–311; and M. A. Vogt and A. E. Ekoko (eds.), *Nigeria in International Peacekeeping 1960–1992* (Lagos: Malthouse Press, 1993).

[5] Sanda, 'Nigeria's Global Role', pp. 88–9.

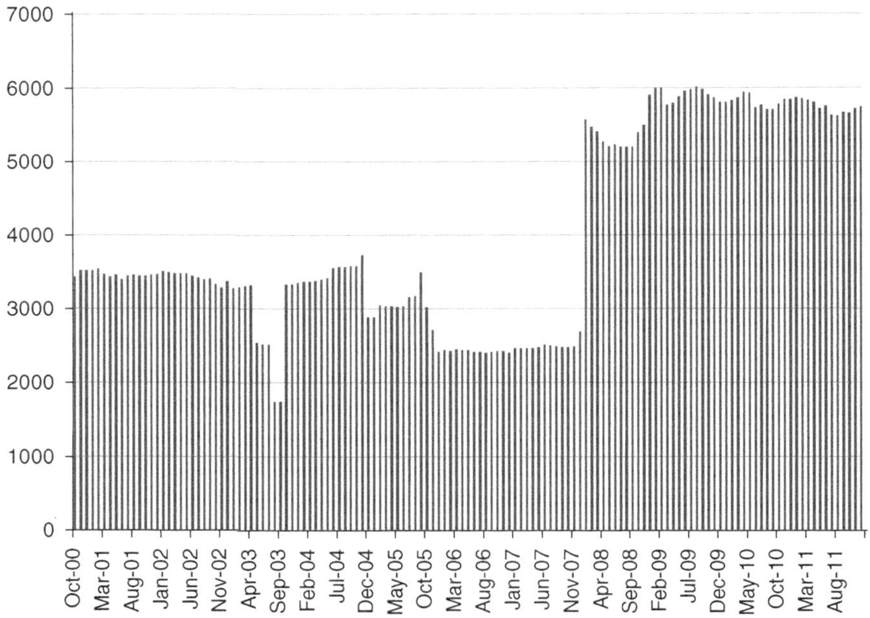

Figure 11.1 Nigerian Uniformed Personnel in UN Peacekeeping Operations, 2000–2011

formative experience that resulted in consistent support for these missions at the very highest political level.[6]

Nigerian governments have, however, been criticized for not incorporating UN peacekeeping into broader foreign and security policy goals in a coherent manner.[7] Critics have pointed to the lack of a strategic approach to peacekeeping and poor coordination between key policy-makers in Nigeria's ministries of foreign affairs, defence, and police affairs, which has led to a lack of a clearly articulated rationale of the national interest involved in UN peacekeeping. While Nigeria's prime minister under the First Republic (1960–6), Abubakar Tafawa Balewa, his cabinet, and the national parliament were directly involved in decision-making on deploying troops to UN

[6] See Chuks Iloegbunam, *Ironside: The Biography of General Aguiyi-Ironsi, Nigeria's First Military Head of State* (London: Press Alliance Network, 1999), pp. 42–57; J. Isawa Elaigwu, *Gowon: The Biography of a Soldier-Statesman* (Ibadan: West Book Publisher, 1986), pp. 35–6; and John Iliffe, *Obasanjo, Nigeria and the World* (Suffolk, UK and Rochester, NY: James Currey and Boydell & Brewer, 2011), pp. 14–15.

[7] Telephone interview with Joy Ogwu, Permanent Representative of Nigeria to the UN, 17 May 2012.

missions, Nigerian policy analyst Julie Sanda has noted that the decision-making circle has since become much smaller as a direct result of military rule.

Decisions on peacekeeping are usually meant to be taken by the Ministry of Foreign Affairs through Nigeria's permanent mission to the UN in New York, before being passed on to the Ministry of Defence. The defence ministry plays a technical role, receiving political guidance from the Nigerian foreign ministry.[8] It has been alleged that commitments on peacekeeping have sometimes been made by Nigeria's permanent mission to the UN without consulting the defence ministry. There is a high-level military adviser at the permanent mission in New York, but he reports directly to the defence ministry rather than to the permanent representative who serves as his host.[9] During Ibrahim Gambari's tenure as Nigeria's permanent representative to the UN (1990–9), he worked with the military advisers in New York who served as back-channels between the mission and the defence ministry.[10] The relationship between the permanent representative and the head of state in Abuja has also sometimes come into play. During the Nigerian deployment of troops to the UN mission in Somalia in 1993, UN Secretary-General, Boutros Boutros-Ghali, worked directly with Ibrahim Gambari to secure agreement for the deployment of Nigerian troops by telephone with General Ibrahim Babangida.[11]

Military officials are also said to have made decisions on peacekeeping deployments without consulting the police, while police officials have acted likewise, with all these decisions taken without proper political guidance. Nigeria's foreign ministry has thus not always been able to play the chief coordinating role in this process, and the National Defence College has sometimes been left to play this role by default.[12] Nigeria has historically been poor at inter-ministerial coordination.[13] Parliamentary oversight of the country's UN contributions is also weak due to a lack of expertise and research capacity within the national legislature, and the dominant role of the executive, particularly under the presidency of Olusegun Obasanjo (1999–2007). Others have criticized the lack of battle-readiness of the Nigerian military, with its obsolete weapons and an airforce cannibalized and grounded by the regime of General Ibrahim Babangida following its central role in an alleged coup plot in December 1985. Nigeria has been slow to modernize its weaponry

[8] Telephone interview with General Chikadibia Isaac Obiakor, former Force Commander of UNMIL, 12 May 2012.

[9] Interview with Joy Ogwu, 17 May 2012.

[10] Telephone interview with Ibrahim Gambari, Nigeria's Permanent Representative to the UN (1990–9), 18 May 2012.

[11] Interview with Ibrahim Gambari, 18 May 2012.

[12] I have relied for these points on Sanda, 'Nigeria's Global Role', pp. 92–5.

[13] Interview with Ibrahim Gambari, 18 May 2012.

and lacks the capacity to repair and service them, leading President Obasanjo to seek US support in professionalizing his army after 1999.[14]

By the time of the return to civilian rule in 1999, the Nigerian military was in a state of decay after nearly two decades of corrupt neglect and politicization which had eroded its professionalism. Plans announced in 1999 by then defence minister, General Theophilus Danjuma, to reduce the military from about 94,500 to 50,000 were shelved due to concerns about the socio-economic impact of demobilizing 44,500 soldiers with insufficient alternative employment prospects. The Army was also not short of trouble spots to police: nearly one-third of the army was being used during Obasanjo's first presidential term (1999–2003) for missions in Sierra Leone and the Nigeria/Cameroon border as well as in the Niger Delta and various parts of the country where conflicts resulted in an estimated 12,000 deaths between 1999 and 2007.

According to Nasir El-Rufai, in March 2012, the Nigerian military and police contingents in UNAMID could not meet 20 per cent of the needs of the contingent-owned equipment (COE) required by the UN, while less than seven out of forty-five Nigerian Armoured Personnel Carriers (APCs) in the mission were functional.[15] Less than 30 per cent of these APCs were serviceable.[16] The country also experienced similar problems with its APCs deployed in Liberia.[17] Nigeria was never able to meet the equipment needs in pre-deployment agreements signed with the UN Secretariat, causing much frustration in New York. More positively, Nigeria's National Defence College and its Army Peacekeeping School have incorporated UN standardized modules into their teaching curricula. Some critics have linked abuses by Nigerian peacekeepers abroad to the tactics adopted in quelling armed insurrections at home.[18] While such a crude link is unconvincing, the need for proper training of Nigerian soldiers deployed to foreign peacekeeping missions remains a major challenge.

In recent debates at the UN, Nigerian officials have pushed for greater coordination between the UN and African regional institutions such as the AU and ECOWAS as well as more predictable funding to support their efforts. They have also called for better coordination between troop-contributing countries (TCCs), the UN Security Council, and its Secretariat to ensure that troop-contributing countries are involved in the planning, review, reduction, and termination of peacekeeping missions. Nigerian officials have

[14] W. Alade Fawole, 'Militaries, Militias and Mullahs: National Security in Nigeria's Foreign Policy', in Adebajo and Mustapha (eds.), *Gulliver's Troubles*, pp. 108–11. See also Joy Ogwu, 'We Need a Doctrine on National Security', *The Punch* (Nigeria), 17 June 2005, p. 32.

[15] Nasir El-Rufai, 'Failing State, Fading Peacekeepers', *This Day* (Nigeria), 16 March 2012.

[16] Interview with Ibrahim Gambari, 18 May 2012.

[17] Interview with General Obiakor, 12 May 2012.

[18] See for example, J. N. C. Hill, 'Thoughts of Home: Civil–Military Relations and the Conduct of Nigeria's Peacekeeping Forces', *Journal of Military Ethics*, 8:4 (2009), pp. 289–306.

also supported both the civilian protection agenda and the notion of 'robust' peacekeeping.[19]

11.2 RATIONALES FOR NIGERIA'S UN PEACEKEEPING ROLE

There is no mono-causal explanation for Nigeria's decisions to provide peacekeepers. Politically, there is a belief that peacekeeping enhances Nigeria's national prestige and could strengthen its efforts to acquire a permanent seat on an expanded UN Security Council. There is also a widespread belief that peacekeeping is in Nigeria's national security interest. This was true for the key twenty-first century missions in Liberia, Sierra Leone, and Darfur, not least because two of them were in West Africa. Part of the official rationale, especially after the ECOMOG missions of the 1990s, was to have the UN share the burden of peacekeeping, thus, in a sense, helping to subsidize Nigeria's foreign policy aims.

In terms of economics, Nigeria lost more than it gained from UN peacekeeping missions, particularly during the 2000s, due to the poor quality of its equipment which deprived it of UN reimbursements. Nigerian soldiers and police increasingly lobby to be deployed on lucrative UN peacekeeping missions where their salaries are boosted, professionalism sometimes enhanced, and promotions can result from good performances. Certain members of the military chain of command have also reportedly benefited personally from UN reimbursements that were not paid to the treasury, but the country as a whole has not made a profit from these missions. Nigeria's soldiers, though, were receiving the entire $1,028 monthly allowance from UN peacekeeping missions in May 2012.[20] General Martin Luther Agwai, the Nigerian former military chief of staff, the former Force Commander of UNAMID, and former deputy Force Commander of the UN mission in Sierra Leone (UNAMSIL), has argued that the country should be capitalizing more on its contributions to UN peacekeeping. Noting that a few other countries were practically running their armies based on their investments in UN peacekeeping, Agwai argued that, if Nigeria kept ten APCs in Darfur (maintained to UN standards), it

[19] See, for example, Joy Ogwu, 'UN Security Council debate on Civilian Protection', S/PV.6354, 7 July 2010, p. 29; Joy Ogwu, 'Debate on the New Horizon report on Peacekeeping', S/PV.6178 (Resumption 1), 5 August 2009, pp. 18–19; Security Council 6427th Meeting, 22 November 2010, SC/10089; UN General Assembly, Special Committee on Peacekeeping Operations, 222nd and 223rd meetings, 21 February 2012, GA/PK/209; UN General Assembly, Special Committee on Peacekeeping Operations, 224th and 225th meetings, 22 February 2012, GA/PK/210; and UN Security Council, 6650th Meeting, 9 November 2011, S/PV.6650.

[20] Interview with General Obiakor, 12 May 2012.

could earn $720,000 annually, while a well-maintained battalion could fetch the country $14.4 million each year.[21] Though the UN is notoriously slow at providing compensation payments to TCCs, the views of this UN insider are worth carefully considering in terms of how some members of the military view peacekeeping as a wasted financial opportunity for Nigeria. Similarly, General Joseph Owonibi, the Nigerian former Force Commander of the UN mission in Liberia (UNMIL) lamented the fact that the UN's largest TCCs—Pakistan, Bangladesh, and India—were able to deploy troops within a month due to well-functioning national systems that led to these countries benefiting more from UN peacekeeping than Nigeria. This situation had not been remedied by May 2012 even as the defence minister, Bello Haliru Mohammed, announced that Abuja would deploy troops to Guinea-Bissau as part of a 600-strong ECOWAS battalion following a military coup there (it arrived in the country on 28 May 2012). Bello also talked of the possibility of deploying another ECOWAS mission to Mali following a military coup in that country.

Focusing on institutional rationales, as part of the belief in Nigeria's leadership role as a regional power, UN peacekeeping was traditionally supported by sections of the country's army, police, press, and public who have generally viewed the UN in a favourable light. This is in stark contrast to the ECOMOG missions in Liberia and Sierra Leone which were widely seen as profligate (even within sections of the military), and the AU Mission in Sudan (AMIS) which was also criticized as ineffectual. Confirming greater acceptance of the UN than regional missions, a 2006 poll of 1,000 Nigerians by Globescan reported that while 77 per cent expressed much or some trust in the UN and 17 per cent expressed not much or no trust at all, 58 per cent expressed much or some trust in the AU, while 34 per cent expressed not much or no trust at all in the continental body.[22]

11.3 THE ROOTS OF PAX NIGERIANA[23]

As the largest black state in the world with over 140 million citizens it is not surprising that Nigeria's foreign policy has exhibited a 'missionary zeal'—an enthusiasm that has claimed a special responsibility to protect, or at least speak on behalf of, black people in apartheid South Africa, pre-civil rights America, and contemporary Brazil (which has a large Nigerian-descended black population). The expression *Pax Nigeriana* was coined in 1970 by Bolaji

[21] Cited in Sanda, 'Nigeria's Global Role', pp. 90–1.
[22] Globescan, *Africa in the New Century* (Washington, DC, 2005 and 2006).
[23] This section draws on Adekeye Adebajo, *Liberia's Civil War* (Boulder, CO: Lynne Rienner, 2002).

Akinyemi, Nigeria's foreign minister between1985 and 1987, to describe the country's leading role in the founding of the Organization of African Unity (OAU). The concept can help explain the rationale behind Nigeria's operations in Liberia and Sierra Leone under the auspices of ECOWAS and the UN, as well as in Sudan's Darfur region under the auspices of the AU and later the UN.

In essence, *Pax Nigeriana* describes the country's ambition to play a political, economic, and military leadership role in Africa or on issues related to Africa. Politically, Nigeria has sought to exert its leadership at the UN and OAU as well as within the Non-Aligned Movement (NAM), and to speak loudest for African concerns. Militarily, it has sent peacekeepers to Congo, Chad, Liberia, Sierra Leone, Somalia, and Darfur, and provided military assistance to Tanzania and Gambia, as well as to liberation struggles in Southern Africa in the 1970s and 1980s. Economically, Nigeria has tried to exert its leadership through ECOWAS and also through its 'oil diplomacy', by providing economic assistance to its poorer neighbours.[24] These moves represent, in a real sense, elements of a historical 'responsibility to protect' doctrine in the country's foreign policy.

Pax Nigeriana is reflected in the utterances of Nigeria's soldiers, diplomats, politicians, journalists, and students, who seem to share a common belief in the country's 'manifest destiny' to take on special responsibilities as a regional 'big brother'. The metaphor of a benevolent older brother who is more experienced and thus responsible for protecting his younger siblings has often been employed in Nigeria's diplomatic and popular parlance.[25] However, the 'big brother' syndrome also smacks of paternalism and has often irritated the country's neighbours. Although smaller countries recognize the inevitability of Nigeria's leadership role, they often question its unilateral style. Nigeria's dominance of the ECOMOG military commands in Liberia and Sierra Leone remains a source of much unease in West Africa.[26]

Although *Pax Nigeriana* has not involved military expansionism, this is not to suggest that it is purely altruistic. Since its civil war between 1967 and 1970, Nigeria has sought to loosen France's neo-colonial ties in the region and to gain more security and larger markets for itself. But Nigeria's peacekeeping role in Liberia, Sierra Leone, and Darfur between 1990 and 2012 represents a form of long-term political, rather than short-term military, aggrandizement. The aim is not to win military control of these territories but to build long-term political and economic influence in Africa that can help promote Nigeria's security interests and help win a permanent seat on an expanded

[24] See, for example, Adebajo and Mustapha (eds.), *Gulliver's Troubles*.

[25] Interview with Sule Lamido, 'I Will Surprise My Critics', *This Day*, 8 August 1999, p. 10.

[26] Author's interviews with diplomatic and military officials in Burkina Faso, Côte d'Ivoire, Guinea, Liberia, Nigeria, and Sierra Leone, July–August 1999.

UN Security Council, as well as to fulfil a historical sense of responsibility as a regional 'big brother'.

A cultural analysis of the self-image held by the country's military rulers can help understand this rationale. Many of its leaders have a profound concern for their place in history and some have even tried to write this history themselves. Olusegun Obasanjo and the late Joseph Garba and Emeka Ojukwu have all written books about their own experiences. Ibrahim Babangida and Joshua Dogonyaro have authorized others to write their mostly laudatory biographies. Yakubu Gowon did both. Many Nigerian military officers see their institution as exemplifying positive values of self-discipline, camaraderie, honesty, and patriotism. They have also often seen themselves as guardians of national unity and integrity, with a responsibility to save the country from the decadence of corrupt politicians. However, the idea of honest military messiahs saving the country from decadent politicians appears threadbare in light of the staggering corruption witnessed during successive military administrations between 1984 and 1999, with an estimated $380 billion said to have been pilfered by the country's post-independence leaders.[27] The next section turns from the theory of *Pax Nigeriana* to its practice in the three peacekeeping cases of Liberia, Sierra Leone, and Darfur.

11.4 THE PRACTICE OF PAX NIGERIANA[28]

11.4.1 Nigeria in Liberia

In explaining Nigeria's role in Liberia's civil war, one is also explaining why the ECOMOG operation (1990–8) occurred, since without Nigeria's 12,000 troops (out of a total of 16,000), there would have been no ECOMOG. Nigeria was the only contingent whose withdrawal would have meant the end of the mission and had the capacity and resources to undertake the operation alone. However, Nigeria recognized the importance of involving other ECOWAS members in the mission in a subregion already profoundly suspicious of its hegemonic ambitions.

Most analysts have identified some combination of four main reasons for Nigeria's decision to intervene in Liberia: first, the Nigerian leader, General Babangida's close relationship with Liberian autocrat, Samuel Doe; second, the holding of Nigerian hostages by Charles Taylor's rebel National Patriotic

[27] 'Big Men, Big Fraud and Big Trouble', *The Economist*, 26 April 2007, p. 46.

[28] The next two sections on Liberia and Sierra Leone draw on Adekeye Adebajo, 'Mad Dogs and Glory: Nigeria's Interventions in Liberia and Sierra Leone', in Adebajo and Mustapha (eds.), *Gulliver's Troubles*, pp. 177–202.

Front of Liberia (NPFL); third, Nigeria's fear of Libyan adventurism in Liberia; and fourth, Nigeria's suspicion of French political motives and economic interests in orchestrating an anti-ECOMOG alliance.[29] On the first point, General Babangida was, in fact, condescending towards Samuel Doe and, having initially sent him arms to quell the rebellion, withdrew support from him as required by the ECOWAS peace plan. Doe was also killed within a month of ECOMOG's deployment in 1990 without a precipitate Nigerian withdrawal, suggesting other factors were at play. Regarding the second explanation, Nigeria could surely have simply evacuated its citizens (as it eventually did) and withdrawn its peacekeepers (which it did not). Nigerian diplomats familiar with this case dismissed the third explanation of fears of Libyan adventurism, as they did the fourth explanation of suspicions of the French, as Liberia was historically not part of its Gallic sphere of influence.

These explanations are therefore off the mark. More convincing explanations are found with reference to the cultural assumptions embedded in *Pax Nigeriana*. First, is the idea of *Pax Nigeriana* and Nigeria's leadership aspirations in West Africa; second, General Babangida's image of himself as a great leader and his desire to leave an indelible mark on Nigeria's history; and third, the aspirations of the Nigerian Army to enhance its status and prove its worth as a national and subregional asset. Thus Nigeria, Babangida, and the Army wanted to make history through the operation in Liberia. As Babangida explained, 'participation in ECOMOG fell in line with Nigeria's foreign policy over the past three decades'.[30] The changed international environment after the Cold War made the pursuit of *Pax Nigeriana* possible. With less external interest in Africa, Nigeria could intervene in Liberia where previously American interests would have made this impossible.

The second reason for Nigeria's participation was Babangida's self-image. Where every Nigerian military ruler had adopted the title of head of state, the unelected Babangida insisted on being referred to as 'President'; where every Nigerian military leader was *primus inter pares* in the ruling junta (Murtala Mohammed/Olusegun Obasanjo; Obasanjo/Shehu Yar'Adua/Theophilus Danjuma; and Muhammad Buhari/Tunde Idiagbon) or relied on other power centres like the civil service (Johnson Aguiyi-Ironsi and Yakubu

[29] See Ademola Adeleke, 'The Politics and Diplomacy of Peacekeeping in West Africa', *Journal of Modern African Studies*, 33:4 (1995), pp. 569–93; Stephen Ellis, *The Mask of Anarchy* (London: Hurst, 1999);Terry Mays, 'Nigeria's Foreign Policy and Its Participation in ECOMOG', in Karl Magyar and Earl Conteh-Morgan (eds.), *Peacekeeping in Africa: ECOMOG in Liberia* (Basingstoke: Macmillan, 1998); W. Ofuatey-Kodjoe, 'Regional Organizations and the Resolution of Internal Conflicts: The ECOWAS Intervention in Liberia', *International Peacekeeping*, 1:3 (1994), p. 273; Max Sesay, 'Civil War and Collective Intervention in Liberia', *Review of African Political Economy*, 23:67 (1996), pp. 35–52; William Reno, 'Reinvention of an African Patrimonial State: Charles Taylor's Liberia', *Third World Quarterly*, 16:1 (1995), p. 115.

[30] Quoted in Mays, 'Nigerian Foreign Policy', p. 112.

Gowon), Babangida, for a while, reigned supreme, shuffling even the most senior officers around like a pack of cards and dissolving the cabinet and Armed Forces Ruling Council at will.[31]

Having amassed more power than any other Nigerian leader at home, Liberia was to be Babangida's foreign policy showpiece. He adopted a 'hands on' approach to policy over Liberia, stamping his personal authority on decision-making, and exacerbating the already strained relationship with Charles Taylor rather than presenting himself as a statesman in contrast to Taylor's warlordism. The Nigerian Ministry of Foreign Affairs was merely an instrument rather than originator of policy, used as much or as little as was required, and no one in this key ministry knew how much Nigeria was spending on Liberia.[32] Babangida's quest for international recognition was clearly evidenced by his chairmanship of ECOWAS for an unprecedented three consecutive terms between 1985 and 1988, and his chairmanship of the OAU in 1991.

General Sani Abacha joined the Nigerian Army aged nineteen and established himself as an infantryman with training in Nigerian and British military institutions. He was involved in his first coup d'état in 1966, fought bravely to keep the country united during its civil war (1967–70), and was instrumentally involved in two further coups in 1983 and 1985, with the second eventually propelling him to the position of chief of defence staff and *khalifa* (king-in-waiting) to General Ibrahim Babangida.[33] He eventually took advantage of a weak, illegitimate interim government to seize full power following the annulment of elections by the military in June 1993. Although less articulate and more openly ruthless than Babangida, Abacha shared his predecessor's belief in Nigeria's regional peacekeeping responsibilities.

Most of the Nigerian military was excluded from decision-making on Liberia and many soldiers privately opposed the operation. However, some senior members of the Nigerian Army eventually became keen to prove their worth to a country that had long questioned its professionalism.[34] Prominent members of this elite bureaucracy wished to demonstrate that the Army was more than an avenue for coup-making soldiers to embark on political careers. As General Ishola Williams, who was Commander of the Nigerian Army's

[31] See Shehu Othman, 'Nigeria: Power for Profit—Class, Corporatism and Factionalism in the Military', in Donal Cruise O'Brien et al. (eds.), *Contemporary West African States* (Cambridge: Cambridge University Press, 1989), pp. 142–3. See also the excellent J. Bayo Adekanye, 'The Military', in Larry Diamond, Anthony Kirk-Greene, and Oyeleye Oyediran (eds.), *Transition Without End: Nigerian Politics and Civil Society Under Babangida* (Boulder, CO: Lynne Rienner, 1997), pp. 55–80; and Wole Soyinka, *The Open Sore of a Continent* (Oxford: Oxford University Press, 1996).

[32] Personal interviews, Nigerian Ministry of Foreign Affairs, Abuja, November and December 1995.

[33] See Ifeanyi Ezeugo, *Abacha: Another Evil Genius?* (Lagos: El-Rophekah International, 1998).

[34] Author's interviews with Nigerian military officers, Lagos, January 1997.

Training and Doctrine centre in Minna in 1990, put it, 'Nigeria is the superpower of the subregion.... Here you have a situation in which you do not want to lose face.'[35]

Before the Nigerian civil war (1967–70), the Nigerian Army had 6,000 soldiers, its Air Force had no frontline jets or airlift capability, and its Navy could not provide support for its Army. Babangida was determined to professionalize the Army and succeeded where many of his predecessors had failed in reducing the military from 140,000 to 94,500.[36] By 1990, the Nigerian military's Air Force had ninety-five fighter jets, including Hercules C-130s, Jaguars and Alpha jets, and had developed close air-support capability; the Army had two mechanized divisions, two light rapid deployment divisions, one armoured division, modern artillery pieces, anti-aircraft guns, fighting vessels, and 257 armoured battle tanks; while the Navy had acquired a flagship, a landing ship, a fast patrol craft, mine sweepers, and Lynx helicopters. The Nigerian military was also particularly concerned with developing its maritime capacity in order to defend its vulnerable offshore oil in the possible event of conflict.[37]

In the early 1990s, the Nigerian Army had sent troops on international peacekeeping missions with the UN in the Balkans, Lebanon, Kuwait, Western Sahara, Somalia, and Rwanda.[38] Seeking a permanent seat on a reformed UN Security Council to enhance Nigeria's self-image as a regional power and its desire for others to recognize it as such, Nigeria's military rulers wished to portray the country as a responsible global citizen. But there were also practical considerations behind the Nigerian military establishment's support for ECOMOG. As Adedoyin Jolaade Omede noted in 1995, 'It is felt within the Nigerian Army, that the ECOMOG mission will be used as a testing ground for both the effectiveness and viability of its arsenals and act also as a deterrent to any hypothetical enemy.'[39]

Having embarked on a twenty-year arms build-up fuelled by the oil boom of the 1970s, some senior members of the Nigerian Army were keen to test out both their new weaponry and the battle-preparedness of their troops: an estimated 75 per cent of Nigeria's soldiers in 1990 had not been involved in armed combat.[40] It was also felt that the intervention could help deter

[35] Author's interview with General Ishola Williams, 6 January 1997.

[36] Adekanye, 'The Military', p. 76.

[37] Brigadier R. M. Kupolati, 'Strategic Doctrines: Joint Operations', in A. E. Ekoko and M. A. Vogt (eds.), *Nigerian Defence Policy* (Lagos: Malthouse Press Ltd, 1990), p. 327.

[38] See Charles Dokubo, 'Nigeria's International Peacekeeping and Peacebuilding Efforts in Africa, 1960–2005', and Julie Sanda, 'Nigeria's International Peacekeeping Efforts outside of Africa, 1960–2005', both in Bola Akinterinwa (ed.), *Nigeria and the United Nations Security Council* (Ibadan: Vantage Publishers, 2005), pp. 205–92.

[39] Adedoyin Jolaade Omede, 'Nigeria's Military-Security Role in Liberia', *African Journal of International Affairs and Development*, 1:1 (1995), p. 51.

[40] Author's interview with a former ECOMOG officer, Lagos, 7 January 1997.

countries like Cameroon and Chad with which Nigeria had had clashes over disputed border areas. Senior members of the Nigerian Army, led by Babangida, thus staked their honour and professional reputation on success in Liberia. General Sani Abacha conducted the mission with similar determination between 1993 and 1998, also using Nigeria's leadership role to try to ward off punitive sanctions against his regime. This helps to explain Nigeria's determination to bring peace to Liberia even at great economic cost to itself at a time when the country had an external debt of $30 billion and against a growing tide of domestic public opposition.

Due to the importance of individuals in driving Nigeria's peacekeeping operations, it is important to describe the experiences that shaped Nigeria's third powerful general, Olusegun Obasanjo, who continued Nigeria's peacekeeping roles in Sierra Leone (1999–2005) and Liberia (2003–present) under UN auspices, and extended this peacekeeping role to Sudan's Darfur region in 2004.[41] Obasanjo had served as part of the Nigerian contingent with the ONUC mission (1960–4) and developed a strong anti-colonial outlook as a result. He was also a strong nationalist who believed fervently in Nigeria's unity and leadership role in Africa, having played a prominent role during the country's civil war between 1967 and 1970. These experiences were later captured in Obasanjo's self-aggrandizing *My Command* published in 1980.[42] After serving as military head of state between 1976 and 1979 and dispatching peacekeeping troops to Lebanon (under the UN) and Chad (under the OAU), Obasanjo sought to carve out a role as an elder statesman joining the Commonwealth Eminent Person's Group to South Africa in 1986. On assuming power as a civilian leader in 1999, he forged a strategic alliance with South African President Thabo Mbeki that helped to build the institutions and peacekeeping capacity of the African Union.[43] He assumed the African Union chair between 2004 and 2005 and adopted a strong focus on conflict resolution. Even after leaving power in 2007, Obasanjo served as the UN Secretary-General's Special Envoy to the Great Lakes region between November 2008 and June 2009.

Despite ECOMOG's peacekeeping presence in Liberia (1990–8), the lack of security sector reform and reintegration of ex-combatants into local communities, as well as Charles Taylor's autocratic rule and the transformation of his NPFL rebel movement into a private security force to protect his regime, eventually triggered the second civil war in a decade when Liberians United

[41] See Reuben Abati, 'Obasanjo: A Psychoanalysis', *The Guardian* (Lagos), 8 July 2001, p. 57.

[42] Olusegun Obasanjo, *My Command* (London: Heinemann, 1980).

[43] See Adekeye Adebajo, 'South Africa and Nigeria: An Axis of Virtue?' in Adekeye Adebajo, Adebayo Adedeji, and Chris Landsberg (eds.), *South Africa in Africa* (Scottsville: University of Kwazulu-Natal Press, 2007), pp. 213–35; and Chris Landsberg, 'An African "Concert of Powers"? Nigeria and South Africa's Construction of the AU and NEPAD', in Adebajo and Mustapha (eds.), *Gulliver's Troubles*, pp. 203–19.

for Reconciliation and Democracy rebels attacked Liberia from Guinea in 1999. The conflict threatened to spread across the subregion. After fighting between Taylor's government and rebels in June and July 2003 that killed an estimated 1,000 civilians in Monrovia, the warlord-turned-president was pressured by regional leaders and the United States to go into exile in Nigeria in August 2003. In the same month, a Comprehensive Peace Agreement was signed by all of Liberia's parties that called for the establishment of the National Transitional Government of Liberia under businessman Charles Gyude Bryant.

Under General Obasanjo's civilian regime, a Nigerian battalion deployed to Liberia shortly after Taylor's departure as the advanced units of a 3,600-strong ECOWAS mission in Liberia (ECOMIL). This became part of a UN peacekeeping mission, UNMIL, to which Ghana, Senegal, Mali, Benin, Gambia, Guinea-Bissau, and Togo also contributed troops.[44] Chastened by Nigeria's earlier difficulties in securing external financial and logistical support for ECOMOG in Liberia and Sierra Leone, Obasanjo agreed to deploy troops to Liberia in August 2003 on the condition that the UN took over the force three months later. The Security Council mandated UNMIL to support the implementation of the cease-fire agreement and peace process, to provide assistance for security sector reform, and to facilitate humanitarian and human rights assistance. By May 2004, 14,131 troops had arrived in Liberia with UNMIL's largest contingents coming from Bangladesh, Ethiopia, Nigeria, and Pakistan. While UN peacekeepers were able to avert the imminent bloodshed in Monrovia and to increase stability in the country, sporadic incidents continued throughout UNMIL's stay as did rampant corruption within the interim government.[45]

Although Liberia held elections on schedule in October and November 2005, won by Ellen Johnson-Sirleaf, a former Liberian finance minister and former head of the UN Development Programme's Africa Bureau, the Security Council wisely decided to maintain UNMIL's presence in Liberia and only gradually drawdown its troops. UNMIL peacekeepers helped to quell tensions involving ex-combatants in Maryland, Nimba, Grand Cape Mount, and Grand Geddeh counties between 2008 and 2009, as well as religious violence in Lofa county in 2010. Tensions remained over the trial of Charles Taylor for war crimes in Sierra Leone (for which he was convicted in 2012 for helping Revolutionary United Front rebels), and between members of the Armed Forces of Liberia and the national police, and widespread youth

[44] The presence of ECOWAS and US troops was authorized by UN Security Council resolution 1497, 1 August 2003. UNMIL was established by Security Council resolution 1509, 19 September 2003.

[45] See, for example, Comfort Ero, 'UN Peacekeeping in West Africa', in Adekeye Adebajo (ed.), *From Global Apartheid to Global Village* (Scottsville: University of KwaZulu-Natal Press, 2009), pp. 283–304.

unemployment remained. UNMIL also had to cope with the arrival of some 100,000 refugees fleeing instability following Côte d'Ivoire's post-election crisis in March and April 2011. And in October 2011, Johnson-Sirleaf won a controversial election process shortly after being awarded the Nobel Peace Prize. Nigerian peacekeepers played an important role in calming tensions in Monrovia during the election period, though some of their protective equipment that should have arrived to assist the electoral process never did.[46] Once again, this underlined the lack of effective management and degraded state of the country's military. By April 2012, Nigeria contributed 1,577 of UNMIL's 7,922 peacekeepers. The pride that the country took in its contributions to this mission was expressed by General Chikadibia Isaac Obiakor, the Nigerian Force Commander of UNMIL (2006–8), who noted that 'The Nigerian contingent has carved its name in gold in Liberia.'[47]

11.4.2 Nigeria in Sierra Leone

Nigeria provided 12,000 of 13,000 troops in the ECOMOG operation in Sierra Leone (1998–9), and its treasury released nearly $400 million a year for the mission. Seven main arguments have been commonly advanced to explain Nigeria's presence in Sierra Leone: first, Nigeria's domineering ambitions to control West Africa; second, its desire to protect President Ahmed Tejan Kabbah's regime in Freetown; third, its desire to protect General Lansana Conté's regime in Conakry; fourth, its bid to prevent an alliance of warlords in the three Mano river states of Sierra Leone, Liberia, and Guinea; fifth, its need for a strategic presence in this corner of West Africa; sixth, the desire of Nigeria's soldiers to profit from Sierra Leone's diamonds; and finally, General Sani Abacha's need to avoid domestic instability and a threat to his regime by diverting his soldiers to another peacekeeping mission. Once again, more convincing explanations for Nigeria's role in Sierra Leone flowed from the cultural dimensions of *Pax Nigeriana*.

Many observers have erroneously described ECOMOG as simply a vehicle for the pursuit of Nigeria's parochial interests in West Africa.[48] Most scholars have also ignored or underplayed the fact that many ECOWAS states were grateful to Nigeria for its sacrifices in an attempt to restore stability to the subregion. Several ECOWAS states, particularly Guinea and Liberia, which

46 Confidential interview.

47 Interview with General Obiakor, 12 May 2012.

48 Eric Berman and Katie Sams, *Peacekeeping in Africa* (Geneva: UN Institute for Disarmament Research, 2000), p. 25; 'Nigeria Imperatrix', *The Economist*, 7 June 1997, p. 50; and Robert Mortimer, 'From ECOMOG to ECOMOG II', in John Harbeson and Donald Rothschild (eds.), *Africa in World Politics* (Boulder, CO: Westview Press, 3rd edn., 2000), p. 188.

shared common borders with Sierra Leone, had far more of an interest in stabilizing the situation than Nigeria. Even Charles Taylor, who had been fuelling Sierra Leone's war by backing the rebels, eventually realized the importance of secure borders after incursions into Liberia by rebels from Guinea in April 1999.

Others have failed to elaborate Nigeria's concrete interests in Sierra Leone and to assess whether Nigeria actually lost or gained from the operation. Nor did they separate the parochial and self-serving interests of General Abacha from Nigeria's broader interests. If ECOMOG was indeed simply an instrument of Nigeria's domineering foreign policy to control West Africa, one would have expected subsequent Nigerian leaders to continue the country's commitments in Sierra Leone. Surely, imperial interests do not simply disappear with the advent of a new regime. But both General Abdulsalaam Abubakar (1998–9) and Obasanjo's civilian regime (1999–2007) preferred to cut Nigeria's losses and withdraw most of their troops from a protracted and costly civil war, before handing the mission over to the UN.

Three main factors explain Nigeria's involvement: first, the mission represented Nigeria's historic quest for leadership in its own subregion; second, it helped Nigerian leader, General Abacha, ward off the threat of severe international sanctions against his regime; and third, some of Nigeria's generals personally benefited from revenues written off as ECOMOG expenses.

As in Liberia, many of Nigeria's generals were pursuing their historic quest for *Pax Nigeriana* in Sierra Leone as part of a cultural mission to bolster the country's self-image as a regional power. As General Abdulsalaam Abubakar noted, 'Nigeria can claim a fair share of the glory for peace that is enjoyed in Sierra Leone today.'[49] In a similar guise, General One Mohammed, ECOMOG's Nigerian chief of staff in Sierra Leone, argued 'We had to put out the fire in order to stop it from extending to our own houses.'[50]

General Abacha was also attempting to break his diplomatic isolation by demonstrating his regime's indispensability to peacekeeping in a region that most Western states sought to avoid. They were thus thankful for Nigeria's sacrifices. Finally, by restoring democracy to Sierra Leone, Abacha and his generals could continue to make billions of dollars from supposed ECOMOG expenses charged to Nigeria's treasury. The staggering level of corruption under the Abacha regime, involving billions of dollars, was subsequently exposed by the two regimes that followed—with Abacha's family forced to return $700 million (out of a reported $3 billion) from Swiss bank accounts in August 2006.[51]

[49] Quoted in Sanda, 'Nigeria's Global Role', p. 89.

[50] Quoted in Berman and Sams, *Peacekeeping in Africa*, p. 26 footnote 173.

[51] See, for example, M. Chris Alli, *The Federal Republic of Nigerian Army* (Lagos: Malthouse Press, 2001); and Agwuncha Arthur Nwankwo, *Nigeria: The Stolen Billions* (Enugu: Fourth Dimension, 1999).

Nigeria intervened in Sierra Leone to restore Kabbah to power in 1998, not just because General Abacha regarded him as a 'staunch ally', but due to the Nigerian leader's need to break his diplomatic isolation, amidst limited sanctions imposed on Nigeria by the US, the Commonwealth, and the European Union. Abacha also sought to burnish his image by maintaining stability in, and restoring democratic rule to, Sierra Leone. International opinion was strongly opposed to the military coup in Freetown in 1997, and Britain, in particular, encouraged the ousting of the military regime. Nigeria also had commercial interests with the Kabbah regime: Sierra Leone's oil refinery had been sold to the Nigerian National Petroleum Corporation, and there were persistent rumours of diamond deals between Abuja and Freetown, which some analysts saw as too lucrative to surrender.[52] But Abacha could simply have cut a deal with the military officers who had toppled Kabbah in order to protect these interests. Nigeria had, after all, continued to support two military regimes in Sierra Leone between 1992 and 1996.

Both ECOMOG missions between 1990 and 1998 were, therefore, undertaken by powerful, idiosyncratic military rulers—Generals Babangida and Abacha—for similar reasons. Babangida, who was keen on leaving a historical legacy, sought to achieve military glory for himself and his country. Abacha, whose soldiers had successfully helped disarm Liberia's factions and who, as ECOWAS chairman, had played a prominent part in Liberia's disarmament and elections between 1996 and 1997, was keen to portray himself as a promoter of peace and democracy in his subregion, despite the ironies involved in retarding democracy in Nigeria. Abacha sought to break out of his diplomatic isolation while simultaneously believing that Nigeria should live up to its subregional commitments. Nigeria had signed a military agreement with the Kabbah government pledging to provide it with military assistance. Both ECOMOG operations were essentially children of circumstances, born out of the desire of two strong-willed Nigerian autocrats to further their own personal ambitions, while burnishing Nigeria's leadership aspirations in West Africa.

During presidential elections in Nigeria in 1999, all the candidates called for Nigeria's withdrawal from Sierra Leone. Three months after taking office in August 1999, Nigeria's new president, General Obasanjo, wrote to Ghanaian UN Secretary-General Kofi Annan, informing him of his country's intention to withdraw 2,000 of its peacekeepers from Sierra Leone every month. Obasanjo, however, offered to subsume some of Nigeria's 12,000 troops under a new UN mission.[53] He began the phased withdrawal on 31 August 1999 and suspended the process only after a plea by Sierra Leonean President Ahmed

[52] See, for example, Berman and Sams, *Peacekeeping in Africa*, p. 26.

[53] Eighth Report of the Secretary-General on the UN Observer Mission in Sierra Leone, S/1999/1003, 23 September 1999, p. 6.

Tejan Kabbah and Annan not to leave a security vacuum in Sierra Leone. As Obasanjo noted during an address to the UN General Assembly in September 1999, 'For too long, the burden of preserving international peace and security in West Africa has been left almost entirely on the shoulders of a few states in our subregion . . . Nigeria's continual burden in Sierra Leone is unacceptably draining Nigeria financially. For our economy to take off, this bleeding has to stop.'[54] Obasanjo, unlike Babangida and Abacha, now faced pressure from an elected parliament and from within his own ruling People's Democratic Party to end the lavish spending abroad and focus resources closer to home. Unlike Babangida and Abacha, Obasanjo could not ignore a hostile press and public opinion that had been consistently critical of the ECOMOG expenses.

Nigeria's withdrawal pressured the Security Council to authorize a UN peacekeeping mission in Sierra Leone (UNAMSIL) in October 1999 to take over from ECOMOG. Obasanjo rejected a UN Security Council proposal that ECOMOG continue to protect Freetown and undertake enforcement actions against rogue rebel elements, in part because this might leave ECOMOG as a useful scapegoat if things went wrong in Sierra Leone and in part because of the challenges of maintaining two peacekeeping missions in the country with different mandates, commands, and conditions of service.[55] The UN Secretariat turned down ECOMOG's request for the Security Council to finance the entire ECOMOG force, though about 4,000 West African peacekeepers were subsumed into UNAMSIL. The UN's Department of Peacekeeping Operations (DPKO) in New York was also unhappy about the presence of Nigerian peacekeepers, as many officials insisted on a reduced Nigerian role while overselling the new UN mission to Sierra Leoneans who were told that the Blue Helmets would be prepared to fight the country's rebels.[56]

In order to fill the vacuum left by the departure of Nigerian peacekeepers, UNAMSIL was expanded to 12,455 troops by December 2000, of which roughly a quarter were Nigerian. Other key contingents came from India, Jordan, Kenya, Bangladesh, Guinea, Ghana, and Zambia. The mission was eventually expanded to 17,500 peacekeepers. Oluyemi Adeniji, a Nigerian diplomat who had served as the UN Special Representative in the Central African Republic, was appointed as the UN Special Representative in Sierra Leone. This appointment compensated Nigeria for not gaining the Force

[54] Olusegun Obasanjo, 'Nigeria, Africa and the World in the next Millennium', address at the 54th Session of the UN General Assembly, 23 September 1999, reproduced in U. Joy Ogwu and W. O. Alli (eds.), *Years of Reconstruction: Selected Foreign Policy Speeches of Olusegun Obasanjo* (Lagos: Nigerian Institute of International Affairs, 2007), p. 40. (The second part of this quote is missing from the version in this book which differs slightly from the original speech obtained from Nigeria's permanent mission to the UN in New York.)

[55] James Jonah, 'The United Nations', in Adekeye Adebajo and Ismail Rashid (eds.), *West Africa's Security Challenges* (Boulder, CO: Lynne Rienner, 2004), p. 330.

[56] Jonah, 'The United Nations', p. 331.

Commander position that Obasanjo had wanted, but which had been strongly resisted within the UN Secretariat and Security Council and was given to India.[57] (Adeniji later went on to be Obasanjo's trusted foreign minister between 2003 and 2006, ensuring a strong pro-UN peacekeeping voice within the cabinet.)

Despite Nigeria's reduction of troops, following various challenges that UNAMSIL faced at the hands of the Revolutionary United Front rebels, it agreed to some of its soldiers forming part of a 3,000-strong ECOWAS rapid reaction force to bolster the UN force. About 500 UN peacekeepers were held hostage in May 2000 before a brief British intervention stiffened the resolve of the UN mission which adopted a more aggressive stance towards the rebels. Nine UN peacekeepers died as a result of these missions, including seven Nigerians.[58] With the end of the civil war in early 2002, the completion of the UN's disarmament programme for 72,000 Sierra Leonean combatants, and Kabbah's landslide re-election as President in May 2002, UNAMSIL began to withdraw. In September 2004, UNAMSIL completed the transfer of primary responsibility for maintaining peace and security to the government of Sierra Leone, and by December 2005 the mission was brought to a close.

11.4.3 Nigeria in Sudan's Darfur Region[59]

In the Darfur case, General Obasanjo, who served as AU chair between 2004 and 2005, was the main driver of Nigeria's decision to provide peacekeepers; first to an AU mission, and later as part of an AU–UN hybrid force. As international attention on the war and human suffering in Darfur increased in early 2004, Nigeria became involved for both military and diplomatic reasons. Following a cease-fire negotiated in N'Djamena between all sides in April 2004, the AU sent sixty military observers and a 300-strong protection force to keep the observers safe. Nigerian and Rwandan troops made up the bulk of the personnel in what was known as AMIS I. Abuja adopted the AU—and UN—approach that, though crimes were being committed in Darfur, they did not constitute 'genocide'.

An expanded AU mission in Darfur (AMIS II), again composed mainly of soldiers from Nigeria and Rwanda, was authorized by the AU Peace and Security Council in October 2004. This included civilian police units to protect displacement camps, with the UN dispatching a handful of human rights

[57] Jonah, 'The United Nations', p. 330.

[58] See Trevor Findlay, *The Use of Force in UN Peace Operations* (Oxford: Oxford University Press, 2002), pp. 296–314; and Funmi Olonisakin, *Peacekeeping in Sierra Leone: The Story of UNAMSIL* (Boulder, CO: Lynne Rienner, 2008).

[59] This section builds on Adekeye Adebajo, *UN Peacekeeping in Africa* (Boulder, CO: Lynne Rienner, 2011), pp. 202–16.

monitors. The mission's mandate was to monitor and observe compliance with the cease-fire, build confidence among the parties, help establish a secure environment to deliver humanitarian relief, facilitate the return of internally displaced persons (IDPs) to their homes, and contribute to improving security in Darfur.

In 2005, based largely on the recommendations of an AU-led assessment mission to Darfur, the force was increased to 6,170 military personnel and 1,560 civilian police.[60] Its mandate was expanded to protecting civilians in areas in which it was deployed. By this stage AMIS had a Nigerian Force Commander, General Festus Okonkwo, while a Nigerian diplomat, Baba Gana Kingibe, served as the AU Special Representative in Darfur.

In practice, however, AMIS II was hampered by a failure to devise a sound logistics plan; weak capacity for financial management; lack of vehicles, furniture, oil, stationery, and communication equipment; bureaucratic red tape; lack of strategic intelligence and a clear mandate to use force; lack of relevant linguistic and driving skills; and difficulties with securing accommodation. The United States, Britain, the Netherlands, and Canada assisted AMIS with meals, accommodation, vehicles, and helicopters, though not to the required extent.

Nigeria also played a leading role in a joint commission involving the Sudanese parties, the AU, the UN, and regional governments which continued to meet regularly to seek implementation of countless peace accords, all of which failed. Seven rounds of inter-Sudanese peace talks were held in the Ethiopian capital of Addis Ababa and then mostly in the Nigerian capital of Abuja between 2004 and 2006, many of them while Nigerian President Obasanjo chaired the AU.[61] The Abuja talks eventually produced the Darfur Peace Agreement (DPA) signed in May 2006, but only by the government in Khartoum and the rebel faction headed by Minni Minnawi. The atmosphere at the talks was not helped by President Obasanjo's scolding of the rebels like a hectoring schoolmaster. Unsurprisingly, the DPA accord collapsed almost immediately.[62]

By July 2007, after discussing various forms of assistance packages to AMIS, the UN Security Council and the new UN Secretary-General, Ban Ki-moon, supported the idea of an AU–UN hybrid force which would retain an 'African character' to assuage the concerns of Omar al-Bashir's government in Khartoum. Ban sought to confirm Khartoum's acceptance of the refined three-

[60] See Cdr. Seth Appiah-Mensah, 'AU's Critical Assignment in Darfur: Challenges and Constraints', *African Security Review*, 14:2 (2005), pp. 7–21.

[61] See Dawit Toga, 'The African Union Mediation and the Abuja Peace Talks', in Alex de Waal (ed.), *War in Darfur and the Search for Peace* (Cambridge, MA: Harvard University Press, 2007), pp. 214–44.

[62] For an insider perspective of the peace talks, see Alex de Waal, 'Darfur: The Inside Story', *NewAfrican*, 461 (April 2007), pp. 28–33.

phase UN support of AMIS: first, the provision of a small number of advisers; second, the delivery of a 'heavy' support package to AMIS involving 2,250 military personnel, three police units, as well as transport and engineering units, aircraft, and helicopters; and, third, the deployment of a full hybrid force, UNAMID, with an authorized strength of 26,000 peacekeepers. UNAMID officially took over from AMIS in early 2008. Nigeria's respected former deputy UN Force Commander in Sierra Leone, General Martin Luther Agwai, was appointed UNAMID's Force Commander, arriving in the mission area in July 2007. UNAMID's main mandate was to oversee the implementation of the Nigerian-brokered Darfur Peace Agreement of May 2006 and to protect civilians.[63] Its main contingents were retained from AMIS, namely, four battalions each from Nigeria and Rwanda; one each from South Africa and Senegal; and additional troops from Ethiopia, Egypt, Burkina Faso, Gambia, Tanzania, Sierra Leone, as well as Bangladesh, Nepal, China, and Thailand. Nigeria had the largest contingent in the mission with 3,322 troops in February 2012 (out of 23,287 uniformed personnel) as well as a military hospital. In recognition of Nigeria's large contributions to UNAMID, in January 2010, Ibrahim Gambari was appointed as the UN Special Representative in Darfur.

There were rarely any public debates within Nigeria over the domestic costs of the Darfur mission. In a June 2005 poll of 10,809 people (including 1,300 Nigerians) in eight African countries published by Globescan, no Nigerian respondent cited Darfur as being one of the major problems facing the world, while only 8 per cent of Nigerians polled claimed great knowledge of the Darfur conflict, 16 per cent a fair amount, and 60 per cent had heard not very much or nothing at all about the conflict.[64] There were press reports of the seven Nigerians killed in Haskanita in October 2007 and the then Chief of Defence Staff, General Andrew Azazi, paid tribute to the men who were described as 'gallant soldiers who died in the pursuit of peace in Africa'. Then president, Umaru Yar'Adua, also sent a message read at their funeral, pledging Nigeria's commitment to regional peace and security especially in West Africa.[65] The deaths of twenty-nine Nigerian peacekeepers in Darfur have, however, rarely elicited major debates in the country's media and among its opinion-shapers, and the fact that the UN effectively took over funding of the mission from the AU by late 2007 has made the mission an easier financial and logistical burden to bear. Much of the information on Darfur remains within a very small group of defence experts, and even senior politicians and

[63] UN Security Council resolution 1769, 31 July 2007.
[64] World Public Opinion, *Africa in the New Century*.
[65] Juliana Taiwo, 'Nigeria: Tears As Soldiers Killed in Darfur Get Heroic Burial', *This Day* (Nigeria), 6 October 2007.

members of the general public do not seem to realize the level of Nigeria's peacekeeping commitment there.[66]

The lack of sustained debate on the Darfur mission continued under the presidency of Goodluck Jonathan (2010–present). This was potentially damaging to the country as the performance of the four Nigerian battalions in Darfur was increasingly seen as poor. In January 2012, the arms and four vehicles of a Nigerian platoon in Darfur were stolen from them by local militias without any resistance. A month later, a similar incident saw Nigerian peacekeepers being disarmed.[67] The equipment of Nigerian peacekeepers in Darfur had also become so degraded that by May 2012 there was talk of withdrawing one of the country's battalions from the country due to poor performance. These challenges were related to the increasing politicization of the Nigerian Army with constant rotation of senior military officials which negatively affected its professionalism. Many senior members of Nigeria's armed forces were themselves particularly unhappy with the country's poor performance in Darfur. There were continuing reports of procurement of equipment being riddled with mismanagement and corruption and a lack of proper oversight, leading to the wrong types of equipment being sent or no equipment at all.[68]

Some action was taken to address these problems by May 2012. Following consistent prodding by Ibrahim Gambari during his visits to Abuja, a team was sent to repair some of this equipment, with spare parts also flown to Darfur. The UN DPKO was invited to help assess Nigeria's pre-deployment training in order to improve the situation of its under-performing troops. Part of the problem was also that some of the most able Nigerian infantry battalions were being used to police trouble spots in Nigerian cities such as Kano and Maiduguri as well as the Niger Delta, resulting in less well-trained troops being deployed to Darfur.[69]

11.5 CONCLUSIONS: THE FUTURE OF PAX NIGERIANA

This chapter has argued that cultural factors related to Nigeria's national identity and its pursuit of *Pax Nigeriana*, combined with the idiosyncratic decisions of some of its key military leaders—Generals Babangida, Abacha, and Obasanjo—offer the best explanations of its historical role in UN peacekeeping as exemplified in the three key theatres of Liberia, Sierra Leone, and Darfur. In comparison, institutional priorities and official policies do

[66] Confidential interview.
[67] Interview with Ibrahim Gambari, 18 May 2012.
[68] Confidential interviews.
[69] Interview with Ibrahim Gambari, 18 May 2012.

not sufficiently explain Nigeria's operations in these countries. Members of the bureaucracies of Nigeria's defence, foreign affairs, and police affairs ministries, as well as the press and informed general public, shared many of the beliefs about Nigeria's leadership role in providing security as the public good of a responsible regional hegemon in its perennial quest for a permanent seat on an expanded UN Security Council. But their influence on decision-making was often limited, particularly under the military regimes of Generals Babangida and Abacha. General Obasanjo, under more pressure from these domestic constituencies—as well as parliament and his party—continued Nigeria's activist peacekeeping role, but shifted the burden from ECOWAS and the AU to the UN, which made the missions more financially bearable and politically palatable.

While Nigeria clearly has both economic and political interests in stabilizing West Africa, its domestic political and economic problems will continue to take up much of its attention and resources.[70] Nigeria's decision not to contribute troops to the ECOMOG missions in Guinea-Bissau (1999) and its decisions to reduce significantly its troops in Sierra Leone (1999–2000) and subsume missions in Liberia, Sierra Leone, and Darfur under a UN umbrella between 1999 and 2007, were signs of a growing wariness at the costs and frustrations with regional peacekeeping, even among Nigeria's leaders. It is unlikely that civilian administrations will be able to sustain these casualties and costs without some loss of political support. More recently, the government of Goodluck Jonathan decided not to deploy troops to the AU mission in Somalia in 2011 following an assessment by Nigeria's defence ministry.[71] This is another sign of growing caution about over-committing troops abroad amidst Nigeria's own domestic security challenges, especially related to those in the Niger Delta and concerning *Boko Haram*'s terrorist activities.[72] Nevertheless, in May 2012, Nigeria deployed peacekeepers to Guinea-Bissau as part of a 600-strong ECOWAS mission and was considering sending troops to Mali. The argument of this chapter suggests that as long as Abuja still hopes to gain a seat on an expanded UN Security Council as part of a historical *Pax Nigeriana* and Africa remains a major theatre of UN peacekeeping, Nigeria is likely to continue providing peacekeepers, albeit under greater levels of domestic pressure.

[70] See Stephen Wright and Julius Emeka Okolo, 'Nigeria: Aspirations of Regional Power', in Stephen Wright (ed.), *African Foreign Policies* (Boulder, CO: Westview Press, 1999), pp. 125–30.

[71] Interview with General Obiakor, 12 May 2012.

[72] Telephone interview with Martin Uhomoibhi, Permanent Secretary in the Nigerian Foreign Ministry, 12 May 2012.

12

Ghana

Kwesi Aning and Festus K. Aubyn

United Nations (UN) peacekeeping operations have changed significantly since Ghana's first President, Kwame Nkrumah, initially contributed troops to the UN Operation in the Congo (ONUC) in 1960.[1] In spite of the difficulties and controversies engendered by that decision, Ghana has consistently continued to provide UN peacekeepers in many different part of the world including Lebanon, Afghanistan, Côte d'Ivoire, East Timor, Cambodia, Kosovo, Sudan, Rwanda, the Balkans, and Pakistan. For close to fifty years, it has remained one of the largest and consistent troop-contributing countries (TCC) in UN peacekeeping operations. Since its debut engagement in ONUC, over 80,000 Ghanaian men and women have rotated in and out of more than thirty UN and other multilateral peacekeeping missions.[2]

This chapter argues that Ghana's unwavering support for UN peacekeeping stems from its first engagement in the Congo. As a newly independent small state, 'Ghana's involvement in Congolese affairs was . . . deep: they [sic] inspired the Congolese to play their part in their own nationalist drama . . . and their Commander and troops played an important role in the UN command (ONUC) at several points.'[3] There is no doubt that this experience continued to shape Ghana's understanding and perception of peacekeeping irrespective of the type of ruling regime in Accra. However, while Ghana's contribution of personnel grew in parallel with the expansion in UN peacekeeping operations as a whole, there are several unanswered questions relating to why Ghana

[1] See Kwame Nkrumah, *Challenge of the Congo* (London: Panaf, 1967); Kwame Nkrumah, *Africa Must Unite* (London: Panaf, 1964); Walter Rooney, *Kwame Nkrumah: Vision and Tragedy* (Accra: Sub-Saharan Publishers, 2007), pp. 280ff.; Scott W. Thompson, *Ghana's Foreign Policy 1957–1966* (Princeton, NJ: Princeton University Press, 1969), especially pp. 117–61.

[2] Brigadier Samuel Odotei, past Chief of Staff of the Ghana Armed Forces, remarks at 'International Day of the Peacekeeper Today', 29 May 2003. At http://www.modernghana.com/news/35319/1/international-day-of-the-peacekeeper-today.html

[3] Thompson, *Ghana's Foreign Policy*, p. 119.

continues to deploy so many troops and police officers.[4] Focusing on the period from 2000 until 2010, we argue that Ghana's unwavering support for UN peacekeeping is motivated by multiple rationales, principally: to keep its neighbourhood safe and peaceful, a principled commitment to the UN's peace and security architecture, and the operational and financial benefits that stem from providing peacekeepers.[5]

The chapter proceeds in six sections. The first sketches the historical background to Ghana's involvement in UN peacekeeping, highlighting the country's willingness to contribute peacekeepers regardless of different domestic regimes and difficult financial circumstances. Consequently, the second section explores some of the motivations behind Ghana's troop contributions to UN peacekeeping operations around the world. Since independence, but particularly since the early 1980s, Ghana has faced stringent resource constraints. This raises questions as to why it has continued to provide troops. Scott Thompson argues that 'small states play small roles in settling international crises'.[6] Yet Ghana continues to contribute large numbers of the troops needed by the UN to maintain international peace and security. The third section evaluates Ghana's decision-making processes and mechanisms for peacekeeping both at the strategic and operational levels. At both levels Ghanaian decision-makers have sought to disprove the notion that a small, resource constrained state cannot make meaningful contributions to international crisis management. Between 2000 and 2010, Ghana experienced two different governments. The fourth and fifth sections analyse their policies with respect to peacekeeping requests, demonstrating that in spite of their ideological differences, these political parties consistently supported UN peacekeeping requests. We conclude by discussing the broader lessons that can be learnt from Ghana's experiences in UN peacekeeping.

12.1 GHANA'S PARTICIPATION IN UN PEACEKEEPING

Ghana's involvement in UN peacekeeping spans its entire independence period. It was driven and inspired by the Pan-Africanist ideals of its late

[4] For a discussion, see Kwesi Aning, 'Unintended Consequences of Peace Support Operations for Troop-Contributing Countries from West Africa: The Case of Ghana', in Chiyuki Aoi, Cedric de Coning, and Ramesh Thakur (eds.), *Unintended Consequences of Peacekeeping Operations* (Tokyo: UN University Press, 2007).

[5] Aning, 'Unintended Consequences'.

[6] Thompson, *Ghana's Foreign Policy*, p. 119.

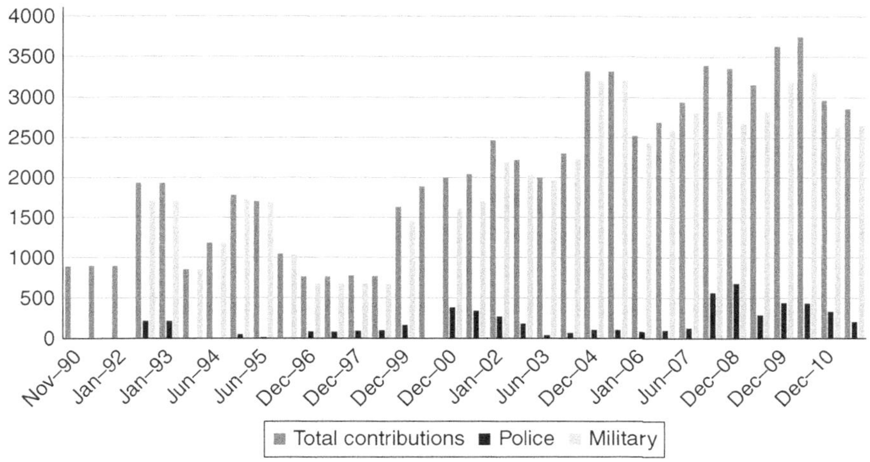

Figure 12.1 Ghana's Uniformed Personnel in UN Peacekeeping, 1990–2011
Source: UN DPKO figures.

President, Kwame Nkrumah.[7] Shortly after attaining independence in 1957, Ghana was admitted into the membership of the UN as the 81st member state and has since remained committed to the ideals that inspired its creation.[8] As an active member of the UN, Ghana has participated in almost every peacekeeping and observer mission since 1960. In other words, for Ghana, UN peacekeeping activism has become a habit.[9] Figure 12.1 shows the trends in Ghana's contribution of uniformed UN peacekeepers since November 1990.

As Figure 12.1 illustrates, Ghana's contribution has been fairly consistent though there have been peaks and troughs since the 1990s, which largely follow more general trends in UN peacekeeping. It also indicates that the majority of the country's peacekeepers have been drawn from the Ghana Armed Forces (GAF) and Ghana Police Service (GPS). But Ghana has also made extensive contributions on the political and diplomatic front. In particular, whereas members of the military serve as observers and perform other tasks including military patrols, de-mining, and cease-fire monitoring, its politicians and diplomats have regularly been engaged in negotiating peace

[7] Some historians have traced the roots of this commitment to the period of the Gold Coast Regiment (GCR), which was part of the West African Frontier Force and the precursor to the modern Ghana Armed Forces. During the First World War, the GCR fought in defence of the British Empire in German Togoland, Cameroons, and East Africa. It also fought on the side of the Allies during the Second World War. See Ghana Armed Forces, 'International Peacekeeping'. At http://www.gaf.mil.gh/index.php?option=com_content&view=category&layout=blog&id=32&Itemid =54

[8] Ministry of Foreign Affairs, Regional Integration and NEPAD, 'Ghana and the UN'. At http://www.ghanadiplomaticguide.com/ghanaforeignpolicy.php

[9] Davis B. Bobrow and Mark A. Boyer, 'Maintaining System Stability: Contributions to Peacekeeping Operations', *Journal of Conflict Resolution*, 41:6 (1997), p. 731.

Table 12.1 Ghanaians in Senior Leadership Positions in UN Peacekeeping Operations

Name	Mission	Position
Ambassador James Victor Gbeho	UN Operation in Somalia (UNOSOM II)	Special Representative of the Secretary-General (July 1994–April 1995)
Chief Superintendent Selwyn Mettle	UNOSOM II	Police Commissioner (June 1994–February 1995)
Robert K. A. Gardiner	UN Operation in the Congo (ONUC)	Officer-in-charge (February 1962–May 1963)
Brig. Gen. Henry Kwami Anyidoho	UN Assistance Mission for Rwanda (UNAMIR)	Deputy Commander
J. Joseph Dankwa	UNAMSIL	Police Commissioner (December 1999–February 2003)
Major-General Timothy K. Dibuama	UN Iraq–Kuwait Observation Mission (UNIKOM)	Chief Military Observer (July 1992–August 1993)
James Oppong-Boanuh	African Union/UN Hybrid operations in Darfur (UNAMID)	Police Commissioner
Henrietta Joy Abena Nyarko Mensa-Bonsu	UN Mission in Liberia (UNMIL)	Deputy Special Representative of the Secretary-General for rule of law

in countries that are being affected by conflicts.[10] Personnel from the GPS have also performed functions such as training the police forces of war-torn states, encouraging respect for human rights in the administration of justice, and maintaining law and public order in countries such as Sudan, Kosovo, Côte d'Ivoire, Sierra Leone, and Liberia. Equally, other civilians employed by the UN have played important roles in extending democracy through the preparation and monitoring of elections in countries such as Afghanistan and East Timor.[11] Thus, at all levels of peacekeeping, Ghanaian personnel have contributed to a wide range of complex and multidisciplinary tasks, serving in leadership positions as commanders, police commissioners, special representatives of the Secretary-General, and chief military observers.[12] Table 12.1 lists some of the Ghanaians who have occupied leadership positions in UN peacekeeping missions.

Increasingly, as a result of the courage, initiative, loyalty, humility, and professionalism that Ghanaian peacekeepers continue to display, they have been recognized internationally as some 'of the finest in the world'.[13] As of July

[10] For more information, see Kwesi Aning, Evelyn Avoxe, and Fiifi Edu-Afful, 'Breaking up a Monolithic State: Reflections of Unarmed Ghanaian Military Observers in Kosovo and Bosnia' (unpublished paper, 2011).

[11] Leah Marchuk, 'The Faces of Ghana's Peacekeepers', *Daily Graphic*, 4 August 2008. At http://leahmarchuk.blogspot.com/2008/08/faces-of-ghanas-peacekeepers.html

[12] See 'Ghana celebrates 50 years participation in UN peacekeeping', Ghana News Agency, 25 May 2010. At http://www.ghananewsagency.org/details/Politics/Ghana-celebrates-50-years-participation-in-UN-peacekeeping/?ci=2&ai=15998

[13] UN Information Centre, 'Ghana marks the International Day of United Nations Peacekeeping', 29 May 2009. At http://unic.un.org/imu/recentActivities/post/2009/05/Ghana-marks-the-International-Day-of-United-Nations-Peacekeepers.aspx

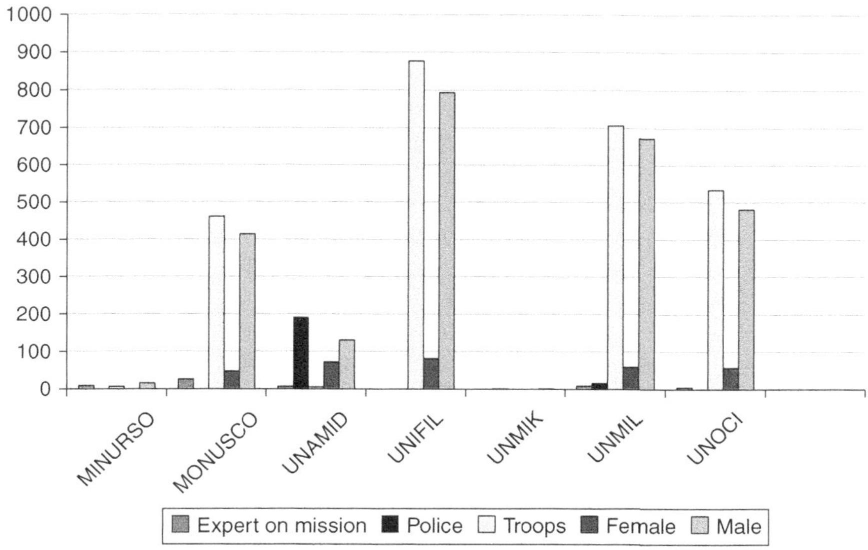

Figure 12.2 Ghana's UN Peacekeepers, July 2011

2011, Ghana was involved in seven UN peacekeeping missions with significant contributions (see Figure 12.2).

12.2 EXPLAINING GHANA'S UN PEACEKEEPING CONTRIBUTIONS

This section identifies the major motivations behind Ghana's contributions to UN peacekeeping operations.

12.2.1 Security Rationale: Keep the Neighbourhood Safe and Peaceful

Africa, and in particular the West African subregion, has been pivotal to Ghana's external relations since independence.[14] Ghana shares cultural history and ties of blood especially with its immediate neighbours and given the

[14] N. C. Coleman, 'Defence Policy in Ghana: The Past, Present and Way Forward', in Gilbert K. Bluwey and Kofi Kumado (eds.), *Ghana in Search of National Security Policy* (Accra: LECIA, University of Ghana and Ministry of Defence, 2007); Ministry of Foreign Affairs and Regional Integration, 'Aims and Objectives'. At http://www.ghana.gov.gh

spate of civil wars that have engulfed the subregion, there has always been the fear of a spillover of proximate conflicts and instability into Ghana.[15] This is because the effects of conflicts often transcend national boundaries. To promote a safe and peaceful neighbourhood, Ghana therefore participates in international peacekeeping efforts to control and suppress the spread of these conflicts, prevent them from jeopardizing its security and developmental agenda, sometimes to extricate Ghanaian expatriates who may be caught up in the conflicts,[16] to stop conflicts sparking a regional conflagration which might undermine the region's security, prosperity, and stability, and to stem the humanitarian crises that are often associated with such conflicts. The assumption here is that Ghana's security and economic development are best supported by a peaceful region.[17]

Ghana's commitment to provide UN peacekeepers in Côte d'Ivoire, Sierra Leone, and Liberia are good examples of this approach.[18] The Liberian conflict, for instance, posed an immediate threat to stability in Ghana.[19] Ghana had to accommodate about 13,000 refugees from Liberia in 1992 at the Buduburam and Krisan camp in its central and western region.[20] Since then, more than 40,000 Liberian refugees moved to Ghana until 2004, when a tripartite agreement between the refugees, UN High Commissioner for Refugees (UNHCR), and the Ghana refugee board was signed to manage a process of voluntary repatriation. As of August 2011, 11,585 Liberian refugees remained in Ghana.[21]

12.2.2 A Principled Commitment to Support the UN Peace and Security Architecture

Ghana's engagement in UN peacekeeping is also driven by a deep-rooted commitment to help maintain international peace and security as enshrined in the UN Charter.[22] Ghana's President Mills reiterated this commitment at the 66th UN General Assembly meeting in 2011 stating that 'Ghana will remain

[15] Michael E. Brown (ed.), *The International Dimensions of Internal Conflicts* (Cambridge, MA: MIT Press, 1996). See also Kwesi Aning, *International Dimensions of Internal Conflict: The Case of Liberia and West Africa* (Copenhagen: Centre for Development Research, 1997).

[16] Eboe Hutchful, *The ECOMOG Experience with Peacekeeping in West Africa* (Pretoria: ISS Monograph No. 36, April 1999).

[17] Interview with Hon. Papa Owusu Ankomah, Former Minister of Interior, 12 July 2011.

[18] See, for example, Kwesi Aning, 'Ghana, Liberia and ECOWAS: An Analysis of Ghana's Policies in Liberia', *Liberian Studies Journal*, 21:2 (1996).

[19] Festus B. Aboagye, *ECOMOG: A Sub-Regional Experience in Conflict Resolution, Management and Peacekeeping in Liberia* (Accra: Sedco Publishing Limited, 1999).

[20] Abeeku Essuman-Johnson, 'Ghana's Response to the Liberian and Sahelian Refugees Influx', paper prepared for the 4th IRAP conference on Refugees at Somerville College, University of Oxford, 2004.

[21] Figures from UNHCR, Ghana Office.

[22] Interview with Col. M'Bawine Atintande, Director, Public Relations/Spokesman, GAF, 15 July 2011.

unwavering in its commitment to the ideals and objectives of the United Nations.'[23] But Ghana's commitment to the UN is also found in its domestic legal principles and values as set out in the country's Constitution of 1992. Specifically, Article 40 (c) (d) of the Constitution states that Ghana should:

> promote respect for international law and treaty obligations and the settlement of international disputes by peaceful means; and adherence to principles enshrined in or as the case may be, the aims and ideals of (i) the Charter of the United Nations, (ii) the Charter of African Union, (iii) the Commonwealth, (iv) the Treaty of the Economic Community of West African States, and any other International Organizations of which Ghana is a member.

Participation in peacekeeping, therefore, demonstrates Ghana's commitment to sustain global peace, security, and stability.[24] It also serves as one of the opportunities through which Ghana can demonstrate its influence in world affairs and enhance its image and prestige in the international system.[25] Thus, peacekeeping serves as a public good in terms of Ghana's efforts to contribute to the maintenance of international peace and stability.[26]

12.2.3 Operational Gains and Financial Benefits

Ghana's participation in UN peacekeeping is also motivated by the operational and economic benefits that accrue from such activities. In particular, peacekeeping has served as an avenue for the military and police to acquire overseas experience and training.[27] Through their continued engagement in peacekeeping, the GAF has benefited from capacity-building initiatives and training assistance programmes such as the US African Crisis Response Initiative (ACRI) and African Contingency Operation Training and Assistance (ACOTA), France's Reinforcement of African Peacekeeping capabilities

[23] See President Mills's Keynote Address at the 66th UN General Assembly Meeting, 23 September 2011. At http://www.ghana.gov.gh/index.php/information/speeches/7674-speech-delivered-by-his-excellency-john-evans-atta-mills-president-of-the-republic-of-ghana-at-the-66th-general-assembly-of-the-united-nations-on-friday-23rd-septeber-2011-

[24] Ghana News Agency, 'Ghana's peacekeeping—a demonstration of commitment to peace—Smith'. At http://www.ghananewsagency.org/details/Social/Ghana-s-peacekeeping-a-demonstration-of-commitment-to-peace-Smith/?ci=4&ai=29337, accessed 12 July 2011.

[25] Aning, 'Unintended Consequences', p.140; 'Police boil over recruitment exercise . . . for AU peace mission in Sudan', *Ghanaian Chronicle*, 4 March 2005; Baby Ansabah, 'Presidential jet scandal: who faces the music?', *Daily Guide*, 6 January 2004, pp. 1, 8; Eboe Hutchful, 'Military Policy and Reform in Ghana', *Journal of Modern African Studies*, 35:2 (1997), p. 258. See also *Defending Democracy: A Global Survey of Foreign Policy Trends 1992–2002*, summary of a Council on Foreign Relations meeting, January 2003. At http://www.cfr.org/international-organizations/defending-democracy-global-survey-foreign-policy-trends-1992—2002/p5610

[26] Bobrow and Boyer, 'Maintaining System Stability', p. 726.

[27] Interview with Col. Emmanuel Kotia, GAF Command and Staff College, 11 July 2011.

programme (RECAMP), and Canada's Military Training Assistance Programme (MTAP).[28] Such collaborative training and assistance programmes have also offered opportunities for the GAF to accumulate military equipment and technology by retaining the supplies provided by the UN and other donors.[29] Through pre-deployment training, the police have also gained broader perspectives on different policing methods and issues such as human rights, rule of law, crowd control measures, crime scene management, investigations and administration.[30] Given the resource constraints faced by the GAF and GPS, these training programmes have enabled them to improve their skills and knowledge to advanced international military and policing standards.[31] This has impacted positively on their professional expertise and capabilities and enhanced their operational performance both at home and abroad.

Besides training and experience-sharing, peacekeeping has also brought pecuniary rewards to serving personnel and the country as a whole through the compensation packages offered by the UN.[32] In 2010, for instance, Ghana received $74,336,121.42 compensation for all peace support operations while its total expenditures incurred were $42,100,576.47, resulting in a 'profit' of $32,235,544.95.[33] Some of these financial gains were used to purchase aircraft and other military equipment. A classic example of such spin-offs occurred in 1998 and 1999, when $2,450,000 from the GAF peacekeeping account in New York was reportedly used by the government to finance the acquisition of a Gulf Stream Gill aircraft for the presidency.[34]

12.3 DECISION-MAKING PROCESSES AND MECHANISMS

This section analyses how Ghana decides to deploy its troops or otherwise and the multiple actors involved by evaluating the decision-making processes and

[28] Kwesi Aning, Thomas Jaye, and Samuel Atuobi. 'The Role of Private Military Companies in US–Africa Policy', *Review of African Political Economy*, 35:118 (2008), pp. 613–28; Alhaji Sarjoh Bah and Kwesi Aning, 'US Peace Operations Policy in Africa: From ACRI to AFRICOM', *International Peacekeeping*, 15:1 (2008), pp. 118–32.

[29] Kwesi Aning, *Military Imports and Sustainable Development: Case Study Analysis—Ghana* (African Security Dialogue and Research, 2004) At http://allafrica.com/download/resource/main/main/idatcs/00010208:3a9e8d3c4b4e360b8546ea500dae6beb.pdf

[30] Interview with SUPT/Mr Henry Otto, IRD, GPS, 15 July 2011.

[31] Interview with Col. M'Bawine Atintande, Director, Public Relations/Spokesman, GAF, 15 July 2011.

[32] Interview with Col. A. K. Asare, Director, Army Peacekeeping Operations (DAPKOP), 13 July 2011.

[33] See *Historical on GAF's Participation in International Peace Support Operations* (Accra: GAF, IPSO internal document, 2011).

[34] See 'Peprah in Hot Soup Again', Ghana News Agency, 12 May 2003. At http://www.modernghana.com/news/34580/1/peprah-in-hot-soup-again.html

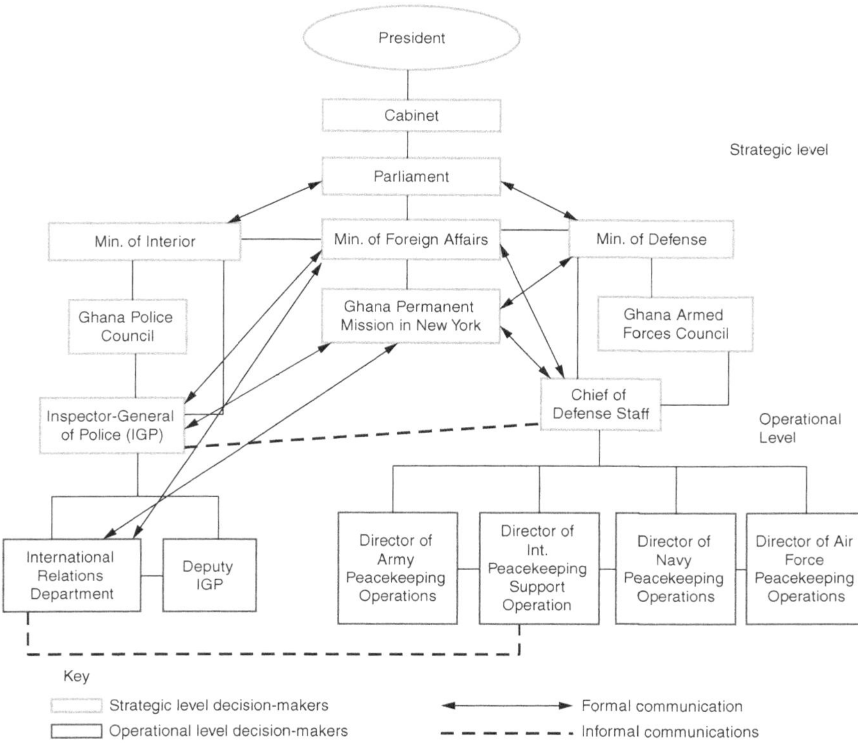

Figure 12.3 Ghana's Peacekeeping Decision-Making Processes: Institutions and Actors
Source: Compiled by authors.

mechanisms at the strategic and operational levels. To avoid repetition, the strategic level decision-making processes at the GAF and GPS are examined in tandem. But for the purpose of clarity and understanding, the operational level decisions are discussed separately.

12.3.1 Strategic Level

The key actors involved at the strategic decision-making level include the President, Cabinet, Parliament, Minister of Defence, Minister of Interior, Minister of Foreign Affairs, Ghana Armed Forces Council (GAFC) and Ghana Police Council, Chief of Defence Staff (CDS), and the Inspector-General of Police (IGP) (see Figure 12.3).[35] The decision on whether to supply troops and police to UN peacekeeping operations is taken at this level. But this

[35] Interview with Col. A. K. Asare, 13 July 2011.

remains the sole prerogative of the President, who is the Commander-in-Chief of the GAF according to the 1992 Ghana Constitution.[36] The Cabinet, Minister of Defence, Minister of Interior, Armed Forces and Police Councils, Chief of Defence Staff, and the Inspector-General of Police only act as advisers to the President in the decision-making processes. The Minister of Foreign Affairs through the Ghana Permanent Mission in New York negotiates the logistical and operational details of Ghana's participation with the UN.[37] Parliament, especially, the Parliamentary Select Committee on Defence and Interior (PSCD&I), which is not active in the actual decision-making process, also plays an important role in terms of oversight over defence budgeting and procurements.[38] It has to approve all budgets meant for peacekeeping procurements and expenses. In January 2003, for instance, Parliament had to approve $55 million for the Ministry of Defence to acquire equipment including helicopters to facilitate Ghana's participation in peacekeeping activities in the Democratic Republic of Congo.[39]

More significantly, before a decision is made to contribute troops or police to any UN mission, an internal threat assessment is conducted. The rationale is to ensure that the absence of the forces will not have any adverse effect on the country in terms of quelling any internal conflict and preventing any major national security crisis.[40] This is mainly carried out by the CDS, IGP, Armed Forces and Police Councils with the support of the GAF International Peace Support Operation (IPSO) Office and International Relations Department (IRD) of the GPS.[41] It is after these threat assessments have been conducted that the decision is taken to supply a particular number and type of troops and police. Both the GAF and GPS undertake their own internal threat assessments as to how acceding to such requests might impact on the institution.

Essentially, in carrying out the internal threat assessment, a number of critical factors are taken into consideration. The first is the mission mandate: whether it is in line with the national interest and the extent to which it has an effective command and control structure as well as clearly defined rules of engagement for every situation.[42] For instance, is deployment going to be *deployment in contact* or otherwise?[43] This issue is important

[36] The Constitution of the Republic of Ghana 1992, Chapter 8, Article 57(1).

[37] Interview with DSP/Mrs Regina Antwiwaa Tengey, IRD, GPS, 15 July 2011.

[38] Eboe Hutchful, 'Ghana', in Wuyi Omotoogun and Eboe Hutchful (eds.), *Budgeting for the Military Sector in Africa* (New York: Oxford University Press, 2006).

[39] Kwesi Aning and Ernest Lartey, 'Parliamentary Oversight of the Security Sector: Lessons from Ghana', in Jake Sherman (ed.), *Strengthening Security Sector Governance in West Africa* (New York: Center on International Cooperation, 2009).

[40] Emma Birikorang, *Ghana's Regional Security Policy* (Accra: KAIPTC Paper No. 20, September 2007).

[41] Interview with Col. A. K. Asare, 13 July 2011.

[42] Interview with Col. A. K. Asare, 13 July 2011.

[43] Which means peacekeepers will enter to engage rebels or government forces and for this kind of deployment casualties may occur which might be detrimental to the country's interest.

because there are missions that are considered detrimental to the nation's interest. Ghana, for instance, declined a request by the African Union (AU) to participate in a peacekeeping mission in Somalia primarily due to issues of national interest as the mission mandate put its personnel in unacceptable danger.[44] Likewise in Côte d'Ivoire, the President's decision during the election crises in early 2011 not to commit troops to ECOWAS was based on the country's security interest.[45] It is worth noting that Ghana places significant emphasis on force protection in its participation in UN peacekeeping operations.[46]

The next critical consideration has to do with the internal political situation in the host country. The threat assessment process takes into account the domestic security conditions with respect to the internal security requirements, political climate, and potential ethnic tensions in the country to ensure whether the number of personnel on the ground can contain any emergency when they occur in the aftermath of deployment.[47] Whenever there is a conflict between domestic and international interest, emphasis is placed on domestic interests. Indeed, Ghanaian security officials claimed that during election periods for instance, Ghana does not contribute new deployments of soldiers or police officers to peacekeeping duties due to the operational strains on the security services during such periods.[48] However, this claim is not borne out by the evidence depicted in Figure 12.1.

The level, size, and expertise of the troops and police contributions demanded in the UN request or memorandum of understanding (MOU) are other factors that are assessed. The analytical significance of such an exercise is to appreciate the number of soldiers requested, the tasks to be performed, how many soldiers the country can contribute, and in the case of the police, the specific expertise that is needed for the mission. For the police service, for instance, in situations where the expertise or skills set attached to the mission mandates is in high demand locally and scarce, either a limited contribution is made or the request is declined.[49] Similarly in the armed forces, when the

[44] The mandate put Ghanaian troops in danger because it was likely they would have to engage in combat operations against al-Shabaab. Confidential interview with a senior officer at the GAF.

[45] Ghana's non-involvement, argued by President Mills and Gen. Henry Smith, the Minister of Defence, stems from its overstretched armed forces, internal security requirements, and potential reprisals against Ghanaians resident in Côte d'Ivoire and on the oil rigs. See 'GAF Won't Commit Troops to Cote d'Ivoire'. At http://www.graphic.com.gh/news/page.php?news=11176

[46] Interview with Lt. Col Salifu, IPSO, GAF, 26 July 2011.

[47] Birikorang, *Ghana's Regional Security Policy*.

[48] Interview with Col. A. K. Asare, 13 July 2011; and see Ernest Lartey and Kwesi Aning, 'The 2008 Ghana Elections: A Model that Unraveled?', *African Renaissance*, 6:1 (2009).

[49] Interview with DSP/Mrs Regina Antwiwaa Tengey, IRD, GPS, 15 July 2011.

number of soldiers requested is high and beyond the country's capabilities, the request is either declined or limited numbers of troops are deployed.

Another important concern is the country's capacity in terms of the requisite human, financial, and logistical resources needed to support the operation. According to the UN's contingent owned equipment (COE) system, the troop-contributing country has to be self-sufficient in terms of providing rations, petrol, oil, water, etc. in the mission areas for the first 30 to 90 days of an operation.[50] So a needs assessment is carried out to find out whether the country can finance the requested mission within this self-sufficiency period. Logistical difficulties, for instance, can be a major impediment to the effective deployment of troops. But sometimes in cases where Ghana lacks the equipment or logistics needed for the mission, the UN either provides them or helps Ghana to secure them from a third country.[51] Once this threat assessment is completed, the conclusions are forwarded to the President who decides what Ghana can contribute, and then the process for selection and training at the operational level for peacekeeping or enforcement duties commences.

12.3.2 Operational Level

The process of selection and training for peacekeeping or enforcement duties is undertaken by the decision-makers at this level. It is carried out as soon as the President decides to contribute troops or police. For the purpose of clarity and understanding, this section separately discusses the operational level decisions of the armed forces and police service.

12.3.2.1 Ghana Armed Forces

The key players involved at this level are the Director of International Peacekeeping Support Operation (DIPSO), Director of Army Peacekeeping Operations (DAPKOP), Director of Navy Peacekeeping Operations, and the Director of Air Force Peacekeeping Operations.[52] While the DIPSO coordinates the peacekeeping activities of the GAF in general, the Directors of Peacekeeping operations of the three service headquarters (i.e., Army, Navy, and Air Force) supervise the selection processes of their individual headquarters. Usually, because most peacekeeping operations are on land, the DIPSO and DAPKOP perform most of the operational level tasks.[53] But this is not to

[50] See 'Introduction to contingent owned equipment (COE) system'. At http://www.un.org/en/peacekeeping/sites/coe/referencedocuments/Booklet%20Handout%20Intro%20to%20COE.pdf

[51] Interview with Col. A. K. Asare, 13 July 2011.

[52] Interview with Lt. Col. Salifu, 26 July 2011.

[53] Interview with Lt. Col. John H. K. Buntuguh, Chief Coordinator, KAIPTC, 9 July 2011.

say that Ghana does not contribute much in terms of naval and air assets. The reality is that most of the requests from the UN have been largely confined to the provision of land contingents/infantry. Perhaps this is best explained by the lack of logistical capacity among most African TCCs, of which Ghana is no exception. When the government decides to contribute troops, the information is widely circulated among the various service headquarters by the IPSO office for the nomination of eligible officers.[54] The Directors of Peacekeeping Operations at the Army, Navy, and Air Force carry out the process of nominations at their various service headquarters. The type and number of officers to be nominated in Army, Navy and Air Force categories is based on the specifications required in the UN request. But generally, there are two kinds of groupings that can be deployed for peacekeeping operations. This can either be a unit or a composite battalion or taskforce. A unit is formed around an existing battalion that would serve as the nucleus of the Ghanaian peacekeeping battalion usually called *Ghanbatt* in the mission areas, and the composite battalion or taskforce is created by bringing together personnel from different units and assigning a commander.[55] The decision as to whether to mobilize a unit or a taskforce is determined by factors such as the internal security needs of the country at the time. Usually, shortlisted officers undertake a written examination after which successful candidates are nominated.

A medical examination is then organized by IPSO to select successful candidates for training. Diseases that could disqualify an individual from participation in a peacekeeping operation include HIV/AIDS, tuberculosis, diabetes, hypertension, and chronic alcoholism. All successful candidates congregate at Bondase training facility where they undergo pre-deployment training for a month or more.[56] The pre-deployment training which is delivered by a field training team from the KAIPTC covers three broad areas: tactical training towards peace support roles, mission specific training, and UN modules. The tactical aspect involves among other things training on how to conduct VIP escort duties, checkpoint duties, search operations, curfew enforcement, observation post duties, crowd control, ambushes, raids, land navigation or map reading, endurance/physical training, and weapon training. The mission specific training deals with the background to the conflict, geopolitical situation in the operational zone, the climate, people, and culture, and the mission mandate of the peacekeepers. The training in UN modules includes topics such as introduction to UN peacekeeping operations,

[54] IPSO coordinate all the peacekeeping activities of the GAF and facilitate the correspondence between the Ghana Permanent mission in New York and GAF.

[55] Kwesi Aning and Evelyn Avoxe, 'A Comparative Study of Ghanaian Police and Military Experiences in United Nations Peacekeeping: 1960–2010', unpublished paper, 2011.

[56] Bondase is a peacekeeping training camp established by the GAF for training both military and police officers earmarked for peacekeeping operations. The camp is currently managed by the Kofi Annan International Peacekeeping Training Centre (KAIPTC).

international humanitarian law, international human rights law, conduct and discipline, the civilian dimensions of peace operations, and sexual exploitation and abuse (SEA).[57] The purpose of all these pre-deployment training exercises is to bring personnel up to standard with international best practices on peacekeeping. Because there are assigned dates to each deployment, after training all candidates are dispersed to their various service sectors.

It is important to note that this selection process is a very competitive exercise that is sometimes fraught with allegations of corruption and favouritism. There are instances where some officers are even believed to have paid bribes to senior commanders in order to be selected. However, most of these allegations have been denied by the GAF command and they cannot be substantiated.[58]

12.3.2.2 The Ghana Police Service

When the government decides to contribute police to the UN, the GPS International Relations Directorate (IRD) takes up the responsibility of selecting and preparing officers for the requested mission. The IRD, per its mandate, undertakes all the peacekeeping activities of the police service.[59] It does this in concert with the deputy IGP in charge of administration and UN DPKO.[60] First, the information is sent through all twelve regional police commands in Ghana to all the 51 police divisions, 179 police districts, and 651 police stations in the country for nominations of qualified officers.[61] This is done to ensure that all regions are fairly represented. A quota of police nominations is given to each region based on the size of police strength. These nominations are to be based on the specific qualifications and expertise required by the UN. But most often, nominations are based on the experience of personnel, usually a minimum of seven years' service for junior officers and five years for senior officers, peacekeeping experience, abilities in shooting and driving, and unblemished record. As soon as the IRD gets the full list of nominees from all the regions, the pre-selection of eligible officers begins.[62] The pre-selection phase starts with a screening exercise that assesses the competence of successful nominees for the mission tasks. Its purpose is not only to dispel institutional perceptions of corruption, but also to obtain the full

[57] For more information see Aning and Avoxe, 'A Comparative Study'.

[58] 'Corruption in the selection of peacekeepers', *Ghanaian Chronicle*, 25 March 2005.

[59] Ghana Police Service, 'International Relations Directorate (IRD): Set Up, Establishment, Functions and Achievements'. At http://www.ghanapolice.info/international_relations.htm

[60] Interview with SUPT/Mr Henry Otto, 2IC, IRD, GPS, 15 July 2011.

[61] Apart from the ten regions in Ghana, for effective policing and maintenance of rule of law, the police service has added the General Headquarters and Tema to the regions, making 12 regions in all. Interview with DSP/Mrs Regina Antwiwaa Tengey, 15 July 2011.

[62] Interview with SUPT/Mr Henry Otto, 15 July 2011.

list of eligible officers before the actual UN Selection Assessment Test by DPKO officials. The DPKO tests the police officers based on the skills set specified in the peacekeeping mandate. The areas of expertise or skills that are most often assessed or tested are driving, language proficiency (French or English), computer skills, and some specialized expertise required by the mission mandates. Once the testing is completed, successful candidates are selected for training.

These training programmes include pre-deployment training, advance driving, and information communication technology (ICT).[63] The training ends with a medical screening exercise for the final selection of candidates. Candidates who emerge successful after the medical examinations wait for UN assigned dates for deployment. The IRD uses what they call *deployment tracking*, which illustrates where, how, and when an officer will be due for deployment according to the UN. Once a police officer is deployed the maximum period he or she can spend is one year after which he or she is rotated.

Like the selection process in the GAF, the process confronts many challenges. In recent times, there have been allegations of corruption, favouritism, and unfairness in the nomination of personnel. While some police officers accuse the senior officers at the IRD and police administration of taking bribes, others complain that the circulation of messages to create awareness of the exercise among interested personnel is sometimes done in secret.[64] But these allegations have been denied by the police administration who state that when some personnel fail to be nominated, they resort to tarnishing the image of senior officers and that of the service.[65]

12.4 PERSPECTIVES ON CURRENT TRENDS IN UN PEACEKEEPING OPERATIONS

This section analyses the government's perspective on some important current developments in UN peacekeeping, notably the protection of civilians, rule of law, use of military force, relation with host states, and legal accountability for crimes committed by peacekeepers.

[63] Usually, most of these training programmes are offered and sponsored by the KAIPTC, the Norwegian government, the German Technical Cooperation (GTZ), and the Pearson Peacekeeping Centre (PPC).

[64] See 'Peacekeeping for sale at Police Headquarters', *Ghanaian Chronicle*, 4 April 2011. At http://ghanaian-chronicle.com/news/other-news/peacekeeping-for-sale-police-headquarters/

[65] 'Peacekeeping for sale at Police Headquarters'.

12.4.1 Protection of Civilians

Ghana recognizes the vulnerability of civilians and supports all efforts by the UN to protect civilians during armed conflicts.[66] Ghana believes that the protection of civilians should begin with a culture of prevention encompassing all phases of armed conflict.[67] This should include the strengthening of early warning systems, rapid response in the early stages of conflicts, and the establishment of mechanisms for peacebuilding after war.[68] An effective sanctions regime is also important for the prosecution and punishment of perpetrators to deter attacks on innocent civilians. With sufficient political support, the International Criminal Court could contribute towards containing and combating crimes against innocent populations in conflict areas.[69] Moreover, peacekeepers and humanitarian agencies need to be adequately resourced to fulfil their mandates, and to achieve this the UN needs to work with regional organizations to strengthen regional mechanisms designed to enhance the protection of civilians in armed conflict.[70]

12.4.2 Rule of Law

Ghana sees its role in peacekeeping as emphasizing the significance of the rule of law both at home and abroad.[71] It considers establishing respect for the rule of law and democracy to be fundamental prerequisites for achieving durable peace in the aftermath of conflicts. The country is wholly supportive of this agenda and to further demonstrate this commitment, Ghana celebrated

[66] This statement was made by Hon. Dr Addo Kufuor, former Minister of Defence, during an expert meeting in Accra in 2007 to fashion ways to protect civilians in conflict areas. See 'Experts fashion ways to protect civilians in conflict areas' at http://www.businessghana.com. See also Kwesi Aning and Samuel Atuobi, 'Responsibility to Protect in Africa: An Analysis of the African Union's Peace and Security Architecture', *Global Responsibility to Protect*, 1:1(2009), pp. 90–113.

[67] This was contained in a Statement made by Ghana's delegation on the 'Protection of Civilians in Armed Conflict' to the UN Security Council meeting on Wednesday, 11 November 2009.

[68] Statement made by Ghana's delegation on the 'Protection of Civilians in Armed Conflict'.

[69] The deputy representative of Ghana to the UN, H.E. Mr Leslie Kojo Christian, made this statement in the Security Council open debate on the Protection of Civilians in Armed Conflict on 28 June 2006. At http://www.iccnow.org/documents/SCExcerpts_ProtectionofCivilians_28-Jun06.pdf

[70] See, for example, Kwesi Aning and Naila Salihu, 'Accountability for Intervention: Negotiating Civilian Protection Dilemmas with Respect to the Economic Community of West African States and African Union Interventions', *African Security*, 4:2 (2011), pp. 81ff.

[71] The Minister for Foreign Affairs, Hon. Alhaji Mohammed Mumuni, made this statement at a press conference in Accra to mark the official launching of the International Day of UN Peacekeepers. See 'International Day of UN Peacekeepers Launched', 24 May 2011. At http://ghana.gov.gh/index.php?option=com_content&view=article&id=6012:international-day-of-un-peacekeepers-laun

the 2011 UN day with events on the theme of 'peacekeeping within the rule of law: challenges of the Ghanaian Peacekeepers'.[72] Nevertheless, strengthening the rule of law in peacekeeping missions continues to be hampered by the collapse of governance institutions, lack of professional and bureaucratic capacities, uncooperative political elites, and the activities of criminal groups.[73] The existence of functional, effective, and transparent legal and judicial frameworks is therefore critical to consolidating peace, restoring and strengthening rule of law, preventing impunity, and instilling public trust in state institutions.

12.4.3 Legal Accountability for Crimes Committed by Peacekeepers

Peacekeeping operations in recent years have been marked by allegations of peacekeepers exploiting the very people they were sent to protect.[74] This has ranged from stealing and the exchange of food, money, or goods for sex to the sexual exploitation of minors.[75] Since 1999, when UN peacekeepers in Bosnia were implicated in sex trafficking, the UN has in recent years faced charges of rape and sexual violence by peacekeepers in the Democratic Republic of Congo, Haiti, and Sudan.[76] This damages the credibility and effectiveness of peacekeeping operations. Although this challenge has prompted considerable efforts by the UN, such as the issuance of the UN's zero-tolerance policy on sexual exploitation and abuse, Ghana underscores the importance of additional support from TCCs in that respect. Specifically, TCCs need to support the UN's efforts by taking appropriate disciplinary measures and, where necessary, legal action when their personnel serving on missions breach UN rules, codes of conduct, and any other applicable international laws.[77] The GAF and GPS have outlined stringent punishment or disciplinary measures such as withdrawing perpetrators from the mission areas and sometimes banning them from taking part in any peacekeeping activities in the future.[78] Being banned from participation in peacekeeping operations is a particularly

[72] Statement by Minister for Foreign Affairs, Hon. Alhaji Mohammed Mumuni, 24 May 2011.

[73] Statement by Minister for Foreign Affairs, Hon. Alhaji Mohammed Mumuni, 24 May 2011.

[74] For more information see Catherine E. Sweetser, 'Providing Effective Remedies to Victims of Abuse by Peacekeeping Personnel', *New York University Law Review*, 86 (November 2008), pp. 1643–77.

[75] Lauren Hunter, 'Should We Prosecute the Prosecutors? Holding Peacekeepers Accountable in Cases of Sexual Exploitation and Abuse', *Carleton Review of International Affairs*, 1 (2009), pp. 15–34.

[76] Peter Mameli, 'The Blue Helmets: Sexual Exploitation, Sex Trafficking and Organizational Culture in UN Peacekeeping Operations', *Journal of Social Issues*, 15:1 (2011).

[77] Interview with Col. M'Bawine Atintande, Director, Public Relations/Spokesman, GAF, 15 July 2011.

[78] Interview with Lt. Col. Salifu, IPSO, GAF, 26 July 2011.

significant penalty for Ghanaian soldiers because they are usually permitted to deploy to multiple UN missions during their career. The UN needs to support TCCs by undertaking regular and systematic training of their soldiers and police in the relevant UN codes of conduct *before deployment*. Moreover, mechanisms to monitor the excesses that some soldiers and police in mission areas engage in must also be put in place to curb the menace.

12.4.4 Use of Military Force and Relations with Host States

Each peacekeeping operation takes place in accordance with the basic principles of consent, impartiality, and the non-use of force except in self-defence and in defence of the mandate.[79] The interpretation and application of these core principles has undergone significant transformation. While wide gaps exist between consent at the strategic, operational, and tactical levels between parties to the conflict, with respect to impartiality, Ghana underscores the position that the UN must not stand by when civilians are in danger. Sometimes, the UN's responsibility to protect civilians will require the application of force, as has happened on numerous occasions during the first decade of the twenty-first century.[80] In situations where the minimum use of force is required, it is imperative that peacekeepers have the capacity and mandate to counter serious threats to themselves and those they have been asked to protect. But the mandates should reflect the elements contained in either Chapter VI or VII of the UN Charter, as well as the interest and goals of Ghana.

12.5 FUTURE TRENDS AND GHANA'S UN PEACEKEEPING POLICY

Understanding the historical developments of Ghana's peacekeeping contributions is useful in extrapolating and gauging the future trends in its national policies. Ghana has been a consistent and long-standing supporter of UN peacekeeping, maintaining a position as a top ten contributor of troops and police for close to fifty years. Therefore, based on past and current foreign policy, together with the present stable political climate, it is highly likely that

[79] UN, *United Nations Peacekeeping Operations: Principles and Guidelines* (New York: DPKO/DFS, 2008).

[80] Victoria Holt and Glyn Taylor with Max Kelly, *Protecting Civilians in the Context of UN Peacekeeping Operations* (New York: UN DPKO/OCHA, 2009).

Ghana will maintain and even perhaps increase its contributions in the foreseeable future. Ghana's President Mills confirmed this in his speech at the 66th UN General Assembly meeting in New York in 2011. According to Mills, Ghana recognizes the need to equitably share the burden and costs of peacekeeping and as such, the country will continue to provide personnel and resources in support of UN peacekeeping and peacebuilding efforts.[81] But certainly, as the President mentioned in his speech, Ghana's continuing support will depend on the extent to which the numerous challenges that hinder or impede such peacekeeping contributions, such as financial, material, and human resource capacity constraints, are remedied.[82]

The lack of logistical capacity and critical enabling capacities such as vehicles, weapons, communication equipment, and aircraft in particular is perhaps the major source of threat to Ghana's future peacekeeping contributions. Most of this equipment, especially the aircraft, has been in service for thirty years without replacements and now their spare parts, in addition to being very expensive, are very hard to come by.[83] The lack of aircraft has affected Ghana's capacity to rapidly deploy troops to mission theatres. Moreover, the shift from the Dry Lease to the Wet Lease reimbursement system at the UN (see the Introduction to this volume), although beneficial to developing countries like Ghana, demands an upgrading of military equipment to be able to support peacekeeping operational requirements.[84] However, because the GAF lack the UN standardized operational and logistical equipment needed in operational areas, it has not been able to benefit from the system.

In terms of capacity constraints, there are several additional issues. The first issue is the education and training of the military and police for peace support operations. The KAIPTC is helping in that regard, but the centre needs adequate financial support to meet its training requirements and running costs. Other issues include the need for training in ICT and language

[81] See 'Ghana's President Mills Keynote Address at the 66th UN General Meeting in New York', 23 September 2011. At http://www.ghana.gov.gh/index.php/information/speeches/7674-speech-delivered-by-his-excellency-john-evans-atta-mills-president-of-the-republic-of-ghana-at-the-66th-general-assembly-of-the-united-nations-on-friday-23rd-september-2011-

[82] 'Ghana's President Mills Keynote Address'.

[83] See 'Government to replace GAF's ageing fleet of aircraft', 23 December 2009. At http://www.modernghana.com/news/256003/1/government-to-replace-gafs-ageing-fleet-of-aircraft.html

[84] Dry lease is the contingent-owned equipment reimbursement system where the TCC provides the equipment and the UN assumes responsibility for its maintenance. Wet lease means the TCC provides the equipment and assumes responsibility for its maintenance and support for the deployed major or minor equipment and is entitled to reimbursement. See UN General Assembly Sixty-third session, Fifth Committee Agenda item 132 on 'Administrative and budgetary aspects of the financing of the United Nations peacekeeping operations', a letter dated 22 February 2008 from the Chairman of the 2008 Working Group on Contingent-Owned Equipment to the Chairman of the Fifth Committee.

proficiency, especially French for police officers. The second problem is the lack of technical expertise needed to manage and maintain equipment in mission areas. Because personnel lack the technical expertise to manage some of the new equipment supplied by the UN or used in the mission areas, often they have to depend on external expertise, which is very expensive.

Another crucial challenge is the human resource constraints facing the security services. As at 2010, the GAF had an estimated total strength of 10,000 while the size of the police force was slightly over 23,000 with a police to civilian ratio of about 1:1,200.[85] Contrasting this number with the country's internal security needs and police to civilian ratio, and considering the fact that at any given time about 25 per cent of the military are deployed to peacekeeping missions, these circumstances are probably unsustainable for supporting large contributions. More soldiers, in particular, will need to be recruited in order to deal with internal security requirements and leave a surplus for UN peacekeeping operations.

Quite apart from these internal challenges, external factors such as the full operationalization of the African Standby Force security architecture might also impact on Ghana's contribution to UN. Although this might not be significant, Ghana will have to supply a number of troops to the 6,500 ECOWAS standby force brigade. Ghana has pledged to contribute an engineering company of 150 individuals, a level-II field hospital of 75 personnel, and a helicopter squadron.[86] What this implies is that Ghana will have to diversify its troop and police contributions to both UN and ECOWAS due to human resource constraints.

12.6 KEY LESSONS LEARNT FROM GHANA'S PARTICIPATION IN PEACEKEEPING

A number of constructive lessons can be learnt from Ghana's extensive engagement in UN peacekeeping operations. First, it can be argued that Ghana's involvement in peacekeeping has contributed to the country's stability and the consolidation of its democracy. Since independence, one of the factors that have accounted for the military engagement in Ghanaian politics has been grievances over poor economic conditions in terms of salaries and housing facilities.[87] Although successive governments since 1992 have

[85] Ghana Police Service, 'Broad Formation'. At http://www.ghanapolice.info/broad_formation.htm. Statistics for the current strength of GAF were obtained at the Headquarters in Accra.

[86] This information was obtained from IPSO, GAF headquarters, Accra.

[87] Bjorn Hettne, 'Soldiers and Politics: The Case of Ghana', *Journal of Peace Research*, 17:2 (1980), pp. 173–93.

implemented policies to improve the economic status of security officers, their impact has been minimal.[88] In this context, the UN daily reimbursement package for peacekeepers in mission areas offers an important alternative supplement to their income at home.[89] Most military and police officers can afford to build their own houses, buy good cars, and provide sufficiently for their family in part because of the financial rewards they get from peacekeeping. The unintended consequence is that this has reduced the possibility that the military or police will be tempted to overthrow a democratically elected government over economic grievances and thereby undermine the democratic process.

Moreover, peacekeeping has improved civil–military relations at home and contributed to greater professionalism within the military and police through the training that is given before pre-deployment. Another important lesson that can be learnt from the Ghanaian experience is the approach its peacekeepers have adopted to local customs and traditions in mission areas. Because the environments where peacekeepers most often work are hostile and unpredictable, Ghanaian peacekeepers try in every mission to first establish a strong relationship and trust with the local populace. They do this by respecting the customs, taboos, and traditions of the local people and not imposing their culture upon them. Their generosity towards the local people cannot be overemphasized here. There have been instances where Ghanaian peacekeepers have paid the school fees of local children, helped teach in community schools with a shortage of teachers, helped to arbitrate disputes between locals, and even provide healthcare facilities for the sick.[90] In turn, this trust and relationship-building has proved important for the success and safety of the Ghanaian peacekeepers.

The commitment to the peacekeepers' welfare is yet another lesson that can be learnt from Ghana. The payment of Ghanaian troops for peacekeeping service has been equitable.[91] Before deployment, personnel are made aware of what they are supposed to be earning daily and when they get to the mission areas, even before the UN reimburses personnel, they are given money to take care of their immediate needs. This tends to strengthen the morale of officers and increases levels of trust with their commanders. As a result, the many years of involvement in peacekeeping have not witnessed any confrontation

[88] The current public sector pay policy is the single spine salary structure (SSSS), which is a unified salary structure that places all public sector employees on one vertical structure with incremental pay points from the lowest to the highest level. It is meant to promote fairness and equity in public sector pay and salary administration.

[89] As of 2010, the average police peacekeeper received over $100 per diem and the corresponding payment for the military was $30 a day. See 'History of Ghana's Participation in International Peace Support Operations', GAF, IPSO document, 2011.

[90] Interview with Col. A. K. Asare, DAPKOP, 13 July 2011.

[91] Interview with Lt. Col. Salifu, IPSO, GAF, 26 July 2011.

between commanders and troops or even the government. This is something other countries can learn from.

The last important lesson has to do with professional training and education for peacekeepers. Through the extensive experiences gathered from the many UN and regional deployments to ongoing peace missions, the GAF and GPS can proudly share their experiences with other states. The establishment of the KAIPTC is ample testament to this rich experience. Since its establishment, the KAIPTC has trained thousands of military, police, and civilian personnel across Africa and other parts of the world for UN, AU, and ECOWAS peace operations. The centre has also produced many research works and policy papers on conflict, peace, and security issues in Africa, particularly in the West African subregion.

12.7 CONCLUSION

Since its first operation in 1960, Ghana has made significant contributions to UN peacekeeping in countries such as Lebanon, Liberia, East Timor, Cambodia, Bosnia, Kosovo, Somalia, DR Congo, Sudan, Rwanda, and Sierra Leone. In these missions, Ghanaian personnel have contributed to a wide range of complex and multidisciplinary tasks. Their distinguished service and high sense of responsibility has earned Ghanaian peacekeepers accolades and commendations from the UN system. As a member of the UN, Ghana's activism in UN peacekeeping has been dominated by motivations to keep its neighbourhood safe and peaceful, a deep-rooted commitment to the UN's peace and security architecture, the system of financial rewards attached to UN peacekeeping, and the non-tangible benefits derived from training assistance and operational experience. Against this backdrop, decisions to deploy troops to specific missions have also been influenced by domestic interests and the safety of Ghanaian peacekeepers abroad.

Ghana's consistent support for UN peacekeeping irrespective of financial constraints and regime type also suggests that it will continue to strengthen its contributions of troops and police to the UN. However, this will depend on its capacity to address the logistical, material, financial, and human resource limitations affecting the GAF and GPS. The GAF, in particular, has not been able to benefit from the UN's Wet Lease reimbursement system, basically due to logistical constraints. Peacekeeping is still evolving and so the constant upgrading of military equipment and capacity-building of the military and police needs to be given particular attention.

13

Nepal

Arturo C. Sotomayor

Nepal is a relatively small state with few global aspirations. Nepal's foreign affairs have traditionally been determined by its geopolitical situation, between China and India. As a buffer state between two great powers, Nepal has 'sought to balance Chinese and Indian interests, successfully maintaining its autonomy in the face of this dual competition'.[1] In 1961 it joined and helped found the Non-Alignment Movement precisely to anchor its neutral and non-aligned status. The promotion of trade, tourism, hydropower, investment, and overseas employment defines its foreign policy agenda. According to Kedar Bhakta Shrestha, a retired senior Nepali diplomat, 'Trade, aid and developmental issues have a direct bearing in the formulation of Nepal's foreign policy.'[2]

However, Nepal has substantially increased its troop commitment to the United Nations (UN) in the past decade and has become a major contributor to peacekeeping operations worldwide. According to the Ministry of Foreign Affairs, since 1958 Nepal has participated in twenty-nine UN peace missions, suffering sixty-nine fatalities in the process.[3] Between 2000 and 2010, Nepal was the seventh largest troop contributor to UN peacekeeping. In relation to its population (approximately 26 million), Nepal is the second largest overall troop-lending country per capita in the world (after Uruguay) and the largest contributor per capita in its region (South Asia). In 2010, Nepal had the third

[1] See 'South Asia: External Affairs-Nepal', document produced by Jane's Sentinel Security Assessment, Englewood, Colorado, 19 October 2011.

[2] Kedar Bhakta Shrestha, 'Nepal's Foreign Policy: Tied Up with Course of China–India Relations', presentation at an Institute of Foreign Affairs Seminar, published in *The Telegraph Weekly*, 14 November 2011. At http://www.telegraphnepal.com/national/2011-12-01/nepals-foreign-policy:-tied-up-with-course-of-china-india-relations

[3] See 'Nepal and the United Nations', Ministry of Foreign Affairs, February 2006. At http://www.mofa.gov.np/nepalUN/statement7.php. See also *Ekantipur*, 'Put Nepali Peacekeepers at the Helm, PM tells UN', *Ekantipur*, 27 September 2011. At http://www.ekantipur.com/2011/09/26/top-story/put-nepali-peacekeepers-at-helm-pm-tells-un/341433.html

largest contingent in the UN Stabilization Mission in Haiti (MINUSTAH), after Brazil and Uruguay, and the fifth largest troop commitment to the UN Stabilization Mission in the Democratic Republic of the Congo (MONUSCO), after India, Pakistan, South Africa, and Uruguay. This is interesting, given that Nepal has no strategic interests in the western hemisphere or in Africa. In 2008, these contributions prompted UN Secretary-General Ban Ki-moon to send a message of thanks to Nepal on its fiftieth anniversary of providing peacekeepers: 'More than half of all the Member States of the United Nations', he said 'contribute troops and police to peacekeeping operations. We are grateful to every one of them. But our special thanks go to the top contributors, among which Nepal ranks in the first five. Over the past 50 years, Nepal has contributed 60,000 peacekeepers in some 40 peacekeeping missions. Today, Nepal and four other nations of the South together contribute nearly half of the United Nations peacekeepers around the world.'[4]

Nepal's peacekeeping trajectory is even more remarkable given that during this same period it experienced a civil war and dramatic political transition. In the context of a decade-long civil war (1996–2006), the country went from being a monarchy to a parliamentary monarchy to a republican system in less than twenty years. It also hosted a UN political mission (UNMIN) that has monitored a fragile peace agreement since 2007.[5] Ironically, while the UN deployed personnel in Nepal, Nepalese soldiers were deployed in large numbers to UN missions elsewhere.

This raises the questions addressed in this chapter: Why has such a small country volunteered such a large military force to peacekeeping efforts and increased its troop commitment in the past decade? Drawing on the rationales for contributing to UN peacekeeping identified in this volume, I argue that normative, political, and security rationales played little, if any, role in Nepal's peacekeeping trajectory. Instead, political (regional), institutional (military), and economic factors largely explain this experience. Politically, a diffusion pattern has developed in South Asia, in which India, Pakistan, and its proximate states (Bangladesh, Nepal, and Sir Lanka) have emulated and imitated each other's peacekeeping practices, leading to large troop commitments to the UN operations system. Domestically, the decision-making process is led by the Nepalese Army, an institution that has experienced its own transition and has found in peacekeeping a valuable and sustainable source of income for its troops. In fact, much like the case of Uruguay, peacekeeping policy in Nepal is, in essence, decided in the military domain. Within Nepal, there is a notable

[4] Ban Ki-moon, 'Thanking Every Nepalese Peacekeeper Past and Present', UN Secretary-General, document SG/SM/11638 PKO/187, New York, 12 June 2008. At http://www.un.org/News/Press/docs/2008/sgsm11638.doc.htm

[5] On the role of UNMIN see Astri Suhrke, 'Virtues of a Narrow Mission: The UN Peace Operation in Nepal', *Global Governance*, 17:1 (2011), pp. 37–56.

absence of civilian interest in peacekeeping affairs, in which various political authorities have implicitly ceded space and provided autonomy to the military to exert influence over peacekeeping policies.

This chapter addresses these issues in five sections. The first analyses the evolution of Nepal's peacekeeping contribution, especially since its political liberalization in the early 1990s. The second, third, and fourth sections examine the motivating factors behind Nepal's increasing role in UN peacekeeping, focusing mainly on political, institutional, and economic rationales. Section 13.5 examines the military and political challenges that Nepalese soldiers have often encountered when assuming their Blue Helmet roles.

13.1 NEPAL AND UN PEACEKEEPING

During the Cold War, Nepal was a minor contributor to UN peacekeeping, supplying only military observers. It joined the UN in 1955 but first participated in peacekeeping efforts in 1958, when it committed a handful of observers to the UN Observation Group in Lebanon (UNOGIL). In 1965 it was chosen to supervise the UN Military Observer Group in India and Pakistan (UNMOGIP), which represented the apex of its peacekeeping contribution during the bipolar era.[6]

The country's involvement in peace missions slowly increased in 1993, after its initial move towards democratization. In fact, its peacekeeping trajectory, illustrated in Figure 13.1, shows two different paths. First, there was an initial phase, from 1990 to 2004, when Nepal's troop commitment was relatively significant, but inconsistent, in part due to the consequences of the civil war and the Maoist insurgency. The years between 2004 and 2006, however, marked the beginning of a second phase, when the country more than tripled its peacekeeping commitment, a decision that coincided with the peace process and the establishment of UNMIN.

For the majority of its history, Nepal was governed by a monarchy. In 1959, the country experienced a brief flirtation with democracy when the king established an authoritarian regime, based on a system of one-party rule, which was referred to as the *Rashtriya Panchayat* regime. However, in 1990, massive demonstrations forced King Birendra to redraft the Constitution and modify the political system to grant extensive democratic rights. Nepal was

[6] For a brief overview of Nepal's peacekeeping contribution in the Cold War see Surendra Singh Rawal, *United Nations Peacekeeping Participation and Civil–Military Relations in Troop Contributing Countries* (Monterey, CA: Naval Postgraduate School, Master of Arts in Security Studies, March 2010), p. 72. At http://edocs.nps.edu/npspubs/scholarly/theses/2010/Mar/10Mar_Rawal.pdf

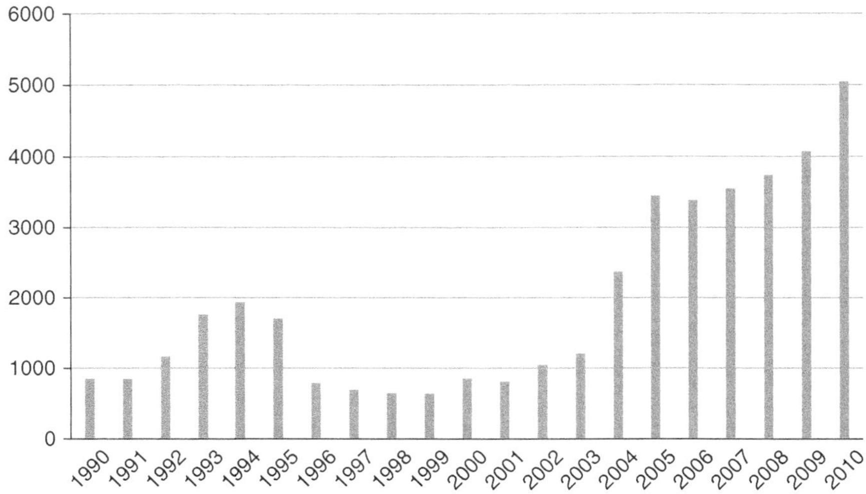

Figure 13.1 Nepali Uniformed Personnel in UN Peacekeeping Operations, 1990–2010[7]

also declared a multiethnic, multilingual, and parliamentary monarchy, and in 1991 suffrage was recognized and democratic elections introduced.[8]

While democratization generated high expectations, the country experienced great political instability. Between 1991 and 1999, Nepal went through six different governments, but the Nepalese Royal Army was not dismantled and remained loyal to the king, even though it faced accusations of resorting to the unrestrained use of force.[9] Just as Nepal was undergoing its first experience of democracy, the Maoists launched an insurgent movement in 1996, which first affected rural areas, but then spread across the country. The guerrillas enjoyed some degree of support, but they also generated violence, and more than 13,000 people were killed. At first, they targeted law enforcement and police agencies, but by 2001 army barracks were also under attack. By then,

[7] The UN does not report a yearly ranking of troop contributions to its operations. Instead, it reports monthly data on the size of individual peacekeeping activities. The data in this figure represent the sum of a yearly average for Nepal's monthly contributions to UN peacekeeping operations, including troops, military observers, and police from 1990–2010. Data were obtained from *UN Department of Peacekeeping Operations, Facts and Figures for Troop Contributors, 2000–2010*. At http://www.un.org/en/peacekeeping/resources/statistics/

[8] For an analysis of Nepal's transition to democracy in the 1990s, see Ramje P. Parajulee, *The Democratic Transition in Nepal* (New York: Rowman & Littlefield, 2000); Maya Chadda, *Building Democracy in South Asia: India, Nepal, Pakistan* (Boulder, CO: Lynne Rienner, 2000), pp. 111–42; and Mahendra Lawoti, 'Democracy, Domination and Exclusionary Constitutional Engineering Process in Nepal, 1990', in Mahendra Lawoti (ed.), *Contentious Politics and Democratization in Nepal* (London: Sage, 2007), pp. 48–72.

[9] See Madhav Joshi and T. David Mason, 'Peasants, Patrons, and Parties: The Tension Between Clientelism and Democracy in Nepal', *International Studies Quarterly*, 55:1 (2010), pp. 151–75.

both the Maoists and the military were responsible for gross human rights violations.[10]

Nepal contributed troops to the UN in spite of, or perhaps because of, its political instability. During the early process of democratization, the country's contribution to peacekeeping went from just a handful of observers in 1991 to almost 2,000 soldiers in 1994. Most of Nepal's Blue Helmets were concentrated in the UN Interim Force in Lebanon (UNIFIL) and the UN Protection Force for Yugoslavia (UNPROFOR).

Nevertheless, its commitment to UN peacekeeping was volatile at this stage. When the Maoist insurgency emerged, Nepal progressively reduced the number of its UN peacekeepers from close to 2,000 in 1994 to less than 600 soldiers in 1999. Although this coincided with a general decline in UN peacekeepers, Nepal's decision appears to have been in direct response to the demand for counter-insurgency security forces at home. During the civil war (1996–2006), the country maintained an average force of less than 800 Blue Helmets per year. The decline in peacekeeping participation occurred in spite of the fact that in 2003 the Royal Nepalese Army increased its manpower ceiling from 50,000 to nearly 65,000.[11] In other words, Nepal had more soldiers available during this period, but committed less to UN missions.

This decline in peacekeeping participation overlaps with the country's democratic breakdown. In 2001, King Gyanendra took over the throne after the crown prince Dipendra gunned down ten members of his own family, including his father, King Birendra Shah, before shooting himself.[12] In early 2005, chaos appeared to dominate the political spectrum, with the Maoists increasing their influence and military presence. Amidst the turmoil, the newly crowned king suspended parliament and appointed a government led by himself, effectively instigating a legislative coup. The Nepalese Royal Army remained loyal to the crown and assumed its classic role as guardian of the monarchy, becoming increasingly involved in cordon, search and destroy operations across the country.[13] Allegations of human rights abuses by both the Maoists and the Army peaked during this period, as close to 100,000 people were killed in less than a decade.[14]

The breakdown of democracy did not last very long. The king's assumption of power in 2005 generated massive discontent among the middle classes and

[10] Shisir Khanal, 'Committed Insurgents, a Divided State and the Maoist Insurgency in Nepal', in Lawoti (ed.), *Contentious Politics and Democratization in Nepal*, pp. 75–94.

[11] See Stuart Gordon, 'Evaluating Nepal's Integrated "Security" and "Development" Policy', *Asian Survey*, 45:4 (2005), p. 594.

[12] See Ishaan Tharoor, 'Revisiting Nepal's Palace Massacre', *Time Magazine* 8 April 2009. At http://www.time.com/time/world/article/0,8599,1890047,00.html#ixzz1tlYv9IB0

[13] See Gordon, 'Evaluating Nepal's Integrated "Security" and "Development" Policy'.

[14] See Mahendra Lawoti, 'Contentious Politics in Democratizing Nepal', in Lawoti (ed.), *Contentious Politics and Democratization in Nepal*, p. 35.

political parties. Once again, street protests forced the king to cede power to the last elected government. At that point, the Maoists came out from the jungle and turned themselves into a political party. Elections were held and, for the first time, the Maoists joined the government. They demanded that the king be removed and voted to transform the country into a republic, effectively putting an end to a 240-year-old monarchical institution.[15]

The process culminated with the Comprehensive Peace Agreement signed in November 2006, which put an end to the armed struggle. It was then that the UN was invited to participate as a peace guarantor and to monitor the cease-fire and disarmament processes (through UNAMIN).[16] Interestingly enough, this coincided with Nepal's increasing involvement in UN peace operations, leading to the second phase of its recent peacekeeping trajectory. In 2005, the Army started to provide a large number of UN peacekeepers, averaging more than 3,000 soldiers per year, which was almost triple the number deployed during the first phase. In 2010, it reached its historical peak, deploying a yearly average of more than 5,000 Blue Helmets, becoming the fifth largest troop-contributing country that year.

In 2010, for example, Nepal sustained full battalions in four concurrent UN missions: MINUSTAH, MONUSCO, UNIFIL, and UNAMID (the African Union/UN hybrid operation in Darfur). In early 2011, Nepal had 3,491 soldiers abroad, of which 1,075 were in Haiti (9 per cent of the UN force, the largest non-Latin American troop-lending country in MINUSTAH), 1,047 in the DRC (5 per cent of the UN force), 1,014 in Lebanon (8.5 per cent of the UN force there), and 637 in Darfur. In addition to these large deployments, Nepal also contributed a handful of observers—or token contributions—to five UN missions: UNAMI (UN Assistance Mission to Iraq), UNMIL (UN Mission in Liberia), UMIT (UN Mission in East Timor), UNOCI (UN Mission in Côte d'Ivoire), and UNTSO (UN Truce Supervision Organization in the Middle East).[17]

Nepal's emergence as a major UN peacekeeping contributor appears, in principle, to have been motivated by a desire to send credible international signals. In fact, it welcomed peacekeepers, which was interpreted as a sign, both of its credibility and its commitment to settle peace once and for all. As Page Fortna argues, 'willingness to accept intrusive monitoring by peacekeepers sends a credible sign of commitment to peace'.[18] In fact, the most important component of the 2006 Comprehensive Peace Agreement was the

[15] See Somini Sengupta, 'Nepal Reborn as a Republic', *The New York Times*, 29 May 2008. At http://www.nytimes.com/2008/05/29/world/asia/29nepal.html

[16] See Nishchal Nath Pandey, *New Nepal: The Faultines* (London: Sage, 2010), pp. 6–10, 92–7.

[17] See UN Department of Peacekeeping Operations, 'Country Contributions Detailed by Mission'. At http://www.un.org/en/peacekeeping/resources/statistics/contributors.shtml

[18] Virginia Page Fortna, *Does Peacekeeping Work? Shaping Belligerents' Choices after Civil War* (Princeton, NJ: Princeton University Press, 2008), p. 95.

integration of the former Royal Nepalese Army and the former Maoist combatants into the newly created People's Liberation Army of Nepal. Participation in peacekeeping would thus have created an ideal opportunity to reshape the armed forces by providing a non-contentious and unifying external mission.

However, the peace agreement has never been fully implemented, in part because of a dispute regarding the rehabilitation package. The Maoists demanded a large cash payment for every departing soldier. Those demands were rejected and the insurgents then agreed to proceed with the discharges by accepting a UN-sponsored package that included educational support, business, vocational training, and financial help to start a business.[19] A similar package, however, has not been negotiated with the Army. At the time of writing it remained unclear how the forces would be merged in order to implement the peace agreement. The stalemate over the integration process has been harmful for peace and democratization efforts. Both armies remain intact, resistant to civilian oversight and increasingly testy.[20]

Hence, Nepal's UN peacekeeping troop contribution has never included former Maoist insurgents or other forces (such as the Gurkha soldiers).[21] Nor has it significantly influenced the democratic reform process. In fact, the country's peacekeeping commitment involves mostly Army personnel and a handful of police forces. For example, in December 2011, Nepal contributed with 3,597 uniformed personnel, of whom 5.7 per cent were individual police forces, 13.5 per cent formed police units, and the remaining 80.8 per cent included Army troop contingents, military observers, and experts on the mission.[22] What

[19] See Jim Yardley, 'Nepal Waits as 2 Armies, Former Foes, Become One', *The New York Times*, 4 February 2010. At http://www.nytimes.com/2010/02/04/world/asia/04nepal.html

[20] See Tilak Pokharel, 'Nepal's Premier Resigns After Power Struggle Over Army Chief', *The New York Times*, 5 May 2009. At http://www.nytimes.com/2009/05/05/world/asia/05nepal.html; and see Kiran Chapgain, 'Nepal Releases Thousands of Former Fighters as Part of Peace Deal', *The New York Times*, 3 February 2012. At http://www.nytimes.com/2012/02/04/world/asia/nepal-releases-thousands-of-former-maoist-fighters.html?ref=nepal

[21] The Nepalese Army is not to be confused with the Nepalese Gurkhas. Not only are these two institutions different in terms of instruction, training, and recruitment, but they also have different systems of loyalty and institutional affiliation. Gurkha soldiers are recruited mostly from an ethnic minority in central Nepal. They serve the British Army (not the Nepalese Army) and are considered as a private force or 'mercenaries' by the Nepalese government. They do not participate in UN peacekeeping operations as part of the Nepalese troop contribution and the Nepalese Army does not train them. For detailed information on the nature and history of the Gurkhas see http://www.gwt.org.uk/about-gurkhas/

[22] According to UN official statistics, in December 2011 Nepal's individual police contribution was distributed as follows: 133 in UNAMID, 29 in MINUSTAH, 25 in UNMIL, 11 in UNMIL, and 7 in UNMISS. Similarly, Nepal contributed with police force units in the following missions: 126 in MINUSTAH, 128 in UNAMID, and 234 in UNMIL. See UN Department of Peacekeeping Operations, 'Country contributions detailed by mission', December 2011. At http://www.un.org/en/peacekeeping/resources/statistics/contributors_archive.shtml

motivates such participation? I argue that political, institutional, and economic incentives motivate the Army's interest in UN peace operations.

13.2 POLITICAL RATIONALES AND NEIGHBOURHOOD EFFECTS ON PEACEKEEPING CONTRIBUTIONS

Evidence from South Asia suggests that peacekeeping policies are subject to what appears to be a 'diffusion wave', whereby neighbouring states have adopted similar peacekeeping patterns. According to the theoretical literature on International Relations, international diffusion patterns are often geographically clustered, suggesting that proximity prompts imitation, leading to a strong pattern of regional policy diffusion, in which states factor in the choices of their neighbours without any previous notion of mutual coordination.[23] This is what Zachary Elkins and Beth Simmons refer to as uncoordinated interdependence, which includes imitation, band-wagoning, emulation, and mimicry.[24]

Indeed, the ranking of top ten UN troop contributors includes four of the seven South Asian states (Pakistan, Bangladesh, India, and Nepal), followed by Sri Lanka (26th in the ranking). The exceptions are Bhutan and the Maldives, which have yet to provide any UN peacekeepers. The 'peacekeeping wave' spread first between the two regional rivals (India and Pakistan) and then among the smaller neighbouring states. This is also a subregion of Asia where states interact regularly via trade and through various diplomatic networks. They also share a common history and culture, having experienced similar patterns of colonialism, independence, and even conflict processes. The four leading South Asian states have not only contributed with troops; they have also established their own peacekeeping training centres and have occasionally participated in joint peace operations. In the case of Nepal, specifically, the Army established its peacekeeping centre, known as the Birendra Peace Operations Training Centre, in 2002, amidst the counter-insurgency war.[25]

[23] Stephen M. Walt used the metaphor of political contagion in 'Fads, Fevers, and Firestorms', *Foreign Policy*, 121 (2000), pp. 34–42.

[24] Zachary Elkins and Beth Simmons, 'On Waves, Clusters, and Diffusion: A Conceptual Framework', *Annals of the American Academy*, 598 (2005), p. 35.

[25] According to *Jane's Military*, the centre was established with financial assistance from the United Kingdom and the United States. Great Britain provided close to £210,000, while Washington funded an electronic classroom and other equipment, including a driving simulator. The army suspended international training and exercises temporarily in 2003, when the state of emergency was declared, but activities were soon resumed in 2005, when Nepal increased its peacekeeping commitment. See Jane's Sentinel Security Assessment—South Asia, 'Nepal: Army', *Jane's Military*, 30 April 2009.

An intense regional rivalry might have prompted India and Pakistan to supply an increasing number of Blue Helmets; but the competition for influence and primacy had a contagion effect that reached the neighbouring countries (Bangladesh and Nepal). Indeed, what started as a regional diffusion pattern soon morphed into a political imperative, merging regional and prestige effects. For a small state such as Nepal, peacekeeping offered international and diplomatic exposure that was readily available in regional forums. In a region rife with intense political and military competition, Nepalese decision-makers found it easier to participate in UN peacekeeping missions than in other diplomatic circles. For instance, Nepal seldom participated in the UN Security Council as a non-permanent member, serving in such a capacity only twice in its history (1969–70 and 1988–9). Competition for a non-permanent seat in the Council has become so intense for the Asian group (with India, Pakistan, and Japan regularly engaged in diplomatic disputes for a single seat) that smaller states often feel excluded from the process.

In this context, peacekeeping participation offered a global role for small South Asian states. For instance, in 2005, Nepal became a member of the UN Peacebuilding Commission, which gathers all relevant actors to marshal resources and provide recommendations on peacebuilding. This appointment was achieved through military activism in peacekeeping. Membership of the Peacebuilding Commission was automatically given to the top five providers of military and police personnel to UN missions, of which Nepal was one (the others were Bangladesh, India, Nigeria, and Pakistan).[26] Peacekeeping thus allowed Nepal to be seen as a relevant player vis-à-vis its larger neighbours, while pursuing an independent and even autonomous foreign policy. As the Nepali National Contingent Commander in Haiti put it, 'we have been the true diplomats and representatives of Nepal'.[27] This implies that Nepalese national interests were equally represented by its military commitments overseas. Hence, regional dynamics created political imperatives to participate in peacekeeping, as it provided a rationale to assert an independent foreign policy in a competitive regional environment.

Similarly, South Asia has a feature that no other region possesses, namely, a critical mass of soldiers, mostly infantrymen, which can be committed for missions overseas. True, Nepal is one of the top ten UN troop contributing countries; yet the contribution represents only a small part of the Army's force at home, which now totals close to 100,000 individuals (95,753). Ironically, the Army has increased its strength since peace was formally signed. As a former

[26] Detailed information about the role of the PBC and its membership can be obtained directly from the UN website at http://www.un.org/en/peacebuilding/mandate.shtml

[27] Author's interview with Colonel Ratindra Khatri, Chief Military Personnel Officer of MINUSTAH Force Headquarters and the Nepali National Contingent Commander in Haiti, Nepalese battalion (NEP BATT), Port-au-Prince, 21 September 2010.

UN diplomat and native Nepali told *The New York Times* during an interview in 2010, 'the Nepalese army is twice as large today, with 96,000 soldiers, as it was when the guerrilla war began, and the number of police and paramilitary police officers has steadily risen to roughly 80,000 . . . That's more than all the country's civil servants combined, minus teachers.'[28] By comparison, in 2010 Nepal was deploying less than 5,000 soldiers abroad per month to UN peace missions, around only 5 per cent of its total force. Some critics considered that even sending a handful of soldiers abroad was too risky for a country facing so many security threats at home. In an interview for the *Nepali Times* in 2004, the then Army's spokesperson, Brigadier General Rajendra Thapa, dismissed these criticisms. Instead, he argued that peacekeeping only affected 'a small portion of the army, and does not affect our full operational strength . . . The army's strength has grown and is now approaching 80,000 . . . We have a larger force today, enough to spare for non-military activities like maintenance, disaster relief and Maoist rehabilitation programs.'[29]

Regional and political considerations, however, only provide the context under which Nepal contributes uniformed personnel to UN peacekeeping operations. For example, regional diffusion patterns cannot account for why Nepal increased its commitment in 2004–6; for that purpose we need to explore institutional and economic rationales, which are analysed in the next two sections.

13.3 INSTITUTIONAL RATIONALES: MILITARY AND PROFESSIONAL MOTIVATIONS

Civil–military and bureaucratic considerations affect the final decision on whether or not to deploy soldiers abroad. As I argue elsewhere, 'Although short from war, peacekeeping entails a military dimension of foreign policy, in which uniformed personnel are deployed to accomplish diplomatic and political means. As such, decisions to commit troops to UN peacekeeping must have the implicit support of the armed forces.'[30] In Nepal, civilian control of the armed forces and foreign policy succumbed to the prevailing political instability. Repeated coups and the absence of clear leadership naturally

[28] See Jim Yardley, 'Nepal Waits as 2 Armies, Former Foes, Become One', *The New York Times*, 3 February 2010. At http://www.nytimes.com/2010/02/04/world/asia/04nepal.html

[29] Naresh Newar, 'Peacekeeping Away from Home: Can Nepal Afford to Keep the Peace Elsewhere When There is No Peace at Home?' *Nepali Times*, 27 May 2004. At http://www.nepalitimes.com/issue/2011/09/09/Nation/18542

[30] Arturo C. Sotomayor, 'Why Some States Participate in UN Peace Missions While Others Do Not: An Analysis of Civil-Military Relations and its Effects on Latin America's Contributions to Peacekeeping Operations', *Security Studies*, 19:1 (2010), p. 162.

affected the foreign affairs establishment. A comprehensive study of Nepal's peacekeeping policy by Surendra Singh Rawal found that instability and short-lived regimes impeded the formulation of a long-term foreign policy agenda. As Singh Rawal argued, 'The political parties were always focused on making and breaking the government, and almost all of the sectors were politicized . . . the country leaders ignored the internationalist aspect of foreign policy . . . Since political attention to the internationalist approach was not sufficient, the Nepalese Army's participation in UN peacekeeping continued without meaningful political-diplomatic congruity.'[31]

Indeed, within the military establishment there was a generalized perception that Nepal's diplomacy had been ineffective in setting out the country's political independence and inconsistent in its multilateral approach. According to Rabinra Mishra, 'This can be attributed partly to Nepal's Foreign Ministry, which, in the words of Kumar, is "regrettably useless", and partly to the politicians, who, in the words of Pan-dey, use nationalism opportunistically "in respect of relation with India" and to seek its blessings to feel "secure".'[32]

In Nepal there has been widespread apathy about scrutinizing military and peacekeeping matters, especially as they relate to the deployment, organization, and training of troops. This civilian deficit probably reinforces militarization, as it affords an opening for the armed forces to monopolize the decision-making process on UN troop commitments. The unstable nature of domestic politics in Nepal in fact enabled the Army to formulate defence and military policies with relative autonomy. On paper, the President is the chief commander and assumes leadership of the Army, with the prime minister and defence minister acting as managers of defence policy. In practice, however, civilians have conceded institutional autonomy. According to Singh Rawal's study on Nepal's peacekeeping policy:

> The government treats Nepalese peacekeeping participation as the sole prerogative of the Nepalese Army, showing a lack of enthusiasm to control, coordinate and supervise these activities. The Ministry of Defense has not been competitive enough in managing peacekeeping efforts. The process of selecting, training, equipping, projecting and maintaining peacekeepers in conflict zones has not been effective.[33]

It is safe to assert that Nepal's peacekeeping participation has therefore been assessed independently of political and civilian imperatives, in which the Army has a virtual monopoly on the decision-making process.

[31] Surendra Singh Rawal, 'United Nations Peacekeeping Participation', p. 73.

[32] Rabindra Mishra, 'India's Role in Nepal's Maoist Insurgency', *Asian Survey*, 44:5 (2004), p. 646.

[33] Singh Rawal, 'United Nations Peacekeeping Participation', p. 65.

What interests does the Army pursue in peacekeeping operations? Army officials often claim that engagement in international operations increases professionalism, in part because it provides an environment in which soldiers can be trained to conduct a variety of tasks abroad. The acquisition of such expertise is thought to generate positive changes in military leadership and management systems at home. One positive, professional acquired skill identified by Nepali officers includes the added flexibility, adaptability, and versatility gained through their participation in UN peace missions. Indeed, Nepal's exposure to multiple and diverse peace operations—from Haiti, Darfur, and the DRC to Yugoslavia and East Timor—has contributed to the development of a hybrid force that is extremely adaptable to different operational environments. As the national force commander in MINUSTAH explained, 'We can go everywhere and adapt ourselves to the mission; we are very versatile in peacekeeping.'[34]

Similarly, the Nepalese Army highly values the so-called diplomatic skills acquired through peacekeeping. From this perspective, additional professional skills are acquired by engaging the armed forces in situations that require conflict resolution. In an era dominated by globalization and diffused threats, the armed forces are increasingly being tasked with multiple missions that go beyond fighting conventional wars or insurgency. New military missions thus help generate the basis for a new military ethos in Nepal, in which peacekeeping has occupied a central position. From the Nepalese perspective, peacekeeping has helped to transform 'the war manager' into 'the soldier diplomat' who is more focused on preventing wars than on fighting them.[35]

For instance, in interviews conducted in Haiti at the Nepalese battalion one of the peacekeepers mentioned that their approach towards peacekeeping was essentially diplomatic: 'We do not have geopolitical interests, we are not from the region, and we are not here to influence anyone. People can trust us because we are neutral and impartial to the conflict.'[36] Indeed, what Nepal offers to the UN peacekeeping system is mostly a neutral and impartial force. Certainly, neutrality is the cornerstone of traditional UN peace-observation missions, which is the forte of the Nepalese military.

[34] Author's interview with Colonel Ratindra Khatri, Chief Military Personnel Officer of MINUSTAH Force Headquarters and the Nepali National Contingent Commander in Haiti, Nepalese battalion (NEP BATT), Port-au-Prince, 21 September 2010.

[35] On the 'soldier diplomat' see Charles Moskos, *Peace Soldiers: The Sociology of a United Nations Military Force* (Chicago: University of Chicago Press, 1976); Charles C. Moskos, John Allen Williams, and David R. Segal (eds.), *The Postmodern Military* (New York: Oxford University Press, 2000); and Tony Corn, 'From War Managers to Soldier Diplomats: The Coming Revolution in Civil-Military Relations', *Small Wars Journal*, 5:6 (2009), pp. 1–33. At http://smallwarsjournal.com/blog/journal/docs-temp/259-corn.pdf

[36] Author's interview with a Nepalese peacekeeper, Port-au-Prince, 21 September 2010.

UN officials have indeed noticed the professional and highly flexible attributes of the Nepalese Blue Helmets. For example, Nepalese forces were instrumental in Haiti, especially in the immediate aftermath of the earthquake, in 2010. There, Blue Helmets participated in the rescue mission in Port-au-Prince, where they were able to quickly produce information about who was missing near Camp Charlie, the UN headquarters, which collapsed and killed over 100 UN staff members, including the head of the mission, his deputy, and the police commissioner.[37] According to Colonel Ratindra Khatri, who served as the Nepali force commander at the time: 'the reason the Nepali forces could function so efficiently was also because the Nepali battalion did not suffer any casualties, let alone fatalities . . . Those military contingents who suffered losses, it was difficult for them. Not only did they have to rescue and recover their own, but they also naturally fell into a grieving period.'[38] Nepali soldiers had one key advantage: they were fluent in English and could thus communicate with UN staff and international NGOs in ways that Brazilian and other Latin American troops could not (because they were not fully conversant or fluent in English).

The core of the Nepalese peacekeeping contingent is made up of infantry, in which only a handful of officers are involved in observing posts. Although these soldiers have institutional incentives to join peace missions, their subsequent chances of promotion are very limited, because their participation in peacekeeping does not contribute to the likelihood of promotion. As one of the Blue Helmets indicated, 'Our career plan has its own requirements separate from participation in peacekeeping.'[39] In fact, those who are recruited for UN missions, including officers, are not volunteers, but are chosen by the Nepalese Army and the military staff of the headquarters.

These issues and the fact that an army at civil war could hardly be said to be lacking operational experience suggest that, while certainly present, 'military professional incentives' were not necessarily the driving force behind the army's decision to embrace UN peacekeeping.

13.4 ECONOMIC INCENTIVES: INSTITUTIONAL AND INDIVIDUAL

This might lead to the conclusion that economic factors played a significant role in the Nepalese case. Three factors drive the military's appetite for economic

[37] See 'Haiti quake death toll rises to 230,000', *BBC News*, 11 February 2011. At http://news.bbc.co.uk/2/hi/8507531.stm

[38] Kashish Das Shrestha, 'Haiti's Nepali UN Peacekeepers', *República: The Week*, 17 December 2010. At http://archives.myrepublica.com/portal/index.php?action=news_details&news_id=26239

[39] Author's interview with a Nepalese peacekeeper, Port-au-Prince, 21 September 2010.

resources. First, the abolition of the monarchy created enormous uncertainty for the Army. For centuries it had been a staunch supporter of the king. In 2006, the Royal Nepalese Army was renamed the People's Liberation Army and was placed under parliament's control. The prospect of a Maoist defence minister or commander-in-chief created uncertainty within the Army and placed it in the difficult position of having to surrender itself to a former foe. Hence, in this uncertain environment, there has been a strong imperative to find a justification for the establishment of a force of over 90,000 individuals.

Second, according to Stuart Gordon, the Army found itself starved of funds as government budgets shrank with the collapse of the tourist industry. Public funding was suddenly cut by nearly 75 per cent.[40] Little was done to reduce, integrate, and modernize the force, as requested by the peace agreement.[41] As a consequence, peacekeeping provided an important alternative source of income, while making it possible for force levels to be maintained. As an officer revealed in an interview with the *Nepali Times*, 'many join the army with a dream of participating in peacekeeping. In six months they earn more than what they would make in 10 years of service at home. We used international peacekeeping as a reward for our troops and yes, it is an important source of revenue for the army as well.'[42]

For those chosen to join a UN mission, there is a substantial monetary—not professional—incentive to participate. The UN monthly allowance of approximately $1,000 per soldier is almost equal to Nepal's GDP/per capita ($1,200 per year). While the Army retains a portion of these allowances (see below), soldiers still earn substantially more on peacekeeping missions than at home. This cascades nationally as the money returns to Nepal in the form of remittances.

Third, peacekeeping is not only a source of individual income, but also a supplier of funds for the Army as an institution. Unlike some of the country cases examined in this book, where allowances are directly paid to the Blue Helmets, a large proportion of the pay and allowances accrued by soldiers on UN service is paid to the Nepalese Army Welfare Fund, which then has the power to disburse it. Before 2004, close to 80 per cent of UN allowances went straight into the welfare fund. This rate was eventually reduced to 50 per cent in 2004 and is currently at 25 per cent.[43] In 2010, alone, close to 5,000 Nepalese soldiers were deployed every month to different UN missions, which amounts to $5 million dollars per month ($1,000 dollars per month per soldier) or $60 million per year. In proportion to the defence budget, this

[40] Gordon, 'Evaluating Nepal's Integrated "Security" and "Development" Policy', p. 581.
[41] See Yardley, 'Nepal Waits'.
[42] See Newar, 'Peacekeeping Away from Home'.
[43] See Newar, 'Peacekeeping Away from Home'.

represents close to a quarter of the 2010 Nepalese defence budget ($245 million).[44]

Certainly, peacekeeping represents a very small portion of the Army's operational strength, but its value resides in the money it generates and the foreign currency it attracts. In fact, peacekeeping reimbursements help finance Nepal's defence budget, effectively providing the necessary incentives to keep the force as it is. Hence, Nepal provides an example of a case in which UN peacekeeping offers financial rewards to both the defence sector and individual soldiers. UN reimbursements have provided resources to sustain operational costs, while helping sustain force levels amidst demands for modernization and force restructuring in the wake of the civil war.

13.5 CHALLENGES AND OBSTACLES: CORRUPTION, RECRUITMENT, AND CHOLERA

Nepal has participated in UN peacekeeping operations above and beyond the line of duty. Some states make primarily financial contributions to support UN missions, while others provide mainly uniformed personnel. Though both types of participation (financial and military) are important for the functioning and success of peace missions, the major burden of carrying out these operations in the field is borne by a small number of troop-contributing countries, of which Nepal is among the top ten. However, Nepal's peacekeeping efforts have been subject to serious criticisms too, ranging from allegations of institutional corruption to human rights violations. This, in turn, raises questions about the quality of Blue Helmets being provided by small and developing states.

First, there is evidence that the military's engagement in peacekeeping has generated institutional corruption. As Singh Rawal explains, 'The Ministry of Defence has not been competitive enough in managing peacekeeping efforts . . . Although the Nepalese Army has made efforts to make the welfare fund activities transparent and better managed, these efforts are seen inadequate for projecting a positive image of the army and enhancing the effectiveness and efficiency of Nepalese peacekeeping efforts.'[45]

Indeed, as indicated in the previous section, the Welfare Fund provides the army with the powers of disbursement and enables it to have direct access to resources without proper means of accountability. Ultimately, this has

[44] For Nepal's defence budget see International Institute for Strategic Studies, *The Military Balance 2011* (New York: Routledge, 2011), p. 261.

[45] Rawal, 'United Nations Peacekeeping Participation', pp. 65–6.

generated an environment propitious for corruption. In 2010, the UN discovered that Nepalese peacekeepers serving in Sudan (most of them police units) were poorly equipped for the mission. This prompted an internal investigation, which found that 'armoured personnel carriers bought in 2009 were of poor quality and had parts missing . . . They were bought at much cheaper prices and the remaining funds were siphoned off.'[46] In total, $4 million dollars had been embezzled for the procurement of armoured vehicles to supply Nepali Blue Helmets in Darfur. In an unprecedented move, the UN requested that Nepal replace the equipment or risk being pulled out of the mission and losing all reimbursement benefits. The Nepalese government did comply, but it did not identify the corrupt officials. The Nepalese anti-corruption body (known as the CIAA) was tasked with investigating and charging any officials responsible in the 'Sudan scam' (as it is known in Nepal). However, the CIAA could not question or charge politicians. Most officials who have been charged have blamed the security forces' chain of command. According to one of the reports, 'Dilli Raman Acharya, the CIAA lead investigator assigned to the case, said he lacked sufficient time to investigate the details of the Sudan scam.'[47]

Similarly, the recruitment process by which soldiers are chosen to serve in peace missions has also alarmed the UN and some NGOs. For example, in December 2009, Amnesty International criticized the Nepalese government after it found serious shortcomings in the vetting process leading to the selection of Blue Helmets. In particular, Amnesty International discovered that a Nepalese Army major accused of human rights abuses, torture, and murder during the civil war had been later selected to serve as an observer in the UN mission in Chad. In a letter addressed to the Prime Minister, Sam Zarifi, Amnesty International's Asia Director asserted that: 'The Nepali government had failed to provide accountability for the many atrocities committed by Nepali security forces as well as Maoist cadres during Nepal's civil war. The resulting culture of impunity undermines the rights of victims and their families, and potentially carries over to the Army's involvement in UN missions and threatens the rights of those they have been assigned by the UN to protect.'[48]

[46] See 'Nepal Vows to Punish the Corrupt in UN Defense Deal', *Reuters*, 14 February 2011. At http://in.reuters.com/article/2011/01/14/idINIndia-54155720110114

[47] See Bhadra Sharma, 'Sidelined Peacekeepers and a Headless, Toothless Anti-Corruption Body', *Ekantipur*, 5 April 2012. At http://www.ekantipur.com/2012/04/05/intl-coverage/sidelined-peacekeepers-and-a-headless-toothless-anti-corruption-body/351834.html

[48] Amnesty International, 'Nepal Must Bar Human Rights Violators from UN Peacekeeping Missions', *Amnesty International* document, 18 December 2009. At http://www.amnesty.org/en/news-and-updates/nepal-must-bar-human-rights-violators-un-peacekeeping-missions-20091218

The UN eventually expelled the officer involved in this scandal from the mission, but the Army then shielded him by refusing to hand him over to the civilian authorities. The Army not only protected its officer, it also accused Amnesty International of orchestrating a smear campaign. An official for the Nepalese army declared that:

> At some juncture when the country was in the midst of the internal conflict, a few human rights activists even lobbied against Nepal's participation in UN peacekeeping operations. Due to persevering efforts of the government to counter the logic of the activists, the embarrassing situation of non-deployment of Nepali security personnel in the UN Peacekeeping Operations has not occurred as yet. We need to be very alert in ensuring that such campaigning against Nepal's interests does not gain momentum.[49]

Finally, Nepal has been at the eye of the storm regarding a cholera outbreak in Haiti, which has debilitated some 300,000 Haitians and killed over 6,000 people between 2010 and 2011.[50] As indicated above, in 2010 Nepal had the third largest peacekeeping contingent in Haiti. This troop commitment included two battalions with close to 600 soldiers each. One was in Port-au-Prince (also known as NEP BATT), and another was located in Mirebalais, in the centre of the country, about 60 kilometres north of the capital. A report published by the medical journal *Emerging Infectious Diseases* (and made public through the US Center for Disease Control and Prevention) indicated that in mid-October Cuban doctors first identified acute cases of watery diarrhoea in the village of Meille, two kilometres south of Mirebalais, where Nepali troops had a camp. This coincided with the arrival of new Nepalese soldiers on 9, 12, and 16 October. A group of epidemiologists then observed sanitary deficiencies in the Nepalese camp, which included a pipe discharging sewage from the camp into the Meille river. The water stream from the river was used by villagers for cooking and drinking. The Meille, in turn, flowed into Haiti's longest and most important river, the Artibonite. The journal strongly suggested that the disease originated from the Nepalese peacekeeping camp, which spilled raw sewage into the river. As the report indicates:

> The start of the cholera epidemic was explosive in Lower Artibonite. It peaked within 2 days and then decreased drastically until October 31 . . . There was an exact correlation in time and places between the arrival of a Nepalese battalion from an area experiencing a cholera outbreak and the appearance of the first cases in Meille a few days after. The remoteness of Meille in central Haiti and the

[49] Hira Bahadur Thapa, 'Nepal Army: Contributions to UN Peacekeeping', op-ed page reproduced by the International Institute for Strategic Studies, 6 September 2007. At http://nepal-democracy.blogspot.co.uk/2007/09/nepal-army-contributions-to-un.html

[50] See 'Haiti's Continuing Cholera Outbreak', *The New York Times*, 10 May 2011. At http://www.nytimes.com/2011/05/11/opinion/11wed3.html

absence of report of other incomers make it unlikely that a cholera strain might have been brought there another way.[51]

A different study conducted by American epidemiologists also indicated that the cholera strain found in Haiti was identical to the strain found in Nepal, where a similar outbreak of cholera had recently occurred.[52] Haiti had not seen a case of cholera in more than a century.[53]

The cholera outbreak soured relations between locals and NEP BATT. Violence erupted in the autumn of 2010, as residents from Mirebelais and Hinche attacked the Nepali contingent. Peacekeepers became targets and some soldiers had to be transported by medical helicopters after sustaining injuries.[54] Shortly thereafter, locals elsewhere in Haiti began attacking other UN peacekeepers, including the Chilean battalion. In response, Chilean peacekeepers fired tear-gas to disperse the crowds and one demonstrator was killed.[55]

Concerned to protect one of its largest troop contributors, the UN's response was muted at best. Secretary-General Ban Ki-moon appointed a panel to 'carefully consider' the sources of the epidemic and convened a 'task force within the UN system, to study the findings and to ensure prompt and appropriate follow-up'.[56] A year later nothing had been done. The UN institutional context contributed to creating an environment of concealment and denial, in which a lack of accountability and transparency prevailed. Although the origin of the crisis was unintentional, the response by the Nepali military authorities was not. A month into the cholera crisis the Nepalese Army rejected the scientific claims and denied that it was responsible. Brigadier General Ramindra Chhetri, a representative of the Army, declared that:

> Until now, whatever investigations have been carried out so far, there is no evidence to conclude that the disease has been caused or carried by the Nepalese peacekeepers . . . No cholera bacteria was found in those samples collected inside and outside the barracks of the Nepalese peacekeepers . . . all soldiers had undergone a medical check-up before being sent to Haiti. Up until now, no Nepalese soldier has tested positive for cholera or shown any symptoms.[57]

[51] Renaud Piarroux, Robert Barrais, Benoît Faucher, Rachel Haus, Martine Piarroux, Jean Gaudart, Roc Magloire, and Didier Raoult, 'Understanding the Cholera Epidemic, Haiti', *Emerging Infectious Diseases*, 17:7 (2011). At http://dx.doi.org/10.3201/eid1707.110059

[52] Associated Press, 'Cholera in Haiti Matches Strains Seen in South Asia, U.S. Says', *The New York Times*, 1 November 2010. At http://www.nytimes.com/2010/11/02/world/americas/02haiti.html

[53] 'Haiti's Needless Cholera Deaths', *The New York Times*, 6 September 2011. At http://www.nytimes.com/2011/09/07/opinion/haitis-needless-cholera-deaths.html

[54] See Shrestha, 'Haiti's Nepali UN Peacekeepers'.

[55] 'Haiti protester shot dead by UN peacekeepers', *BBC News*, 16 November 2010. At http://www.bbc.co.uk/news/world-latin-america-11761941

[56] See UN Department for Peacekeeping Operations, 'Cholera outbreak in Haiti', UN, New York, October 2010. At http://www.un.org/en/peacekeeping/missions/minustah/

[57] See Nita Bhalla, 'U.N. peacekeepers not to blame for Haiti's cholera—Nepalese army', *Reuters AlertNet*, 2 November 2010. At http://reliefweb.int/node/373244

At the same time, the military official admitted that Blue Helmets from Nepal were not tested for cholera, since the UN did not require such medical examination.[58]

By the summer of 2011, Nepali soldiers had clearly become a liability for the UN mission. Instead of doing peacebuilding, patrolling, and policing, they themselves had to be policed and secured against the locals. As a result, the military contingent from Nepal could no longer be involved in helping secure the elections and had to be quartered, effectively impeded from having any direct interactions with locals. This, along with an alleged case of sexual abuse committed by Uruguayan peacekeepers, contributed to the development of an anti-MINUSTAH sentiment in Haiti. According to Arthur Boutellis, a senior policy analyst at the International Peace Institute and a former staff member of MINUSTAH, this 'undermined the ability of UN humanitarian agencies and NGOs to carry out cholera response, both because of deteriorating security and because they are conflated in the public mind with MINUSTAH'.[59] In November 2011 a group of human rights activists and lawyers filed claims in New York and Haiti against MINUSTAH on behalf of 5,000 cholera victims.[60]

This crisis prompted Nepal to progressively withdraw troops from Haiti and other UN missions, effectively reducing its peacekeeping commitment. By February 2012, Nepal had reduced its presence in MINUSTAH by almost 65 per cent, sustaining a force of only 365 soldiers. A similar trend took place in UNAMID, where there was a troop reduction of almost 50 per cent (from 637 to 345 soldiers). Nepal thus went from deploying an average of 5,000 Blue Helmets a month in 2010 to less than 3,000 peacekeepers per month in 2012. Although this is still a large commitment, it is also a substantial reduction from previous years, casting doubt about the future of Nepal's contributions to UN peace operations.

The reputational effects of these scandals had a negative impact on Nepal's peacekeeping contribution. In a critical review of Nepal's foreign policy published by *The Telegraph Week* (Nepal's leading foreign policy forum), Keshav Raj Jha, a former ambassador to France and UNESCO, argued that 'Nepal had a grand prestige among the community of nations because of our

[58] See Associated Press, 'Nepali troops blamed for Haiti cholera', reported in *The Himalayan*, 7 January 2011. At http://www.thehimalayantimes.com/fullNews.php?headline=Nepali+troops+blamed+for+Haiti+cholera&NewsID=293934

[59] See Arthur Boutellis, 'Cholera, Haiti and MINUSTAH: What Implications for Peacekeeping?' Comment and Analysis, International Peace Institute, New York, 11 January 2011. At http://www.ipacademy.org/news/comment-a-analysis/211-cholera-haiti-and-minustah-what-implications-for-peacekeeping.html

[60] See Pooja Bhatia, 'Haiti: Group Seeks $250 Million from U.N. Over Cholera Epidemic', *New York Times*, 8 November 2011. At http://www.nytimes.com/2011/11/09/world/americas/haiti-group-seeks-250-million-from-un-over-cholera-epidemic.html

peacekeeping forces. However, with the Haiti cholera episode, our prestige took a dangerous slide. In addition, in Sudan, the Darfur APC scam too has caused immense damage to Nepal's prestige in the international community.'[61]

13.6 CONCLUSION

My analysis of Nepal suggests additional arguments for why small, developing, and transitioning states provide large military contingents to UN peacekeeping operations. Certainly, the UN monetary allowances for soldiers provide an incentive to use such operations as a source of income for the military. In Nepal, participation in UN peacekeeping missions has increased salaries, motivated troops, enticed new recruits, and even helped sustain operational costs and purchase equipment. But none of these material incentives would exist if there was certainty about Nepal's political and economic stability. Ironically, it was domestic instability and political uncertainty in the face of democratization which increased the military's interest in peacekeeping. Reduced military expenditures and budgets, especially after the downfall of the Nepalese economy and the end of the insurgency war, created further anxiety among the armed forces. Fearing that the UN-brokered peace process would actually increase pressures to downsize, the Nepalese Army followed the example set by its neighbours in South Asia and increased its participation in UN peacekeeping. This did not necessarily eliminate all the challenges posed by the arrival of the Maoists to power or the transition to a republican system, but the UN's operations did provide the military with an alternative mission to help sustain troop numbers. Hence, Nepal's increased role in peacekeeping stemmed from motives related to the country's security sector and regional dynamics (institutional, economic, political, and regional rationales).

The effects of such policies can be felt beyond the institutional and bureaucratic dynamics, all of which could be significant for future troop deployments. Indeed, the resources generated by UN peacekeeping can pose a serious oversight challenge for civilian leaders, especially when they adopt laissez-faire attitudes. Institutional corruption is just one of the many problems that peacekeeping can encourage with insufficient accountability and weak civilian control. Hence, the Nepalese case illustrates how UN economic benefits can have unintended consequences for troops.

However, UN peacekeeping has done little to improve the quality and even transparency of the armed forces. In the face of scandals attributed to the recruitment process and even the health status of its Blue Helmets, the response

[61] See Keshav Raj Jha, 'Nepal's Lopsided Foreign Policy', *Telegraph Weekly*, 3 December 2011. At http://www.telegraphnepal.com/views/2011-12-03/nepals-lopsided-foreign-policy

of the Nepalese Army has been obfuscation and withdrawal. UN peacekeeping has thus failed to either socialize or compel the Army to accept international standard norms about human rights, democracy, accountability, and transparency. This ultimately creates problems not only for troop-contributing countries, but also for the UN itself. The absence of transparency converted Nepalese Blue Helmets from assets to liabilities in MINUSTAH, forcing UN and Nepal's authorities to withdraw Nepali soldiers from Haiti and other missions. The scandals in Haiti and Sudan in fact have created disincentives to contribute more troops in the future and add political and reputation costs to contributing forces. In sum, the challenge posed by large UN troop-contributing states, such as Nepal, is not one of quantity per se, but also one of quality.

14

Uruguay

Arturo C. Sotomayor

In 1982, Uruguay participated in only two peace missions, the United Nations Military Observer Group in India and Pakistan (UNMOGIP) and the Multinational Force Operation in Sinai (MFO). In 2010 this small South American state was involved in nine different peacekeeping operations.[1] By late 2011, over 24,335 of the country's soldiers had been involved in at least one UN peacekeeping mission. In relation to its population (less than four million people), there is one Uruguayan peacekeeper for every 280 citizens, making Uruguay the world's largest UN troop contributor per capita. As UN Secretary-General Ban Ki-moon said during a visit to Montevideo in June 2011, 'Uruguay's commitment to global peacekeeping is without rival . . . When adjusted for population, no country contributes more troops than Uruguay.'[2] In fact, more than half of Uruguay's Army officers and around one-third of its non-commissioned officers have some kind of UN peacekeeping experience. On any given day, more than 10 per cent of Uruguay's total armed forces are deployed as UN peacekeepers around the world.[3]

[1] The missions in which Uruguay participated in 2010 include: UN Mission for the Referendum in Western Sahara (MINURSO), UN Mission Stabilization in Haiti (MINUSTAH), UN Organization Stabilization Mission in the Democratic Republic of the Congo (MONUSCO), UN Assistance Mission in Afghanistan (UNAMA), UN Mission in Liberia (UNMIL), UN Mission in Nepal (UNMIN), UN Integrated Mission in Timor-Leste (UNMIT), UN Military Observer Group in India and Pakistan (UNMOGIP), and UN Operation in Côte d'Ivoire (UNOCI). See UN Department of Peacekeeping Operations (DPKO), 'Missions detailed by country', 30 December 2010. At http://www.un.org/en/peacekeeping/resources/statistics/contributors_archive.shtml. See UN Department of Peacekeeping Operations (DPKO), 'Missions detailed by country', 30 December 2011. At http://www.un.org/en/peacekeeping/resources/statistics/contributors.shtml

[2] See 'UN Secretary General praises Uruguay's contribution to peace keeping worldwide', *MercoPress*, 16 June 2011. At http://en.mercopress.com/2011/06/16/un-secretary-general-praises-uruguay-s-contribution-to-peace-keeping-worldwide

[3] Personal interview with General Héctor R. Islas, Director General of the School of the Arms and Services and Lt. Colonel Pablo Pintos, Director of the School of Peacekeeping Operations at the School of the Arms and Services, Uruguayan Army, Montevideo, Uruguay, 8 August 2003.

In absolute terms, Uruguay was the eighth largest UN troop contributor between 2000 and 2010 (see Figure 14.1).[4] It was also Latin America's leading supplier of Blue Helmets. In 2011, Uruguay sustained three battalions in two concurrent missions, deploying almost three times more soldiers than Argentina and almost twice as many as neighbouring Brazil. According to UN sources, close to 92 per cent of Uruguay's UN Blue Helmets were evenly distributed between the UN Mission Stabilization in Haiti (MINUSTAH) and the UN Organization Stabilization Mission in the Democratic Republic of Congo (MONUSCO). The remaining 8 per cent were military experts and observers (or so-called 'token contributions') deployed to the UN Mission for the Referendum in Western Sahara (MINURSO), the UN Military Observer Group in India and Pakistan (UNMOGIP), and the UN Operation in Côte d'Ivoire (UNOCI).[5]

Why does this small South American state supply such a large number of soldiers to UN peacekeeping operations? Realist and power-based accounts which focus on security dynamics cannot properly explain Uruguay's behaviour. Unlike neighbouring Brazil and Argentina, Uruguay has never had an appetite for primacy or world political status; quite the opposite, it has been the victim of regional rivalries between powerful nations. In fact, Uruguay has

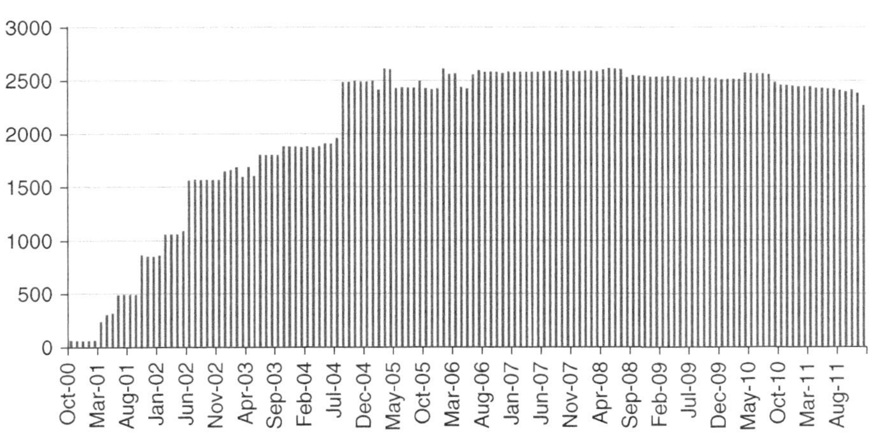

Figure 14.1 Uruguayan Uniformed Personnel in UN Peacekeeping Operations, 2000–2011

[4] Data were obtained from UN Department of Peacekeeping Operations, *Facts and Figures for Troop Contributors, 2000–2010*. At http://www.un.org/en/peacekeeping/resources/statistics/

[5] Uruguay is a reliable supplier of troops and infantrymen (2,214 soldiers as of December of 2011) and a small supplier of military experts and observers (47 in late 2011). Data were obtained from the UN Department of Peacekeeping Operations, *Troop and Police Contributors*. At http://www.un.org/en/peacekeeping/resources/statistics/contributors.shtml

been historically vulnerable to political events in Brasília and Buenos Aires.[6] Because of this vulnerable position Uruguay has had no geostrategic or geopolitical ambitions beyond national defence. Hence, Uruguay has little interest in using peacekeeping as a mechanism to dominate or influence UN policies or troop recipient states.

Nor can Uruguay be considered as a middle power. In fact, unlike Canada or Sweden, middle powers that actively participate in the UN system, Uruguay has been part of the UN Security Council as a non-permanent member only once (in 1965–6). According to an Uruguayan diplomat, 'we are a small country that does not have strategic interests abroad. Being in the Security Council exposes state-members to enormous international pressures.'[7] As described by the editors in the Introduction to this volume, the expectation of the public goods and middle-power theories was that countries like Canada, the Scandinavian states, and the Netherlands would supply UN Blue Helmets for an indeterminate number of years; yet their commitment has eroded since the end of the Cold War, while Uruguay's contribution has dramatically increased over the same period.

In this chapter, I argue that domestic politics rather than international status or security concerns have played an important role in shaping Uruguay's motivations to provide UN peacekeepers. Uruguay's democratization process, which began in 1984, generated greater domestic interest in international affairs. Indeed, democratization became a 'critical juncture' for Uruguayans, providing an initial impetus to reform the armed forces and re-shape their traditional inward-looking orientation. Within this context, Uruguay's initial engagement with UN peacekeeping missions came about because of important institutional reasons, namely, it was an attempt to modify the perverse strategic national culture that dominated the armed forces. For decades, the dominant strategic culture in the Uruguayan military was focused on internal missions, including counter-insurgency, control of labour protests, strikes, peasant land seizures, and other civic action and development functions. Peacekeeping provided sufficient incentives to modify old doctrines by providing the armed forces with a new, externally oriented mission.

So, why did the armed forces allow such a radical change of mission to occur? Why did they accept a new mandate without contestation? As I describe below, the internal weakness of the military and the urge for a strategic mission contributed to facilitating the transition towards peacekeeping. Once this institutional logic developed, peacekeeping then took on a life of its own. By 2000, the policy had been effectively institutionalized and rationalized in

[6] Tanisha M. Fazal argues that buffer states like Uruguay—states caught between two rivals—are particularly vulnerable to being coerced. Although Uruguay was not invaded by either Argentina or Brazil, its politics, including defence, security, economic, and financial policies, is vulnerable to pressures from both Brasília and Buenos Aires. See Tanisha M. Fazal, 'State Death in the International System', *International Organization*, 58:2 (2004), p. 311.

[7] Author's interview, Uruguayan Ministry of Foreign Affairs, Montevideo, Uruguay, 18 August 2003.

the military's organizational ethos. Not only did peacekeeping become the Army's central mission; it also provided the resources and economic benefits to subsidize national defence policies and salaries. Peacekeeping became bureaucratized as the military deployed not only soldiers, but was also heavily engaged in providing services for several UN peacekeeping missions. In other words, peacekeeping became institutionalized into Uruguay's national defence policy. This has not been without controversy, in part because such measures were introduced with little or no accountability and transparency. Uruguayan peacekeepers have also been charged with serious violations and misconduct in the field, raising concerns about the extent to which peacekeeping has actually fostered corruption within the armed forces. This may eventually erode Uruguay's commitment to providing peacekeepers.

To address these issues, this chapter proceeds in three sections. The first analyses the early phase of democratization, from 1992 to approximately 1999 when, in the face of a serious military identity crisis, the country deployed a large number of military staff members to UN missions in Cambodia and Angola. A transformation of the national strategic culture was the prime motivating factor during this first phase. The second section analyses Uruguay's participation in UN peacekeeping from 2002 to the present day, during which time the country engaged in major deployments in the Democratic Republic of Congo (DRC) and Haiti. Economic incentives and bureaucratization provide the main impetus for participation in this second phase. The final section provides a critical assessment of Uruguay's current commitment and its implications for future contributions.

14.1 URUGUAY'S INITIAL ENGAGEMENT WITH PEACEKEEPING, 1992–1999

Understanding Uruguay's involvement in UN peacekeeping during the 1990s requires an assessment of its domestic process of democratization. In fact, Uruguay would probably not have volunteered Blue Helmets had it not been for two fundamental crises within the armed forces themselves, namely, an identity crisis and a budgetary emergency, both of which were brought on by democratization.

The re-democratization of Uruguay stemmed from domestic and international pressures that forced the military government to withdraw from direct rule and to hold extrication elections.[8] Civilian opposition from the

[8] See Juan Linz and Alfred Stepan, *Problems of Democratic Transition and Consolidation* (Baltimore: Johns Hopkins University Press, 1996), p. 159; Gerardo Caetano and José Rilla, *Breve*

left and the right forged alliances that, in turn, led to massive street demonstrations against the dictatorial regime in 1983. One such demonstration took place in late November 1983, when approximately half a million people (almost 17 per cent of Uruguay's total population) demonstrated in Montevideo's Obelisk, demanding that the military return to their barracks. The military was then forced to engage in negotiations with the opposition, which produced the Naval Club Accord and culminated with the democratic election of Julio Maria Sanguinetti as President in 1985. Fifteen years after the establishment of an authoritarian-bureaucratic regime and after five years of intense negotiations with the military Uruguay re-established liberal democracy and the rule of law.[9]

The circumstances of Uruguay's democratization in 1985 afforded civilians both political leverage and influence. In contrast to Brazil, where the military and its conservative allies in part handled the transition, in Uruguay the democratization process ultimately remained in the hands of civilians. Juan Linz and Alfred Stepan explain that the erosion of military influence was due, in part, to the strength of political parties as well as to the relative institutional weakness of the armed forces. In their account, 'one of the reasons that the military was not very powerful in Uruguayan politics after free elections was that they had virtually no allies'.[10] Hence, the democratization process did not provide the military with the degree of autonomy required to proactively assume the role it deemed necessary.

Slowly but surely, civilians began to introduce an unprecedented number of initiatives that diminished the role of the military. For instance, the Uruguayan police forces were demilitarized and the military was unable to award itself constitutional responsibilities for the maintenance of law and order, as it had originally envisioned in the 1980 constitutional proposal. The National Security Council was abolished, as was the Commission for Political Affairs, both of which were formerly managed by the intelligence services and the military.[11]

One consequence was that the Army experienced an identity crisis, which in large part stemmed from its incapacity to define its political mission. This was exacerbated by the absence of leftist guerrilla movements, which rendered obsolete the Communist threat that the military had devoted years to

Historia de la Dictadura [Brief History of the Dictatorship] (Montevideo: Ediciones Banda Oriental, 1987), pp. 65–75.

[9] Charles Guy Gillespie, *Negotiating Democracy: Politicians and Generals in Uruguay* (Cambridge: Cambridge University Press, 2006), pp. 128–238; Luis González, *Estructuras políticas y democracia en Uruguay* [Political Structures and Democracy in Uruguay] (Montevideo: Fundación de Cultura Universitaria, 1993), pp. 88–128.

[10] Linz and Stepan. *Problems of Democratic Transition*, pp. 158–9.

[11] Alfred Stepan, *Rethinking Military Politics: Brazil and the Southern Cone* (Princeton, NJ: Princeton University Press, 1988), pp. 116–18.

combating and defeating.[12] Military reform in Uruguay has thus always been debated, not only in terms of re-orientation, but also in terms of changing tactics, doctrine, and national security culture. By the time the re-democratization began in 1985, the communist guerrillas had been defeated, so the military had no explicit domestic threats to combat.

Mercosur, South America's regional integration project, played its part too, since Uruguay joined the organization and its capital, Montevideo, became the headquarters of the new regional institution. In this new era of regional integration Uruguayans began to seriously question the need for armed forces. This effectively transformed the conventional national security doctrine and altered the national security culture that prevailed within the armed forces.

To make things worse for the military, a budgetary crisis emerged. Politicians and soldiers clashed over the size of military budget shares in Uruguay's new democracy. Defence spending proved to be a very low priority for most politicians. In its pre-authoritarian era, Uruguay was widely known and acknowledged for its strong welfare system and when the country returned to democracy, legislators were eager to reintroduce federal funds for socio-economic programmes that ultimately re-established the welfare system. Year after year, politicians diverted funds from the military to other areas that were more highly valued by their constituents. According to data from the US Arms Control and Disarmament Agency, defence spending in terms of percentage of the gross national product (GNP) decreased from 2.7 per cent in 1985 to 1.3 per cent in 1999. In 1981, at the peak of the dictatorial regime, the central government was spending 15.4 per cent of its budget on the military. This represented 4.0 per cent of GNP. By 1999, military expenditures amounted to just 4.1 per cent of the total government's expenditures, i.e. 1.3 per cent of GNP.[13]

It is thus safe to assert that the Uruguayan military was caught in a severe crisis. It found itself with a shrinking budget and a relatively large force that needed to be fed and paid. The absence of purpose, low salaries, and decreasing budgetary allocations led to a downward spiral of morale. For the civilian politicians alone, economic constraints compelled the military to implement

[12] It is worth noting that the country experienced bloody urban guerrilla and counter-insurgency warfare in the 1960s and 1970s. The Tupamaros, a radical Uruguayan guerrilla movement, ceased to be a threat to the country in large part because the army relied on mass arrests, torture, and large cordon-and-search operations. Juan Rial, *Las Fuerzas Armadas: Soldados-Políticos Garantes de la Democracia* [The Armed Forces: Political Soldiers Guarantors of Democracy] (Montevideo: Ediciones Banda Oriental, 1986); Caetano and Rilla, *Breve Historia de la Dictadura* [Brief History of the Dictatorship]; Selva López Chirico, *El Estado y las fuerzas armadas en el Uruguay del Siglo XX* [The State and Armed Forces in Twentieth Century Uruguay] (Montevideo: Ediciones Banda Oriental, 1985).

[13] US Arms Control and Disarmament Agency, *World Military Expenditures and Arms Transfers* (Washington, DC: US Department of State, Bureau of Verification and Compliance, 2000). At http://www.fas.org/asmp/profiles/wmeat/WMEAT99-00/WMEAT99-00.pdf

reforms. Civilian leaders reasoned that, in the face of scarcity, the armed forces should be reorganized and restructured.[14] For military officers, however, the economic constraints translated into operational and professional decay.

It is in this critical domestic context that participation in UN peacekeeping provided an opportunity to cope with the institutional crisis in the military. The need to reform the national security culture of the armed forces prompted an interest in peacekeeping affairs, and a small window of opportunity emerged in 1991. That year, Venezuela accepted a UN invitation to join the mission in Cambodia (UNTAC) by sending a contingent of approximately 1,000 peacekeepers. The following year, a failed military coup organized by then Colonel Hugo Chávez prevented Venezuela from deploying its troops to UNTAC.[15] This gave Uruguay the justification to assume Venezuela's role. Hence, in 1992 *Batallón Uruguay I* was deployed; a battalion of close to 1,200 individuals that included Army officers and non-commissioned officers, as well as Navy personnel. Uruguayan peacekeepers were positioned across four Cambodian provinces, with military units occupying six border-patrol positions.[16] This represented one of Uruguay's largest peacekeeping contributions, both for the number of soldiers deployed as well as for the logistics required. The operation entailed transporting forces, vehicles, ships, hospitals, and aircraft sorties from Montevideo, via Bangkok, to Boung Long, in the providence of Ratanakiri, in the northeast side of Cambodia.[17]

The decision to allow the armed forces to participate in UNTAC was made by President José Alberto Lacalle in consultation with his Minister of Defence, Mariano Brito. The government was prompted by economic and military considerations. Military advisers in Uruguay reasoned that UN peacekeeping was a relatively inexpensive mission that could divert the focus of the armed forces away from domestic politics and budgets to external roles; thus effectively transforming the dominant national security culture of the armed forces (which had focused mostly on internal missions). Peacekeeping thus provided an ongoing role that was more likely to be funded by some sort of international assistance.

[14] David Pion-Berlin, *Through Corridors of Power: Institutions and Civil–Military Relations in Argentina* (Pennsylvania: Pennsylvania State University Press, 1997), pp. 190–4.

[15] On Venezuela's failed attempt to participate in UN peace missions and the attempted coup organized by Hugo Chávez, see Carlos A. Romero, 'Exporting Peace by Other Means: Venezuela', in Jorge I. Domínguez (ed.), *International Security and Democracy: Latin America and the Caribbean in the Post-Cold War Era* (Pittsburgh: University of Pittsburgh Press, 1998), pp. 151–66.

[16] Ejército de la República Uruguay [Army of the Republic of Uruguay], *El Ejército Uruguayo en Misiones de Paz* [The Uruguayan Army in Peacekeeping Missions] (Montevideo: Ejército de la República del Uruguay, 1999).

[17] Author's interview with Ambassador Pablo Sader, General Director for Political Affairs and former Deputy Ambassador to the United Nations in 1991–3, Uruguayan Ministry of Foreign Affairs, Montevideo, Uruguay, 18 August 2003.

Decision-makers in Uruguay thought that UN peacekeeping would also help alleviate budgetary ailments by providing additional salaries and perhaps operational resources. Indeed, individual military personnel had strong monetary incentives to join UN efforts because their salaries can be more than tripled during peacekeeping service. For example, a lieutenant colonel is paid roughly US$700 per month in Uruguay but while on a UN mission, the same officer can make up to US$6,000 per month; which is more than four times his or her normal salary because of all the extra incentives the state provides, such as a 50 per cent pay hike. Likewise, a Navy non-commissioned officer makes US$100 per month, but while on a UN mission, the same soldier can make up to US$1,000 per month.[18] Certainly, initial expectations about the automatic economic benefits of peacekeeping participation were unrealistic. The government did not realize that UN payments were slow and that it could take up to two years to be fully reimbursed. As Brito, the former Minister of Defence, revealed in an interview, 'we prepared the material, including vehicles, and we even painted the equipment; but the UN paid with some delay'.[19]

After UNTAC, Uruguay engaged in two other deployments in Africa. In February 1993, Uruguay sent an infantry battalion to the southern region of Mozambique as part of the ONUMOZ mission. In January 1996, Uruguay followed in Brazil's footsteps, deploying an infantry battalion to the UN mission in Angola (UNAVEM II and III). In total, 96 military observers (UNMOs) and 2,389 Army officers and non-commissioned officers were sent to help verify a cease-fire agreement and an electoral process. However, in 1997 the UN ordered all peacekeepers to withdraw, leading to a drastic decline in participation by Uruguayan Blue Helmets. This marked the end of the first phase of Uruguay's peacekeeping history, in which a declining military institution progressively embraced UN peacekeeping as an alternative mission.

14.2 FROM DOCTRINAL CHANGE TO BUREAUCRATIZATION AND PROFITEERING, 2000–2010

Uruguay had not fully recovered from UNAVEM III when, in February 2000, the UN Security Council expanded the mandate and objective of its mission in

[18] Author's interviews with former peacekeepers conducted at the Army's General Staff's Office and at the Navy's Peacekeeping Operations Directorate, Montevideo, Uruguay, 5 and 20 August 2003.

[19] Author's interview with Dr Mariano Brito Checchi, Rector of the Universidad de Montevideo and former Minister of Defence between 1990 and 1993, Montevideo, Uruguay, 27 August 2003.

the DRC (MONUC). Given Uruguay's peacekeeping experience in Africa, UN Secretary-General Kofi Annan requested that Uruguayan Blue Helmets should form part of the mission. After domestic deliberations, Jorge Battle, the newly elected president of Uruguay, accepted the invitation and deployed his country's fourth largest peacekeeping force. Between 2000 and 2004, close to 5,400 Uruguayan soldiers participated in MONUC. By 2004, Uruguay became the leading troop contributor to MONUC, providing 21.32 per cent of all UN military personnel there. Since this deployment, Uruguay has maintained close to 11 per cent of its military strength in UN peacekeeping operations.[20]

Slowly but surely, the armed forces transitioned from being an inward-oriented institution (focused mostly on anti-guerrilla tactics) to an outward-oriented military, committing troops abroad, while assuming an entrepreneurial role in the provision of peacekeeping services. In interviews conducted in 2003, several Uruguayan officers rejected the idea that peacekeeping had de facto become the military's main mission. As Colonel Roberto Urrutice explained, 'we continue to value our traditional mission. We still defend the national sovereignty, as described in our Constitution.'[21] Certainly, if attention is focused exclusively on formal institutions and written documents, there seems to be very little evidence that peacekeeping had become a strategic mission. In Uruguay, there is no White Book on National Defence, there are no peacekeeping manuals, nor is there an official peacekeeping doctrine. Indeed, the Army's official website specifies that its mission is to 'guarantee, in all circumstances and against all forms of aggression, the security and integrity of the nation, its institutions and its inhabitants'. The website does have a link for peacekeeping, but it appears as part of what the army calls 'solidarity missions', which involve providing assistance to local communities and international peace missions.[22]

Nevertheless, it is difficult to dispute the claim that, since 1992, peacekeeping has become the military's *raison d'être*, especially when more than 11 per cent of the military's personnel are serving in nine different UN missions, including the DRC and Haiti (where close to 2,500 Uruguayan soldiers are currently deployed). In addition to those 2,500 troops, an equal number of soldiers are presently training for the next peacekeeping tour as troops are rotated every six months: troops are sent abroad for half a year and then returned home to be replaced by a different unit. In compliance with UN regulations, peacekeepers are volunteers from the various military branches. Uruguay is actually one of the few Latin American countries that have an

[20] Author's interviews with Col. Raúl Gloodtdofsky, Military Attaché at the Permanent Mission of Uruguay to the United Nations, New York, 3 July 2003; and with Col. Picabea, Army's General Staff's Office, Uruguayan Army, Montevideo, Uruguay, 5 August 2003.

[21] Author's interview with Col. Roberto Urrutice, Sub-Director of the School of Peacekeeping Operations at the School of the Arms and Services, Uruguayan Army, Montevideo, 8 August 2003.

[22] See http://www.ejercito.mil.uy/conozca.htm

all-volunteer and professional force. Yet, Uruguay does not have a specialized peacekeeping unit. Instead Blue Helmets are enlisted from different services and military divisions nationwide, which poses challenges for military cohesion. Ultimately, this means that close to 25 per cent of Uruguay's military is fully committed to peacekeeping missions every year.[23]

Furthermore, peacekeeping is a truly joint effort involving members of three military services (Army, Navy, and Air Force). Indeed, Uruguay is one of the few Latin American states that can conduct maritime and aerial peacekeeping operations, involving naval diplomacy, port management, medical evacuation, enforcement of sanctions, escort and protection of civilian vessels, in-shore pollution control, environmental programmes in public beaches, as well as air support. For instance, in MINUSTAH, Uruguay volunteered a naval force (known as URUMAR) to safeguard Haiti's coasts. The fleet included 187 sailors and about 21 ships, mostly patrol boats. For the Uruguayan Navy, the mission provided an opportunity to put its naval and coastal guard capabilities in practice and to project force into an area beyond Uruguay's shores, all while collaborating with the Haitian police and customs service.[24] Likewise, Uruguay's Air Force joined Argentina and Chile by providing a small unit of 40 Air Force pilots in support of UNFLIGHT.

There is therefore no doubt that UN peacekeeping is now part of the military's role. The organizational purpose of the military, as an institution, is focused on addressing issues related to logistics, deployment, training, and budgeting for peace missions that take place miles away from Uruguay's borders. In other words, UN peacekeeping has become 'institutionalized' within the armed forces.

Nevertheless, the deployment in the DRC began a gradual transformation of Uruguay's engagement with UN peacekeeping. Whereas in the first phase Uruguay supplied troops, in the second the country assumed a much more active, logistical role as a peacekeeper, taking over tasks that included not only the deployment of observers and units, but also the provision of services for the UN peacekeeping system. For instance, in MONUC, Uruguay maintains three battalions responsible for air and river transportation. A corps of Army engineers has also been responsible for installing water treatment

[23] For Uruguay's force strength and commitment to peacekeeping see RESDAL, 'Uruguay', in *A Comparative Atlas of Defence in Latin America and the Caribbean* (Buenos Aires: RESDAL 2010), pp. 284–91.

[24] See La Armada Nacional de la República de Uruguay [The Navy of the Republic of Uruguay], 'La Armada Nacional y las Misiones de Paz' [The Navy and Peace Missions], Montevideo, Uruguay, 12 December 2011. At http://www.armada.mil.uy/armada-misiones-de-paz.html; and 'La Armada Nacional y su participación en el Contingente Naval de Haití' [The Navy and its Participation in the Naval Contingent in Haiti], Montevideo. At http://www.armada.mil.uy/comar/repar/Noticias/contingente_haiti/contingente_haiti.html

plants, which supply drinking water to all UN units in the DRC.[25] Nowadays, there are six operating plants in the DRC and four in Haiti.[26] Gradually, Uruguay established not only a way of keeping its armed forces busy, but also a niche speciality area in the UN peacekeeping system that generates additional sources of income.

According to Julián González, a Uruguayan expert in civil–military relations, the number of Uruguayan soldiers abroad has increased since 2004, mainly as a result of the country's contribution to MINUSTAH. In fact, Uruguay doubled its military strength by deploying 1,136 soldiers to Haiti, while also maintaining 1,360 peacekeepers in MONUC and a handful of observers in other UN missions.[27] By 2010, Uruguay had become the second largest troop-lending country in Haiti, second only to Brazil, yet larger than Argentina and Chile.[28]

The irony is that Uruguay was not originally included in the core group of South American states involved in MINUSTAH, i.e., Argentina, Brazil, and Chile. This group coordinated the political aspects of participating in MINUSTAH and was formalized into a coordination mechanism. This excluded Montevideo from the bargaining table, in part because the country believed that it was already overcommitted in the DRC. MINUSTAH was by no means a Mercosur initiative, although its members converged in Haiti by chance and then cooperated in an ad hoc manner. Chile (a non-Mercosur member) was the lead state on Haiti, when it joined the UN Multinational Interim Force (MIF) in 2004, which included US Marines, as well as French and Canadian troops. Brazil and Argentina followed suit. Uruguay, the largest Latin American peacekeeper, was left aside. In fact, it did not join the mission until late in 2005 when its government offered water treatment plants for Haiti—almost two years after the MINUSTAH mission was approved. Since then, the ABC (Argentina, Brazil, Chile) mechanism has expanded into the ABC + U (U for Uruguay) and the so-called 2×9 (ABC + Bolivia, Ecuador, Guatemala,

[25] On the Uruguayan treatment plants see Coronel Carlos O. Angelero, 'Origen de las plantas potabilizadoras compactas y transportables' [Origin of the Water Treatment Plants], *Revista El Soldado* [Soldier, the Magazine], November 2008. At http://www.ingenierosmilitares.org.uy/cronicas/Cronica21.htm

[26] See RESDAL, *Comparative Atlas of Defence in Latin America and Caribbean 2010 Edition* (Buenos Aires: SER 2010). At http://www.resdal.org/atlas/atlas10-ing-25-uruguay.pdf

[27] Julián González, 'The *Frente Amplio* in Government and the Military Situation: After Five Years, the Most Complex Challenges Arrive', in *Comparative Atlas of Defence in Latin America and Caribbean 2010 Edition* (Buenos Aires: SER 2010), p. 293. At http://www.resdal.org/atlas/atlas10-ing-25-uruguay.pdf

[28] According to the data available from the UN DPKO published in December 2010, Brazil, Uruguay, Nepal, Argentina, Jordan, and Chile are the largest troop-lending countries in MINUSTAH. See United Nations Department of Peacekeeping Operations, *Facts and Figures for Troop Contributors*, December 2010. At http://www.un.org/en/peacekeeping/resources/statistics/contributors_archive.shtml

Paraguay, Peru, and Uruguay).[29] The emerging policy convergence and defence coordination amongst South American peacekeepers have led scholars to believe that the region has now become an exporter of peace.[30]

But why did Uruguay join MINUSTAH when it was already fully committed in MONUC? Perhaps because it was drawn into peacekeeping by its neighbours, following a regional diffusion pattern that prompted 'contagious' behaviour, in which proximate states emulate and imitate the strategies, policies, and practices of their fellow neighbours.[31] But Uruguayan peacekeepers were deployed at a time when regional relations and integration within Mercosur were at their worst. Uruguay was knocked off course by Argentina's economic collapse in 2001, which led to a run on its banks and a deep recession in 2002–3. By 2004, Uruguay began exporting elsewhere, away from its own subregion. That year, Uruguay signed a Bilateral Investment Treaty (BIT) with the US and it even considered a complete withdrawal from Mercosur in order to negotiate a free trade agreement with Washington (which the rules of Mercorsur do not permit as it binds its member states to negotiate as a regional bloc).

Furthermore, 2004 was also the year that a diplomatic conflict emerged between Argentina and Uruguay, because the latter authorized the construction of two paper mills on the banks of a river that both states share. Eventually, Buenos Aires took the case to the International Court of Justice and sued Uruguay in 2006, leading to a freezing of diplomatic relations between these two South American neighbours.[32] It is thus not surprising that most of the coordination efforts in Haiti were conducted exclusively by Argentina, Brazil, and Chile, while Uruguay played a secondary role at best. If

[29] See Rut Diamint, 'El 2×9 una incipiente comunidad de seguridad en América Latina?' [The 2×9, an emerging security community in Latin America?] (Santiago: Friedrich Ebert Stiftung, Policy Paper no. 18, December 2007). At http://library.fes.de/pdf-files/bueros/la-seguridad/50501.pdf; Danilo Marconedes de Souza Neto, 'A Participaçâo e a Cooperaçâo entre os Países de Cone Sul em Operaçôes de Paz: O Caso da MINUSTAH' [The Participation and Cooperation between the Southern Cone Countries in Peace Operations: The Case of MINUSTAH], in Eduardo Svartman, Maria Celina D'Araujo, and Samuel Alves Soares (eds.), *Defesa, Segurança Internacional e Forças Armadas: II Encontro da Abed* [Defense, International Security and Armed Forces: II Abed Meeting] (Campinas: Mercado Letras, 2009), pp. 169–96.

[30] Rut Diamint, 'Security Communities, Defence Policy Integration and Peace Operations in the Southern Cone: An Argentine Perspective', *International Peacekeeping*, 17:5 (2010), p. 666; Monica Herz, 'La intervención sudamericana en Haití' [The South American Intervention in Haiti] (FRIDE Commentario, April 2007), p. 336.

[31] On policy diffusion see Beth A. Simmons and Zachary Elkins, 'Globalization and Policy Diffusion: Explaining Three Decades of Liberalization', in Miles Kahler and David A. Lake (eds.), *Governance in a Global Economy* (Princeton, NJ: Princeton University Press 2003), pp. 275–304.

[32] See 'Uruguay: The next Chile. If only it allowed itself to be', *The Economist*, 1 February 2007; United States, 'Uruguay signs Bilateral Investment Treaty', US Embassy Montevideo. At http://archives.uruguay.usembassy.gov/usaweb/paginas/220-00EN.shtml

anything, bad neighbourhood relations (not neighbourhood effects) distanced Montevideo from the rest of its regional peacekeeping counterparts.

In Uruguay peacekeeping is not a diplomatic or foreign policy mission, but a military endeavour. In fact, peacekeeping is part of the military's exclusive area of influence or reserve domain. The core of the decision-making process resides in the National Defence Council and its National System for the Support of Peacekeeping Operations (SINOMAPA in Spanish). SINOMAPA coordinates peacekeeping policies between military organizations and governmental agencies. It also ensures that the units are prepared for the mission and guarantees economic, political, and technical support, once participation in a peacekeeping mission has been decided upon by the President and the Ministry of Defence.[33] However, civilians are underrepresented; the President chairs SINOMAPA, but its regular attendees are the service commanders. The statutory director of the system is the Joint Chief of Staff, who reports directly to the Army's commander-in-chief. The heads of other executive departments and agencies (such as the Ministry of Foreign Affairs and the Ministry of Economics), as well as other senior officials, are invited to attend meetings, but only when appropriate.[34]

SINOMAPA guarantees the centralization of the decision-making process within the Ministry of Defence, mostly staffed by military officers.[35] As mentioned above, diplomatic or civilian input is virtually non-existent. There is, in fact, no concrete correlation between Uruguay's foreign policy and its peacekeeping strategy. Peacekeepers are deployed to countries with which Uruguay has no diplomatic or bilateral relations, and in regions that are beyond its national interests. As indicated above, to date most Uruguayan Blue Helmets are concentrated in the DRC and Haiti, yet Uruguay does not have embassies in either of these countries. Similarly, the coordination of

[33] See also Jorge W. Rosales, 'Uruguay: Meeting the Challenges of Modern Peacekeeping Operations', in John T. Fishel and Andrés Sáez (eds.), *Capacity Building for Peacekeeping: The Case of Haiti* (Washington, DC: National Defense University Press, 2007), pp. 140–4; and Eduardo Ulery, 'The Uruguayan Armed Forces and the Challenge of 21st Century Peacekeeping' (unpublished MA Thesis, Department of National Security Affairs, Naval Postgraduate School, Monterey, California, December 2005), p. 39.

[34] See Comando General del Ejército [General Command of the Army], *Ejército Nacional: Desde 1811 al servicio de la patria, desde 1935 al servicio de la paz mundial* [The Army: Serving the Country since 1811, Serving World Peace since 1935] (Montevideo: Comando Nacional del Ejército, 2003), pp. 153–4; and Cristina Zurbriggen, 'Política exterior, defensa y las operaciones de paz, ¿una estrategia coherente? El caso de Uruguay' [Foreign Policy, Defence and Peacekeeping Operations: A Coherent Strategy? The Case of Uruguay], *Revista Fuerzas Armadas y Sociedad* [Journal of Armed Forces and Society], 19:1(2005), pp. 93–107.

[35] Studies conducted by Pion-Berlin in 1995 found that 91.4 per cent of all employees in the ministry were military, 7.8 per cent were retired officers, and only 0.8 per cent were civilians. With regard to leadership positions (advisers and head of departments), 85.5 per cent were military, 11.3 per cent were retired officers, and only 3.2 per cent were civilians. See Pion-Berlin, *Through Corridors of Power*, p. 184.

peacekeeping policies between Montevideo and New York is dealt with mostly by the military attachés, who serve as liaison officers between the Ministry of Defence and the UN DPKO, developing links and contacts between military organizations and the UN system. Hence, peacekeeping deployments are mostly influenced and shaped by military dynamics and preferences.

In the case of Haiti specifically, the country did not withdraw from the DRC in order to go to MINUSTAH; instead it increased its peacekeeping commitment for predominantly economic and institutional/military reasons. The 2002–3 financial crisis almost drained the country's foreign-exchange reserves, forcing the government to close banks and negotiate a loan with the International Monetary Fund. Public spending was drastically cut, again impacting the budget of the armed forces. As in the previous phase, peacekeeping served to cushion the impact of this recession. In 2003, Yamandú Fau, then Uruguay's Minister of Defence, declared in testimony to Congress that the country had received US$129 million over the past eleven years for its troop contributions. As explained by an official: 'Peacekeeping provides jobs that are needed when the country is facing its worst economic crisis.'[36] In 2002 alone, the government received US$20 million for supplementary peacekeeping salaries of participants in the UN mission in the DRC.[37] Peacekeeping became the second source of foreign income, after beef exports. By 2004, the Uruguayan economy was still recovering and the UN mission in Haiti offered yet more resources and foreign currency.

There are no public data available on how much money is paid to Uruguay for its peacekeeping services, but it does receive a generous amount of money in terms of UN allowances. In 2010 alone, Montevideo had, on average, close to 2,300 soldiers abroad, participating in different peace missions. This translates into US$2.3 million per month or US$27.6 million a year in UN allowances, which compared to its defence budget represents close to 8 per cent of the total budget for 2010 (US$375 million).[38] This figure does not include the reimbursement for equipment that had depreciated in value, nor does it take into account the compensation soldiers received for services, such as water treatment, provided to the UN. But, given that at any time 11 per cent of the Uruguayan armed forces are abroad, while another 11 per cent are training for the next deployment (with troops are rotated every six months), it

[36] Author's interview, School of Peacekeeping Operations at the School of the Arms and Services, Uruguayan Army, Montevideo, Uruguay, 8 August 2003.

[37] See Instituto de Ciencia Política de la Universidad de la República [Political Science Institute of the Republic University], 'Informe Semanal Uruguay' [Weekly Report Uruguay], *Observatorio Cono Sur de Defensa y Fuerzas Armadas* [Armed Forces Observatory for the Southern Cone], 96 (19–25 July 2003). At http://www.cee-chile.org/resumen/urug/uru054-099/semuru96.htm

[38] See RESDAL, *Comparative Atlas of Defence in Latin America and Caribbean 2010 Edition.*

appears that UN peacekeeping partially helps maintain individual salary incentives for at least a quarter of the force.

Uruguayan peacekeeping therefore appears to be primarily motivated by institutional/military and economic imperatives. Its military has been keen to derive individual salary incentives and some organizational benefits (mostly from the provision of services to the UN) through peacekeeping participation. In this sense, UN peacekeeping has become a true military profession, since its practitioners are being generously paid for performing their duties.

14.3 CRITICAL ISSUES IN URUGUAY'S PEACEKEEPING CONTRIBUTIONS

In spite of its large troop commitment, recent trends in Uruguay suggest that its peacekeeping contribution might have reached a plateau. Once again, economic and military factors are influencing outcomes. First, the Uruguayan economy, like those of its nearby neighbours, is experiencing an economic boom. In this context, the incentives to join a peacekeeping force are less enticing today than they were in the recent past. In fact, according to the Defence Minister, Luis Rosadilla, it has become increasingly difficult to recruit staff for peacekeeping missions because there is less unemployment and wages in the country are now better.[39] Specifically, the Air Force, which provides air support in Port-au-Prince as part of UNFLIGHT, has found itself in a dilemma as most of its pilots have joined commercial airlines as soon as they have returned from their peacekeeping assignment. Hence, it has become increasingly difficult to recruit volunteers for future UN missions.[40]

Similarly, in 2009, a Uruguayan military plane crashed near the border between Haiti and the Dominican Republic, killing eleven Blue Helmets (six from Uruguay and five from Jordan).[41] The accident raised concerns about the conditions of the Uruguayan fleet, which some suspected of being out-dated. In fact, a 2010 routine inspection by a UN delegation in Haiti found that 70

[39] See América Economía [America Economy], 'Gobierno uruguayo enfrenta falta de interés en participar en misiones del paz' [Uruguayan Government Faces Lack of Interest in Participating in Peace Missions], *América Economía*, 14 February 2011. At http://www.americaeconomia.com/politica-sociedad/politica/gobierno-uruguayo-enfrenta-falta-de-interes-para-participar-en-misiones-d

[40] See Infodefensa, 'Uruguay no participará en Misiones de Paz de la ONU por falta de pilotos militares' [Uruguay Will Not Participate in Peacekeeping Missions Due to Lack of Military Pilots], *Revista Poder Militar* [Magazine of Military Power], 13 (26 December 2010). At http://podermilitar.blogspot.com/2010/12/uruguay-no-participara-en-misiones-de.html

[41] El País, 'Un Avión militar uruguayo se estrelló en Haití: 11 muertos' [An Uruguayan Military Plane Crashes in Haiti: 11 Deaths], *El País*, 20 October 2009. At http://www.elpais.com.uy/091010/pinter-447143/americalatina/un-avion-militar-uruguayo-se-estrello-en-haiti-11-muertos

per cent of Uruguay's battalion equipment was not operational.[42] Uruguay's peacekeeping commitment could thus be jeopardized unless it modernizes its force. Peacekeeping, however, has not been able to subsidize such modernization effort, since the UN only refunds equipment depreciation costs.

Second, a series of scandals and abuse cases committed by Uruguayan peacekeepers have placed the military, literally, in the eye of the storm. The first signs of controversy appeared in the UN mission in the DRC, where violence resurged in the summer of 2003 and the UN Security Council modified the mandate of the operation. Here, Uruguayan soldiers were accused of corruption and improper behaviour. Seven Uruguayan soldiers were put under investigation for allegedly stealing sacred objects from a church in Bunia. According to an internal UN report, the Uruguayan soldiers 'alleged that the material was removed purely for safekeeping'. The report also said, 'Evidence supports extensive looting by the local population, and the Uruguayan soldiers had indeed stolen some items of value.'[43] A month later, Uruguayan troops, who tried to contain the fighting in Bunia itself, were accused by other factions and NGOs of violations of human rights. According to Amnesty International, 'Uruguayan soldiers from MONUC arrested Willy Benguela, an official from the National Intelligence Service and consultant to the UN . . . The soldiers took him to the camp, undressed him, beat him, and then tied his hands and legs.'[44]

This type of misconduct does not appear to be generalized or systemic among Uruguay's forces, but it has affected the image of the armed forces. The Army did suspend the soldiers and the top officers heading the battalion in the DRC. However, Congress did not conduct a formal investigation and no official report was published or released by the Army. Furthermore, the events in Bunia included misbehaviour of a criminal nature, in which the Blue Helmets should have been subject to criminal proceedings and not just liable for punishment. The UN, as an international body controlled by sovereign states, is limited to denouncing acts of misbehaviour, but has virtually no authority to enforce domestic law when criminal misconduct occurs. It is then the responsibility of each country participating in the mission to impose a sanction when their national contingents infringe the law of another state

[42] Pablo Melgas, 'Haití: Batallón uruguayo no superó inspección de ONU; 70 per cent inoperativo' [Haiti: Uruguayan UN battalion does not pass inspection; 70 per cent is non-operative], *El País*, 21 September 2010. At http://www.elpais.com.uy/100921/pnacio-516703/sociedad/haiti-batallon-uruguayo-no-supero-inspeccion-de-onu-70-inoperativo/

[43] 'Seven UN Uruguayan Peacekeepers Probed for Stealing Sacred Objects in Democratic Republic of Congo', *UN Integrated Regional Information Network*, 12 September 2003.

[44] Personal translation from news note in: 'Acusan a cascos azules de Uruguay por torturas en África' [Uruguayan Peacekeepers Accused of Torture in Africa], *Clarín*, 21 September 2003, El Mundo [The World]. At http://old.clarin.com/diario/2003/09/21/i-02201.htm

while performing peacekeeping.[45] Ironically, in the DRC incident, the Uruguayan military proceeded in the same way as when it was accused of human rights abuse at home, that is, with secrecy, denial, and no trials of any type.

A second scandal erupted in 2011, when five Uruguayan peacekeepers in Haiti were accused of sexual abuse and assault on a teenage boy.[46] The media revealed this scandal through a one-minute video that showed images captured by a mobile phone camera. The footage, filmed at a UN base and then posted on the internet, showed 'several men in camouflage uniforms laughing and saying "no problem" in Spanish as they pinned a young man down on a mattress with his hands behind his back'.[47] The mother of the alleged victim, an 18-year-old resident of Port Salut, then told Haitian radio stations that Uruguayan Marines had raped her son inside the UN base.

The case prompted a crisis in Uruguay and Haiti, forcing President José Mujica, himself a victim of torture during the Uruguayan dictatorship, to publicly apologize to the Haitian people. In a letter addressed to the Haitian President Michel Martelly, Mujica wrote: 'We apologize for the outrage that some soldiers from my country have perpetrated . . . Although the damage is irreparable, be assured that we will fully investigate the matter and apply the harshest sanctions to those responsible.'[48]

The scandal prompted Uruguayan authorities to dismiss URUMAR's commander, while the five sailors accused of alleged sexual assault were withdrawn from the mission, decommissioned and then put under military justice. An initial investigation by the UN, the Uruguayan Navy, and the Ministry of Defence determined that the complaints of alleged sexual abuse were only acts of misconduct. As one of the reports indicated: 'Sailors are only responsible for engaging in misconduct by acting on facts that are not consistent with the guidelines of the Mission . . . The military used offensive language against a local citizen and his family.' The Navy investigation added the word 'joke' to refer to the 'relationship of proximity and relative friendship' between sailors and the alleged victim. The report stated: 'The incident did not involve aberrant or sexual acts.'[49]

[45] On peacekeeping accountability, see Françoise J. Hampson and Ai Kihara-Hunt, 'The Accountability of Personnel Associated with Peacekeeping Operations', in Chiyuki Aoi, Cedric de Coning, and Ramesh Thakur (eds.), *Unintended Consequences of Peacekeeping Operations* (New York: UN University Press, 2007), pp. 195–220.

[46] See 'Uruguayan peacekeepers in Haiti accused of abuse', *BBC News Online*, 4 September 2011. At http://www.bbc.co.uk/news/world-latin-america-14783538

[47] See Robin Yapp, 'Uruguayan peacekeepers investigated over Haiti sexual assault', *The Telegraph*, 5 September 2011. At http://www.telegraph.co.uk/news/worldnews/centralamericaandthecaribbean/haiti/8742878/Uruguayan-peacekeepers-investigated-over-Haiti-sexual-assault.html

[48] BBC Latin America, 'Uruguayan peacekeepers in Haiti accused of abuse', *BBC News*, 4 September 2011. At http://www.bbc.co.uk/news/world-latin-america-14783538

[49] Personal translation. See *El Observador* [The Observer], 'Tres informes descartan abuso sexual y hablan de mala conducta' [Three Reports Dismiss Sexual abuse and Talk About

The measures taken by both the UN and Uruguay's government, however, proved to be insufficient. The reports were not welcomed in Haiti, where public demonstrations and outrage broke out in the streets. The angriest protests were reported in Port Salut, where residents demanded the complete withdrawal of Uruguayan Blue Helmets. Locals also complained about the filthy conditions of the naval base and women who apparently had to engage in 'food for sex' with peacekeepers raised new unconfirmed sexual abuse allegations.[50]

Mariano Fernández, the Special Representative of the Secretary-General and head of MINUSTAH, minimized the incident and argued that the 'acts of a few should not also tarnish [the image] of thousands of military, police, and civilian personal serving MINUSTAH and Haiti impeccably since 2004'.[51] Certainly, acts of misconduct are likely to take place when such a large military force is deployed overseas. The problem, however, was that this incident took place in a context in which UN peacekeepers had been consistently accused of sexual abuse in Haiti. In 2007, some 100 Sri Lankan Blue Helmets—10 per cent of an entire brigade—were repatriated because they were giving small amounts of cash, food, and sometimes mobile phones in exchange for sex with underage girls.[52] The Uruguayan incident thus confirmed the belief that a culture of institutional impunity, which tolerated sexual abuse, had developed within the UN mission.

In Uruguay, the incidents involving Blue Helmets have led critics to argue that peacekeeping missions have merely transferred military anti-guerrilla tactics from domestic to international environments.[53] The fact that human rights abuses took place while Uruguayan peacekeepers were performing peace missions has raised concerns about how they are being trained. The incidents in the DRC and Haiti suggest that perhaps the Army was training its

Misconduct], *El Observador* [The Observer], 9 September 2011. At http://www.elobservador.com.uy/noticia/208839/tres-informes-descartan-abuso-sexual-y-hablan-de-mala-conducta/

[50] For a journalistic description of how the video was discovered and then released to the media see interview with Amy Goodman, from *Democracy Now*, and Ansel Herz, an independent journalist who broke the story in the international press, in 'As UN Mission Mandate Faces Renewal: UN Soldiers' Sexual Assault of Haitian Man Provokes Outrage and Protest', transcribed in *Haïti Liberté*, 6 September 2011. At http://www.haiti-liberte.com/archives/volume5-8/As%20UN%20Mission%20Mandate.asp

[51] Keane Bhatt and Greg Grandin, 'The Nation: Why the U.N. Troops Should Leave Haiti', *National Public Radio*, 29 September 2011. At http://www.npr.org/2011/09/29/140914125/the-nation-why-the-u-n-should-leave-haiti

[52] See also 'Sri Lanka troops "abused Haitians"', *BBC News*, 2 November 2007. At http://news.bbc.co.uk/2/hi/south_asia/7075866.stm

[53] Selva López Chirico, 'Las FF.AA Uruguayas en la democracia post-dictatorial: notas sobre misión y estrategias política' [The Uruguayan Armed Forces in the Post-Dictatorial Democracy: Notes on Mission and Policy Strategies], in Rut Diamint (ed.), *Control civil y fuerzas armadas en las nuevas democracias latinoamericanas* [Civilian Control and the Armed Forces in the New Latin American Democracies] (Buenos Aires: Grupo Editorial Latonoamericano, 1999), pp. 276–9.

peacekeeping personnel with some of the old doctrines used during the authoritarian era, such as counter-insurgency and anti-guerrilla tactics. As a former UN civil servant and Uruguayan native said during an interview, 'For peacekeeping to be effective, human rights training is required. Most of our peacekeepers, however, have no understanding whatsoever of international or humanitarian law.'[54]

Ultimately, these incidents may erode Uruguay's commitment to peacekeeping, especially since Haiti is where Uruguay has its largest troop contribution to date. In fact, during a meeting in Montevideo, held on 8 September 2011, Latin American states agreed to a 15 per cent cut in the peacekeeping force, which effectively translates into a gradual withdrawal of Latin American troops in Haiti. The Haitian Senate, however, voted and demanded that all peacekeepers (including those from Uruguay) depart by October 2012.[55] The incidents in MINUSTAH may also undermine future contributions, especially if Uruguayan commanders fail to implement changes to the way they train their peacekeepers. Peacekeeping policies are thus becoming much more scrutinized and critical voices within Uruguay may in fact ask for their troops to return home after two decades of large UN troop contributions.

In fact, a National Defence Act, which would radically transform and strengthen the Ministry of Defence by eradicating the National Defence Council and its other agencies (including SINOMAPA), was approved by Congress in December of 2010. However, the administration of President José Mujica has yet to enact and implement the law. According to Julián González, if the new government does implement the approved legislation, then 'it might be the basis for the Uruguayan civil-military relation re-definition process'.[56] This could bring some changes to current military and peacekeeping policies. In other words, the UN mission in Haiti might be seen as a critical policy juncture, which could prompt a radical change within the defence establishment. This conjecture must nevertheless be treated with caution, as similar incidents in the DRC did not appear to impact government or military policies. The current crisis could well translate into policy inertia. The future of Uruguay's peacekeeping contributions is thus uncertain.

[54] Author's confidential interview with a government official at the Office of International Human Rights at the Ministry of Foreign Affairs and former civil servant at a UN peacekeeping operation, Montevideo, 22 August 2003.

[55] 'Haiti's Senate votes to request end of MINUSTAH by October 2012; Martelly says the force should stay', *Canadian Haitian Action Network*, 30 September 2011. At http://www.canadahaitiaction.ca/content/haitis-senate-votes-request-end-minustah-oct-2012-martelly-says-force-should-stay; Raul Garces, 'Brazil wants Haiti peacekeeping force cut 15 per cent', *The Guardian*, 8 September 2011. At http://www.guardian.co.uk/world/feedarticle/9837340

[56] See Julián González Guyer, 'The Frente Amplio in Government and the Military Situation: After Five Years, the Most Complex Challenges Arrive', in *A Comparative Analysis of Defense in Latin America and the Caribbean* (Buenos Aires: RESDAL), p. 293.

In sum, political, economic, and institutional considerations or rationales explain Uruguay's contribution to UN peace operations. First, a political democratizing process in Uruguay served as a critical stimulus to involve military personnel in missions abroad. Peacekeeping, indeed, provided an opportunity to reorient the Army away from internal roles and towards external missions at a time when civilian elites were attempting to institutionalize democracy. Second, budgetary considerations also played a role in shaping the incentives to participate in peacekeeping operations. UN reimbursements offered resources, however minimal, to cover individual military salaries and even sustain operational costs. The incentive to earn money in a foreign currency helped motivate troops and even served as an enticement to recruit capable young men and women into the armed forces when Uruguay's economy experienced a recession. Finally, institutional considerations have been consequential for Uruguay. Military motivations and bureaucratized interests within the services have traditionally shaped policy preferences and predispositions regarding UN peace missions.

Part IV

Rising Contributors?

15

Brazil

Kai Michael Kenkel

Once an inward-looking, regionally focused power, Brazil has grown into an economic—and increasingly a political—powerhouse. Despite still being burdened with the constraints that accompany commodity dependence and a decrepit transportation infrastructure, the country's economy recently overtook that of the United Kingdom as the world's sixth largest by nominal GDP, and its growing regional domination has led to incipient tensions with its neighbours.[1] As its economy grows, Brazil's policy-makers have sought to transform this newfound prosperity into greater global political and strategic influence. Peace operations play a key part in attaining this goal: these missions offer the possibility to make Brazilian virtues—which predominantly lie in other areas such as development—fit the necessities of demonstrating the capacity and responsibility inherent to the more influential security arena. The country's role in peace operations cannot therefore be understood in isolation from the foreign policy goals inherent to its emerging power status.

As Brazil becomes a larger contributor to peace operations, gaining a deeper understanding of its motivations is paramount to guaranteeing the stable provision of peacekeepers overall. This chapter describes Brazil's instrumentalist, yet still inchoate, approach to peace operations, outlining the cornerstones of those motivations in several steps. It begins by providing the institutional and political context in which the country's decisions regarding peace operations are made, including the nature of the legal decision-making process, the key players involved in it, and the nature of the coordination between them. These actors' preferences are grounded in specific preferences

[1] 'Brazilian economy overtakes UK's, says CEBR', *BBC News*, 26 December 2011. At http://www.bbc.co.uk/news/business-16332115; Simon Romero, 'Brazil's Long Shadow Vexes Some Neighbors', *New York Times*, 4 November 2011. At http://www.nytimes.com/2011/11/05/world/americas/brazils-rapidly-expanding-influence-worries-neighbors.html; David Rothkopf, 'Brazil's New Swagger', *Foreign Policy*, 28 February 2012. At http://www.foreignpolicy.com/articles/2012/02/28/brazil_s_new_swagger

anchored in the context of foreign and domestic policy, which are brought into line with those that underpin this volume's analysis.

This is followed by an overview of Brazilian positions on current trends in the evolution of peacekeeping practice, particularly as they relate to norms of intervention, which are a fundamental determinant of the country's level of support for, and participation in, today's peace operations. Subsequently, the prospects and conditions for continued Brazilian commitment to UN missions is assessed, followed by concluding lessons from the country's lengthy experience in peacekeeping deployments. The country is likely to continue to follow an instrumentalist course on contributing to peace operations, participating where its presence might showcase the exportability of its domestic political success stories and increase its global profile. A disjointed policy process still hampers the formulation of a fully coherent policy on peace operations; nevertheless, in keeping with its traditions of foreign conduct, Brazil will continue to seek ways to contribute to peacekeeping and the debates around it without abandoning its repudiation of the use of force, including a focus on development issues and civilian capacities.

15.1 THE DECISION-MAKING PROCESS AND KEY PLAYERS

In Brazil's political system, the long-term success of policy initiatives depends on sustained, informed action by the President. As this cannot be permanently maintained across the entire agenda, ministries enjoy significant autonomy—and some, considerable specialist sophistication—in their policy areas and coordination between them is weakly institutionalized and impermanent. This has negative effects on the continuity, rationality, effectiveness, and internal cohesion of Brazilian policy in areas such as peacekeeping participation, which require coordination and cooperation among several ministries and other actors.

Security policy-making in general, and peace operations policy with it, is influenced by two key factors deriving from this context. First, the Ministry of External Relations (MRE) or *Itamaraty*, as it is colloquially known, has traditionally enjoyed an almost total monopoly over the formulation of foreign policy. While this exclusivity has begun to erode with increasing issue complexity and the democratization of governance, the MRE's institutional culture remains fiercely resistant to attempts to infringe on this prerogative.[2] As a result, peace operations policy is heavily influenced by

[2] See, *inter alia*, Jeffrey Cason and Timothy Power, 'Presidentialization, Pluralization, and the Rollback of Itamaraty: Explaining Change in Brazilian Foreign Policy Making from Cardoso to Lula', paper presented at the conference on 'Regional Powers in Asia, Africa, Latin America, the Near and Middle East', 11–12 December 2006, GIGA German Institute of Global and Area

the entrenched values of Brazilian diplomacy, which impose a conservative continuity of tradition.

Second, civilian governance has been slow to consolidate following the establishment of democracy in 1988. While overall Brazil's democratic fundamentals are quite solid, true civilian control over military affairs has been sluggish in developing; tellingly, a civilian-led Ministry of Defence (MOD) was created only in 1999 and still lacks an attendant civilian career path. As a result, while there is a high level of development of doctrine—and strongly held policy positions—within the armed forces, the MOD still articulates the civilian voice on these issues weakly. In the absence of detailed presidential guidelines, both the MRE and the armed forces (despite the existence of the MOD) remain highly independent and produce policy preferences in relative isolation—and, as will be shown, on the basis of divergent criteria and motivations.

This has resulted in two hallmarks of Brazilian peace operations policy. First, despite the fact that both the armed forces and the foreign ministry[3] have extensive, coherent, and sophisticated doctrines and guidelines which orient their attitude towards peacekeeping policy, the lack of coordination during policy formulation has resulted in vague documents that fail to provide concrete priorities or implementation benchmarks.[4] Brazil's formal security policy documents are of little help in providing guidance. Article 4 of the 1988 Brazilian Constitution establishes the key principles of foreign policy, which include the defence of human rights, non-intervention, self-determination, the defence of peace, and the peaceful settlement of disputes. In light of recent debates on intervention, these principles have the potential to be contradictory;

Studies, Hamburg. At http://www.giga-hamburg.de/dl/download.php?d=/content/forumregional/pdf/giga_conference_RegionalPowers_0612/giga_RegPowers0612_paper_cason-power.pdf

[3] On the armed forces see, for example, Brazil Ministry of the Army, *Manual de Campanha: Operações de Manutenção da Paz* [Field Manual: Peacekeeping Operations] (Brasília: Ministry of the Army, 1998); Brazil Ministry of Defence, *Manual de Operações de Paz* [Manual for Peace Operations] (Brasília: Ministry of Defence, 2006). At http://www.coter.eb.mil.br/html/cepaeb/CEPAEB%20WEB%20SITE/Docs/manuais/ManualOpPaz_MD33_M_01.pdf. Itamaraty thinking on peace operations is outlined eloquently in Eduardo Uziel, *O Conselho de Segurança, as operações de manutenção da paz e a inserção do Brasil no mecanismo de segurança coletiva das Nações Unidas* [The Security Council, Peacekeeping Operations and Brazil's Participation in the United Nations' Mechanism for Collective Security] (Brasília: Instituto Rio Branco/Ministry of External Relations, 2009) and Filipe Nasser, *Pax Brasiliensis: solidariedade e projeção de poder na construção de um modelo de engajamento do Brasil em operações de paz da ONU* [Pax Brasiliensis: Solidarity and the Projection of Power in the Construction of a Model for Brazil's Engagement in UN Peace Operations] (Brasília: Instituto Rio Branco/Ministry of External Relations, 2009).

[4] Fernando Cavalcante, 'Rendering Peacekeeping Instrumental? The Brazilian Approach to United Nations Peacekeeping during the Lula da Silva Years (2003–2010)', *Revista Brasileira de Política Internacional*, 53:2 (2010), pp. 142–59 at 149–51.

the Constitution does not, however, establish a hierarchy between them, leaving the article per se ambiguous as a guideline for policy generation.[5]

Similarly, past documents such as the 1996 and 2005 National Defence Policies, drafted by inter-ministerial working groups, amount to little more than an amalgam of the involved actors' positions, and lack the capacity to serve as true policy guidelines. The Defence Ministry has published a number of documents, not the least of which is the National Defence Strategy of 2008.[6] This sets more concrete guidelines but applies them only to the immediate ambit of the armed forces. The country's recently published Defence White Paper similarly does not raise hopes of consistent concrete guidance for peacekeeping policy.[7] This lack of guidance is manifested in peacekeeping policy through the absence of clear criteria for selecting operations for participation or the goals to be achieved through them. As a result, decisions remain reactive and vary according to calculations of short-term political expediency.

This lack of consistency is exacerbated by a byzantine and under-institutionalized decision-making process. The process is governed by imprecise legislation issued in 1956 (on the occasion of the country's contribution to UNEF).[8] Indicative of a pervasive culture of under-formalization (often valued for the malleability it allows), what was initially meant as a stopgap solution has become permanent.

Under the democratic Constitution of 1988, the process begins with an informal query by the UN Department for Peacekeeping Operations (DPKO) to the Brazilian Permanent Mission to the UN, which is forwarded to the MRE together with an initial *prise de position* from the Mission. After conferring with the President as to domestic political backing for the mission, the MOD is consulted concerning the availability of troops, and the Ministries of Planning and Finance regarding funding. Given positive responses, UN DPKO is asked to prepare a formal request for troops. On the basis of this request, the MOD and the MRE draw up a Joint Exposition of Motives, which is forwarded with a Presidential Message to the National Congress. If a legislative decree authorizing participation is approved by the Congress, the President, again by decree,

[5] Constitution of Brazil 1988, Article 4. At http://www.v-brazil.com/government/laws/titleI.html

[6] Brazil Ministry of Defence. *Estratégia Nacional de Defesa* (Brasília: Ministry of Defence, 2008). At http://www.mar.mil.br/diversos/estrategia_defesa_nacional_portugues.pdf

[7] On the vagueness of Brazilian policy documents see Kai Michael Kenkel, 'Brazil and R2P: Does Taking Responsibility Mean Using Force?' *Global Responsibility to Protect*, 4:1 (2012), pp. 5–32 and Cavalcante, 'Rendering'.

[8] Brazil Presidency, *Lei No. 2.953 de 17 de novembro de 1956. Fixa normas para remessa de tropas brasileiras para o exterior* [establishes norms for the sending of Brazilian troops abroad]. At http://www.planalto.gov.br/ccivil_03/Leis/1950-1969/L2953.htm

authorizes the Ministry of Defence to organize and carry out the deployment.[9] Operational matters such as the size and type of forces are under the competence of the Defence General Staff, which coordinates the activities of the Army, Navy, and Air Force.[10] Several efforts have been undertaken to formalize and institutionalize this process; foremost among these was the creation of an Inter-Ministerial Working Group in 1993. However, no proposals ever made it to a vote.

Among the most urgent issues is the need to increase parliamentary involvement in the process: legislative competence on defence matters is almost non-existent, which leads to the danger of decisions in this area—including peace operations—being made based on personal preferences or those from other issue areas, and of a lack of understanding of the deeper implications of defence policy decisions, leading potentially to sharp reactions to unexpected situations foreseeable to those with more specialist knowledge.[11] Politicians' interest is further limited by a stigma on military matters rooted in the excesses of military rule (1964–85).

As a corollary to this, public interest in defence issues in Brazil is minimal. Only recently, and in part as a result of the decline of *Itamaraty*'s monopoly, have foreign policy debates begun to reach a broader public. Indeed much of the burgeoning interest in security issues results from what is perceived as Brazil's successful participation in the UN Stabilization Mission in Haiti, MINUSTAH, beginning in 2004. This interest has not, however, reached a level where the government needs to justify its decisions regarding UN peace operations to the public. Nevertheless, as participation in robust peace

[9] See the Ministry of Defence, *Manual for Peace Operations*; Osvaldo Peçanha Caninas, 'Enquadramento Jurídico-Normativo Nacional das Operações de Manutenção da Paz: Situação Atual e Proposta de Mudanças' [The Domestic Legal-Normative Framework for Peacekeeping Operations: Current Situation and Proposal for Change] (Thesis, Escola de Guerra Naval [Naval War College], Rio de Janeiro, 2007), p. 7; Marcello Yoshida, 'Cenário político, social e econômico para a desmobilização do componente militar da MINUSTAH: uma proposta' [Political, Social and Economic Scenario for the Demobilization of the Military Component of MINUSTAH] (Ph.D. Thesis, Escola de Comando e Estado-Maior do Exército [Army Command and Staff College], Rio de Janeiro, 2011), p. 115. It is indicative that the sources listed for the study of this aspect originate in the military ambit, as civilian research has not focused on decision-making.

[10] This is regulated, once again, by decree. See http://www.jusbrasil.com.br/legislacao/110954/decreto-3080-99.

[11] The literature on the deleterious effects of a lack of parliamentary participation in decision-making regarding peace operations—both in terms of reliability and consistency of decisions and especially in terms of democratic legitimation—is well developed, for example, in the German context. See, for example, Dieter Wiefelspütz, *Das Parlamentsheer: Der Einsatz bewaffneter deutscher Streitkräfte im Ausland, der konstitutive Parlamentsvorbehalt und das Parlamentsbeteiligungsgesetz* [The Parliamentary Army: The Deployment of the German Armed Forces Abroad, the Parliament's Constitutional Reservation and the Parliamentary Participation Act] (Berlin: Berliner Wissenschafts-Verlag, 2005) and Dieter Wiefelspütz, *Der Auslandseinsatz der Bundeswehr und das Parlamentsbeteiligungsgesetz* [Bundeswehr Missions Abroad and Parliamentary Participation Act] (Frankfurt am Main: Verlag für Polizeiwissenschaft, 2008).

operations as part of an emerging foreign policy paradigm is new to the Brazilian public, the domestic consensus remains quite risk-averse and susceptible to casualties and high costs, especially given the country's ongoing domestic problems with underdevelopment and violence.

Given these institutional characteristics, prior to 2004 Brazilian participation in peace operations consisted—bar a few quite notable exceptions—of 'token' contributions. This changed when President Lula da Silva identified these missions as a key component in his quest to match Brazil's emerging economic power with political clout. This objective provided the key normative and political rationales that drove increased participation in UN peacekeeping, which were matched by the predominantly institutional imperatives motivating the military's support of greater engagement.

15.2 FOREIGN POLICY, DOMESTIC ISSUES, AND PEACEKEEPING PARTICIPATION

In terms of the five broad rationales for providing peacekeepers outlined in the introduction to this book—political, security, economic, institutional, and normative—in the Brazilian case, motivations for participating in peace operations fall almost exclusively into the political, normative, and institutional categories. Financial and security concerns play a negligible role. Indeed the story of the country's changing participation over the last decade is one of a shift from normative to political considerations, as well as a growing fit between peace operations and the institutional concerns of the armed forces.

The growing literature on Brazil's role in UN peacekeeping has generated relatively consistent lists of factors to explain the country's increasing participation. These factors were helpfully summarized by Eduardo Uziel as being:

1. Insert the country fully into the UN system of collective security (political/normative).
2. Increase Brazilian influence in UN decision-making bodies (political).
3. Fulfil the principles that govern Brazil's international relations, outlined in Article 4 of the Brazilian Constitution (normative).
4. Reinforce the very idea of multilateralism and insert Brazilian interests among those that orient decisions, including with a view to minimizing issues such as the Security Council's double standards (normative/political).
5. Validate Brazil's candidacy for permanent membership in the Security Council (political).

6. Make use of opportunities for cooperation during the implementation of peace processes (political).
7. Provide greater international experience for the armed forces (institutional).[12]

Another analyst, W. Alejandro Sánchez Nieto, identified the following five factors, which spanned a similar terrain but were distinct in some important respects:

1. 'International Good Samaritan Syndrome', centred on the provision of public goods (such as peace) in areas not associated with the national interest (normative).
2. Strategic national interest, as embodied in progress towards a permanent seat on the United Nations Security Council (political).
3. Monetary compensation from the UN (financial).
4. Live-combat training for the armed forces (institutional).
5. National pride: prestige and image (political).[13]

Interestingly, the differences between these two sets of lists echo the divide between the foreign policy establishment and the armed forces and Defence Ministry.[14] Here, the Foreign Ministry follows an overwhelmingly political rationale, with some normative overtones, while the military has, with equal clarity, identified a number of institutional advantages to seconding troops to the UN.[15] Financial compensation plays at best a negligible role. The rise in Brazil's peacekeeping profile is the result of a hitherto unique juxtaposition of factors spurring interest in these missions within both of these communities.

[12] Eduardo Uziel, *O Conselho de Segurança, as operações de manutenção da paz e a inserção do Brasil no mecanismo de segurança coletiva das Nações Unidas* [The Security Council, Peacekeeping Operations and Brazil's Participation in the United Nations' Mechanism for Collective Security] (Brasília: Instituto Rio Branco/Ministry of External Relations, 2009), p. 82.

[13] W. Alejandro Sánchez Nieto, 'Brazil's Grand Design for Combining Global South Solidarity and National Interests: A Discussion of Peacekeeping Operations in Haiti and Timor', *Globalizations*, 9:1 (2012), pp. 161–78.

[14] On this divide see Gisele Lennon de Albuquerque Lima e Figueiredo Lins, 'A (des)articulação entre o Ministério da Defesa e o Ministério das Relações Exteriores na MINUSTAH' (MA Thesis, Political Science Department, Federal University of Pernambuco, Recife, 2007).

[15] This division mirrors the difference between the competing logics set forth in James March and Johan Olsen's 'The Institutional Dynamics of International Political Orders', *International Organization*, 52:4 (1998), pp. 943–69. Whereas a 'logic of consequences' is taken to follow a rational analysis of cost and benefit, the 'logic of appropriateness' is ostensibly guided by values and the perception of a given policy course being 'the right thing to do'. In the Brazilian peacekeeping context, Itamaraty putatively adheres to a 'logic of appropriateness' while the armed forces have followed a 'logic of consequences'. See Kai Michael Kenkel, 'Interests, Identity and Brazilian Peacekeeping Policy', *Tempo do Mundo* [Perspective of the World Review], 3:2 (2011), pp. 9–36. At http://ipea.gov.br/portal/images/stories/PDFs/120822_rtmv3_portugues02.pdf.

15.2.1 The Foreign Policy Establishment: Shifting from Normative to Political Motivations

Brazilian policy towards UN peace operations cannot be understood outside the context of the foreign policy programme implemented by President Lula da Silva between 2003 and 2010. Particularly during his second term, Lula embarked on a quest to transform Brazil's growing economic prowess into strategic clout at the global level. The quest for influence brought with it a series of departures from previous practice.

Historically, the guiding principles of Brazilian foreign policy have embodied predominantly normative, but also political, explanations for peacekeeping participation: non-intervention and the equation of sovereignty with the inviolability of borders; the pacific resolution of disputes and the non-use of force, coupled with a strong penchant for legal normativism; an emphasis on multilateral institutions; a strong focus on its immediate geographic environs in South America; and the importance of advancing the country's economic development.[16] Many of these are elements of a specific South American security subculture rooted in the region's political and military history.[17]

The legal principle of non-intervention, seen as a bulwark against intervention by larger powers (principally the US)—a recurrent phenomenon in the past—is perhaps the strongest norm of South American international relations. Most relevantly for peace operations, this principle has generated ancillary precepts such as the repudiation of the use of force, emphasis on the pacific resolution of disputes, and a penchant for legal normativism.[18] Another prominent manifestation of this principle is a pronounced 'Grotian' predilection for multilateralism and support for global governance, both as a way to promote public goods and primarily as a means of furthering interests

[16] This section is intended to provide a very brief overview of selected key aspects of Brazilian foreign policy, and builds on earlier work by the author. See 'South America's Emerging Power: Brazil as Peacekeeper', *International Peacekeeping*, 17:5 (2010), pp. 644–61; 'Brazil and R2P'; 'New Missions and Emerging Powers: Brazil's Involvement in MINUSTAH', in Christian Leuprecht, Jodok Troy, and David Last (eds.), *Mission Critical: Smaller Democracies' Role in Global Stability Operations* (Montréal/Kingston: McGill-Queen's University Press, 2010), pp. 125–48.

[17] See Kenkel, 'South America's Emerging Power', pp. 650ff.; Kenkel, 'New Missions', pp. 130ff.; and the first section in Kenkel, 'Brazil and R2P'. On the regional security subcultures, including a view on their South American manifestation, see Barry Buzan and Ole Wæver, *Regions and Powers: The Structure of International Security* (Cambridge: Cambridge University Press, 2003) and Monica Herz, 'Concepts of Security in South America', *International Peacekeeping*, 17:5 (2010), pp. 598–612.

[18] See Jorge Heine, 'The Responsibility to Protect: Humanitarian Intervention and the Principle of Non-intervention in the Americas', in Ramesh Thakur, Andrew F. Cooper, and John English (eds.), *International Commissions and the Power of Ideas* (Tokyo: UN University Press, 2005), pp. 221–45.

in an arena where inequalities between states are reduced.[19] While these normative motivations provide the historical basis for the region's involvement in peace operations, several studies point to the advent of a more instrumental *démarche*.[20]

As these precepts relate to how peace operations are contemplated, Brazil's diplomats over the years crafted for the country a pacific, structurally satisfied international identity supportive of public goods such as multilateralism, focused on its immediate neighbourhood, and neither facing nor posing meaningful threats in the military ambit. Little contemplation, if any, was given to the idea of using the armed forces as a component of foreign policy; rather, emphasis was placed on diplomacy: 'With its ability to form consensuses, Brazilian diplomacy offsets the armed forces' scarce means of dissuasion and defense.'[21]

President Lula's drive for political power commensurate with Brazil's new-found economic clout led to a series of ruptures with established principles; specifically with relevance to peace operations, these include the adoption of a global political horizon and the need to balance regional and global priorities; the shift towards a more outward-looking international identity; a more ambiguous posture towards international institutions and their underlying distribution of power; and a more assertive international presence as a political actor.[22] This new posture is strongly tied to Lula's own political position.

The iconic goal of this new approach is the revival of a long-standing Brazilian foreign policy goal: a permanent, veto-wielding and prestige-endowed seat in a reformed UN Security Council.[23] The focus on Security Council membership, and the clear link made to this objective in officials' statements on participation in MINUSTAH, favour theories that attribute Brazilian motivations to participate in peace operations to a realist-inspired preoccupation with prestige.[24]

[19] Gustavo Sénéchal de Goffredo Jr., *Entre poder e direito: A tradição grotiana na política externa brasileira* [Between Power and Law: The Grotian Tradition in Brazilian Foreign Policy] (Brasília: Instituto Rio Branco/FUNAG, 2005).

[20] See Sean Burges and Jean Daudelin, 'Brazil: How Realists Defend Democracy', in Thomas Legler, Dexter Boniface, and Sharon F. Lean (eds.), *Promoting Democracy in the Americas* (Baltimore: Johns Hopkins University Press, 2007), pp. 107–32; and Jean Daudelin, 'Le Brésil Comme Puissance', *Problèmes d'Amérique Latine*, 77 (2010), pp. 27–45; and Cavalcante, 'Rendering Instrumental'.

[21] Amado Luiz Cervo, 'Brazil's Rise on the International Scene: Brazil and the World', *Revista Brasileira de Política Internacional*, 53, special edition (2010), p. 17.

[22] See, for example, Rafael Antonio Duarte Villa and Manuela Trindade Viana, 'Security Issues during Lula's Administration: From the Reactive to the Assertive Approach', *Revista Brasileira de Política Internacional*, 53, special edition (2010), pp. 91–113.

[23] See Daniel Flemes, 'Brazilian Foreign Policy in the Changing World Order', *South African Journal of International Affairs*, 16:2 (2009), pp. 161–82.

[24] See Villa and Viana, 'Security Issues', pp. 96–7.

In analytical terms many of these policy shifts reflect a textbook case of emerging power behaviour, and peace operations typically occupy pride of place in the international strategies of middle and emerging powers.[25] Emerging powers like Brazil typically support multilateral arrangements that allow them to 'punch above their weight', but are actively revisionist towards those that do not. Brazil has consistently stated that the Security Council is the only body with the power to dispatch legitimate intervention forces; at the same time, however, it questions the legitimacy of selected Council decisions based on what it considers the Council's lack of representativeness.[26] Declarations by Brazilian officials betray a revisionist orientation critical of the West that clearly shapes the country's overall stance on norms of intervention (see below) and overall participation in peace operations. Overall, with conformity to the role of emerging power has come a shift from normative to political orientations towards peacekeeping participation.

15.2.2 The Brazilian Military: The Institutional Rationale

The Brazilian armed forces are a highly professional military establishment which has constantly updated its strategic thinking in both normative and tactical terms. As it does so, it adopts a rationalist approach, based on widely adopted concepts from the US which hues closely to institutional explanations for the utility of peace operations.

Due to historical circumstances, the Brazilian armed forces—in particular the Army—have been tasked with a number of internal missions, such as infrastructure provision, medical programme delivery, and, more controversially, the maintenance of law and order, which require high levels of contact with the population and are thought to increase their effectiveness in the context of peacebuilding.[27] This proximity of purpose has contributed to

[25] For an analysis that provides more a more detailed description of the liberal functionalist approach to emerging power foreign policy, see Kenkel, 'South America's Emerging Power'. On middle powers in general, see, indicatively, Laura Neack, 'UN Peace-Keeping: In the Interest of Community or Self?', *Journal of Peace Research*, 32:2 (1995), pp. 181–96, as well as Adam Chapnick, 'The Middle Power', *Canadian Foreign Policy*, 7:2 (1999), pp. 73–82; Eduard Jordaan, 'The Concept of a Middle Power in International Relations', *Politikon* (Pretoria), 30:2 (2003), pp. 165–81; David Black, 'Addressing Apartheid: Lessons from Australian, Canadian and Swedish Policies in Southern Africa', in Andrew F. Cooper (ed.), *Niche Diplomacy* (New York: Palgrave Macmillan, 1997), p. 103.

[26] Celso Amorim, 'Brazilian Foreign Policy under President Lula (2003–2010): An Overview', *Revista Brasileira de Política Internacional*, 53, special edition (2010), p. 221.

[27] An estimated 90 per cent of army troops sent to conduct a prominent occupation of a favela in November 2010—the Complexo do Alemão—have served in MINUSTAH. The existence of cooperation and tactical sharing between the Brazilian armed forces contingents in Haiti and the Rio de Janeiro military police are the object of increasingly open investigation (personal communication with occupation participants).

perceptions of the forces' aptitude for peace operations, and highlighted the perceived institutional benefits of Blue Helmet deployments.

The armed forces have largely been left to develop tactics and strategy, as well as relationships, with other militaries in the absence of strong civilian policy guidelines. This is partly the result of weak democratic control since the negotiated transition from uniformed rule in 1985. As the country democratized, however, steps were increasingly taken to integrate the armed forces into the toolbox of an emerging civilian security policy, though there is no pervasive tradition of coordination, much less the subordination of defence to foreign policy.[28]

As a result, the armed forces have approached peacekeeping from the standpoint of maximizing institutional gains. These include first and foremost the opportunity for long-term deployment in a theatre providing training resembling combat experience; the provision of a new, positive, and most importantly external mission following the loss of the Cold War-era Communist enemy and the need to abandon internal counter-insurgency;[29] and finally the opportunity to enhance training through the establishment of a specialized training centre for peace operations. This latter element further provides, in Brazilian eyes, the opportunity to exercise leadership in peacekeeping training at the regional level, through the Brazilian Joint Centre for Peace Operations Training, CCOPAB.

Finally and perhaps most notably, peace operations—though doubtless financially beneficial to the individual troops deployed, who receive substantial bonuses for foreign deployment—do not seem to represent budgetary gains for the armed forces. The Defence Ministry has not been spared the same sensitive cuts as have been applied across the government apparatus;[30] extensive purchasing programmes have been centred on protecting newly discovered offshore oilfields; and at least until recently, payment for personnel and equipment has come from the military budget but been reimbursed to the general treasury. Brazilian representatives estimate that UN compensation payments reimburse no more than 40 per cent of the country's total expenditures in contributing to peace operations.

[28] See James H. Lebovic, 'Uniting for Peace? Democracies and United Nations Peace Operations after the Cold War', *Journal of Conflict Resolution*, 48:6 (2004), pp. 910–36. On the lack of policy integration, see Arturo C. Sotomayor Velásquez, 'Why Some States Participate in UN Peace Missions While Others Do Not: An Analysis of Civil-Military Relations and its Effects on Latin America's Contributions to Peacekeeping Operations', *Security Studies*, 19:1 (2010), pp. 170–2; and Lins, *A (des)articulação entre o Ministério da Defesa*, pp. 62–9.

[29] João Roberto Martins Filho, and Daniel Zirker, 'The Brazilian Military Under Cardoso: Overcoming the Identity Crisis', *Journal of Interamerican Studies and World Affairs*, 42:3 (2000), pp. 143–70.

[30] O Estado de São Paulo, 'Corte no Orçamento da Defesa será de R$4 bilhões', 15 February 2011. At http://economia.estadao.com.br/noticias/economia,corte-no-orcamento-da-defesa-sera-de-r-4-bilhoes,55170,0.htm

15.2.3 Past Participation in UN Peace Operations: MINUSTAH as Watershed

MINUSTAH represents a clear turning point in both the conceptual justifications and the political objectives of Brazilian participation in UN peace operations, as well as in the size and type of contingents deployed. The country places key importance on peace operations in its search for greater global strategic profile, and has sent its largest contingent ever to Haiti, supplying not only the lead contingent for the mission but also—in a break with the UN's usual rotational practice—an uninterrupted string of general officers to serve as its military force commander.

Prior to 2004, with four notable exceptions, Brazilian contributions had amounted to what Katharina Coleman has described elsewhere in this volume as 'token' contributions (see Figure 15.1). The country's first contribution to a collective security effort consisted of the sending of one officer to the League of Nations' Leticia Commission in 1933–4. In the UN context, this was followed by two officers sent to UNSCOB in 1947.[31] Participation began in earnest with

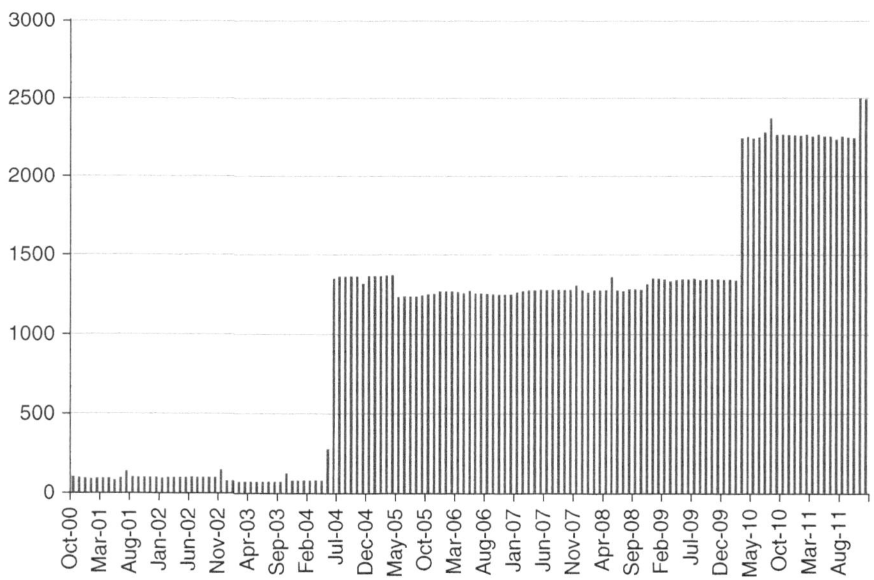

Figure 15.1 Brazilian Uniformed Personnel in UN Peacekeeping Operations, 2000–2011

[31] Paulo Roberto Campos Tarrisse da Fontoura, *O Brasil e as Operações de Manutenção da Paz das Nações Unidas* [Brazil and UN Peacekeeping Operations] 2nd edn. (Brasília: FUNAG, 2005), p. 197. At http://www.funag.gov.br/biblioteca/index.php?option=com_docman&task=-doc_download&gid=25&Itemid=41. See also Afonso José Sena Cardoso, *O Brasil nas Operações de Paz das Nações Unidas* [Brazil in UN Peace Operations] (Brasília: FUNAG, 1998).

UNEF, where the country maintained a contingent of 600–800 troops from 1957–67. The country participated in twenty-three peacekeeping operations from 1957 to 1999, including a 200-strong force to the United Nations Operation in Mozambique (ONUMOZ, 1992–4), and a large contingent deployed to the United Nations Angola Verification Mission III (UNAVEM III, 1995–7), consisting of 800 infantry troops, 200 engineers, and two field hospitals.[32] This was followed by a substantial contribution to the successive operations sent by the Organization to alleviate the crisis in East Timor. Of the 11,669 total military positions filled by Brazilian citizens between UNEF and the first Timor mission, UNAMET, to which the country seconded only a small number of observers and policemen, these three missions account for over 10,800.[33] From 1999 to 2004, the country's contribution was focused on East Timor as well as the established flow of individual observers and staff officers.

In terms of the normative underpinnings for participation, both Brazilian voting behaviour as a non-permanent member of the Security Council and its contribution of troops were strictly limited to supporting action under Chapter VI of the Charter. In keeping with the historical traditions outlined above, firmly based on the principle of non-intervention and the non-use of force, Brazilian deployments were limited in scope and objective. In keeping with another aforementioned element of the country's foreign policy, apart from UNEF the largest contingents of this period were deployed to Portuguese-speaking countries in Africa and Asia. Peace operations were viewed during this time as a means of contributing to the normative objective of global governance as a public good. Peacekeeping policy during the Cold War era was reactive and not a function of consistent motivations or policy, with the exception of linguistic solidarity demonstrated in Angola, Mozambique, and Timor-Leste.

The country's participation in MINUSTAH followed a decidedly different pattern. Though the Foreign Ministry has parsed the language of Resolution 1542 (which establishes MINUSTAH's three-pillared mandate under Chapter VII) somewhat uniquely in the interest of minimizing the appearance of a rupture with tradition, particularly during its first two years, the UN's mission in Haiti clearly involved robust peace enforcement—in whose implementation the Brazilian contingent played a crucial role. Following deployment in June 2004, Brazilian commanders in Haiti, including several force commanders, were initially loath to enter the capital's shantytowns by force, acquiescing only after strong pressure from Canada and the United States. This rupture between Brazil's traditional understanding of the principles that should guide peacekeeping and its actions in MINUSTAH can be explained by changes in the expected returns in terms of influence and prestige

[32] Fontoura, *Brazil and UN Peacekeeping Operations*, p. 200.
[33] Fontoura, *Brazil and UN Peacekeeping Operations*, pp. 201–2.

accompanying a shift from a continental focus to a global one.[34] Special attention here should be given to the implied connection between the use of force in UN peace operations and perceived eligibility for Security Council membership.

From 2004 until January 2010, Brazil supplied contingents of 1,300 troops to MINUSTAH. When the mission was enlarged in response to a devastating earthquake, Brazil contributed an additional 900 troops. These troops currently consist of two battalions, with the second, which arrived after the January 2010 earthquake, pursuing purely humanitarian tasks. The Brazilian Marine Corps contributes a joint battle group of approximately 230 men, and the army has provided an engineering company of about the same size. The Brazilian troops' area of responsibility (AOR) is urban Port-au-Prince, including the majority of problem areas such as Cité Soleil and Bel-Air; prior to the earthquake this area was home to over 1.5 million people.

Brazil's commitment to MINUSTAH further provides it the opportunity to exercise a coordination and leadership role at the regional level. Latin American troops make up about half of MINUSTAH's military component, and the coordination of these efforts outside the UN has to an extent set a precedent for multilateral defence policy cooperation in South America, which previously was almost non-existent.[35] Inasmuch as there is clarity about what Brazil seeks to achieve in Haiti, it is clear that a central position is occupied by the development of a specific Brazilian approach to peacebuilding, touted to an extent as a counter-proposal to weaknesses in 'liberal peacebuilding' practice (discussed below).

Rounding out current Brazilian contributions to UN peace missions, as of the end of 2012, Brazilian Admirals have since 24 February 2011 exercised command of the UNIFIL's Maritime Task Force. This position was enhanced by the dispatch of a frigate with 300 Marines in November 2011. This appointment marks the first time that the UNIFIL Task Force has been commanded by an officer from a non-NATO country. Similar appointments elsewhere have produced difficulties, however, owing to the ambiguity of

[34] For more on rupture and continuity with regard to Brazil's role in MINUSTAH, alongside the author's work see Eugênio Diniz, 'Brazil: Peacekeeping and the Evolution of Foreign Policy', in John T. Fishel and Andrés Sáenz (eds.), *Capacity Building for Peacekeeping: The Case of Haiti* (Washington, DC: National Defense University Press, 2007), pp. 94–5.

[35] For an introductory look at this topic, see Kai Michael Kenkel, 'Military–Military Cooperation, Regional Integration and Training for Peacekeeping Operations: Brazil and the Southern Cone', in Henrik Fürst and Gerhard Kümmel (eds.), *Core Values and the Expeditionary Mindset* (Baden-Baden: Nomos, 2011), pp. 149–63. For more detail see Danilo Marcondes de Souza Neto, 'A participação e a cooperação entre os países do Cone Sul em operações de paz: o caso da MINUSTAH' [Participation and Cooperation between South Cone States in Peace Operations: The Case of MINUSTAH], in Eduardo Svartman, Maria Celina D'Araujo, and Samuel Alves Soares (eds.), *Defesa, Segurança Internacional e Forças Armadas* [Defence, International Security and Armed Forces] (Campinas: Mercado de Letras, 2009), pp. 169–98.

Brazil's stance on robust peacekeeping. After a Marine Corps officer was selected to fill the position of Chief of Staff in UNOCI in Côte d'Ivoire in 2011, the Foreign Ministry withdrew the country's offer to fill the position over concerns about losing its neutral standing in the African nation.[36]

15.3 BRAZIL AND RECENT TRENDS IN PEACE OPERATIONS: INTERVENTION NORMS

Perhaps the most important critical factor likely to shape Brazil's positioning with regard to peace operations is its stance on changing norms of international intervention. The country's policy is deeply anchored in traditions which abjure the use of force and interpret sovereignty almost exclusively in its horizontal manifestation as the inviolability of borders. Nevertheless, as it seeks to transfer its influence to the international security arena, Brazil has been confronted with the need to engage with the association between armed intervention and international responsibility. In keeping with its revisionist project, in doing so it has sought to broaden the definition of security issues to suit its strengths rather than conforming to a reading equating a constructive international stance exclusively with acceptance of the recourse to military force.

Brazil has been a particularly active contributor, since 2009, to the global conversation about humanitarian intervention norms and the responsibility to protect (R2P). In doing so it has addressed, mostly through statements during debates in the UN General Assembly, issues related to R2P such as the protection of civilians, the use of force, and the notion of host-country consent. Once overtly hostile to concepts such as R2P, the country's diplomats have managed to do more than simply object to principles and specific interventions brought forward by Western states, instead integrating their contributions on the intervention issue neatly into the overall revisionist stance the country has adopted since the second Lula administration.

Brazil's evolving response to changes to international intervention norms encompasses two features with specific impact on peace operations. First, in reacting to R2P, Brazilian representatives have always resisted the way the principle has been implemented by the West more than the norm's actual content, which is grounded in widely accepted legal principles. The country's diplomats mistrust the principle's potential for what they consider misuse in contexts such as the 2011 NATO action in Libya. This became evident with

[36] Brazil had previously criticized an attack by UNOCI on then-President Laurent Gbagbo in April of 2011. Agência Angola Press, 'Brasil reprova ataque da ONU a Laurent Gbagbo', 7 April 2011. At http://www.portalangop.co.ao/motix/pt_pt/noticias/africa/2011/3/14/Brasil-reprova-ataque-ONU-Laurent-Gbagbo,857fd622-6fd6-4418-ad73-3f5d6c2f24ad.html

Brazil's issuance of the principle of the 'responsibility while protecting' in late 2011, which admonishes UN member states to use force for R2P purposes only very sparingly. The document effectively demonstrates that mistrust of Western intentions at least equals the felt obligation to act to put an end to human rights violations.[37] What recent Brazilian contributions to the debate on norms of intervention have made clear is that the country will not support peace operations and other interventions considered to serve the 'Western agenda' (see Daniel's chapter in this volume), and despite rhetorical service to UN principles it will not actively support—with votes or troops—missions whose raison d'être is indebted to the protection of civilians or human rights.

The second element of Brazilian engagement specifically with R2P is its increasing effort to mould the concept to fit its own priorities. Beginning with the debates that followed the Secretary-General's Implementation Report, the country's representatives expressed limited support for the first (primary state responsibility) and second (international assistance) pillars, which lend themselves more to Brazil's foreign policy aims.[38] The third pillar, which potentially legitimates armed intervention, continues to be rejected. Of particular interest are recent initiatives to bring development issues to the R2P conversation, which fit well with Brazil's export of its own successful domestic policies for development, agricultural innovation, and poverty reduction within an incipient new approach to peacebuilding.

15.4 FUTURE TRENDS: A BRAZILIAN PEACEBUILDING MODEL FOR THE FUTURE?

Due to its close tethering to an overarching foreign policy project that seeks increased global profile on strategic issues, Brazil's future participation in peace operations will be influenced by opportunities for enhanced prestige and positive international exposure. Brazil's strengths as a contributor to these missions clearly lie where its own advantages come to bear: in activities associated more with developmental and institutional aspects of peacebuilding, and less with the use of force and peace enforcement. Peace operations—particularly peacebuilding—provide Brazil with a means to contribute to defining international responsibility in terms more amenable to emerging powers and those in the global South. Grassroots peacebuilding has been

[37] Brazil, Permanent Mission to the United Nations, 'Responsibility while protecting: elements for the development and promotion of a concept', 9 November 2011. At http://www.globalr2p.org/media/pdf/Concept-Paper_RwP.pdf.

[38] Report of the UN Secretary-General, *Implementing the Responsibility to Protect* (New York: UN A/63/677, 2009).

identified as just such a niche within the ambit of UN peace operations.[39] Indeed, Brazil has been actively involved in UN debates on peacebuilding for over a decade.[40]

As is the case with many troop contributors, there is a strong current of exceptionalism in Brazilian attitudes on peacekeeping, and the country's criterion for future troop and other contributions will be to identify contexts where that exceptionalism will attain its maximum result, including by gaining the greatest international audience. Brazil's contribution to MINUSTAH has served as a laboratory for the development of an approach to peacebuilding that unites a number of foreign policy objectives into a project that underscores Brazil's revisionist stance towards global structures of power and its own place in them. The utility of Brazil's perceived success in Haiti to the country's critical stance towards established powers' role in intervention is made clear in Brazilian representatives' explicit distancing of their approach from that of the West:

> For this reason, Brazil's unprecedented participation in Haiti, as well as that of other South American states, does not consist only of troops: it is a stabilization operation different from others, which, in our understanding, must be based on three factors: promoting stabilization via the peace force; dialogue between the various political factions; and institutional, social and economic capacity-building.... We are trying something new, seeking to learn lessons from the previous interventions which were based on an essentially repressive vision of the problem.[41]

In a pattern also employed by other emerging powers, in Haiti Brazil has couched its military and financial contribution to MINUSTAH within an overarching bilateral assistance programme which also foments cooperation through the India–Brazil–South Africa (IBSA) Fund and other emerging variable-geometry arrangements. The specific elements of this approach have been touted by a rapidly growing epistemic community in Brazil as a counter-proposal to established Northern reconstruction models of liberal peacebuilding. Concretely, while it cannot yet be said to have taken the

[39] In accordance with the functionalist theoretical approach to emerging powers' international conduct, thematic niches provide criteria for states to maximize returns on their investment of resources, both material and political, in terms of diplomatic influence and positive publicity. See Kenkel, 'Brazil as Peacekeeper'.

[40] On Brazil's role in UN peacebuilding debates, see Brazilian diplomat Gilda Motta Santos Neves, *Comissão das Nações Unidas para Consolidação da Paz-Perspectiva Brasileira* [The UN Peacebuilding Commission: A Brazilian Perspective] (Brasília: FUNAG/Ministry of Foreign Affairs, 2010). At http://igepri.org/pesquisa/index.php?option=com_docman&task=doc_download&gid=1729&Itemid=60

[41] Celso Amorim, 'Política Externa do Governo Lula: os dois primeiros anos' [The Lula Government's Foreign Policy: The First Two Years], *Análise de Conjuntura OPSA* 4 (2005). At http://www.gedes.org.br/downloads/992abee1f32006ceb57149d0d659f132.pdf

shape of a cohesive paradigm, the core of the Brazilian approach is based on specific policies and projects which have been successful at home.

The approach is based on reducing the need for the use of force in pacification through continuous close contact with the population; nevertheless, in something of a breach with diplomatic rhetoric, Brazilian troops have not hesitated to use force where deemed necessary in the Haitian context. Its focus on smaller-scale development projects and socio-economic goals such as hunger and poverty reduction allows Brazil to pursue an outward-looking exportation of its own successes, couched in South–South cooperation models unburdened by the whiff of colonialism the country admonishes in Northern models. Indeed, there is a sense that the model compensates for its material and financial limitations through the political legitimacy of a Southern origin and the magnifying effect of a domestic experience with underdevelopment.

Key to the Brazilian model is the integration of input from domestically successful agencies, coordinated by the Brazilian Cooperation Agency (ABC), which is subordinated to the Foreign Ministry. These include *inter alia* the Brazilian Agricultural Research Corporation (EMBRAPA), the National Service for Industrial Apprenticeship (SENAI), and, importantly, civil society organizations such as the NGO Viva Rio, which contributes its experience in conflict reduction in the favelas of Rio de Janeiro.

While these factors themselves are located outside the immediate purview of UN peacekeeping, future large-scale Brazilian deployments are very likely to be limited to where the capacity and will exist to implement the entire broad approach in its entirety. Based on the growing importance of development issues and of South–South solidarity in its foreign policy, Brazil has also focused considerable diplomatic resources in Africa, and may be more likely to contribute to development-based operations there. While there are certain to be relatively limited exceptions—as the UNIFIL deployment has demonstrated—Brazilian representatives have made clear that the country, rather than providing peacekeepers as a contribution to a normative public good, will follow an instrumentalist policy of getting more impact for their reais, including through the further development of the peacebuilding model.

15.5 CONCLUSION

As Brazilian foreign policy adapts to new parameters and horizons, the country's policy is in a state of flux. The typical emerging-power shift from a regional to a global horizon brings with it the move from a predominantly normative middle-power motivation in peace operations to more politically oriented preoccupations with prestige and influence. As a result, the country's approach to peacekeeping participation—a key part of the profile-seeker's toolbox—has become increasingly instrumental and defiant of dominant powers' interpretations of the goals and scope of peace operations. Brazil—and here the country is emblematic of other rising powers—will contribute to peace operations where these combine two main characteristics. First, the opportunity must exist for Brazil's strengths to come to bear without its weaknesses becoming handicaps—in other words, the focus will be on development-heavy peacebuilding missions where the very robust use of force is not necessary and where the country can take on a leading role. Second, Brazil will likely participate only in those missions which do not openly align with established 'Western powers' agendas. It is unlikely to participate for the sake of participation; safeguarding the continuing provision of peacekeepers from this type of theatre requires their full inclusion in shaping the coming peacekeeping agenda as well as accommodation of an exceptionalist and increasingly instrumental impetus to contribute.

Brazil and a number of other emerging powers have come a long way towards making a virtue of necessity. As actors with extensive experience at the nexus of security and development, they have emphasized this connection and sought to bring their strengths in the developmental ambit to bear in the security realm, where international influence is more concrete. Its focus on developmental aspects of peacebuilding provides not only a way for the country to contribute actively and continuously to UN peace operations, but has led, in incipient fashion, to the inclusion of these aspects in global debates on intervention issues such as those regularly conducted by the General Assembly. This is likely to change the face of UN peace operations as guaranteeing a steady flow of personnel and financial contributions will come to depend on the involvement of emerging powers. The inclusion of developmental approaches to the root causes of conflicts has the potential to strengthen both the normative underpinnings of peace operations, such as R2P, and practices such as peacebuilding, in terms of both efficacy and legitimacy.[42]

Finally, in practical terms, the concomitant rise of powers such as Brazil—with increasing interest and capacities in peace operations, a clear focus on development, and restrictions on the use of force—and increased proclivity for the use of force to protect civilians, suggest that it is appropriate to contemplate a more fixed division of labour in peace operations. For example, the use of force for human rights—including outside the UN system—might be left to those Western powers with greater military means and normative inclination,[43] and developmental peacebuilding and longer-term alleviation of root causes to emerging 'Southern' powers able to bring to bear their own

[42] See Alex J. Bellamy, *Global Politics and the Responsibility to Protect* (New York: Routledge, 2011), pp. 93–121.

[43] See Alex J. Bellamy and Paul D. Williams, 'The West and Contemporary Peace Operations', *Journal of Peace Research*, 46:1 (2009), pp. 39–57.

domestic experience.[44] As a state that seeks to take on global responsibility without the dictation of its terms, Brazil is uniquely placed to contribute to the definition of such a distribution of tasks. As it continues to identify ways in which peace operations provide opportunities to advance its quest for global influence, given the right incentives, Brazil is poised to remain a key contributor of Blue Helmets in the future.

[44] On the notion of a division of labour and the regionalization of peacekeeping, see Fred Tanner, 'Addressing the Perils of Peace Operations: Toward a Global Peacekeeping System', *Global Governance*, 16:2 (2010), pp. 209–17.

16

Turkey

Nil S. Satana

Turkey, with its strong military, the second largest in the NATO alliance after the United States, participates in United Nations (UN) peacekeeping operations all over the world. Turkey's incumbent government led by the Justice and Development Party (*Adalet ve Kalkınma Partisi*, AKP) came to power in 2002 with the stated aim of pursuing a more active foreign policy. Although Turkey's principal priorities in terms of military crisis management in the last decade were its contributions to NATO's missions in Afghanistan and later Libya, part of Ankara's new foreign policy agenda involved greater contributions to UN peacekeeping operations. Consequently, Turkey provided peacekeepers to eleven UN operations during the 2000s: from Kosovo and Lebanon to Haiti, Timor-Leste, Burundi, Liberia, the Democratic Republic of Congo (DRC), Côte d'Ivoire, Sierra Leone, Sudan, and the Central African Republic and Chad.

Turkey started contributing troops and police to UN missions only after the threat of the Soviet Union receded with the end of the Cold War. While the trend of the 1990s set a positive tone for further peacekeeping efforts, the contributions markedly increased during the 2000s (see Figure 16.1). Nevertheless, the Turkish contribution remained limited except for the mission in Lebanon. Thus, this chapter examines two major questions: why did Turkish contributions to UN peacekeeping rise in the 2000s and why did its contributions remain limited when put in the context of the potential capacity of the Turkish Armed Forces (TAF) and the Turkish National Police Force (TNPF).

By the end of 2011, Turkey participated in nine UN peacekeeping operations with about 500 uniformed personnel, roughly one-quarter of which were police officers. This chapter argues that the rationales behind Turkey's provision of UN peacekeepers have changed significantly from the 1990s to the 2000s. While its UN peacekeeping contributions could be explained by normative and security-based explanations in the 1990s, Turkey's more recent rising contributions are a consequence of its political aspirations to become a regional and global player. Bolstered by its growing economy and social transformation, Turkish foreign policy sought to improve the country's

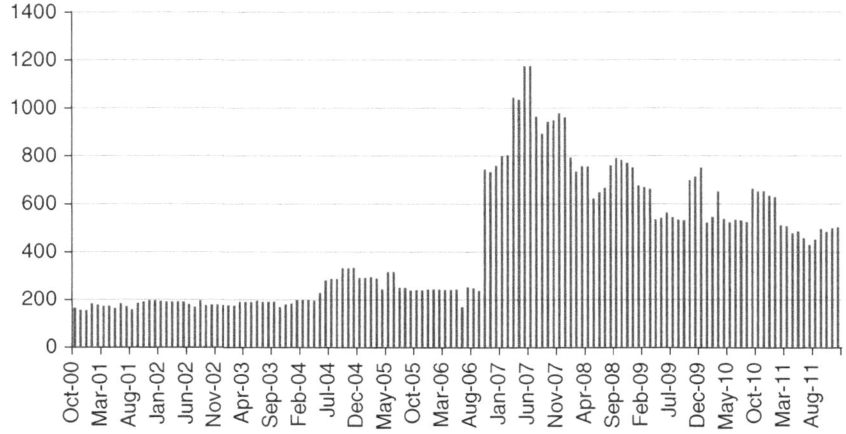

Figure 16.1 Turkish Uniformed Personnel in UN Peacekeeping Operations, 2000–2011

standing in international society. The AKP government saw UN peacekeeping as one instrument to help attain that goal.

After examining the decision-making mechanisms in Turkish peacekeeping and discussing the various rationales for providing UN peacekeepers, this chapter shows that despite some obstacles, Turkey has the potential to increase its contributions still further. Significant constraints include the perceptions of both politicians and bureaucrats that equate UN-led operations with UN-mandated NATO operations, the disconnect between civilians and the military on security-related issues, the limited reward structures for participating in UN operations, particularly within the military, and the fight against the PKK (Kurdistan Workers' Party) that has engaged Turkish security forces since 1984.

The literature on Turkish contributions to UN peacekeeping remains very limited, confined mostly to more general evaluations of the participation of the Turkish Armed Forces in regional and global security and to the work of military officers who have served in peace operations.[1] Moreover, media coverage of Turkey's peacekeeping contributions is rare and generally limited to the loss of life in such operations, a topic deemed to be newsworthy. Since most casualties have occurred in NATO missions, these have received the most coverage. In addition, reportage about what Turkish peacekeepers

[1] See Mehmet Öcal, 'Türk Silahlı Kuvvetleri'nin Bölgesel ve Küresel Güvenlik ve Barışa Katkısı' [Contributions of the Turkish Armed Forces to Regional and Global Security], *Sosyal Bilimler Enstitüsü Dergisi*, 28 (2010/11), p. 282. For a comprehensive analysis of Turkey's military contributions to peace missions in the 1990s, see Uğur Güngör, 'The Analysis of Turkey's Approach to Peacekeeping' (unpublished Ph.D., Bilkent University, 2007) and Uğur Güngör, *Why States Contribute to Peace Operations: Motivations Behind Turkey's Involvement* (New York: Lambert Academic Publishing, 2011).

actually do and public opinion about this issue is often unreliable.[2] As a result, this chapter relies on confidential interviews conducted with military and police personnel that have served in at least one UN peacekeeping operation as well as with bureaucrats involved in processes related to peacekeeping missions. Parliamentary records of decisions to send troops to particular missions are also utilized.

The chapter proceeds in five sections. The first summarizes Turkey's contributions to UN peacekeeping operations since 1990 but with a focus on the 2000s. The second section analyses why Turkey provided peacekeepers with reference to security-based, normative, institutional, economic, and political rationales. The decision-making process for Turkish contributions to UN peacekeeping is the focus of the third section, while the fourth shows that Turkey's contributions remain well below its potential and asks why this is the case. The chapter concludes by reflecting on the future of Turkish peacekeeping for policymakers.

16.1 TURKEY'S CONTRIBUTIONS TO UN PEACEKEEPING OPERATIONS: A BRIEF OVERVIEW

Turkey contributed more uniformed personnel to UN peacekeeping in the first decade of the twenty-first century than it did in all of the previous fifty-plus years of UN peacekeeping combined. Turkey's first operation was the UN-authorized war in Korea (1950–3) where it dispatched a 4,500 strong brigade and deployed some 15,000 troops throughout the course of the conflict. It suffered a total of 733 'martyrs'—as they are commonly called.[3] In contrast, Turkey refrained from getting involved in UN peacekeeping missions during the Cold War since these were deemed 'missions empowered to "manage" conflicts rather than "resolve" them'.[4] Further Turkish participation was inhibited by concerns about the potential for a Soviet invasion. Because of this concern, Turkey's foreign policy during the Cold War was

[2] 'The media in the 1980s and 1990s self-censored and refrained from writing military-related issues as a result of the notorious after-effects of the 1980 coup. In some security-related issues such as the PKK attacks, the military summoned the media owners and asked not to publicize the casualties.' Confidential interview with a senior military officer, April 2011. Nevertheless, the media now complains that AKP rule in the 2000s represents a civilian dictatorship as opposed to the tutelary role of the military in the 1980s and 1990s. See for example, Ömer Taşpınar, 'Turkey's General Dilemma', *Foreign Affairs*, 8 August 2011. At http://www.foreignaffairs.com/articles/68019/omer-taspinar/turkeys-general-dilemma?page=2

[3] A. Kadir Varoglu and Adnan Bicaksiz, 'Volunteering for Risk: The Culture of the Turkish Armed Forces', *Armed Forces and Society*, 31:4 (2005), p. 587.

[4] Tarık Oğuzlu and Uğur Güngör, 'Peace Operations and the Transformation of Turkey's Security Policy', *Contemporary Security Policy*, 27:3 (2007), p. 474.

cautious and conservative, particularly when it came to activities related to international peace and security. Consequently, Ankara focused on national defence and economic development, and did not see much added value in peacekeeping. It sought security primarily through a strategic alliance with the United States and NATO membership, which was denied twice before accession was finally granted in 1952, in part because of its contributions in Korea.

The end of the Cold War reduced Turkey's geostrategic importance.[5] However, the subsequent turmoil in the Balkans and the Caucasus encouraged Turkish leaders to engage more actively in regional and global affairs, including through UN peacekeeping operations. This new emphasis on regional security policy resulted in the TAF's participation in the UN Iran–Iraq Military Observer Group (1988–91), its first UN-led peacekeeping mission. This was quickly followed by its participation in the UN Iraq–Kuwait Observation Mission (UNIKOM, 1991–2003) and other missions in the Balkans. Such activities led the official General Staff policy to claim that since the 1990s, 'Turkey has participated in peace support missions at the greatest level in parallel with her international responsibilities, national interests and capabilities.'[6] While this is a vague definition of how the General Staff understands Turkish peacekeeping efforts, the TAF and the police were consistent, if relatively minor, participants in UN peacekeeping operations during the 1990s.[7] While these contributions were mainly focused on the Balkans due to ethnic and historical ties with the Bosnian Muslims especially, troops were also sent to African missions (e.g., Somalia and the DRC) mainly because of Turkey's aspirations to show that it could be an important player in the post-Cold War security environment.[8] It was a much-celebrated development for Turkey's international prestige when Turkish Lieutenant-General Çevik Bir assumed the role of Force Commander in UNOSOM II in Somalia.[9] In 1998,

[5] Duygu Bazoğlu Sezer, 'Turkey's Grand Strategy Facing a Dilemma', *The International Spectator*, 27:1 (1992), pp. 17–32.

[6] Official website of the Turkish Armed Forces at http://www.tsk.tr/4_uluslararasi_iliskiler/4_1_turkiyenin_barisi_destekleme_harekatina_katkilari/konular/turk_silahli_%20kuvvetlerinin_barisi_destekleme_harekatina_katkilari.htm

[7] Thirty police officers were sent to Bosnia-Herzegovina for the first time in 1996 for the UN Police Task Force (IPTF), which later became the UN Mission in Bosnia and Herzegovina (UNMIBH) together with the UN Civilian Office operations. Since 1996, 'over 1,000 Turkish policemen have participated in some of the UN missions (Kosovo, Bosnia-Herzegovina, Liberia, Congo D.C., Sierra Leone, Eastern Timor, Afghanistan, Ivory Coast, Haiti, Burundi and Sudan)'. See http://www.disiliskiler.pol.tr/en/TNP/Pages/InternationalPolice.aspx

[8] See http://www.disiliskiler.pol.tr/en/TNP/Pages/InternationalPolice.aspx. It should also be noted that the 1990s were frustrating years for Turkey's foreign policy decision-makers not only due to regional conflicts but also the constant struggle for European Union accession, which resulted in Turkey's candidacy in 1999.

[9] 'Yeni Bir Somali' [A New Somalia], *Milliyet*, 28 March 1993. While a generally accepted conviction in Turkey is that a Turkish general was given the command at the request of the United States, there is little reliable evidence to confirm this belief. Still, the motivation of

Turkey committed to training peacekeepers by offering courses at a training centre under the Partnership for Peace initiative. The centre remains active to this day.

The 2000s witnessed Turkey's continuing participation in UN peacekeeping missions in Kosovo and the DRC, as well as newer missions in Central African Republic and Chad, Liberia, Burundi, Côte d'Ivoire, Sudan, Haiti, Timor-Leste, and Lebanon. Moreover, Turkey sent one frigate to assist in counter-piracy operations off the coast of Somalia and provide surveillance under the Combined Task Force 151 (CTF-151) established under UN Security Council resolutions 1816, 1838, 1844, 1846, and 1851.[10] Turkey also assumed command of CTF-151 from May to August 2009 and September to December 2010.[11]

While Turkey sent troops to UN peacekeeping operations in both the 1990s and the 2000s, it also contributed military observers to UNIKOM (1991–2003), the UN Mission of Support in East Timor (UNMISET, 2000–4), the UN Mission in Bosnia and Herzegovina (UNMIBH, 2001–2), the UN/EU coordinated effort (EU Police Mission in the DRC, 2006–7), and the UN Observer Mission in Georgia (UNOMIG, 1994–2009).[12]

Turkey's more active peacekeeping policy since the end of the Cold War has not been limited to UN-led peacekeeping. It also participated in UN-authorized NATO operations such as the Implementation/Stabilization Force (IFOR/SFOR) in Bosnia-Herzegovina where it remained until 2004. In the 2000s Turkey participated in other UN-authorized NATO operations such as *Essential Harvest*, *Amber Fox*, *Allied Harmony*, *Concordia*, and *Proxima* in Macedonia between 2001 and 2005. The TAF has also been part of the NATO-led Kosovo Force (KFOR) since 1999. In 2001, Turkey sent troops to Afghanistan under the UN-authorized International Security Assistance Force (ISAF), assuming command of the operation in 2003, 2007, and 2010–11. In 2004, Ankara started partaking in NATO's Training Mission in Iraq (NTM-I). The TAF also participated in EU operations such as *Althea* in Bosnia (2004–), the OSCE Kosovo Verification Mission (1999), the OSCE Border Monitoring Operation in Georgia (2000–4), and the OSCE Georgia Observer Mission (2006–9).

Turkey's active participation in these NATO, EU, and OSCE missions is important to note since its commitments to multiple regional and international

keeping the US as a close ally might have been influential in Turkey's involvement in Somalia in the 1990s.

[10] 'Yeni Bir Somali' [A New Somalia].

[11] 'Turkish frigate sails for Gulf of Aden against Somali pirates', *World Bulletin*, 27 July 2010. At http://www.worldbulletin.net/index.php?aType=haber&ArticleID=61856

[12] Official website of the Turkish Armed Forces at http://www.tsk.tr/4_uluslararasi_iliskiler/4_1_turkiyenin_barisi_destekleme_harekatina_katkilari/konular/turk_silahli_%20kuvvetlerinin_barisi_destekleme_harekatina_katkilari.htm

organizations have limited its UN peacekeeping efforts. Turkish military and police have had to provide forces to several NATO operations as well as UN peacekeeping missions, which has stretched its forces thin considering Turkey's internal problems that also require troops at home.

As a result, Turkey has become a 'serial token contributor' to UN peacekeeping missions.[13] In other words, although Turkey actively started providing more UN peacekeepers after the end of the Cold War, it has preferred to contribute to several UN operations with only a few personnel deployed to each one. Ankara did, however, pledge its support to the UN Standby Arrangements System (UNSAS) in 2000. In this vein, on 3 December 2003, Turkey passed Law No. 5010 to legalize its previous commitment to the UNSAS and promised the provision of a medical evacuation team, a mechanized infantry battalion, police forces, military observers, officers, and the equipment that these personnel would use.[14] To date, however, no units have been deployed since parliament passed this law.[15] The official enthusiasm evident in some of the political discourse on peacekeeping has thus not been adequately reflected in Turkey's actual contributions of uniformed personnel, which have only rarely gone beyond 500.

The following sections elaborate on Turkey's decision-making mechanisms for peacekeeping operations and discuss why Turkey has not lived up to its potential in this area.

16.2 PEACEKEEPING OPERATIONS AND THE DECISION-MAKING PROCESS IN TURKEY

Turkish civil–military relations experienced a significant transformation in the 2000s, in part because of the start of Turkey's candidacy for EU membership in 1999.[16] Until this recent (and ongoing) transformation, Turkey's peacekeeping decisions were military-dominated despite the occasional presence of strong civilian governments after 1983, which forced the military to accept certain foreign policy decisions.[17] At these times, the government and the

[13] See Katharina Coleman's chapter in this volume.

[14] Official parliamentary website at http://www.tbmm.gov.tr/kanunlar/k5010.html

[15] Author's confidential interview with a commissioned TAF officer, October 2011.

[16] For the causes and consequences of this transformation see, Nil S. Satana, 'Transformation of the Turkish Military and the Path to Democracy', *Armed Forces and Society*, 34:3 (2008), pp. 357–88. For a comparison of Turkish civil–military relations with European and Middle Eastern paradigms, see Nil S. Satana, 'Civil–Military Relations in Europe, the Middle East and Turkey', *Turkish Studies*, 12:2 (2011), pp. 279–92.

[17] A good example is the decision to send troops to Somalia in the 1990s despite the military's objection along with protests by the opposition for 'sending Turkish soldiers to die in a conflict-torn country'.

military acted as two separate actors in peacekeeping matters: the government dominated not only the decision-making process but also decisions about where to send peacekeeping forces while the military remained relatively autonomous in deciding how to handle the job on the ground. The 2000s saw firmer civilian control of the military and thus decisions about UN peacekeeping.

Turkey's UN peacekeeping policy is determined by two documents. The first is the 1982 Constitution, Article 92 of which rules that upon the UN's request for peacekeepers, Turkey's National Security Council (NSC) will advise the government, and the Council of Ministers will send the proposal to the Parliament, which is responsible for the decision to send troops.[18] The parliament specifies the number of the troops that will be sent to a mission and sets other conditions to govern Turkey's contribution to that particular operation.

The second document is the *Concept on Turkey's Contribution to Peacekeeping and Peacebuilding Operations*, issued by Prime Minister Tayyip Erdoğan on 15 March 2005. This paper sets out principles to guide Turkish decision-making on peacekeeping. The first principle it identifies is that the peacekeeping operation in question must be seen as internationally legitimate, which means that it should have authorization from the UN Security Council. Missions sent to certain regions such as the Balkans, Central Asia, and the Middle East are to be prioritized over others. Moreover, certain international organizations are prioritized: NATO, EU, UN, and OSCE, usually in that order. This shows that UN peacekeeping is not a priority focus for Turkey and that, like several other states, Turkey prefers to work outside UN-led operations.[19] Finally, the paper demands that mission objectives be clearly defined to enable the government to evaluate costs and the benefits of sending Turkish troops.[20]

16.3 EXPLAINING TURKEY'S CONTRIBUTIONS TO UN PEACEKEEPING OPERATIONS

The limited literature on Turkey's contributions to UN peacekeeping missions focuses mainly on ideational explanations and national security and economic

[18] Turkish police officers are contracted in UN and non-UN missions under Article 77 of Law No. 657. See official website of the Turkish National Police at http://www.turkishnationalpolice.gov.tr/peace.html

[19] Since Turkey's bid for EU membership lost its significance in the eyes of the Turkish public, UN missions may now become a priority after Turkey's NATO commitments.

[20] Confidential interview at the Ministry of Foreign Affairs, 17 January 2012.

concerns.[21] Some argue that these two sets of motivations are closely related.[22] However, these explanations are based primarily on analysis of UN and non-UN-led missions in the 1990s. While they still remain valid to a certain extent, the main motivation for Turkish contributions to UN peacekeeping in the 2000s has been political and related to Turkey's self-image as a global player. Moreover, while most studies focused solely on military contributions, this chapter discusses both police and military contributions to UN mandated and led peacekeeping operations.

16.3.1 Security Rationales

The Turkish government and military have often employed security rationales to justify participation in UN peacekeeping operations.[23] In fact, such concerns have often been invoked to explain Turkey's relatively small contribution as a product of priority being given to security over other concerns in foreign policy.[24] During the Cold War, Turkey's security concerns stemmed from geographic proximity to the Soviet Union and the perceived threat to Turkish territorial integrity. Thus, the decision to contribute troops to the UN-mandated intervention in Korea (1950–3) was a direct consequence of Turkey's aspirations for NATO membership which was, in turn, seen as the best guarantor of security from the Soviet threat.[25] Therefore, a realist argument would see the need to prioritize NATO membership as the driving force behind Turkey's reluctance to provide UN peacekeepers during the Cold War.[26] Accordingly, while seven of the thirteen UN peacekeeping operations during the Cold War years took place in the Middle East, Turkey refrained from taking part in these operations.[27]

According to Öcal, Turkey's security concerns were once again exacerbated with the fall of the Soviet Union and the conflicts in the Balkans, Middle East,

[21] See Güngör, *The Analysis of Turkey's Approach to Peacekeeping* and Öcal, 'Türk Silahlı Kuvvetleri'nin Bölgesel ve Küresel Güvenlik ve Barışa Katkısı' [Contributions of the Turkish Armed Forces to Regional and Global Peace], p. 306.

[22] Oğuzlu and Güngör, 'Peace Operations'.

[23] For a comprehensive critique of this security-based approach, see Güngör, *Why States Contribute to Peace Operations*.

[24] Pınar Bilgin, 'Only Strong States Can Survive in Turkey's Geography: The Uses of "Geo-political Truths" in Turkey', *Political Geography*, 26:7 (2007), pp. 740–56.

[25] Güngör, *The Analysis of Turkey's Approach to Peacekeeping*.

[26] Güngör, *The Analysis of Turkey's Approach to Peacekeeping*.

[27] Uğur Güngör, 'Türk Dış Politikası ve Barışı Koruma'[Turkish Foreign Policy and Peace-keeping]ers]ping Operations.as a new asl rationales section. ul and the civilians mostly sumi [Turkish Foreign Policy and Peacekeeping], in Yelda Demirağ and Özden Çelebi (eds.), *Türk Dış Politikasının Son On Yılı* (Ankara: Palme Yayınları, 2011).

and Turkic republics in Turkey's periphery.[28] Consequently, this rationale would suggest that global and regional security concerns and Turkey's geopolitics explain Ankara's peacekeeping contributions in the post-Cold War era.

A fear of the spillover effects of conflicts in its neighbourhood might have been a driving force for Turkey's involvement in the peacekeeping operations in the Balkans and the Middle East in the 1990s, and its extensive contribution to UNIFIL II deployed in Lebanon in 2006. However, decisions to send troops to Somalia (1992–4) and Sudan in 2007 cannot be explained this way. Indeed, the dispatch of over 300 soldiers to Somalia in December 1992 was widely perceived as an unnecessary burden on Turkey's military, which at the time was engaged in active combat against the PKK at home.[29] Still, according to Baskın Oran, Turkey's security concerns and national interests were deemed at stake after the developments in the Balkans, which motivated Turkish foreign policy-makers to send troops to Somalia.[30] The main objective for this deployment, according to Oran, was to gain leverage for getting involved in UN peacekeeping in Bosnia, where Turkey's contribution was opposed by the Serbs, Greeks, and Russians.[31]

In sum, the Turkish military did not believe that Turkey's involvement in Somalia in the 1990s or 2000s (or the other missions to Africa) was urgently necessary from a security perspective. Until the transformation of civil–military relations in the 2000s, the Turkish military was politically strong enough to force the government's hand in various political matters including peacekeeping decisions, while the politicians in general succumbed to the military's perspective on security-related issues with hardly any civilian debate.[32] Nevertheless, despite its reluctance, the Turkish military complied with political decisions to deploy peacekeepers in Africa for various reasons including economic and ideational concerns that will be further discussed in the following sections.[33]

[28] Öcal, 'Türk Silahlı Kuvvetleri'nin Bölgesel ve Küresel Güvenlik ve Barışa Katkısı' [Contributions of the Turkish Armed Forces to Regional and Global Peace], p. 306.

[29] Although the military struggle against the PKK has depleted Turkey's economic and human resources since 1984, conscription provides Ankara with a very large pool of military forces. Thus, it is rather speculative to argue that PKK attacks significantly constrained Turkey's participation in UN peacekeeping during the 1990s or after the 2003 invasion of Iraq. Nevertheless, below, I briefly discuss how the ongoing conflict with the PKK has at times limited Turkey's contributions to UN peacekeeping.

[30] Baskın Oran, 'Türk Dış Politikası: Temel İlkeleri ve Soğuk Savaş Ertesindeki Durumu Üzerine Notlar' [Turkish Foreign Policy: Notes on Main Principles and the Implications of the Post-Cold War], *Ankara Üniversitesi Siyasal Bilgiler Fakültesi Dergisi*, 51:1 (1996), p. 362.

[31] Oran, 'Türk Dış Politikası', p. 362.

[32] Civil–military relations in Turkey are discussed in more detail in the institutional rationales section.

[33] The same is true for police forces that are sent to Africa in token contributions.

16.3.2 Normative/Ideational Rationales

Ideational factors, especially Turkey's evolving national identity, are also important in understanding its peacekeeping contributions. Güngör argues that in the 1990s Turkey's peacekeeping efforts were first and foremost about siding with the West, defined as NATO in the past and more recently the EU, in order to gain endorsement of the Turkish state's 'Western' credentials.[34] Turkey was established in 1923 from the ashes of the Ottoman Empire and the founder, Mustafa Kemal Atatürk, adopted a Western developmental approach. Arguably, Atatürk viewed the most significant reason for the collapse of the Empire as the backwardness of state structures and the prevalent social culture. Thus, the official state ideology—Kemalism—pursued Western standards of civilization through a secular and statist republic. In this context, some argue that Turkey's main motivation for providing UN peacekeepers in the 1990s was to prevent its Western identity being questioned by certain states within the EU. As a result, it is argued that 'active involvement in peace operations has been seen as a near-panacea to reinforce the country's Western identity in the West'.[35]

In this vein, through operations such as the ones in Africa in the 1990s, 'Turkey's contribution to peace operations helped the members of the western community understand that Turkey is a security producing country in the region and is always a part of the solutions, rather than the problems.'[36] Moreover, according to this view, the dynamics of Turkey's security relations with Western powers help explain Ankara's decision to send peacekeepers to Somalia.[37] While this motivation would explain why Turkey prefers contributing to NATO and EU peacekeeping more than it does to UN missions, it does not explain why UN peacekeeping is thought to help enhance Turkey's Western image, considering that the UN is not a 'Western' organization and deploys fewer Western peacekeepers than it once did. Moreover, Turkey's ideational identification with Europe has declined in the 2000s as a result of its repeated rejection from the EU after its candidacy in 1999.

Another ideational explanation may be related to Atatürk's foreign policy principle of 'peace at home, peace abroad' which aims to enhance Turkey's identity as a 'contributor to world-peace'. This notion has been a central tenet of Turkish foreign policy for decades. However, the meaning and practice of this principle have changed from early Republican times throughout the 1990s: 'Whereas at the time of formulation it was meant to contribute to world peace through a passivist [sic], status quo oriented foreign

[34] Güngör, *The Analysis of Turkey's Approach to Peacekeeping.*
[35] Oğuzlu and Güngör, 'Peace Operations', p. 472.
[36] Güngör, *The Analysis of Turkey's Approach to Peacekeeping*, p. 226.
[37] Güngör, *The Analysis of Turkey's Approach to Peacekeeping*, p. 177.

policy—mainly to consolidate the newly-established regime—in the 1990s it was seen as a basis for a more proactive contribution to the maintenance of world peace in general and maintenance of peace in Turkey's neighbourhood in particular.'[38] Thus, in this view, contributions to UN peacekeeping (even small ones) hold symbolic importance for a country trying to internalize the principle of 'peace at home and abroad'. Accordingly, in the 2000s, Turkey cultivated a self-image as a peacekeeper and mediator between West and East (as part of its emerging global power role), an approach driven by both normative and self-interested concerns.[39] For example, Yanık argues that after the end of the Cold War, Turkey's 'bridging' geopolitical location between West and East was highlighted particularly in its foreign policy-making relating to the Middle East and Eurasia.[40]

A more constructivist perspective would posit that Turkey's national interests are shaped by constructions of identity. In the 1990s, this was primarily Western oriented and thus it used UN peacekeeping to realize this goal during the 1990s; during the 2000s it began to recraft its identity and to see itself as an emerging global power, which also had implications for its policy on UN peacekeeping. In fact, the decision to send troops to Lebanon/UNIFIL II after heated debates and protests 'was a victory for Prime Minister Recep Tayyip Erdoğan, who called Turkey's participation a moral duty that would contribute to regional stability and raise Turkey's profile on the international stage'.[41] Peacekeeping, therefore, may have become instrumental in shaping Turkey's identity as a bridge between West and East in the 1990s or as a central power that helps other states in times of need during the 2000s.

16.3.3 Institutional Rationales

Similar to several Latin American states, a possible cause of Turkish participation in UN peacekeeping during the 2000s is civil–military relations.[42] As in the case of the Somalia operations (1992–5), UN peacekeeping has become at times an issue where the civilian government imposed its will on the military

[38] Hüseyin Bağcı and Şaban Kardaş, 'Exploring Turkey's Role in Peace Operations: Towards a Framework of Analysis', in Foreign Policy Institute (ed.), *Contemporary Issues in International Politics: Essays in Honour of Seyfi Tashan* (Ankara: Foreign Policy Institute, 2004), p. 131.

[39] Accordingly, Turkey's reconstruction of its status as a global player and its relevance for UN peacekeeping contributions will be discussed in the following political rationales section.

[40] Lerna Yanık, 'The Metamorphosis of Metaphors of Vision: "Bridging" Turkey's Location, Role and Identity After the End of Cold War', *Geopolitics*, 14:3 (2009), pp. 531–49.

[41] George E. Gruen, 'Turkey's Role in Peacekeeping Missions', *American Foreign Policy Interests*, 28:6 (2006), p. 435.

[42] Arturo C. Sotomayor Velázquez, 'Why Some States Participate in UN Peace Missions While Others Do Not: An Analysis of Civil–Military Relations and Its Effects on Latin America's Contributions to Peacekeeping Operations', *Security Studies*, 19:1 (2010), pp. 160–95.

despite unpreparedness for this first peacekeeping mission that Turkey participated in.[43] While Turkey has struggled in the realm of civil–military relations until the considerable transformation which occurred over the last decade, peacekeeping decisions became civilian-dominated in the 2000s.[44] For example, in response to protests from the opposition and public about the government's decision to send troops to Lebanon in 2006, former Chief of General Staff Yaşar Büyükanıt argued that the Turkish military would act upon parliament's decision to fulfil its mandate in Lebanon, which he assessed as 'low risk'.[45] Moreover, in 2006, Cemil Çiçek, former speaker of the government, stated that the government made the decision to participate in UNIFIL after receiving positive feedback from the military, Ministry of Foreign Affairs, and the National Intelligence Agency.[46]

However, one common theme that my interviews with military officers reflect is that the TAF has never fought an international war since its independence and UN operations provide invaluable experience overseas. Moreover, peacekeeping operations are deemed useful by both military and police personnel, providing valuable experience that can be used by forces later committed to the struggle against the PKK. Moreover, the experience gained in this conflict at home helped Turkish forces to lead missions in places such as Somalia and Sudan where the terrain or circumstances are rough. Both military and police interviewees noted that Turkish peacekeepers were more trained and capable compared to peacekeepers from less developed countries. Interestingly, both police and military personnel raised the issue of the relative importance of quality over quantity and suggested that token contributions of Turkish peacekeepers were sometimes more helpful to UN missions than larger numbers of less experienced peacekeepers.

Finally, at the individual level, while the TAF has modernized its technology and training as a result of Turkey's NATO membership, UN peacekeeping missions are considered an opportunity to effectively use acquired skills and capacity in arduous missions such as UNIFIL. Moreover, all interviewees pointed to the value of practising their language skills in UN missions, since they do not find such opportunities in their work environment in Turkey.

[43] Taner Tanesen, 'Kore'den Afganistan'a Türkiye'nin Uluslararası Barışı Koruma Operasyonlarına Katkıları' [Turkey's Contributions to International Peacekeeping Missions from Korea to Afghanistan] (unpublished Master's Thesis, Yıldız Teknik Üniversitesi, 2006), p. 39.

[44] See Satana, 'Transformation of the Turkish Military' and author's interviews with military and police officers and officials in the Ministry of Foreign Affairs.

[45] 'Büyükanıt: Bize orada kimse emir veremez' [Büyükanıt: No one can order us around], *Radikal*, 7 September 2006.

[46] See Cemil Çiçek's interview with Fikret Bila at http://www.milliyet.com.tr/2006/08/30/yazar/bila.html

16.3.4 Economic Rationales

The explanatory power of traditional economic accounts, which claim that states pursue UN peacekeeping for economic gains, is weaker than other rationales in the Turkish case. Turkey desperately needed financial aid throughout the Cold War years; however, it refrained from partaking in peace operations due to overriding security concerns. On the other hand, the Turkish economy has performed much better after 2001 than in the 1990s and it was in that period that the country stepped up its contributions to UN peacekeeping. In fact, Turkey's financial contribution to UN peacekeeping and peacebuilding operations has increased more than five times from 2006 to 2012.[47]

From the perspective of the individual peacekeepers themselves, the Turkish police seem to be more motivated by financial incentives than the commissioned military personnel participating in UN peace missions.[48] This is mostly due to the lower salaries paid to police officers and the difficulties of police duties within Turkey. Furthermore, police officers are quite motivated for UN missions since these missions are perceived to be less demanding than the working environment in Turkey. Military officers claim that serving in UN peace missions was more beneficial financially in the 1990s than in the 2000s, which may be related to the fact that UN reimbursement rates have not kept pace with rising prices and Turkish wages.

At the national level, it is harder to argue that Turkey's contributions have anything to do with economic considerations. Where there is an economic rationale, its contributions have been used instrumentally to expand Turkey's trade partners and gain prestige in the international arena and to strengthen Turkey's thriving economy after the 2001 economic crisis. Turkish business circles have discovered new trade opportunities in the Middle East and Africa and started pushing the AKP government to strengthen political relations with these regions.[49] Consequently, the government declared 2005 the 'Africa year'.[50] In this vein, UN peacekeeping missions along with investments of

[47] The exact numbers allocated by the Turkish state for UN peacekeeping operations (other than the official annual dues) are difficult to reach and the data include both UN-mandated and UN-led operations, including NATO missions such as ISAF in Afghanistan and the Libya operation. Nevertheless, I was able to confirm in interviews with officials from various ministries that the budget allocated for expenditures of the military and the police forces in UN mandated (and led) operations has significantly increased from 2006 on ($33,491,036 in 2006 to $130,340,410 in 2011). The major reason for the increase is Turkey's contributions to UNIFIL and ISAF. Unfortunately, the numbers are not available for the period before 2006.

[48] Conscripts or non-commissioned officers are financially very motivated for UN peace missions.

[49] Mustafa Kutlay, 'Economy as the "Practical Hand" of "New Turkish Foreign Policy": A Political Economy Explanation', *Insight Turkey*, 13:1 (2011), pp. 67–88.

[50] Tom Wheeler, 'Ankara to Africa: Turkey's Outreach since 2005', *South African Journal of International Affairs*, 18:1 (2011), pp. 43–62.

the Turkish International Cooperation and Development Agency (TİKA) have become instrumental in showing African states that Turkey invests in their security and welfare. Parliamentary documents, for instance, show that the continuation of Turkish contributions to MONUC/MONUSCO in the DRC is directly connected to the goal of increasing trade relations with African countries.[51] It was also a consequence of Turkey's campaign (2003–8) for election to a non-permanent seat on the UN Security Council for 2009–10. As far as it is possible to tell, Turkey received the votes of most if not all African and Middle Eastern member states, which shows that its strategy worked well.

One interesting insight generated by interviews with military officers was that Turkey has only recently started learning about the 'tricks' of using UN logistics services for the transportation of its troops to theatres of UN peacekeeping operations. Tanesen supports this finding by indicating that Turkey failed to negotiate such terms during the UNOSOM II operation despite the fact that a Turkish general became the force commander.[52] As a result, whether due to miscommunication or disinformation, Turkish forces were sent to Somalia in late 1992 by sea. Only later was it realized that the UN permits and funds air transfers and it would have been much more efficient to use this mode of transport. The General Staff did not opt for this option since air transfer was deemed too expensive. Only in the 2000s did Turkey start using UN resources more efficiently, which makes the economic rationale more plausible for the last decade. However, it would be fair to argue that economic concerns have never been a direct cause of Turkey's contributions to UN peacekeeping operations. At most they have been considered a useful instrument to increase trade relations with host states.

16.3.5 Political Rationales

Political rationales are the most important factor behind Turkey's provision of UN peacekeepers in the 2000s, especially after the Justice and Development Party (AKP) came to power in 2002. While Turkish foreign policy became more dynamic in the mid-1990s before the AKP's reign, the country could not steer clear of economic and political instabilities in the late 1990s, which

[51] Genel Kurul Tutanağı, 22. Dönem 4. Yasama Yılı 120. Birleşim 27 Haziran 2006 Salı [General Assembly Minutes, 22nd Period, 4th Legislative Year, 120th Convention, 27 June 2006]. At http://www.tbmm.gov.tr/develop/owa/tutanak_g.birlesim_baslangic?P4=17205&P5=H&page1=41&page2=41

[52] Taner Tanesen, 'Kore'den Afganistan'a Türkiye'nin Uluslararası Barışı Koruma Operasyonlarına Katkıları' [Turkey's Contributions to International Peacekeeping Missions from Korea to Afghanistan] (unpublished Master's Thesis, Yıldız Teknik Üniversitesi, 2006), p. 39.

constrained Turkey's aspirations for a more active foreign policy in the post-Cold War international environment. Bayer and Keyman argue that

> the economic reforms that Turkey embarked upon starting in the 1980s have allowed Turkey's economy to benefit increasingly from the global economy. Not only does the state draw upon the tax basis and commercial leverage of a much bigger GDP, which it can use abroad in various peacebuilding tasks, but at the same time, Turkish civil society has (slowly) grown, including organizations interested in humanitarian assistance internationally.[53]

Moreover, in the 2000s, Turkey 'replaced its long-standing security-driven objectives of foreign policy with ones stemming from an economy-oriented pragmatic mindset'.[54] In fact, Kutlay argues that the last decade of Turkish foreign policy has seen 'cooperation in the low politics (or the trade and economy-related issues)' as 'the practical hand of Turkish policy makers to solve the disputes in high political issues via functional spill-over mechanisms, which can be seen as material interests, multiple dialogue channels and perceptions'.[55]

As a result of Turkey's economic revival, social awakening, and an economy-oriented mindset, an active foreign policy, under Davutoğlu's principles laid out in his book *Strategic Depth*, aimed to make Turkey a major regional power, especially in the Middle East.[56] Turkey's new goal of constructing for itself an identity as an emerging power was clearly presented in Davutoğlu's writings where he pointed to Turkey's long historical legacy and ties to the Middle East, Africa, Asia, and Europe as an asset that has unfortunately not been sufficiently utilized in the past.[57] Davutoğlu's objective was also to show Europe that Turkey is a global player: 'using an analogy of a bow and arrow, he argues that the more Turkey strains its bow in Asia, the further and more precisely will its arrow extend into Europe'.[58] Thus, a more proactive and multidimensional foreign policy has been enacted during the AKP's reign with a special emphasis on zero-problems with neighbours and Turkey's contribution to conflict resolution in the world.[59]

As Hart and Jones argue, 'emerging powers often make large contributions on issues central to the UN's mandate, such as peacekeeping'.[60] Indeed, in a

[53] R. Bayer and E. F. Keyman, 'Turkey: An Emerging Hub of Globalization and Internationalist Humanitarian Actor?' *Globalizations*, 9:1 (2012), pp. 73–90.

[54] Kadri Kaan Renda, 'Turkey's Neighborhood Policy: An Emerging Complex Interdependence?' *Insight Turkey*, 13:1 (2011), p. 94.

[55] Kutlay, 'Economy as the "Practical Hand"', p. 85.

[56] Ziya Öniş and Şuhnaz Yilmaz, 'Between Europeanization and Euro-Asianism: Foreign Policy Activism in Turkey during the AKP Era', *Turkish Studies*, 10:1 (2009), pp. 7–24.

[57] Ahmet Davutoğlu, *Stratejik Derinlik. Türkiye'nin Uluslararası Konumu* [Strategic Depth: Turkey's International Status] (Istanbul: Küre Yayınları, 2010), pp. 45–65.

[58] Öniş and Yilmaz, 'Between Europeanization and Euro-Asianism', p. 9.

[59] Bayer and Keyman, 'Turkey'.

[60] Andrew F. Hart and Bruce D. Jones, 'How Do Rising Powers Rise?' *Survival*, 52:6 (2010), p. 75.

UN General Assembly speech in September 2011, Turkey's aspirations were portrayed by its Prime Minister 'as vying for global power'.[61] Accordingly, Turkey's participation in UN and other peace operations is seen as part of its identity construction as an emerging power. Middle Eastern states' preference for Turkey, as a Muslim country, in peace missions as opposed to Western powers made the construction of this role easier.[62] For example, less than a week after the UN Security Council decision that authorized NATO's intervention in Libya for human protection purposes, the Libyan government declared a cease-fire on 18 March 2011 and asked Turkey and Malta to observe and coordinate it.[63] The Turkish Foreign Ministry declared in September 2011 that it was ready and willing to contribute to UN Support Mission in Libya (UNSMIL).[64] As a reflection of its self-image as an 'emerging global player', Turkey has been very willing to contribute peace missions especially in the context of the so-called Arab Spring.

Similarly, in 2006 when public opinion was almost uniformly against sending troops to UNIFIL II due to the conflictual environment in Lebanon and the publicly perceived risks of the mission, Prime Minister Erdoğan declared that Turkey would help establish peace in the Middle East on its own terms—with the two caveats of not getting into hot pursuit and not helping Hezbollah's disarmament.[65] The missions were extended twice in 2009 and 2011, and the Turkish prime minister has occasionally used Turkey's participation in UNIFIL as a sign of its growing soft power and a tool for increasing Turkey's visibility and prestige in the international arena.[66] Moreover, Güngör argues that Turkey's election as a non-permanent UN Security Council member in 2009–10 (its fourth time) was partly because of its deployment of peacekeepers to missions such as Sudan and Lebanon.[67] Tanesen supports this notion for the 1990s as well by arguing that Turkey's decision to provide UN peacekeepers despite political opposition and public opinion

[61] 'PM Erdoğan reaffirms Turkey's role as global player with UN speech', *Today's Zaman*, 23 September 2011.

[62] Ünsal Sığrı and Mustafa Kemal Topçu, 'Barış Gücü Operarasyonlarında Kullanılan Kültürlerarası Bütünleştirme Yöntemlerinin Kültürel Boyutlar Bağlamında İncelenmesi: UNIFIL Örneği' [A Study on Cross-Cultural Integration Mechanisms Employed in Peacekeeping Operations within the Context of Cultural Dimensions: The UNIFIL Case], *Ankara Üniversitesi SBF Dergisi*, 67:1 (2012), p. 229.

[63] 'Libya Türkiye'den yardım istedi' [Libya Asks for Turkey's Help], 18 March 2011. At http://www.ntvmsnbc.com/id/25193823/

[64] 'Türkiye BM'nin Libya misyonuna katkı yapmaya hazır' [Turkey is Ready to Participate in UN's Libya Mission], *Show Haber*, 19 September 2011. At http://www.showhaber.com/turkiye-bmnin-libya-destek-misyonuna-katki-yapmaya-hazir-481555.htm

[65] 'Lübnan için iki "caveat"'[Two Caveats for Lebanon], *Sabah*, 8 September 2006.

[66] 'Türk askerinin görev süresi uzatıldı' [Term of Office Extended for Turkish Soldiers], *Bugün*, 9 July 2011.

[67] Uğur Güngör, 'Günümüzde Barış Operasyonları' [Contemporary Peace Operations], *Güvenlik Stratejileri Dergisi*, 4:8 (2008), p. 8.

concerns enhanced it international prestige.[68] In sum, Turkish decision-makers have deemed UN-mandated and UN-led operations prestigious and an indication of becoming an emerging power. There is also little doubt that NATO and EU peace missions are viewed in a similar vein.

On a different note, ethnic and religious ties are used to expand Turkey's sphere of political influence as exemplified in the case of strong support for sending troops to Bosnia-Herzegovina and Kosovo in the 1990s.[69] Turkey's involvement in the UN peacekeeping missions in Sudan in 2005–10 (both UNMIS and UNAMID) is another case in point. Before Sudan's government consented to UNAMID, Larry Rossin from 'Save Darfur Coalition' highlighted Turkey's Muslim identity and its membership at the Organisation of Islamic Cooperation as significant assets for helping cease violence in Sudan in 2007.[70] Indeed, Turkey decided to contribute to the mission once the UN deployed forces into Darfur.[71]

16.4 LIMITS AND FUTURE POTENTIAL

Although official Turkish discourse claims Turkey is already a very active peacekeeper, a brief overview of Turkey's potential and the actual contributions indicates that Ankara could significantly increase its contributions to UN peacekeeping operations both in terms of quantity and quality.

In 2011, Turkey's armed forces were the sixth largest in the world with 612,900 personnel actively serving and the number of active reserves at 429,000.[72] Turkey has a total population of nearly 79 million, available manpower of nearly 42 million, some 35 million fit for military service, and with roughly 1.3 million men of military age that are eligible for conscription.[73] The defence budget amounts to $25 billion, which has slightly declined since 2000 although Turkey is still one of the top military spenders in the world.[74] On the other hand, by 2010, 'approximately 1,200 Turkish police officers, most of whom are highly qualified ranking officers holding middle or

[68] Taner Tanesen, 'Kore'den Afganistan'a' [From Korea to Afghanistan], p. 39.

[69] Taner Tanesen, 'Kore'den Afganistan'a' [From Korea to Afghanistan], p. 39.

[70] İpek Yezdani, 'Türkiye, Darfur'da ağırlığını koysun' [Turkey Should Exert its Authority in Darfur], *Milliyet*, 1 June 2007.

[71] Bağcı and Kardaş, 'Exploring Turkey's Role', argue that one reason Turkey might be so active in UN peacekeeping missions in the Middle East and Africa is the USA's influence on Turkey's regional policies.

[72] 'Turkey Military Strength', http://www.globalfirepower.com/country-military-strength-detail.asp?country_id=Turkey. This website gathers national defence data from US Library of Congress and the Central Intelligence Agency.

[73] 'Turkey Military Strength'.

[74] 'Turkey Military Strength', and Lale Sarıibrahimoğlu, 'Turkey spends more on defence', *Today's Zaman*, 16 June 2008.

high level managerial positions in the TNP, have been deployed in multinational police missions'.[75] Moreover, the 'TNP has a total of 14,335 ranking police officers' and the '1,200 ranking officers committed to peacekeeping operations constitute over 10 per cent of the eligible ranking officers (11,076)'.[76] Clearly, Turkey has the capacity to field a large number of uniformed personnel and could therefore extend its contributions to UN peacekeeping.

Nevertheless, according to the official Department of Peacekeeping Operations data, in January 2012, 358 military and 148 police officers and 2 military experts—a total of 508 uniformed personnel—served in UN peacekeeping operations and Turkey ranked 36th in the world by contributing to eleven of eighteen UN operations.[77] These data show that while the official military, police, and ministerial sources highlight Turkey's significant contributions to UN peacekeeping, Turkey remains a serial token contributor to these missions despite its increasing financial contributions.[78] Turkish potential for sending uniformed personnel to UN peace missions is much larger than its actual participation to date.

While the police force seems to be very enthusiastic about contributing to UN peace missions, views held within sections of the military point to why Turkish contributions to UN peace missions are more limited than the potential:

1. *Lack of internal reward mechanisms.* Turkish police and military officers sent to UN missions are not efficiently utilized once they return from their tours. In particular, the TAF does not fully assess the value of UN missions and the experience that its officers gain in these missions. In line with the perception held by the country's leaders, NATO and EU missions are deemed more important. Thus, some military officers see UN tours as a waste of their time because they do not improve their career paths. Revising the military's promotion system to take account of this would only be possible if the government pushes the General Staff in that direction. Since Turkish civil–military relations have only recently begun to transform, the military's view that UN tours are largely redundant for their officers' career paths might have reduced the number of troops who might otherwise volunteer for UN service.[79]

[75] Ahmet Çelik, 'Assessment of Post-Deployment Reintegration Attitudes among Turkish Police Peacekeepers and its Associations with Organizational Commitment' (unpublished Ph.D., Rutgers University, 2010), p. 7.

[76] Çelik, 'Assessment of Post-Deployment Reintegration Attitudes', p. 7.

[77] See the official Department of Peacekeeping Operations website at http://www.un.org/en/peacekeeping/contributors/2012/feb12_1.pdf

[78] All interviewed officials highlighted the difference between quantity and quality of contributions, and argued that Turkey's contributions are of high quality, which will be discussed in more detail below.

[79] There are still major changes that are required to normalize civil–military relations in Turkey. One such change is to hold the General Staff responsible to the Ministry of National Defence, which is at the moment directly responsible to the Prime Minister.

2. Disconnect between the military and the civilian government. Some military officers point out that the recent transformation of Turkish civil–military relations has not caught up with peacekeeping decisions and actions. Although decisions about UN peacekeeping are made by the civilian government and approved by the parliament, the military continues to exert significant clout over decision-making. While in principle the TAF is committed to all peace operations, in practice NATO operations are considered more important than UN missions. Consequently, the government needs to communicate the importance of UN missions more effectively to its military personnel. All other things being equal, better communication between civilians and the military and the consolidation of civilian control of the military is likely to contribute to future increases in the Turkish contribution to UN peacekeeping.

3. Intolerance towards human losses. 'Martyrdom' is both a financial and cultural phenomenon in Turkey. Uniformed personnel who lose their lives are considered martyrs in Turkish culture since they die in defence of their country and people. They are accorded sacred status in the public conscience and the state provides financial help to their families. Lives lost in the fight against the PKK are politically justifiable in Turkey in a way that losing Turkish soldiers and police in UN and NATO peace missions are not. This explains why Turkey is more willing to contribute limited numbers of personnel to safer, observer missions.[80] According to UN DPKO data, Turkey has so far lost six personnel in UN peace missions (as of 29 February 2012).[81] While this is not an intolerable number for a country participating in several peace missions, any loss is magnified in the public conscience.

4. The perception that priority should be given to counter-insurgency at home over UN peacekeeping operations. As previously noted, UN peacekeeping is not a strategic priority for Turkey. This explains why its police forces are more active in UN peacekeeping—because the fight against domestic terrorism has been under the strict supervision of the TAF for decades, not the national police force. This perception of the primacy of homeland defence plays a powerful role in limiting the TAF's willingness to commit more significant numbers of troops to UN peacekeeping operations.

5. Turkish military tradition is not geared to sustained expeditionary deployments. A common view of military officers is that since the TAF has

[80] During an interview, one officer mentioned that Turkey lost enthusiasm for serving in the Temporary International Presence in Hebron (TIPH), that it contributed to from 1997–2008, after one of its officers was killed along with a Swiss observer off duty in their vehicle in 2002. Apparently, this was not taken well in the top ranks of the military and the experience was generalized to all peace missions. This incident was interestingly not extensively publicized in the Turkish media.

[81] Three of the Turkish casualties were lost in the UNPROFOR mission and one each in the UNIFIL, UNOSOM, and UNOMIG missions.

not fought a war abroad since independence in 1923, peace operations, which demand sustained expeditionary deployments, are not viewed favourably by the military. Interestingly, while NATO operations where 'fighting' is part of the mission are still not desired but more prestigious, UN missions which are less prone to casualties are not as respected in the eyes of the participant military officers. Thus, losses are not well tolerated and there is not significant demand from military officers to serve in outside missions. If they have to choose between NATO and UN missions, they prefer the former.

Some military officers argued in the interviews that they were paid better for foreign postings in the 1990s than in the 2000s, thereby reducing individual incentive for participating in UN missions. Moreover, studies corroborate the interview data that domination of officers from a couple of countries over all the others in leadership roles demoralizes Turkish personnel, who only serve around six months and hardly find time to adapt to the mission circumstances.[82]

6. Turkey's peacekeeping commitments to non-UN led operations. As discussed above, the peacekeeping and building concept document accepted in 2005 prioritized NATO and EU missions over UN operations. In fact, after highlighting how committed Turkey is to UN peacekeeping, Baki İlkin, former Ambassador to the UN, highlights this limitation:

> given the magnitude and complexity of the challenges to peacekeeping, we also believe that the capabilities of regional organizations should always be taken into account, and cooperation between such organizations and the UN should be further enhanced. This is actually a commitment that we need to fulfil under article 170 of the World Summit Outcome. We therefore support the call for the establishment of effective arrangements between the UN and regional organizations, including also the provision of regional capacities in support of UN peace operations.[83]

Taken together, these obstacles constrain Turkey's contributions to UN peacekeeping and explain why, despite its pro-UN policy stance, Turkey's contribution to UN peacekeeping has remained well below its military capacity. However, none of these obstacles appears insurmountable.

[82] For the effect of cultural interactions on individual officer motivation for UNIFIL, see Sığrı and Topçu, 'Barış Gücü Operarasyonlarında Kullanılan Kültürlerarası Bütünleştirme Yöntemlerinin Kültürel Boyutlar Bağlamında İncelenmesi: UNIFIL Örneği' [A Study on Cross-Cultural Integration Mechanisms Employed in Peacekeeping Operations within the Context of Cultural Dimensions: The UNIFIL Case], p. 229.

[83] Statement at the General Debate of the UN's Special Committee on Peacekeeping Operations, 27 February 2006. At http://turkuno.dt.mfa.gov.tr/ShowSpeech.aspx?ID=1351

16.5 CONCLUSIONS

Political rationales appear to offer the best explanation for Turkey's consistent but rather limited contributions to UN peacekeeping operations, especially the new foreign policy initiatives of the AKP government and its goal to establish Turkey as an 'emerging power' in world politics. Turkey's traditionally status quo-oriented foreign policy has gradually been replaced with one that takes international risks and targets the twin goals of establishing Turkey as a benign regional hegemon and asserting its status as a global player. Turkey's economic revival in the 2000s and its social transformation made these goals more achievable than during the 1990s. In this context, UN peacekeeping is perceived as reinforcing the AKP's foreign policy objectives of extending Turkish influence and building international prestige to enhance Turkey's identity as a major power. Turkey also has the potential to contribute more to UN missions with its large military and police base and its growing economy. In addition, souring relations with the EU in the last few years have made the UN a more attractive international institution for Turkey to work through in order to realize its stated foreign policy goals. This has also encouraged Turkey to push for another term as a non-permanent member of the UN Security Council. It would therefore be to the UN's advantage to understand Turkey's current foreign policy goals and to develop strategies of engagement that will enable it to capitalize on Ankara's new role in its search for more and better peacekeepers.

17

South Africa

Cedric de Coning and *Walter Lotze*

Since the end of apartheid, South Africa has undergone a radical transformation from international pariah to a prominent, albeit somewhat controversial international actor. The country has swiftly assumed a significant role in various international forums and became a vocal advocate for multilateral diplomacy, via subregional, continental, and global organizations. It has contributed to a broad range of issue areas including human rights, environmentalism, international arms control, and the trade in conflict diamonds. South Africa also played a leading role in the transition from the Organization of African Unity (OAU) to the new African Union (AU), and in the creation of the New Partnership for Africa's Development (NEPAD). It is the only African member of both the BRICS (Brazil, Russia, India, China, South Africa) and the IBSA (India, Brazil, and South Africa), and has been a regular member of the AU's Peace and Security Council, while to date serving twice in the UN Security Council.

Within this context, it is South Africa's role in the UN Security Council that has generated most controversy, particularly Pretoria's votes which have been interpreted as sometimes defending regimes accused of human rights abuses. While critics talk of deep contradictions in South African foreign policy, the government maintains that it has voted, as a matter of principle, against the Council dictating matters which are best dealt with by other competent bodies (such as the UN Human Rights Council, for instance). Indeed, South Africa has relatively consistently argued that matters that do not threaten international peace and security should be dealt with by the General Assembly, the Human Rights Council, and other relevant bodies. This position is part of a larger strategy to build a more just international order, which includes reforming the Security Council. While changes in the membership and procedures, such as the veto powers, are a long-term objective, in the short to medium term, South Africa has tried to use its non-permanent membership of the Security Council to shape the way the Council works. Perhaps the most prominent action South Africa took during its second term on the Council was to vote in favour of resolution 1973 (17 March 2011), which sanctioned the use of force to protect civilians in Libya, but later to object to the way the Council, and the implementing coalition, ignored the political solution proposed by the AU and ousted Gaddafi's regime. It has been this willingness to boldly pursue its own positions that has made South Africa's emerging international role somewhat controversial.

Within this broader context, one of South Africa's most prominent and constructive international activities has been its contributions to several peace processes in Africa, including in Burundi, the Comoros, Côte d'Ivoire, the Democratic Republic of Congo (DRC), Zimbabwe, Sudan, and Madagascar. Peace diplomacy, understood as the country's involvement in peacemaking, peacekeeping, and peacebuilding, thus plays a critical, if not dominant, role in South Africa's foreign policy towards Africa.[1]

Indeed, as this chapter highlights, South Africa's contributions to UN and African peacekeeping operations have been closely linked to its involvement in peacemaking initiatives. This was in stark contrast to its activities during the apartheid years when its sole participation in a UN-authorized mission was the Korean War.[2] In the period immediately after apartheid, the new South African National Defence Force (SANDF) and South African Police Service (SAPS) were preoccupied with their own security sector reform processes, and thus it was only from 2001 that Pretoria started to contribute to international peacekeeping. Despite initial constraints, South Africa's engagement developed rapidly, and after ten years of peacekeeping experience it has served in no fewer than fourteen international peace operations and has been consistently among the UN's top fifteen troop-contributing countries (TCCs). This evolution in South Africa's contribution to peace missions has been interpreted by some observers as motivated increasingly by economic self-interest.[3] While South Africa's economic interests are certainly linked to its political interests, its foreign policy seems to be primarily aimed at securing an important political role for South Africa in Africa and the world. It is assumed that a prominent political position will also generate economic spin-offs for the country. Thus, while economic interest is a guiding principle of South African foreign policy, the driving factor seems to be a desire to increase the country's political footprint and influence in Africa and

[1] Anthoni van Nieuwkerk, 'South Africa and Peacekeeping in Africa', *African Security*, 5:1 (2012), p. 45.

[2] South Africa contributed a fighter plane squadron to the operations in the Korean peninsula. Dermot Moore and Peter Bagshawe, *South Africa's Flying Cheetahs in Korea* (Johannesburg: Ashanti Publishing, 1991).

[3] Van Nieuwkerk, 'South Africa and Peacekeeping in Africa', p. 58.

internationally, so that it is better able to shape and influence the changing world order and thereby to protect its national interests.

In this regard, apart from contributing uniformed personnel in the field, South Africa has also provided personnel to the UN's Department of Peacekeeping Operations (DPKO), the AU Commission's Peace Support Operations Division (PSOD), and the planning element of the Southern African Development Community's (SADC) Standby Force. South Africa's contribution to UN peacekeeping thus forms only one dimension of its overall support to international peace operations. Pretoria has also been an important player at the normative level, working to strengthen and reform UN, AU, and SADC peace operations and the relevant institutional architecture. At home, it has developed a whole-of-government approach to peacekeeping through the establishment of a National Office for the Coordination of Peacekeeping Missions (NOCPM).

South Africa has therefore laid the groundwork to sustain its contribution to international peace operations, not least because it forms a central aspect of its international identity and represents a mechanism for influencing the international environment. Pretoria's contributions to peace operations are seen as a tool to protect itself from instability in its immediate region, including conflict, migration, and negative economic trends. But such contributions are also seen as a tool to project power in regional and international forums. Specifically, South Africa views its position as a major UN TCC as a prerequisite for making a successful bid for a permanent seat on a reformed UN Security Council, and as part of its strategy to retain a prominent emerging power identity. But peace operations are not just about advancing narrow national interests. A broad range of South African opinion-makers suggest that the country has a responsibility to contribute to international peace and security, and that drawing benefit from an international rules-based system necessitates contributions to its upkeep.[4]

In this context, some critics have suggested South Africa still punches below its weight: given its prominent political and peacemaking role, the relative strength of South Africa's economy, and the size and specialized capabilities of its armed forces, Pretoria should be the largest contributor, or at least among the top three contributors, to peace operations in Africa. Yet, several African countries that have smaller economic and political footprints contribute more troops, including Ghana, Kenya, Rwanda, and Ethiopia.

This criticism raises a question that is central to this volume, namely, what are the key factors shaping the nature and size of a country's contribution to peace operations? This chapter grapples with this question by analysing South Africa's military contribution to international peace operations over the past

[4] Laurie Nathan, 'Interests, Ideas and Ideology: South Africa's Policy on Darfur', *African Affairs*, 110:438 (2010), pp. 55–74.

decade, assessing the factors that explain its willingness to make substantial contributions to select peace processes, as well as those factors that inform decision-making on the levels and types of its contributions. Although South Africa also contributes civilians and police, including formed police units, to UN and AU peace operations, this chapter considers only South Africa's military contributions. However, it should be noted that one of the distinguishing features of South Africa's policy towards international peace missions is the degree to which it attempts to integrate its approach to peacemaking, peacekeeping, and peacebuilding engagements.[5] This chapter analyses the decision-making process within the South African government, the role of domestic and foreign audiences and politics, and how support to peace operations relates to the national identity that South Africa has sought to promote in world politics, particularly within the AU and the UN. The chapter also investigates the institutional, resource, and political factors that inhibit South Africa from playing an even more prominent role in international peacekeeping.

17.1 SOUTH AFRICA'S EMERGENCE AS A CONTRIBUTOR TO INTERNATIONAL PEACE OPERATIONS

In the immediate post-apartheid years, the new African National Congress (ANC)-led government focused heavily on its pressing domestic agenda. While it promoted a strongly multilateralist and African-centred foreign policy, it was cautious not to become engaged in cumbersome and expensive commitments. As a result, while South Africa became substantively involved in promoting peace and security on the African continent, this did not immediately translate into a willingness to contribute troops to international peace operations. In the late 1990s, however, Pretoria increasingly recognized that South Africa's stability and prosperity were linked to the political and economic development of the African continent as a whole, reflecting a growing appreciation of the nexus between national interest and regional stability.

It was obvious, however, that South Africa's domestic context was not yet geared towards providing peacekeepers. After the transition of power in 1994, the previous South African Defence Force (SADF) was transformed into the National Defence Force (SANDF), amalgamating the SADF with the four armed forces of the previously independent homelands and the two armed

[5] Van Nieuwkerk, 'South Africa and Peacekeeping in Africa', p. 48.

wings of the ANC and the Pan-Africanist Congress (PAC). Consequently, by the late 1990s, the SANDF was still facing the challenge of redefining its role under a democratic dispensation.[6] It was thus not clear in which direction the SANDF should develop or what roles it should play in terms of South Africa's new foreign policy. South Africa's new Constitution stipulated that the SANDF was to act both in defence of the republic and in fulfilment of international obligations.[7] However, the Defence White Paper of May 1996 and the subsequent Defence Review of 1998 argued that the primary role of the SANDF was to protect the territorial integrity of the country, and that only limited resources should be set aside for international peace operations.[8]

To bridge these differences, and to prepare South Africa for what was (domestically and internationally) expected to become a growing role in the prevention and resolution of conflicts, particularly on the African continent, the South African Department of Foreign Affairs in 1997 drafted the *White Paper on South African Participation in International Peace Missions* (the White Paper). Approved by the Cabinet in 1999, the White Paper promoted a holistic and multidisciplinary approach, embracing political, military, and humanitarian considerations in support of the deployment of the SANDF outside South Africa's borders.[9] Importantly, the White Paper recognized that participation in peace support operations was increasingly becoming a prerequisite for international respectability and for developing an authoritative voice in international debates about conflict management and the reform of multilateral organizations such as the UN, the OAU (now the AU), and SADC.[10] The White Paper envisaged that support to international peace missions would become a foreign policy priority, and therefore the Department of Foreign Affairs (DFA)—now the Department of International Relations and Cooperation (DIRCO)—should assume lead responsibility in overseeing and coordinating South African involvement in such operations.[11] On this basis, and subsequent to the endorsement of the White Paper, the National Office for the Coordination of Peacekeeping Missions (NOCPM) was established within the Africa Multilateral Section of the DFA in 1999. The DFA, through the NOCPM, was mandated to coordinate South African engagement in international peace operations, and maintain political

[6] *South Africa's Peacekeeping Role in Burundi* (ACCORD Occasional Paper Series, Vol. 2, No. 2, 2007), p. 12.

[7] Constitution of the Republic of South Africa, 1996, section 201(2).

[8] T. M. Jorgensen, 'You Do Need a Stick to be Able to Use it Gently', in L. Buurs, S. Jensen, and F. Stepputat (eds.), *The Security-Development Nexus: Expressions of Sovereignty and Securitization in Southern Africa* (Cape Town: HSRC Press, 2007), pp. 40–1.

[9] *White Paper on South African Participation in International Peace Missions* (Pretoria: South African Department of International Relations and Cooperation (DIRCO), 1999).

[10] *White Paper*, p. 20.

[11] Cedric de Coning, 'The White Paper on SA Participation in Peace Missions: A Unique Beginning', *Conflict Trends*, 2 (April 1999).

oversight of such missions. The NOCPM was further mandated to lead the development of a whole-of-government approach to South Africa's engagement in international peace operations, leading the combined planning efforts of the Department of Defence, the Department of Safety and Security, and the National Treasury.[12] Despite these preparatory efforts, South Africa was ill-prepared for the shock of its first international deployment to Lesotho.

17.1.1 Lesotho: An Unfortunate Start

On 22 September 1998, a South African force entered Lesotho to prevent mutinous soldiers of the Royal Lesotho Defence Force (RLDF) from staging a military coup and to create a safe and stable environment for a diplomatic initiative to find a peaceful solution to the crisis. The South African contingent was part of a SADC Combined Task Force, but when the operation commenced, only South African forces entered Lesotho, as the expected contingent from Botswana had not arrived in time. The operation eventually achieved all of its objectives: the mutineers were disarmed, the situation was eventually stabilized, and the political parties in Lesotho reached agreement on the establishment of a multiparty Interim Political Authority that oversaw the government until fresh elections were held following eighteen months of transitional rule.

However, in the first thirty-six hours after South African soldiers crossed the border into Lesotho, forty-nine people lost their lives and the capital city of Lesotho, Maseru, was severely damaged by riots.[13] The mutineers offered fierce resistance, resulting in a large number of casualties, with eight South African soldiers, forty mutineers, and one civilian losing their lives.[14] Due to the manner in which the operation was authorized, planned, and deployed, the opposition parties and the mutineers initially saw the SADC Task Force as a South African invasion, aimed at entrenching the rule of the governing Lesotho Congress for Democracy (LCD) party, and as a result they resisted the deployment, spilling over into spontaneous mass protest action in the streets of Maseru. The protest action deteriorated into rioting, the burning of government buildings and shops, especially those identified with South Africa, and widespread looting, resulting in a number of refugees crossing over into South Africa. With many businesses destroyed or closed, almost no basic commodities were available in Maseru for several days, and it was estimated that more than 8,000 people lost their jobs as a result of their places of

[12] *South Africa's Peacekeeping Role in Burundi*, p. 35.

[13] Sechaba ka'Nkosi, 'SANDF's Chaotic Invasion', *Mail & Guardian* (Johannesburg), 25 September–1 October 1998, p. 4.

[14] Operation Boleas Media Release One, 23 September 1998.

employment being destroyed or closed. The rioting and looting that followed in the wake of the operation left a scar on the Lesotho economy, and placed even greater pressure on an already fragile political system.[15]

This operation represented post-apartheid South Africa's first foreign military action.[16] It was a rude entry, and an unfortunate reminder that interventions are highly sensitive affairs that can easily have negative unintended consequences if not carefully planned and managed.[17] Questions have been raised as to the legality of the intervention, and whether it can be regarded as a SADC operation. For instance, Katharina Coleman points out that the proper procedures were not followed and she argues that the operation can therefore not be said to have been formally authorized by SADC.[18] However, the governments involved claimed that they acted under the authority of SADC, and this claim has not been challenged subsequently by any SADC body or member state. South Africa and SADC drew many lessons from the Lesotho operation, including its implications for the level at which SADC needed to obtain authorization for operations that have the authority to use force, the clarity and transparency of the mandate that such missions need to operate with, the multinational identity of SADC operations, the need for political-strategic mission leadership, the need for clear rules of engagement, and the kind of specific demands that peace operations place on equipment, operational readiness, and training.[19]

17.1.2 Burundi: From VIP Protection to Peacekeeping

Throughout the late 1990s, South Africa played a key role in the negotiation of the Arusha peace process which sought to bring to an end decades of civil conflict in Burundi. The final stages were overseen by former President Nelson Mandela, following the death of Tanzanian President Julius Nyerere. They concluded with the signing of the Arusha accords on 28 August 2000. However, the peace process threatened to unravel because two of the principal armed movements were not included.

[15] Cedric de Coning, 'Conditions for Intervention: DRC and Lesotho', *Conflict Trends*, 1 (October 1998).

[16] It can also be said to have been the first SADC intervention, depending on whether or not one regards the so-called Allied Forces in the DRC to have been a duly authorized SADC operation.

[17] Chiyuki Aoi, Cedric de Coning, and Ramesh Thakur (eds.), *Unintended Consequences of Peacekeeping Operations* (Tokyo: UN University Press, 2007).

[18] Katharina P. Coleman, *International Organizations and Peace Enforcement* (Cambridge: Cambridge University Press, 2007), pp. 167–9.

[19] SADC has not deployed a peace operation since Lesotho, but it has taken a number of steps to further clarify these issues in the SADC Protocol on Politics, Defence and Security Cooperation, and other peace operations-related policies and guidelines.

Mandela pushed hard for the deployment of international forces to Burundi to secure the peace process, yet the UN proved reluctant to do so until a comprehensive cease-fire agreement had been signed. Mandela decided that South Africa should lead by example, and pushed newly elected President Thabo Mbeki to send South African troops to Burundi to provide protection to the returning political leadership.[20] Mbeki, who had become involved in initiatives to reach a peace agreement in the Democratic Republic of Congo (DRC), viewed a viable peace process in Burundi as essential to attaining stability in the Great Lakes region. He also thought the deployment of international forces ahead of the installation of Burundi's transitional government in November 2001 was the key to success. On 21 October 2001, Mbeki deployed 754 troops—the South African Protection Service Detachment (SAPSD)—to Burundi with a mandate to provide protection to the returning political leadership charged with the implementation of the Arusha accords.[21]

Given the limited mandate of the SAPSD—it could only provide protection to the returning political leadership—it was unable to play a broader peacekeeping role in support of the transition in Burundi, or to provide protection to the civilian population which was bearing the brunt of the ongoing civil conflict, not least because the SAPSD was based solely in Bujumbura. South Africa therefore continued to argue for the deployment of a larger peace support operation, which eventually arrived in the form of the African Union Mission in Burundi (AMIB).[22] By the end of April 2003, the South African force strength in Burundi was raised to 1,800. Later that year, the South Africans were joined by 858 troops from Ethiopia and 228 troops from Mozambique, bringing the total AMIB force strength to 2,860.[23] While the Ethiopian and Mozambican contingents were financially supported by contributions from the United States and the United Kingdom, South Africa, as the lead nation, continued to carry the bulk of the mission's operating costs. By the time AMIB took over, the cost of the SAPSD mission to South Africa was an estimated $21 million, and by 2003 AMIB's operational cost to South Africa soared to an estimated $110 million.[24]

Following the inclusion of the remaining armed movements into the peace process in 2003, South Africa again played a leading role in advocating and negotiating for the deployment of a UN peacekeeping force to Burundi. On 21 May 2004, the UN Security Council adopted resolution 1545, authorizing the deployment of the *Operation de Nations Unies au Burundi* (ONUB) in support of

[20] *South Africa's Peacekeeping Role in Burundi*, p. 25.

[21] *South Africa's Peacekeeping Role in Burundi*, pp. 26–7.

[22] AMIB was deployed for one year, and ultimately grew to 3,335 military and civilian personnel. It was intended as an interim mission pending the deployment of a UN peacekeeping operation.

[23] *South Africa's Peacekeeping Role in Burundi*, p. 33.

[24] *South Africa's Peacekeeping Role in Burundi*, p. 29.

the 2001 Arusha accords. The South African, Ethiopian, and Mozambican AMIB troops were re-hatted and became the vanguard of the new ONUB mission.

Following elections in 2005 and the conclusion of Burundi's political transition period, the UN in 2007 drew down its peacekeeping operation, and established the *Bureau Integré des Nations Unies au Burundi* (BINUB), a political office mandated to support the peacebuilding process. The AU argued that a need to safeguard the peace process remained, and following negotiations with Burundi and South Africa, in late 2006 authorized the deployment of the AU Special Task Force (STF), mandated to provide protection to the leadership of the last armed movement which was entering into the peace process. As the UN operation withdrew, South Africa maintained 752 troops in Burundi, this time under the banner of the AU STF. Although the AU had wanted a larger presence, it did not have the requisite financial and logistical capacity and South Africa proved the only country willing to conduct the operation and support it financially.[25] South African forces remained in Burundi until June 2009 (termed *Operation Curriculum* by the SANDF), when the AU STF completed its mandate, and the last South African troops left Burundi in December 2009, after eight years of maintaining a permanent presence in that country.

South African deployments to Burundi proved instrumental in securing the Arusha peace process and the political transition, and paved the way first for an AU and then for a UN operation in Burundi. Indeed, South Africa provided the backbone for both the AU and the UN operations that followed the deployment of the SAPSD, and (until late 2009) the only foreign forces to secure the peacebuilding process following ONUB's withdrawal. Pretoria's first deployments to AU and UN peace operations in Burundi thus proved crucial to keeping the peace process on track. They also paved the way for subsequent South African engagements in international peace operations elsewhere.

Two preliminary observations can be drawn from the South African deployments in Burundi. First, South Africa's peacekeepers were used to backstop a major peacemaking commitment. It therefore became a matter of national prestige and power-projection (the political and normative rationales referred to in this book's Introduction) to ensure the conclusion of a successful peace agreement. When international security guarantees were not as forthcoming as had been hoped, South Africa deployed its own forces to provide them. Second, as South Africa became more deeply involved in Burundi it also became willing to lead the AU's first peace support operation and to carry the bulk of the mission's costs.[26] This highlights that direct national political

[25] *South Africa's Peacekeeping Role in Burundi*, p. 32.

[26] Whereas the UN uses the term 'peacekeeping', the AU prefers 'peace support operations'. This chapter uses the UN term or the more general 'peace operations', except when referring specifically to AU operations.

interests were at stake and South Africa was willing to commit its forces and the resources of its treasury to secure them. As discussed below, this pattern continued to inform South Africa's decisions to contribute to AU and UN peace operations.

17.1.3 DRC: South Africa's Second Contribution to a UN Peacekeeping Operation

Building on South Africa's prominent role in the Lusaka negotiations and its subsequent hosting of the Sun City negotiations on the DRC, in May 2000, President Thabo Mbeki publicly pledged to provide troops to the *Mission de l'Organisation des Nations Unies au Congo* (MONUC), which was mandated to observe the Lusaka cease-fire agreement of July 1999. While South Africa initially provided staff officers to assist in the planning for the mission, it was not until 2003 that the first batch of ninety-six staff officers actually arrived in the DRC. South Africa soon expanded its contribution, however, via the SANDF's *Operation Mistral*, which consisted of a Task Force Headquarters, an infantry battalion, engineering elements, a logistics unit, a medical unit, a military police unit, and a headquarters support unit, totalling 1,192 personnel.[27] This support remained more or less constant throughout MONUC's presence in the DRC, and continued with the transition of MONUC into the *Mission de Stabilisation de l'Organisation des Nations Unies au Congo* (MONUSCO) in 2010.

In addition to *Operation Mistral*, South Africa also deployed sixteen personnel to support the reconstruction of the *Forces Armées de la Republique Democratique du Congo* (FARDC), known as *Operation Teutonic*, and eleven personnel to assist in the development of a rapid reaction battalion for the FARDC, known as *Project Thebe*.[28]

South Africa's deployment to the DRC included specialized logistics, engineering, medical and signal capabilities, military observers, staff officers, as well as helicopters, highlighting the country's ability to contribute to peacekeeping operations across a broad spectrum of requirements. Further, through its bilateral programme to assist with security sector reform efforts,[29] South Africa combined its bilateral peacebuilding efforts with its support to peace operations.[30]

[27] Lindy Heinecken and Rialize Ferreira, 'Fighting for Peace: South Africa's Role in Peace Operations in Africa (Part 1)', *African Security Review*, 21:2 (2012), pp. 20–35.

[28] Heinecken and Ferreira, 'Fighting for Peace'.

[29] Apart from its military deployments, South Africa also helped reform and develop the capacity of different line ministries in the DRC government, and supported the country's electoral processes, partly through its African Renaissance Fund.

[30] This trend has not been consistent. South Africa has played an important role in support of strengthening governance in South Sudan, but has not contributed troops or other resources to the UN peacekeeping operations in that country.

While South Africa's deployments in the DRC therefore generated several valuable lessons and highlighted the country's willingness and ability to be a serious actor in international peacekeeping, the MONUC experience also brought challenges. For instance, the SANDF had difficulty in maintaining the quality of its deployments in the DRC. A limited number of operational commanders and officers were deployed frequently, and this proved unsustainable. Due to the high level of HIV in the SANDF (at the time of the DRC deployments official levels of HIV were 23 per cent), and the SANDF policies not to deploy soldiers that were HIV positive, the SANDF found it difficult to deploy whole battalions, and the composite battalions that were deployed brought all kinds of integration challenges with them. Some South African peacekeepers were also undisciplined and engaged in sexual misconduct, which harmed the reputation of not only South Africa, but also of MONUC and UN peacekeeping in general. South Africa also had a problem with the age and serviceability of its equipment, especially its vehicles. It was not always able to maintain the UN's minimum levels of operational capability, and as a result, the SANDF was not able to claim full reimbursement for the equipment it had brought into the mission area, making the MONUC deployment a relatively expensive one for the South African government. Yet, South Africa barely had time to factor the lessons learned in the DRC into its preparations for peace operations, as by 2004 the SANDF was already preparing for its next international deployment.

17.1.4 Darfur: Expanding Contributions to Peacekeeping

South Africa's next international deployment came through the AU Mission to the Darfur region of Sudan in 2004 (AMIS). Initially conceived as an observer mission with a protection force, AMIS was expanded into a peace support operation which ultimately reached 7,200 military personnel by 2007. Its expanded mandate included facilitating delivery of humanitarian assistance, providing protection to the civilian population, and supporting a fragile fledgling peace process. Finding troop contributing countries willing to deploy their forces into a very hostile environment proved challenging: initially only Nigeria and Rwanda provided three battalions each, while Senegal and South Africa each contributed one battalion. South Africa's contribution (dubbed *Operation Cardite* by the SANDF) commenced in July 2004 with the deployment of 794 military personnel. This commitment remained more or less consistent until AMIS, concluded on 31 December 2007. The South African troops were then re-hatted into the hybrid AU–UN Mission in Darfur (UNAMID) on 1 January 2008. In addition, South Africa also for the first time contributed police officers to a peacekeeping operation: initially in 2005 to AMIS and then from 2008 onwards continued such deployments to

UNAMID, with a total of 1,094 members of the SAPS, including 311 women, deployed to UNAMID at the end of 2010.[31]

When AMIS was transitioned into UNAMID, the UN asked South Africa to increase its contingent to a standard UN-sized battalion. However, financial constraints and logistical considerations related to the lack of infrastructure in the mission area left South Africa unable to oblige. Indeed, the deployment to Darfur had posed a series of logistical challenges for the SANDF, and the extreme weather conditions had taken their toll on both personnel and equipment. The South African contingent's lack of armoured personnel carriers also left it exposed to attack by armed groups in Darfur and it repeatedly suffered assaults, kidnappings, hijackings, ambushes, and forced disarmament, fortunately without loss of life.[32]

Curiously, whereas in Burundi and the DRC South Africa's role as a peacekeeper evolved from its role as a peacemaker, in the case of Darfur this rationale appears to have been inverted. Indeed, South Africa deployed its forces to Darfur from 2004 onwards, while its political role only emerged following the appointment of Thabo Mbeki as the chairperson of the AU's High-Level Panel on Darfur in July 2008. After this, South Africa became a prominent peacekeeper *and* peacemaker in Darfur, thus reversing the order in which it adopted these roles in both Burundi and the DRC. The main motive for Pretoria's contribution to AMIS was a strong sense of commitment to AU conflict resolution and peace operations, and the sense that, as a leading member of the AU, South Africa should play a significant role in the AU's peace support operation in Sudan. There was also a strong sense of solidarity with the people of Sudan and the need to contribute to finding an 'African solution' to a crisis that had drawn widespread international attention at the time.[33]

As of February 2012, South Africa was sustaining its deployments in the DRC and Darfur. It also provides personnel to the SADC Standby Force planning element, the AU's Peace Support Operations Division (PSOD), and the UN's Department of Peacekeeping Operations (DPKO).[34] South Africa also plays an important role in supporting the development of the African Standby Force, hosting in 2009 the SADC Standby Force regional peacekeeping exercise, known as *Exercise Golfinho*, in the Kalahari Desert.

[31] Elrena Van der Spuy, 'Policing Beyond the Domestic Sphere', *African Security Review*, 20:4 (2011), pp. 34–44.

[32] Heinecken and Ferreira, 'Fighting for Peace'.

[33] See, for example, Thabo Mbeki's comments in Susan E. Rice, 'Why Darfur Can't Be Left to Africa', *Washington Post*, 7 August 2005, p. B4. See also Nathan, 'Interests, Ideas and Ideology', p. 55.

[34] South Africa provides senior military (at the level of major-general) and police (at the level of director) personnel on an ongoing basis to the SADC Standby Force Planning Element and has, since 2006, provided senior officials to head the AU PSOD, as well as fill other positions within the division.

In a relatively short period of time, compared to countries like Ghana, Kenya, and Nigeria (Ethiopia and Rwanda emerged as troop contributors in the same period), South Africa became a significant troop contributor to international peacekeeping. Since the end of apartheid, South Africa has contributed staff officers, military observers, and units to fourteen international peace operations. Over and above the battalion sized contributions discussed above, South Africa's contributions included personnel deployed to Côte d'Ivoire, Ethiopia/Eritrea, the Central African Republic (CAR), the Comoros, and Liberia. Significantly, and in line with the policy direction spelled out in the *White Paper on Participation in International Peace Missions* and other policies, South Africa is the TCC which contributes the most female peacekeepers to UN and AU peace operations.[35] By late 2011, South Africa was one of the top five troop contributors to AU peace support operations, and consistently remained among the top fifteen UN troop-contributing countries. Moreover, South Africa has also been willing to deploy troops to bilateral missions. For instance, at the time of writing, South Africa had deployed 100 military personnel to the Central African Republic (CAR) in response to a bilateral request from that country to assist with security sector reform and training initiatives.

The exception so far has been the African Union Mission to Somalia (AMISOM). Given South Africa's commitment to AU peace operations, its political role on the continent, and its ambitions at the UN Security Council, it is perhaps surprising that South Africa did not contribute to AMISOM. This anomaly can perhaps be explained on two counts. First, South African politicians and senior military personnel were reluctant to commit to the mission, arguing that it lacked the conditions set out in Pretoria's White Paper for contributions. The mission was also thought to lack a clear political process and thus also a clear exit strategy or end-state. These were thought particularly important given that South Africa saw no clear strategic interests in Somalia. Second, the Somalia operation has been a regionally driven process, with East African states directing the political-strategic direction of the mission and, by 2012, was still providing all its troops. There was thus no subregional imperative for South African involvement in AMISOM.

As illustrated in Figure 17.1, South Africa's support to peace operations grew rapidly between 2001 and 2005, and remained relatively consistent since that time, declining only slightly in 2007 before returning to previous levels in early 2008. Given these commitments, it could reasonably be expected that South Africa's contribution to international peace operations would remain consistent for the near future. However, if recent policy pronouncements are indicative, South Africa might come to play an even more prominent role in

[35] Maxie Schoeman, *South African Female Peacekeepers on Mission in Africa: Progress, Challenges and Policy Options for Increased Participation* (Nordic Africa Institute, Policy Notes 2010/1).

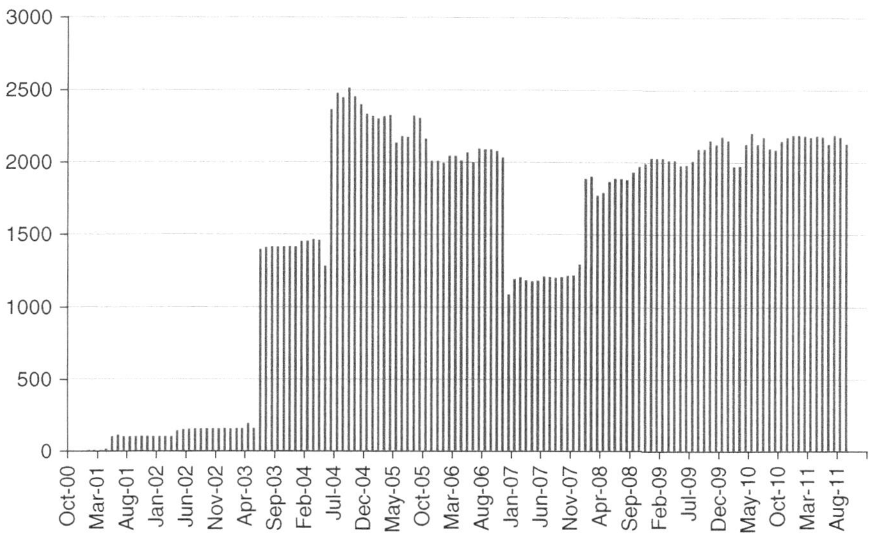

Figure 17.1 South African Uniformed Personnel in UN Peacekeeping Operations, 2000–2011

international operations. This view was expressed by the Chief of the SANDF, General Siphiwe Nyanda, in 2003, when he stated that 'South Africa has just recently become involved in peace missions in Africa, and more deployments are on the horizon. After a healthy pause, post-1994, during which time the SANDF integrated and transformed, the SANDF is on the march—a march for peace, development and prosperity.'[36]

In February 2011, the South African Minister of Defence and Military Veterans, Lindiwe Sisulu, echoed similar sentiments, announcing that South Africa would increase its international peacekeeping commitments. Addressing the media, Sisulu noted that in 2012 South Africa would contribute a total of 2,240 personnel to operations, including 1,271 to the DRC, 850 to Sudan, and 100 to the CAR. Sisulu also argued that South Africa would not be limited to military deployments, but would also increase its focus on police, and especially civilian, deployments. South African personnel would also be seconded to the AU and SADC in an effort to strengthen regional approaches to peacekeeping.[37]

Indeed, given South Africa's political ambitions, the relative size of South Africa's economy, the size and capability of its armed forces, and its potential

[36] Quoted in Theo Neethling, 'The SANDF as an Instrument for Peacekeeping in Africa: A Critical Analysis of Three Main Challenges', *Journal for Contemporary History*, 36:1 (2011), pp. 134–53.

[37] 'SA to Step Up International Commitments', *DefenceWeb*, 28 February 2011.

to contribute civilian personnel and expertise, it would seem likely that South Africa's contributions to international peace operations should expand further in the next decade. Until now, however, financial, equipment, and human resource constraints have left South Africa's contributions remaining relatively stable at what are approaching its maximum levels, given current constraints. As mentioned earlier, some argue that at a total deployment level of approximately 2,200 military personnel—compared to the contributions made by African countries like Ethiopia, Ghana, Kenya, and Rwanda—South Africa is punching below its weight. However, Pretoria has given no indication that it will invest in changing these constraints in the short to medium term.

17.2 CHALLENGES TO SUSTAINING AND EXPANDING SOUTH AFRICA'S CONTRIBUTIONS

South Africa's growing contributions to international peacekeeping have raised several challenges. Some revolve around its national decision-making process for deploying personnel and assets in support of peacekeeping operations. Although the White Paper provided a policy framework for a whole-of-government approach to South African engagement in international peace operations, it has never been fully implemented. The NOCPM has been reduced to a DIRCO desk dealing with peace operations, and the ways in which the various missions have been considered and approved have rarely, if ever, followed the path foreseen in the White Paper. In most cases, the decision to deploy South African forces was taken by the presidency. It did not follow the decision-making process envisaged in the White Paper, and the legislature was, in most if not all cases, informed, in writing, after the troops had already been deployed.[38] South Africa will need to revisit the White Paper, given the lessons that have been identified to date in the planning and conduct of international deployments, and assess whether the policy framework still adequately supports the national decision-making process. At the time of writing, such a review of the White Paper was already underway.

In addition, the White Paper will need to be updated to incorporate provisions for the effective deployment not only of soldiers, but also of police and civilian personnel to AU and SADC operations. The current White Paper does make provision for the deployment of police and civilian personnel, but since it was drafted the African Standby Force has developed. This means the revised White Paper must become much more specific about how South

[38] *South Africa's Peacekeeping Role in Burundi.*

Africa will generate its military, police, and civilian contributions to the SADC Standby Force.

Another set of challenges relate to the cost of South Africa's contributions. Since the mid-1990s the SANDF, as with most other armed forces, has witnessed consistent budget cuts, resulting in a reduction in both personnel and the SANDF's ability to maintain its operational capability. By March 1999, the Minister of Defence approved plans to reduce military personnel from 93,000 to 70,000 permanent posts (including civilian posts), and many observers argue that subsequent budget cuts have had serious implications on the state of force readiness of the SANDF.[39] Given a decline in the defence budget, and on the basis of the 1998 Defence Review, the Cabinet determined that the SANDF force design should be based on a high-technology core force, sized for peacetime operations, which could be rapidly expanded to meet an emerging threat.

On this basis, the South African Air Force (SAAF) and the South African Navy (SAN) were reinvigorated through the purchase of light fighter aircraft, fighter-trainer aircraft, light utility helicopters, patrol corvettes, and submarines. While these purchases did serve to strengthen the ability of the SANDF to ensure territorial security, they were not in line with the SANDF's requirements for peace support operations. Indeed, a multibillion dollar deal to secure eight Airbus A400M military transport aircraft, required by the SANDF to transport troops and equipment into mission areas in line with its existing peacekeeping obligations, was cancelled in 2010 because the deal became too costly. South Africa therefore remains reliant on nine Lockheed Martin C-130 Hercules transports, of which only four were operational in 2011.[40]

The operating costs of the newly purchased equipment for the SAAF and the SAN also soared. This was in a context where defence spending had declined to an estimated 3.9 per cent of government expenditure in financial year 2009–10.[41] As one observer noted, it had become increasingly clear that a mismatch existed between defence funding and the purchase of costly equipment vis-à-vis what was required or demanded from the SANDF.[42]

Noting these challenges, in 2003 the Chief of Joint Operations of the SANDF, Lieutenant-General Godfrey Ngwenya, urged caution against overstretch by deploying more troops to peacekeeping operations. Ngwenya highlighted that by July 2003 approximately 2,500 personnel were deployed in operations in the DRC, Burundi, and Ethiopia/Eritrea, and that the SANDF's force structure and logistical capabilities did not allow for more foreign

[39] Neethling, 'The SANDF', p. 139.

[40] 'South Africa: paper tiger of African peacekeeping operations', *IRIN News*, 6 January 2012. At http://www.irinnews.org/report.aspx?ReportId=94597

[41] Neethling, 'The SANDF', p. 139.

[42] Neethling, 'The SANDF', p. 139.

deployments. Ngwenya was effectively arguing that South Africa had reached a ceiling as far as its contributions to peace support operations were concerned.[43] His projection seems to have been accurate, as almost a decade later, South Africa is still maintaining the same approximate deployment levels.

Under ideal circumstances, it is estimated that for South Africa to deploy three battalions, it would need to maintain nine battalions at operational deployable capability. Estimates in 2005 were that this would require a sustained expenditure of around 2 per cent of gross domestic product (GDP) allocated to the SANDF on an annual basis.[44] However, as noted above, defence expenditure is currently far below these levels. Whereas defence expenditure averaged 16.4 per cent of the national budget in the mid-1980s, a decade later this had been reduced to less than 10 per cent. In real terms, this amounted to a 50 per cent cut between 1989 and 1997. Since the late 1990s, defence expenditure has been pinned down to approximately 1.6 per cent of GDP, or between 6 and 7 per cent of government expenditure, and by 2010 had declined to 3.9 per cent of government expenditure.[45]

Claiming reimbursement after costs has also been an issue in relation to the international organizations under whose mandate the SANDF has deployed (i.e., the UN and AU). In the DRC, for instance, the South African contingent-owned equipment (COE) was deemed unsuitable and did not meet UN standards; hence South Africa did not receive reimbursement for it.[46] In Burundi, it was only in October 2011 that a Memorandum of Understanding between the South African government and the AU Commission outlined how reimbursements for costs incurred by the South African deployment should be handled, and it is unlikely that the AU will find the funds to reimburse South Africa for costs incurred a decade earlier in Burundi. The financial incentive for South African contributions to international peace support operations therefore seems very limited at best. The only financial benefit appears to be for the individual peacekeepers who collect AU or UN allowances, as well as being paid their monthly salaries in full at home. Despite these financial constraints, and despite the likelihood that South Africa will not be in a position to significantly increase its defence expenditure in the near to mid-term, it has been able to sustain its level of deployments at a more or less stable level for over a decade, and there is nothing to suggest that it will not be able to continue to do so until 2020.

[43] Neethling, 'The SANDF', p. 141.

[44] H. R. Heitman, 'Is SANDF Falling Apart?', *Daily News*, 31 August 2005. At http://www.dailynews.co.za/general/print_article.php?articleid=2858224

[45] Neethling, 'The SANDF', p. 139.

[46] Neethling, 'The SANDF', p. 144.

One way in which South Africa can enlarge the cake is to partner with one or more Western countries. Several are keen to return to UN peacekeeping, but most lack the troop numbers to deploy the battalion-sized configurations favoured by the UN. A 'South–North' partnership could provide South Africa with the financial and material resources it lacks, and provide a Northern partner with the matching numbers it needs to contribute to peacekeeping. A similar partnership arrangement can be envisaged for highly specialized contributions such as airframes. Helicopters are a critical shortcoming in most UN missions, especially military-capable tactical helicopters. A South–North partnership that can result in South Africa deploying a squadron of its Rooivalk attack helicopters to South Sudan would, for instance, be a very significant contribution to a particular mission, as well as a high profile symbol of both South Africa's military capability and the utility of such South–North partnerships.

A further challenge is the low levels of professionalism and discipline among South Africa's peacekeepers. Currently the level of preparation of South African peacekeepers leaves room for improvement. In Burundi and the DRC, for instance, South African peacekeepers were found guilty of more than 1,000 cases of misconduct between 2002 and 2006. More than half of these violations involved absence without leave, disobeying lawful commands, and drunkenness. Included in these statistics are also 230 criminal cases, in which South African peacekeepers were found guilty of assault, indecent assault, theft, rape, and murder. According to statistics at the time, several further cases were pending, which also involved several high-ranking officers, including six lieutenant-colonels, four colonels, and a general.[47] In contrast to other contributors to international peacekeeping, such as Kenya for instance, this high number of violations (approximately 170 per annum for the reporting period) has proved embarrassing for the South African government and the UN. There is a proposal floating in New York to blacklist countries that have a poor track record when it comes to sexual exploitation and abuse, and if South Africa were to ever find itself on such a blacklist, it would effectively end its campaign for a Security Council seat.

At current budget levels South Africa can sustain the quantity of its deployments, but not improve the quality of its equipment and the preparation and training of its personnel. While it may be possible, within current budgetary levels, to generate a highly professional and disciplined cadre of peacekeepers, this has not happened to date, and there is nothing in the pipeline that suggests the situation is likely to improve in the short to medium term.

47 Neethling, 'The SANDF', p. 147.

Despite these challenges, South Africa's foreign policy goals, as formulated in the DIRCO Strategic Plan for 2009–12, explicitly states that peace, security, and stability are prerequisites for Africa's socio-economic development, and that within this context, Pretoria will continue to help operationalize the institutions of the African Peace and Security Architecture (APSA).[48] Taking note of the clear articulation of South Africa's foreign policy objectives and its outdated defence policy (published in 1996), in 2010 the Minister of Defence and Military Veterans, Lindiwe Sisulu, mandated a review of the defence policy to consider major changes in the defence environment over the course of the next fifteen years, and align it more closely with South Africa's foreign policy priorities.[49] At the time of writing, the Defence Review Committee was concluding its deliberations, and the review of defence policy is expected to be released in 2012. The findings of this review, and the manner in which these are taken on board by the South African government, will significantly influence South Africa's future role in international peacekeeping.

17.3 CONCLUSION

South Africa's contribution to UN and African peace operations is closely related to its identity as a peace broker and its ambitions to be a leading influence in Africa, an important emerging power in the wider world, and ultimately, to gain a permanent seat on the UN Security Council. Almost all of South Africa's peacekeeping deployments have thus been closely linked to those peace processes where it played a leading role in the negotiations, or can otherwise be explained in terms of these foreign policy objectives.

South Africa's peacekeeping record also shows that its current capacity falls short of its ambitions. Despite the significant contribution South Africa has made in a relatively short period of time, and despite the fact that it has contributed not just in terms of numbers, but also in terms of various specialized capabilities, including helicopters, and despite the fact that it is the leading contributor of female peacekeepers, its critics persist in the view that given South Africa's prominent political and peacemaking role, the relative strength of its economy, and the size and specialized capabilities of its armed forces it should be the largest, or at least among the top three African contributors to peace operations on the continent. However, several African countries that have a smaller economic and political footprint than Pretoria provide more peacekeepers, such as Ethiopia, Ghana, Kenya, Rwanda, Uganda, and Burundi.

[48] *Strategic Plan 2009–2012* (Pretoria: Department of International Relations and Cooperation, 2010), p. 9.

[49] Neethling, 'The SANDF', p. 142.

A strategic gap thus remains between South Africa's foreign policy goals and its capacity to provide the peacekeepers necessary to achieve those objectives. In order to sustain its current levels of deployments South Africa needs, at a minimum, to invest more resources in the professionalization and discipline of its peacekeepers, as well as the quality of their equipment.

It seems that for the moment, South Africa's ceiling is approximately 2,500 troops. Having attained this level in 2004 it is difficult to see how Pretoria can break through that ceiling without a considerable increase in defence spending, which is unlikely any time before 2020. Under exceptional circumstances, South Africa could deploy more soldiers for a short period of time, but it will not be able to sustain such a deployment for more than a year.

The current strategy of maintaining this approximate ceiling of 2,500 troops and then carefully choosing the missions to which South Africa deploys seems effective and efficient because Pretoria has enjoyed high levels of political recognition internationally. South Africa has over recent years enjoyed the leadership of SADC and has been a member of both the AU Peace and Security Council and the UN Security Council. It is also a member of IBSA, the BRICS, the G20, and other powerful groupings.

The wild card is the professionalism and discipline of South Africa's peacekeepers. If South Africa were to be, for instance, blacklisted as a UN troop-contributing country, it would signal the end of its campaign for a permanent seat on a reformed Security Council. If nothing else, South Africa would have to find the means to invest in the professionalization and discipline of its peacekeepers. As South Africa further matures as a peacekeeping contributor, it is possible that its troops may increase in professionalism, and the country may deploy more of its specialized capabilities. If the past record is an indication of things to come, then South Africa's peacekeeping contributions are likely to closely follow its peacemaking commitments on the African continent.

18

Japan

Katsumi Ishizuka

Japan's contribution to UN peacekeeping is relatively recent. Its first deployment of troops occurred only in 1992 when some 600 military engineers of the Japanese Self-Defence Forces (SDF) were dispatched to the UN Transitional Authority in Cambodia (UNTAC). The principal reason for this is that Japanese policy towards UN peace operations has been complicated by several domestic factors, especially the national Constitution which prohibits the use of the SDF for anything but national self-defence. Paradoxically, however, Japanese foreign policy has tended to focus on the UN, creating an ambition in some parts of the policy-making community for the country to make a more active contribution to UN peacekeeping operations. These ambitions were reflected to some extent by legal reforms in 1992 and 1998 aimed at facilitating the provision of peacekeepers by Japan. Nevertheless, despite modest signs of progress, Japan still does not respond in a consistently positive fashion to requests to provide UN peacekeepers and its overall contribution remains relatively small.

This chapter evaluates the factors that have influenced the level and type of Japan's contributions to UN peacekeeping. It starts with a brief history of Japan's approach to UN peacekeeping which examines how Tokyo first became engaged in peacekeeping through the enactment of the 'Peacekeeping Operations Law' in 1992 and its amendment in 2001. The second section explains the decision-making process behind these contributions, in which the International Peace Cooperation Headquarters (IPCHQ) plays a central role. The third section considers the rationales that influence this decision-making. The main rationale for Japan's commitment to UN peacekeeping is political, while normative, security, and institutional factors are also relevant. The fourth section identifies factors that inhibit the Japanese government from contributing more, especially the legal restriction. The fifth section recommends policy options for strengthening Japan's peacekeeping contribution. Such options include legal reform, developing a training system, establishing a rapid deployment capability, and enhancing civilian capacity. While Japan's contribution to UN peacekeeping operations is still modest, this chapter will argue that Japan has the potential to become a more significant contributor.

18.1 JAPAN AND UN PEACEKEEPING: A BRIEF HISTORY

In the immediate post-Second World War environment, Japan confronted two dilemmas. First, it possessed competent military forces but there was a widespread (domestic and international) consensus that disapproved of their use abroad. Second, the country's political elite was torn between the desire among the more internationalist-minded elements to join and support the emerging UN system and the constitutional restrictions placed on Japan's contribution. Although Japan became a contributor to UN peacekeeping only after the Cold War ended, Tokyo expressed a commitment to the ideals of the UN and its peacekeeping activities soon after the end of the Second World War. Indeed, Japan's first direct engagement with UN-authorized military force was its secret support for the enforcement mission in Korea (1950–3). This involvement could probably be explained by the fact that Japan was still under US military occupation at the time.[1] Nonetheless, in 1952—before Japan joined the UN (it joined in 1956, and was elected a non-permanent member of the Security Council in 1958)—Foreign Minister Katsuo Okazaki stated in a letter to the UN Secretary-General that Japan would fulfil the obligations of a UN member with all the means at its disposal. However, Japan was formally precluded from joining UN peacekeeping by Article 9 of its post-Second World War Constitution, which prohibited the possession of significant military forces.[2] This was confirmed in June 1954 when the House of Councillors passed a resolution not to allow the SDF to be dispatched abroad. While some legal scholars suggested that this did not preclude participation in missions authorized by the UN, this claim was not widely examined by policy-makers.[3]

Election to the UN Security Council in 1958 gave new urgency to some of these debates. In response to the crisis in Lebanon that emerged that year, Japan supported the basic idea of peacekeeping, arguing in the Council that the UN should enable 'a withdrawal of the United States forces from Lebanon'.[4] It also advocated an increase in the strength of the UN

[1] Milton Leitenberg, *The Participation of Japanese Military Forces in UN Peacekeeping Operations* (Maryland: Maryland/Tsukuba Papers on US–Japan Relations, 1996), p. 6. Leitenburg pointed out that 'during the Korean War, Japan . . . sent mine sweepers to operate off the Korean coast in assistance to the UN forces in response to a request from the United States. The ships were technically part of the Japanese coast guard, and the deployment was made secretly, and even incurred casualties.'

[2] Article 9 (1): 'Aspiring sincerely to an international peace based on justice and order, the Japanese people forever renounce wars as a sovereignty right of the nation and the threat or use of force as means of setting international dispute. (2) In order to accomplish the aim of the preceding paragraph, land, sea and airforces, as well as other war potential, will never be maintained. The right of belligerence of the state will not be recognized.'

[3] Kozai Sigeru, *Kokuren no heiwa iji katsudou* [UN Peacekeeping Operations] (Tokyo: Yuhikaku, 1991), pp. 474–81.

[4] S/4055/rev 1, 22 July 1958.

Observation Group in Lebanon (UNOGIL) deployed to monitor the situation in preference to supporting the use of US troops, which it argued would have violated the UN's spirit of neutrality.[5] This line of argument prompted UN Secretary-General Dag Hammarskjöld to request that Japan contribute ten SDF officers to UNOGIL as military observers. The request prompted another debate within Japan about the wisdom of dispatching its soldiers as UN peacekeepers. Director-General of the Defence Agency, Sato, wanted to respond in the affirmative. However, in the *Diet* (national parliament) the Foreign Minister stated that the Japanese government was not considering dispatching the SDF to UNOGIL because Article 3 of the 'SDF Law' did not permit such deployments. The next day, the government decided to decline Hammarskjöld's request.[6] This decision met with some criticism within the *Diet*.[7] It also put Japan's UN representatives in New York in a difficult position due to the apparent contradiction between the country's stated support for the UN and its deep reluctance to make even small contributions to UN peacekeeping.

The issue resurfaced in 1961. Ambassador Koto Matsudaira was reported to have stated 'it is not consistent for Japan to adhere to UN cooperation on the one hand and refuse all participation in the UN armies on the other'. He insisted that because Japanese foreign policy emphasized diplomacy through the UN, it should participate in the UN mission in Congo, ONUC. Matsudaira's suggestion caused controversy in the *Diet* and opposition parties demanded his resignation. In the end, Matsudaira withdrew his statement.[8] The issue returned again four years later when Japan was elected once more as a non-permanent member of the UN Security Council. According to the *Tokyo Shimbun*, in February 1966, the Ministry of Foreign Affairs drafted a 'UN Resolutions Cooperation Bill', which specifically mentioned deploying personnel, including members of the SDF, as part of Japan's contribution to UN missions. However, the bill did not make much progress. Indeed, it was not until 1980 that the government clarified that the dispatch of the SDF to UN peacekeeping operations would not be prohibited if the mission did not entail the use of armed force.[9]

In 1982, the Japanese government submitted to the UN General Assembly a resolution that highlighted the need to strengthen the role and effectiveness of the UN in maintaining international peace and security. As a response, the

[5] The Japanese sponsored draft resolution was not passed due to a Soviet veto.

[6] L. William Henrich, Shibata Akiho, and Soeya Yoshihide, *United Nations Peace-keeping Operations: A Guide to Japanese Politics* (Tokyo: UN University Press, 1999), p. 9.

[7] Sigeru, *Kokuren no heiwa*, p. 485.

[8] See Tanaka Akihiko, 'The Domestic Context: Japanese Politics and UN Peacekeeping', in Harrison Selig and Nishihara Masashi (eds.), *UN Peacekeeping: Japanese and American Context* (Washington, DC: Carnegie Endowment for International Peace, 1995), pp. 90–1.

[9] Heinrich, Akiho, and Yoshihide, *United Nations Peace-keeping Operations*, p. 7.

Secretary-General asked each member state to submit concrete proposals for strengthening the UN. The Japanese government formed an advisory panel chaired by a former UN ambassador, including academics such as Sadako Ogata, Shigeru Kozai, and Hidejiro Kotani. The group's final report included the issue of Japan's contribution to the UN. On this, it concluded: 'The commitment of our country to the UN has been apt to be restricted to financial aspects. However, our country should participate in UN peacekeeping operations in terms of the following sections positively and extensively: provision of funds and materials, election supervision, medical assistance, transport and communications activities, police activities, logistic support, and observation and patrol activities.'[10] Although this proposal did not specifically mention the SDF, it was obvious that tasks such as logistical support and observation and communication activities could be conducted only by the SDF. However, facing serious criticism from the opposition and a large section of the public, Prime Minister Nakasone publicly dismissed the report, calling it 'merely one view put forward by a private study group'.[11] The ambition of the Ministry of Foreign Affairs, which was consistently supportive of the idea of Japan's participation in UN peacekeeping operations as a diplomatic tool, was undermined by pressure from the opposition parties and the Japanese public. From the mid-1980s, various academics began to urge the Japanese government to consider participating in UN peacekeeping operations that did not involve the use of force. Drawing on neutral Austria's *Bundesverfassungesetz* (International Service Law), which allowed Austria to participate in peacekeeping operations, Ribot Hatano claimed it was contrary to logic that a state like Japan which supported 'peace' could not participate in UN peacekeeping operations because of the SDF law.[12] Similarly, Yoshio Hirose argued that the internationalism evident in other parts of the constitution limited the effects of the articles relating to the SDF, such that it could participate in peacekeeping operations provided that they did not include military enforcement measures.[13] Another proposal was that the SDF should be reformed into a dedicated peacekeeping force.[14] However, there

[10] Ishizuka Katsumi, 'The Evolution of Japan's Policy towards UN Peace Operations', paper presented at the Fifteenth Annual Meeting for the Academic Council on the United Nations System (ACUNS), Cascais, Portugal, 21–23 June 2002, pp. 7–8.

[11] Heinrich, Akiho, and Yoshihide, *United Nations Peace-keeping Operations*, p. 16.

[12] The Japan Institute of International Affairs, a discussion meeting titled 'The United Nations as a Dispute Settlement Organ', *Kokusai Mondai* (*International Affairs*), July 1984, p. 66. At http://www2.jiia.or.jp/retrieval/search.php (accessed 20 April 2012).

[13] Quoted in Hirose Yoshio, 'Zoku Kokusai Shakai no Komyunitika no Joken (1)' [The Conditions for Changing International Law into International Community Law (continued)], *Meiji Gakuin Ronso Hogaku Kenkyu* [*The Meiji Gakuin Law Review*], 33 (1985), pp. 18–19.

[14] Quoted in Wada Hideo, Kobayashi Naiko, Fukase Tadakazu, and Furukawa Atsushi (eds.), *Heiwa Kenpo no Sozoteki Tenkai* [A Comprehensive Peace Strategy of the Japanese Constitution] (Tokyo: Gakuyu Shobo, 1987), pp. 461–73.

remained little public interest in international peacekeeping. According to an opinion poll conducted by the Ministry of Foreign Affairs in 1982, only 44 per cent of respondents said Japan should cooperate with UN peacekeeping operations, whilst 18 per cent said Japan should not and 38 per cent selected 'No idea'.[15]

However, as the Cold War came to an end, the Japanese government's focus on being a good international citizen and increased public awareness pushed the SDF towards closer cooperation with the UN. In 1988, Prime Minister Noboru Takeshita proposed an 'International Cooperation Initiative' and identified five areas in which Japan could have a role on the world stage: active pursuit of diplomatic efforts aimed at strengthening political dialogue and international cooperation; increased contributions for UN-sponsored activities seeking to prevent the outbreak of conflicts; active involvement in international efforts to resolve disputes peacefully (such as dispatching civilian personnel to trouble spots to assist with the supervision of elections or provide transportation, communications, or medical services); strengthened assistance to refugees through both bilateral and multilateral efforts; and vigorous contributions to international cooperative efforts aimed at reconstruction once a conflict has been peacefully resolved.[16] That same year, Japan dispatched civilian personnel to UN peacekeeping operations. It sent a political officer to the UN Good Office Mission in Afghanistan and Pakistan (UNGOMAP), and another to the UN Iran–Iraq Military Observer Group (UNIIMOG). In 1989, Japan dispatched twenty-seven election observers to the UN Transition Assistance Group (UNTAG) in Namibia.[17] Moreover, the government began seriously to consider dispatching the SDF to UN mandated operations. In November 1989, the Director-General of the Japan Defence Agency, Juro Matsumoto, told the *Diet* that he was considering authorizing the use of troops for anti-terrorist operations, protecting Japanese nationals overseas, and international peacekeeping activities.[18]

[15] Ishizuka Katsumi, 'The Evolution of Japan's Policy towards UN Peace Operations', p. 9.

[16] Heinrich, Akiho and Yoshihide, *United Nations Peace-keeping Operations*, p. 18.

[17] The Ministry of Foreign Affairs, *Building Peace: Japan's Participation in United Nations Peace-keeping Operations* (Tokyo: The Ministry of Foreign Affairs, 1994), p. 9. Meanwhile, in 1988 and 1989, Japan's financial contribution to UN peacekeeping also grew significantly. In 1988 Japan made voluntary contributions of $5 million to the establishment of UNGOMAP, and $10 million to the formation of UNIMOG. In 1989 it contributed $14.1 million and $3.1 million in assessed contributions to the Interim Force in Lebanon (UNIFIL) and the Disengagement Observer Force (UNDOF), respectively. In addition, Japan made a voluntary contribution of $13.6 million to the UNTAG. See Akaha Tusneo, 'Japan's Comprehensive Security Policy', *Asian Survey*, 31:4 (1991), p. 329.

[18] Leitenberg, *Participation of Japanese Military Forces*, p. 12.

18.2 JAPAN'S PEACEKEEPING LAW AND THE SDF

Although Japan refused to make a military contribution to the Gulf War (1990–1), pressure from the US prompted it to advance its thinking on peacekeeping. As a result, on 16 October 1990 the Japanese government submitted a 'Bill Concerning Cooperation to the UN Peace Effort (UN Peace Cooperation Bill)',[19] which would enable the SDF to be dispatched abroad. This bill called for the creation of a UN Peace Cooperation Corps (UNPCC), consisting of non-SDF government employees, private citizens directly subordinate to the Prime Minister, and members temporarily transferred from the SDF. The proposed law specified that the proposed corps would be mandated to conduct non-combat peacekeeping-related tasks such as overseeing cease-fire agreements, monitoring elections, medical activities, disaster relief measures, and the provision of transportation, telecommunications, and other logistical support.

US pressure also persuaded Japan to contribute $13 billion to the US-led international coalition in the Gulf. To raise this, the government imposed special taxes on its citizens.[20] Despite this, however, Japan's policy of not contributing troops drew much criticism from the international community.[21] The government succumbed to the pressure and dispatched SDF minesweepers to the Persian Gulf without any further legislation in April 1991. This was then criticized as being 'too little too late' by the opposition.[22] In addition to Gulf War pressure, there was also evidence around this time that the Japanese public was becoming more positive about the idea of contributing forces to peacekeeping. According to an opinion poll by *Yomiuri Shimbun* in 1992, 67.8 per cent of the respondents supported the SDF's participation in UN peacekeeping operations, whereas 24.4 per cent did not support it.[23]

In response to these pressures, a 'Peacekeeping Operations Bill' was introduced in September 1991 which identified five principles that would guide the participation of Japanese contingents in UN peacekeeping operations.[24] These were:

[19] In this context, it is well known that James Baker, former US Secretary of State, said during a speech to the Japan Institute for International Affairs in Tokyo in November 1991, 'your checkbook diplomacy like our dollar diplomacy of an earlier era is clearly too narrow'. *The Daily Yomiuri*, 12 February 1992.

[20] Ito Mayumi, 'Expanding Japan's Role in the United Nations', *Pacific Review*, 8:2 (1995), p. 285.

[21] The US Ambassador to Japan, Michael Armacost, urged the dispatch to the Gulf at a meeting of the *Diet* members of the Liberal Democratic Party (LDP). Hugo Dobson, *Japan and United Nations Peacekeeping* (London: RoutledgeCurzon, 2003), pp. 70–1.

[22] *The Daily Yomiuri*, 12 February 1992.

[23] Ishizuka Katsumi, 'A Japanese Perspective to the UN Peacekeeping Operations' (MA Dissertation, Department of Politics, University of Nottingham, 1996), p. 78.

[24] The Defense Agency, *Defense of Japan: The White Paper of the Defense Agency* (Tokyo: Japan Times, 1995), p. 99.

1. Agreement on the cease-fire shall have been reached among the parties to the conflicts.
2. The parties to the conflict shall have given their consent to deployment of the peacekeeping force and Japan's participation in the force.
3. The peacekeeping force shall strictly maintain its impartiality.
4. Should any of the above guideline requirements cease to satisfy the government of Japan, it may withdraw its contingent.
5. Use of weapons shall be limited to the minimum necessary to protect the lives of personnel.

The Socialist and Communist parties opposed the bill on the grounds that it was unconstitutional. However, the three largest political parties—the Liberal Democratic Party (LDP), the Socialists, and Komeito—contained factions that favoured the SDF's participation in UN peacekeeping, as well as ones that opposed it. Public opinion was also divided. A poll conducted just before the vote in the *Diet* indicated that 41.6 per cent of respondents favoured SDF participation in UN peacekeeping operations, while 36.9 per cent did not.[25] After much deliberation, the bill became law in June 1992. This became the legal authority for SDF participation in all subsequent UN peacekeeping operations. Consequently, the Japanese government dispatched 600 military engineers to UNTAC in September 1992. UNTAC was ideal in many ways, in particular because the SDF wanted a mission in its own region, UNTAC wanted to recruit troops from the region, and the mission had a large civilian component.

Following their participation in UNTAC, SDF members were deployed to Mozambique (ONUMOZ) in December 1992, and later to Zaire and Tanzania as part of the mission in Rwanda (UNAMIR). In Mozambique, five SDF personnel were assigned as staff officers to the ONUMOZ headquarters. It should be noted that the SDF's deployment in Zaire was not requested by the UN Secretary-General, nor was it a joint mission with other countries. It was rather an independent and voluntary mission by the SDF in order to enhance Japan's UN peacekeeping record. In addition to these missions, the SDF has contributed personnel to the Golan Heights (UNDOF) since March 2002. However, Japan's role in UNDOF, which monitors the separation of forces between Israel and Syria, was limited to providing transportation services.

Coincidentally, it was on 11 September 2001 that the Japanese government decided to send a logistical unit to the UN operation in East Timor (UNTAET). This modest contribution soon came under review, however, for a number of reasons. Most notably, in the wake of the '9/11' attacks the government expected that the United States would ask it to play a broader role in Afghanistan and in nation-building elsewhere in Asia. For example, the

[25] *The Asahi Shimbun*, 12 June 1992.

Director of UNHCR's Pakistan office stated that he expected that the Japanese SDF would play a major role in Afghanistan in the field of mine-clearance.[26] Around the same time, a director of the UN Department of Peacekeeping Operations urged the government to amend the 1992 peacekeeping law, arguing that 'UN peacekeeping operations require each participating state's co-operation. Strict restrictions among states would lose flexibility in operating peacekeeping units.'[27]

A bill to amend the 1992 law was passed in the upper house on 7 December 2001 to expand the scope of the SDF's participation in UN peacekeeping. The bill was supported by the three ruling parties and a majority of the largest opposition Democratic Party. It lifted a 'freeze' on SDF participation in UN peacekeeping forces engaged in such activities as monitoring cease-fires, disarming local forces, patrolling demilitarized zones, inspecting the transport of weapons, and collecting and disposing of abandoned weapons. It authorized the SDF to use weapons to protect 'those under their control', such as troops from other countries, refugees, government officials, and personnel from the UN and other international organizations. The revision also lifted a ban on the application of Article 95 of the SDF Law, which stipulated that force may be used to protect weapons stores.[28]

In summary, Japan's contribution to UN peacekeeping needs to be seen in the context of its unusual domestic political and constitutional situation. Debates about contributing forces to UN peacekeeping are tied together with concerns about changing the Constitution, the role of the SDF, and the legitimacy of deploying forces overseas for tasks other than self-defence. Although there has long been a constituency of politicians and experts prepared to argue for greater involvement, they have tended to be in the minority though recent evidence suggests that this is beginning to change. The legal restrictions on the use of the SDF overseas have gradually been relaxed, however, largely as a result of international pressure, increasing the potential for Japan to make a larger contribution of personnel to UN missions.

18.3 DECISION-MAKING AND MOTIVATIONS

This section briefly examines Japan's decision-making process in relation to UN peacekeeping and the country's main rationales for responding positively to requests from the UN. It argues that the principal rationales are political, but that security and military-institutional rationales also play a role.

[26] *The Yomiuri Shimbun*, 7 December 2001.
[27] *The Yomiuri Shimbun*, 29 December 2001.
[28] *The Japan Times*, 8 December 2001.

The decision-making process with regard to Japan's contributions to UN peacekeeping is long and complex, involving many of the key arms of government as well as the *Diet*. The process formally begins with the receipt of a request or invitation from the UN. However, in practice, formal invitations tend to be based on understandings reached during informal discussions between UN and government officials.[29] In Japan's case, these informal discussions are conducted between the UN and the International Peace Cooperation Headquarters (IPCHQ) situated in the Cabinet Office. The IPCHQ reviews the request and determines whether the proposed operation would satisfy the conditions of the basic framework of the PKO Law. If the judgement is positive, the IPCHQ forwards the proposal to the Chief Cabinet Secretary. The Secretary forms his or her own judgement as to whether the proposal can expect political support from parliament and the Japanese public. If positively inclined, the Secretary would order a fact-finding mission to be dispatched to the potential operational area charged with examining the situation, the mandate, and the relevant military requirements and modalities. If the fact-finding mission confirms that the Japanese SDF or civilian police could comply with the 'PKO Law' and the 'five principles' (see above), it issues a report to the *Diet* recommending that a deployment be approved. While the Chief Cabinet Secretary requires approval from the *Diet*, the IPCHQ completes an implementation plan, which specifies the details of the tasks of the Japanese staff, the duration of the mission, and the types of equipment, such as weapons to be used. Finally, the IPCHQ requests that the UN issue a formal request of Japan's dispatch to the UN peacekeeping operation. Only then, after officially receiving the request from the UN (itself possible only after the IPCHQ, Cabinet Secretary, fact-finding mission, and *Diet* have indicated their approval of the proposal), can the Chief Cabinet Secretary obtain Cabinet approval to implement the plan. Once this process is completed, the SDF is entitled to prepare for the deployment.[30]

The main rationale for Japan's commitment to UN peacekeeping is political. In particular, Japan sees peacekeeping as a way of enhancing its international prestige, identifying itself as a benign civilian power, and supporting its diplomacy—especially in relation to the promotion of human security. In this, Japanese motivations are similar to those of Canada and Ireland during the Cold War, where consistent use of UN peacekeepers was part of a policy designed to help them stake out an original diplomatic policy. UN peacekeeping operations are a particularly attractive way of doing this because they can be deployed without the direct participation of the superpowers, enjoy the

[29] Katsumi Ishizuka, *Ireland and International Peacekeeping Operations, 1960–2000* (London: Frank Cass, 2005), p. 2.

[30] Inoue Mari, 'Japan's Contributions to International Peacekeeping in the 21st Century' (unpublished MA thesis, George Washington University, May 2011), pp. 19–20.

legitimacy of Security Council authorization, and are associated with the pursuit of core common goals such as peace and security, good governance, human security, and poverty reduction. Therefore, Japan's activism in peacekeeping operations should be seen as part of an effort to balance its bilateral relationship with the US and present an independent face to the world. Japan's commitment to UN peacekeeping also broadens its diplomatic options on the international political stage and gives it a more influential voice at the UN. This is particularly important for Japan, as it has maintained a UN-centred foreign policy drawn from two principal sources. First, as mentioned earlier, the post-Second World War Japanese Constitution prohibits the possession of military forces, which in Japan is seen as compatible with the basic spirit of the UN Charter, which focuses on the pursuit of peaceful means for responding to political or military disputes. Second, in the early period after the foundation of the UN, many Japanese viewed the UN as a symbol of US power and prestige, owing to the central role that the US played in its foundation. This basic 'UN-centred policy orientation' has remained important for Japan. As the US veered towards unilateralism in the post-9/11 environment, taking Japan with it to some extent, participation in UN operations provided a useful counterbalance in Japanese foreign policy.

A further political rationale relates to Japan's pursuit of a permanent seat on a reformed UN Security Council and the government's belief that being a consistent contributor to UN peacekeeping would positively influence its chances of success. For example, the SDF's commitment to UNDOF was partly motivated by a desire to create a positive image of Japan as a suitable candidate for permanent membership of the Security Council. In 2003, the US Senate also passed a resolution threatening not to support Japan's bid for a permanent seat unless it lived up to its full commitment to peacekeeping.[31] On the occasion of the UN's sixtieth anniversary and in the framework of the High-Level Plenary Meeting in September 2005, Japan and other major candidates for permanent membership of a reformed Security Council, including India, Brazil, and Germany, launched their campaign for Security Council reform. At that time, Japan referred to the contribution of the SDF to the maintenance of international peace and security in the global fight against terrorism and in eight UN peacekeeping operations as evidence of its qualification for permanent membership of the Council.[32]

An additional rationale is related to security. Japan's geopolitical position is a significant factor in shaping Japanese attitudes towards the UN. The political difficulties related to North Korea, Afghanistan, India–Pakistan, China–Taiwan, and the territorial disputes in the South China Sea and East China

[31] Dobson, *Japan and United Nations Peacekeeping*, p. 140.

[32] Arturo Duplancher, 'The Evolution of Japan's Peacekeeping Policy Explained' (unpublished MSc thesis, Institute of International Relations, Leiden University, June 2011), p. 52.

Sea mean that Asia is one of the most potentially volatile areas in the world.[33] As a result, serious arms races are emerging among and between China, Japan, South Korea, Indonesia, India, and Australia.[34] Moreover, more than 80 per cent of Japan's total oil requirements come from the Middle East and Southeast Asia and Japanese exports require secure sea lines. The South China Sea and its surrounding area hold around 40 per cent of global maritime trade.[35] The UN is therefore seen as a potential dampener of regional instability and avenue for the peaceful resolution of disputes that could fundamentally threaten Japanese interests. The National Defence Programme Guidelines, approved by the Japanese Cabinet on 17 December 2010, mentioned North Korean and Chinese military modernization as destabilizing factors in Japan's national security. The guidelines then stressed that 'Japan will participate in international peace cooperation activities in a more efficient and effective manner.'[36] In Japan's view, regional stability is key to its economic and political interests and can be promoted through commitment to UN peacekeeping. This partly explains why Japan's major commitments to date have been to missions in its own region, in Cambodia and Timor-Leste.

Another set of rationales are related to the institutional concerns of the armed forces. Since its establishment, the SDF has not fought a conventional war. As a result, participation in UN peacekeeping provides a useful way in which the SDF can acquire operational experience. Specific benefits that have been identified include:

- operational experience, which cannot be gained by training in Japan;
- opportunities to develop and evaluate the leadership of SDF officers under operational conditions;
- reinforcement of home training, enabling personnel to practise and develop individual and team skills;
- opportunities to evaluate strengths and weaknesses vis-à-vis other national militaries; and
- positive effects on morale.

It should also be noted that one SDF officer commented on the confidence-building effects of participation in UNMISET. He argued that the successful mission in Timor-Leste boosted morale by proving the worth of training on

[33] The main territorial dispute in the South China Sea is one over the Spratly Islands, involving six sovereign states within the region, namely, China, Taiwan, the Philippines, Vietnam, Malaysia, and Brunei. One of the territorial disputes in the East China Sea is over the Senkaku Islands between China, Taiwan, and Japan.

[34] *Yomiuri Shimbun*, 21 November 2011.

[35] Yamaguchi Noboru, 'Regional Stability in the post-Cold War Periods', in Kimura Masaho (ed.), *What are Japan's Security Issues?* (Tokyo: PHP, 1996), p. 43.

[36] Duplancher, *The Evolution of Japan's Peacekeeping*, p. 58.

national soil.[37] Finally, the SDF's positive attitude towards peacekeeping is shaped by the fact that its most significant contributions were to quite successful UN operations in Cambodia and Timor-Leste.

In summary, partly as a response of its restrictive constitution and legal context, Japan has an extremely complex decision-making process in relation to peacekeeping that involves several arms of government, including the *Diet*. The primary rationales for participation in UN peacekeeping are political and relate to prestige, the country's identity as a pro-UN 'civilian power', and pursuit of foreign policy goals. Security rationales also play a role, as Japan sees the UN system as a crucial way of navigating a particularly dangerous regional context, and the military is generally well disposed to participating in peacekeeping because of the operational experience it delivers.

18.4 THE WEAKNESSES OF JAPAN'S UN PEACEKEEPING POLICY

Since the enthusiasm for UN peacekeeping operations that characterized the 1990s and the early 2000s, Japan's record of participation in peacekeeping has diminished (see Figure 18.1). After the withdrawal of the SDF from UNMISET in

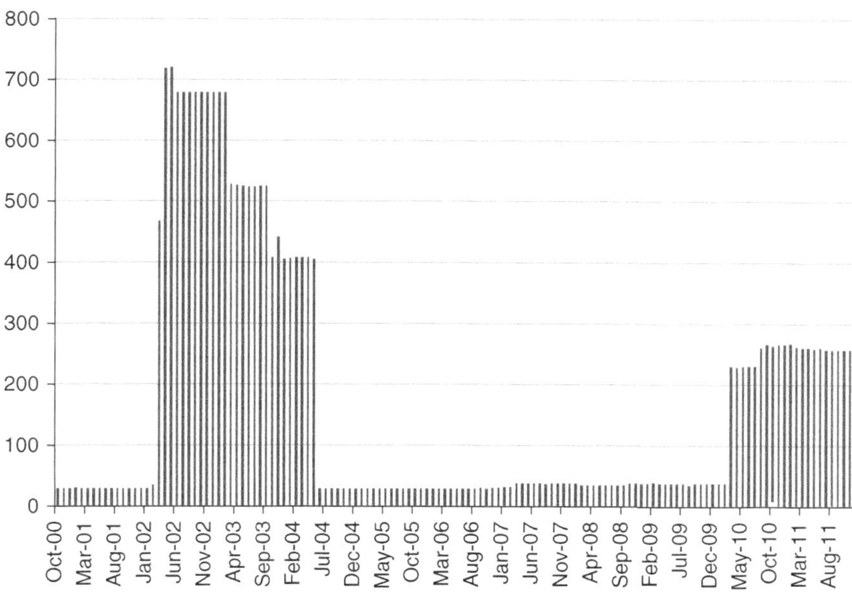

Figure 18.1 Japan's Uniformed Personnel in UN Peacekeeping Operations, 2000–2011

[37] Asahi Hideaki, *Experiencing Nation-building in the 21st Century* (Tokyo: Japan Institute of International Affairs Working Paper, March 2007), p. 38.

May 2004, Japan dispatched a small number of election observers, military observers, and headquarters staff to UN missions to the Democratic Republic of Congo (MONUC), Nepal (UNMIN), and Sudan (UNMIS). During this period, only around 30 to 40 SDF personnel were deployed on UN missions, until March 2010, when 192 troops were sent to MINUSTAH in Haiti to conduct humanitarian work after the devastating earthquake there. In 2011, the number of Japanese uniformed personnel in UN peacekeeping hovered around 250. This means that Japan's contribution to UN peacekeeping was merely 0.26 per cent of the UN's total uniformed personnel. This is well below its contribution of 12.5 per cent of the UN's peacekeeping budget.[38] This low level of commitment stands in sharp contrast with the country's stated desire to pursue a 'UN-centred policy'.

There are a number of reasons why Japan's enthusiasm for UN peacekeeping has diminished in the twenty-first century. First, the changing international strategic environment created new priorities and placed new demands on the SDF—emanating from the US in particular. After the 9/11 attacks, domestic debates about the external use of the SDF moved from a focus on UN peacekeeping to one on the 'War on Terror', which was framed much more in terms of the Japan–US alliance. This effectively sidelined UN peacekeeping.[39] In October 2001 the government adopted a new anti-terrorism law and immediately thereafter dispatched the Japanese Maritime Self-Defence Force (MSDF) to the Indian Ocean for oil-fuelling missions to support the US-led intervention in Afghanistan. The five MSDF corps deployed in the Indian Ocean was the second largest contribution to the effort after the US itself. The refuelling missions in the Indian Ocean continued for eight years until January 2010, when the new Democratic Party of Japan (DPJ) allowed the anti-terrorism law to expire.[40] The Japanese SDF was also dispatched to Iraq for humanitarian and reconstruction work between late 2003 and early 2009. Thus, Japan was more concerned about counter-terrorism missions than UN peacekeeping from 2001 to 2010 and about 1,000 SDF personnel were deployed at any one time in Iraq and Afghanistan. Although several hundred Japanese SDF members were deployed to UNMISET in Timor-Leste, participation in UN peacekeeping operations was considered to be a secondary priority for the Japanese government.

Second, the constitutional issue has still not been resolved. Peacekeeping forces which are not legally permitted to engage in combat operations in

[38] *Annual Review of Global Peace Operations 2011* (Boulder, CO: Lynne Rienner/Centre for International Cooperation, 2011), p. 139.

[39] Author's communication with Professor Hugo Dobson, University of Sheffield, England, 26 November 2011.

[40] Ishizuka Katsumi, 'Japan's Policy towards the War on Terror in Afghanistan', paper presented to 'Expert Workshop: Ready or Not? Assessing Recent Changes in Japan's International Crisis Management Capabilities', University of Duisburg-Essen Germany, 28–29 October 2011, pp. 15–16.

emergency situations, like those of the SDF, are not welcomed into UN peacekeeping operations which might require their personnel to engage in a unified use of force in accordance with common rules of engagement. There are good reasons for this, notably that SDF deployments with caveats increase the security burdens on other contributing countries. For example, when the SDF engineering unit deployed in Timor-Leste in UNTAET and UNMISET (2000–4), it was unarmed and unprepared for combat in areas viewed as security risks. As a result, Japanese peacekeepers had to rely for protection on the New Zealand battalions in Covalima, the Portuguese in Bobonaro and Dili, and the Koreans in Oecusse.[41]

Third, although its foreign policy is UN-centred, Japan's peacekeeping policy is shaped more by domestic considerations than international concerns. As noted above, the controversy about Japan's participation in UN operations was triggered by foreign pressure during the Gulf Crisis (1990–1). The government's decision to review the 1992 law was encouraged by the terrorist attacks of 11 September 2001. In other words, Japan's peacekeeping policy has been influenced more by political considerations unrelated to peacekeeping itself. Domestically, participation in peacekeeping has also been consistently linked with Japan's desire for permanent membership of the UN Security Council. As debate about Security Council reform has fallen off the international agenda, so too has Japanese interest in peacekeeping.

Fourth, since the 9/11 attacks on the US, Japanese foreign policy has begun to move away from its UN-centredness towards a focus on national security. This was evidenced by debates about Japanese contributions to US-led activities in Afghanistan. In November 2007, debate on Japan's policy towards peace and security operations was provoked by a paper written by Ichiro Ozawa, leader of the opposition Democratic Party of Japan (DPJ). Ozawa argued that the Japanese SDF should be dispatched to the UN-authorized International Security Assistance Force (ISAF) in Afghanistan.[42] Responses to the paper were mainly critical. Shigeru Ishiba, the then Minister of Defence, argued that state power should not be emasculated by UN authorization.[43] More in keeping with traditional concerns about the use of force, Masahiro Sakata argued that it was unreasonable to interpret the Japanese Constitution as requiring the use of force to fulfil the 'desire to occupy an honored place in an international society striving for the preservation of peace'.[44] Similarly, Akira Kodera, an expert on international law at Tokyo University, concluded

41 Author's field research, Dili, Timor-Leste, September 2002.

42 Ozawa Ichiro, 'The Principles of the International Security System Should be Created in Japan Now', *Sekai*, November 2007, pp. 148–53.

43 Ishiba Sigeru, 'One Consideration on the Overseas Dispatch of the SDF', *Sekai*, December 2007, pp. 142–7.

44 Sakata Masahiro, 'The Interpretation of the Japanese Government and the Ozawa Theory', *Sekai*, December 2007, pp. 153–6.

that the use of force by the SDF in multinational forces such as ISAF was unconstitutional.[45]

The debates surrounding the question of the SDF's participation in ISAF only served to confirm that Japanese politicians, scholars, and the wider public were not ready to accept the use of the SDF in multinational forces such as ISAF even if they were authorized by the UN Security Council. Thus, the use of the SDF in unarmed roles in UN-commanded peacekeeping operations appears to be the limit of what can be tolerated politically. Moreover, it is telling that debates on the possibility of Japan's participating in UN peacekeeping focused mainly on domestic legal issues, indicating that for all the apparent change, debates about the role of the SDF have not changed significantly in Japan since the 1960s.

18.5 STRENGTHENING JAPANESE CONTRIBUTIONS TO UN PEACEKEEPING

This section examines potential factors likely to strengthen Japan's contribution to UN peacekeeping and the potential for this in the foreseeable future. It focuses on legal reforms, better peacekeeping training, commitment to rapidly deployable capacities, and the need for more national debate on peacekeeping. It then goes on to identify one area—civilian capacities—where Japan might be expected to increase its participation.

18.5.1 Legal Reform

Japanese law remains a critical inhibitor to Japanese peacekeeping. In particular, the 'five principles' contained in Japan's peacekeeping law have not only presented a significant barrier to Japanese participation in UN peacekeeping, but have also negatively affected the SDF's performance in operational areas. Indeed, in September 2011, former Minister of Foreign Affairs, Seiji Maehara, commented on the necessity of easing legal regulations on the use of force by the SDF in overseas operations. There are some nascent signs of public debate on the need to reform the relevant laws. In June 2010, the Japan Association for United Nations Studies (JAUNS) issued a report which recommended that Japan consider adopting a permanent law which enables Japanese personnel in

[45] Kodera Akira, 'From the Viewpoint of International Law', *Sekai,* December 2007, pp. 156–60.

UN operations to conduct their missions more effectively and rationally.[46] However, ultimately, a constitutional amendment, especially to Article 9 of the Japanese Constitution, will be necessary if Japan wants to be a consistent and fully-fledged UN peacekeeper.

18.5.2 Training

Historically, the legal issues have stymied military training related to peacekeeping, but here again there are early signs of change. In November 2009, Japan co-hosted the 'US–Japan Global Peace Operations Initiative Senior Mission Leaders Course' (GPOI SML). The GPOI SML course was one of the action programmes launched by the Global Peace Operations Initiative, initiated as the US contribution to the broader G8 Action Plan for Expanding Capability for Peace Support Operations, adopted at the 2004 G8 Sea Island Summit. The GPOI SML course was the first such experience for senior mission leaders and its content reflected the curriculum and training guidelines developed by the UN. The course participants, comprising twenty-six military, police, and civilian personnel from thirteen countries in the Asia-Pacific region, underwent training in the multiple tasks of UN peacekeeping.[47] A second GPOI SML course was conducted in Tokyo in September 2011.[48] In keeping with this broader engagement with peacekeeping, in 2011 Japanese peacekeeping instructors from the SDF taught at training institutes in Mali, Egypt, Ghana, and Malaysia. The then Japanese Prime Minister, Naoto Kan, also announced that the government was studying new ways to increase the SDF's peacekeeping contributions.[49]

18.5.3 Rapid Deployment

A second area related to peacekeeping that has seen some important developments in recent times is in capability for rapid deployment. In March 2007, the

[46] The Japan Association for United Nations Studies (JAUNS), *Towards a Diplomacy that Strengthens the United Nations: Proposal for Japan's UN Policy*, July 2010, p. 11.

[47] These are integrated planning; mediation; public affairs; disarmament, demobilization and reintegration, peace-building; rule of law; protection of civilians; gender based violence; security management; humanitarian affairs; and human rights in the context of peace support operations. The participants were: Japan, Australia, Bangladesh, Cambodia, Indonesia, South Korea, Malaysia, Mongolia, Nepal, New Zealand, Pakistan, the Philippines, and Thailand.

[48] Ministry of Foreign Affairs of Japan. At http://www.mofa.go.jp/announce/event/2011/9/0901_01.html (accessed 25 November 2011).

[49] Duplancher, *The Evolution of Japan's Peacekeeping*, p. 58.

Ministry of Defence (MOD) decided to create the Central Readiness Force (CRF) in order to respond to any situation on either Japanese or foreign soil by direct actions, including peacekeeping operations and unconventional warfare. SDF personnel selected as members of the CRF received additional training, part of which aimed to provide SDF personnel with the knowledge and skills necessary for their participation in UN peacekeeping operations. The CRF, consisting of about 4,000 soldiers, is the first programme for the SDF to provide special education on international missions for its personnel.[50] Furthermore, in 2009 the SDF also agreed to participate in the UN Standby Arrangement System (UNSAS). The SDF applied for Level 1 of UNSAS, requiring it to submit a list of the type of tasks, and the duration and the size of the support the SDF can provide to UNSAS. The SDF applied for tasks related to logistics missions such as transportation, engineering, military observers, and commanding officers. The members of Level 1 are expected to deploy their troops within 180 days of a request from UNSAS.[51]

18.5.4 Future Directions: Civilian Capacity

Although there are modest signs that Japan might be preparing to engage more fully with UN peacekeeping, it is unlikely that the SDF will contribute armed units in the near future. Whilst my own field research in Timor-Leste in 2003 records that the Japanese SDF's engineer unit in UNMISET earned a good reputation for its standard of skills, its inability to provide its own security imposed burdens on other contributors which makes this approach unviable as a long-term strategy and unappealing to the UN.[52] A more likely area of growth is the contribution of civilian personnel. As the place of civilian personnel in UN peacekeeping grows, Japan could be expected to train and recruit personnel in fields such as governance, administration, human rights, and civilian police missions. In 2007 the Ministry of Foreign Affairs (MOFA) established a peacebuilding training programme for work at the UN and other international institutions in the future.[53] At present, however, Japanese

[50] Isobe Koichi, 'International Missions and the SDF' [in Japanese], *Journal of International Security*, 36:1 (2008), pp. 21–41.

[51] Ministry of Foreign Affairs. At http://www.mofa.go.jp/mofaj/gaiko/pko/unsas.html (accessed 26 November 2011).

[52] Katsumi Ishizuka, 'Japan and UN Peace Operations', *Japanese Journal of Political Science*, 5:1 (2004), p. 155.

[53] In the programme, the trainees receive several lectures as domestic seminars in Tokyo for about 45 days and then move on to overseas seminars as practical training in the Asian and African countries for 12 months. Afterwards, many of them find positions at UN peacekeeping operations, UN headquarters, international NGOs, etc. See http://www.mofa.go.jp/mofaj/gaiko/peace_b/pdfs/h21_ji_gai.pdf (accessed 22 April 2012).

contributions to the UN are skewed towards a disproportionately high number of headquarters staff, while Japan's civilian field presence remains relatively modest. In 2010, there were five Japanese officials in the UN's Department of Field Support (DFS), and ten in the DPKO, making Japan the tenth most represented state at UN headquarters. Meanwhile, Japan was not ranked within the top twenty contributors of civilian personnel in UN field missions for 2010.[54] This is partly due to Japan's negative tradition of passive commitment to field missions in UN peacekeeping operations. To redress this problem, the MOFA peacebuilding training programme has organized public events to encourage young Japanese people and university graduates to apply for UN field positions.

In relation to policing, Japanese commitment was negatively affected by a policing fatality during the UNTAC operation in Cambodia and has not recovered since. Nonetheless, there has been some discussion of expanding Japan's role in policing. In December 2002, a report of the Conference on International Peace and Cooperation, which were advisory panels directed by the Japanese government and chaired by former Under-Secretary-General Yasushi Akashi, encouraged the Japanese police force to play a larger role in UN peacekeeping operations. The report called for recognition of international peace and cooperation activities conducted by Japanese civilian police as a principal duty and for the Japanese police force to establish a special unit for international peace and cooperation activities.[55]

Finally, although not strictly 'civilian', an additional area where the Japanese SDF might develop a fuller contribution to UN peacekeeping is in capacity-building and security sector reform. In 2011, the Ministry of Defence advocated a capacity-building assistance project in Asia. Its purpose is to support the enhancement of defence capacity in the non-traditional security sector in developing countries in Asia, and subsequently to contribute to stabilization. Japanese officials see the project as an innovative new activity for creating regional stability by building national capacity to tackle non-traditional security threats through a continuous supply of training and technical assistance. Japan's Defence Plan in 2010 also supported capacity-building in the region. In 2011, the Ministry of Defence opened a special section for the capacity-building assistance project.[56]

18.6 CONCLUSION

Japan's policy towards UN peacekeeping operations has been caught in a contradiction between the country's stated preference for a 'UN-centred'

[54] *Annual Review of Global Peace Operations 2011*, pp. 131–2.

[55] The Report of the Round-Table Conferences on International Peace and Cooperation, 18 December 2002. At http://www.kantei.go.jp/jp/singi/kokusai (accessed 20 April 2012).

[56] Author's interview with Dr Susumu Takai, former Professor at the National Institute for Defense Studies, Tokyo, September 2011.

foreign policy and its constitutional restrictions on the overseas deployment of armed forces. At different times, the Japanese government, individual politicians, legal experts, and scholars have voiced an ambition to contribute more to UN peacekeeping missions. These views seemed to be in the ascendancy in the early 1990s, as the SDF made a major contribution to UNTAC and participated in UN peacekeeping in Mozambique, Rwanda, the Golan Heights, and East Timor. However, Japan's enthusiasm towards UN operations diminished in the twenty-first century, just as its neighbours China and South Korea strengthened their own contributions. This was partly due to the limited performance of the SDF in operational areas caused by its inability to bear arms, the re-emergence of domestic inhibitions to deploying troops overseas, and, paradoxically, the priority afforded to counter-terrorism operations in Afghanistan in the context of the Japan–US security alliance. The SDF's oil-fuelling missions in the Indian Ocean ended in 2010 after the new DJP government allowed the anti-terrorism law to expire, and it was no coincidence that in November 2011 the Japanese government then decided to send several hundred SDF engineers to the UN peacekeeping operation in the newly independent state of South Sudan (UNMISS).[57] By February 2012, this nearly doubled Japan's contribution of uniformed UN peacekeepers, bringing the total to nearly 470.

Overall, though, the principal barrier to larger Japanese contributions to UN peacekeeping remains the legal restriction on the deployment of SDF forces overseas and this seems unlikely to change in the near future, despite some subtle moves to increase engagement in training and rapid deployment. Because of these restrictions, the SDF will remain unable to implement key parts of most contemporary peacekeeping mandates, such as the protection of civilians and provision of area security. Therefore, attention—both in Japan and at the UN—should focus on other areas where Japan could make a larger contribution, notably in the fields of civilian personnel, the use of defence personnel for capacity-building, and policing. Once again, however, Japan's potential far outstrips its provision of peacekeepers to date. Moving debate away from constitutional reform and the provision of armed units towards a focus on these civilian and unarmed capacities might be one way of beginning to better harness Japan's potential as a peacekeeper.

[57] *The Japan Times*, 5 November 2011.

Part V

Conclusions

19

Explaining the National Politics of Peacekeeping Contributions

Alex J. Bellamy and *Paul D. Williams*

This book's preceding chapters make clear that the composition of an individual state's peacekeeping 'portfolio'—to borrow Coleman's phrase—is comprised of more than a simple binary decision about whether or not to contribute. First, states have multiple choices related to peacekeeping contributions. They choose *what* to contribute—do they contribute what the UN asks for, do they make a niche or specialized contribution, a token contribution, or no contribution at all? There are also demand-side issues because states have choices about *where* to contribute. Geographic proximity or regional affiliation can be an important positive influence (e.g., Brazil in Haiti, Nigeria in West Africa, or Russia in its 'near abroad'), but it can also work in the opposite direction—inhibiting states in peaceful neighbourhoods from contributing. Similarly, there are supply-side issues because states have choices about with *whom* to contribute. African and European states in particular have several institutional options when it comes to conducting peace operations and our case studies revealed some clear preferences. Most notably, perhaps, they identified a strong European preference for working through NATO and the European Union. An additional supply-side issue is the relatively fixed pool of capabilities and its zero-sum nature: capability employed for one task (national defence, a NATO mission, etc.) is not available for another (i.e., UN peacekeeping). A country's institutional preferences matter a lot, therefore.

Second, a country's peacekeeping portfolio is often the product of dozens of different decisions. Of the countries examined in this book, only a handful of determined contributors (Nepal, Bangladesh, Uruguay, and Ghana) explicitly assigned parts of their armed forces for UN peacekeeping duties. The great majority approached the question in an ad hoc manner. In several cases, including France, Japan, Nigeria, and Brazil, relatively ad hoc decisions about particular missions in their own neighbourhood (Bosnia and Herzegovina, Cambodia, Liberia, and Haiti respectively) had a profound effect on their overall peacekeeping profile. Third, in all our case studies, the ebb and flow of domestic politics was absolutely critical in shaping both general attitudes towards UN peacekeeping and decisions about individual missions.

This chapter highlights some of the key findings that emerged from the case studies and develops a new framework for understanding and comparing the national politics of UN peacekeeping contributions. It proceeds in three parts. First, we highlight common themes that emerged in the case study chapters, focusing especially on the factors that inhibited states from providing UN peacekeepers. Second, we outline a framework which accounts for both the general *dispositions* states hold towards the UN and peacekeeping in general, as well as the specific *decisions* they make about particular missions. It does this by focusing on the roles played by culture, institutions, and national policies. Third, we briefly reflect on why and how national policies might change.

19.1 RATIONALES AND INHIBITORS

Each of the case study chapters found evidence of at least some of our identified rationales (political, security, economic, institutional, and normative) influencing national decisions about whether and what to contribute. Significantly, the case studies showed that decisions were usually influenced by multiple rationales, the relative salience of which fluctuated depending on the context and the mission under consideration. In the book's introduction, we noted that most analyses of UN peacekeeping contributions tended to gloss over the specific factors that inhibited states from providing peacekeepers. When asked to identify such factors, the case study authors pointed to a combination of predispositions and specific policy issues that was just as complex as the motivating rationales. Decisions about whether and what to contribute are therefore best understood as products of a competition between motivating and inhibiting factors, the result of which is determined by political leaders who are presented by the context in question with limited options, preferences, and expected payoffs. We described the motivating rationales in the book's introductory chapter and so focus here on the inhibitors. Several inhibiting factors were evident across multiple cases and for purposes of comparison we categorize them as political, security, economic, institutional, and normative types. We found that most of the inhibitors were political in nature, though economic, security, institutional, and normative factors could also militate against providing peacekeepers.

19.1.1 Political

The case studies helped us identify five distinct political inhibitors to peacekeeping contributions. First, is the presence of alternative political or strategic priorities. Some states decided that their foreign and security policy interests were not well served by tying up resources in UN peacekeeping or that these other concerns were more pressing than UN peacekeeping. One of the alternatives identified was national security concerns that placed demands on military and/or police resources, especially fear of a direct security threat, regional insecurity, internal instability, and secessionism. Another was a desire to focus state policies on certain parts of the world; hence only peacekeeping missions in those areas were given serious consideration. The willingness of European states to send large numbers of UN peacekeepers to the Balkans and Lebanon while avoiding UN commitments in Africa is a case in point. Several of the countries examined in this book developed formal decision-making processes or White Papers which insisted that the government apply a national interest test when deciding whether or not to provide UN peacekeepers. These tests usually involved assessing the degree of risk associated with the mission and the extent to which the mission helped further national priorities.

A second set of inhibitors revolved around the politics of exceptionalism. A surprising number of the states examined here—including the US, UK, France, Russia, Brazil, and to some extent South Africa—viewed themselves as 'exceptional' and this inhibited their willingness to become regular major providers of UN peacekeepers. In some countries, an influential strand of exceptionalism promoted a self-image of possessing unique interests, responsibilities, capabilities, and/or perspectives. These states tended to see UN peacekeeping as usually somebody else's job, or in instrumental terms as a foreign policy tool, a vehicle for advancing regional or global interests, or as a means of supporting diplomatic/peacemaking activities. Exceptionalism reinforced a state's tendency to see the UN as only one among several potential mechanisms to pursue conflict management policies, to be highly selective about the missions it participated in, to expect senior positions in missions and to be able to influence mission design, and to expect an influential role in shaping peacekeeping doctrine and guidelines. When these expectations were confronted with the reality of official UN policies or objections by other member states, lingering disillusionment or frustration could result, inhibiting greater contributions to UN peacekeeping.

The third political inhibitor was the absence of serious international pressure to provide more peacekeepers. Officials from several states that are not among the UN's largest troop or police contributors observed that their governments did not feel under pressure to contribute more. Some officials from different countries reported that their governments were not seriously asked to contribute more, making it easy for them to maintain only token contributions and avoid national debate about playing a larger role. Additionally, outside South Asia, where there is a degree of informal peer pressure, many states feel limited or no serious pressure from their peers to provide more UN peacekeepers.

Fourth, many governments also experienced an absence of domestic pressure to contribute more to UN peacekeeping. In some cases, the domestic political environment was overtly hostile to such contributions. While the prestige associated with UN peacekeeping is a significant motivating factor in some countries, in others, especially in Western Europe and North America, strengthening contributions to UN peacekeeping is not actively promoted by publics and parliaments. Aversion to potential casualties in UN peacekeeping is also widespread, as these are not typically operations associated with national defence or core security interests where casualties may be tolerated. In theory, this makes it politically risky for leaders to provide more UN peacekeepers. In practice, it often means that the question of contributing more is not seriously raised and debated.

A fifth political inhibitor was the potential for peacekeeping to damage the national reputation. The UN's move towards a zero tolerance stance on discipline issues and the greater attention paid to crimes and abuses committed by peacekeepers has exposed poor discipline and standards among some contributors, giving rise to national embarrassment that might inhibit future peacekeeping contributions. In addition, long-standing concerns about HIV/AIDS infection rates in the armed forces of some contributing countries weakens their suitability for peacekeeping duties. Other health-related problems—such as the role that Nepalese peacekeepers played in introducing cholera to Haiti (see Chapter 13)—can cause profound national embarrassment and potentially inhibit contributors.

An additional consideration is that states are often concerned about damaging their reputation by deploying troops to operations that are likely to fail. Negative experiences such as those of Belgium in Rwanda, the Netherlands in Srebrenica, and the UK in Bosnia and Herzegovina have made some states more risk averse with regards to UN peacekeeping. In deciding whether or not to contribute to a particular mission, some states assess the political quality of the mission and its chances for success. Some contributors are inhibited from deploying to missions that lack a clear political strategy supported by the local parties, are deployed into hostile environments, or lack a clear exit strategy (see also Chapter 20). We observed earlier that some officials in European and North American states believe these features to be hallmarks of all UN operations and as a result, prefer to use alternative arrangements when deploying their own forces.

19.1.2 Security

Governments have choices about which institutions to utilize to address particular problems and they will usually work through those they believe will further their security goals at minimum cost. Some governments clearly prefer to work through alternative international organizations, alliances, or ad hoc coalitions. Sometimes, states may choose to operate unilaterally. Such preferences arise not just from a country's close relationship with its own regional institutions, as in the case of Turkey's strong preference to work through NATO. They also—perhaps mainly—emerge from negative assessments about the UN's capability. As a result of high profile failures in the 1990s, especially the troubled UNPROFOR mission in Croatia and Bosnia and Herzegovina, many European and North American military and political elites are highly sceptical about the UN's command and control mechanisms and have expressed deep institutional antipathy towards the UN. Some of these governments have informal rules of thumb dictating that only in exceptional circumstances would they place anything other than token contributions under UN command. As the case studies on the US, the UK, and France revealed, some Western states will only contribute significant forces when they can exercise direct operational control, whether through unilateral action, ad hoc coalitions, alliances such as NATO, or when special arrangements are established (e.g., the Strategic Military Cell in UNIFIL in 2006).

19.1.3 Economic

Financial arrangements are an additional disincentive for many Western states in particular because the UN's compensation payments do not fully reimburse the costs of deploying their military or police officers. The past decade has seen the gap increase between the UN's rates of compensation and actual deployment costs. In an era of increasing financial austerity in the West, these governments will be less likely to accept the financial burdens associated with UN deployments. (On the other hand, the UN's system of compensation payments for member states that provide peacekeepers might make the UN a more attractive vehicle for peacekeeping than other organizations which adopt the 'costs lie where they fall' approach.) As their economies grow and their militaries become increasingly sophisticated and therefore expensive, emerging powers such as India and Brazil will also find that any national financial benefits of UN peacekeeping become marginal at best. Financial considerations are increasingly becoming a consideration for developing states too. The UN's move towards enforcing minimum standards of training, capability, and equipment is increasing the costs associated with UN peacekeeping, squeezing the margins for some countries. It was reported that some contributors, such as Pakistan, were concerned that delays in reimbursement forced them to assume financial risk, which is becoming more difficult given increasing costs and falling margins.

19.1.4 Institutional

Civil–military relations were a key part of the institutional rationales described in this volume's introduction. One aspect that should be given greater prominence, however, is overt resistance to participating in UN peacekeeping within some military establishments (e.g., Britain, the United States, Russia, and Turkey). Sometimes, as in the British and French cases, this stems from past negative experiences and/or scepticism about UN command and control mechanisms and force structures, especially for robust, multidimensional operations. Sometimes it stems from a concern that training soldiers to be peacekeepers detracts from their war-fighting capabilities. As former US Secretary of State Condoleezzaa Rice famously put it with explicit reference to peacekeeping in the Balkans, 'We don't need to have the 82nd Airborne escorting kids to kindergarten.'[1] In other cases, such as Turkey, the military might not be encumbered with negative views but may have simply not factored UN peacekeeping into their internal rewards system, with the result that troops and units have few career incentives for becoming UN peacekeepers. In the Russian case, arguments over the interpretation and implementation of certain UN mandates encouraged the view that UN operations could be dominated by Western agendas.

19.1.5 Normative

Some contributing countries are uncomfortable with some elements of the expanding UN peacekeeping agenda. States are more likely to contribute to UN peacekeeping operations if they support the political values these missions promote. If consensus over these values breaks down, states which feel marginalized are less likely to make major contributions. Although arguments about a fundamental clash between Western and 'rising' powers are overblown, as Thierry Tardy has pointed out and this book's case studies confirm, there are clearly elements of the contemporary UN peacekeeping agenda which some states see as controversial.[2] For example, this book's chapters

[1] Quoted in Michael R. Gordon, 'The 2000 Campaign: The Military', *New York Times*, 21 October 2000.

[2] Thierry Tardy, 'Peace Operations: The Fragile Consensus', in *SIPRI Yearbook 2011* (Oxford: Oxford University Press, 2011), pp. 87–109.

on India and Brazil showed that the governments were cautious about the concept of 'robust peacekeeping' and preferred a traditional approach. Brazil even advocated its own approach to peacekeeping which downplayed the role of force and emphasized consent, impartiality, and peacebuilding. To some extent this places them at odds with current thinking and practice in the UN Secretariat, many Western states, and others on matters such as the protection of civilians, use of force, human rights, and consent acquisition and management. Although this has not yet had a major impact on contributions, these concerns did play a role in persuading India to withdraw from UNAMSIL and Dipankar Banerjee warned that unless India's view is taken seriously this discord might have negative effects in the future (see Chapter 10).

19.1.6 Summary

Explaining why states do (or do not) provide UN peacekeepers requires an account of both the rationales motivating contributions and the inhibitors constraining them. This book's case studies help us understand some of the key inhibitors and illustrate that sometimes factors which motivate contributions can also work in the opposite direction. Table 19.1 summarizes the key general motivating and inhibiting factors. It is equally important to recognize

Table 19.1 Rationales and Inhibitors for Providing Peacekeepers

Sector	Rationale	Inhibitor
Political	• National prestige • Voice in international affairs/UN • Peer pressure • Further other foreign policy goals	• Alternative priorities • Exceptionalism • Absence of international pressure • Difficult domestic politics • Damage to national reputation
Security	• Resolve regional conflicts • Contribute to global peace • Support a conflict party	• Preference for non-UN solutions
Economic	• Financial rewards: states, ministries, militaries, individuals, and firms	• Imposes additional costs
Institutional	• Gain operational experience • Prevent military involvement in domestic politics • Improve interoperability • Legitimize armed forces	• Military antipathy to UN • No internal incentives for UN peacekeeping
Normative	• Good Samaritan/Humanitarian • Support UN system	• Discomfort with normative agenda • Discomfort with 'robust' peacekeeping

that the relative value attached to the rationales and inhibitors and the effect this has on actual decision-making is contingent, i.e., it is deeply influenced by not only the domestic, political and institutional, but also the international context in question. The following section outlines a way of understanding the role that context plays in decision-making about UN peacekeeping.

19.2 A FRAMEWORK FOR ANALYSIS

This section sketches a framework for understanding how states make decisions about providing UN peacekeepers (see Figure 19.1). It identifies three elements organized into a two-stage process. The first two elements—*cultures* and *institutions*—influence a state's predisposition towards providing UN peacekeepers. A disposition, however, does not determine individual decisions about contributing to particular missions. This is the outcome of our framework's third element, *policies.*

Cultures are prevailing beliefs and habits about fundamental elements of a state's identity, including how it views its place in the world, the nature of international society, and the role of military power, as well as the potential of UN peacekeeping to achieve important goals, etc. Institutions are bureaucratic processes and practices that shape the advice given to decision-makers and therefore influence how they understand the realm of the possible. Together, the prevalent culture and institutions will affect a state's disposition towards providing UN peacekeepers. Our framework's third element, state policies, are informed by the country's strategic culture and institutions, as well as by prevailing policy standpoints, demand-side factors,

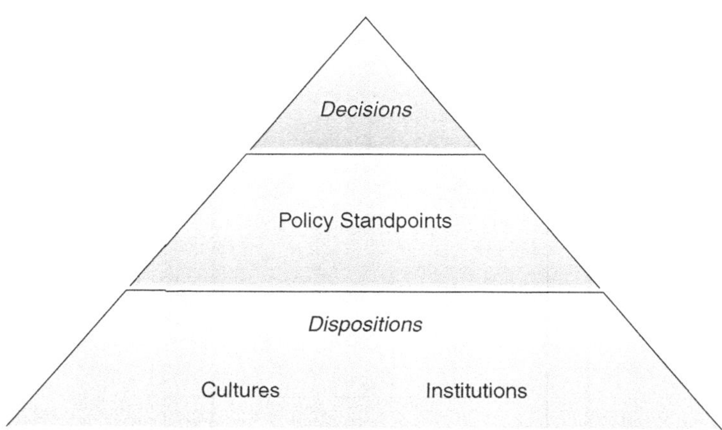

Figure 19.1 Providing UN Peacekeepers: A Framework for Analysis

and prevalent interpretations of the political context. It is the interaction between a state's disposition and its policies that produces a concrete decision on whether to provide UN peacekeepers based on judgements about the relative importance of specific rationales and inhibitors. This section elaborates this framework in more detail.

19.2.1 Cultures

General theories about peacekeeping contributions often assume that states think alike or are interest-maximizing rational actors that have similar conceptions of their interests, make decisions in similar ways, and face similar constraints. But interests are not natural; they are constructed and reconstructed over time, and this process necessarily occurs in a specific cultural context. We define culture as the sum of prevailing attitudes, beliefs, and habits shared by a state's policy elite. Of particular relevance here are shared beliefs about the nature of international society, a country's identity and role in the world, the presence of existential threats and challenges, the desirability and efficacy of UN peace operations both generally and in terms of private costs and benefits, the legitimacy of contributing to those operations, the role of the armed forces, and the proper relationship between military and civilian power. Countries might be disposed to provide peacekeepers because it fuels their self-image as 'global Good Samaritans', 'good international citizens', or as part of a 'non-aligned' group of states that supports the UN as an alternative to great power hegemony. Some 'Good Samaritans' contribute to collective peacekeeping efforts, in part, because it promotes what they regard as universal goods. Canada (periodically), the Netherlands, Japan, Norway, and Sweden have been identified as 'Good Samaritans' but this list is not exhaustive.[3] Alternatively, some states identify themselves as being normatively committed to the UN's system of conflict management because, like Ghana, they see it as the most legitimate framework and wish to be 'good international citizens', or, like India, see it as a fairer and more preferable alternative to great power hegemony and provide peacekeepers to support that system.

The idea that culture influenced security policy was first mooted in the 1970s by strategists who believed that American ethnocentrism 'skewed' its strategic thinking. In a now famous study for RAND, Jack Snyder warned that US nuclear strategy was premised on flawed assumptions about Soviet rationality which had led Americans to believe that the Soviets saw the issues in the same way that they did. This type of thinking created expectations about Soviet behaviour that were not grounded in a deep understanding of how the Soviets

[3] Alison Brysk, *Global Good Samaritans* (Oxford: Oxford University Press, 2009).

actually thought about the relevant issues. Instead of 'rational man', Snyder argued that Soviet thinking about nuclear issues was shaped by a combination of history, ideology, and institutional learning. For Snyder, this 'strategic culture' was a collection 'of ideas, conditioned emotional responses, and patterns of habitual behaviour that members of a national strategic community have acquired through instruction or imitation and share with each other'.[4]

This idea was developed in the 1980s and 1990s by realists and constructivists alike. Colin Gray, for instance, argued that 'national style' always influenced a state's security policies and defined strategic culture as 'modes of thought and action with respect to force, which derive from perceptions of the national historical experience, from aspirations for responsible behaviour in national terms . . . [and] the civic culture and way of life'.[5] Similarly, Ken Booth identified the role that the 'fog of culture' played in strategic policy in his call for the rational actor model to be replaced by an approach to strategy that encompassed culture, perception, and identity.[6] More recent accounts have shown that security policies can also be influenced by international norms, or what Jürgen Haacke and Paul Williams describe as 'regional security cultures', namely dispositions and habits about the most appropriate and effective ways of approaching security challenges shared by members of a regional organization.[7]

So rather than being driven by natural, a priori interests and putatively self-evident material facts, security policies are shaped by culture. Culture does not determine behaviour, but it does enable and constrain particular ways of thinking and acting. According to Gray, strategic cultures exercise a 'semi-permanent influence upon policy behaviour' that provides states with an enduring set of ideas through which to organize and explain their strategic behaviour in the absence of 'new historical experience'.[8] Cultures are not static but they do tend to be 'sticky' because they are embedded in historical experience, identity, and perceptions of geography, among other things.

Two different elements of strategic culture are directly relevant for understanding decisions to provide UN peacekeepers. The first might be described as 'frames'—intersubjective understandings that formulate roles and interpret objects. Michael Barnett has usefully defined frames as 'specific metaphors, symbolic representations and cognitive cues used to render or cast behaviour

[4] Jack L. Snyder, *The Soviet Strategic Culture* (Santa Monica, CA: RAND Corporation, 1977), p. 8.

[5] Colin S. Gray, *Nuclear Strategy and National Style* (Lanham, MD: Hamilton Press, 1986), pp. 36–7.

[6] Ken Booth, *Strategy and Ethnocentrism* (London: Croon Helm, 1979).

[7] Paul D. Williams and Jürgen Haacke, 'Regional Approaches to Conflict Management', in Chester Crocker, Fen Osler Hampson, and Pamela Aall (eds.), *Rewiring Regional Security* (, DC: US Institute of Peace Press, 2011), pp. 49–74.

[8] Gray, *Nuclear Strategy*, p. 37.

and events in an evaluative mode of action'.[9] Understood in this manner, frames do not *determine* a particular policy—much less a specific course of action—but they do influence the types of actions believed to be appropriate, legitimate, and effective in a given situation.[10]

Table 19.2 provides a caricature of how three fictional countries of similar size and wealth and with similar political systems might use different frames to evaluate whether or not to provide UN peacekeepers, both in general and in relation to a particular crisis.

In Table 19.2, Country A would be averse to providing UN peacekeepers because its policy-makers see them as a futile waste of military resources and are sceptical about the utility of multilateral cooperation. Country B's disposition is hesitant towards peacekeeping, but it might be prepared to contribute to traditional peacekeeping to strengthen and promote rules of coexistence

Table 19.2: Frames and the Decision to Provide UN Peacekeepers

Issue	Country A	Country B	Country C
Nature of international society	Realist: states pursue own interests; little chance for cooperation.	Pluralist: states can agree on basic rules and cooperate to maintain society.	Cosmopolitan: there are universal principles of peace and justice which states can uphold through cooperation.
National identity	Exceptionalist: the state is exceptional and justified in promoting its own values.	Nationalist: the state is inward-looking, protects its citizens, and focuses on national well-being.	Cosmopolitan: the state is outward-looking and believes it can be a force for good in the world.
View of war and peace	Conflict is endemic and hence warfare inevitable.	Conflict is a product of imperialism, aggression, or underdevelopment.	Conflict is a product of injustice and human rights abuse.
Role of the UN	The UN is largely ineffective.	The UN can help maintain peace between states with their consent.	The UN can promote universal goods and foster cooperation.
Use of military force	The armed forces should serve the national interest.	The armed forces should focus on national defence.	The armed forces should perform many functions.

[9] Michael Barnett, 'Culture, Strategy and Foreign Policy Change: Israel's Road to Oslo', *European Journal of International Relations*, 5:1 (1999), p. 17.

[10] There is a sizeable literature on framing. The classic statement is Erving Goffman, *Frame Analysis: An Essay on the Organization of Experience* (Cambridge, MA: Harvard University Press, 1974). In relation to the framing of political violence see, *inter alia*, Pippa Norris, Marion Just, and Montague Kern (eds.), *Framing Terrorism* (London: Routledge, 2003); Phillip Hammond, *Framing Post-Cold War Conflicts* (Manchester: Manchester University Press, 2007); Robert Entman, *Projections of Power* (Chicago: University of Chicago Press, 2004). On 'frames' in the context of peacebuilding, see Séverine Autesserre, 'Hobbes and the Congo: Frames, Local Violence, and International Intervention', *International Organization*, 63:2 (2009), pp. 249–80.

between states. Country C, on the other hand, is well disposed to contribute troops to the full range of UN peace operations. In reality, these frames are less clear-cut, are usually the subject of political contestation, and they do not determine policy. Nevertheless, a politician in Country B would find it harder to justify to his/her own public sending 5,000 troops to UNAMID than one in Country C.

The second relevant element of strategic culture is 'embedded practices'—long-standing policies, procedures, and habits that enable or inhibit troop-giving. Embedded practices likely to facilitate positive dispositions to UN peacekeeping include: the identification of peacekeeping as a legitimate military function in national defence strategy papers; the presence of a working relationship with the UN in force generation, including habitual commitment to assigning standby forces; positive working relations with UN officials; and the integration of peacekeeping into the roles and duties assigned to regional organizations of which the country is a member. Conversely, embedded practices might work in the opposite direction if military and political leaders are habitually focused on internal security issues or national defence; there are policies insisting that national troops not be placed under foreign command or deployed outside their immediate neighbourhood; there is no or little experience of cooperation with the UN; or there is deep-seated reticence towards contributing national resources to multilateral bodies. In democratic states, embedded practices will often transcend political differences and withstand changes of government. For example, the US' reluctance to deploy its troops under foreign command was apparent under the administrations of Bill Clinton, George W. Bush, and Barack Obama. Likewise, Canada continues to train its armed forces in peacekeeping despite being governed by a party that is deeply sceptical about both peacekeeping and the UN.

These insights about strategic cultures—and their respective frames and embedded practices—yield two important points for those interested in influencing UN peacekeeping contributions. First, in most cases, persuading new states to provide peacekeepers or current contributors to significantly and regularly increase their contribution across different missions is likely to require significant reform of the state's strategic culture. This will not happen overnight. In the absence of external shocks or coercion (see below), attempts to alter state behaviour without the requisite cultural change are likely to meet significant resistance. Where states succumb to external pressure to provide peacekeepers but do not undergo a requisite change in strategic culture, they are likely to engage only in surface-level changes to existing behaviour resulting in small/symbolic or irregular contributions. This may already be the default position for many states and may partly explain why so many have portfolios comprised primarily of token contributions (see Chapter 2). Nevertheless, the second insight is that even within the confines of existing strategic cultures, disputes over how to respond to specific crises are common. As a consequence, it is always worth articulating why providing peacekeepers might be a good idea in a particular mission even if such arguments run against the grain of a state's strategic culture, as they might convince key policy entrepreneurs or decision-makers.[11]

19.2.2 Institutions

Bureaucracies, whether civilian or military, are not simply neutral instruments of government policy. Rather, they shape the policy process in important ways. David Beetham has identified four shared features of bureaucracies: First, they are hierarchic in that each official has a specific role to play and is answerable to a superior. Second, they display continuity inasmuch as they provide ongoing full-time employment and the possibility of career progression usually irrespective of the political fortunes of individual governments. Third, they are impersonal inasmuch as work is conducted according to prescribed rules and procedures designed to eliminate arbitrariness. Finally, they possess expertise in that officials are organized according to technical functions and control access to knowledge on the basis of similar criteria.[12] According to Max Weber, bureaucratic efficiency derives from the fact that they are impersonal and rules-oriented actors that display a shared culture, rules, working procedures, and worldview, and where individual success is measured in relation to these values.[13]

How do these bureaucratic cultures and systems impact on decisions to provide UN peacekeepers? In their work on international bureaucracies, Michael Barnett and Martha Finnemore have identified some general effects that are directly relevant to foreign and security policy decision-making.[14] Three are particularly useful for our purposes.

First, bureaucratic rules prescribe 'standard operating procedures' that allow the organization to fulfil its role efficiently and delineate appropriate and inappropriate ways of responding to problems. Thus, organizations with limited experience in cooperating with UN peacekeeping missions and without procedures to establish and guide such cooperation are less likely to

[11] On the concept of policy entrepreneurs see James M. Goldgeier, *Not Whether but When: The U.S. Decision to Enlarge NATO* (Washington, DC: Brookings Institution Press, 1999).

[12] David Beetham, *Bureaucracy* (Minneapolis, MN: University of Minnesota Press, 2nd edn. 1996), pp. 9–12.

[13] Max Weber, 'Bureaucracy', in H. H. Gerth and C. Wright-Mills (eds.), *From Max Weber: Essays in Sociology* (Oxford: Oxford University Press, 1978).

[14] See Michael N. Barnett and Martha Finnemore, 'The Politics, Power and Pathologies of International Organizations', *International Organization*, 53:4 (1999), pp. 699–732; Michael N. Barnett and Martha Finnemore, *Rules for the World: International Organizations in Global Politics* (Ithaca, NY: Cornell University Press, 2004).

provide troops than organizations with experience, designated officials, and procedures for handling this relationship.

Second, bureaucracies foster their own organizational culture which shapes the way their officials see the world and understand the problems that they confront. This is not always consistent with a country's prevailing strategic culture because bureaucrats may, for instance, prioritize organizational interests. Hence, even in a country that is culturally well disposed towards peacekeeping, defence officials might oppose contributing to a particular mission because of the risks to their personnel, because they believe the armed forces are overstretched, because they worry that peacekeeping might degrade their ability to conduct high-intensity combat operations, or because they do not want to participate in multinational command structures.

Third, bureaucracies are competitive and tend towards self-promotion. This can affect peacekeeping in two ways. On the one hand, military bureaucracies facing a loss of purpose at the end of the Cold War did not argue that there was a diminished need for military expenditure and capacity. Instead, they set about finding new roles and expanding into new areas. For Whitworth, this partly explains the arrival of new peacekeepers in the 1990s.[15] On the other hand, however, bureaucracies might recognize that higher political, social, and economic value is attached to national defence than to peacekeeping and that the prospects for growth are greater in addressing putative internal and external threats than in UN peacekeeping. An additional dimension of this issue is contestation within bureaucracies. Particularly relevant to peacekeeping are inter-service rivalries—peacekeeping tends to prioritize armies and may draw resentment from navies and air forces—and interdepartmental rivalries—ministries of foreign affairs and defence may have different priorities and worldviews. Bureaucratic advice may therefore reflect a particular departmental view or one arm of the armed forces.

Another way in which bureaucracies influence decision-making about peacekeeping is through path-dependency or what might be understood as the evolution of 'peacekeeping habits'. Whichever rationale or combination of rationales leads a country to provide UN peacekeepers, once it contributes above a certain level, path-dependency can help sustain that state's commitment as a contributor.[16] Once states commit to UN peacekeeping, they can internalize the peacekeeping role and are more likely to develop institutionalized processes and habits that support an ongoing commitment across multiple missions.[17] Moreover, the UN Department of Peacekeeping Operations

[15] Sandra Whitworth, *Men, Militarism and UN Peacekeeping* (Boulder, CO: Lynne Rienner, 2004), p. 25.

[16] Of course, there are no guarantees, as the significant drop in UN contributions during the 2000s by Kenya, Ukraine, and Poland, among others, illustrates.

[17] Davis B. Bobrow and Mark A. Boyer, 'Maintaining System Stability: Contributions to Peacekeeping Operations', *Journal of Conflict Resolution*, 41:6 (1997), p. 731.

also gets into the habit of approaching certain countries for peacekeepers, notably those with which it has personal relationships and prior experience of positive cooperation. To the extent that the UN focuses its requests on established contributor states, this reinforces the degree to which some states feel almost no pressure to provide some or more peacekeepers. The effects of path-dependency are particularly evident in South Asia, but it is also a factor in Ghana and Uruguay, which have developed the 'habit' of regularly providing UN peacekeepers. The tendency towards path-dependency has been facilitated by the increasing number of peacekeeping training centres established around the world since the mid-1990s. These help foster peacekeeping habits and give states a pool of trained peacekeepers that they then see a need to employ.

19.2.3 Policies

National strategic culture and bureaucratic institutions create a general disposition that either enables or constrains decisions to provide UN peacekeepers. But dispositions do not determine individual decisions about particular missions or the level of contribution that might be made. These are most immediately influenced by 'policy standpoints', demand-side factors, and the political context.

What Kerry Longhurst has called 'policy standpoints' are 'the contemporary, widely accepted interpretations as to how best core values are to be promoted through policy channels'.[18] This might be described as prevailing 'common sense' within the establishment, which sets the default position of bureaucrats and politicians when confronted with armed conflict or requests for peacekeepers. Take the case of the policy elite of a Nordic country that 'frames' itself as a 'Good Samaritan' and has embedded practices that include frequent and active cooperation with UN peacekeeping missions. Here, the state's default policy standpoint when confronted by armed conflict would be to work through the UN or other relevant bodies and explore the options for deploying peacekeepers. The deeper cultural elements frame issues in particular ways and make certain types of behaviour appear more appropriate, effective, and feasible than other courses of action. Naturally, policy standpoints can also inhibit troop-contributing behaviour. For example, many states hold as 'common sense' the view that they ought to prioritize contributions to missions in their own region because the mix of national interest and community interest is stronger in these cases.

Demand-side factors that influence decisions about whether to contribute to particular missions include the geographic distribution of conflict and peace

[18] Kerry Longhurst, *Germany and the Use of Force* (Manchester: Manchester University Press, 2004), p. 17.

operations, the degree to which the host environment is thought to be hostile, and whether the host state will consent to troops from particular countries.[19] There are many cases of host states refusing to accept troops from particular contributors. An important recent example occurred in Sudan when the authorities demanded that UNAMID retain its 'predominantly African character' and placed considerable barriers to the deployment of peacekeepers from certain non-African countries.

Deployment decisions will also be shaped by the political context. Myriad domestic and international political considerations impact on individual decisions to provide peacekeepers and may work to reinforce or mitigate the background factors. These include the level of domestic support for a mission, the degree of international political support, the degree of local support in the theatre of operations, operational issues such as the type and clarity of a mandate and expected exit strategies, the availability of forces, and historical connections between the contributing country and the host state.

Another significant political factor is the actual decision-making process for peacekeeping. This book's case studies illustrate the wide variation in how states take decisions about providing UN peacekeepers. Only a minority of them had formal procedures for making decisions and in several cases where formal procedures existed they were seldom used except to rubber-stamp decisions adopted elsewhere. Nonetheless, the relative roles of the executive and legislature and the relationship between relevant ministries were frequently identified as significant factors. In almost every case, decisions to contribute were taken by the president or head of government—though in Japan several arms of government have a say and an effective veto, including both the executive and the legislature. Sometimes, decisions were made on the basis of advice after the UN request had been considered by relevant government departments. In other cases, most notably Brazil and Nigeria, it was almost solely down to the president. In one Russian deployment in Transdnestria, the decision to deploy was taken by two generals.

Domestic political considerations are therefore always a factor in decision-making, as are considerations about other demands placed upon the armed forces and/or police, political attitudes towards the UN and assessment of its peacekeeping record, the feasibility of the proposed mission, and the politics associated with the mission. These factors appeared more salient in cases where legislatures assumed a more active role. Although they often had the formal right to oversee decisions about peacekeeping deployments and the appropriation of resources to that end, in all but a small number of cases

[19] For a broader discussion of demand-side issues see Virginia Page Fortna and Lisa L. Martin, 'Peacekeepers as Signals: The Demand for International Peacekeeping in Civil Wars', in Helen Milner and Andrew Moravscik (eds.), *Power, Interdependence and Nonstate Actors in World Politics* (Princeton, NJ: Princeton University Press, 2009), pp. 87–107.

parliaments were not central to decision-making about individual UN requests. This might help by streamlining the political process, but the absence of parliamentary engagement might also weaken domestic support for contributions and limit public debate and awareness of the relevant issues.

It is also notable that different countries gave the leading role on peacekeeping requests to different departments/ministries and the armed forces had different degrees of latitude. This affected the priority given to different issues. In some states, a presidential style dictated that the head of government took an early decision and the rest of government then had to implement it. In most of this book's case studies though, UN requests were handled either by the foreign affairs department or by the defence ministry and subsequent discussion was based on the initial assessment by that department. Anecdotally, when it came to declining UN requests for peacekeepers, the initial assessment was also often the final assessment. In many cases, requests were not seriously considered in national capitals or were handled by the country's permanent mission to the UN. Permanent missions themselves played greater or lesser roles in different countries, but usually tended to be much more engaged with these issues than national capitals. The exceptions were those contributor countries that had established a strong 'path-dependency' (see above) and hence, permanent missions did not appear to play a decisive role in decision-making. In some cases, the military itself played a key role in shaping policy on UN peacekeeping, either in a supportive manner, as in Uruguay, or by displaying significant antipathy, as in Turkey and the US.

19.2.4 Summary

No general theory provides an adequate explanation of why states provide UN peacekeepers. Instead of developing another problematic general theory, our approach was to identify some broad rationales and inhibitors and outline a framework for analysis that provides a basis for identifying trends and comparing cases by illuminating the contextual factors that impact on particular decisions. Our framework emphasizes the interplay between the *dispositions*, which emerge from a state's strategic culture and its bureaucratic institutions, and the *policy standpoints* which together produce specific *decisions*. Table 19.3 illustrates how existing explanations might fit within this framework.

19.3 HOW MIGHT POLICIES CHANGE?

Why do states change their position on providing UN peacekeepers? One useful way of thinking about change is to distinguish between 'fine-tuning' and

Table 19.3 Explaining UN Troop Contributions: An Indicative Framework

	Element	Factor
Cultures	Frames	- Identity - Democracy - Worldview (realist, pluralist, cosmopolitan, etc.) - Regional solidarity (security community, regional security cultures, etc.)
	Embedded practices	- Pursuit of prestige - Cooperation with regional and/or multilateral organizations - Outward/inward disposition
Institutions	Bureaucratic rules	- National interest test - Willingness to place personnel under foreign command - Presence/absence of procedures for handling troop requests
	Bureaucratic culture	- Outward-/inward-looking - Extent to which peacekeeping is seen to aid/endanger personnel - Extent to which bureaucrats believe they profit from peacekeeping
	Bureaucratic competition	- Fit between peacekeeping and bureaucratic interests
Policies	Policy standpoint	- National interest test - Habit of cooperation with UN - Beliefs about utility of peacekeeping - Peacekeeping enhances prestige
	Demand-side	- Geographic location of conflict - Host state consent - Hostile/benign environment
	Political context	- Domestic support for individual mission - Regional and global political context - Suitable mandate/exit strategy - Availability of forces/other commitments

'fundamental' changes.[20] 'Fine-tuning' involves the reinterpretation of already existing cultures, institutional practices, and policies to address newly perceived challenges or lessons learned from past experience. With regard to contributions to UN peacekeeping, 'fine-tuning' might involve recalibrating contributions to accommodate new doctrines such as the protection of civilians, pooling resources with neighbouring countries to provide multinational packages to the UN, or deciding to concentrate peacekeeping contributions in a particular geographic area. Although such changes are important, they remain consistent with prevailing beliefs about the role of peace operations, the merit of contributing, and the desirability of working through the UN system.

[20] This distinction is drawn from Longhurst, *Germany and the Use of Force*, p. 18.

The literature on policy change suggests that there are at least three key drivers of 'fine-tuning' changes. The first is 'institutional learning', which occurs where bureaucracies learn to develop more effective ways of pursuing established goals in a context where measures of effectiveness remain relatively constant.[21] The second is 'convergence', where cultures, bureaucracies, and policies are adapted, but not fundamentally altered, to better reflect shared regional and global understandings of 'desirable and acceptable' forms of behaviour.[22] This may reflect deeper cultural shifts in international society or be prompted by guidance, lessons learning, standard setting, mandate drafting, or capability requests by the UN itself.[23] The third is 'recalibration', where pre-existing beliefs, institutional arrangements, and policies are applied to new external issues, producing new types of practice. These fine-tuning changes are relatively frequent and part of the routine of bureaucratic politics within and between states and international organizations.

'Fundamental' changes, in contrast, are rare and involve the alteration or removal of a core aspect of a prevailing culture, institutional practice, or policy, sometimes in a dramatic fashion. For example, a fundamental change might involve moving from participating in UN operations to participating only in coalitions of the willing as a matter of stated policy, or a shift from a situation where the armed forces are not permitted to operate abroad to one where they can deploy overseas to carry out certain peacekeeping tasks. Sometimes, fundamental change might involve the collapse of cultural beliefs that enabled or inhibited contributions to UN peace operations.

Fundamental changes tend to be brought about by one or more of the following processes. First, a rapid proliferation of fine-tuning changes may ultimately undermine a central tenet of the prevailing culture, bureaucratic practice, or policy. For example, a state that is generally opposed to 'robust' peacekeeping but which contributes forces to many operations with protection mandates may find that its forces are compelled to adopt robust postures or face criticism for failing to protect civilians and that this, in turn, prompts it to rethink its policy stance.

Second, an external shock (i.e., external to the national bureaucracy) or environmental change may render a core tenet of a culture or institutional practice redundant. This might include internal political instability, economic

[21] Peter Haas, 'Introduction: Epistemic Communities and International Policy Coordination', *International Organization*, 46:1 (1992), pp. 1–35. See also, Lise Howard, *UN Peacekeeping in Civil Wars* (Cambridge: Cambridge University Press, 2007) and Thorsten Benner, Stephan Mergenthaler, and Philipp Rotman, *The New World of UN Peace Operations* (Oxford: Oxford University Press, 2011).

[22] Richard Higgott, 'Beyond Embedded Liberalism', in Philip Gummett (ed.), *Globalization and Public Policy* (Cheltenham: Edward Elgar, 1996), p. 21.

[23] On the role of global culture see Roland Paris, 'Peacekeeping and the Constraints of Global Culture', *European Journal of International Relations*, 9:3 (2003), pp. 441–73.

shocks, or environmental disasters that inhibit capacity to contribute or provide new reasons to seek international recognition by contributing. Alternatively, this might result from something more mundane like the election of a new government that is more or less well disposed to peacekeeping. The most dramatic example might be that of Yugoslavia, which ceased to be a troop contributor when the country literally fell apart.

Third, a legitimacy crisis may cause a cultural belief, institutional practice, or policy to lose its domestic consensus. Such crises can only be resolved by the recalibration of legitimacy through the reconfiguring of the belief, practice, or policy in question.[24] For example, the loss of peacekeepers to hostile action, accusations of widespread sexual misconduct, or the adoption of peacekeeping practices inimical to national policies and attitudes might dramatically reduce the domestic legitimacy of contributing UN peacekeepers, forcing the government to rethink its stance. A fourth potential source of fundamental change is foreign imposition by force, bribery, or coercion.

19.4 CONCLUSION

The national politics of peacekeeping contributions are shaped by both rationales motivating a state to provide UN peacekeepers and inhibiting factors. Decisions as to whether and what to contribute result from competition between the rationales and inhibitors in each of the five sectors we identified, i.e., political, security, economic, institutional, and normative. Because the relative weight of the factors and their impact on policies and decisions is context-dependent, our framework views the decision to provide UN peacekeepers as essentially a two-level game. First, cultural and bureaucratic factors influence a state's general predisposition towards providing UN peacekeepers. However, they do not determine the decision on whether or not to contribute to a particular UN operation or what to contribute. These decisions are informed by cultural and bureaucratic factors but mediated by policy standpoints, demand-side issues, and the contemporary political context. Finally, there are several possible mechanisms by which such policies might change.

Since decision-making about UN peacekeeping contributions is contingent, analysis will be necessarily complex and the search for general theories quixotic. But this also means there are opportunities for the UN to influence the politics of peacekeeping contributions, even if only marginally. In the final chapter we analyse the contemporary challenges facing the UN and how it might positively influence the politics of providing peacekeepers.

[24] See Christian Reus-Smit, 'International Crises of Legitimacy', *International Politics*, 44:2–3 (2007), pp. 157–74.

20

UN Force Generation: Key Lessons and Future Strategies

Alex J. Bellamy and *Paul D. Williams*

We opened this volume with the challenges confronting UN peacekeeping in the twenty-first century and noted the UN's need to 'expand the base' of troop- and police-contributing countries. Persuading states to contribute more and better peacekeepers would be easier if we understood why they contribute, the key impediments to contributing, and how the two sets of issues relate in different contexts. As the preceding chapters make clear, although domestic politics played the primary role in shaping a state's willingness to provide peacekeepers, some scope remained for the UN to influence the outcome to its own advantage.

The contemporary challenge confronting the UN is not simply one of attracting the right number of uniformed peacekeepers. Indeed, UN officials report that they are often able to recruit sufficient numbers of basic infantry soldiers for their missions. The challenge lies in recruiting the right sort of personnel and force multiplier capabilities. As Donald Daniel pointed out (in Chapter 1), the past decade or so has seen unprecedented growth in the number of troops contributed to peacekeeping operations, a dramatic rise in the number of contributing countries, and compared to other institutional vehicles for deploying peacekeepers, the UN has a good recruitment record. On the downside, however, Daniel found that the UN is more heavily reliant on contributors with limited military capacities than non-UN operations and that as a result, the UN has proved less able than non-UN operations to secure the key specializations needed for multidime nsional and/or robust operations.

In theory at least, 'expanding the base' of UN peacekeeping contributors should increase the pool of expertise available and may, in the longer term, increase the quality of even basic infantry by creating a degree of competition for places among contributing states. This chapter considers ways in which the

UN might influence member states' choices and encourage them to contribute more and better peacekeepers to UN-led operations. It does so in two parts. First, we outline three contemporary challenges that affect the UN's ability to generate forces for peacekeeping. Second, we offer some suggestions that might help the UN to positively influence the national politics of providing peacekeepers.

20.1 UN FORCE GENERATION: THREE CONTEMPORARY CHALLENGES

As several of the preceding chapters pointed out, the global financial crisis, the difficulty level of several current UN missions, and the problem of tokenism pose significant challenges for UN force generation. Expanding the pool of capabilities for peacekeeping will require the UN to develop ways of alleviating these challenges.

20.1.1 Global Financial Crisis

Although highly uneven in its effects, the global financial crisis has increased the economic pressures on many current and potential troop- and police-contributing countries. On the one hand, it has increased the likelihood that many states will reduce their defence budgets and cut personnel numbers. While this may bring other benefits, it reduces the pool of available resources for UN peacekeeping and increases potential for competition between international organizations for deployable capabilities. In this context, it is notable that East Asia has not seen cuts in defence spending, but instead, several states rapidly modernizing their armed forces. Indeed, 2011 was the first year when East Asian states spent more on defence than European countries. At the current rate of growth it will not be long before several Asian states are capable of fielding the sorts of specialized capabilities that have traditionally been the preserve of Western states. South Korea, Singapore (albeit in relatively small numbers), and Japan already can, but China, Malaysia, Thailand, Indonesia, and Vietnam will not be far behind. The global financial crisis should therefore prompt analysts to 'look east' for potential sources of peacekeeping capability.

There is another important way in which the financial crisis could present the UN with new opportunities. Several of our case studies, especially Bangladesh, Uruguay, and Nepal, highlighted the potential for militaries to embrace UN peacekeeping as a way of securing legitimacy, protecting their budgets, and earning additional income. In each of these cases, the military embraced peacekeeping after a period of profound instability and in the face of serious challenges to the armed forces themselves. Speculation is rife that with the drawdown of forces from Afghanistan, several Western militaries might seek to re-engage with UN peacekeeping for similar reasons but, as yet, there is little hard evidence to support this view.

20.1.2 Difficult Missions

This book's case studies demonstrate that many UN member states are highly sensitive to the nature of particular peacekeeping operations and that this influences contribution decisions. Naturally, all contributing countries want to avoid casualties and hence exhibit greater reluctance to contribute troops to missions that are thought overly dangerous. Contributing states thus typically assess the degree of host government consent for a mission and might be deterred from participating in operations where this is questionable (e.g., UNAMID, UNMIS, but see also the AU Mission in Somalia). National publics are also frequently intolerant of casualties sustained on peacekeeping operations. This poses a particular challenge to the emerging concept of 'robust peacekeeping'. Potential contributors might also be deterred by controversies associated with individual missions, be they political controversies of the sort experienced by UNOCI or UNMEE, or those associated with indiscipline as occurred in MONUC/MONUSCO and UNAMSIL.

An associated issue—and one that relates to broader questions about the public image of UN peacekeeping—is that contributing countries are often sensitive to the credibility of exit strategies.[1] Except perhaps where economic motivations are paramount, states tend to be more comfortable contributing to missions that have clear goals, feasible political benchmarks, and a viable exit strategy, than to missions that lack these basic elements. It is noteworthy that almost all of the countries surveyed in this book that established formal decision-making structures or guidelines included criteria relating to the viability of the political process, the mission's aims, and exit strategies. States are also likely to be more sceptical about participating in missions that are perceived to be either treading water or lacking the conditions for success. Several UN member states have learned from experience that participation in a failed mission damages national standing and can incur domestic political costs.

[1] For a discussion see Richard Caplan (ed.), *Exit Strategies and State Building* (Oxford: Oxford University Press, 2012).

20.1.3 Token Contributions

When responding to UN requests for peacekeepers, states have multiple options: contribute forces as requested, make a specialized contribution, make a token contribution, or decline the request. The prevalence of token contributions presents a particular set of challenges for the UN, i.e., the deployment of less than forty uniformed personnel who are not normally deployed as formed specialized units. Where small numbers are deployed in specialized teams, these contributions are not best described as 'token' because they add significant value to a mission's capabilities, usually in areas such as communications, engineering, information-gathering and analysis, logistics, mobility (aerial or surface), medicine, mine-clearance, and units capable of high intensity operations (see below). As Coleman pointed out in Chapter 2, token contributions are now remarkably common in UN peacekeeping and often represent a deliberately chosen and distinctive mode of participation rather than being simply products of resource constraints.

From the outside, token contributions appear to be a highly inefficient way of providing peacekeepers. They are popular among member states, Coleman found, because they satisfy certain political and sometimes pecuniary interests at minimal cost to the contributing state. Politically, they are useful because they expand the options available to states and offer low-risk ways of participating in UN peacekeeping; they establish a country as a mission contributor—which gives it access to privileged information about the operation, membership of the C34, and the right to attend meetings on the mission; and they create prestige both domestically and within the UN because prestige derives in part from contributing per se, not from the size (or quality) of that contribution. Token contributions allow individuals to be placed into key positions of influence or rewarded with staff office or military observer postings that have much higher allowances than regular military peacekeepers. Token contributions also allow developed states to participate in missions without taking on the financial burden of supporting deployments of fully formed troop contingents.

UN officials are reluctant, however, to dismiss token contributions as wholly negative. Viewed in a more positive light, they might also provide new and emerging contributors with a way to familiarize themselves with the relevant UN procedures and mechanisms and hence act as a stepping stone to more significant contributions in the future. While this is certainly true—as attested by recent cases such as Mongolia which came to peacekeeping through token contributions and is gradually expanding its participation—and may provide a useful opportunity for the UN to influence national decision-makers, the great majority of token contributors are not new to peacekeeping and have not used tokenism as a stepping stone to bigger and/

or better contributions. UN officials also point out, however, that token contributions of staff officers can be a significant force multiplier. There is a large academic literature on the value of military leadership that has not yet translated into a similar literature on leadership in peacekeeping. But clearly strong and effective leaders play an important role in shaping missions and contributing to effectiveness. Thus, the careful placing of one or two highly effective officers into leadership positions can add much more value to a mission than the numbers alone might suggest.

20.2 FUTURE STRATEGIES FOR THE UN

We conclude this book by proposing some ways in which the UN might positively influence national peacekeeping politics by encouraging and facilitating the provision of more and better peacekeepers. In light of this volume's preceding chapters, we argue that the UN should adopt a force generation strategy based on four core elements. First, continue the shift of focus in force acquisition from numbers to capabilities and offer different ways for contributing countries to provide capabilities for UN missions. Second, disseminate positive images of and narratives about UN peacekeepers to help promote national cultures and political contexts which are more positively disposed to UN peacekeeping. Third, make it easier for member states to participate by building stronger working relations between the UN Department of Peacekeeping Operations (DPKO) and national capitals. Fourth, develop medium- and long-term force generation strategies by identifying, augmenting, and building the capabilities required for UN peacekeepers to successfully complete their mandates.

20.2.1 From Numbers to Capabilities and Partnerships

The UN has been less successful than some other organizations in securing specialized contributions. This is a problem because today's multidimensional peace operations have complex mandates that extend well beyond the skill sets of infantry troops with basic training. One of the principal reasons why the UN has not secured sufficient specialized capability for its missions is that this capability is held primarily by Western states, which prefer to operate outside UN command and control and have had alternative strategic priorities. As the case studies on the US, UK, and France demonstrated, Western governments often view their militaries as too highly trained and equipped to be used as rank and file UN peacekeepers. When combined with the other inhibiting factors outlined in Chapter 19, this makes it unlikely that Western states will contribute large infantry contingents to UN peacekeeping. It is possible, though, that they might consider contributing specialized capabilities relating to heavy lift, mobility, intelligence, medevac and hospital provision, as well as rapid reaction, high-intensity, and over-the-horizon deterrence tasks. In the medium term, mission specialization and the use of partnership arrangements could be used to forge a practical division of labour to achieve the UN's peacekeeping mandates without having to persuade Western governments to place significant assets under UN command and control—something which our case studies suggest is a long way from being a realistic prospect. This suggests the need for a shift in emphasis in UN force generation away from the acquisition of certain numbers of troops/police towards the acquisition of mission capabilities through a combination of direct recruitment into UN-led missions and partnerships with contributors who prefer that their assets remain outside UN command and control and—we might add—the UN's system of finance.

Operationally, it is useful to distinguish between 'tightly coupled' and 'loosely coupled' partnerships. In 'tightly coupled' missions, such as KFOR/UNMIK in Kosovo, the UN and non-UN components are jointly mandated and share some common command or political decision-making structure. 'Loosely coupled' partnerships, in contrast, are ad hoc and the different components do not share formal institutional structures, though the UN and non-UN elements may cooperate very closely. Partnerships can also be distinguished on the basis of timing: some arrangements might be sequenced such that non-UN operations precede or follow a UN mission, while others might be conducted in parallel with a UN peacekeeping operation.

Four types of potential partnerships between Western states and UN missions can be identified:

- 'Spear-head/vanguard' operations where a Western-led multinational force deploys first and prepares the security environment for a follow-on UN peacekeeping mission, e.g., INTERFET in East Timor or the Multinational Force in Haiti.
- 'Stabilization operations' in which Western forces work alongside UN and/or other international peace operations to provide military security, e.g., *Operation Licorne* (Côte d'Ivoire) or *Operation Palliser* (Sierra Leone).
- 'Fire-fighting' operations in which Western troops provide in-theatre military support to a UN mission, particularly by providing enforcement capabilities, e.g., SFOR in Bosnia and *Operation Artemis* in the DRC.
- 'Over-the-horizon' operations whereby Western forces are dispatched close to the theatre in question to perform a deterrent role or provide enforcement capability if required, e.g., the US Joint Task Force in

Liberia, and the European Union Force in the Democratic Republic of Congo.[2]

This is not an exhaustive list of possible partnerships but they provide potential models for harnessing relatively large-scale specialized contributions from countries that might be reluctant to place major troop contingents under UN command and control.

20.2.2 Stronger Relationships

Promoting UN peacekeeping as a general, global good faces two principal challenges. First, there must be positive stories about UN peacekeeping so that member states and their publics understand that these operations usually work, i.e., they actually promote international peace and security and save lives. The UN needs to tell a better public story about its peacekeepers and establish relations with troop- and police-contributing countries—and, just as importantly, with their publics—that are distinct from relations concerning force generation for particular missions. In particular, UN public diplomacy should aim to increase awareness among governments (executives and parliaments) and publics of the positive contribution that peacekeeping makes to international peace and security. Academic research has demonstrated that 'peacekeeping works' by reducing the frequency of armed conflict—governments and publics need to be made aware of this basic fact.[3] A second task is increasing the prestige associated with making large and high quality contributions to UN peacekeeping operations.

Given the immense size of the task associated with promoting peacekeeping to almost two hundred UN member states and their publics, two forms of targeting would help. First, the strategy should target both established contributors (to help create prestige as a reward for their participation and encourage them to maintain and improve their contributions) and countries identified as potential or emerging contributors (see below). Second, the strategy should identify national champions for UN peacekeeping and encourage and facilitate these champions in the promotion of peacekeeping. Candidates might include military officers who served in past missions or other visible personalities. This would help give the UN message a national character and increase the extent to which politicians and publics relate to and feel ownership over the peacekeeping enterprise.

[2] See Alex J. Bellamy and Paul D. Williams, 'The West and Contemporary Peace Operations', *Journal of Peace Research*, 46:1 (2009), pp. 47–9.

[3] For example, Virginia Page Fortna, *Does Peacekeeping Work? Shaping Belligerents' Choices after Civil War* (Princeton, NJ: Princeton University Press, 2008) and Joshua S. Goldstein, *Winning the War on War: The Decline of Armed Conflict Worldwide* (New York: Dutton, 2011).

Public diplomacy should be conducted separately from discussions about specific force generation requests in order to build positive attitudes about UN peacekeeping and change the context (if only slightly) in which national decisions about contributing are taken. Potential initiatives might include appointing an 'ambassador for peacekeeping' to promote the headline figures about peacekeeping's contribution to peace and security and highlight good work, and/or developing a 'friends of UN peacekeeping' mechanism.[4] Such initiatives could be accompanied by the public release of more information about who contributes what and by civil society initiatives to monitor and publicize contributors, and publicly recognize the best contributors. Public diplomacy could also be used to send generic messages about enabling pathways to countries that are potential contributors. This might include advising new or minor contributors about the merits of even modest contributions and sensitizing states to the fact that the UN needs equipment, enabling assets, and specialist capabilities as well as large numbers of troops and police.

Civil society must also be harnessed to disseminate positive messages. The Washington-based 'Partnership for Effective Peacekeeping' (PEP) provides one model for how this might be done.[5] Other countries could be encouraged to establish PEPs with an international network of PEPs established in order to strengthen this type of work. It is worth stressing here that our case studies revealed that very few contributing countries have active civil society or academic networks working to promote the field of peacekeeping. This contributes to the sense among governments that there is little pressure to provide peacekeepers and that, much more often than not, domestic politics works against UN peacekeeping rather than in its favour. Facilitating the emergence of national networks of academics, civil society groups, former peacekeepers, and other interested individuals might begin to shift this balance. More work is thus needed to build the civil society support structure for peacekeeping in many contributing countries.

Ideas and cultures are important, but so too are material considerations. As Coleman noted in Chapter 2, the UN's incentive structure makes token contributions an attractive option for member states. Indeed, the current incentive structures encourage states to make multiple token contributions, resulting in a situation wherein most contributing countries make nothing but token contributions. There are only limited incentives for a state to go from being a token to a major contributor of more and better quality troops/police. Given the importance of economic rationales for some developing states, financial incentives might be the best way of encouraging movement beyond

[4] George Clooney fulfils some of the more public aspects of this role in his capacity as a UN 'Messenger for Peace' but this could be augmented with more focused bilateral discussion with contributing countries and potential contributors.

[5] The PEP website is at http://www.effectivepeacekeeping.org/

tokenism, but budgetary cutbacks in light of the global financial crisis make it unlikely that the UN General Assembly would approve spending additional resources on allowances, salaries, and reimbursements. Moreover, financial incentives would do little to encourage developed states to move beyond tokenism and provide specialized contributions. As such, a more fruitful avenue might be to focus on measures that attach greater prestige to larger but also better contributions. Clearly, this is politically difficult for the UN Secretariat to achieve—and past proposals that election to the Security Council and other diplomatic honours be made contingent on a member state's willingness to be an active and substantive contributor to peacekeeping have not flourished. One modest step that might be considered is asking the Security Council to make greater use of presidential statements to commend major contributors and highlight the good work done by UN peacekeepers. The Council might also be encouraged to conduct more site visits to operational theatres in order to draw attention to the work of field personnel and convey the Council's gratitude to the contributing countries. Civil society initiatives to track and assess peacekeeping contributions based on both quantitative and qualitative factors might help generate publicity and prestige for effective contributions.[6] By themselves, such steps are unlikely to radically reconfigure the way in which international prestige is accumulated or dramatically alter the balance of incentives in favour of larger and better contributions over smaller and less good ones but they might nudge things in the right direction.

Another way of thinking about the incentives attached to UN peacekeeping is to focus on the development of capabilities themselves. Once member states have developed certain capabilities, they can employ them on both UN and national missions. Attaching peacekeeping contributions to the development of relevant capacity might be one way of creating additional incentives. Of central importance here are measures aimed at lowering the entry costs to providing UN peacekeepers and building relevant national capacity. One recent proposal was that new or emerging contributors might voluntarily partner with a leading contributor for guidance on deployment and training routines.[7] In terms of assistance for capacity-building, it would be worth enhancing existing bi- and/or multilateral 'train and equip' programmes such as the Global Peace Operations Initiative (US funded), African Contingency Operations Training and Assistance (US funded), *Renforcement des Capacités Africaines de Maintien de la Paix* (RECAMP, French funded), the European Union African Peace Facility, the UK's Peace Support Teams,

[6] Such as the 'Providing for Peacekeeping' project run by the International Peace Institute, the Elliott School of International Affairs at the George Washington University, and Griffith University. See http://www.ipinst.org/peace-operations/providing-for-peacekeeping/ programslist.html

[7] Fatemah Ziai, 'Broadening the Base of Contributors to UN Peacekeeping' (International Forum on the Challenges of Peace Operations, 9 November 2009), paragraph 8c.

Norway's 'Training for Peace' programme, and Canada's Global Peace Operations Programme. These initiatives help strengthen key military and some policing capacities which can then be employed in peacekeeping, but in so doing, they also help states to develop capabilities that can be used for other national purposes. Ensuring that, once developed, the relevant capabilities are deployed when the UN needs them is more difficult. Politically, it is probably best to separate out capacity-building from direct requests to provide UN peacekeepers for a particular mission, but it would make sense for external programmes to channel greater assistance to those states that have demonstrated a strong commitment to UN peacekeeping.

20.2.3 Reform the Request

The UN should also revisit how it communicates its requests for peacekeepers to its member states. These have typically been sent via informal oral communication with permanent missions or faxing *notes verbales*. Unfortunately, these are not effective ways of empowering domestic champions, creating pressure to respond positively, or encouraging governments to consider seriously the requests. Although the permanent missions to the UN are an important part in the diplomatic chain, our case studies consistently reported that key decisions about providing peacekeepers are made in national capitals, not by permanent missions. UN DPKO must therefore do more to reach out directly to capitals. Faxing requests or sending only *notes verbales* requesting personnel makes it too easy for member states to decline or avoid serious consideration of requests. It also reinforces DPKO's tendency to only talk seriously about contributions with a relatively small pool of existing committed contributors. In our view, there is no substitute for building bilateral ties with contributing countries that are separate from specific requests and then subsequently visiting potential contributors in their national capitals to request peacekeepers for particular missions.

20.2.4 Force Generation Strategy

Finally, the UN needs to think strategically about force generation. To do so, the DPKO must understand its current capability needs (as well as those for the foreseeable future), where those capabilities are situated or are likely to be situated, and the prerequisites for securing their release for UN duties.

As we noted above, public diplomacy and strengthening ties with contributing countries are important precursors to requesting personnel and equipment for a specific mission. However, these activities should be guided by analysis of the key, emerging, and potential future contributing countries.

This could take the form of 'donor profiling' analysis based on information about the member states' past history with peacekeeping, its UN and non-UN commitments, how its government takes decisions about peacekeeping, key motivating rationales and inhibiting factors, and other relevant issues. Such analysis should also provide an understanding of the evolving operational capacities of potential contributors with regard to their deployable assets, concepts, and approaches.

Understanding its potential contributors is important, but the UN must also know its own capability requirements. The DPKO must therefore develop a comprehensive and prioritized assessment of its critical capability gaps. A recent assessment of the DPKO 'gap lists' found that member states appreciated the utility of systematically identifying and communicating the technical needs of each mission and their utility for the capabilities-driven approach.[8] However, states have not made widespread use of the gap lists because they lacked a clear vision, mode of communicating that vision, and a means of relaying information in a transparent and easily accessible fashion. The assessment recommended that DPKO utilize more efficient methods of updating and disseminating the information and that it foster more effective communication between stakeholders and capacity-building donors. It also proposed the development of an online mechanism—a 'Gap Map'—combined with a quarterly Gap Report and concomitant briefing on key trends and issues to member states. This would facilitate more efficient and effective communication of the uniformed and specialized personnel and asset gaps in UN peacekeeping operations to Member States. The Gap Map would also make the information instantly and easily accessible to permanent missions in New York and, importantly, national officials in their capitals.

In sum, in order to 'expand the base' of peacekeeping contributors and secure more and better peacekeepers, the UN must understand its own needs, the domestic politics of peacekeeping decisions in contributing countries, and the ways in which it can influence those processes. To achieve this important goal, there is no substitute for careful analysis of individual contributors, forging strong bilateral relations with those countries outside of the specific force generation process, and developing long-term force generation strategies.

[8] Authors' interview with UN officials, New York, February 2012.

Index